Cases on AI Innovations in Occupational Health and Safety

Martha Chadyiwa
University of Johannesburg, South Africa

Olanrewaju Oladimeji
Sefako Makgatho Health Sciences University, South Africa

IGI Global
Scientific Publishing
Publishing Tomorrow's Research Today

Vice President of Editorial | Melissa Wagner
Director of Acquisitions | Mikaela Felty
Director of Book Development | Jocelynn Hessler
Production Manager | Mike Brehm
Cover Design | Jose Rosado

Published in the United States of America by
IGI Global Scientific Publishing
701 East Chocolate Avenue
Hershey, PA, 17033, USA
Tel: 717-533-8845
Fax: 717-533-7115
Website: https://www.igi-global.com E-mail: cust@igi-global.com

Library of Congress Cataloging-in-Publication Data

Names: Chadyiwa, Martha, 1979- editor.
Title: Cases on AI innovations in occupational health and safety / edited by: Martha Chadyiwa.
Other titles: Cases on artificial intelligence innovations in occupational health and safety
Description: Hershey, PA : IGI Global Scientific Publishing, [2025] | Includes bibliographical references and index. | Summary: "The objective of the book is to explore how AI technologies can enhance workplace safety and health"-- Provided by publisher.
Identifiers: LCCN 2024060439 (print) | LCCN 2024060440 (ebook) | ISBN 9798369393017 (hardcover) | ISBN 9798369393024 (paperback) | ISBN 9798369393031 (ebook)
Subjects: LCSH: Industrial hygiene--Technological innovations--Case studies. | Industrial safety--Technological innovations--Case studies. | Artificial intelligence--Industrial applications--Case studies.
Classification: LCC HD7261 .C365 2025 (print) | LCC HD7261 (ebook) | DDC 658.3/82--dc23/eng/20250328
LC record available at https://lccn.loc.gov/2024060439
LC ebook record available at https://lccn.loc.gov/2024060440
British Cataloguing in Publication Data
A Cataloguing in Publication record for this book is available from the British Library.

Table of Contents

Detailed Table of Contents

Occupational illnesses presents a considerable difficulty in both clinical and non-clinical environments, mainly due to their prolonged latency conditions, illustrated by ailments such as pneumoconiosis, silicosis, asbestosis, lung cancer, and chronic obstructive pulmonary chronic obstructive pulmonary disease (COPD), frequently making comprehensive management more difficult. Recent developments in AI algorithms utilizing deep learning (DL) functionality have demonstrated significant potential in processing lung images, creating a notable influence on illness identification relying on plain radiographs. As artificial intelligence (AI) increasingly influences occupational health and safety, the ethical issues linked to its incorporation are becoming more glaring. This chapter explores and examines the ethical challenges in AI development and AI assimilation with a glimpse of methods to enhance transparency, fairness, and accountability, especially in occupational health and safety.

The integration of artificial intelligence (AI) in diagnostic X-ray quality assurance (QA) represents a transformative advancement medical imaging. This paper explores the application of AI algorithms in enhancing the accuracy and efficiency of QA processes in X-ray diagnostics. We discuss various AI techniques, including machine learning and deep learning, that automate the assessment of image quality and detect anomalies, thereby reducing the reliance on manual evaluations. The implementation of AI-driven systems not only improves diagnostic accuracy but also streamlines workflows, minimizes radiation exposure, and supports radiologists in clinical decision-making. Challenges such as data quality, algorithm interpretability, and regulatory compliance are also addressed. Our findings suggest that AI-based QA systems can significantly enhance patient outcomes and operational efficiency in diagnostic radiology, paving the way for future innovations in medical imaging.

as protective measures or adjustments to work schedules. The system also integrates real-time alerts, which are generated when exposure levels exceed predefined limits, ensuring workers receive immediate safety instructions.

This chapter examines the incorporation of Artificial Intelligence (AI) into Occupational Health and Safety (OHS), representing a significant change in workplace safety management. It highlights the importance of AI technology in reducing risks, improving worker satisfaction, and increasing operational effectiveness in the workplace. Consideration is given to the functions of significant AI technologies in unsafe work automation, ergonomic assessments, health monitoring, and hazard identification. Some processes include predictive analytics, computer vision, machine learning, and natural language processing. Additionally, innovations that are altering safety training and skill development include wearable technology, augmented reality, and virtual reality. Alongside focusing on issues including employment displacement, regulatory gaps, and ethical problems, the chapter suggests multidisciplinary collaboration and strategic partnerships for AI-driven safety solutions.

In recent years, X ray imaging has emerged as a promising non-invasive technique for detecting osteoarthritis. However, existing techniques for osteoarthritis detection in thermal images suffer from several limitations, such as low accuracy, limited generalizability, and lack of interpretability. To address these challenges, we propose a novel approach for osteoarthritis detection in x ray images using the SqueezeNet model deep learning architecture. The proposed approach involves pre-processing the X-ray images to enhance their features, followed by segmentation to extract the region of interest. The segmented region is then fed into the SqueezeNet model, which is trained to classify the thermal image as normal or abnormal based on the presence of osteoarthritis. The parameter of SqueezeNet is tuned using grey wolf optimizer to reach maximum accuracy. We evaluated the performance of the proposed approach on a dataset of thermal images collected from patients with osteoarthritis and healthy controls.

South Africa's informal sector, including street vendors, faces significant occupational health and safety challenges, including exposure to air pollution, extreme weather, and limited sanitation. Current legislative frameworks, offer limited protections for these workers, leaving substantial gaps in regulatory coverage. Artificial Intelligence (AI) presents a promising solution by enabling real-time environmental monitoring, predictive analytics, and health alerts tailored to high-risk conditions. This chapter explores various AI applications for improving vendor safety, such as wearable devices for air quality and vital signs monitoring, and mobile apps delivering real-time health information. However, barriers to implementation exist, including financial constraints, digital literacy gaps, and data privacy concerns. To address these, the chapter recommends targeted interventions like public-private partnerships and subsidies, and digital literacy initiatives alongside robust policy frameworks that expand OHS protections to include AI-driven health solutions.

This chapter explores how Artificial Intelligence (AI) is transforming risk management in moving and handling tasks, particularly within nursing and geriatric care. By integrating AI-powered technologies—such as wearable sensors, predictive analytics, and real-time decision support systems—organisations can identify biomechanical hazards, predict musculoskeletal injuries, and personalise care strategies. The chapter offers clinical insights from nursing practice, including safe patient handling in long-term care facilities, and illustrates how AI enhances ergonomic assessment, staff training, and risk mitigation. Drawing on current research and international practice guidelines, it positions AI as a crucial innovation in safeguarding both patients and healthcare workers. Practical applications, ethical considerations, and case studies from eldercare nursing are critically examined to showcase how AI aligns with occupational health and safety (OHS) standards.

This chapter explores the application of Artificial Intelligence (AI) in addressing demographic-specific challenges in manual handling safety, focusing on age, gender, and physical capability variations in the workforce. The chapter examines AI-driven ergonomic solutions, predictive analytics, and adaptive training programs. It highlights case studies showcasing AI's role in reducing injury rates and enhancing safety protocols tailored to diverse worker demographics. The discussion concludes with the potential

Preface

In the face of rapidly evolving workplace environments, *Cases on AI Innovations in Occupational Health and Safety* illuminates the transformative capacity of artificial intelligence to redefine how hazards are identified, risks are assessed, and incidents are prevented. Under the stewardship of Martha Chadyiwa of the University of Johannesburg, this volume assembles a diverse set of case studies showcasing AI's practical impact on occupational health and safety (OHS) across sectors and geographies.

This collection pursues two complementary goals. First, it advances research by presenting empirically grounded, rigorously documented studies that expand the frontier of knowledge in AI-enabled OHS. Examples range from machine-learning models that detect ergonomic stress in manufacturing to computer-vision systems deployed on construction sites for real-time behavior analysis. Each contribution offers new data, methodologies, and lessons learned. Second, it emphasizes practical applications, detailing not only the underlying algorithms and system architectures but also the organizational strategies, stakeholder engagement processes, and governance frameworks that underpin successful implementation.

Organized into thematic sections, the book opens with explorations of AI in risk assessment, where natural-language processing and deep-learning techniques uncover latent patterns in incident reports. It proceeds to predictive analytics for incident prevention, highlighting dynamic forecasting tools that enable proactive resource allocation and targeted interventions. Subsequent chapters examine AI-driven safety training, wearable technologies, and ergonomic optimization, before turning to real-time environmental and health monitoring and enhanced emergency response protocols. The final sections address critical data privacy and ethical considerations and conclude with a forward-looking discussion on future trends and innovations in AI-driven OHS.

CHAPTER OVERVIEWS

Chapter 1: Addressing the Ethical and Data Privacy Concerns Related to AI in Occupational Health and Safety

This opening chapter delves into the ethical and privacy challenges that arise as deep-learning and other AI methods are applied to occupational health—particularly in diagnosing long-latency illnesses such as pneumoconiosis, asbestosis, and COPD from radiographic images. It surveys emerging concerns around algorithmic fairness, data consent, and transparency, and proposes governance frameworks and design principles to ensure accountability at every stage of AI development and deployment in OHS settings. privacy safeguards to strengthen organizational resilience.

Chapter 2: AI-Based Diagnostic X-ray Quality Assurance

This chapter examines how machine-learning and deep-learning algorithms can automate and enhance quality-assurance processes in diagnostic radiology. By assessing image clarity, detecting anomalies, and reducing manual review burdens, AI-driven QA systems not only improve diagnostic accuracy but also streamline radiology workflows, lower radiation exposure, and support regulatory compliance—paving the way for more efficient, patient-centered care.

Chapter 3: AI-Powered Ergonomics: Transforming Workplace Health and Safety

This chapter explores the use of AI-enabled wearables, motion sensors, and analytical platforms to monitor posture, movement, and environmental conditions in real time. Predictive models identify musculoskeletal and repetitive-strain risks before they manifest as injuries, while personalized recommendations and adaptive workstation designs improve comfort, productivity, and long-term employee well-being.

Chapter 4: Artificial Intelligence Innovation and Safety in Biotechnology Research

This chapter surveys the convergence of AI and biotechnology, highlighting applications in agriculture, medicine, and environmental management that raise unique safety and regulatory questions. It discusses AI-driven risk assessments, customized training programs, and the need for robust ethical frameworks and intellectual-property safeguards to ensure that AI innovations advance both scientific discovery and workforce protection.

Chapter 5: Automated Health and Safety Recommendations Using LSTM in Hazardous Workplaces

This chapter introduces a Long Short-Term Memory (LSTM)–based recommendation engine designed for hazardous environments. By ingesting sequential exposure and health data, the model forecasts risk thresholds and issues personalized safety advisories—supplemented by real-time alerts when exposures exceed safe limits—thereby enabling timely preventive measures and enhanced regulatory compliance. equity goals.

Chapter 6: Future Trends and Innovations

This chapter offers a forward-looking survey of emerging AI applications in OHS—from automated hazard detection and augmented-reality training to AI-infused wearables and natural-language-processing tools. It also addresses workforce displacement, regulatory gaps, and the imperative for cross-sector collaboration to realize AI's full potential in workplace safety.

Chapter 7: Hybrid Approach for Osteoarthritis Detection in X-Ray Images

This chapter introduces a novel pipeline combining a lightweight deep-learning architecture and Grey Wolf Optimizer tuning to detect osteoarthritis in X-ray images. Through image enhancement, segmentation, and parameter optimization, the hybrid model achieves high classification accuracy, demonstrating a scalable approach for non-invasive diagnostic screening.

Chapter 8: Impact of Workplace Factors on Nurse Well-Being

This chapter presents a multivariate study of mental-health outcomes among nurses, analyzing survey data from over 1,400 actively employed practitioners. Using natural-language processing preprocessing, Principal Component Analysis, and Bayesian-optimized regression, it identifies key psychosocial stressors—informing targeted support programs to mitigate anxiety, depression, and burnout in healthcare settings.

Chapter 9: Integrating Robotics and AI into Workplace Biorisk Management

This chapter outlines how AI-driven predictive analytics, coupled with robotic monitoring platforms, can enhance biorisk assessment—particularly in under-resourced settings—through continuous surveillance, adaptive response protocols, and ethically grounded governance structures.

Chapter 10: Predictive Analytics for Incident Prevention in the Transportation of Dangerous Goods

This chapter explores how integrating AI into hazardous-materials transport systems enables proactive safety measures, preventing incidents before they occur. It examines predictive models that use sensor data and driver-behavior analytics, and concludes with recommendations for improving model accuracy and addressing data-privacy concerns.

Chapter 11: Preventing Accidents—A Hybrid Approach to Workplace Safety Prediction and Risk Management

This chapter employs Particle Swarm and Remora Optimization techniques for feature selection, followed by Convolutional Neural Network models to predict accident severity. It demonstrates how hybrid optimization-ML frameworks can accurately forecast injury outcomes, enabling more strategic allocation of safety resources.

Chapter 12: Real-Time Personal Noise Measurements' Contribution to Hearing Deterioration for Mineworkers in South Africa

This chapter details the use of cutting-edge noise dosimetry and big-data audiometric surveillance to monitor and predict hearing loss among mineworkers. By integrating continuous noise tracking with machine-learning trend analysis, it advocates for proactive intervention tools that safeguard auditory health in high-risk industries.

Chapter 13: Strengthening Sensors and Wearable Technologies in Gauging Healthcare

This chapter surveys AI-augmented wearables—from biosensors and fitness trackers to smart exoskeletons—that enable continuous health monitoring, fatigue detection, and ergonomic support. It highlights how these innovations democratize preventive care, enhance workplace safety, and open new frontiers in human augmentation and telehealth.

Chapter 14: The Potential of AI in Enhancing Occupational Health and Safety for Urban Informal Vendors

This chapter examines AI solutions such as air-quality monitors, vital-sign wearables, and mobile health apps to address the precarious conditions faced by informal street vendors. It proposes public-private partnerships, subsidy models, and digital-literacy initiatives to bridge implementation gaps and extend OHS protections to this underserved workforce.

Chapter 15: The Role of AI in Revolutionizing Risk Management for Moving and Handling Tasks

This chapter explores AI-powered ergonomic assessments, predictive analytics, and decision-support tools tailored for nursing and eldercare. By integrating sensor data, biomechanical modeling, and best-practice guidelines, it demonstrates how AI can personalize safe-handling protocols and reduce musculoskeletal injury risks.

Chapter 16: Using AI to Address Demographic-Specific Challenges in Manual Handling Safety

This concluding chapter investigates how AI can tailor manual handling interventions to demographic variables such as age, gender, and physical capacity. Through adaptive training programs, ergonomic modeling, and targeted analytics, it illustrates pathways to more equitable, personalized safety protocols that accommodate workforce diversity.

Designed for researchers, practitioners, and policymakers, this book offers a bridge between academic theory and operational practice. Contributors—from industry leaders and academic scholars to regulatory experts—provide a comprehensive perspective on how AI can be integrated responsibly and effectively into workplace safety strategies. It is hoped that the insights contained herein will inspire further interdisciplinary collaboration and guide the development of safer, healthier, and more resilient work environments worldwide.

Martha Chadyiwa
University of Johannesburg, South Africa

Olanrewaju Oladimeji
Sefako Makgatho Health Sciences University, South Africa

Chapter 1
Addressing the Ethical and Data Privacy Concerns Related to AI in Occupational Health and Safety:
Ethical Issues in OHS

Pheyiye Mapungwana
https://orcid.org/0000-0001-7351-9936
University of Johannesburg, South Africa

ABSTRACT

Occupational illnesses presents a considerable difficulty in both clinical and non-clinical environments, mainly due to their prolonged latency conditions, illustrated by ailments such as pneumoconiosis, silicosis, asbestosis, lung cancer, and chronic obstructive pulmonary chronic obstructive pulmonary disease (COPD), frequently making comprehensive management more difficult. Recent developments in AI algorithms utilizing deep learning (DL) functionality have demonstrated significant potential in processing lung images, creating a notable influence on illness identification relying on plain radiographs. As artificial intelligence (AI) increasingly influences occupational health and safety, the ethical issues linked to its incorporation are becoming more glaring. This chapter explores and examines the ethical challenges in AI development and AI assimilation with a glimpse of methods to enhance transparency, fairness, and accountability, especially in occupational health and safety.

INTRODUCTION

The past decade has seen an unmatched increase in the creation and implementation of artificial intelligence (AI) technologies. AI has permeated numerous spheres of life, including occupational health and safety. It is seriously replacing humans in daily tasks and decisions. The application of AI has brought about different opportunities from improving efficiency and productivity to facilitating new services and boosting human creativity. From machine learning techniques to sophisticated neural networks, AI has infiltrated occupational health and safety. As an example AI chatbot can give answers to patients 24 hours

DOI: 10.4018/979-8-3693-9301-7.ch001

a day, leading to customer satisfaction. Doctors can serve patients in distant places using telemedicine services, courtesy of AI. This swift expansion is driven by the growing accessibility of extensive datasets, improvements in computing capabilities, and advancements in algorithmic innovation (Dwivedi et al, 2021). The shift from conventional rule-based systems to advanced learning models has enabled AI to thrive in areas like image recognition, natural language processing, and decision-making.

The rapid growth of AI applications has resulted in significant shifts in our lifestyles and work environments, offering improvements in efficiency, creative solutions, and better decision support systems (Steyvers & Kumar, 2023). Nevertheless, alongside the significant progress in AI technology arise ethical issues that require thoughtful attention. For example, 2016 saw a Tesla Car killing its driver after its Auto-pilot mode failed to recognise an oncoming truck.Tay.ai, a Microsoft Chat bot was de-commissioned because it exhibited racism and sexism in a few hours after joining Twitter now X. Too many instances exist where privacy, fairness, bias and many other ethical issues become prominent. On a divergent note, criminals have started to use AI in ways that injure society. Fraudsters are impersonating peoples' voices for political and financial mileage. In this sense, ethical issues must be dissected. Therefore, it is urgent and critical to address ethical issues and or risks associated with AI.

The inherent characteristics of AI, frequently defined by sophisticated algorithms and elaborate decision-making methods, present various ethical challenges (Lysaght, Lim, Xafis & Ngiam,2019). Concerns like algorithmic bias, where AI tools might reinforce or intensify current social prejudices, prompt inquiries regarding equity and justice. The absence of clarity on how AI systems make decisions, often called the "black box" issue, heightens worries about responsibility and user confidence. These ethical issues highlight the necessity for a thorough assessment of AI development practices to guarantee responsible and ethically appropriate deployment in occupational health safety. A comprehensive approach combining technological innovation with ethical and regulatory strategies is essential for ensuring the protection of individual privacy in AI development and deployment (Radanliev & Santos,2023).

The primary objective of this book chapter is to examine the ethical issues associated with the development and application of AI technologies in occupational health and safety. The development and deployment of AI technologies pose a variety of ethical dilemmas. These challenges are complex and encompass multiple parties, such as developers, users, and regulatory agencies. The chapter emphasizes the primary ethical concerns noted in various research studies. There is a worldwide agreement on fundamental ethical principles like transparency, justice and equity, non-maleficence, accountability, and privacy. Nevertheless, there is considerable variation in the interpretation and application of these principles among various domains and actors. The absence of uniform ethical standards and the existence of ambiguous principles create difficulties in the real-world implementation of AI ethics. Converting broad ethical principles into specific actions is challenging. This encompasses the requirement for particular indicator systems to evaluate the ethical implications of AI design traits, which differ among various AI applications. The lack of strong legal and professional accountability systems in AI development, when contrasted with areas such as medicine, makes enforcing ethical guidelines more challenging. In the healthcare sector, ethical issues involve machine precision, patient safety, data confidentiality, and the risk of AI reinforcing current disparities. These challenges require multifaceted solutions and the creation of specialized ethical frameworks. Employing AI in critical areas like healthcare necessitates thoughtful evaluation of ethical concerns to avoid serious repercussions for individuals. The development of ethical AI necessitates the participation of various stakeholders, such as researchers, developers, and regulatory agencies. There is a demand for clear, ethical, and socially responsible AI methods. AI developers and corporations have ethical obligations that involve tackling concerns related to bias, fairness, and the broader societal effects of AI technologies (Martin, Schmidt & Hillerbrand, 2023).

By examining critical issues such as bias, transparency, and accountability, we seek to illuminate the ethical implications that surface as AI systems become essential to decision-making in different areas (Lysaght et al,2019). By conducting a detailed examination of real-world instances and case studies, we will highlight the ethical complexities related to AI applications. This presentation will enhance comprehension of the ethical framework and guide conversations on responsible practices in AI development. Alongside examining ethical dilemmas, the paper aims to suggest approaches designed to enhance transparency, fairness, and accountability in AI development. Acknowledging that ethical issues cannot be solved solely through technological progress, we will examine diverse strategies that include technical, regulatory, and organizational aspects (Lussier & Sherman,2022). By outlining effective strategies, we seek to offer direction for AI developers, policymakers, and organizations to crisscross the intricate ethical landscape. The suggested approaches aim to achieve a harmony between technological advancement and ethical accountability, ensuring that AI progress is consistent with societal values and standards. The advancement of artificial intelligence (AI) presents numerous ethical issues that create considerable obstacles to the responsible implementation of these technologies. Bias and Fairness, AI algorithms, especially those powered by machine learning, can be influenced by biases found in the training data. If the historical data utilized for training contains societal biases, the AI system might continue or even worsen these biases in its decision-making process. For example, biased facial recognition technologies have sparked worries regarding racial and gender differences in identification precision (Scheuerman, Paul & Brubaker,2019). Tackling bias demands a sophisticated comprehension of its origins, be they historical, cultural, or systemic. Furthermore, it emphasizes the need to create methods for identifying and reducing bias during both the training and implementation stages of AI systems.

BACKGROUND

Designing AI ethics in occupational health and safety should be preceded by an understanding of the definition of ethics. Ethics incorporates judgements on what is right or wrong including the consequences of such. Julia Driver (2011) mentions that the ethical theory of consequentialism presumes that deeds are ethically right, unjust, or unsocial due to their consequences. However, the ethical theory of consequentialism is one of the typical, normative virtuous theories. Normative means that this ethical theory leans on promoting norms that are not only common but also help humans with guidelines when facing "ought" in human action. The understanding is that an action is right if and only if its total outcome remains the best alternative. This is the simple form of consequentialism; there are, however, many variations. The definition illustrates that it is more concerned about the immediate and subsequent effects occasioned by an action. As mentioned by Christian Seidel (2018:4), the issues of being futuristic and satisfying are not limited to consequentialism. These constructions remain the foundation stones of Aristotelian ethics. Putting consequences as a prime benchmark of ethical judgment by default supports the future in which those consequences transpire. By worrying about what is going to happen due to an act, there is a sense of being futuristic in doing the act, which tries to predict the aftermaths of an action. Pre-emption is essential to realize appropriate consequences and henceforth permits the actor to place consequentialism into practice. Due to this reason, consequentialism is considered to have its origins in the Aristotelian ethic on teleology, which incorporates the futuristic component, and eudemonia, which embraces the pleasurable or desirable action, as mentioned by Seidel (2018). There are four types of consequentialism namely: rule consequentialism; utilitarianism; act consequentialism; and indirect consequentialism. For Julia Driver (2011), utilitarianism is an ethical theory that says that the rightness or wrongness of an act is realized through the goodness or badness of the products of the act. The products of the acts may either bring or encourage pleasure or pain. Utilitarianism intends to promote pleasure through the "utility/ Happiness Principle" where happiness comes intending to achieve pleasure. Seidel (2018) states that Act-consequentialism encompasses consideration of a sequence of actions and then picking up an act that would produce the best consequences. Rule consequentialism follows certain guidelines to realize the best consequences. Indirect consequentialism holds that the moral qualities of something depend on the consequences of something else. A different form of consequentialism which is important for this study is "subjective consequentialism" or "utilitarianism". With utilitarianism, the intrinsic value that we seek to maximize pertains to utility. Seidel (2018) mentions that action is believed to be moral if its consequences contribute to the goal of promoting and achieving happiness and lasting benefits for the greatest number, and it is morally wrong if its consequences produce pain and misery to the majority.

CONSEQUENCES OF AI ON MARGINALIZED COMMUNITIES

Identifying occupational illnesses presents a considerable difficulty in clinical environments, mainly due to their prolonged latency conditions, illustrated by ailments such as pneumoconiosis, silicosis, asbestosis, lung cancer, and chronic obstructive pulmonary chronic obstructive pulmonary disease (COPD), frequently making comprehensive management more difficult. Recent developments in AI algorithms utilizing deep learning (DL) functionality have demonstrated significant potential in processing lung images, creating a notable influence on illness identification relying on plain radiographs. AI algorithms can evaluate lung images, such as chest X-rays (CXRs), CT scans, or magnetic resonance imaging (MRI) scans, resulting in precise identification and assessment of different lung disorders for enhanced making decisions. They are capable of identifying and categorizing irregularities, and detecting nodules, masses, or patterns suggestive of conditions such as mesothelioma, chronic obstructive pulmonary disease, and silicosis.

However, the existence of AI algorithm biases that frequently have a greater impact on marginalized and underrepresented groups, can worsen existing disparities (Cardenas & Vallejo-Cardenas,2019). Therefore, it is essential to guarantee that AI technologies are created and evaluated with a dedication to fairness and equity, taking into account various demographic groups and preventing discriminatory results in occupational health and safety. As mentioned earlier, the absence of clarity in AI systems, commonly known as the "black box" issue, presents a major ethical dilemma (Konkov,2023). Numerous AI models function as intricate, unclear systems, making it difficult for users and stakeholders to grasp or even follow how decisions are made. This absence of transparency may diminish user confidence, impede accountability, and restrict the capacity to recognize and correct biases. Solutions to tackle the black box issue include creating explainable AI (XAI) methods, making sure AI systems are understandable, and offering detailed documentation regarding the decision-making procedures. Clarification is essential for allowing users, regulators, and the general public to comprehend and evaluate AI systems. Clear decision-making processes allow stakeholders to evaluate the ethical consequences of AI results, confirm the lack of bias, and understand the rationale for particular suggestions or actions. Attaining explainability requires creating models that offer understandable justifications for their choices, making certain that AI development methods emphasize transparency as a core ethical value.

Accountability and Responsibility

AI technologies have also made their way into occupational health finding applications in diverse areas, such as coordinating machinery and industrial processes, workforce management (especially from a human resources [HR] perspective), customer risk assessment, benefits analysis, and staff safety evaluation. The assignment of decision-making in AI systems presents difficulties in determining who is responsible for actions or outcomes. In contrast to human decision-makers, AI does not possess consciousness or intentionality, making it challenging to determine accountability. This further brings up concerns regarding legal and ethical accountability, especially in situations where AI choices result in major societal consequences. Creating frameworks for accountability requires specifying the roles and responsibilities of different stakeholders, such as developers, organizations, and regulatory authorities. It also requires the creation of legal and ethical guidelines that outline accountability in the realm of AI. The absence of well-defined legal structures and ethical standards for AI development makes accountability issues even more complex. With AI systems becoming essential in key decision-making areas like healthcare including occupational health and safety, a lack of strong regulations may result in unforeseen outcomes and difficulties in tackling ethical issues. To tackle accountability, it's essential to create detailed legal structures that define responsibilities and liabilities, alongside ethical standards that promote responsible AI creation and implementation. Ethical challenges in AI development, including bias and fairness, insufficient transparency, and accountability, require extensive strategies to address and reduce these issues.

Approaches for Transparency in AI Development for Occupational Health and Safety

Guaranteeing transparency in AI development is crucial for establishing trust, promoting accountability, and tackling ethical issues. This part examines three essential approaches designed to improve transparency in AI systems which are: Explainable AI (XAI), Open Data Sharing, and Ethical AI Frameworks.

Explainable AI (XAI) is an essential approach to tackle the opacity in AI decision-making. Transparent models allow users to comprehend how AI systems reach particular results, offering insights into the elements affecting their choices. This openness is crucial for establishing trust among users, stakeholders, and regulatory organizations (Jermutus, Kneale Thomas & Michie,2022). Gaining interpretability requires the creation of AI models that offer clear and comprehensible explanations for their predictions or decisions. Methods like decision trees, rule-based frameworks, and model-independent strategies enhance the understanding of AI systems. Incorporating XAI principles into AI development processes necessitates a transition towards creating models that emphasize interpretability while maintaining performance standards. Developers ought to adopt techniques like model-agnostic interpretability approaches, attention mechanisms, and layer-wise relevance propagation to improve the transparency of intricate neural networks (Guillemot, Heusele, Korichi, Schubert & Chen, 2020).

Additionally, it is vital to offer users intuitive interfaces that explain AI decisions clearly to guarantee transparency in practical applications. Sharing open data is a crucial approach to improve transparency and minimize bias in AI systems. By using varied and representative datasets, developers can reduce the likelihood of biased algorithms that could continue discrimination (Cerrato, Halamka & Pencina,2022). Sharing open data facilitates external examination, allowing researchers, developers, and the public to evaluate the integrity and equity of datasets utilized for training AI models (Brundage et al., 2020). Open data initiatives must focus on inclusivity, guaranteeing that datasets encompass various demographic groups and are frequently refreshed to align with changing societal standards. Although open data sharing provides various advantages, it also introduces challenges, such as issues tied to privacy, security, and proprietary data. Achieving a balance between data transparency and protecting sensitive information necessitates the creation of strong data anonymization methods, secure data-sharing platforms, and explicit guidelines for responsible data utilization (Shahbazi, Lin, Asudeh & Jagadish 2022).

Highlighting the advantages of data transparency in promoting ethical AI development is essential for addressing possible concerns and guaranteeing broad acceptance. Ethical AI frameworks offer an organized method for incorporating transparency into AI development. Numerous organizations and initiatives have proposed guidelines to tackle ethical issues, including fairness, accountability, and transparency. Significant instances feature the IEEE Global Initiative on Ethics of Autonomous and Intelligent Systems as well as the European Commission's Ethics Guidelines for Trustworthy AI (Nikolinakos, 2023). These frameworks highlight principles like transparency, fairness, and accountability as essential cornerstones for ethical AI development. Ethical AI frameworks act as guides for developers and organizations, helping them incorporate ethical aspects into all phases of AI development. Establishing ethical AI frameworks necessitates a comprehensive approach that takes into account not just technical factors but also the wider societal effects of AI applications. Approaches for transparency in AI creation, such as Explainable AI, Open Data Sharing, and Ethical AI Frameworks, are crucial for tackling ethical challenges. These approaches help in promoting responsible and accountable AI systems, guaranteeing that the creation and implementation of AI adheres to ethical standards and societal values. The upcoming sections will examine approaches to enhance fairness and accountability in AI development.

ADVANCING EQUITY IN AI ALGORITHMS

Tackling bias and advancing equity in AI algorithms is essential for guaranteeing just results and averting discriminatory actions. This segment explores three essential strategies: Fairness Metrics and Assessment, Varied and Representative Training Data, and Ongoing Monitoring and Iterative Enhancement.

Fairness Metrics and Evaluation

Fairness metrics provide quantitative assessments of AI algorithms' performance regarding bias and equity. Multiple metrics, such as disparate impact, equalized odds, and demographic parity, are utilized to assess the distribution of results among various demographic groups. Grasping these metrics aids developers in recognizing and measuring possible biases in algorithmic decision-making (Pagano et al. 2023; Zhou, Zhang, Nair, Singhal & Chen,2022; Wong, 2019). Choosing suitable fairness metrics relies on the application context and the particular objectives of the AI system. Clarity regarding the selected metrics and their significance is crucial for stakeholders to understand the fairness assessment. Incorporating fairness metrics into the assessment process is essential for detecting and addressing bias. Model evaluation ought to emphasize not only conventional accuracy but also the varying effects on distinct subpopulations. An equitable and impartial AI model must show reliable performance among various demographic groups, reducing differences in predictive accuracy (Cherian, Candès,2023; Paulus and Kent, 2020; Barda, Yona, Rothblum, Greenland, Leibowitz, Balicer, Bachmat & Dagan 2020). This strategy highlights the necessity of implementing a comprehensive assessment method that values equity alongside conventional performance indicators.

Varied and Inclusive Training Data

Biases found in training data can transcend AI models, resulting in biased results. To enhance fairness, it is essential to tackle biases within training data, which can arise from historical inequities, cultural factors, or systemic injustices. For instance, prejudiced training data in facial recognition technologies can lead to imprecise and unjust identification results, particularly for marginalized groups (Wehrli et al., 2022; Khalil, Ahmed, Khattak & Al-Qirim,2020; Yucer, Akçay, Moubayed & Breckon,2020). Recognizing and addressing biases in training data demands careful curation, data enhancement methods, and cooperation with varied communities to guarantee representation. To create equitable AI models, developers need to intentionally pursue diversity in their training datasets. This entails gathering information that reflects a wide range of demographic traits, steering clear of both over-representation and under-representation of particular groups. Working alongside domain experts, community stakeholders, and various user groups can aid in developing inclusive and representative training datasets (Chen, Clayton, Novak, Anders & Malin 2023; Mehrabi, Morstatter, Saxena, Lerman & Galstyan,2019). Achieving a balance between the quality and representativeness of training data is crucial for developing models that generalize effectively across various populations. D-BIAS is an interactive visual tool that assesses and reduces social biases in tabular datasets through a graphical causal model, enhancing trust, interpretability, and accountability in AI systems (Ghai & Mueller,2022). The TARA method employs training and changes in representation to reduce AI bias, effectively or entirely debiasing baseline models and surpassing rival debiasing techniques (Paul, Hadžić, Joshi, Alajaji & Burlina,2020)

Ongoing Monitoring and Progressive Enhancement

Fairness is not a singular factor but a continual endeavour. Ongoing surveillance of AI systems is crucial to detect and correct biases that might develop over time. The performance of AI models can be affected by real-world conditions and user interactions, highlighting the importance of ongoing monitoring as a key aspect of responsible AI development (Li, Qi, Li, Di, Liu, Pei, Yi & Zhou,2021). Creating feedback loops with consistent evaluations, user input, and audits guarantees that AI systems evolve with shifting contexts and uphold fairness throughout their operational duration. Including Feedback Loops in AI Systems and embedding feedback loops into AI systems enables ongoing enhancements based on user feedback and changing societal standards. These loops allow developers to tackle new challenges, improve models, and tackle unexpected biases that can arise during deployment (Suryadevara, Rangineni, & Venkata,2023). User input, ethical evaluations, and outside assessments play a role in an ongoing enhancement process that aligns AI systems with fairness goals (Pagan, Baumann, Elokda, Pasquale, Bolognani & Hann'ak,2023).

Promoting responsibility in AI development is essential to tackle ethical issues, guarantee responsible usage, and foster trust among users and society at large. This segment examines three essential strategies: Regulatory Actions, Ethical AI Oversight, and Human-in-the-Loop Techniques. The framework for AI regulation is changing, as different nations and areas evaluate or enforce actions to manage AI creation and usage. Current regulations, however, frequently have difficulty keeping up with the swift progress in AI technology. Though certain industries, like healthcare and finance, have particular regulations, broad and universally applicable AI regulations remain in early development (Dwivedi et al., 2021). Recognizing the shortcomings of existing regulations emphasizes the necessity for an active strategy to tackle ethical issues that extend beyond legal obligations. Suggestions for enhancing AI regulations focus on creating thorough frameworks that tackle ethical issues, responsibility, and openness. The goal is to establish a regulatory framework that directs AI developers, safeguards users, and sets up systems for accountability in the event of misuse or negative outcomes. Proposals such as the European Commission's suggested Artificial Intelligence Act detail standards for high-risk AI systems, conformity evaluations, and sanctions for non-compliance (Almeida, Mendes, Doneda & Almeida (2023). The creation of strong regulatory frameworks requires cooperation among policymakers, technologists, and ethicists. AI Governance includes forming committees or boards focused on monitoring the ethical dimensions of AI development in organizations. These committees encompass diverse expertise, encompassing technical, ethical, legal, and social viewpoints. Their responsibility is to create, apply, and uphold ethical standards for AI development, making sure they align with organizational principles and societal norms (Birkstedt, Minkkinen, Tandon & Mäntymäki,2023). The makeup of these committees ought to be inclusive, reflecting a diverse array of stakeholders to promote a comprehensive approach to ethical decision-making (Urmeneta,2023. Ethical AI governance encompasses more than just internal committees; it involves the creation and compliance with ethical standards by AI developers and organizations. These guidelines ought to include principles like transparency, fairness, accountability, and user privacy. Developers ought to receive ethical training, and organizations must implement systems for ethical evaluations and audits during the AI development process (Amugongo et al.2023). Ethical guidelines act as a code of behaviour, directing AI professionals in making choices that conform to ethical norms and social expectations.

Human-in-the-Loop Methods

Carley & Price (2021) mentioned that Human-in-the-Loop (HITL) methods entail integrating human supervision into AI systems, particularly in crucial decision-making scenarios. This guarantees that human evaluation is a vital component of the decision-making process, enabling the adjustment of possible biases, ethical factors, and intricate contextual comprehension that AI systems might not possess. HITL methods find an equilibrium between automation and human involvement, reducing risks linked to entirely automated systems. Human supervision is especially important in situations where AI choices greatly affect society, like in healthcare, criminal justice, and autonomous systems. Finding the right balance between automation and human input entails establishing distinct roles and responsibilities for individuals within AI frameworks. This involves setting up guidelines for human involvement when AI systems face unclear situations, exceptions, or cases beyond their training scope. Human-in-the-loop methods improve accountability by avoiding unregulated automation and making certain that AI systems conform to ethical and societal standards (Buckley et al., 2021). Designing HITL systems necessitates thoughtful evaluation of autonomy levels, the type of human involvement, and escalation protocols when necessary. Guaranteeing accountability in AI development requires managing regulatory frameworks, creating ethical AI governance systems, and including human supervision to complement automation. These approaches form a structure that ensures AI developers and organizations are responsible for the ethical consequences of their technology, promoting accountable AI creation and implementation.

Organizing Ethical Problems Into Groups

To further understand AI ethics in occupational health and safety, Table 1 groups ethical dimensions into different dimensions;

Table 1. Categorising ethical consequences

Narrow classification	Ethical problem
AI-induced moral dilemmas.	Security of data, Privacy, Autonomy, Malice, Responsibility.
Human factors moral factors	Ethical standards, Accountability, Human rights, Laws.
Impacts of Ethics of AI on Society	Job losses due to machines taking over, Democracy, civil rights
Vulnerabilities Brought by AI	AI needs data, Garbage in/Garbage out, Errors of algorithms, Black box.
Vulnerabilities of Humans	Abuse of AI, Human replacement, Robots' friendship with humans.
Algorithm ethical issues	Security of algorithms, Explainability, Algorithm decision dilemma
Data-related ethical issues	Protection of privacy, Understanding the protection of individual personal information.
Application ethical issues	Unwanted discrimination, Abuse of algorithms
Inherent Risks in Ethics	Ownership, Competition, employment, responsibility,
Impact on society	The employment market, equity, privacy, Dignity, Bias, Democracy.
Human psychological impact	Connections, individualism
Impact on Justice	Criminal law, Law of tort, statute law.
Personalised ethical matters	Secrecy, Safety, Freedom of choice, Dignity
Societal matters	Justice & fairness, Accountability and responsibility, Freedom, Controllability of AI, Job replacement, accountability, and Human relations.

Concerns about breach security of data, invasion of privacy, autonomy, malice and responsibility come about due to the fact algorithms require large amounts of data to function optimally hence there are risks of overlooking these matters. Ethical matters induced by human factors include the need for developers to follow ethical standards, to be accountable and to be knowledgeable about human rights. Ethical issues depicted in the realm of societal impact include but are not limited to job losses due to AI taking over jobs that would be normally done by humans. A simple categorisation where ethical issues can be labelled according to vulnerabilities created by AI cannot be ignored. In this category, we all know that AI needs data and as such if wrong prompts are given then AI may also hallucinate hence the issue of garbage in and garbage out comes to fore. Vulnerabilities of humans to AI include humans' exposure to manipulation due to the use of AI, humans' exposure to replacement by AI and robots' friendship with humans which all raise eyebrows on ethical issues. When data-related ethical issues are raised, they refer to breaches of data privacy whether in storage or its use. Algorithm ethical issues include but are not limited to the black box issues and the need for explainable AI. Furthermore, decision-making may not be left in the hands of AI without human control. Application ethical issues incorporate biases that are brought about by the training data that was used. Inherent risks in AI ethics take cognisance of ownership matters, the issue of competition, the suffocation of employment opportunities and the ambiguous issue of assigning responsibility once something goes wrong. Needless to say, AI impacts society through job losses, prejudices in accessing it and so forth. As depicted in Table 1, AI ethics can be further categorised into human psychological impacts, the impact of AI on justice, personalised ethical matters and societal matters.

Practical Examples of AI Usage in Health and Safety

Analysing real-world instances of the usage of AI technologies in occupational health and safety is essential in linking the pre-emptied ethical considerations. Identifying occupational diseases presents a considerable difficulty in medical environments, mainly due to their prolonged latency phases, illustrated by ailments such as pneumoconiosis, silicosis, asbestosis, lung cancer, and chronic obstructive pulmonary disease (COPD), frequently complicating overall treatment. AI techniques utilizing deep learning (DL)functionality have demonstrated significant potential in processing lung images, creating a notable effect on disease identification based on basic radiographs. AI systems can examine lung images, such as chest X-rays (CXRs), computed tomography (CT) examinations, or magnetic resonance imaging (MRI) scans, resulting in precise identification and assessment of different lung disorders for enhanced decision-making. Trivedi & Alqahtani (2024) observed the progress of Artificial Intelligence (AI) in Occupational Health and Safety (OHS) within high-risk sectors. They pointed out that the mining industry is marked by its significant risk factors, often involving incidents with heavy machinery, explosives, and dangerous materials. Such events often lead to injuries, fatalities, or permanent disabilities. Workers in this field are also subjected to dust, gases, and fumes that can result in serious lung diseases like silicosis, coal workers' pneumoconiosis, asbestosis, and various tumours that impact hearing and cause occupational hearing loss. Therefore, managing these risks is essential, and implementing AI might enhance the effectiveness of these management efforts.

Recent developments in AI have significantly improved automation in machinery and vehicle functioning. Significantly, one of the most cutting-edge applications of AI entails creating anti-collision systems based on computer vision. Specific innovations involve advanced sensor technologies, including high-resolution cameras and LIDAR, utilizing sophisticated deep-learning algorithms to track and recognize people's and machines' movements in mining settings. This ability is vital for improving safety, as it facilitates the delivery of prompt warnings and alerts to operators and workers, which may help avert accidents and injuries. In addition, the mining industry is progressively utilizing virtual and augmented reality (VR/AR) technologies. Moreover, VR/AR is advantageous for simulating crises, enhancing employees' response times and their overall readiness for safety. Moreover, these technologies enable remote surveillance and upkeep activities, permitting equipment inspections without the need for workers to be physically present thus minimizing the chances of accidents. A significant advancement is a Bluetooth-enabled system created for underground navigation and oversight of mining activities, backed by a comprehensive underground setup.

Table 2. Some applications of AI in mining industry

AI Technique	Application	Comment
Artificial neural network	Estimation	Neural networks demonstrate their appropriateness. for surface modelling sinking, providing a trustworthy approach for forecasting geological adjustments.
Artificial neural network, Fuzzy Inference System	Forecasting of Hazards by FME	Merging ANN and Fuzzy systems improve the accuracy of predictions of sinking hazards, enhancing extraction security
Hyperion Picture Examination	Iron Ore Mapping	Hyperion picture evaluation efficiently iron ore maps distributions, supporting in management of resources and removal tactics.
Artificial neural network	Estimating the amount of Dust in Coal Mines	Neural networks efficiently forecast dust concentrations in surface coal mines, assisting with ecological and wellness management
Internet of Things (IoT)	Preemptive Safety Alerts System for Subterranean Mines	Systems based on IoT improve safety in subterranean coal mines via successful occasion reporting and initial cautions.
Hybrid CNN-LSTM Model	Dangers in coal mining oversight and forecast	System based on IoT for live tracking and forecasting
Deep Convolutional Neural Network (CNN)	Protected wireless audio interaction for subterranean mines	Protected wireless audio interaction for subterranean mines

The use of exoskeletons, robotic suits worn on the body designed to improve the movement of limbs and joints, has surfaced as a method to enhance productivity and safeguard employee welfare. Several research studies show an increase in the use of different artificial neural network (ANN) architectures in contemporary Exoskeleton-associated technologies. Furthermore, conventional control techniques are merged with smart or adaptive optimizers to create robust or hybrid systems. Throughout the history of bio mechatronics and smart systems, ANNs have been a fundamental component. These networks have enabled the expansion of smart healthcare aid tools such as brain-computer prostheses controlled by interfaces and sophisticated robotic exoskeletons intended for rehabilitation purposes. Exoskeletons assist biometric evaluation and recovery following injuries, and they can reduce tension on the spine, leading to improved physical well-being for workers. Exoskeletons in occupational settings present both opportunities and ethical challenges. While they can reduce muscle activity and decrease the risk of injury, their mandatory use raises ethical concerns related to worker autonomy, privacy, and safety. The imposition of exoskeletons by employers can infringe on worker autonomy, especially if employees are uncomfortable or unable to use them. Ethical frameworks suggest offering adjustable models and allowing job transfers for those unwilling to use exoskeletons. The requirement for body measurements for exoskeleton fitting raises privacy concerns. Employers must balance the need for data with respect for employee privacy. While exoskeletons aim to reduce work-related musculoskeletal disorders (WRMSDs), their long-term health effects are not fully understood. There is a need for more research to ensure they do not introduce new health risks. There is a potential for employers to increase workloads due to the enhanced capabilities provided by exoskeletons, which could lead to ethical issues regarding fair labour practices. Conducting pilot studies and gathering user feedback can help tailor exoskeleton use to individual needs and improve acceptance. Developing clear regulations and standards for exoskeleton use can help address safety and ethical concerns, ensuring they are used responsibly as personal protective equipment. Ensuring that exoskeletons are comfortable and easy to use is crucial for user acceptance and effectiveness. Design improvements should focus on ergonomics and user feedback (Pote, Asbeck & Asbeck,2023).

With the emergence of intelligent PPE and wearable tech, it becomes viable to collect information about both the employees and their environment. This method based on data offers the possibility to reduce the occurrence of accidents and job-related health issues, thus bringing about a significant improvement in overall workplace conditions. Innovations in intelligent PPE allow for the monitoring of crucial health metrics and the evaluation of industrial environments. Various approaches are available for the integration of wearables into work environments, enabling an exploration of how networks of devices that are connected can help protect people. Smart helmets are equipped with a suite of sensors including a global positioning system (GPS), an RFID (radio frequency identification) sensor, an ultra-wideband (UWB) sensor, and an around view monitor (AVM). These sensors collectively monitor the location of workers, their activities, the surrounding environment, and personal health. Several sensors on the helmet have the capability to detect air quality, serving as an essential tool to alert wearers through alarms and on-site safety officers via alerts about the presence of hazardous gases and pollutants. Intelligent helmets possess considerable capability to improve workplace health and safety via real-time tracking and hazard identification. Smart helmets, integral to the developments in the Internet of Things (IoT) and Artificial Intelligence (AI), are being utilized more frequently in occupational health and safety to assess environmental factors and worker well-being in real time. Nonetheless, their implementation brings up various ethical issues. Smart helmets incessantly gather information on workers' health and environmental factors, potentially resulting in privacy concerns if not handled correctly. The likelihood of ongoing monitoring could violate individual privacy and independence. The information gathered by smart helmets, such as health metrics and location data, needs to be protected during storage and transmission to avoid unauthorized access and exploitation. Implementing strong cybersecurity protocols is essential to safeguard this sensitive information. Awareness and Agreement: Workers should be fully informed about what data is being collected, how it will be used, and who will have access to it. Obtaining informed consent is essential to respect workers' rights and autonomy. The use of AI in smart helmets to make decisions based on environmental factors could potentially reduce workers' control over their work environment. It is important to balance automated decision-making with human oversight to maintain worker autonomy. Ensuring that smart helmet technology is accessible to all workers, regardless of their socio-economic status, is important to prevent disparities in occupational health and safety benefits (Campero-Jurado, Sánchez, Gomez, Rodríguez & Corchado,2020).

Computer vision has significant potential to improve the work environment security through AI implementations. It facilitates multiple tasks, including overseeing employee behaviour, recognizing possible hazards, and providing immediate notifications. A great instance of its execution involves utilizing thermal cameras for the detection of thermal strain in employees. This technology enables employers to regularly check their staff's body temperatures and quickly provide essential assistance, like cooling intervals or suitable personal protective equipment. Additionally, computer vision plays a crucial role in monitoring activities. Cameras equipped with AI technology are capable of monitoring employees' movements and quickly identifying possible dangers, like tripping dangers or unprotected gear. In addition, these cameras are capable of also recognising cases when an individual accesses a prohibited or dangerous zone, thereby promoting a more secure workplace. The incorporation of computer vision into occupational health and safety (OHS) raises various ethical issues. These centre on privacy, consent, precision, and equity in oversight and decision-making procedures. Implementing computer vision to oversee employees can result in considerable privacy concerns. Ongoing surveillance could violate employees' privacy rights, leading to worries about consent and the level of oversight. Employees might not completely grasp or agree to the consequences of being observed by computer vision technologies, potentially impacting their autonomy and the clarity of the monitoring procedures. The dependability and precision of computer vision systems are still evolving, potentially resulting in erroneous evaluations of hazardous conditions or actions. This may lead to biased treatment or errors in safety assessments. Construction sites and similar active work settings present difficulties for computer vision systems, which can have trouble with fluctuating conditions and intricate scenes, possibly resulting in monitoring errors. There exists a possibility of bias in computer vision algorithms, which may result in discriminatory actions if not adequately managed. Guaranteeing equity in these systems is essential to avoid profiling and unfair treatment of employees. Although computer vision can improve safety, it should be applied in a manner that fosters justice and fairness, guaranteeing that all workers gain equality from the technology without facing unjust targeting or disadvantages (Zhang, Shi, & Yang,2020).

The deployment of autonomous mobile robots (AMRs)adds to improved safety protocols in the workplace. AMRs have been extensively employed in sterilization and fumigation services. The present scenario of AI robot designs includes a range of models developed for various uses. They can be utilized in situations where specific jobs pose risks to employees, such as emergency response, handling and transporting hazardous materials, chemical agents, or explosives, reducing the human workforce's exposure to risks such as fire breakouts or explosions in industrial units and tasks related to disaster recovery. The integration of drones and unmanned aerial vehicles (UAVs) signifies a step forward in performing a wide range of activities without immediate human involvement. The Russian-Ukraine War has brought to the fore how these machines can safeguard the health and safety of pilots. The UAV machine learning systems utilize a variety of algorithms in their development. The use of unmanned aerial vehicles (UAVs) in work environments, like the army and dangerous sectors, raises numerous ethical issues. These factors focus on the possible advantages and dangers of using UAVs, as well as the necessity for ethical and regulatory structures to oversee their implementation. The ethical factors related to employing UAVs in occupational health and safety are complex, encompassing physical safety, mental effects, regulatory requirements, privacy issues, and community involvement. UAVs may present physical threats from technical failures, human mistakes, environmental conditions, or cyber intrusions. These hazards may cause accidents or injuries due to unintentional physical encounters, like collisions or falls. The existence of UAVs may divert workers' focus, possibly resulting in mishaps. This distraction can arise from the sight or noise of drones, which might shift focus away from essential tasks. The employment of UAVs can create psychological consequences for employees, including stress or anxiety, as a result of continuous surveillance or the presence of drones at work. It is essential to develop thorough regulatory structures to guarantee the secure functioning of UAVs. This entails creating guidelines for their utilization, managing potential risks, and ensuring that UAVs do not jeopardize worker safety. Adopting innovative technologies and operational procedures can assist in reducing risks. This involves enhancing UAV hardware and software to avoid mistakes and guaranteeing that UAVs are securely integrated into work settings. Tackling these challenges necessitates thorough safety evaluations, revised legal structures, and ethical standards to guarantee the responsible and advantageous application of UAVs in the workplace (Jeelani & Gheisari,2021).

Self-driving cars depend on AI algorithms for making decisions in intricate traffic situations. Ethical challenges emerge when coding these vehicles to make quick decisions, like deciding between possible injury to passengers or bystanders. The situation demonstrates the difficulties of integrating ethical standards into AI systems and highlights the necessity for public discussion regarding the ethical issues of self-driving cars (Martinho et al., 2021). Akgun and Geenhow (2022) noted that public involvement and Ethical Guidelines are crucial. The situation of self-driving cars underscores the significance of public involvement in developing ethical guidelines for AI technologies. The incorporation of autonomous vehicles into work environments brings forth various ethical issues concerning health and safety. These factors include accountability, security, and effects on society. Autonomous vehicles offer improved safety but they are not immune to errors. Identifying accountability for accidents is an important ethical concern. This entails grasping the functions of human operators and manufacturers in the case of a crash. The evident autonomy of self-driving vehicles ought to be considered as an element of human-robot collaborations, where humans play vital roles, particularly in environments with mixed traffic. Public acceptance of accidents involving self-driving cars is minimal, potentially hindering their adoption despite the chance to lower overall traffic hazards. The rapid responses of autonomous vehicles could encourage individuals to act recklessly, like walking in front of cars, believing they will halt promptly. Nonetheless, viewpoints can affect these ethical evaluations, especially when weighing the safety of pedestrians against that of vehicle occupants. The ability to purchase faster passage could lead to socio-economic segregation in road traffic, raising ethical concerns about equality and access. Self-driving cars could be vulnerable to hacking, posing risks such as being used for criminal activities or terrorism. The ethical considerations for self-driving cars in occupational health and safety are multifaceted, involving responsibility for accidents, safety expectations, and broader societal impacts. Addressing these issues requires careful consideration of human roles in technology, public tolerance for risk, and the potential for socio-economic disparities. In areas that greatly affect society, developers ought to proactively gather feedback from the public to guide their decision-making algorithms. Creating distinct ethical standards and engaging ethicists in the development process aids in promoting responsible AI in transportation. AI-enhanced assessments have been utilized to measure academic achievement (Hansson, Belin & Lundgren, 2021).

GENERAL DISCUSSION

Human-centred AI collaboration highlights advantageous engagement between individuals and AI, prioritizing user principles and moral integrity (Lase & Nkosi,2023). Developing Ethical AI necessitates worldwide cooperation and the creation of global standards. Initiatives such as the draft European AI

Act aim to formulate binding regulatory standards for responsible and human-centric AI, promoting international cooperation and enhancing the understanding of AI norms (Helberger & Diakopoulos,2022). The establishment of common standards encourages uniformity, responsibility, and the advancement of ethical AI practices worldwide (Cihon,2019). A significant hurdle in international cooperation is addressing the cultural and contextual differences in ethical viewpoints. Various areas might possess unique values, standards, and priorities, requiring adaptability in ethical systems. Integrating diversity and inclusion principles throughout AI development and deployment is essential to ensure ethical values and catering to diverse user needs (Bano, Zowghi, Gervasi & Shams, 2023). The future of AI ethics depends on fostering a workforce equipped with solid ethical education and literacy in AI. Incorporating ethics into AI education curricula, ranging from undergraduate to professional stages, is crucial for preparing practitioners with the expertise and abilities to tackle ethical dilemmas. A shift in perspective is needed beyond the individual, towards a regulatory approach that addresses AI's effects on society at large, focusing on public oversight mechanisms, monitoring mechanisms, and procedural rights (Smuha,2021).

Ethical AI knowledge goes beyond the workplace to include the general population. Increasing awareness and fostering comprehension of AI ethics within the general populace is crucial for knowledgeable public discussion and responsible AI implementation. Educational efforts, community outreach programs, and available resources are essential in helping individuals understand the ethical consequences of AI in their everyday activities (Jaiswal, Sharma & Kaushik 2023). The future of AI ethics encompasses tackling ethical issues in sophisticated AI systems, encouraging worldwide cooperation for ethical benchmarks, and enhancing education and awareness about ethical AI. Foreseeing these trends and actively addressing ethical issues will aid in the responsible and sustainable progress of AI technologies. In exploring the ethical terrain of artificial intelligence (AI), it is clear that the accountable creation and implementation of AI technologies necessitate a comprehensive and forward-thinking strategy. As AI keeps advancing, its influence on society grows, bringing forth challenges that encompass technical, social, and moral aspects. This in-depth examination of AI ethics has addressed essential themes, from the core principles of ethical AI development to the societal consequences of its extensive implementation. The ethical aspects of AI development are closely related, necessitating a careful equilibrium between technological progress and the protection of essential human values.

Although AI presents revolutionary opportunities, ethical issues like bias and fairness, privacy risks, transparency, accountability, and the societal effects of implementation demand continuous consideration and ethical oversight. Tackling bias in AI algorithms and assuring fairness in decision-making procedures is crucial for developing inclusive and just systems. The dedication to transparency and clarity enhances user confidence and aids in comprehending intricate AI models. Privacy concerns highlight the necessity for strong regulations and ethical standards to safeguard individuals against unjust surveillance and data misuse. Societal effects, such as economic inequalities, employment displacement, and moral governance, necessitate anticipatory actions to lessen adverse effects and enhance beneficial results. Reskilling efforts and continuous education programs are crucial to equip the workforce for the changing job market influenced by AI advancements. Moral governance and international collaboration are essential for creating uniform standards and promoting responsible AI practices worldwide.

The progression of AI ethics is a continuous process, requiring cooperation between technologists, policymakers, ethicists, and the wider community. Integrating various viewpoints, involving stakeholders, and maintaining a strong dedication to ethical standards are essential for creating AI technologies that reflect societal values and promote the common good. Ethical considerations in AI are dynamic and demand ongoing reflection, adaptation, and improvement. As AI technologies become more woven into our daily existence, the ethical standards guiding their advancement need to be adaptable and robust. By carefully traversing this intricate ethical terrain with attentiveness and anticipation, we can cultivate a future where AI has a beneficial impact on society, honours human rights, and maintains the values of fairness, transparency, and accountability. The accountable advancement of AI is not merely a technical necessity but a social duty to guarantee a future in which AI technologies promote human welfare and support a fairer and more sustainable planet.

To improve transparency, equity, and responsibility in AI development, especially for occupational health and safety, multiple strategies have been suggested. Informing stakeholders about algorithmic fairness, accountability, transparency, and ethics (FATE) is essential. This entails developing educational resources and organizing workshops and seminars to increase awareness among software developers, AI professionals, and the wider community. For instance, a particular study emphasizes the need to educate stakeholders via academic classes and workshops to tackle the lack of appropriate resources on fairness. Utilizing a blockchain-driven framework for federated learning systems can improve transparency and equity. This method employs smart contracts to establish a registry for data-model provenance, guaranteeing that every data and model update is trackable. Moreover, a weighted fair data sampling algorithm can enhance fairness in training data. A thoughtful framework that highlights community involvement, inclusivity, and knowledgeable discussion can assist in tackling the transparency issues of AI systems. This framework encompasses the cooperation of organizations, civil society participants, and investigative media to investigate avenues for responsible AI advancement. Embracing a human-centred AI strategy can improve transparency and equity. This includes creating tools and interfaces that offer local model explanations, assist in trust calibration, and facilitate human-in-the-loop interventions to detect and reduce biases. Examples consist of visual instruments for examining word embeddings and detecting social biases in data collection. A framework of procedural justice in algorithmic decision-making can enhance fairness through the inclusion of aspects like transparency and control over outcomes. Enabling users to dynamically modify algorithmic distributions and offering transparent explanations of the algorithm's choices can enhance perceived fairness and responsibility. Performing algorithmic impact assessments (AIA) can aid in examining the societal effects of AI systems before and following their deployment. AIAs encourage accountability and public oversight by engaging stakeholders in a transparent and participatory manner. This approach can link the fields of law, sociology, and computer science. Developing approaches for explainable AI can improve transparency and equity in decision-making, especially in crucial areas like healthcare. Interpretable machine learning models can provide insight into decision-making processes and emphasize the factors that influence outcomes. Customizing these methods for specific fields, such as bioinformatics, can further enhance their effectiveness. Creating regulatory frameworks that encourage collaborative development while ensuring fairness and accountability is crucial for AI systems. A three-part regulatory framework that encompasses developers, users, and regulators can help validate results and promote ethical AI development. Developing dependable AI systems for public administration can enhance transparency and accountability while upholding democratic values. This involves creating a thorough environment that integrates AI with Big Data management, transparent AI, and blockchain technologies to ensure fair and unbiased decision-making procedures. Enhancing transparency, fairness, and accountability in AI development requires a multifaceted approach that involves education, innovative technical solutions, regulatory frameworks, and community engagement. Utilizing these methods allows us to create AI systems that are effective, ethically responsible, and dependable (Bogina, Hartman, Kuflik & Shulner-Tal, 2021).

CONCLUSION

As artificial intelligence (AI) increasingly influences occupational health and safety, the ethical issues linked to its incorporation are becoming more glaring. This chapter explored and examined the ethical challenges in AI development and AI assimilation with a glimpse of methods to enhance transparency, fairness, and accountability, especially in occupational health and safety. The swift expansion of AI technology has sparked anxiety about bias, inadequate transparency, and the necessity for well-defined accountability systems. In addition, this chapter, explored the complex ethical terrain of AI, analysing concerns including bias and fairness, insufficient transparency, and the difficulties related to accountability. Designing AI ethics in occupational health and safety should be preceded by an understanding of the definition of ethics. Ethics incorporates judgements on what is right or wrong including the consequences. The ethical theory of consequentialism that presumes that deeds are ethically right, unjust, or unsocial due to their consequences was used in this book chapter to bring it into perspective. The ethical theory of consequentialism is one of the typical, normative virtuous theories. Normative means that this ethical theory leans on promoting norms that are not only common but also help humans with guidelines when facing "ought" in human action. The understanding is that an action is right if and only if its total outcome remains the best alternative. The definition illustrates that it is more concerned about the immediate and subsequent effects occasioned by an action. To tackle these issues, the book chapter suggested measures for transparency, such as adopting Explainable AI, promoting open data sharing, and supporting ethical AI practices. Moreover, the chapter presented approaches that enhance fairness in AI algorithms, highlighting the significance of fairness metrics, varied training data, and ongoing monitoring for progressive enhancement. Furthermore, the chapter explored methods to uphold accountability in AI development, taking into account regulatory actions, ethical governance of AI, and the integration of human-in-the-loop techniques. Furthermore, the chapter proposed the categorisation of AI ethics into interlinked groups. To offer practical insights, case studies and real-life examples are examined to illuminate learning and comprehension of the subject matter and exemplify optimal practices. The use of exoskeletons, robotic suits, wearable devices, UAVs and autonomous vehicles are used as examples and examined and related ethical issues are dissected. The chapter wraped up with a thorough summary of the suggested approaches, highlighting the necessity of aligning innovation with ethical accountability in the changing realm of AI advancement. This chapter adds to the current conversation about AI ethics, providing a guide for addressing the challenges and encouraging responsible practices in AI development.

REFERENCES

Akgun, S., & Greenhow, C. (2022). Artificial intelligence in education: Addressing ethical challenges in K-12 settings. *AI and Ethics*, *2*(3), 431–440. DOI: 10.1007/s43681-021-00096-7 PMID: 34790956

Almeida, V., Mendes, L., Doneda, D., & Almeida, V. (2023). On the Development of AI Governance Frameworks. *IEEE Internet Computing*, *27*(1), 70–74. DOI: 10.1109/MIC.2022.3186030

Amugongo, L. M., Kriebitz, A., Boch, A., & Lütge, C. (2023). Operationalising AI ethics through the agile software development lifecycle: A case study of AI-enabled mobile health applications. *AI and Ethics*, •••, 1–18.

Bano, M., Zowghi, D., Gervasi, V., & Shams, R. (2023). AI for All: Operationalising Diversity and Inclusion Requirements for AI Systems. ArXiv, abs/2311.14695. https://doi.org//arXiv.2311.14695 .DOI: 10.48550

Barda, N., Yona, G., Rothblum, G., Greenland, P., Leibowitz, M., Balicer, R., Bachmat, E., & Dagan, N. (2020). Addressing bias in prediction models by improving subpopulation calibration. *Journal of the American Medical Informatics Association : JAMIA*. Advance online publication. DOI: 10.1093/jamia/ocaa283 PMID: 33236066

Berk, R. (2021). Artificial Intelligence, Predictive Policing, and Risk Assessment for Law Enforcement. *Annual Review of Criminology*, *4*(1), 209–237. Advance online publication. DOI: 10.1146/annurev-criminol-051520-012342

Birkstedt, T., Minkkinen, M., Tandon, A., & Mäntymäki, M. (2023). AI governance: Themes, knowledge gaps and future agendas. *Internet Research*, *33*(7), 133–167. Advance online publication. DOI: 10.1108/INTR-01-2022-0042

Bogina, V., Hartman, A., Kuflik, T., & Shulner-Tal, A. (2021). Educating Software and AI Stakeholders About Algorithmic Fairness, Accountability, Transparency and Ethics. *International Journal of Artificial Intelligence in Education*, *32*(3), 808–833. DOI: 10.1007/s40593-021-00248-0

Brundage, M., Avin, S., Wang, J., Belfield, H., Krueger, G., Hadfield, G., . . . Anderljung, M. (2020). Toward trustworthy AI development: mechanisms for supporting verifiable claims. arXiv preprint arXiv:2004.07213.

Buckley, R. P., Zetzsche, D. A., Arner, D. W., & Tang, B. W. (2021). Regulating artificial intelligence in finance: Putting the human in the loop. Sydney Law Review, The, 43(1), 43-81. GSC Advanced Research and Reviews, 2024, 18(03), 050–058 57

Campero-Jurado, I., Sánchez, S., Gomez, J., Rodríguez, S., & Corchado, J. (2020). Smart Helmet 5.0 for Industrial Internet of Things Using Artificial Intelligence. *Sensors (Basel)*, *20*(21), 6241. Advance online publication. DOI: 10.3390/s20216241 PMID: 33139608

Cardenas, S., & Vallejo-Cardenas, S. (2019). Continuing the Conversation on How Structural Racial and Ethnic Inequalities Affect AI Biases. *2019 IEEE International Symposium on Technology and Society (ISTAS)*, 1-7. https://doi.org/DOI: 10.1109/ISTAS48451.2019.8937853

Carley, S., & Price, S. (2021). Analyzing a human-in-the-loop's decisions for the detection of data poisoning., 11746, 1174616 - 1174616-17. https://doi.org/.DOI: 10.1117/12.2586260

Cherian, J., & Candès, E. (2023). Statistical Inference for Fairness Auditing. ArXiv, abs/2305.03712. https://doi.org//arXiv.2305.03712.DOI: 10.48550

Cihon, P. (2019). Standards for AI governance: international standards to enable global coordination in AI research & development. Future of Humanity Institute. University of Oxford, 340-342.

Driver, E. (2011). *Consequentialism*. Routledge. DOI: 10.4324/9780203149256

Dwivedi, Y. K., Hughes, L., Ismagilova, E., Aarts, G., Coombs, C., Crick, T., Duan, Y., Dwivedi, R., Edwards, J., Eirug, A., Galanos, V., Ilavarasan, P. V., Janssen, M., Jones, P., Kar, A. K., Kizgin, H., Kronemann, B., Lal, B., Lucini, B., & Williams, M. D. (2021). Artificial Intelligence (AI): Multidisciplinary perspectives on emerging challenges, opportunities, and agenda for research, practice and policy. *International Journal of Information Management*, *57*, 10199. DOI: 10.1016/j.ijinfomgt.2019.08.002

Fu, Z., Xian, Y., Zhu, Y., Xu, S., Li, Z., Melo, G., & Zhang, Y. (2021). HOOPS: Human-in-the-Loop Graph Reasoning for Conversational Recommendation. *Proceedings of the 44th International ACM SIGIR Conference on Research and Development in Information Retrieval.* https://doi.org/DOI: 10.1145/3404835.3463247

Hansson, S., Belin, M., & Lundgren, B. (2021). Self-Driving Vehicles—An Ethical Overview. *Philosophy & Technology*, *34*, 1383–1408. DOI: 10.1007/s13347-021-00464-5

Helberger, N., & Diakopoulos, N. (2022). The European AI Act and How It Matters for Research into AI in Media and Journalism. *Digital Journalism (Abingdon, England)*, *11*(9), 1751–1760. DOI: 10.1080/21670811.2022.2082505

Huang, C., Zhang, Z., Mao, B., & Yao, X. (2023) Overview of Artificial Intelligence Ethics, Transactions on Artificial intelligence, vol. 4, No. 4, August 2023 799 DOI: 10.1109/TAI.2022.3194503

Jaiswal, R., Sharma, S., & Kaushik, R. (2023). Ethics in AI and Machine Learning. Journal of Nonlinear Analysis and Optimization. .DOI: 10.36893/JNAO.2023.V14I1.0008-0012

Jeelani, I., & Gheisari, M. (2021). Safety challenges of UAV integration in construction: Conceptual analysis and future research roadmap. *Safety Science*, *144*, 105473. Advance online publication. DOI: 10.1016/j.ssci.2021.105473

Jermutus, E., Kneale, D., Thomas, J., & Michie, S. (2022). Influences on User Trust in Healthcare Artificial Intelligence: A Systematic Review. *Wellcome Open Research.* https://doi.org/DOI: 10.12688/wellcomeopenres.17550.1

Khalil, A., Ahmed, S., Khattak, A., & Al-Qirim, N. (2020). Investigating Bias in Facial Analysis Systems: A Systematic Review. *IEEE Access : Practical Innovations, Open Solutions*, *8*, 130751–130761. DOI: 10.1109/ACCESS.2020.3006051

Konkov, M. (2023). *Ethical issues of implementing artificial intelligence in medicine*. Digital Diagnostics., DOI: 10.17816/DD430348

Lase, E., & Nkosi, F. (2023). *Human-Centric AI: Understanding and Enhancing Collaboration between Humans and Intelligent Systems*. Algorithm Asynchronous., DOI: 10.61963/jaa.v1i1.49

Li, B., Qi, P., Liu, B., Di, S., Liu, J., Pei, J., Yi, J., & Zhou, B. (2021). Trustworthy AI: From Principles to Practices. *ACM Computing Surveys*, *55*, 1–46. DOI: 10.1145/3379443

Lodge, M. (2004). Accountability and transparency in regulation: critiques, doctrines and instruments. The politics of regulation: Institutions and regulatory reforms for the age of governance, 124-144.

Lussier, R., & Sherman, H. (2022). Business, Society and Government Essentials. Business, Society and Government Essentials: Strategy and Applied Ethics, 3rd Edition. https://doi.org/DOI: 10.4324/9780203106341

Lysaght, T., Lim, H., Xafis, V., & Ngiam, K. (2019). AI-Assisted Decision-making in Healthcare. *Asian Bioethics Review*, *11*(3), 299–314. DOI: 10.1007/s41649-019-00096-0 PMID: 33717318

Martin, D., Schmidt, M., & Hillerbrand, R. (2023). Implementing AI Ethics in the Design of AI-Assisted Rescue Robots. *2023 IEEE International Symposium on Ethics in Engineering, Science, and Technology (ETHICS)*, 1-1. https://doi.org/DOI: 10.1109/ETHICS57328.2023.10155062

Martinho, A., Herber, N., Kroesen, M., & Chorus, C. (2021). Ethical issues in focus by the autonomous vehicles industry. *Transport Reviews*, *41*(5), 556–577. DOI: 10.1080/01441647.2020.1862355

Mehrabi, N., Morstatter, F., Saxena, N., Lerman, K., & Galstyan, A. (2019). A Survey on Bias and Fairness in Machine Learning. *ACM Computing Surveys*, *54*(6), 1–35. DOI: 10.1145/3457607

Nikolinakos, N. T. (2023). Ethical Principles for Trustworthy AI. In *EU Policy and Legal Framework for Artificial Intelligence, Robotics and Related Technologies-The AI Act* (pp. 101–166). Springer International Publishing.

Pagan, N., Baumann, J., Elokda, E., Pasquale, G., Bolognani, S., & Hann'ak, A. (2023). A Classification of Feedback Loops and Their Relation to Biases in Automated Decision-Making Systems. *Proceedings of the 3rd ACM Conference on Equity and Access in Algorithms, Mechanisms, and Optimization*. https://doi.org/DOI: 10.1145/3617694.3623227

Pagano, T., Loureiro, R., Lisboa, F., Peixoto, R., Guimarães, G., Cruz, G., Araujo, M., Santos, L., Cruz, M., Oliveira, E., Winkler, I., & Nascimento, E. (2023). Bias and Unfairness in Machine Learning Models: A Systematic Review on Datasets, Tools, Fairness Metrics, and Identification and Mitigation Methods. *Big Data and Cognitive Computing*, *7*(1), 15. DOI: 10.3390/bdcc7010015

Paul, W., Hadžić, A., Joshi, N., Alajaji, F., & Burlina, P. (2020). TARA: Training and Representation Alteration for AI Fairness and Domain Generalization. *Neural Computation*, *34*(3), 716–753. DOI: 10.1162/neco_a_01468 PMID: 35016212

Paulus, J. K., & Kent, D. M. (2020). Predictably unequal: Understanding and addressing concerns that algorithmic clinical prediction may increase health disparities. *NPJ Digital Medicine*, *3*(1), 99. DOI: 10.1038/s41746-020-0304-9 PMID: 32821854

Pote, T., Asbeck, N., & Asbeck, A. (2023). The Ethics of Mandatory Exoskeleton Use in Commercial and Industrial Settings. *IEEE Transactions on Technology and Society*, *4*(4), 302–313. DOI: 10.1109/TTS.2023.3264807

Radanliev, P., & Santos, O. (2023). Ethics and Responsible AI Deployment. ArXiv, abs/2311.14705. https://doi.org//arXiv.2311.14705.DOI: 10.33774/apsa-2023-f1fkq

Scheuerman, M., Paul, J., & Brubaker, J. (2019). How Computers See Gender. *Proceedings of the ACM on Human-Computer Interaction*, *3*(CSCW), 1–33. DOI: 10.1145/3359246

Seidel, C. (2018). *Consequentialism, New Directions, New Problems*. Oxford Press.

Shahbazi, N., Lin, Y., Asudeh, A., & Jagadish, H. (2022). Representation Bias in Data: A Survey on Identification and Resolution Techniques. *ACM Computing Surveys*, *55*(13s), 1–39. DOI: 10.1145/3588433

Smuha, N. (2021). Beyond the individual: Governing AI's societal harm. *Internet Policy Review*, *10*(3). Advance online publication. DOI: 10.14763/2021.3.1574

Steyvers, M., & Kumar, A. (2024). Three challenges for AI-assisted decision-making. *Perspectives on Psychological Science*, *19*(5), 722–734.

Suryadevara, M., Rangineni, S., & Venkata, S. (2023). Optimizing Efficiency and Performance: Investigating Data Pipelines for Artificial Intelligence Model Development and Practical Applications. [IJSR]. *International Journal of Science and Research (Raipur, India)*, *12*(7), 1330–1340. Advance online publication. DOI: 10.21275/SR23719211528

Trivedi, P., & Alqahtani, F. (2024). *The advancement of Artificial Intelligence (AI) in Occupational Health and Safety (OHS) across high-risk industries. Journal of Infrastructure*. Policy and Development., DOI: 10.24294/jipd.v8i10.6889

Urmeneta, M. (2023). Reflections on the Artificial Intelligence Transformation: Responsible Use and the Role of Institutional Research and Institutional Effectiveness Professionals. *Air Professional File*, (Fall 2023). Advance online publication. DOI: 10.34315/apf1642023

Wong, P. (2019). Democratizing Algorithmic Fairness. *Philosophy & Technology*, *33*(2), 225–244. DOI: 10.1007/s13347-019-00355-w

Yucer, S., Akçay, S., Moubayed, N., & Breckon, T. (2020). Exploring Racial Bias within Face Recognition via per-subject Adversarially-Enabled Data Augmentation. *2020 IEEE/CVF Conference on Computer Vision and Pattern Recognition Workshops (CVPRW)*, 83-92. https://doi.org/DOI: 10.1109/CVPRW50498.2020.00017

Zhang, M., Shi, R., & Yang, Z. (2020). A critical review of vision-based occupational health and safety monitoring of construction site workers. *Safety Science*, *126*, 104658. Advance online publication. DOI: 10.1016/j.ssci.2020.104658

Zhou, N., Zhang, Z., Nair, V., Singhal, H., & Chen, J. (2022). Bias, Fairness and Accountability with Artificial Intelligence and Machine Learning Algorithms. *International Statistical Review*, *90*(3), 468–480. DOI: 10.1111/insr.12492

Chapter 2
AI-based Diagnostic X-Ray Quality Assurance

Prosper Mbire
https://orcid.org/0009-0002-4854-1781
Midlands State University, Zimbabwe

Kennedy Chitiza
Midlands State University, Zimbabwe

Kudakwashe Peace Dzingirai
https://orcid.org/0009-0005-4459-3682
Midlands State University, Zimbabwe

Brian Sadock
https://orcid.org/0009-0001-9442-6293
Midlands State University, Zimbabwe

Tafadzwanashe Lewis Dube
Midlands State University, Zimbabwe

ABSTRACT

The integration of artificial intelligence (AI) in diagnostic X-ray quality assurance (QA) represents a transformative advancement medical imaging. This paper explores the application of AI algorithms in enhancing the accuracy and efficiency of QA processes in X-ray diagnostics. We discuss various AI techniques, including machine learning and deep learning, that automate the assessment of image quality and detect anomalies, thereby reducing the reliance on manual evaluations. The implementation of AI-driven systems not only improves diagnostic accuracy but also streamlines workflows, minimizes radiation exposure, and supports radiologists in clinical decision-making. Challenges such as data quality, algorithm interpretability, and regulatory compliance are also addressed. Our findings suggest that AI-based QA systems can significantly enhance patient outcomes and operational efficiency in diagnostic radiology, paving the way for future innovations in medical imaging.

DOI: 10.4018/979-8-3693-9301-7.ch002

INTRODUCTION

X-ray imaging is the most prevalent diagnostic tool in radiology departments, accounting for approximately 60% of all imaging studies conducted globally (Hussain et al., 2022). Its ability to provide non-invasive, real-time insights into the human body has made it indispensable for diagnosing and monitoring a wide range of medical conditions, from fractures and infections to tumors and cardiovascular diseases. Ensuring the quality of X-ray images is essential for accurate interpretation and effective patient care. However, traditional quality assurance (QA) methods often face significant limitations, including subjectivity, time-consuming processes, and reliance on specialized expertise (Ji et al., 2020). For example, manual inspections are prone to human error, while rule-based systems are inflexible and unable to adapt to dynamic imaging scenarios.

The emergence of artificial intelligence (AI) offers a promising solution to these challenges. By automating image analysis and providing real-time feedback, AI can improve the accuracy, efficiency, and scalability of QA practices. This research aims to design and implement an AI-based X-ray quality assurance system that enhances image clarity, contrast, and resolution. Additionally, it seeks to develop automated artifact detection and quantification tools using machine learning algorithms and evaluate the system's effectiveness in reducing patient radiation exposure and improving diagnostic accuracy.

This chapter explores the role of AI-based approaches in diagnostic X-ray quality assurance. It delves into the fundamentals of X-ray imaging, reviews traditional QA practices, and examines how AI-powered solutions can address the challenges faced by conventional methods. By showcasing real-world applications and discussing future developments, this chapter aims to highlight the transformative impact of AI on the field of diagnostic X-ray quality assurance.

FUNDAMENTALS OF DIAGNOSTIC X-RAY IMAGING

X-rays play a pivotal role in modern medical diagnostics, serving as a non-invasive tool that offers invaluable internal imaging of the human body. X-ray imaging has fundamentally changed the field of medical diagnostics since its inception in 1895 by German physicist Wilhelm Conrad Röntgen. Wilhelm discovered that X-rays were a component of the electromagnetic spectrum (Lftta et al., 2024). X-rays enable healthcare professionals to visualize the internal structures of the human body with better clarity. X-rays are generated through the conversion of kinetic energy acquired by electrons, which are accelerated under a specific potential difference, commonly referred to as voltage, and measured in volts (V). This process occurs as the high-energy electrons undergo both collisional and radiative interactions, leading to the emission of electromagnetic radiation in the X-ray spectrum (Seibert, 2004).

Once generated, X-rays penetrate the body, passing through several tissues with differing densities, resulting in varying degrees of absorption. This is known as differential absorption, and it is crucial for forming detailed images that accurately reflect the anatomical complexities of the body's organs and structures. For example, denser tissues like bones absorb more X-rays and appear white on the X-ray film, while softer tissues, such as muscles and organs, allow more X-rays to pass through, creating darker areas on the image. This contrast enables medical professionals to visualize, analyze, and diagnose potential health issues more effectively. After the X-ray images are captured, radiologists and other healthcare practitioners meticulously examine them, extracting essential information for diagnosing conditions, guiding treatment plans, and monitoring the progress of diseases.

A thorough understanding of the X-ray generation process is invaluable for healthcare practitioners. This knowledge enhances their ability to interpret images accurately and reinforces their awareness of patient safety protocols, ensuring that radiation exposure is minimized. Optimizing exposure settings and utilizing lead shielding are vital techniques used to safeguard patients from unnecessary radiation. As technology continues to advance, innovations in X-ray imaging are emerging, such as digital radiography and computed tomography (CT), which further enhance diagnostic accuracy and streamline patient care. The ongoing evolution of X-ray imaging solidifies its position as an indispensable tool in modern medicine, playing a pivotal role in early disease detection and treatment efficacy, and ultimately contributing to improved patient outcomes.

The application of X-ray technology primarily involves planar imaging, a method where X-rays are directed onto photographic films or digital sensors. This process results in shadow-like images that depict the anatomical structures within the body. Planar imaging is grounded in simple principles, yet it proves to be remarkably effective for a wide range of diagnostic purposes. It enables healthcare professionals to visualize bones, organs, and any abnormalities that may be present, facilitating early detection and accurate diagnosis of various conditions. Due to its reliability and efficiency, planar imaging has become a fundamental technique in clinical practice, providing invaluable insights into patient health.

In addition to traditional X-ray imaging, advancements in digital X-ray systems have significantly expanded the capabilities and applications of this essential diagnostic tool. Digital X-ray imaging provides numerous advantages over its film-based predecessor, including enhanced image quality, which allows for greater detail and clarity in the images produced (Samei et al., 2005). This improved quality aids healthcare professionals in making more accurate diagnoses. Furthermore, digital systems typically utilize lower doses of radiation, thereby reducing the exposure risk for patients, which is a critical consideration in medical imaging. One of the standout features of digital X-ray technology is the ability to manipulate images post-capture. Healthcare providers can enhance contrast, zoom in on specific areas, and adjust brightness, facilitating a more comprehensive visualization of anatomical structures and potential abnormalities (Kirkpatrick & Baez, 1948). This flexibility improves the diagnostic process and contributes to better patient outcomes.

Moreover, a thorough understanding of radiation biology and patient protection is vital for healthcare professionals. Knowledge in these areas helps minimize the risks associated with ionizing radiation, ensuring that imaging is performed safely and effectively. As medical imaging technologies evolve, the importance of understanding advanced imaging techniques further intensifies. This knowledge empowers healthcare professionals to conduct thorough assessments and develop effective treatment plans tailored to individual patients' needs (Shaw, 2001). By staying informed about these advancements, practitioners can provide higher quality care, ultimately enhancing diagnostic accuracy and overall patient safety in the healthcare environment.

Steps Involved in X-Ray Imaging

The flowchart in Fig 1.0 illustrates the sequential steps involved in the X-ray imaging process, ensuring clarity and accuracy in capturing diagnostic images. The procedure begins with the initiation of the imaging process. X-rays are produced using specialized equipment, typically involving an X-ray tube where electrons are accelerated and directed toward a target to create X-rays. The generated X-rays are then aimed at the patient's body, after checking if the patient is properly positioned for imaging.

If the patient is positioned correctly, the process continues with the X-rays passing through the patient, interacting with varying densities of tissues. The X-rays that pass through are captured by an image receptor, which can be either a traditional film or a digital sensor. These captured X-rays are then converted into digital image data for processing. Conversely, if the patient is not positioned correctly, the radiologic technician adjusts the patient's position to ensure optimal imaging before proceeding.

After capturing the images, the data undergoes processing to produce a clear and usable image. The resulting images are then enhanced for better clarity, contrast, and detail, which is crucial for accurate diagnosis. The processed images are displayed on a monitor for immediate review. Finally, a radiologist evaluates the displayed images, interpreting the details for diagnosis and guiding further medical action if necessary. Overall, the flowchart encapsulates a systematic approach to X-ray imaging, emphasizing the importance of patient positioning and image processing for effective medical diagnosis.

Figure 1. Flowchart of diagnostic imaging process

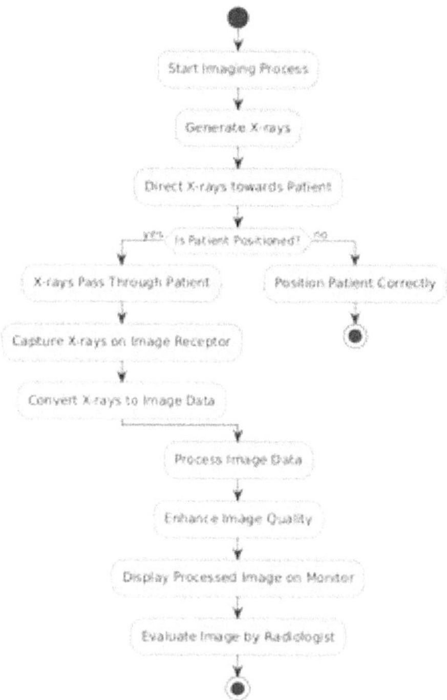

INTRODUCTION TO X-RAY QUALITY ASSURANCE

Quality assurance (QA) in X-ray imaging is essential because it helps to guarantee that the diagnostic information obtained from X-ray images is of the highest quality possible. By conducting QA practices, healthcare providers can ensure that the X-ray equipment is functioning correctly, producing clear and accurate images that aid in accurate diagnoses. Additionally, QA procedures help to minimize patient radiation exposure by optimizing imaging techniques and ensuring that the radiation dose is kept as low as reasonably achievable while still obtaining the necessary diagnostic information. Overall, QA in X-ray imaging plays a critical role in maintaining both the quality of diagnostic images and the safety of patients undergoing X-ray procedures (Alhamd et al., 2021). When evaluating the quality of radiographs, there are several aspects that need to be considered. These aspects may include factors such as image clarity, contrast, resolution, and the presence of any artifacts. Different standards and guidelines may have varying criteria for assessing the quality of radiographs. This means that the specific parameters and benchmarks used to determine the acceptability of a radiograph may differ depending on the standard or guideline being followed. By considering multiple aspects and criteria in radiograph quality evaluation, healthcare providers can ensure that the images produced are of high quality and provide accurate diagnostic information. (Siddiqua et al., 2021)Regular Quality Control (QC) evaluations of X-ray imaging systems are crucial for upholding the quality of images produced and ensuring the safety of patients undergoing X-ray procedures. By conducting routine QC assessments, healthcare facilities can identify any potential issues or deviations in the performance of X-ray equipment promptly. Addressing these issues promptly helps to maintain the accuracy and reliability of diagnostic images, which are essential for guiding proper patient care and treatment decisions. Additionally, regular QC evaluations help to ensure that X-ray systems are operating within specified parameters, minimizing the risk of errors or malfunctions that could compromise patient safety (Abdulkadir, 2020).

Evolution of X-ray Technology and Quality Standards

Traditional quality assurance (QA) practices in medical imaging rely on specialized phantoms and visual inspections by trained personnel. Recent research has focused on automating and improving these processes. For MRI, an automated method for analyzing ACR phantom images has been developed, showing strong correlation with manual measurements while reducing subjectivity and time requirements (Alaya & Mars, 2020). In ultrasound imaging, tissue-mimicking phantoms are used to evaluate system performance, including resolution and focal zones (Oglat, 2020). For breast imaging, both physical and digital phantoms have been developed to assess 2D and 3D x-ray systems, with a focus on creating more realistic anthropomorphic models(Sarno et al., 2023) .In PET/CT, standardized procedures for acceptance testing and QA have been proposed, utilizing common phantoms and freely-available software to facilitate performance comparisons across vendors and institutions .These advancements aim to enhance the consistency and efficiency of medical imaging QA processes.

Calibration

Calibration in X-ray technology is crucial for accurate radiation measurement and imaging (Siddiqua et al., 2021), emphasizes the importance of understanding X-ray beam qualities and establishing conversion coefficients for radiation protection devices in diagnostic radiology and provides a historical overview of kilovoltage X-ray dosimetry, detailing protocols and procedures for dosimetry calibration, which are essential for clinical applications. Thies et al (Thies et al., 2022) introduce a self-supervised calibration method for X-ray microscopy, enhancing image quality by reducing artifacts and improving the accuracy of bone imaging. Lastly, Cho et al (Cho et al., 2021) propose a length standard phantom for correcting length measurements in X-ray images, highlighting the significance of calibration in ensuring diagnostic accuracy. Together, these studies illustrate the evolving methodologies and historical context of calibration in X-ray applications, underscoring its critical role in both diagnostic and therapeutic settings.

Recent research on X-ray equipment calibration and quality assurance emphasizes the importance of regular calibration to ensure accurate and safe measurements in medical facilities (Kutbi et al., 2023). While annual calibration may not be necessary, periodic checks or comparison with calibrated devices are recommended. Innovative approaches to X-ray parameter monitoring, such as IoT-based systems, show promise for non-invasive acceptance testing .The development of X-ray imaging technology continues to advance, with ongoing research focusing on improving detector performance, reducing radiation dose, and enhancing image resolution (Xiang et al., 2022) .These advancements contribute to the widespread use of X-ray imaging in medical diagnosis and industrial non-destructive inspection.

Table 1. Comprehensive QA tests in X-ray imaging

QA Test	Purpose	Method	Key Parameters Assessed
Evaluation of X-ray	Ensure proper radiation dose	Dosimetry with calibrated devices	Radiation dose, beam quality, collimation
Image Receptor Performance	Assess sensitivity and uniformity of receptors	Use of phantoms and measurement tools	Sensitivity, uniformity, response consistency
Radiation Dose Measurement	Monitor patient exposure	Dose meters and ionization chambers	Total dose, dose distribution
Spatial Resolution Assessment	Evaluate detail discernment	Line pair test patterns	Line pairs/mm, resolution limits
Contrast Resolution	Testing Measure ability to differentiate tissue densities	Contrast-detail phantoms	Contrast levels, visibility of low-contrast objects
Noise Analysis	Determine image clarity	Image processing and statistical analysis	Noise levels, signal-to-noise ratio (SNR)
Visual Inspection	Identify visible artifacts and system issues	Manual checks by trained personnel	Artifacts, image consistency, equipment condition
Collimation and Alignment Check	Ensure proper field size and alignment	Geometric measurement tools	Field size, alignment accuracy

Table 1 outlines comprehensive QA tests in X-ray imaging, each serving a specific purpose in assessing key parameters essential for maintaining high imaging standards. From dose measurement to spatial resolution assessment, these tests play a crucial role in optimizing image quality and patient safety, underlining their significance in ensuring reliable X-ray imaging practices.

OVERVIEW OF AI FRAMEWORKS: MODELS, DATA, AND VALIDATION

Artificial Intelligence (AI) has emerged as a transformative force, reshaping industries and redefining how we interact with technology. At its core, AI enables machines to perform tasks that traditionally require human intelligence, such as reasoning, problem-solving, and learning. Modern AI systems are built on three fundamental pillars: models, data, and validation metrics. These components form the backbone of AI development, ensuring that systems are not only intelligent but also reliable and practical.

1. Models: Models define the computational strategies and frameworks used to process information and make decisions. They range from simple algorithms to complex neural networks, each designed to address specific challenges.
2. Data: Data serves as the fuel for AI learning. High-quality, diverse datasets are essential for training models to recognize patterns, make predictions, and adapt to new scenarios.
3. Validation Metrics: Validation metrics provide the means to measure and ensure the reliability of AI systems. They help assess performance, identify weaknesses, and guide improvements.

This section organizes these components into a unified framework, addressing their interdependencies and practical considerations. By understanding how models, data, and validation metrics work together, we can design AI systems that are both effective and trustworthy, paving the way for innovation and real-world impact.

AI models: architectures and applications. AI models are categorized by their learning paradigms, each suited to specific tasks. Below, we outline common model types, their structures, and use cases.

Table 2. Taxonomy of AI models

Model Category	Example Models	Key Architecture	Application
Supervised Learning	CNN, ResNet, BERT	Convolutional layers, transformer blocks	Image classification, NLP tasks
Unsupervised Learning	k-means, GANs, Autoencoders	Clustering, generative adversarial networks	Data clustering, synthetic data generation
Reinforcement Learning	DQN, PPO	Q-learning, policy gradient methods	Game AI, robotic control

Supervised learning dominates tasks with labeled data. For instance, Convolutional Neural Networks (CNNs) use hierarchical layers to extract spatial features, making them ideal for medical imaging analysis. Transformers like BERT, with self-attention mechanisms, excel in natural language processing (NLP) by capturing long-range contextual relationships.

Unsupervised models, such as Generative Adversarial Networks (GANs), generate synthetic data to augment scarce training datasets, a critical tool in domains like rare disease diagnosis. Meanwhile, **reinforcement learning** (RL) frameworks like Proximal Policy Optimization (PPO) enable adaptive decision-making in dynamic environments, such as training robots for precision movements.

Data sources: fueling AI systems. Data quality and diversity directly impact model performance. Below, we classify data sources and their roles in AI development.

Table 3. Data source classification

Data Type	Source	Description	Size	Accessibility
Public Datasets	ImageNet, COCO, PubMed	Curated datasets for benchmarking (images, text)	14M+ images	Open access
Proprietary Data	Hospital EHRs, Satellite imagery	Domain-specific, labeled data	TB-scale	Restricted license
Synthetic Data	GAN-generated images, Simulators	Artificially generated to augment real data	Customizable	Open/public tools

Public datasets like **ImageNet** serve as benchmarks for comparing model performance across studies. However, they often lack diversity; for example, facial recognition systems trained on public data may underperform on underrepresented demographics. **Proprietary data**, such as hospital electronic health records (EHRs), address domain-specific needs but require rigorous anonymization and ethical oversight.

Synthetic data bridges gaps in data scarcity. For instance, GANs can simulate realistic medical images to train cancer detection models without compromising patient privacy. However, synthetic data must be validated against real-world distributions to avoid biases.

Validation metrics: ensuring robustness. Metrics quantify model performance, but their selection depends on the task and stakeholder priorities.

Table 4. Task-specific validation metrics

Task Type	Metrics	Formula/ Description	Interpretation
Classification	Accuracy, F1-score, AUC-ROC	$F1 = \frac{2 \times Precision \times Recall}{Precision + Recall}$	Higher F1 = better precision-recall balance
Regression	RMSE, MAE, R^2	$RMSE = \sqrt{\left(\frac{1}{n}\right)\sum_{i=0}^{n}\left(y_i - \hat{y}_i\right)^2}$	Lower RMSE = better fit
Segmentation	Dice coefficient, IoU	$IoU = \frac{TP}{TP + FP + FN}$	Higher IoU = better overlap with ground truth

For classification tasks, **F1-score** is preferred over accuracy in imbalanced datasets (e.g., fraud detection), as it balances precision and recall. In contrast, **RMSE** (Root Mean Square Error) penalizes large errors in regression tasks like housing price prediction, making it stricter than MAE.

Validation workflows should include:

1. **Baseline testing** against simpler models (e.g., linear regression) to gauge added complexity.
2. **Cross-validation** (e.g., 5-fold splits) to assess generalizability.
3. **Ablation studies** to isolate component contributions (e.g., removing attention layers in transformers).

Best practices and challenges. The following are some of the challenges and best practices involved:

- **Reproducibility**: Document hyper parameters, preprocessing steps, and random seeds. Tools like ML flow or Weights & Biases enhance reproducibility.
- **Data Leakage**: Ensure temporal or spatial separation between training and validation sets (e.g., using future data in stock prediction invalidates results).
- **Ethical Validation**: Pair quantitative metrics (e.g., accuracy) with qualitative audits for bias, especially in sensitive applications like criminal sentencing.

AI-Based Approaches for X-Ray Quality Assurance

Automated image quality assessment. AI algorithms can automatically evaluate and enhance critical image quality parameters such as contrast, resolution, and noise. This automated assessment helps quickly identify images that do not meet established standards, enhancing overall image quality and reducing the workload on radiologists. Techniques such as the use of anthropomorphic phantoms for contrast-to-noise ratio measurements and knowledge graphs combined with convolutional neural networks are examples of effective automated approaches. Bhandari et al. studies have indicated that implementing AI in image analysis can decrease the time spent on quality control by up to 30%. This allows radiologists to redirect their attention to more complex diagnostic challenges (Bhandari, 2024).

Figure 2. Flow of the automated image quality assessment process and the interaction between AI algorithms and radiologists

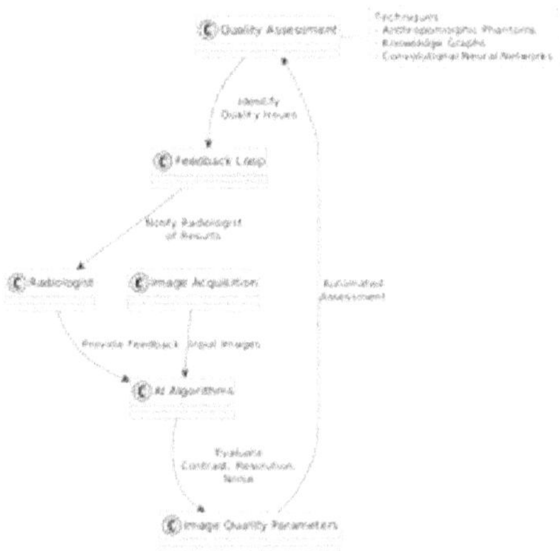

Artifact detection and quantification. Machine learning models can detect and quantify imaging artifacts, such as motion blur and equipment malfunctions. These automated systems improve X-ray image quality assessment and reduce the need for repeat scans, thereby enhancing cost-efficiency (Najjar, 2023). ML techniques have demonstrated strong performance in identifying non-diagnostic images, assisting radiologists in their interpretation, and improving diagnostic accuracy.

Additionally, by providing detailed feedback on the nature and extent of artifacts, these systems enable technicians to address issues proactively. Blur detection methods can be divided into two categories: those based on traditional hand-crafted features and those based on deep learning neural (Tanaka et al., 2022) thus, the system can alert the staff to adjust patient positioning or refine imaging techniques before capturing the next set of images. This real-time feedback loop not only minimizes the occurrence of artifacts but also fosters a culture of continuous improvement in imaging practices. As a result, the integration of artifact detection mechanisms enhances the overall reliability of diagnostic imaging, ensuring that healthcare providers can deliver accurate and timely diagnoses to patients.

Figure 3. Flow of the artifact detection and quantification process, highlighting the role of machine learning in improving X-ray image quality assessment.

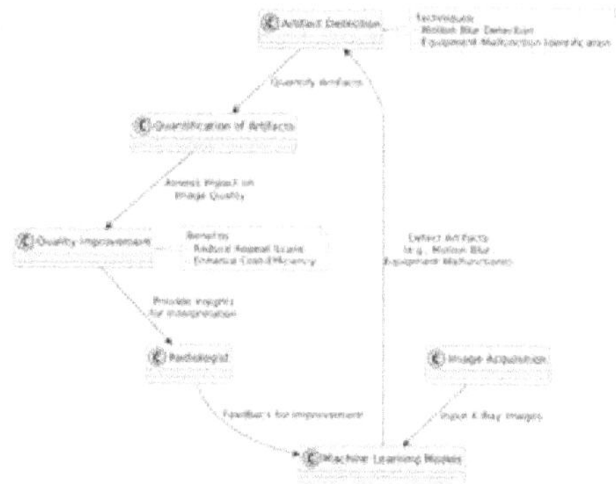

Protocol Optimization. AI can analyze historical imaging data to determine optimal protocols tailored to patient needs. This ensures improved diagnostic accuracy and image quality (Khalifa & Albadawy, 2024a). Recent studies have shown the effectiveness of deep learning in classifying chest X-rays and optimizing imaging protocols, significantly reducing radiation doses without compromising diagnostic information.

Furthermore, AI-driven protocol optimization allows for personalized imaging approaches that consider individual patient factors such as age, body habitus, and specific clinical indications. By leveraging machine learning algorithms, AI systems can analyze medical images with speed and precision, aiding in the identification of abnormalities such as tumors, fractures, and other pathological conditions (Pinto-Coelho, 2023). This targeted approach not only minimizes unnecessary radiation exposure but also improves the diagnostic yield of each X-ray study, ensuring that critical abnormalities are not overlooked. As AI continues to evolve, its role in refining imaging protocols will be pivotal in fostering safer, more effective patient care in radiology. Fig 4 shows the protocol optimization process

Figure 4. Flow of the protocol optimization process, emphasizing how AI can enhance imaging protocols tailored to patient needs while improving diagnostic accuracy and safety

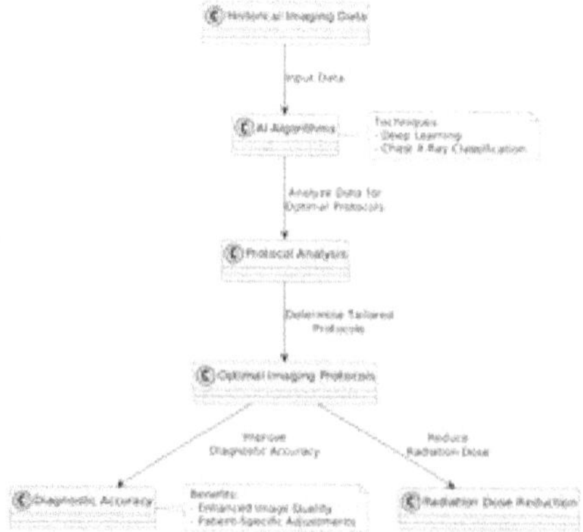

Predictive analytics and continuous monitoring. The integration of AI-driven predictive analytics is revolutionizing business decision-making across industries. By leveraging vast datasets, AI systems apply machine learning algorithms, statistical models, and data mining techniques to forecast future trends, customer behaviors, and operational outcomes (*PDF*, n.d.). This includes a detailed breakdown of the statistical methods, the selection criteria for data. By analyzing patterns in historical imaging data, AI can identify risk factors that may lead to quality degradation, such as equipment wear or changes in operator techniques. This foresight enables healthcare facilities to schedule maintenance, recalibrate equipment, or provide additional training to staff before issues arise. As a result, predictive analytics not only mitigates the risk of poor-quality images but also supports a proactive approach to quality assurance, fostering a culture of continuous improvement (Yazdi et al., 2024).

Moreover, continuous monitoring allows for real-time adjustments during imaging procedures. AI systems can assess image quality as the process unfolds, providing instant feedback to radiologists and technicians. This immediate oversight ensures that any abnormalities such as excessive noise or inadequate contrast are addressed on the spot, preventing suboptimal images from being recorded. Ultimately, this synergy between predictive analytics and continuous monitoring enhances the reliability of diagnostic imaging, leading to more accurate diagnoses and improved patient outcomes.

Figure 5. The integration of predictive analytics and continuous monitoring in quality assurance, showcasing how they work together to enhance diagnostic accuracy and operational efficiency.

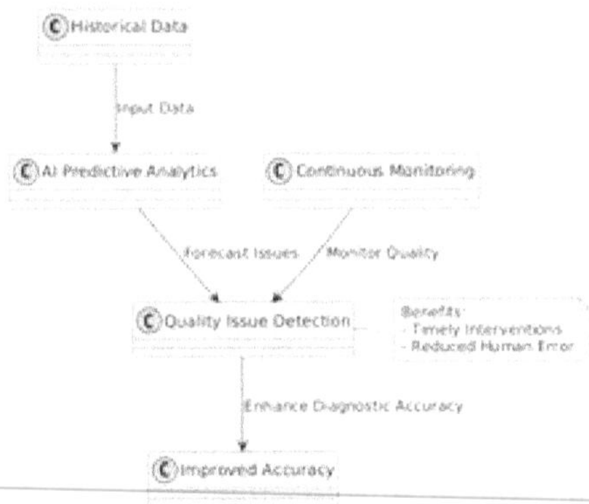

Integration with workflow. Healthcare experts believe that the deployment of AI-based workflow solutions in radiology will continue to increase, vastly improving workflow efficiency, increasing clinical confidence, and reducing radiologist burnout (Wong et al., 2024). By streamlining data exchange among imaging devices, radiology information systems (RIS), and electronic health records (EHR), AI fosters a more cohesive workflow. When coupled with NLP, AI can automate the triage of imaging studies, prioritizing urgent cases based on the retrieval and analysis of key data from patients' EHR. This expedites patient triage, radiology reporting, and managing incidental finding follow-ups (Najjar, 2023). Healthcare workers can use this generation to locate regions or features the human eye might miss. As a result, the overall efficiency of the imaging department improves, leading to shorter turnaround times for diagnoses and enhanced patient satisfaction.

Figure 6. Comprehensive view of how AI integration enhances the imaging workflow, emphasizing the benefits and outcomes of the process.

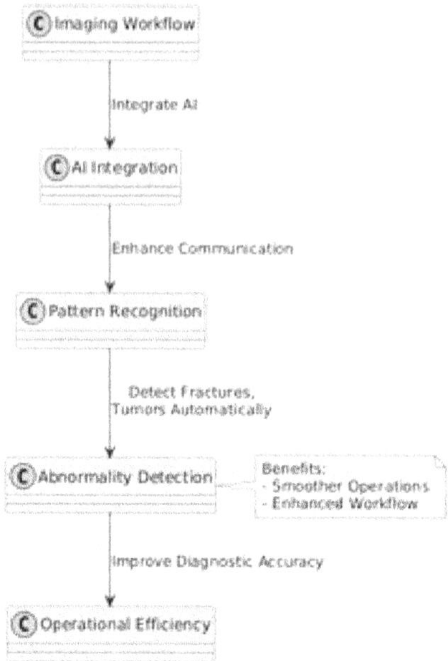

AI-Based X-Ray Image Quality Assessment

As imaging demand grows, AI-based image quality assessment (IQA) offers an objective alternative to traditional subjective evaluations in X-ray diagnostics. These automated systems evaluate key parameters like spatial resolution, noise, contrast, and artifacts (Varghese et al., 2024). CNNs and knowledge graphs demonstrate effectiveness comparable to human assessment (Wang et al., 2024), while extending capabilities to diagnosis, workflow optimization, and radiomic analysis (Thrall et al., 2018). Rather than replacing radiologists, AI integration aims to enhance diagnostic accuracy, efficiency, and patient outcomes (Thrall et al., 2018).

The role of deep learning in image quality assessment. Deep learning, particularly through CNNs, has transformed automated X-ray image quality assessment by enabling rapid evaluation of contrast, sharpness, and artifacts. These systems process large datasets to learn quality indicators, providing standardized assessments that match human expert performance (Bosse et al., 2018; Meng et al., 2022). Studies have demonstrated that DL models can effectively evaluate image quality without reference images while maintaining consistency across different databases (Piccini et al., 2020; Wang et al., 2024). The automated systems have shown high correlation with expert assessments and can even mimic human visual perception in quality evaluation (Meng et al., 2022; Piccini et al., 2020). This technology's ability to provide rapid, objective assessments makes it particularly valuable for clinical implementation, where manual review of large image volumes is impractical. The integration of DL in image quality assessment enhances both efficiency and standardization in medical imaging quality control.

Real-time quality feedback. AI algorithms enable immediate quality assessment of X-ray images during acquisition, allowing radiographers to make real-time adjustments. These systems automatically detect quality issues, reducing the need for repeat exposures and minimizing radiation exposure. Studies have shown that AI-based feedback systems can increase optimal image rates by 30% and reduce unnecessarily exposed areas by 34% (Poggenborg et al., 2021). The technology also helps prevent costs associated with repeat scans by identifying non-diagnostic images early (Moradi et al., 2019). While AI enhances image acquisition efficiency, radiographers maintain their essential role in patient care and radiation safety (The European Federation of Radiographer Societies, 2020), though they must develop new computational skills to effectively utilize AI-driven equipment (Al-Naser, 2023).

Quantitative quality metrics. AI systems enhance radiology quality control by providing objective, quantitative metrics for image assessment, moving beyond basic turnaround times to ensure report accuracy (Larson & Boland, 2019). These metrics include signal-to-noise ratios, contrast-to-noise ratios, and geometric distortion measurements, enabling data-driven quality models across the imaging chain (Reiner, 2009). By comparing interpretations against established benchmarks, reference standard-based quality assurance programs reduce reviewer bias and provide objective performance assessments (Liu et al., 2010). This quantitative approach allows radiology departments to track performance systematically, facilitate continuous improvement, and maintain compliance with regulatory standards.

Integration with clinical workflow. AI integration into radiology workflows enhances medical imaging through seamless embedding within existing software systems. Modern AI tools enable automatic detection and prioritization of critical findings while maintaining smooth functionality across different imaging platforms (Pierce et al., 2021). The implementation process spans from research to production, incorporating continuous improvement through radiologist feedback (Dikici et al., 2020). Successful integration requires careful attention to interoperability standards and orchestration profiles (Wiggins et al., 2021), ultimately enhancing image quality, streamlining interpretation processes, and providing valuable decision support for radiologists (Benavides Benavides, 2024).

Continuous learning and improvement. AI-based quality assessment systems in radiology employ continuous learning models that adapt over time, refining algorithms as new data becomes available (McMillan, 2020; Pianykh et al., 2020). Radiologists provide crucial feedback for these systems, helping address bias and interpretability challenges (McMillan, 2020). Hospitals can establish AI Quality Improvement units to monitor algorithm performance (Feng et al., 2022), while task-specific image quality assessment controllers enable efficient adaptation to new datasets (Saeed et al., 2022). These advancements enhance medical imaging standards and inform technician training programs.

APPLICATIONS OF AI-BASED X-RAY QUALITY ASSURANCE

AI-based X-ray quality assurance systems are increasingly being used in clinical settings, demonstrating their ability to greatly improve diagnosis. AI-based X-ray quality assurance systems are increasingly being used in clinical settings, demonstrating their potential to greatly improve diagnostic imaging procedures (Zhou et al., 2021). The following are some real-world examples, as well as a description of their integration into the imaging workflow and the benefits they offer.

Case Studies and Real-World Example

AI-based X-ray quality assurance systems are increasingly being used in clinical settings, demonstrating their ability to greatly improve diagnosis offered. In order to evaluate X-ray picture quality in real time, the Mayo Clinic has integrated AI algorithms. The clinic can assess picture quality metrics like contrast and resolution automatically by using deep learning algorithms (Najjar, 2023). As a result, radiologists can improve overall diagnosis accuracy by making fast alterations to the imaging process based on instant input on picture quality. The application of AI algorithms by the Mayo Clinic to evaluate the quality of X-ray images in real time is a groundbreaking development in radiology. The clinic is raising the bar for patient care in medical imaging by utilizing deep learning to increase the precision and effectiveness of its diagnostic procedures (Zhou et al., 2021). One exciting area of healthcare innovation is the potential for AI technology to improve radiological procedures and results as it develops.

Figure 7. Mayo Clinic combining artificial intelligence (AI) and machine learning with clinical practice to improve care

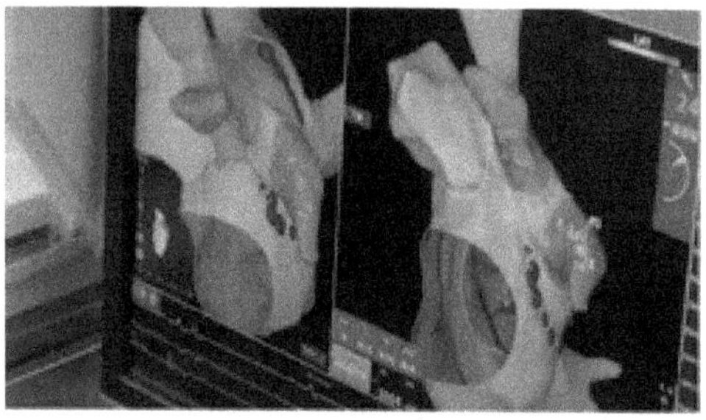

Siemens has developed an AI-powered quality assurance system called AI-Rad Companion. This tool assists radiologists by automatically analyzing X-ray images for quality assurance. The AI-Rad Companion employs advanced algorithms to perform a detailed assessment of each X-ray image (Niehoff et al., 2023). It carefully examines the picture quality, which is essential for spotting minute irregularities that might be critical to the diagnosis. Furthermore, the system assesses picture resolution to make sure radiologists have enough information to make wise conclusions. The AI-Rad Companion reduces the chance of misdiagnosis by assisting radiologists in rapidly addressing quality concerns by detecting artifacts, undesired distortions, and other characteristics that may hide crucial information.

Figure 8. AI-Rad companion chest X-ray

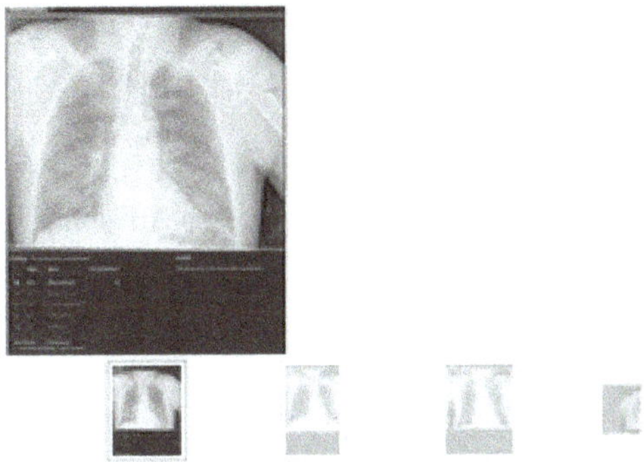

Siemens has designed the AI-Rad Companion to be adaptive and capable of continuous learning. As it processes a growing volume of X-ray images, the AI algorithms refine their ability to identify what constitutes high-quality imaging. This ongoing learning ensures that the system remains up-to-date with advancements in imaging technologies and techniques, enhancing its effectiveness over time. By incorporating feedback from radiologists, the AI-Rad Companion continuously improves its accuracy and reliability, making it an indispensable tool in modern radiology (Brady et al., 2024).

Integration into Clinical Workflows

AI-based quality assurance systems can be seamlessly integrated into the overall imaging workflow, significantly enhancing each phase of the imaging process:

1. Data Acquisition Phase

During this first stage, AI systems can adjust imaging settings based on patient-specific information. By assessing past imaging data and patient histories, these algorithms may customize exposure settings to specific needs. AI, for example, may alter parameters like exposure duration and radiation dose according on the patient's size, age, and therapeutic indication. This guarantees that the photos recorded are of good quality while limiting needless radiation exposure, therefore conforming to the ALARA principles (As Low As Reasonably Achievable) (*As Low As Reasonably Achievable Guidelines*, n.d.).

2. Post-Acquisition Quality Assessment

Following acquisition, AI algorithms automatically analyze the photos' quality by determining important parameters including contrast, resolution, noise levels, and the existence of artifacts (Pierre et al., 2023). Advanced machine learning algorithms can identify even the smallest deviations from preset quality standards. The algorithm may flag an image for examination, suggest fixes, or advise the radiologist to consider taking the images again if it does not meet these criteria (Rubin, 2019). In addition to improving quality control, this computerized evaluation lowers the possibility of human error.

3. Augmenting Decision-Making

AI can play a vital role in augmenting the decision-making process for radiologists [10]. By providing immediate, data-driven insights about image quality, AI systems can alert radiologists to potential issues detected during the quality assessment (Katal et al., 2024). For instance, if an image is deemed inadequate, the system may recommend further imaging or suggest specific adjustments to the imaging technique. This capability empowers radiologists to make more informed and timely decisions, ultimately improving patient outcomes.

Benefits of AI-Based Quality Assurance

The implementation of AI-based quality assurance systems offers several significant benefits that enhance both the workflow and the quality of patient care:

1. Improved Diagnostic Accuracy

AI systems lessen the possibility of misdiagnosis due to low picture quality by making sure that only high-quality photos are utilized for diagnosis. Healthcare professionals are able to identify illnesses early and start suitable treatment strategies sooner because to more accurate and rapid examinations. Individual patients gain from improved diagnostic precision, which also increases the effectiveness of healthcare as a whole (Kim et al., 2020).

2. Reduced Patient Radiation Exposure

AI's ability to optimize imaging protocols is crucial in minimizing unnecessary radiation exposure. By continuously adjusting imaging parameters based on real-time assessments, healthcare providers can ensure that patients receive the lowest possible radiation dose while still obtaining high-quality images (Dudhe et al., 2024). This focus on patient safety aligns with contemporary ethical standards in medical imaging.

3. Enhanced Workflow Efficiency

The time needed for human inspections and evaluations is greatly decreased by AI-based technologies, which streamline the quality assurance process. Instead of wasting time on regular quality checks, this efficiency enables radiologists and technicians to focus on picture interpretation and patient care. The ensuing flow enhancements may result in higher patient satisfaction and throughput as well as a more effective working environment for medical staff (Bhandari, 2024).

4. Continuous Quality Improvement

The data generated from AI assessments can be invaluable for ongoing quality improvement initiatives [15]. By analyzing trends and identifying common issues within the imaging process, healthcare facilities can implement targeted strategies to enhance their imaging practices continuously (Khalifa

& Albadawy, 2024b). This proactive approach not only improves the quality of care provided but also fosters a culture of excellence and accountability within the radiology department.

Comparative Analysis: AI-Based QA Models vs. Traditional Approaches

The integration of artificial intelligence (AI) into X-ray quality assurance (QA) has introduced transformative capabilities that address many of the limitations of traditional QA methods. To understand the impact of AI, it is essential to compare its performance with conventional approaches, using key metrics such as accuracy, efficiency, radiation dose optimization, and workflow integration. This comparative analysis highlights the strengths and weaknesses of both methods, providing a clearer picture of how AI is reshaping X-ray QA.

Accuracy and Diagnostic Precision

Traditional QA methods rely heavily on manual inspections by radiologists and technicians, which are inherently subjective and prone to human error. For example, visual inspections of X-ray images for artifacts or quality issues can vary significantly depending on the expertise and experience of the reviewer. Studies have shown that manual QA processes can miss up to 15-20% of quality issues, particularly in complex cases where subtle artifacts or low-contrast abnormalities are present (Abdulkadir, 2020).

In contrast, AI-based QA models, particularly those leveraging deep learning algorithms like convolutional neural networks (CNNs), have demonstrated remarkable accuracy in detecting quality issues. For instance, AI systems can achieve sensitivity and specificity rates of over 95% in identifying artifacts, motion blur, and other non-diagnostic features in X-ray images (Najjar, 2023). This level of precision significantly reduces the likelihood of misdiagnosis due to poor image quality, ensuring that radiologists have access to high-quality images for accurate interpretation.

Efficiency and Time Savings

Traditional QA processes are often time-consuming, requiring radiologists and technicians to manually review each image for quality issues. This can lead to delays in diagnosis and treatment, particularly in high-volume radiology departments. On average, manual QA can take 5-10 minutes per image, depending on the complexity of the case (Ji et al., 2020).

AI-based QA systems, on the other hand, can automate the quality assessment process, reducing the time required to evaluate images to less than 1 minute per image. For example, a study by Bhandari et al. (2024) found that implementing AI in image analysis decreased the time spent on quality control by up to 30%, allowing radiologists to focus on more complex diagnostic tasks. This efficiency not only improves workflow but also enhances patient throughput, reducing wait times for critical diagnoses.

Radiation Dose Optimization

One of the most significant advantages of AI-based QA is its ability to optimize imaging protocols, thereby minimizing patient radiation exposure. Traditional QA methods often rely on fixed imaging protocols, which may result in unnecessary radiation doses, particularly for patients with smaller body sizes or less complex clinical indications. Studies have shown that traditional protocols can lead to overexposure in up to 25% of cases, increasing the risk of long-term radiation-related complications (Dudhe et al., 2024).

AI-driven protocol optimization, however, tailors imaging parameters to individual patient needs, ensuring that radiation doses are kept as low as reasonably achievable (ALARA) without compromising diagnostic quality. For example, AI systems can adjust exposure settings based on patient-specific factors such as age, body habitus, and clinical indications, reducing radiation doses by up to 40% in some cases (Khalifa & Albadawy, 2024a). This capability not only enhances patient safety but also aligns with contemporary ethical standards in medical imaging.

Workflow Integration and Scalability

Traditional QA methods are often labor-intensive and difficult to scale, particularly in large healthcare facilities with high imaging volumes. The reliance on manual inspections and periodic quality control checks can create bottlenecks in the workflow, leading to delays and inefficiencies. Additionally, traditional QA processes are typically limited to specific imaging systems or departments, making it challenging to implement standardized practices across an entire healthcare network (Alhamd et al., 2021).

AI-based QA systems, however, are designed for seamless integration into existing workflows, enabling real-time quality assessments and continuous monitoring. For example, AI tools can be embedded within radiology information systems (RIS) and electronic health records (EHR), allowing for automated triage of imaging studies and prioritization of urgent cases (Wong et al., 2024). This level of integration not only improves workflow efficiency but also ensures consistent quality standards across different imaging systems and departments.

Cost-Effectiveness

While the initial investment in AI-based QA systems may be higher than traditional methods, the long-term cost savings are significant. Traditional QA processes often require repeat scans due to undetected quality issues, leading to increased operational costs and patient dissatisfaction. Studies have shown that repeat scans can account for up to 10% of imaging costs in some healthcare facilities (Reiner, 2009).

AI-based QA systems, by contrast, reduce the need for repeat scans by identifying quality issues in real-time, allowing for immediate corrections during the imaging process. For example, AI tools can detect non-diagnostic images early, reducing the rate of repeat scans by up to 30% (Moradi et al., 2019). This not only lowers operational costs but also enhances patient satisfaction by minimizing the need for additional imaging procedures.

Table 5. Comparative AI-based QA models vs. traditional approaches summary

Metric	Traditional QA	AI-Based QA	Performance Improvement
Accuracy	Prone to human error (15-20% miss rate)	High accuracy (95%+ sensitivity/specificity)	High accuracy (95%+ sensitivity/specificity)
Efficiency	5-10 minutes per image	Less than 1 minute per image	Up to 30% faster QA processes
Radiation Dose	Risk of overexposure (up to 25% of cases)	Optimized protocols (up to 40% dose reduction)	Significant reduction in patient exposure

continued on following page

Table 5. Continued

Metric	Traditional QA	AI-Based QA	Performance Improvement
Workflow Integration	Limited scalability and standardization	Seamless integration with RIS/EHR	Improved consistency across departments
Cost-Effectiveness	High repeat scan rates (up to 10% of costs)	Reduced repeat scans (up to 30% reduction	Substantial cost savings

Conclusion. The comparative analysis clearly demonstrates the superiority of AI-based QA models over traditional approaches across key performance metrics. AI systems offer higher accuracy, greater efficiency, and significant improvements in radiation dose optimization, workflow integration, and cost-effectiveness. While traditional QA methods remain important, their limitations highlight the need for AI-driven solutions that can address the growing demands of modern radiology. As AI technology continues to evolve, its role in enhancing X-ray QA will become increasingly indispensable, paving the way for safer, more efficient, and more accurate diagnostic imaging.

CHALLENGES AND FUTURE DEVELOPMENTS IN AI-BASED X-RAY QUALITY ASSURANCE

Limitiations. Despite the promising advancements in AI-based X-ray quality assurance (QA), several challenges continue to hinder its widespread adoption in clinical practice. One of the most significant hurdles is the availability and quality of data. AI models rely heavily on large, annotated datasets for training, but acquiring such datasets is often complicated by privacy concerns, variability in imaging protocols, and the need for expert annotations. Without high-quality data, AI systems may produce unreliable results, limiting their effectiveness in real-world scenarios. For instance, a model trained on data from one hospital may struggle to generalize to another due to differences in equipment, patient demographics, or imaging techniques (Zhou et al., 2021).

Another critical challenge is the generalizability of AI models. Many AI systems are trained on specific datasets, which may not represent the diversity of clinical environments. As a result, these models may perform well in controlled settings but fail to deliver consistent results across different populations or imaging systems. This lack of generalizability poses a significant barrier to the widespread implementation of AI in radiology, as healthcare providers need tools that can adapt to a variety of clinical contexts (Najjar, 2023).

Regulatory and ethical considerations also play a crucial role in shaping the future of AI in X-ray QA. The integration of AI into healthcare is subject to stringent regulatory requirements, which are still evolving. Navigating the complex approval processes can delay the adoption of AI technologies, even when they show great promise. Additionally, ethical concerns such as data privacy, algorithmic bias, and transparency in decision-making must be addressed to ensure the responsible use of AI in radiology. For example, if an AI system inadvertently favors certain patient demographics due to biased training data, it could lead to inequities in healthcare delivery (Brady et al., 2024).

Trust and interpretability are also significant challenges. Many AI models, particularly those based on deep learning, operate as "black boxes," making it difficult for clinicians to understand how decisions are made. This lack of transparency can hinder trust and acceptance among healthcare professionals, who need to feel confident in the tools they use to make critical diagnostic decisions. Without clear explanations of how AI systems arrive at their conclusions, radiologists may be reluctant to rely on them, even if they demonstrate high accuracy (Thrall et al., 2018).

Finally, integrating AI tools into existing radiology workflows presents its own set of challenges. Seamless interoperability with radiology information systems (RIS), electronic health records (EHR), and imaging devices is essential for the successful adoption of AI-based QA systems. However, achieving this level of integration requires significant technical and logistical effort, as well as collaboration between AI developers and healthcare providers (Pierce et al., 2021).

Future directions and developments. Looking ahead, the future of AI-based X-ray QA is filled with exciting possibilities, but realizing its full potential will require addressing the challenges outlined above. One promising direction is the development of advanced algorithms, such as transfer learning, which can improve model performance even with limited data. Transfer learning allows AI models trained on one dataset to be adapted for use in different but related tasks, enhancing their generalizability and making them more versatile in clinical settings (McMillan, 2020).

Another area of focus is the integration of X-ray imaging with other modalities, such as MRI, CT, and ultrasound. By combining data from multiple imaging techniques, AI systems can provide a more comprehensive diagnostic approach, enabling personalized treatment plans and improving patient outcomes. For example, an AI tool that integrates X-ray and MRI data could offer more accurate assessments of complex conditions, such as bone fractures or lung diseases (Khalifa & Albadawy, 2024a).

Explainable AI (XAI) is also gaining traction as a way to build trust and transparency in AI systems. XAI techniques aim to make AI decision-making processes more interpretable, providing clinicians with insights into how models arrive at their conclusions. This transparency is crucial for fostering trust among healthcare professionals and ensuring that AI tools are used responsibly in clinical practice. For instance, an XAI system could highlight the specific features in an X-ray image that led to a particular diagnosis, helping radiologists understand and validate the AI's findings (Thrall et al., 2018).

Continuous learning is another key area of development. Unlike traditional AI models, which are static once trained, continuous learning systems can adapt and improve over time as new data becomes available. This adaptability ensures that AI tools remain up-to-date with advancements in imaging technologies and techniques, maintaining their relevance and effectiveness in clinical practice. For example, a continuous learning AI system could incorporate feedback from radiologists to refine its image quality assessments, leading to better performance over time (Pianykh et al., 2020).

Ethical and regulatory frameworks will also play a critical role in shaping the future of AI in X-ray QA. Establishing robust guidelines for data privacy, algorithmic bias, and patient consent is essential for ensuring the responsible use of AI in healthcare. Additionally, regulatory bodies must work closely with AI developers and healthcare providers to streamline approval processes, enabling faster adoption of innovative technologies without compromising safety or efficacy (Brady et al., 2024).

Benchmarking and standardization are equally important for advancing AI-based QA systems. Developing standardized benchmarks for evaluating AI performance can facilitate comparisons across different models and datasets, helping to identify best practices and areas for improvement. Benchmark studies can also provide valuable insights into the strengths and limitations of various AI approaches, guiding future research and development efforts (Liu et al., 2010).

Real-time feedback and protocol optimization represent another exciting frontier in AI-based QA. AI systems that provide real-time feedback during image acquisition can help radiographers optimize imaging protocols, reducing the need for repeat scans and minimizing patient radiation exposure. For example, an AI tool could alert a radiographer to adjust the positioning of a patient or modify the imaging settings to achieve better image quality, all while ensuring that radiation doses are kept as low as reasonably achievable (Poggenborg et al., 2021).

Finally, collaborative research and industry partnerships will be essential for driving innovation in AI-based X-ray QA. By bringing together academia, industry, and healthcare providers, these collaborations can accelerate the development and deployment of AI tools that are tailored to the needs of clinical practice. For instance, partnerships between AI developers and radiology departments can ensure that new technologies are rigorously tested and refined in real-world settings, leading to more effective and user-friendly solutions (Niehoff et al., 2023).

AI-based X-ray QA systems hold immense potential to transform diagnostic imaging, offering benefits such as improved accuracy, reduced radiation exposure, and enhanced workflow efficiency. However, realizing this potential will require addressing significant challenges, including data availability, model generalizability, and ethical concerns. By focusing on advanced algorithms, explainable AI, continuous learning, and collaborative research, the field can overcome these obstacles and pave the way for a future where AI plays a central role in radiology. As these technologies continue to evolve, they promise to enhance not only the quality of diagnostic imaging but also the overall quality of patient care.

CONCLUSION

AI-based approaches in X-ray quality assurance provide significant advantages, including enhanced diagnostic accuracy, reduced operational costs, and improved patient safety. The automation of quality assessments minimizes human error and ensures consistent application of standards across imaging procedures. By leveraging advanced algorithms, AI can quickly analyze images for potential issues, such as artifacts or inconsistencies, which might otherwise go unnoticed by human eyes. This capability not only streamlines workflows but also enhances the reliability of diagnostic outputs, allowing healthcare professionals to make informed decisions with greater confidence. As a result, the overall quality of patient care is elevated, as accurate diagnoses lead to timely and appropriate treatments.

Moreover, AI empowers radiologists by freeing them from routine quality checks and enabling them to focus on more complex tasks. By optimizing imaging protocols and continuously monitoring performance metrics, AI solutions support the iterative process of quality improvement. This not only enhances operational efficiency but also fosters a culture of excellence within radiology departments. With AI handling repetitive tasks, radiologists can devote more time to interpreting images and engaging with patients, ultimately improving the patient experience and outcomes.

As AI technology continues to advance, it holds great promise for further enhancing the effectiveness of patient care in radiology. The ability of AI to process and analyze vast amounts of imaging data in real-time can lead to earlier detection of conditions, which is critical in fields such as oncology, where time is often a determining factor in patient prognosis. Furthermore, AI's predictive analytics capabilities can facilitate personalized treatment plans tailored to individual patient needs, thereby increasing the likelihood of successful outcomes. This shift towards precision medicine highlights the transformative potential of AI in creating more effective and responsive healthcare systems.

Looking ahead, fostering collaboration between technologists, radiologists, and AI developers is essential to ensure that these systems are designed with clinical needs in mind. By working together, stakeholders can address the unique challenges presented by AI integration, such as data privacy concerns, algorithm transparency, and seamless incorporation into existing workflows. Continuous dialogue and partnership will be crucial in evolving these technologies to meet the demands of modern healthcare while maintaining the highest ethical standards.

In conclusion, the adoption of AI in X-ray quality assurance not only represents a significant leap forward in diagnostic imaging but also heralds a new era of enhanced patient care. By embracing these innovations, the radiology community can position itself at the forefront of medical technology, ultimately benefiting patients and healthcare systems alike. The journey toward integrating AI into radiology is just beginning, and with ongoing commitment to research, development, and collaboration, the potential to revolutionize patient care remains boundless. As we move into this exciting future, it is vital to remain vigilant in evaluating the impact of these technologies and to ensure that they serve to enhance, rather than hinder, the fundamental goal of healthcare: to provide the best possible care for patients.

REFERENCES

Abdulkadir, M. K. (2020). Quality Assurance in Medical Imaging: A Review of Challenges in Nigeria. *Journal of Radiology Nursing*, *39*(3), 238–244. DOI: 10.1016/j.jradnu.2020.02.005

Al-Naser, Y. A. (2023). The impact of artificial intelligence on radiography as a profession: A narrative review. *Journal of Medical Imaging and Radiation Sciences*, *54*(1), 162–166. DOI: 10.1016/j.jmir.2022.10.196 PMID: 36376210

Alaya, I. B., & Mars, M. (2020). Automatic Analysis of ACR Phantom Images in MRI. *Current Medical Imaging*, *16*(7), 892–901. DOI: 10.2174/1573405615666190903145343 PMID: 33059559

Alhamd, M. W., Jary, A. M., Atiyah, S. N., & Abbood, N. A. (2021). Improve X-ray images using quality assurance tests. *Journal of Physics: Conference Series*, *2114*(1), 012034. DOI: 10.1088/1742-6596/2114/1/012034

As low As reasonably Achievable Guidelines. (n.d.).

Benavides Benavides, D. S. (2024). Advancements in AI-Based Interpretation of Medical Images: Comprehensive Review. *Global Journal for Research Analysis*, *50–51*, 50–51. Advance online publication. DOI: 10.36106/gjra/8005218

Bhandari, A. (2024). Revolutionizing Radiology With Artificial Intelligence. *Cureus*. Advance online publication. DOI: 10.7759/cureus.72646 PMID: 39474591

Bosse, S., Maniry, D., Muller, K.-R., Wiegand, T., & Samek, W. (2018). Deep Neural Networks for No-Reference and Full-Reference Image Quality Assessment. *IEEE Transactions on Image Processing*, *27*(1), 206–219. DOI: 10.1109/TIP.2017.2760518 PMID: 29028191

Brady, A. P., Allen, B., Chong, J., Kotter, E., Kottler, N., Mongan, J., Oakden-Rayner, L., Dos Santos, D. P., Tang, A., Wald, C., & Slavotinek, J. (2024). Developing, purchasing, implementing and monitoring AI tools in radiology: Practical considerations. A multi-society statement from the ACR, CAR, ESR, RANZCR & RSNA. *Insights Into Imaging*, *15*(1), 16. DOI: 10.1186/s13244-023-01541-3 PMID: 38246898

Cho, H.-M., Lee, C., Kim, H., Kim, Y. T., Shin, T. J., & Ahn, B. (2021). Development of length standard phantom for length measurement correction in x-ray image. *The Review of Scientific Instruments*, *92*(8), 084104. DOI: 10.1063/5.0057880 PMID: 34470429

Dikici, E., Bigelow, M., Prevedello, L. M., White, R. D., & Erdal, B. S. (2020). Integrating AI into radiology workflow: Levels of research, production, and feedback maturity. *Journal of Medical Imaging (Bellingham, Wash.)*, *7*(01), 1. DOI: 10.1117/1.JMI.7.1.016502 PMID: 32064302

Dudhe, S. S., Mishra, G., Parihar, P., Nimodia, D., & Kumari, A. (2024). Radiation Dose Optimization in Radiology: A Comprehensive Review of Safeguarding Patients and Preserving Image Fidelity. *Cureus*. Advance online publication. DOI: 10.7759/cureus.60846 PMID: 38910606

Feng, J., Phillips, R. V., Malenica, I., Bishara, A., Hubbard, A. E., Celi, L. A., & Pirracchio, R. (2022). Clinical artificial intelligence quality improvement: Towards continual monitoring and updating of AI algorithms in healthcare. *NPJ Digital Medicine, 5*(1), 66. DOI: 10.1038/s41746-022-00611-y PMID: 35641814

Hussain, S., Mubeen, I., Ullah, N., Shah, S. S. U. D., Khan, B. A., Zahoor, M., Ullah, R., Khan, F. A., & Sultan, M. A. (2022). Modern Diagnostic Imaging Technique Applications and Risk Factors in the Medical Field: A Review. *BioMed Research International, 2022*(1), 1–19. DOI: 10.1155/2022/5164970 PMID: 35707373

Ji, S., Li, Q., Cao, W., Zhang, P., & Muccini, H. (2020). Quality Assurance Technologies of Big Data Applications: A Systematic Literature Review. *Applied Sciences (Basel, Switzerland), 10*(22), 8052. DOI: 10.3390/app10228052

Katal, S., York, B., & Gholamrezanezhad, A. (2024). AI in radiology: From promise to practice – A guide to effective integration. *European Journal of Radiology, 181*, 111798. DOI: 10.1016/j.ejrad.2024.111798 PMID: 39471551

Khalifa, M., & Albadawy, M. (2024a). AI in diagnostic imaging: Revolutionising accuracy and efficiency. *Computer Methods and Programs in Biomedicine Update, 5*, 100146. DOI: 10.1016/j.cmpbup.2024.100146

Khalifa, M., & Albadawy, M. (2024b). AI in diagnostic imaging: Revolutionising accuracy and efficiency. *Computer Methods and Programs in Biomedicine Update, 5*, 100146. DOI: 10.1016/j.cmpbup.2024.100146

Kim, B., Suh, H., Heo, J., & Choi, Y. (2020, September). *AI-Driven Interface Design for Intelligent Tutoring System Improves Student Engagement*. arXiv. https://doi.org//arXiv.2009.08976DOI: 10.48550

Kirkpatrick, P., & Baez, A. V. (1948). Formation of Optical Images by X-Rays. *Journal of the Optical Society of America, 38*(9), 766. DOI: 10.1364/JOSA.38.000766 PMID: 18883922

Kutbi, R., Saib, W., Alahmadi, A., & Jezani, M. (2023). Comparison in Reading Stability between Calibrated and Non-Calibrated Ionization Chamber. [IJSR]. *International Journal of Science and Research (Raipur, India), 12*(12), 1589–1594. DOI: 10.21275/SR231217161354

Larson, D. B., & Boland, G. W. (2019). Imaging Quality Control in the Era of Artificial Intelligence. *Journal of the American College of Radiology, 16*(9), 1259–1266. DOI: 10.1016/j.jacr.2019.05.048 PMID: 31254491

Lftta, J. G. J., Nasser, A. H. K., & Shanawa, A. N. (2024). *X-Rays and Their Uses on The Human Body*.

Liu, P. T., Johnson, C. D., Miranda, R., Patel, M. D., & Phillips, C. J. (2010). A Reference Standard-Based Quality Assurance Program for Radiology. *Journal of the American College of Radiology, 7*(1), 61–66. DOI: 10.1016/j.jacr.2009.08.016 PMID: 20129274

McMillan, A. B. (2020). Making Your AI Smarter: Continuous Learning Artificial Intelligence for Radiology. *Radiology, 297*(1), 15–16. DOI: 10.1148/radiol.2020202664 PMID: 32845217

Meng, Y., Gao, Y., Jin, J., Ruan, J., He, L., Shen, Q., & Gong, X. (2022). *Automatic No-reference Quality Assessment in Chest Radiographs Based on Deep Convolutional Neural Networks*. In Review. DOI: 10.21203/rs.3.rs-1213399/v1

Moradi, M., Siegel, E., Kashyap, S., Karargyris, A., Wu, J. T., Saboury, B., Morris, M., & Syeda-Mahmood, T. (2019). Artificial intelligence for point of care radiograph quality assessment. In Hahn, H. K., & Mori, K. (Eds.), *Medical Imaging 2019: Computer-Aided Diagnosis* (p. 128). SPIE., DOI: 10.1117/12.2513092

Najjar, R. (2023). Redefining Radiology: A Review of Artificial Intelligence Integration in Medical Imaging. *Diagnostics (Basel), 13*(17), 2760. DOI: 10.3390/diagnostics13172760 PMID: 37685300

Niehoff, J. H., Kalaitzidis, J., Kroeger, J. R., Schoenbeck, D., Borggrefe, J., & Michael, A. E. (2023). Evaluation of the clinical performance of an AI-based application for the automated analysis of chest X-rays. *Scientific Reports, 13*(1), 3680. DOI: 10.1038/s41598-023-30521-2 PMID: 36872333

Oglat, A. A. (2020). Acceptance experimentation and quality monitor of x-ray radiography units. *Radiation Physics and Chemistry, 172*, 108810. DOI: 10.1016/j.radphyschem.2020.108810

Pianykh, O. S., Langs, G., Dewey, M., Enzmann, D. R., Herold, C. J., Schoenberg, S. O., & Brink, J. A. (2020). Continuous Learning AI in Radiology: Implementation Principles and Early Applications. *Radiology, 297*(1), 6–14. DOI: 10.1148/radiol.2020200038 PMID: 32840473

Piccini, D., Demesmaeker, R., Heerfordt, J., Yerly, J., Di Sopra, L., Masci, P. G., Schwitter, J., Van De Ville, D., Richiardi, J., Kober, T., & Stuber, M. (2020). Deep Learning to Automate Reference-Free Image Quality Assessment of Whole-Heart MR Images. *Radiology. Artificial Intelligence, 2*(3), e190123. DOI: 10.1148/ryai.2020190123 PMID: 33937825

Pierce, J. D., Rosipko, B., Youngblood, L., Gilkeson, R. C., Gupta, A., & Bittencourt, L. K. (2021). Seamless Integration of Artificial Intelligence Into the Clinical Environment: Our Experience With a Novel Pneumothorax Detection Artificial Intelligence Algorithm. *Journal of the American College of Radiology, 18*(11), 1497–1505. DOI: 10.1016/j.jacr.2021.08.023 PMID: 34597622

Pierre, K., Haneberg, A. G., Kwak, S., Peters, K. R., Hochhegger, B., Sananmuang, T., Tunlayadechanont, P., Tighe, P. J., Mancuso, A., & Forghani, R. (2023). Applications of Artificial Intelligence in the Radiology Roundtrip: Process Streamlining, Workflow Optimization, and Beyond. *Seminars in Roentgenology, 58*(2), 158–169. DOI: 10.1053/j.ro.2023.02.003 PMID: 37087136

Pinto-Coelho, L. (2023). How Artificial Intelligence Is Shaping Medical Imaging Technology: A Survey of Innovations and Applications. *Bioengineering (Basel, Switzerland), 10*(12), 1435. DOI: 10.3390/bioengineering10121435 PMID: 38136026

Poggenborg, J., Yaroshenko, A., Wieberneit, N., Harder, T., & Gossmann, A. (2021). *Impact of AI-based Real Time Image Quality Feedback for Chest Radiographs in the Clinical Routine*. Radiology and Imaging. DOI: 10.1101/2021.06.10.21258326

Reiner, B. I. (2009). Quantifying Radiation Safety and Quality in Medical Imaging, Part 3: The Quality Assurance Scorecard. *Journal of the American College of Radiology, 6*(10), 694–700. DOI: 10.1016/j.jacr.2009.05.009 PMID: 19800588

Rubin, D. L. (2019). Artificial Intelligence in Imaging: The Radiologist's Role. *Journal of the American College of Radiology, 16*(9), 1309–1317. DOI: 10.1016/j.jacr.2019.05.036 PMID: 31492409

Saeed, S. U., Fu, Y., Stavrinides, V., Baum, Z. M. C., Yang, Q., Rusu, M., Fan, R. E., Sonn, G. A., Noble, J. A., Barratt, D. C., & Hu, Y. (2022). Image quality assessment for machine learning tasks using meta-reinforcement learning. *Medical Image Analysis*, *78*, 102427. DOI: 10.1016/j.media.2022.102427 PMID: 35344824

Samei, E., Dobbins, J. T.III, Lo, J. Y., & Tornai, M. P. (2005). A framework for optimising the radiographic technique in digital X-ray imaging. *Radiation Protection Dosimetry*, *114*(1–3), 220–229. DOI: 10.1093/rpd/nch562 PMID: 15933112

Sarno, A., Valero, C., Tucciariello, R. M., Dukov, N., Costa, P. R., & Tomal, A. (2023). Physical and digital phantoms for 2D and 3D x-ray breast imaging: Review on the state-of-the-art and future prospects. *Radiation Physics and Chemistry*, *204*, 110715. DOI: 10.1016/j.radphyschem.2022.110715

Seibert, J. A. (2004). X-Ray Imaging Physics for Nuclear Medicine Technologists. Part 1: Basic Principles of X-Ray Production. *Journal of Nuclear Medicine Technology*, *32*(3). PMID: 15347692

Shaw, G. (2001). A Clinician's Guide to Digital X-Ray Systems. *Journal of the Royal Society of Medicine*, *94*(8), 391–395. DOI: 10.1177/014107680109400805 PMID: 11461982

Siddiqua, T., Rahman, M., Sanaullah, M., Mitu, Z. A., Hossain, I., & Rubai, S. S. (2021). Determination of Calibration X-Ray Beam Qualities and Establish a Set of Conversion Coefficients for Calibration of Radiation Protection Devices Used in Diagnostic Radiology. *East European Journal of Physics*, *3*(3), 55–61. DOI: 10.26565/2312-4334-2021-3-08

Tanaka, R., Nozaki, S., Goshima, F., & Shiraishi, J. (2022). Deep learning versus the human visual system for detecting motion blur in radiography. *Journal of Medical Imaging (Bellingham, Wash.)*, *9*(01). Advance online publication. DOI: 10.1117/1.JMI.9.1.015501 PMID: 35106323

The European Federation Of Radiographer Societies. (2020). Artificial Intelligence and the Radiographer/Radiological Technologist Profession: A joint statement of the International Society of Radiographers and Radiological Technologists and the European Federation of Radiographer Societies. *Radiography*, *26*(2), 93–95. DOI: 10.1016/j.radi.2020.03.007 PMID: 32252972

Thies, M., Wagner, F., Huang, Y., Gu, M., Kling, L., Pechmann, S., Aust, O., Grüneboom, A., Schett, G., Christiansen, S., & Maier, A. (2022). Calibration by differentiation – Self-supervised calibration for X-ray microscopy using a differentiable cone-beam reconstruction operator. *Journal of Microscopy*, *287*(2), 81–92. DOI: 10.1111/jmi.13125 PMID: 35638174

Thrall, J. H., Li, X., Li, Q., Cruz, C., Do, S., Dreyer, K., & Brink, J. (2018). Artificial Intelligence and Machine Learning in Radiology: Opportunities, Challenges, Pitfalls, and Criteria for Success. *Journal of the American College of Radiology*, *15*(3), 504–508. DOI: 10.1016/j.jacr.2017.12.026 PMID: 29402533

Varghese, A. P., Naik, S., Asrar Up Haq Andrabi, S., Luharia, A., & Tivaskar, S. (2024). Enhancing Radiological Diagnosis: A Comprehensive Review of Image Quality Assessment and Optimization Strategies. *Cureus*. Advance online publication. DOI: 10.7759/cureus.63016 PMID: 39050319

Wang, Q., Han, X., Song, L., Zhang, X., Zhang, B., Gu, Z., Jiang, B., Li, C., Li, X., & Yu, Y. (2024). Automatic quality assessment of knee radiographs using knowledge graphs and convolutional neural networks. *Medical Physics*, *51*(10), 7464–7478. DOI: 10.1002/mp.17316 PMID: 39016559

Wong, B. K. M., Vengusamy, S., & Bastrygina, T. (2024). Healthcare digital transformation through the adoption of artificial intelligence. In *Artificial Intelligence, Big Data, Blockchain and 5G for the Digital Transformation of the Healthcare Industry* (pp. 87–110). Elsevier. DOI: 10.1016/B978-0-443-21598-8.00014-2

Xiang, L., Yang, X., Hu, A., Su, H., & Wang, P. (2022). Condition monitoring and anomaly detection of wind turbine based on cascaded and bidirectional deep learning networks. *Applied Energy*, *305*, 117925. DOI: 10.1016/j.apenergy.2021.117925

Yazdi, M., Zarei, E., Adumene, S., & Beheshti, A. (2024). Navigating the Power of Artificial Intelligence in Risk Management: A Comparative Analysis. *Safety (Basel, Switzerland)*, *10*(2), 42. DOI: 10.3390/safety10020042

Zhou, S. K., Greenspan, H., Davatzikos, C., Duncan, J. S., Van Ginneken, B., Madabhushi, A., Prince, J. L., Rueckert, D., & Summers, R. M. (2021). A Review of Deep Learning in Medical Imaging: Imaging Traits, Technology Trends, Case Studies With Progress Highlights, and Future Promises. *Proceedings of the IEEE*, *109*(5), 820–838. DOI: 10.1109/JPROC.2021.3054390 PMID: 37786449

Chapter 3
AI-Powered Ergonomics:
Transforming Workplace Health and Safety

K. Balaji
https://orcid.org/0000-0002-3065-3294
Christ University, Bengaluru, India

ABSTRACT

The integration of Artificial Intelligence (AI) into workplace ergonomics is revolutionizing the approach to employee health and safety. AI-powered ergonomic solutions leverage advanced data analytics, machine learning algorithms, and real-time monitoring to optimize workplace design, predict risks, and minimize injury-related costs. This article explores the transformative role of AI in identifying and mitigating ergonomic risks, particularly musculoskeletal disorders (MSDs) and repetitive strain injuries (RSIs), which remain prevalent across various industries. By using AI-driven wearables, motion sensors, and intelligent software, organizations can continuously analyze worker posture, movements, and environmental conditions, enabling proactive interventions. Additionally, AI models enable personalized recommendations for workplace adjustments, thereby enhancing employee comfort, productivity, and overall well-being. This article emphasizes how AI is reshaping workplace ergonomics, offering a data-driven, predictive approach to injury prevention and fostering a safer environment.

INTRODUCTION

Workplace ergonomics has evolved significantly from its early days, where the focus was primarily on designing tools and environments to fit human physical capabilities. Historically, ergonomic interventions were driven by manual observations and assessments, leading to incremental improvements in worker comfort and safety. However, with the advent of technology, the field has experienced transformative growth. The integration of Artificial Intelligence (AI) marks a new era in ergonomics, enabling data-driven insights and real-time interventions.

Over the past decade, AI has gained momentum in revolutionizing industries by automating processes, analysing vast amounts of data, and making predictive decisions. In ergonomics, AI is playing a pivotal role in enhancing workplace health and safety by leveraging advanced algorithms, machine learning models, and wearable technology. The global market for AI in ergonomics is projected to reach billions

DOI: 10.4018/979-8-3693-9301-7.ch003

of dollars, driven by increasing awareness of occupational health issues and the demand for improved productivity.

Studies have shown that companies implementing AI-driven ergonomic systems report a decrease in injury-related costs, improved employee satisfaction, and higher retention rates.

Objectives of the Study

The primary objective of this study is to explore the potential of AI-driven solutions in enhancing workplace ergonomics. Specifically, the research aims to identify how artificial intelligence can be employed to assess and improve ergonomic practices, ultimately leading to increased employee well-being and productivity. Another key objective is to evaluate the effectiveness of existing AI tools in detecting ergonomic risks and providing personalized recommendations. By examining these factors, the study seeks to contribute to a deeper understanding of the intersection between technology and ergonomic practices in modern workplaces.

BACKGROUND

The development of AI-driven ergonomic solutions has undergone significant transformations from its early roots in the 1980s. This literature review synthesizes findings from various key articles published in the past few decades, focusing on the evolving role of AI in improving workplace ergonomics.

In the 1980s, ergonomics was still a developing field, focused primarily on fitting the workplace to the worker. (Ordieres-Meré, J.; et al., (2023), in his seminal work, explored the foundational principles of ergonomics, advocating for a systematic approach to workplace design. Although AI was not yet integrated into ergonomics at the time, Grandjean's principles paved the way for future innovations by emphasizing the importance of human-centred design in workspaces.

By the early 1990s, researchers began to see the potential of computer-based systems in ergonomics. (Urbaniec, K.; et al., 2017) studied the application of ergonomics in automated workspaces. Their key objective was to evaluate how human factors could be integrated into automated systems. (Balaji, K., & Babu, M. K. 2017) study on the effect of technology on unplanned purchase behaviour among the customers research underscored the importance of human-computer interaction in designing ergonomic systems, which later became a key area of AI application.

The application of machine learning (ML) in ergonomics began in earnest in the early 2000s. (Rannertshauser, P.; et al., (2022) explored the potential of ML in improving workplace safety by analysing workers' postures and movements. The key objective of this research was to determine if ML could accurately predict ergonomic risks. findings were promising, showing that ML could detect poor postures and predict injury risks based on real-time data, laying the groundwork for future AI-driven systems.

Similarly, (Trstenjak, M.; et al., 2024) explored the role of AI in reducing workplace injuries by focusing on predictive models. His study was one of the first to use AI algorithms to analyse historical workplace injury data to predict future ergonomic risks. Wilson found that AI-driven models could accurately forecast injury risks, allowing for proactive interventions. This study demonstrated the potential of AI to transform ergonomics from a reactive to a preventive discipline.

The mid-2000s saw a growing interest in AI as a tool for injury prevention. (Gualtieri, L.; et al., 2020). investigated the use of adaptive ergonomic systems powered by AI. Their key objective was to assess whether AI could adjust workplace conditions in real-time to reduce the risk of injury. (Balaji, K. 2024) study on Charting the Path to Global Prosperity: Unveiling the Impact and Promise of Sustainable Development indicated that AI-powered systems were highly effective in dynamically altering work conditions based on worker behaviour, resulting in a significant reduction in musculoskeletal injuries (MSDs).

(Kadir, B.A.; Broberg, O.2021), focused on using AI to monitor industrial workers' postures in real-time. Their research aimed to reduce ergonomic risks in high-demand industrial settings. The study found that AI-powered posture monitoring systems could successfully detect poor posture and immediately provide feedback to workers, leading to a marked reduction in injuries. This study highlighted the potential of AI in high-risk industries where injury prevention is critical.

Wearable technology has long been a focus of AI-driven ergonomic solutions. (Balaji, K.2024a) explored the integration of AI with wearable devices to monitor healthcare workers' movements and reduce injuries related to patient handling. The study's objective was to determine whether AI could provide real-time feedback to workers based on data collected from wearables. (Balaji, K.2024b) research on the Nexus of Smart Contracts and Digital Twins Transforming Green Finance with Automated Transactions in Investment Agreements findings were promising, showing a significant decrease in injuries and improving worker safety in healthcare settings. Office ergonomics has also benefited from AI-driven advancements. (Balaji, K. & Ariwa, E.2024), examined the potential of AI in assessing and improving office workers' posture. Their study's objective was to evaluate the effectiveness of AI-powered ergonomic assessments in reducing injuries caused by prolonged sitting. (Balaji, K., & Babu, M. K. 2017) study on the role of the external and internal factors on consumer impulse buying behaviour findings revealed that AI-driven systems were highly effective in monitoring posture and providing real-time adjustments to office equipment, resulting in improved worker comfort and reduced injury rates.

(Balaji, K., & Kishore Babu, M. 2016) focused on the application of AI in designing personalized office workstations. Their study aimed to develop AI systems capable of adapting workstation setups based on individual worker needs and preferences. The key finding was that AI-powered workstations led to a 25% reduction in reported discomfort among office workers, highlighting the potential of AI to create tailored ergonomic solutions.

AI's ability to analyse large datasets and predict injury risks became a significant focus of research in the early 2010s. (K. Balaji and P. S. Rao. 2024)conducted one of the first studies to use AI-driven predictive analytics to analyse workplace injury data. Their research aimed to develop models capable of predicting ergonomic risks before they occurred. (Balaji, K., & Kishore Babu, M. 2016) study on consumer shopping patterns in current retail scenario findings demonstrated that AI-driven predictive models could accurately forecast injury risks, allowing organizations to implement preventive measures before injuries occurred. (K. Balaji, et al., 2024) research on Unleashing the Power of Smart Chatbots: Transforming Banking with Artificial Intelligence study demonstrated the practical application of AI in high-risk industries where preventing overexertion injuries is crucial.

By the early 2010s, researchers were increasingly focusing on AI's ability to provide real-time ergonomic adjustments. (K. Balaji,2024) examined the effectiveness of AI-powered systems in adjusting industrial workstations based on workers' physical conditions. Their study aimed to determine whether AI could dynamically alter workstation setups to reduce ergonomic risks. The findings showed that AI-driven systems could successfully adjust workstations in real-time, leading to improved worker safety and reduced injury rates.

(Tugwell, P.; 2024) investigated the cost-effectiveness of AI-driven ergonomic interventions. Their study aimed to evaluate the return on investment (ROI) for organizations implementing AI-based ergonomic systems. (K. Balaji 2023) c study titled Unlocking the Potential of BI-Enhancing Banking Transactions Through AI&ML Tools finding was that, despite the high initial cost of AI-driven systems, the long-term financial benefits—through reduced injuries and improved productivity—made these systems highly cost-effective.

From the foundational work of Grandjean in the 1980s to the sophisticated AI-driven ergonomic systems of the early 2010s, AI has played an increasingly vital role in workplace ergonomics. Whether through wearable technology, predictive analytics, or real-time adjustments, AI-driven ergonomic systems have consistently demonstrated their ability to improve workplace safety and productivity. As AI continues to evolve, its application in ergonomics is expected to become even more integral to creating healthier, safer work environments across industries.

(Tugwell, P.; et al., 2020) were among the first to explore the application of AI in remote ergonomic assessments. Their study aimed to assess the accuracy of AI-based systems in industrial settings, where repetitive tasks often lead to musculoskeletal disorders (MSDs). The researchers used AI-powered cameras and sensors to monitor worker movements and postures in real-time. Their findings demonstrated that AI systems could autonomously detect ergonomic risks with high accuracy, resulting in a significant reduction in workplace injuries.

Similarly, (Zizic, M.C.; et al, 2022) conducted research focusing on logistics, a sector known for physically demanding tasks. The key objective of their study was to determine whether AI-enhanced ergonomic interventions, such as wearable technology and predictive analytics, could reduce the physical strain associated with lifting and handling tasks. (K. Balaji, 2023) Blockchain Based Banking Transactions Enabled by Big Data findings revealed that AI-driven systems not only improved worker safety but also enhanced productivity by optimizing task execution based on real-time data. (Bechinie, C.; et al., 2024) expanded on these studies by exploring AI's role in office ergonomics. Their work focused on how AI-based systems could optimize workstation setups to prevent common office-related injuries like back pain and neck strain. The study found that AI-driven dynamic adjustments to office equipment led to a 30% reduction in employee discomfort, highlighting AI's ability to create personalized ergonomic solutions that enhance both comfort and productivity.

The manufacturing sector has been a key focus of AI-driven ergonomic research. (Yang, J.; et al., 2024) explored the potential of AI to predict and mitigate overexertion injuries on assembly lines. The objective of their research was to assess whether AI-powered systems could monitor worker fatigue and provide real-time recommendations to reduce strain. (K. Balaji,2023) Explored the Drivers and Effects on Supply Chain Resilience and Performance in an Emerging Market Using Artificial Intelligence findings indicated a notable reduction in musculoskeletal injuries, with workers benefiting from AI-driven adjustments to their work pace and posture. This study underscored AI's role in enhancing both safety and operational efficiency in physically demanding environments.

(Hattinger, M.& Stylidis, K. 2023) examined AI's potential in healthcare ergonomics, particularly in reducing injuries caused by patient handling. The key objective was to determine whether AI-powered wearables could monitor healthcare workers' movements and provide immediate feedback to prevent injury. (Gladysz, B.;2023) results showed a significant decrease in injuries related to lifting and transferring patients, suggesting that AI can provide valuable support in high-risk healthcare settings. (Piccarozzi,

M.; et al. 2024) further explored AI in the construction industry, where the risk of MSDs is particularly high. (Mourtzis, D.; et al. 2024) examined the Potential of Cryptocurrencies as An Asset Class study focused on using AI to predict and prevent injury risks through real-time data analysis from wearable devices. The findings revealed a 25% reduction in reported injuries, reinforcing AI's potential in high-risk sectors like construction. (Fabio, G.; et al. 2025) study also highlighted how AI-driven interventions could proactively address ergonomic challenges, leading to safer and more efficient work environments.

A major trend in recent research has been the use of AI to deliver personalized ergonomic solutions. (Borchardt, M.; et al. 2022) investigated how AI algorithms could be tailored to individual workers based on their unique physical attributes, work habits, and injury history. Their study aimed to develop AI models that could adapt ergonomic interventions to suit specific needs, improving both comfort and safety. The findings demonstrated that personalized AI-driven ergonomic solutions were more effective than traditional approaches, with workers experiencing a 40% reduction in discomfort and fatigue. (Caputo, F.; et al. 2019) conducted a meta-analysis on the effectiveness of personalized AI in workplace ergonomics across multiple industries. Their key objective was to synthesize existing research on the impact of AI-driven ergonomic systems that adjust dynamically to workers' needs. The findings showed consistent reductions in injury rates, as well as increases in worker satisfaction and productivity. (Wang, F.-K.; et al. 2022) meta-analysis emphasized the importance of AI in creating adaptive, real-time ergonomic solutions that cater to individual requirements.

The use of predictive analytics in AI-driven ergonomics has become increasingly prevalent. (Abdous, M.-A.; et al. 2022) examined the role of AI in predicting workplace injuries by analysing historical data on worker movements and posture. The key objective was to develop predictive models capable of identifying ergonomic risks before they manifested as injuries. The study found that AI-powered predictive analytics significantly reduced injury rates, with companies experiencing fewer lost workdays and reduced compensation costs. (Cónego, L.; et al. 2024) built on these findings by investigating the cost-effectiveness of AI-driven ergonomic interventions. Their study analysed the return on investment (ROI) for companies that implemented AI-based ergonomic systems, focusing on industries with high injury rates. The key finding was that, despite high initial costs, AI-driven systems resulted in long-term financial savings by reducing injury-related expenses and improving productivity. This research highlighted the economic value of AI in workplace ergonomics, particularly in sectors where injury prevention is critical.

Wearable technology has been central to many AI-driven ergonomic solutions. Grushko, S.; et al.2021) explored the use of AI-enhanced wearables in monitoring workers' posture and movements in industrial settings. The study aimed to assess whether real-time feedback provided by AI-powered wearables could prevent injuries by encouraging workers to adopt healthier postures. The findings indicated that workers wearing AI-driven devices experienced fewer instances of poor posture, leading to a marked reduction in MSDs. (Muñoz,A.; et al. 2020) extended this research by focusing on the integration of deep learning algorithms into wearable technology. Their study aimed to develop AI systems capable of continuously learning and adapting to workers' behaviours over time. The key finding was that deep learning-enhanced wearables could offer personalized ergonomic recommendations.

As AI technology continues to advance, researchers have begun to explore its future potential in workplace ergonomics. (Rahman,M.H.; et al. 2024) investigated the use of AI-driven robotics in reducing repetitive strain injuries (RSIs) by assisting workers in physically demanding tasks. Their study found that AI-powered robots working alongside human employees significantly reduced the risk of RSIs, offering a promising hybrid approach to workplace ergonomics. (Sgarbossa, F.; et al. 2020) took a broader view, analysing the cross-industry applications of AI in ergonomics. Their objective was to identify sectors that could benefit most from AI-driven ergonomic solutions. The findings highlighted those industries with high physical demands, such as manufacturing, healthcare, and construction, were particularly well-suited for AI-driven interventions.

METHODOLOGY

To achieve the objectives, a mixed-methods research design will be employed, incorporating both qualitative and quantitative approaches. A comprehensive literature review will be conducted to gather existing knowledge on AI applications in ergonomics. Following this, a survey will be distributed to employees across various industries to assess their experiences with ergonomic practices and AI tools. Additionally, case studies of organizations that have successfully integrated AI-driven ergonomic solutions will be analysed to extract insights and best practices. The combination of these methods will provide a holistic view of the current landscape and the potential for future innovations.

Models for AI-Driven Ergonomics

In the realm of AI-driven ergonomics, several models can be utilized to effectively assess and enhance workplace ergonomics (Ordieres-Meré, J.; et al., 2023). These models combine theoretical frameworks with practical applications, providing organizations with structured approaches to implement AI solutions. The below Figure 1 shows the Models for AI-Driven Ergonomics.

Figure 1. Models for AI-driven ergonomics. Source: author compilation.

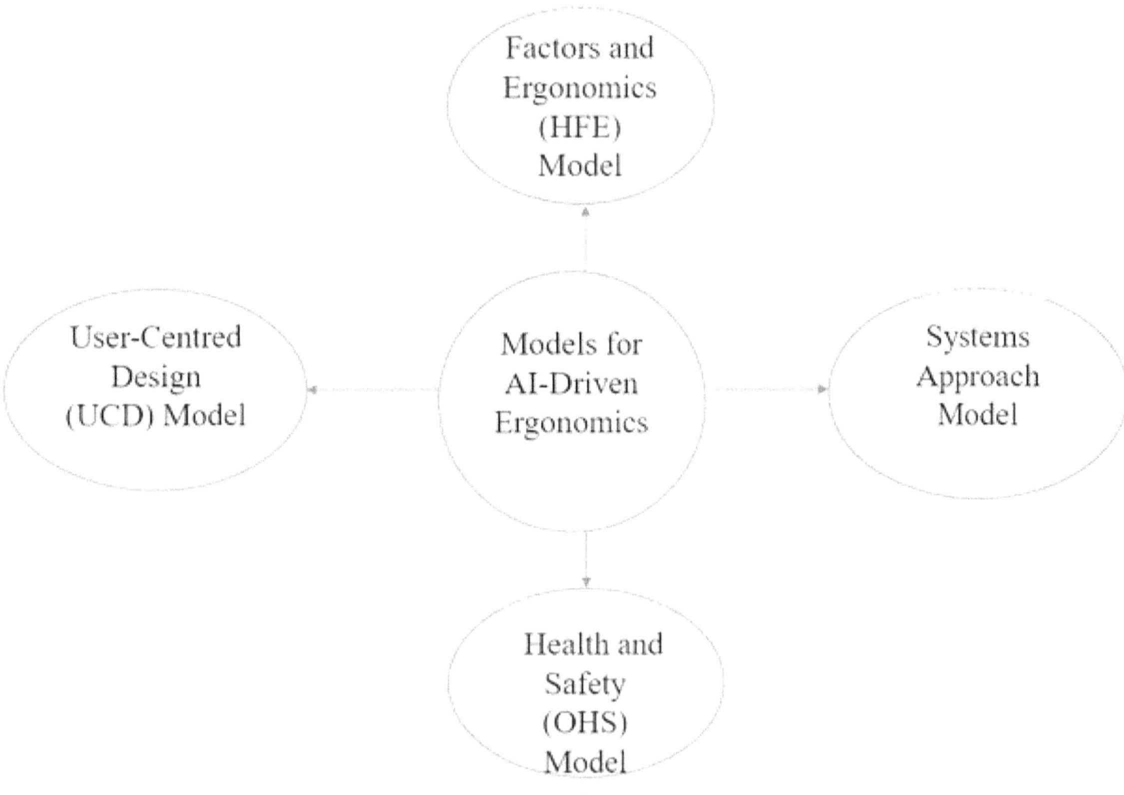

The above Figure 1 shows the Models for AI-Driven Ergonomics. These are detailed discussed here.

Human Factors and Ergonomics (HFE) Model: The Human Factors and Ergonomics (HFE) Model focuses on understanding human capabilities and limitations in relation to their work environment. This model emphasizes the importance of designing tools, tasks, and workspaces that align with human needs (Urbaniec, K.; et al., 2017), thereby optimizing performance and minimizing discomfort. AI technologies, such as predictive analytics and machine learning, can enhance this model by providing real-time assessments of ergonomic risks and delivering tailored interventions based on individual user data.

Systems Approach Model: The Systems Approach Model views the workplace as a complex system composed of interrelated components, including people, tasks, tools, and the environment. This holistic perspective allows for the integration of AI-driven tools that analyze data from various sources, such as wearable devices and environmental sensors. By leveraging AI capabilities, organizations can gain insights into how these components interact, enabling them to identify ergonomic issues and implement comprehensive solutions that improve overall workplace ergonomics.

Occupational Health and Safety (OHS) Model: The Occupational Health and Safety (OHS) Model provides a regulatory framework for maintaining a safe and healthy work environment. This model focuses on the prevention of workplace hazards, including ergonomic risks. AI can enhance the

OHS Model by automating risk assessments and compliance monitoring, ensuring that organizations adhere to ergonomic standards and best practices. By analysing historical data and predicting potential hazards, AI tools enable proactive measures to mitigate risks, ultimately fostering a safer workplace.

User-Centered Design (UCD) Model: The User-Centred Design (UCD) Model emphasizes the importance of involving users in the design and development process of ergonomic solutions. This model prioritizes user feedback and iterative design, ensuring that AI-driven tools are not only effective but also user-friendly. By engaging employees throughout the design and testing phases, organizations can develop AI solutions that address real-world ergonomic challenges, leading to higher acceptance and utilization rates among staff (Rannertshauser, P.; et al., 2022).

By employing these models, organizations can effectively integrate AI into their ergonomic practices, addressing the complexities of workplace ergonomics while enhancing employee safety and productivity.

Tools and Technologies Supporting AI-Driven Ergonomics

Wearable Devices: Wearable devices, such as smartwatches and fitness trackers, play a crucial role in AI-driven ergonomics by monitoring real-time physiological data, including posture, movement patterns, and physical exertion levels. These devices can provide immediate feedback to users, helping them to adjust their positions and movements to prevent ergonomic injuries (Trstenjak, M.; et al., 2024). Advanced wearables equipped with AI algorithms can analyse collected data to identify patterns and recommend personalized adjustments or exercises to enhance workplace ergonomics.

Computer Vision Systems: Computer vision technologies utilize cameras and AI algorithms to assess employee posture and workspace ergonomics. These systems can analyse video footage to detect improper posture or repetitive motions that may lead to injuries. By providing real-time feedback and visual alerts, computer vision tools empower employees to correct their posture and adopt healthier working habits (Gualtieri, L.; et al., 2020). This technology can also be integrated into existing workplace environments to continuously monitor and improve ergonomic practices.

Ergonomic Assessment Software: AI-powered ergonomic assessment software tools are designed to evaluate workstations and tasks systematically. These tools often include features such as digital checklists, risk assessment matrices, and simulation capabilities. By using AI algorithms, these software programs can analyse data from various inputs—such as user feedback, environmental conditions, and task requirements—to identify ergonomic risks and suggest corrective measures. This approach allows organizations to conduct thorough assessments more efficiently and effectively.

Virtual Reality (VR) and Augmented Reality (AR): Virtual reality (VR) and augmented reality (AR) technologies offer immersive training and simulation experiences that enhance ergonomic awareness. Through VR simulations, employees can practice ergonomic techniques in a safe environment, learning to recognize and correct improper postures and movements. AR applications can overlay digital information onto real-world environments, providing real-time guidance and reminders about ergonomic best practices as employees work. These technologies enhance learning and retention, ultimately fostering safer workplace behaviours.

AI-Powered Analytics Platforms: AI-powered analytics platforms aggregate and analyse data from various sources, including employee feedback, wearable devices, and ergonomic assessments. These platforms employ machine learning algorithms to identify trends and patterns related to ergonomic risks, employee productivity, and overall workplace health. By providing actionable insights and data-driven recommendations, these analytics tools empower organizations to make informed decisions about ergonomic interventions and improvements, leading to a healthier work environment.

Case Studies on Successful Applications of AI-Powered Ergonomics

Google (Alphabet Inc.): Google, a pioneer in technology and innovation, has placed significant emphasis on workplace ergonomics as part of its broader commitment to employee well-being. Established in 1998 by Larry Page and Sergey Brin, Google has consistently sought to enhance productivity and comfort within its work environments. One of the company's hallmark initiatives involves the integration of AI technologies to monitor and improve ergonomic practices across its diverse campuses. Through the use of machine learning algorithms, Google has developed systems that analyse data from wearable devices to assess employee posture and movement patterns. This real-time data collection allows the company to identify employees who may be at risk of developing musculoskeletal disorders (MSDs). If the system detects prolonged sitting or improper posture, it sends notifications to employees, prompting them to adjust their posture or take necessary breaks. This proactive approach has significantly reduced the incidence of ergonomic-related injuries, demonstrating Google's commitment to fostering a healthy work environment. In addition to monitoring, Google has invested in ergonomic workstations designed to promote comfort and efficiency. The introduction of adjustable standing desks and ergonomic chairs reflects its understanding of the diverse needs of its workforce. Employees can customize their workspaces to suit their preferences, ensuring that they can work effectively without compromising their health. AI plays a crucial role in this aspect by analysing usage patterns and employee feedback to continually refine these ergonomic solutions (Kadir, B.A.; Broberg, O.2021).

Moreover, Google's initiatives extend beyond physical ergonomics. The company emphasizes mental well-being by providing resources and tools that promote a balanced work-life environment. This holistic approach to ergonomics aligns with Google's core values of innovation and employee satisfaction, resulting in higher levels of engagement and productivity. The impact of these ergonomic practices is evident in Google's business performance. A healthier workforce translates to improved creativity and output, essential components of Google's innovative culture. Furthermore, the reduction in MSD-related costs and absenteeism has positively affected the company's bottom line, reinforcing the financial rationale behind investing in employee health. As a leader in workplace health and safety, Google also shares its findings and best practices with other organizations, advocating for the importance of ergonomics in the tech industry. By promoting the adoption of AI-driven ergonomic solutions, Google aims to influence industry standards and drive broader change. In conclusion, Google's commitment to integrating AI in ergonomics showcases its dedication to enhancing employee well-being and productivity. The successful application of these technologies not only improves health outcomes but also strengthens Google's position as a leading innovator in the global market. As AI continues to evolve, Google's ongoing investment in ergonomic solutions ensures that it remains at the forefront of creating a safe and supportive work environment.

Microsoft: Microsoft, established in 1975, has evolved from a software company to a leader in technology solutions, with a strong commitment to workplace health and safety. Recognizing the importance of ergonomics in enhancing employee productivity, Microsoft has embraced AI-powered tools and technologies to create a healthier work environment. One of the key initiatives Microsoft has implemented is the use of AI analytics to monitor user interactions with its Office 365 suite. By analysing data from millions of users, Microsoft can identify patterns that may lead to ergonomic risks, such as repetitive strain injuries from excessive keyboard use or poor posture during prolonged screen time. This data-driven approach allows the company to develop targeted interventions aimed at promoting healthier work habits among employees (Tugwell, P.; 2024).

Additionally, Microsoft has integrated ergonomic recommendations into its products. For instance, features within Microsoft Teams provide users with insights on meeting durations and suggest breaks to prevent fatigue. These AI-driven suggestions encourage employees to maintain a balanced workflow, fostering a culture of health and well-being. Furthermore, Microsoft has invested in creating ergonomic workspaces in its offices. By providing adjustable desks, ergonomic chairs, and specialized input devices, the company ensures that employees can customize their workstations to suit their individual needs. This emphasis on personalized ergonomic solutions has proven effective in minimizing discomfort and enhancing overall employee satisfaction.

The benefits of these ergonomic initiatives extend beyond individual health. By prioritizing employee well-being, Microsoft has observed increased engagement and productivity, translating into higher levels of innovation and collaboration within teams. The positive impact on employee morale reinforces Microsoft's reputation as an employer of choice in the technology sector. Moreover, Microsoft's commitment to sharing best practices and research findings has positioned it as a thought leader in workplace ergonomics. The company actively participates in industry conferences and collaborates with organizations to promote the importance of ergonomics in the workplace, advocating for the adoption of AI-driven solutions across various sectors. In conclusion, Microsoft's integration of AI-powered ergonomics reflects its dedication to fostering a healthy and productive work environment. By leveraging data analytics and investing in ergonomic solutions, the company not only enhances employee well-being but also strengthens its competitive edge in the technology industry. As Microsoft continues to innovate, its commitment to ergonomics will play a vital role in shaping the future of workplace health and safety.

Amazon: Founded in 1994 by Jeff Bezos, Amazon has grown from an online bookstore to a global e-commerce and technology powerhouse. As one of the largest employers in the world, Amazon recognizes the importance of workplace ergonomics in maintaining employee health and safety. The company has successfully implemented AI-powered ergonomics across its fulfilment centres, revolutionizing how it addresses ergonomic challenges in high-demand environments. Amazon employs advanced AI algorithms to optimize workflows within its fulfilment centres (Zizic, M.C.; et al, 2022). These algorithms analyse employee movements and assess the physical demands of various tasks, allowing the company to identify areas where ergonomic risks may arise. By leveraging data from wearable technology, Amazon monitors the physical exertion of its employees, ensuring that no individual is subjected to excessive strain during their shifts. This proactive approach has led to the implementation of adaptive strategies, such as altering task assignments based on individual capabilities and fatigue levels.

Additionally, Amazon has integrated AI-driven tools to enhance employee safety. For instance, the company utilizes smart sensors that detect signs of fatigue or strain, providing real-time feedback to employees and supervisors. This immediate intervention helps prevent injuries and promotes a culture of safety, reinforcing Amazon's commitment to employee well-being. The company has also invested in ergonomic workstations that are designed to minimize physical strain. By incorporating adjustable equipment and providing training on proper lifting techniques, Amazon empowers employees to work efficiently and safely. These initiatives have resulted in a noticeable reduction in workplace injuries, enhancing overall productivity within the fulfilment centres. Moreover, Amazon's commitment to ergonomics extends to its corporate offices. The company has embraced remote work and flexible scheduling, allowing employees to create work environments that suit their needs. This flexibility has proven beneficial in promoting a healthy work-life balance, which is crucial for maintaining employee morale and job satisfaction.

The financial impact of these ergonomic initiatives is significant. By reducing injury rates and enhancing productivity, Amazon has been able to maintain its competitive edge in the retail sector. The company's ability to efficiently meet customer demands while ensuring employee safety has solidified its position as a leader in the e-commerce industry. In summary, Amazon's successful application of AI-powered ergonomics underscores its dedication to employee health and safety. By leveraging technology to monitor and optimize workplace practices, the company has created a safer and more efficient work environment. As Amazon continues to innovate and expand, its focus on ergonomics will remain a key component of its operational strategy, ensuring the well-being of its workforce and the success of its business model.

IBM: IBM, a stalwart in the technology industry since its founding in 1911, has long recognized the importance of workplace ergonomics in fostering employee productivity and well-being. As part of its commitment to innovation, IBM has effectively integrated AI-driven solutions to enhance workplace health and safety, positioning itself as a leader in the application of technology to improve ergonomic practices.

One of the primary initiatives IBM has undertaken is the development of its Watson AI technology, which analyses vast amounts of data to assess ergonomic risks within the workplace. By collecting data from employee feedback and wearable devices, IBM can identify patterns associated with discomfort or injury. This data-driven approach enables the company to implement targeted interventions that address specific ergonomic challenges, ensuring that employees work in safe and comfortable environments. Additionally, IBM has developed ergonomic assessment tools that allow managers to evaluate workstations and tasks systematically. These tools utilize AI algorithms to provide real-time insights into potential hazards, enabling swift corrective actions. By streamlining the assessment process, IBM ensures that ergonomic best practices are consistently applied across its global operations (Bechinie, C.; et al., 2024).

The company also places a strong emphasis on employee training and awareness. IBM has implemented programs that educate employees about proper ergonomic practices and the use of AI-driven tools to enhance their work environments. This focus on knowledge and empowerment has resulted in increased employee engagement and a shared commitment to workplace safety. Moreover, IBM has made significant investments in ergonomic workstations designed to accommodate the diverse needs of its workforce. By providing adjustable desks, ergonomic chairs, and specialized input devices, IBM promotes a culture of health and well-being. These efforts have led to a noticeable reduction in workplace injuries and a significant improvement in employee satisfaction.

The financial benefits of these initiatives are evident. By reducing the incidence of ergonomic-related injuries and enhancing employee productivity, IBM has seen a positive impact on its operational efficiency and overall performance. The company's commitment to workplace health aligns with its broader goals of innovation and excellence in service delivery. As a thought leader in workplace ergonomics, IBM actively shares its research findings and best practices with industry peers. By advocating for the importance of ergonomics in the workplace, IBM aims to influence industry standards and drive meaningful change across sectors. In conclusion, IBM's strategic application of AI in ergonomics exemplifies its commitment to fostering a healthy and productive work environment. By leveraging technology to assess and improve ergonomic practices, the company not only enhances employee well-being but also strengthens its position as a leader in the technology industry. As AI continues to evolve, IBM's focus on ergonomics will play a vital role in shaping the future of workplace health and safety.

Siemens: Siemens, established in 1847, has emerged as a global leader in technology and engineering solutions. With a commitment to innovation and sustainability, Siemens recognizes the importance of workplace ergonomics in enhancing employee well-being and operational efficiency. The company has successfully integrated AI-driven technologies into its ergonomic practices, transforming its manufacturing environments. Siemens employs advanced AI analytics to assess ergonomic risks in its production facilities. By utilizing data from sensors and wearable devices, the company monitors employee movements and identifies patterns that may lead to physical strain or discomfort. This proactive approach enables Siemens to implement targeted interventions that minimize ergonomic hazards, ensuring a safe and comfortable work environment for its employees (Yang, J.; et al., 2024).

One notable initiative involves the use of virtual simulations to test workstation designs before implementation. By modelling various ergonomic setups, Siemens can evaluate their effectiveness and make necessary adjustments based on data-driven insights. This iterative process not only enhances the safety of the work environment but also promotes employee satisfaction by providing workspaces tailored to their needs. Furthermore, Siemens invests in ergonomic training programs that educate employees about best practices in posture and movement. By empowering employees with knowledge and tools, the company fosters a culture of safety and well-being. This emphasis on education has resulted in increased awareness of ergonomic issues and a shared commitment to maintaining a safe workplace.

Siemens has also integrated AI-driven tools to facilitate continuous monitoring of workplace ergonomics. These tools provide real-time feedback on employee movements and alert managers to potential risks. By streamlining the monitoring process, Siemens ensures that ergonomic best practices are consistently applied, reducing the incidence of workplace injuries. The financial implications of these ergonomic initiatives are significant. By minimizing injury rates and enhancing employee productivity, Siemens has been able to maintain its competitive edge in the technology sector. The company's commitment to workplace health aligns with its broader goals of operational excellence and innovation. In addition to its internal practices, Siemens actively shares its findings and best practices with industry peers, advocating for the importance of ergonomics in manufacturing environments. By promoting the adoption of AI-driven ergonomic solutions, Siemens aims to influence industry standards and drive positive change across sectors. In conclusion, Siemens' successful application of AI-powered ergonomics reflects its dedication to fostering a safe and productive work environment. By leveraging technology to assess and improve ergonomic practices, the company enhances employee well-being while strengthening its position as a leader in the global market. As Siemens continues to innovate, its focus on ergonomics will remain a key component of its operational strategy.

Toyota: Toyota, a leading automobile manufacturer established in 1937, has long been recognized for its commitment to quality and innovation. In recent years, the company has also prioritized workplace ergonomics, recognizing its critical role in enhancing employee safety and productivity. By integrating AI-driven technologies into its manufacturing processes, Toyota has successfully transformed its approach to workplace health. Toyota employs AI analytics to assess and optimize ergonomic practices on its production lines. By analysing data from sensors and employee feedback, the company identifies ergonomic risks associated with specific tasks. This data-driven approach allows Toyota to implement targeted interventions, such as modifying workstation designs and adjusting workflows to minimize physical strain on employees (Hattinger, M.& Stylidis, K. 2023).

One notable initiative involves the implementation of smart technologies that monitor employee movements in real time. These systems provide instant feedback, alerting employees to potential ergonomic hazards. By promoting immediate awareness, Toyota fosters a culture of safety and encourages employees to adopt healthier working habits. In addition to monitoring, Toyota has invested in ergonomic training programs that educate employees about best practices for maintaining proper posture and avoiding repetitive strain injuries. These training initiatives empower employees to take ownership of their health and well-being, reinforcing Toyota's commitment to a safe work environment.

The company's focus on ergonomics extends to the design of its manufacturing facilities. Toyota employs principles of lean manufacturing to create workspaces that minimize unnecessary movements and physical strain. By optimizing workflows and workstation layouts, the company enhances operational efficiency while prioritizing employee health The financial impact of these ergonomic initiatives is significant. By reducing workplace injuries and improving employee morale, Toyota has been able to maintain high levels of productivity and quality in its manufacturing processes. This commitment to workplace health aligns with Toyota's broader goals of sustainability and operational excellence.

Furthermore, Toyota actively shares its research findings and best practices with industry peers, advocating for the importance of ergonomics in the automotive sector. By promoting the adoption of AI-driven ergonomic solutions, Toyota aims to influence industry standards and drive positive change across the manufacturing landscape. In summary, Toyota's successful application of AI-powered ergonomics demonstrates its commitment to fostering a safe and productive work environment. By leveraging technology to assess and improve ergonomic practices, the company enhances employee well-being while reinforcing its reputation as a leader in the automotive industry. As Toyota continues to innovate, its focus on ergonomics will play a vital role in shaping the future of workplace health and safety.

Unilever: Unilever, founded in 1929, is a global consumer goods company that has made significant strides in workplace health and safety through the integration of AI-powered ergonomics. Recognizing the importance of employee well-being in enhancing productivity, Unilever has implemented innovative solutions to create a safer and more comfortable work environment across its manufacturing and corporate facilities. Unilever employs AI analytics to monitor employee health metrics and assess ergonomic risks in its workplaces. By analysing data from wearable devices and sensors, the company identifies patterns that may indicate potential ergonomic hazards. This proactive approach enables Unilever to implement targeted interventions, ensuring that employees are protected from injuries related to poor ergonomics (Gladysz, B.; et al. 2023).

A notable initiative involves the use of AI-driven tools that provide real-time feedback on employee movements. These tools alert employees to adjust their posture or take breaks when they are at risk of physical strain. By fostering a culture of safety, Unilever empowers employees to prioritize their health and well-being while performing their tasks. In addition to monitoring, Unilever has invested in ergonomic workstation designs that cater to the diverse needs of its workforce. By providing adjustable desks, ergonomic chairs, and specialized equipment, the company promotes a comfortable and efficient work environment. These investments have resulted in a significant reduction in workplace injuries and increased employee satisfaction.

Unilever also emphasizes training and awareness programs that educate employees about best practices in ergonomics. By providing resources and tools, the company empowers employees to make informed decisions about their work environments. This focus on education enhances employee engagement and reinforces the importance of ergonomics in maintaining health and safety. The financial benefits of these ergonomic initiatives are evident in Unilever's operational efficiency. By reducing injury rates and enhancing employee morale, the company has been able to maintain high levels of productivity, contributing to its overall market success. This commitment to workplace health aligns with Unilever's broader goals of sustainability and corporate responsibility. Moreover, Unilever actively shares its findings and best practices with industry peers, advocating for the importance of ergonomics in the consumer goods sector. By promoting the adoption of AI-driven ergonomic solutions, Unilever aims to influence industry standards and drive meaningful change. In conclusion, Unilever's successful application of AI-powered ergonomics reflects its dedication to fostering a safe and productive work environment. By leveraging technology to assess and improve ergonomic practices, the company enhances employee well-being while strengthening its position as a leader in the global market. As Unilever continues to innovate, its focus on ergonomics will remain a key component of its operational strategy (Mourtzis, D.; et al. 2024).

Procter & Gamble: Procter & Gamble (P&G), established in 1837, has consistently been recognized for its commitment to quality and innovation in consumer goods. As a leader in the industry, P&G has also prioritized workplace health and safety, integrating AI-driven solutions to enhance ergonomics across its manufacturing and corporate environments. This strategic focus on ergonomics reflects P&G's dedication to fostering employee well-being and operational efficiency. P&G employs advanced AI analytics to assess ergonomic risks in its production facilities. By utilizing data from sensors and wearable devices, the company monitors employee movements and identifies patterns that may lead to physical strain or discomfort. This data-driven approach allows P&G to implement targeted interventions, ensuring that employees work in safe and comfortable environments (Borchardt, M.; et al. 2022).

One notable initiative involves the development of AI-powered tools that provide real-time feedback on employee posture and movements. These tools alert employees when they are at risk of developing musculoskeletal disorders (MSDs), prompting them to adjust their positions or take necessary breaks. By fostering a culture of safety, P&G empowers employees to prioritize their health and well-being. Furthermore, P&G invests in ergonomic workstation designs that accommodate the diverse needs of its workforce. By providing adjustable desks, ergonomic chairs, and specialized equipment, the company ensures that employees can customize their workspaces to suit their individual preferences. This emphasis on personalized ergonomic solutions has proven effective in minimizing discomfort and enhancing overall employee satisfaction.

P&G also emphasizes training and awareness programs that educate employees about best practices in ergonomics. By providing resources and tools, the company empowers employees to make informed decisions about their work environments. This focus on education has resulted in increased awareness of ergonomic issues and a shared commitment to maintaining a safe workplace. The financial impact of these ergonomic initiatives is significant. By reducing the incidence of ergonomic-related injuries and enhancing employee productivity, P&G has seen a positive impact on its operational efficiency and overall performance. The company's commitment to workplace health aligns with its broader goals of sustainability and corporate responsibility.

Moreover, P&G actively shares its research findings and best practices with industry peers, advocating for the importance of ergonomics in the consumer goods sector. By promoting the adoption of AI-driven ergonomic solutions, P&G aims to influence industry standards and drive meaningful change across sectors. In summary, Procter & Gamble's successful application of AI-powered ergonomics showcases its dedication to fostering a safe and productive work environment. By leveraging technology to assess and improve ergonomic practices, the company enhances employee well-being while reinforcing its reputation as a leader in the global consumer goods market. As P&G continues to innovate, its focus on ergonomics will play a vital role in shaping the future of workplace health and safety (Wang, F.-K.; et al. 2022).

Intel: Intel, a leading semiconductor manufacturer established in 1968, has consistently prioritized innovation and quality in its operations. Recognizing the significance of workplace ergonomics in maintaining employee health and productivity, Intel has effectively integrated AI-driven solutions to create safer and more comfortable work environments. Intel employs advanced AI analytics to assess ergonomic risks in its manufacturing facilities. By analysing data from sensors and wearable devices, the company identifies patterns associated with physical strain or discomfort. This proactive approach enables Intel to implement targeted interventions, ensuring that employees work in safe and comfortable environments.

One notable initiative involves the development of AI-powered tools that monitor employee movements in real time. These systems provide instant feedback, alerting employees to potential ergonomic hazards. By promoting immediate awareness, Intel fosters a culture of safety and encourages employees to adopt healthier working habits. Additionally, Intel has invested in ergonomic workstation designs that cater to the diverse needs of its workforce. By providing adjustable desks, ergonomic chairs, and specialized input devices, the company promotes a comfortable and efficient work environment. These investments have resulted in a significant reduction in workplace injuries and increased employee satisfaction (Abdous, M.-A.; et al. 2022).

Intel also emphasizes training and awareness programs that educate employees about best practices in ergonomics. By providing resources and tools, the company empowers employees to make informed decisions about their work environments. This focus on education enhances employee engagement and reinforces the importance of ergonomics in maintaining health and safety. The financial impact of these ergonomic initiatives is significant. By reducing workplace injuries and improving employee morale, Intel has been able to maintain high levels of productivity and quality in its manufacturing processes. This commitment to workplace health aligns with Intel's broader goals of operational excellence and innovation.

Furthermore, Intel actively shares its research findings and best practices with industry peers, advocating for the importance of ergonomics in the technology sector. By promoting the adoption of AI-driven ergonomic solutions, Intel aims to influence industry standards and drive positive change across sectors. In conclusion, Intel's successful application of AI-powered ergonomics exemplifies its commitment to fostering a safe and productive work environment. By leveraging technology to assess and improve ergonomic practices, the company enhances employee well-being while reinforcing its position as a leader in the semiconductor industry. As Intel continues to innovate, its focus on ergonomics will play a vital role in shaping the future of workplace health and safety.

Johnson & Johnson: Johnson & Johnson, founded in 1886, is a multinational corporation known for its commitment to health and wellness. With a diverse portfolio spanning pharmaceuticals, medical devices, and consumer health products, Johnson & Johnson recognizes the critical importance of workplace ergonomics in enhancing employee well-being and productivity. The company has successfully integrated AI-driven solutions to transform its approach to workplace health and safety. One of the primary initiatives Johnson & Johnson has implemented is the use of AI analytics to monitor employee health metrics and assess ergonomic risks in its manufacturing facilities. By analysing data from wearable devices and sensors, the company identifies patterns that may indicate potential ergonomic hazards. This data-driven approach allows Johnson & Johnson to implement targeted interventions, ensuring that employees are protected from injuries related to poor ergonomics (Cónego, L.; et al. 2024).

A notable initiative involves the development of AI-powered tools that provide real-time feedback on employee movements. These tools alert employees to adjust their posture or take breaks when they are at risk of physical strain. By fostering a culture of safety, Johnson & Johnson empowers employees to prioritize their health and well-being while performing their tasks. Furthermore, Johnson & Johnson invests in ergonomic workstation designs that accommodate the diverse needs of its workforce. By providing adjustable desks, ergonomic chairs, and specialized equipment, the company ensures that employees can customize their workspaces to suit their individual preferences. This emphasis on personalized ergonomic solutions has proven effective in minimizing discomfort and enhancing overall employee satisfaction. The company also emphasizes training and awareness programs that educate employees about best practices in ergonomics. By providing resources and tools, Johnson & Johnson empowers employees to make informed decisions about their work environments. This focus on education has resulted in increased awareness of ergonomic issues and a shared commitment to maintaining a safe workplace. The financial impact of these ergonomic initiatives is significant. By reducing the incidence of ergonomic-related injuries and enhancing employee productivity, Johnson & Johnson has seen a positive impact on its operational efficiency and overall performance. The company's commitment to workplace health aligns with its broader goals of sustainability and corporate responsibility (Muñoz,A.; et al. 2020).

Moreover, Johnson & Johnson actively shares its research findings and best practices with industry peers, advocating for the importance of ergonomics in the health and wellness sector. By promoting the adoption of AI-driven ergonomic solutions, Johnson & Johnson aims to influence industry standards and drive meaningful change across sectors. In summary, Johnson & Johnson's successful application of AI-powered ergonomics showcases its dedication to fostering a safe and productive work environment. By leveraging technology to assess and improve ergonomic practices, the company enhances employee well-being while reinforcing its reputation as a leader in the global health and wellness market. As Johnson & Johnson continues to innovate, its focus on ergonomics will play a vital role in shaping the future of workplace health and safety.

Regulatory and Ethical Considerations With AI for Dynamic AI-Powered Ergonomics

When implementing AI-powered ergonomics in dynamic work environments, several regulatory and ethical considerations need to be addressed. On the regulatory front, one of the key issues is data privacy and security. AI-driven ergonomic solutions often rely on continuous data collection through sensors, cameras, or wearable devices to monitor posture, movement, and physical strain. This real-time tracking introduces significant privacy risks, especially concerning the collection of personal and potentially sensitive employee data. Regulatory frameworks like the General Data Protection Regulation (GDPR) in Europe and the California Consumer Privacy Act (CCPA) in the United States emphasize that employees must be informed about the data being collected, how it will be used, and their rights to consent. Moreover, companies must ensure proper data protection measures, including encryption, secure storage, and data minimization practices, to comply with these regulations (Rahman,M.H.; et al. 2024).

AI algorithms must be designed to accommodate different body types, physical abilities, and working conditions, ensuring that solutions do not disproportionately benefit one group of employees while neglecting others. Addressing these regulatory and ethical concerns is crucial to successfully implementing AI-powered ergonomic solutions that enhance workplace well-being without compromising privacy, safety, or fairness.

Recent Issues of AI in Ergonomics

Recent developments in AI-powered ergonomics have opened up opportunities to optimize workplace health and productivity, but they also present several emerging issues. As AI systems become more sophisticated and widely adopted in the workplace, challenges surrounding data privacy, bias, and ethical deployment have gained attention. One of the most pressing issues is the balance between data collection and privacy. AI-driven ergonomic tools, which often rely on wearable devices, cameras, and sensors, collect vast amounts of data on employees' movements, postures, and behaviours. While this data is essential for creating personalized ergonomic solutions, it raises concerns about how much monitoring is acceptable. Invasive tracking could lead to a loss of privacy, making employees feel shrivelled. Companies are grappling with how to ensure that these systems provide value without crossing into invasive surveillance, which could lead to employee discomfort or even legal challenges under regulations such as GDPR or CCPA.

Another issue involves the potential for algorithmic bias in AI ergonomic systems (Sgarbossa, F.; et al. 2020). AI models that are not trained on diverse datasets may fail to account for variations in body types, physical capabilities, or specific ergonomic needs of different demographic groups. This can lead to ergonomic solutions that work well for one segment of the workforce but are less effective or even harmful for others, exacerbating issues related to inclusivity and fairness in the workplace. Ensuring diversity in data used to train these systems is crucial, but achieving it remains a technical and ethical challenge. Finally, the rapid evolution of AI technologies has raised concerns about worker autonomy and consent. AI-powered systems that automatically adjust workstations or suggest posture corrections may diminish employees' sense of control over their own working environments. There is also the risk that these systems could be used to enforce productivity over well-being, with employers potentially focusing on efficiency metrics rather than employee health. Balancing these priorities requires careful regulation and ethical guidelines to ensure that the deployment of AI in ergonomics truly benefits the workforce without compromising individual autonomy.

SOLUTIONS AND RECOMMENDATIONS

The study will propose several AI-driven solutions to enhance workplace ergonomics, including the implementation of real-time monitoring systems that utilize AI to analyse employee posture and movements. Recommendations will focus on developing user-friendly interfaces that provide immediate feedback and suggestions for improving ergonomic practices. Training programs tailored to both employees and management on the effective use of these tools will be emphasized, ensuring that organizations can fully leverage the benefits of AI in their ergonomics strategy. Additionally, fostering a culture of continuous improvement around ergonomics will be essential for long-term success.

IMPLICATIONS OF THE STUDY

The findings of this study will have significant implications for both academia and industry. Academically, it will contribute to the growing body of literature on the application of AI in health and safety, providing a framework for future research in this area. It will also encourage further interdisciplinary studies that merge technology, ergonomics, and organizational behavior. For the industry, the insights gained from this research could lead to the development of innovative ergonomic solutions that enhance employee satisfaction and productivity, thereby reducing costs associated with workplace injuries and absenteeism. The study's recommendations will serve as a guide for organizations seeking to implement AI-driven ergonomic practices effectively.

FUTURE RESEARCH DIRECTIONS

Future research could explore the long-term impacts of AI-driven ergonomic interventions on employee health and organizational performance. Additionally, studies could investigate the effectiveness of different AI algorithms in detecting ergonomic risks across various industries and job roles. There is also potential for research focused on the integration of AI with other technologies, such as wearables, to create comprehensive ergonomic solutions. Finally, examining the ethical implications of using AI in workplace ergonomics will be crucial as organizations adopt these technologies.

CONCLUSION

In conclusion, the study highlights the transformative potential of AI in improving workplace ergonomics, emphasizing that the integration of advanced technologies can lead to enhanced employee well-being and organizational efficiency. By identifying effective AI-driven solutions and providing actionable recommendations, this research not only advances academic discourse but also serves as a practical guide for industries looking to innovate their ergonomic practices. As organizations continue to navigate the challenges of modern work environments, the findings of this study will be invaluable in fostering healthier and more productive workplaces.

REFERENCES

Abdous, M.-A., Delorme, X., Battini, D., & Berger-Douce, S. (2022). Multi-objective collaborative assembly line design problem with the optimisation of ergonomics and economics. *International Journal of Production Research*, *61*(22), 7830–7845. DOI: 10.1080/00207543.2022.2153185

Balaji, K. (2023). Unlocking the potential of BI-enhancing banking transactions through AI & ML tools. *2023 International Conference on Applied Intelligence and Sustainable Computing (ICAISC)*, 1–6. DOI: 10.1109/ICAISC58445.2023.10200018

Balaji, K. (2023). Blockchain based banking transactions enabled by big data. 2023 5th International Conference on Energy, Power and Environment (ICEPE), 1–6. DOI: 10.1109/ICEPE57949.2023.10201613

Balaji, K. (2024). Charting the path to global prosperity: Unveiling the impact and promise of sustainable development. In Ordóñez de Pablos, P., Anshari, M., & Almunawar, M. (Eds.), *Harnessing green and circular skills for digital transformation* (pp. 1–22). IGI Global., DOI: 10.4018/979-8-3693-2865-1.ch001

Balaji, K. (2024). The nexus of smart contracts and digital twins transforming green finance with automated transactions in investment agreements. In Jafar, S., Rodriguez, R., Kannan, H., Akhtar, S., & Plugmann, P. (Eds.), *Harnessing blockchain-digital twin fusion for sustainable investments* (pp. 287–315). IGI Global., DOI: 10.4018/979-8-3693-1878-2.ch012

Balaji, K. (2024). Artificial intelligence for enhanced anti-money laundering and asset recovery: A new frontier in financial crime prevention. *2024 Second International Conference on Intelligent Cyber Physical Systems and Internet of Things (ICoICI)*, 1010–1016. DOI: 10.1109/ICoICI62503.2024.10696100

Balaji, K., & Ariwa, E. (2024). Insurtech disruption: Reshaping the future of insurance in the fintech era. In Jafar, S. H., Shakeb Akhtar, H., Khan, P. A., & El Chaarani, H. (Eds.), *The adoption of fintech: Using technology for better security, speed, and customer experience in finance* (pp. 247–266). Routledge., DOI: 10.4324/9781032644165-16

Balaji, K., & Babu, M. K. (2017). A study on the affect of technology on unplanned purchase behaviour among the customers across selected corporate retail chains of Andhrapradesh, India. *International Journal of Economic Research*, *14*(4), 277–288.

Balaji, K., & Babu, M. K. (2017). A study on the role of the external and internal factors on consumer impulse buying behavior in selected retail outlets of Andhra Pradesh, India. *International Journal of Applied Business and Economic Research*, *15*(4), 171–185.

Balaji, K., Karim, S., & Rao, P. S. (2024). Unleashing the power of smart chatbots: Transforming banking with artificial intelligence. *2024 International Conference on Advances in Computing, Communication and Applied Informatics (ACCAI)*, 1–7. DOI: 10.1109/ACCAI61061.2024.10602456

Balaji, K., & Kishore Babu, M. (2016). A study on consumer shopping patterns in current retail scenario across selected retail stores in Andhra Pradesh, India. *International Journal of Economic Research*, *13*(4), 1629–1640.

Balaji, K., & Rao, P. S. (2024). Artificial intelligence and chatbots: Transforming user experience in e-tailing. 2024 9th International Conference on Communication and Electronics Systems (ICCES), 1375–1379. DOI: 10.1109/ICCES63552.2024.10859474

Bechinie, C., Zafari, S., Kroeninger, L., Puthenkalam, J., & Tscheligi, M. (2024). Toward human-centered intelligent assistance system in manufacturing: Challenges and potentials for Operator 5.0. *Procedia Computer Science*, *232*, 1584–1596. DOI: 10.1016/j.procs.2024.01.156

Borchardt, M., Pereira, G. M., Milan, G. S., Scavarda, A. R., Nogueira, E. O., & Poltosi, L. C. (2022). Industry 5.0 beyond technology: An analysis through the lens of business and operations management literature. *Organizacija*, *55*(4), 305–321. DOI: 10.2478/orga-2022-0020

Caputo, F., Greco, A., Fera, M., & Macchiaroli, R. (2019). Digital twins to enhance the integration of ergonomics in the workplace design. *International Journal of Industrial Ergonomics*, *71*, 20–31. DOI: 10.1016/j.ergon.2019.02.001

Fabio, G., Giuditta, C., Margherita, P., & Raffaeli, R. A. (2025). A human-centric methodology for the co-evolution of operators' skills, digital tools and user interfaces to support the Operator 4.0. *Robotics and Computer-integrated Manufacturing*, *91*, 102854. DOI: 10.1016/j.rcim.2024.102854

Gladysz, B., Tran, T., Romero, D., van Erp, T., Abonyi, J., & Ruppert, T. (2023). Current development on the Operator 4.0 and transition towards the Operator 5.0: A systematic literature review in light of Industry 5.0. *Journal of Manufacturing Systems*, *70*, 160–185. DOI: 10.1016/j.jmsy.2023.07.008

Gualtieri, L., Palomba, I., Merati, F. A., Rauch, E., & Vidoni, R. (2020). Design of human-centered collaborative assembly workstations for the improvement of operators' physical ergonomics and production efficiency: A case study. *Sustainability (Basel)*, *12*(9), 3606. DOI: 10.3390/su12093606

Hattinger, M., & Stylidis, K. (2023). Transforming Quality 4.0 towards resilient Operator 5.0 needs. *Procedia CIRP*, *120*, 1600–1605. DOI: 10.1016/j.procir.2023.12.002

Kadir, B. A., & Broberg, O. (2021). Human-centered design of work systems in the transition to Industry 4.0. *Applied Ergonomics*, *92*, 103334. DOI: 10.1016/j.apergo.2020.103334 PMID: 33264676

Mourtzis, D., Angelopoulos, J., & Panopoulos, N. A. (2022). Literature review of the challenges and opportunities of the transition from Industry 4.0 to Society 5.0. *Energies*, *15*(17), 6276. DOI: 10.3390/en15176276

Ordieres-Meré, J., Gutierrez, M., & Villalba-Díez, J. (2023). Toward the industry 5.0 paradigm: Increasing value creation through the robust integration of humans and machines. *Computers in Industry*, *150*, 103947. DOI: 10.1016/j.compind.2023.103947

Piccarozzi, M., Silvestri, L., Silvestri, C., & Ruggieri, A. (2024). Roadmap to Industry 5.0: Enabling technologies, challenges, and opportunities towards a holistic definition in management studies. *Technological Forecasting and Social Change*, *205*, 123467. DOI: 10.1016/j.techfore.2024.123467

Rannertshauser, P., Kessler, M., & Arlinghaus, J. C. (2022). Human-centricity in the design of production planning and control systems: A first approach towards Industry 5.0. *IFAC-PapersOnLine*, *55*(10), 2641–2646. DOI: 10.1016/j.ifacol.2022.10.108

Trstenjak, M., Hegedić, M., Cajner, H., Opetuk, T., & Tošanović, N. (2024). Cognitive ergonomics in Industry 5.0. In Silva, F. J. G., Ferreira, L. P., Sá, J. C., Pereira, M. T., & Pinto, C. M. A. (Eds.), *Flexible Automation and Intelligent Manufacturing: Establishing Bridges for More Sustainable Manufacturing Systems* (pp. 763–770). Springer., DOI: 10.1007/978-3-031-38165-2_88

Tugwell, P., & Tovey, D. (2021). PRISMA 2020. *Journal of Clinical Epidemiology, 134*, A5–A6. DOI: 10.1016/j.jclinepi.2021.04.008 PMID: 34016443

Urbaniec, K., Mikulčić, H., Rosen, M. A., & Duić, N. (2017). A holistic approach to sustainable development of energy, water and environment systems. *Journal of Cleaner Production, 155*, 1–11. DOI: 10.1016/j.jclepro.2017.01.119

Wang, F.-K., Rahardjo, B., & Rovira, P. R. (2022). Lean Six Sigma with value stream mapping in Industry 4.0 for human-centered workstation design. *Sustainability (Basel), 14*(17), 17. DOI: 10.3390/su141711020

Yang, J., Liu, Y., & Morgan, P. L. (2024). Human-machine interaction towards Industry 5.0: Human-centric smart manufacturing. *Digital Engineering, 2*, 100013. DOI: 10.1016/j.dte.2024.100013

Zizic, M. C., Mladineo, M., Gjeldum, N., & Celent, L. (2022). From Industry 4.0 towards Industry 5.0: A review and analysis of paradigm shift for the people, organization and technology. *Energies, 15*(14), 5221. DOI: 10.3390/en15145221

ADDITIONAL READING

Cónego, L., Pinto, R., Pinto, J., & Gonçalves, G. (2024). Leveraging gamification in Industry 5.0: Tailored solutions for workplace employees. *Procedia Computer Science, 232*, 1769–1778. DOI: 10.1016/j.procs.2024.01.175

Grushko, S., Vysocky, A., Suder, J., Glogar, L., & Bobovsky, Z. (2021). Improving human awareness during collaboration with robot: Review. *MM Science Journal, 2021*(5475). https://doi.org/DOI: 10.17973/MMSJ.2021_10_2021102

Muñoz, A., Martí, A., Mahiques, X., Gracia, L., Solanes, J. E., & Tornero, J. (2020). Camera 3D positioning mixed reality-based interface to improve worker safety, ergonomics and productivity. *CIRP Journal of Manufacturing Science and Technology, 28*, 24–37. DOI: 10.1016/j.cirpj.2020.01.004

Rahman, M. H., Hasan, M. R., Chowdhury, N. I., Syed, M. A. B., & Farah, M. U. (2024). Predictive health analysis in Industry 5.0: A scientometric and systematic review of motion capture in construction. *Digital Engineering, 1*, 100002. DOI: 10.1016/j.dte.2024.100002

Sgarbossa, F., Grosse, E. H., Neumann, W. P., Battini, D., & Glock, C. H. (2020). Human factors in production and logistics systems of the future. *Annual Reviews in Control, 49*, 295–305. DOI: 10.1016/j.arcontrol.2020.04.007

KEY TERMS AND DEFINITIONS

Data Privacy: Refers to the protection of personal information collected by AI systems, ensuring that data is used ethically and in compliance with laws like GDPR, without invading employee privacy.

Algorithmic Bias: Occurs when AI systems produce skewed results due to lack of diversity in training data, leading to ergonomic solutions that may favour certain groups while disadvantaging others.

Wearable Devices: Technology worn by employees to track physical metrics like posture, movement, and strain, which provides data to AI systems for improving ergonomic conditions.

GDPR (General Data Protection Regulation): A European Union regulation that governs how organizations collect, store, and manage personal data, ensuring individual privacy rights are respected in AI applications.

AI-Driven Ergonomics: The application of artificial intelligence to optimize workspaces and improve human comfort and safety by analysing real-time data from sensors and wearables.

Surveillance Concerns: Issues arising from AI-powered systems that may monitor employees excessively, leading to feelings of being constantly watched and reducing workplace autonomy.

Workplace Autonomy: The degree to which employees control their work environment; AI tools that automatically adjust ergonomics may reduce this sense of control.

Ethical AI Deployment: Refers to implementing AI systems in a way that ensures fairness, transparency, and respect for workers' rights, while avoiding harm or bias.

Productivity vs. Well-Being: The tension between using AI to maximize efficiency and ensuring that these systems also prioritize the health and comfort of employees.

Real-Time Data: Information that is collected and processed instantly by AI systems, allowing for immediate adjustments to workplace ergonomics based on current employee movements or postures.

Chapter 4
Artificial Intelligence, Innovation, and Safety in Biotechnology Research

Kehinde Adewole Oyeniran
https://orcid.org/0000-0003-1754-6184
International Centre for Genetic Engineering and Biotechnology, Cape Town, South Africa

Olubukola Helen Oyeniran
https://orcid.org/0000-0001-5262-7487
Federal University, Oye Ekiti, Nigeria

Kolawole Muftau Oladunmoye
Federal University of Technology, Akure, Nigeria

ABSTRACT

Biotechnology research covers different disciplines of life that utilise biological products and systems for scientific research to create innovative products and solutions in industries such as healthcare, agriculture, and environmental management. However, biotechnology research poses challenges of products and workforce safety. Hence, the need for intentional efforts to integrate artificial intelligence (AI) into biotechnology research. This chapter considers the impacts of AI innovation on safety in biotechnology-based agriculture, medicine, environment, and food research areas. AI-driven training programs can markedly improve staff productivity, talent management, and individualised learning experiences. Predictive analytics techniques can confidently assess workplace risk, thereby significantly improving safety. However, non-existent ethical considerations, regulatory frameworks, and intellectual property rights challenges beset effective integration of AI and must be addressed via relevant established stakeholder regulations and ethical practices.

DOI: 10.4018/979-8-3693-9301-7.ch004

1.0 INTRODUCTION

1.1 Overview of Biotechnology Research

Biotechnology research mostly involves the use of plants and animals for rigorous scientific studies with a primary focus of gaining a better understanding of a subject matter for a better society. The field of biotechnology has broad applications in life and medical sciences, with many similarities in scientific experiments or research procedures. Given this fact, it is only intuitive to assume that the process of safety and risk assessments is also similar based on either the nature of the research conducted or the applicable biosafety levels. For instance, healthcare may require a more specific procedure for safety and risk assessment that mainly requires that health workers are protected from exposure to potential infectious agents in addition to the routine sanitary measures that guard against ubiquitous nosocomial infections (Adepoju & Esan, 2023; Banez et al., 2021).

The procedure may be slightly different for the food industry, in which the main goal is to prevent contamination of food products while ensuring the safety of the workforce around machines and equipment. The food industry is also responsible for maintaining the highest standard operating procedure that prevents contaminants of public health concern in food products. Therefore, the concept of safety should be seen from the two perspectives of the concerned workforce, which may include researchers, factory workers, and health personnel in the hospital, to mention but a few, and the products or goods for public consumption (Purwanto et al., 2019; Rosak-Szyrocka & Abbase, 2020; Wang & Wang, 2021).

Long before the advent of science and technology, safety and risk assessment in the workplace were accomplished using the fallible traditional means of manual documentation and ticking of relevant boxes following rigorous workers training from time to time. In the present age, technology can be applied to many endeavours with the intent to either improve or replace the error-prone traditional methods. The continuous developments in artificial intelligence (AI), molecular biology, medicine, genetic engineering, and synthetic biology now play a major role in driving and tracking biotechnology research advances, which have improved significantly in the past few decades (Amore, 2023; Gong, 2023; Kulkarni & Singh, 2023; Mishra*, 2024; Thomas et al., 2021). In addition to expanding our knowledge of life, medical sciences, and biological systems, these developments have budded creative applications in different academic fields, including agriculture, medicine, and environmental science. They have also produced reproducible answers to new global issues like food security, disease control, and long-term sustainability challenges.

1.1.1 Agriculture

Here, biotechnology plays a major role in advancing crop productivity and resilience. For instance, the development of improved crop varieties for better yield and resistance to both biotic and abiotic stressors would not have been made possible without the application of molecular biology techniques, such as gene editing and novel genetic transformation methods. Mamata & Lamichhane (2021) posited that advancements in plant molecular biology have opened avenues for modifying plant genomes to overcome physiological constraints, increasing crop yield potential and resistance to diseases. The production of doubled haploids through gametic embryogenesis has been hailed as a valuable tool for plant improvement, significantly enhancing breeding efficiency and reducing the time required to achieve the desired traits (Aruna et al., 2022). The agricultural sector, more than ever, now needs even more biotechnology innovation due to the necessity of adapting crops to evolving climatic conditions prompted by climate change.

1.1.2 Medicine and Synthetic Biology

Advancements in biotechnology research in the areas of medicine and synthetic biology have facilitated the development of precise, innovative drug delivery systems. The importance of multidisciplinary approaches in enhancing the therapeutic bioavailability of protein and peptide drugs that address the nascent drug solubility and pH change-related challenges are key innovative milestone achievements in precision and molecular medicine (Naz et al., 2020). The ingenious incorporation of nanotechnology in drug delivery systems has enhanced the effectiveness of these medicines, facilitating targeted and controlled release mechanisms (O'Brien & Nelson, 2020; Onugwu et al., 2023; Sahu et al., 2021). The utilisation of microbial cell factories, such as *Bacillus licheniformis* and *Bacillus subtilis*, in biomanufacturing processes has also gained prominence, requiring more adaptive and novel safety protocols (He et al., 2023; Mohsin et al., 2021).

1.2 Safety and Biotechnology Research

The importance of safety in biotechnology cannot be overstated due to its wide range of concerns about human health, environmental integrity, and societal trust in biotechnological innovations. As biotechnology continues to advance and integrate into various sectors, the potential risks associated with safety applications need constant reassessments of measures and regulatory frameworks. Occupational health and safety in biotechnology is a fundamental concern that has garnered attention in recent years because of the high possibility of exposure to infectious agents and other biological health hazards (Chen & Reniers, 2018). Therefore, novel advancements that include the adoption of data-driven sensors to detect hazardous agents and the provision of protective equipment for workers safety can significantly improve workplace safety. Proactive safety measures are important for cultivating a secure working environment in biotechnology, underscoring the potential of AI-based systems in workplace safety, particularly where exposure to biological agents presents considerable health risks.

1.3 How Artificial Intelligence Enhances Safety

Integrating AI into various sectors may notably enhance safety protocols and practices, particularly in healthcare, manufacturing, transportation, and biotechnology. The multifaceted applications of AI may improve operational efficiency and also contribute to risk management and safety assurance. In the healthcare sector, AI has emerged as a pivotal tool in improving patient safety and surgical outcomes (Mohamed et al., 2023; Yu, 2024). This system serves as both a reminder and a regulatory tool, ensuring that critical safety measures are religiously followed during sensitive procedures. AI may also reduce staff workload, allowing workers to focus on their most important duties, and ultimately reduce the risk of workplace accidents (Perez Teixeira, 2023) (Figure 1).

Figure 1. Artificial intelligence and safety enhancement.

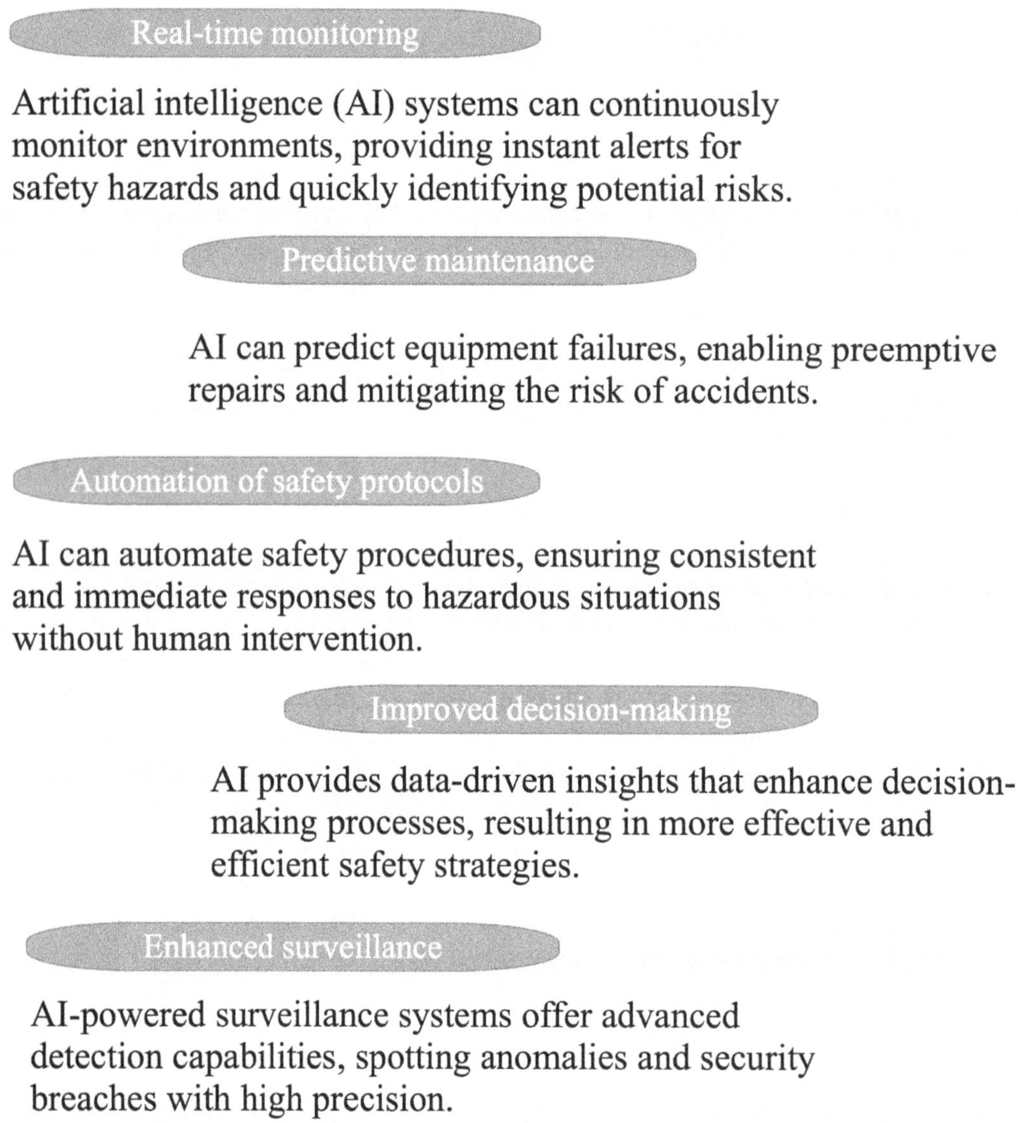

However, we must be cautious, as the rapid advancements in these fields may introduce new risks that must be carefully managed through robust regulatory frameworks. It is essential for AI systems to function properly within the purview of established safety rules for the purpose of building trust in AI applications across multiple sectors. This chapter discusses the concept of AI innovation and safety in biotechnology research under the following headings: key applications, risk management, future perspectives, stakeholder collaborations, and challenges.

2.0 KEY SAFETY APPLICATIONS OF ARTIFICIAL INTELLIGENCE

2.1 Predictive Analytics for Hazard Identification and Safety

Predictive analytics has emerged as a powerful tool for hazard identification in healthcare, biotechnology, food safety, and environmental monitoring frameworks (Agbehadji et al., 2020; Jiang et al., 2020; Misra et al., 2022). Leveraging machine learning algorithms and data-driven approaches for predictive analytics can sharpen our ability to identify potential hazards before they occur, thereby improving safety protocols and risk management strategies. The basic process of predictive analytics workflow is described in Figure 2.

Figure 2. Flowchart for hazard risk assessment utilising predictive analytical artificial intelligence to enhance workplace safety and prevent accidents.

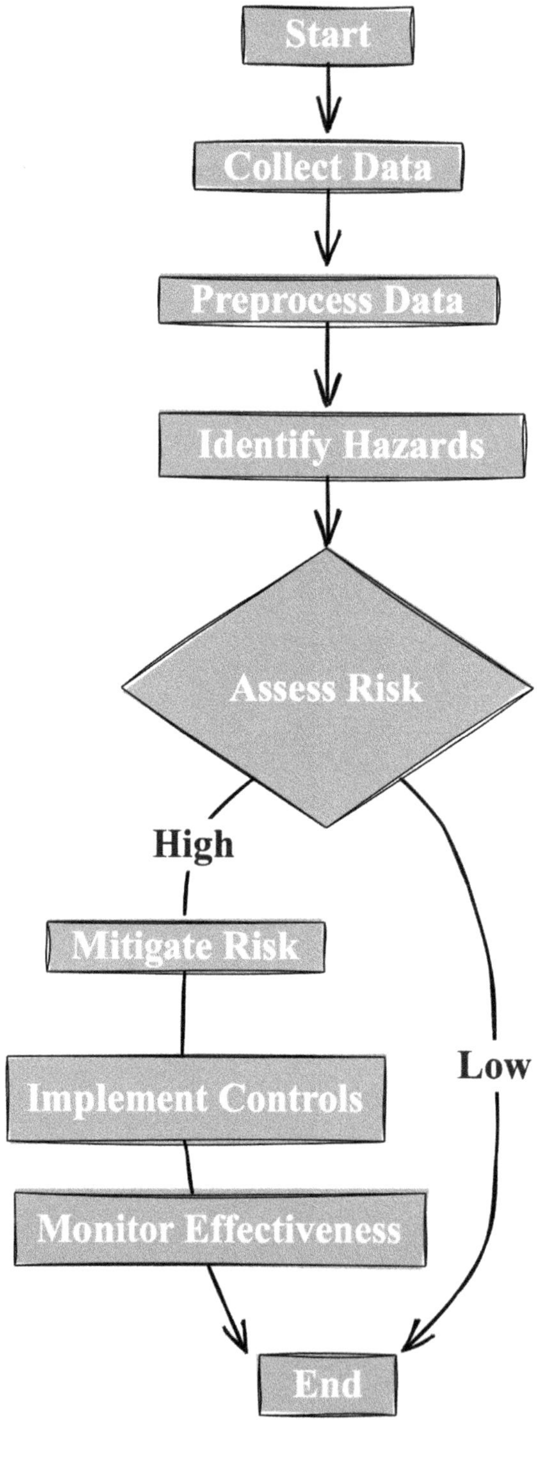

2.1.1 Metabolic Bioindicators

One of the promising applications of predictive analytics is in the identification of bioindicators for biotechnological processes. One of such is the use of machine learning methods for predicting medium-chain carboxylate production performance in anaerobic mixed microbial cultures by identifying specific microbial community data as bioindicators (Liu et al., 2022). Methods like this can significantly improve bioprocess efficiency and safety, enhance our understanding of microbial interactions, and facilitate the optimisation of biotechnological processes via community composition-based results forecasting.

2.1.2 Food Safety

Predictive analytics has been used in food safety to assess hazards associated with cultured meat and seafood products (Ong et al., 2021). While many hazards may not be uncommon, the application of predictive analytics may facilitate the identification of potential contamination risks and residues associated with novel inputs. This proactive approach to hazards assessment is central to developing standardised safety assessment methods, particularly in technologically driven, rapidly evolving industries. Using predictive analytics, we can better anticipate and mitigate risks, hence ensuring new food products are safe. A function-based classification of hazardous biological sequences that classifies biohazards at the individual sequence level has provided a more nuanced understanding of pathogenicity and associated risks (Gemler et al., 2022). Predictive analytics-based assessments of biological sequence functions can identify potential hazards more effectively and develop targeted strategies for risk lessening.

This function-centric approach represents a significant advancement in biohazard identification, away from traditional organism-centric methods. With this approach, food manufacturers can identify significant hazards at each stage of production and also prevent food wastage, ultimately contributing to safer and more sustainable food systems in compliance with acceptable international standards (Lee et al., 2021; Vărzaru, 2024).

Similarly, artificial neural networks (ANN) and Bayesian classification models have been used for the identification of hazardous endocrine-disrupting chemicals (EDCs), and in the assessment of genetically modified organisms (GMOs) for potential allergenicity (Nowicki et al., 2014; Selb et al., 2017). Intelligent AI-based systems such as predictive analytics can provide better assessment for potential allergens, GMO-associated ecological risks, adaptive chemical profile-based hazardous substances identification, and appropriate safety measures.

2.1.3 Environment

The integration of predictive analytics into the environment has been explored for improved bioremediation processes. Precision is important in identifying microbial communities, the design of microbes for effective bioremediation, and the assessment of the differential effectiveness of microbial strains in degrading contaminants for improved bioremediation strategies and environmental health (Chandran et al., 2020; Redfern et al., 2019; Srivastava et al., 2013). Predictive analytics is a critical tool for hazards identification and environmental monitoring purposes. By leveraging intelligent AI systems and data-driven approaches, we can proactively identify potential hazards, optimise processes, and enhance safety protocols.

2.2 Automated Monitoring Systems

Automated monitoring systems (AMS) can be described as autonomous installations that function with little or no human interference and provide critical safety-related data in real time. AMS, particularly those enhanced by AI, are now central to improving safety in various industries for efficiency and compliance (Mehta et al., 2024; Oliveira, 2019; Zhao et al., 2021). These systems rely on advanced technology to continuously monitor environments and processes, thereby identifying potential hazards before they become serious incidents.

AI in food safety monitoring is another area where automated systems play a crucial role, as AI can analyse data from sensors and cameras to detect potential contaminants or hazards in food production chain environments (Taneja et al., 2023; Qian et al., 2023). This capability is essential for preventing foodborne illnesses and ensuring public health via compliance with relevant health regulations for overall food quality improvement.

In healthcare, AMS have revolutionised patient safety and care management, as evident in the AI role in hemodynamic monitoring, where non-invasive AI-driven approaches can predict and manage circulatory failure, thereby improving patient outcomes (Myatra, 2024). These maintain continuous evaluation of patient conditions, facilitating timeous interventions when necessary. AMS can analyse operational data to identify potential anomalies before they lead to safety incidents, thereby ensuring the integrity of critical infrastructure.

Moreover, the integration of AI with Internet of Things (IoT) devices in various sectors can significantly enhance the capabilities of automated monitoring systems (Bhaskar et al., 2023; Borgosz & Dikicioglu, 2024; Panganiban, 2019). This proactive approach positively impacts operational efficiency and safety by ensuring that maintenance crews address critical issues promptly. The use of unmanned aerial systems (UAS) for monitoring *in situ* research or experimental sites is another innovative application of automated monitoring systems, which is of great importance for accessing real-time data on potential hazards (Akinsemoyin et al., 2023). Aerial perspective can enhance situational awareness and facilitate better decision-making regarding safety protocols. AMS have also been used in non-biotechnology industries, such as offshore petroleum and nuclear sites (Russel, 2023).

2.3 Data Management and Analysis

Data management and analysis are key record components in various fields, including healthcare, construction, and urban safety. The integration of AI into these processes enhances the ability to collect, analyse, and utilise data effectively, leading to improved decision-making and safety outcomes. In healthcare, the integration of AI into data management systems has shown significant improvement in enhancing patient safety and operational efficiency. AI can transform integrated risk management (IRM) in hospitals by analysing vast amounts of data to identify patterns and make data-driven predictions (Bozic, 2023).

AI-enabled decision support systems, when implemented correctly, can enhance patient safety by improving prompt error detection and drug management, leading to better clinical outcomes (Choudhury & Asan, 2020). This further emphasises the useful importance of robust data management in healthcare settings. The application of AI in food safety management exemplifies the importance of data analysis in ensuring public health. AI technologies are quite useful for food safety risk prediction and monitoring the supply chain (Qian et al., 2023).

3.0 AI IN RISK MANAGEMENT: IMPROVING SAFETY PROTOCOLS

3.1 Opportunities

The application of AI in risk assessment has gained significant traction across various sectors, including healthcare, aviation, and food safety. AI-driven systems enhance the ability to identify, analyse, and mitigate risks, leading to improved safety outcomes and operational efficiency. In healthcare, AI has been instrumental to developing automated risk assessment systems that enhance patient safety via the implementation of automated fall and pressure injury risk assessment systems, which categorise patients into high, moderate, and low-risk groups based on established criteria (Jin et al., 2020). These systems utilise data from patient assessments to predict risks, allowing healthcare providers to implement timely interventions.

The integration of AI into risk assessment can produce better accuracy of predictions, streamline the documentation process, and enhance overall patient care. Moreover, the development of mobile-based systems for monitoring hypertension risk exemplifies the potential of AI in healthcare risk assessment. Mobile technology can automate the risk assessment of diseases and provide healthcare professionals with real-time data to monitor patients effectively (Egejuru et al., 2019). This increases the efficiency of healthcare delivery and empowers patients to manage their health proactively, ultimately reducing the risk of complications.

The role of intelligent automation technologies in pharmacovigilance drug safety related risk assessment has been studied by Huysentruyt et al. (2021). These technologies can automate routine tasks, improve the quality and consistency of case processing, and facilitate timely assessments of safety signals. The schematic workflow chart of AI-based risk assessments is presented in Figure 3.

Figure 3. Application of data-intensive artificial intelligence-based risk assessments. (A) Schematic representation of a generic risk-based artificial intelligence response to preventing workplace accidents. (B) Enhanced machine learning model-based integrated risk assessment and accident prevention approach.

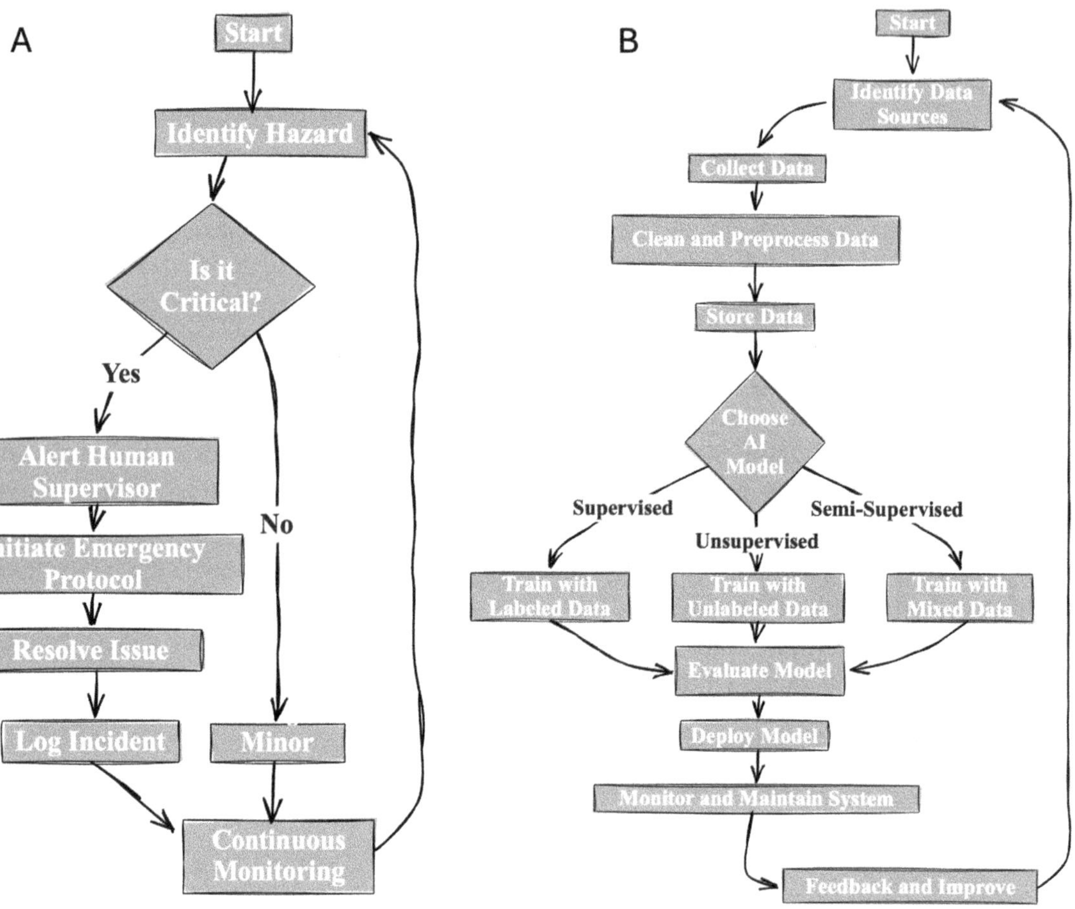

In the food industry, microbiological risk assessment is an essential component of food safety. AI can be deployed to assess microbiological risks by linking foodborne bacteria to risk factors through data analysis, which enables more accurate predictions of hazards, thereby reducing their impact on public health (Li & Wang, 2023). With AI in risk assessment, food safety professionals can make informed decisions with better outcomes on food safety.

3.2 Artificial Intelligence-Based Training Programmes

The integration of AI into training programmes has the potential to revolutionise workforce development across various sectors. AI-based training programmes can enhance learning experiences, improve skill acquisition, and increase overall productivity by improving the workforce, producing a result-orientated implementation of AI technologies within organisations. Training initiatives are key to ensuring that AI implementation translates into enhanced workforce productivity by preparing employees to embrace new technologies effectively, thereby promoting a technologically adept workforce (Nurlia, 2023).

AI plays a major role in talent management by identifying training needs and opportunities for employee growth. AI can help organisations avoid biases in recruitment processes and facilitate the identification of relevant safety-related training needs for existing employees (Rožman et al., 2022). Personalisation is another key advantage of AI-based training programmes. AI-enriched training systems can offer customised training experiences that cater to individual employee preferences and needs (Baki, 2023). This scalable flexibility allows employees to access training materials anytime and anywhere, thereby promoting a culture of continuous learning.

By tailoring training programmes to meet the specific needs of employees, organisations can further enhance engagement and retention of knowledge, ultimately leading to improved performance. In healthcare, AI-based training may enhance the skills of medical professionals, enabling them to adapt to rapidly evolving technologies for patient care. Moreover, AI-driven training programs can facilitate the development of adaptive learning environments. AI-based training systems can intelligently handle queries and adapt to the learning pace of individual users (Upadhyay & Khandelwal, 2019). This adaptability enhances the learning experience by providing timely feedback and support, ultimately leading to better skill acquisition and retention.

However, while automated training systems can increase efficiency, they must be carefully designed to ensure that they meet the specific needs of learners (Birtalan et al., 2020). Concerns about employee resistance to AI-driven training initiatives must be addressed to ensure successful implementation (Baki, 2023).

3.3 Guided AI Use

This includes giving priority to establishing clear guidelines that govern the use of AI in biotechnology, ensuring that safety and efficacy are prioritised. The complexities of intellectual property rights in biotechnology may further complicate compliance efforts. Carefully navigating intellectual property issues, such as in gene and bioprocess patents, is essential for innovative strides while ensuring that ethical standards are upheld (Chazhaev, 2023). The interplay between intellectual property rights and regulatory compliance warrants a clear understanding of how these factors influence research and development in biotechnology. Organisations must be vigilant in managing their intellectual property portfolios while adhering to regulatory requirements to avoid potential disputes and ensure compliance.

4.0 FUTURE PERSPECTIVES: ARTIFICIAL INTELLIGENCE ADOPTION, ETHICS AND PRACTICAL CONSIDERATIONS

4.1 Adoption, Ethical Considerations, Frameworks and Guidelines

The adoption of AI by different countries of the world is a sign that AI has come to stay. These adoptions, being mostly common with the developed nations, are a sign that advanced technology, despite its many applications towards achieving a better society, still remains a luxury that is only affordable by wealthy nations. In the year 2022, the AI in biotechnology market had an estimated market value of $1.2 billion with a projection of $18.9 billion by 2032, demonstrating a potential compound annual growth rate of 31.9% (Holzinger et al., 2023; Xu et al., 2022). Regional assessments show that North America held a valued market share of 41.7% in 2025, most likely driven by a robust pharmaceutical industry and research and development-based government funding (Hewlett Packard Enterprise, 2025; Kesharwani & Krishna, 2021). In Asia Pacific, AI is emerging rapidly with significant spikes in market growth, with countries like China and India investing heavily in AI for biotechnology and electronic-based governance in general (Holzinger et al., 2023). Key country-specific developments include the adoption and integration of AI by pharmaceutical giants in the United States into literacy and training programmes for employees to enhance drug discovery and safety-related regulatory compliance processes (Arnold & Porter, 2024; Hewlett Packard Enterprise, 2025). Likewise in the USA, AstraZeneca plans to invest $2.5 billion in the next five years to support new research and development in Beijing, China, featuring an AI-powered data science laboratory, while in India, Novo Nordisk is building on its operational gains by enhancing and forming AI partnerships with start-ups, leveraging AI for drug development and improved operation efficiency (Holzinger et al., 2023; Xu et al., 2022). Lastly, the United Kingdom (UK) government is investing massively in AI research, with companies like DeepMind getting the 2024 Nobel Prize in Chemistry for their AI-based invention AlphaFold software that predicts protein structure (Hewlett Packard Enterprise, 2025).

These findings substantiate the widespread adoption of AI technologies within the biotechnology industry, particularly in North America and the Asia-Pacific region, which have captured significant market share and experienced substantial growth in this domain. Key nations, such as the United States, China, India, and the United Kingdom, have emerged as leaders in integrating AI to augment research, development, and operational capabilities in the biotechnology field.

Given these possibilities, the development of ethical frameworks and guidelines is important for impactful collaborations and results. Emerging technologies, including explainable artificial intelligence (XAI), federated learning, and inferred learning, present new opportunities and challenges that warrant the establishment of ethical guidelines to ensure responsible AI development (Rama Padmaja, 2024; Srihari, 2020). Collaborative efforts among stakeholders can help create comprehensive ethical frameworks capable of addressing concerns related to bias, transparency, and accountability in AI systems.

4.1.1 Ethics by Design

The concept of "ethics by design" basically emphasises the need to integrate ethical considerations into the design and development of AI systems (Alvi, 2023). This approach encourages developers to consider the ethical implications of their technologies from the outset, ensuring that AI applications align with societal values and ethical norms.

4.1.2 Human-AI Collaboration

The potential of human-AI collaboration in enhancing the accuracy and reliability of AI-powered systems may create a synergistic scenario that can be leveraged for improved safety efficiency (Jiang et al., 2022). As AI technologies become more integrated into decision-making processes, it is essential to incorporate human judgement and expertise to checkmate potential biases and errors. This collaborative approach can improve the results and trust of AI applications among users.

4.1.3 Interdisciplinary Approaches

The complexity of AI technologies necessitates interdisciplinary collaboration to address the multifaceted challenges they present. For instance, collaborative efforts among healthcare professionals, AI experts, and researchers can enhance the development and evaluation of AI systems in healthcare settings (Yelne, 2023). Interdisciplinary workshops and training programmes can foster effective communication and collaboration, ultimately leading to better AI applications and implementations. Collaborations will play a critical role in shaping the impact of AI integration for enhanced safety across various sectors.

4.1.4 Patient Privacy and Autonomy

One of the foremost ethical concerns in the application of AI in biotechnology, particularly in healthcare, is the protection of patient privacy and autonomy. Far (2023) posited that patient privacy-related ethical considerations must be made central to the development and use of AI in precision oncology. Although concerns about data security and the potential for misuse are still quite common.

4.1.5 Bias and Fairness

The risk of bias in AI algorithms is another critical ethical issue. Bozic (2023) discusses the importance of addressing bias in AI algorithms to ensure equitable outcomes in healthcare settings. If AI systems are trained on biased datasets, they may perpetuate existing disparities in healthcare access and treatment outcomes. This emphasises the need for rigorous testing and validation of AI systems for fairness and equity in applications.

4.1.6 Transparency and Accountability

Ensuring transparency in AI algorithms is essential for building trust among stakeholders. Algorithmic transparency is a necessity in healthcare settings where patients and providers must understand, for instance, how AI systems make decisions (Naik, 2024). Establishing clear accountability measures or yardsticks for AI-driven decisions is useful for addressing potential ethical dilemmas and ensuring that stakeholders can hold systems accountable for their actions.

4.2 Practical Considerations

4.2.1 Regulatory Compliance

Ensuring compliance with existing regulations is a common practical challenge for organisations implementing AI in biotechnology. Yazdani (2023) opines that ethical implications can significantly influence consumer trust and acceptance of AI technologies. Furthermore, collaborative efforts between companies and governments are essential for addressing the sustainability challenges and risks associated with AI (Zhao & Fariñas, 2022). Organisation managers must navigate complex regulatory landscapes to ensure that their AI applications comply with relevant laws and guidelines. A proactive regulatory framework supported by rigorous corporate policies can help ensure that AI applications are accountable before being sustainable. Collaborative initiatives may further facilitate the development of harmonised regulations that accommodate more inclusive AI solutions and promote the common good.

4.2.2 Data Governance: Privacy and Security

The integration of AI technologies raises significant concerns regarding data privacy and security. For instance, while AI can enhance customer experience in business, it also poses challenges related to data privacy and ethical considerations (Oyeniran et al., 2025; Tula, 2024). A data governance framework that is both adaptive and strict is key to compliance in AI-enabled biotechnology. A data governance framework that is anything but flexible could be perceived as a regulatory constraint and can hinder the adoption of AI technologies, suggesting a plausible misunderstanding of current frameworks as barriers rather than enablers of innovation (Arigbabu, 2024). This tension between regulation and innovation further informs the need for adaptive and flexible regulatory approaches that foster the responsible use of AI while safeguarding public health and safety. Effective data governance practices must also reflect robust data management with seamless synchronisation among different relevant AI platforms for improved performance and good management practices for data protection and utilisation in compliance with relevant regulations. Regulatory frameworks must ensure a safe and ethical use of biotechnological innovations to gain public acceptance (Kimutai, 2024).

4.2.3 Training and Competency Development

The successful implementation of AI in biotechnology requires a workforce that is skilled in both AI and domain-specific knowledge. It is of utmost importance for healthcare professionals to develop competencies in data literacy and ethical awareness for optimised AI use in integrated risk management (Bozic, 2023). Biotechnology researchers and managers must invest in training programs to equip their employees with the necessary skills for handling AI technologies.

4.2.4 Balancing Innovation and Ethics

The rapid pace of innovation in biotechnology necessitates a careful balance between advancing technology and upholding ethical standards. While AI has the potential to improve research, development, and safety in biotechnology, organisations must remain vigilant in addressing ethical considerations to avoid unintended consequences (Thikare, 2024). Such a balance will increase public trust and ensure the responsible use of AI technologies.

4.3 Emerging AI Technologies

Emerging AI technologies are reshaping various biotechnology sectors by enhancing safety, efficiency, and decision-making processes. As these technologies continue to evolve, it is essential to understand their implications for safety and compliance.

4.3.1 Environmental Health and Public Safety

The transformative potential of AI in environmental health and public safety is huge, as it can readily monitor, predict, and mitigate environmental risks (Adefemi, 2023). AI systems can evaluate extensive environmental databases to identify potential threats, facilitating proactive interventions that improve community safety. For instance, AI can be utilised to predict air quality issues or track the spread of environmental contaminants, thereby informing public health responses and regulatory actions.

4.3.2 Surgical Safety

AI technologies are also making impacts in the fields of medicine and surgery. A study on the use of convolutional neural networks for automated surgical safety evaluation during laparoscopic cholecystectomy underscores the ingenious application of big data analytics to enhance the safety of surgical procedures (Jabbar, 2023). The application of AI in surgical settings can enhance instrument accuracy, safety checks, and anatomical structure recognition, thereby reducing the risk of surgical errors. AI can provide real-time feedback to surgeons, improving patient safety and surgical outcomes.

4.3.3 Pharmaceutical Supply Chains

AI technologies are revolutionising supply chain management in the pharmaceutical industry, with implications for safety and quality control. AI can optimise logistics and production processes, ultimately improving patient safety. Pharmaceutical companies can leverage AI-powered solutions to enhance their ability to track and manage products throughout the supply chain, ensuring that safety standards are met and surpassed and products delivered efficiently (Guo, 2023).

4.3.4 Food Safety

The application of AI in food biotechnology, particularly in food safety, is unfolding in an interesting manner. The role of AI is central to developing new process-aid enzymes and precision fermentation, which can enhance food safety and quality (Amore, 2023). AI systems can draw safety-related insights from data about food production processes in order to detect possible safety hazards and facilitate prompt contamination prevention measures.

5.0 MULTI-STAKEHOLDER ENGAGEMENT AND COLLABORATION

Effective integration of AI technologies necessitates collaboration among diverse stakeholders, including educators, technologists, policymakers, and researchers, to address most challenges of AI adoption for better and credible outcomes. This collaborative approach, given its concerted nature, may specifically ensure alignment with training objectives, ethical standards, and societal values in educational settings (AlAli, 2024). Addressing challenges like privacy, ethical considerations, and scalability in AI research and its applications is crucial, mostly requiring a multidisciplinary community of scientists, clinicians, regulators, and patients having a key role in achieving the desired results in areas like mental health research and practice (Graham et al., 2019). Productive communication and cooperation among these groups are key to addressing the complexities of mental health interventions and ensuring AI applications are well-grounded in clinical realities.

Regulators may consider adopting flexible and adaptive approaches to accommodate the rapid advancements in AI and biotechnology. The intersection of AI and biotechnology presents unique risks that require a razor-sharp assessment and management strategies. Health security specialists must understand the current and emerging risks at this convergence for better performance and management (O'Brien & Nelson, 2020). Robust assessment frameworks must also adequately analyse the risk landscape to ensure compliance measures effectively mitigate potential hazards.

Collaborative efforts in AI must consider ethical, practical, and operational factors to harness the full potential of AI technologies. As AI permeates various sectors, effective collaboration among diverse stakeholders becomes increasingly critical. Cross-sector collaboration in the public sector is essential for overcoming challenges such as information silos, resource constraints, and lack of technical capacity (Mikhaylov et al., 2018). Organisations may likely enhance the efficacy of AI outputs by leveraging a variety of resources and expertise through a collaborative culture.

6.0 NOTABLE CHALLENGES AND SHORTCOMINGS OF AI AND BIOTECHNOLOGY

The integration of AI in risk assessment is not without its challenges. Deep automation bias is common and can lead to over-reliance on AI systems and potential misinterpretations of data (Monteith, 2023; Strauß, 2021; Zou & Schiebinger, 2021). Furthermore, the popular notion that machines may replace humans at work often leaves an anxious impression about the future of regular work settings. While AI models have brought significant improvements to work settings, they are not completely infallible, albeit with great potential for improvement in later versions. Addressing these challenges requires a balanced approach that ensures human oversight and scrutiny remain integral to AI from development to application, including biotechnology-based risk assessment. Communicating risks to relevant stakeholders, such as employers, government organisations, and occupational safety groups, for fairness is also important.

While the application of biotechnology has led to significant advancements in the domain of food security, ethical challenges have sparked concerns from various sectors regarding the potential long-term impacts of gene-edited products on animals (Ghimire et al., 2023; Ricroch et al., 2018). However, it is important to note that gene editing techniques have also excelled in enhancing food security (Ndudzo et al., 2024; Pixley et al., 2022), which is crucial for the peace and wellness of the people worldwide. Furthermore, innovative gene editing techniques, including spray-induced gene interference (SIGI), offer a non-GMO alternative (Akbar et al., 2022; Chaloner et al., 2016; Qi et al., 2019). This approach has proven effective in enhancing virus resistance in monocotyledon and dicotyledon plant species, leveraging the plants' ability to absorb externally applied double-stranded RNA. These methods are now employed to achieve desired objectives without incorporating transgenes, addressing the ethical concerns and potential side effects associated with genetically modified foods.

Ensuring safety in biotechnological research requires carefully considering these challenges to make informed decisions and effectively apply relevant control measures. It also necessitates establishing rigorous validation processes for AI algorithms to ensure their reliability and effectiveness while adhering to applicable ethical guidelines. (Nagbøl et al., 2021; Sætra, 2022).

7.0 CONCLUSION

AI technologies may significantly enhance the dynamic and diverse field of biotechnology research by assessing performance, safety, and risk for worker protection. Automated monitoring systems powered by AI are crucial for enhancing safety in biotechnology and related sectors, as they facilitate real-time data analysis, detect possible hazards, and assure adherence to safety regulations. AI-based training programmes can significantly enhance workforce productivity, talent management, and personalised learning experiences. Ensuring compliance with AI regulations requires navigating complex regulatory frameworks, intellectual property rights, data governance, and stakeholder engagement. Ethical considerations, such as patient privacy, bias, transparency, and regulatory compliance, are major requirements for a responsible AI deployment. Adopting an ethics-centred approach, investing in training, and engaging key stakeholders, organisations can effectively navigate the challenges of AI integration and unlock its full potential.

REFERENCES

Adefemi, A. (2023). *Artificial Intelligence in Environmental Health and Public Safety: A Comprehensive Review of USA Strategies.* World Journal of Advanced Research and Reviews., DOI: 10.30574/wjarr.2023.20.3.2591

Adepoju, O., & Esan, O. (2023). Risk Management Practices and Workers Safety in University of Medical Sciences Teaching Hospital, Ondo State Nigeria. *Open Journal of Management Science (Issn 2734-2107).* DOI: 10.52417/ojms.v4i1.491

Agbehadji, I. E., Awuzie, B. O., Ngowi, A. B., & Millham, R. C. (2020). Review of big data analytics, artificial intelligence and nature-inspired computing models towards accurate detection of COVID-19 pandemic cases and contact tracing. In *International Journal of Environmental Research and Public Health* (Vol. 17, Issue 15, pp. 1–16). MDPI AG. DOI: 10.3390/ijerph17155330

Akbar, S., Wei, Y., & Zhang, M. Q. (2022). RNA Interference: Promising Approach to Combat Plant Viruses. *International Journal of Molecular Sciences 2022, Vol. 23, Page 5312, 23*(10), 5312. DOI: 10.3390/ijms23105312

Akinsemoyin, A., Awolusi, I., Chakraborty, D., Al-Bayati, A. J., & Akanmu, A. (2023). Unmanned Aerial Systems and Deep Learning for Safety and Health Activity Monitoring on Construction Sites. *Sensors (Basel), 23*(15), 6690. Advance online publication. DOI: 10.3390/s23156690 PMID: 37571475

AlAli, R. (2024). Opportunities and Challenges of Integrating Generative Artificial Intelligence in Education. *International Journal of Religion.* DOI: 10.61707/8y29gv34

Alvi, A. (2023). Exploring the Ethical Challenges of Ai in Personalised Marketing in Context of Beauty and Wellness. *International Journal of All Research Education & Scientific Methods.* DOI: 10.56025/IJARESM.2023.120124482

Amore, A. (2023). Artificial Intelligence in Food Biotechnology: Trends and Perspectives. *Front. Ind. Microbiol.* DOI: 10.3389/finmi.2023.1255505

Arigbabu, A. T. (2024). Data Governance in AI - Enabled Healthcare Systems: A Case of the Project Nightingale. *Asian Journal of Research in Computer Science.* DOI: 10.9734/ajrcos/2024/v17i5441

Arnold & Porter. (2024). *AI is Transforming Life Sciences but Raising Risk Concerns, New Benchmark Report Finds | News.* News & Perspectives. https://www.arnoldporter.com/en/perspectives/news/2024/11/ai-is-transforming-life-sciences-but-raising-risk-concerns-new-benchmark-report-finds?utm_source=chatgpt.com

Aruna, S., Rafeekher, M., Gowda, P. P., Anil, A. S., & Anjaly, V. (2022). Double Haploids for Vegetable Crop Improvement: A Review. *Agricultural Reviews (Karnal),* (Of). Advance online publication. DOI: 10.18805/ag.R-2300

Baki, N. U. (2023). Integrating Artificial Intelligence in Human Resource Functions: Challenges and Opportunities. *International Journal of Academic Research in Business & Social Sciences, 13*(8). Advance online publication. DOI: 10.6007/IJARBSS/v13-i8/18071

Banez, C., Carruthers, J. B., Gelmi, S., Kraft, A., Gaulton, C., & Hall, T. (2021). Applying Human Factors Methods to Improve Healthcare Risk Management Tools. *Proceedings of the International Symposium on Human Factors and Ergonomics in Health Care*. DOI: 10.1177/2327857921101124

Barredo Arrieta, A., Díaz-Rodríguez, N., Del Ser, J., Bennetot, A., Tabik, S., Barbado, A., Garcia, S., Gil-Lopez, S., Molina, D., Benjamins, R., Chatila, R., & Herrera, F. (2020). Explainable Artificial Intelligence (XAI): Concepts, taxonomies, opportunities and challenges toward responsible AI. *Information Fusion*, *58*, 82–115. DOI: 10.1016/j.inffus.2019.12.012

Bhaskar, N., Ramana, S., & Kumar, G. M. (2023). Internet of Things for Green Smart City Application Based on Biotechnology Techniques. *Proceedings of the International Conference on Artificial Intelligence and Knowledge Discovery in Concurrent Engineering, ICECONF 2023*. DOI: 10.1109/ICECONF57129.2023.10083965

Birtalan, E., Bánhidi, A., Sanders, J. I., Balázsfi, D., & Hangya, B. (2020). Efficient Training of Mice on the 5-Choice Serial Reaction Time Task in an Automated Rodent Training System. *Scientific Reports*, *10*(1), 22362. Advance online publication. DOI: 10.1038/s41598-020-79290-2 PMID: 33349672

Borgosz, L., & Dikicioglu, D. (2024). Industrial internet of things: What does it mean for the bioprocess industries? In *Biochemical Engineering Journal* (Vol. 201). Elsevier B.V., DOI: 10.1016/j.bej.2023.109122

Bozic, V. (2023). Integrated Risk Management and Artificial Intelligence in Hospital. *Journal of AI*, *7*(1), 63–80. DOI: 10.61969/jai.1329224

Chaloner, T., van Kan, J. A. L., & Grant-Downton, R. T. (2016). RNA 'Information Warfare' in Pathogenic and Mutualistic Interactions. *Trends in Plant Science*, *21*(9), 738–748. DOI: 10.1016/j.tplants.2016.05.008 PMID: 27318950

Chandran, H., Meena, M., & Sharma, K. (2020). Microbial Biodiversity and Bioremediation Assessment Through Omics Approaches. *Frontiers in Environmental Chemistry*, *1*, 570326. Advance online publication. DOI: 10.3389/fenvc.2020.570326

Chazhaev, M. (2023). Economic Potential of Biotechnologies: Challenges and Windows of Opportunity. *Bio Web of Conferences*. DOI: 10.1051/bioconf/20237610002

Chen, C., & Reniers, G. (2018). Risk Assessment of Processes and Products in Industrial Biotechnology. *Advances in Biochemical Engineering/Biotechnology*, *173*, 255–279. DOI: 10.1007/10_2018_74 PMID: 30244300

Choudhury, A., & Asan, O. (2020). Role of Artificial Intelligence in Patient Safety Outcomes: Systematic Literature Review. *JMIR Medical Informatics*, *8*(7), e18599. Advance online publication. DOI: 10.2196/18599 PMID: 32706688

Egejuru, N. C., Ogunlade, O., & Idowu, P. A. (2019). Development of a Mobile-Based Hypertension Risk Monitoring System. *International Journal of Information Engineering and Electronic Business*. DOI: 10.5815/ijieeb.2019.04.02

Far, B. F. (2023). Artificial Intelligence Ethics in Precision Oncology: Balancing Advancements in Technology With Patient Privacy and Autonomy. *Exploration of Targeted Anti-tumor Therapy*, 685–689. Advance online publication. DOI: 10.37349/etat.2023.00160 PMID: 37720345

Gemler, B. T., Mukherjee, C., Howland, C. A., Huk, D. J., Shank, Z., Harbo, L. J., Tabbaa, O. P., & Bartling, C. M. (2022). Function-Based Classification of Hazardous Biological Sequences: Demonstration of a New Paradigm for Biohazard Assessments. *Frontiers in Bioengineering and Biotechnology*, *10*, 979497. Advance online publication. DOI: 10.3389/fbioe.2022.979497 PMID: 36277394

Ghimire, B. K., Yu, C. Y., Kim, W. R., Moon, H. S., Lee, J., Kim, S. H., & Chung, I. M. (2023). Assessment of Benefits and Risk of Genetically Modified Plants and Products: Current Controversies and Perspective. *Sustainability 2023, Vol. 15, Page 1722, 15*(2), 1722. DOI: 10.3390/su15021722

Gong, Z. (2023). Artificial Intelligence in the 21st Century. *Research on Intelligent Manufacturing and Assembly*. DOI: 10.25082/RIMA.2023.01.002

Graham, S., Depp, C. A., Lee, E., Nebeker, C., Tu, X., Kim, H.-C., & Jeste, D. V. (2019). Artificial Intelligence for Mental Health and Mental Illnesses: An Overview. *Current Psychiatry Reports*, *21*(11), 116. Advance online publication. DOI: 10.1007/s11920-019-1094-0 PMID: 31701320

Guo, W. (2023). Exploring the Value of AI Technology in Optimizing and Implementing Supply Chain Data for Pharmaceutical Companies. *Innovation in Science and Technology*. DOI: 10.56397/IST.2023.05.01

He, H., Zhang, Y., Shi, G., & Shi, G. (2023). Recent Biotechnological Advances and Future Prospective of Bacillus Licheniformis as Microbial Cell Factories. *Systems Microbiology and Biomanufacturing*, *3*(4), 521–532. Advance online publication. DOI: 10.1007/s43393-023-00162-7

Hewlett Packard Enterprise. (2025). *Pharmaceutical Companies Embrace AI in Drug Discovery Efforts - Business Insider*. AI in Action. https://www.businessinsider.com/pharmaceutical-companies-embrace-ai-in-drug-discovery-efforts-2025-3?utm_source=chatgpt.com

Holzinger, A., Keiblinger, K., Holub, P., Zatloukal, K., & Müller, H. (2023). AI for life: Trends in artificial intelligence for biotechnology. *New Biotechnology*, *74*, 16–24. DOI: 10.1016/j.nbt.2023.02.001 PMID: 36754147

Huysentruyt, K., Kjoersvik, O., Dobracki, P., Savage, E., Mishalov, E., Cherry, M. J., Leonard, E. B., Taylor, R. C., Patel, B., & Abatemarco, D. (2021). Validating Intelligent Automation Systems in Pharmacovigilance: Insights From Good Manufacturing Practices. *Drug Safety*, *44*(3), 261–272. Advance online publication. DOI: 10.1007/s40264-020-01030-2 PMID: 33523400

Jabbar, S. F. (2023). Automated Stand-Alone Surgical Safety Evaluation for Laparoscopic Cholecystectomy (LC) Using Convolutional Neural Network and Constrained Local Models (CNN-CLM). *Journal of Robotics and Control (Jrc)*. DOI: 10.18196/jrc.v3i6.16201

Jiang, N., Liu, X., Liu, H. K., Lim, E. T., Tan, C., & Gu, J. (2022). Beyond AI-powered Context-Aware services: The Role Of human–AI Collaboration. *Industrial Management & Data Systems*. Advance online publication. DOI: 10.1108/IMDS-03-2022-0152

Jiang, X., Coffee, M., Bari, A., Wang, J., Jiang, X., Huang, J., Shi, J., Dai, J., Cai, J., Zhang, T., Wu, Z., He, G., & Huang, Y. (2020). Towards an artificial intelligence framework for data-driven prediction of coronavirus clinical severity. *Computers, Materials & Continua, 63*(1), 537–551. DOI: 10.32604/cmc.2020.010691

Jin, Y., Kim, H., Jin, T., & Lee, S.-M. (2020). *Automated Fall and Pressure Injury Risk Assessment Systems*. Cin Computers Informatics Nursing., DOI: 10.1097/CIN.0000000000000696

Kesharwani, R. K., & Krishna. (2021). Biotechnology in the Modern Medicinal System. *Biotechnology in the Modern Medicinal System*. https://doi.org/DOI: 10.1201/9781003129783/biotechnology-modern-medicinal-system-rajesh-kesharwani-krishna-misra

Kimutai, E. (2024). Adoption of Biotechnology in Livestock Production. *International Journal of Livestock Policy*. DOI: 10.47941/ijlp.1965

Kulkarni, P. A., & Singh, H. (2023). Artificial Intelligence in Clinical Diagnosis. *Journal of the American Medical Association, 330*(4), 317. Advance online publication. DOI: 10.1001/jama.2023.11440 PMID: 37410477

Lee, J. C., Daraba, A., Voidarou, C., Rozos, G., El Enshasy, H. A., & Varzakas, T. (2021). Implementation of Food Safety Management Systems Along With Other Management Tools (HAZOP, FMEA, Ishikawa, Pareto). The Case Study of Listeria Monocytogenes and Correlation With Microbiological Criteria. *Foods, 10*(9), 2169. Advance online publication. DOI: 10.3390/foods10092169 PMID: 34574279

Li, L., & Wang, C. (2023). Microbiological Risk Assessment and Its Use in Food Industry. *International Journal of Biology and Life Sciences*. DOI: 10.54097/ijbls.v2i1.5163

Liu, B., Sträuber, H., Saraiva, J., Harms, H., Silva, S. G., Kasmanas, J. C., Kleinsteuber, S., & da Rocha, U. N. (2022). Machine Learning-Assisted Identification of Bioindicators Predicts Medium-Chain Carboxylate Production Performance of an Anaerobic Mixed Culture. *Microbiome, 10*(1), 48. Advance online publication. DOI: 10.1186/s40168-021-01219-2 PMID: 35331330

Mamata, K. C., & Lamichhane, A. (2021). Advances in Agricultural Biotechnology. *Nepal Journal of Biotechnology*. Advance online publication. DOI: 10.3126/njb.v9i1.38643

Mehta, A., Niaz, M., Adetoro, A., & Nwagwu, U. (2024). Advancements in Manufacturing Technology for the Biotechnology Industry: The Role of Artificial Intelligence and Emerging Trends. *International Journal of Chemistry. Mathematics and Physics, 8*(2), 12–18. DOI: 10.22161/ijcmp.8.2.3

Mikhaylov, S., Estève, M., & Campion, A. (2018). Artificial Intelligence for the Public Sector: Opportunities and Challenges of Cross-Sector Collaboration. *Philosophical Transactions. Series A, Mathematical, Physical, and Engineering Sciences, 376*(2128), 20170357. Advance online publication. DOI: 10.1098/rsta.2017.0357 PMID: 30082303

Mishra*, S. (2024). Current Trends of Artificial Intelligence in Biotechnology. *Oajda*. DOI: 10.23880/oajda-16000112

Misra, N. N., Dixit, Y., Al-Mallahi, A., Bhullar, M. S., Upadhyay, R., & Martynenko, A. (2022). IoT, Big Data, and Artificial Intelligence in Agriculture and Food Industry. *IEEE Internet of Things Journal*, *9*(9), 6305–6324. DOI: 10.1109/JIOT.2020.2998584

Mohamed, S., El-Rahman Mohamed, M. A., Mahmoud, S. F., & Heggy, E. (2023). The Effect of Educational Program on Nurses' Knowledge and Attitude Regarding Artificial Intelligence. *Egyptian Journal of Health Care*. DOI: 10.21608/ejhc.2023.312617

Mohsin, M., Omer, R., Huang, J., Mohsin, A., Guo, M., Qian, J., & Zhuang, Y. (2021). Advances in Engineered Bacillus Subtilis Biofilms and Spores, and Their Applications in Bioremediation, Biocatalysis, and Biomaterials. *Synthetic and Systems Biotechnology*, *6*(3), 180–191. Advance online publication. DOI: 10.1016/j.synbio.2021.07.002 PMID: 34401544

Monteith, S. (2023). Artificial Intelligence and Increasing Misinformation. *The British Journal of Psychiatry*. Advance online publication. DOI: 10.1192/bjp.2023.136 PMID: 37881016

Myatra, S. N., Jagiasi, B. G., Singh, N. P., & Divatia, J. V. (2024). Role of Artificial Intelligence in Haemodynamic Monitoring. *Indian Journal of Anaesthesia*, *68*(1), 93–99. Advance online publication. DOI: 10.4103/ija.ija_1260_23 PMID: 38406336

Nagbøl, P. R., Müller, O., & Krancher, O. (2021). *Designing a Risk Assessment Tool for Artificial Intelligence Systems*. DOI: 10.1007/978-3-030-82405-1_32

Naik, A. (2024). Assessing the Impact of Climate Change on Global Crop Yields and Farming Practices. *Archives of Current Research International*. DOI: 10.9734/acri/2024/v24i5743

Naz, S., Saeed, S., & Irfan, M. (2020). Approaches and Recent Advances in Protein and Peptide Drug Delivery System. *Pakistan Journal of Medical & Health Sciences*. Advance online publication. DOI: 10.47176/PJMHS.2020.257

Ndudzo, A., Sibanda Makuvise, A., Moyo, S., & Bobo, E. D. (2024). CRISPR-Cas9 genome editing in crop breeding for climate change resilience: Implications for smallholder farmers in Africa. *Journal of Agriculture and Food Research*, *16*, 101132. DOI: 10.1016/j.jafr.2024.101132

Nowicki, P., Klos, J., & Kokot, Z. J. (2014). ANN and Bayesian Classification Models for Virtual Screening of Endocrine-Disrupting Chemicals. *Combinatorial Chemistry & High Throughput Screening*, *17*(5), 407–416. Advance online publication. DOI: 10.2174/1386207317666140219115635 PMID: 24547995

Nurlia, N. (2023). *AI Implementation Impact on Workforce Productivity : The Role of AI Training and Organizational Adaptation*. Escalate., DOI: 10.61536/escalate.v1i01.6

O'Brien, J., & Nelson, C. (2020). Assessing the Risks Posed by the Convergence of Artificial Intelligence and Biotechnology. *Health Security*, *18*(3), 219–227. Advance online publication. DOI: 10.1089/hs.2019.0122 PMID: 32559154

Oliveira, A. L. (2019). Biotechnology, Big Data and Artificial Intelligence. *Biotechnology Journal*, *14*(8), 1800613. Advance online publication. DOI: 10.1002/biot.201800613 PMID: 30927505

Ong, K. J., Johnston, J., Datar, I., Sewalt, V., Holmes, D. C., & Shatkin, J. A. (2021). Food Safety Considerations and Research Priorities for the Cultured Meat and Seafood Industry. *Comprehensive Reviews in Food Science and Food Safety*, *20*(6), 5421–5448. Advance online publication. DOI: 10.1111/1541-4337.12853 PMID: 34633147

Onugwu, A. L., Nwagwu, C. S., Onugwu, O. S., Echezona, A. C., Agbo, C. P., Ihim, S. A., Emeh, P., Nnamani, P. O., Attama, A. A., & Khutoryanskiy, V. V. (2023). Nanotechnology based drug delivery systems for the treatment of anterior segment eye diseases. *Journal of Controlled Release*, *354*, 465–488. DOI: 10.1016/j.jconrel.2023.01.018 PMID: 36642250

Oyeniran, K. A., Tenibiaje, M. O., Oke, M. A., Olowe, B. M., Oyeniran, O. H., & Oladunmoye, M. K. (2025). *Impact of COVID-19 on Electronic-Governance Adoption.*, DOI: 10.4018/979-8-3693-7678-2.ch016

Panganiban, G. G. F. (2019). E-governance in agriculture: Digital tools enabling Filipino farmers. *Journal of Asian Public Policy*, *12*(1), 51–70. DOI: 10.1080/17516234.2018.1499479

Perez Teixeira, R. L. (2023). *Exploring Sustainable Human Manufacturing: Industry 4.0, Manufacturing, and Green Marketing for a Balanced Future.* Concilium., DOI: 10.53660/CLM-1784-23M18

Pixley, K. V., Falck-Zepeda, J. B., Paarlberg, R. L., Phillips, P. W. B., Slamet-Loedin, I. H., Dhugga, K. S., Campos, H., & Gutterson, N. (2022). Genome-edited crops for improved food security of smallholder farmers. *Nature Genetics 2022 54:4, 54*(4), 364–367. DOI: 10.1038/s41588-022-01046-7

Purwanto, A., Asbari, M., & Santoso, P. B. (2019). Inovbiz Influence of Transformational and Transactional Leadership Style toward Food Safety Management System ISO 22000:2018 Performance of Food Industry in Pati Central Java. In *Inovbiz: Jurnal Inovasi Bisnis* (Vol. 7). www.ejournal.polbeng.ac.id/index.php/IBP

Qi, T., Guo, J., Peng, H., Liu, P., Kang, Z., & Guo, J. (2019). Host-Induced Gene Silencing: A Powerful Strategy to Control Diseases of Wheat and Barley. *International Journal of Molecular Sciences 2019, Vol. 20, Page 206, 20*(1), 206. DOI: 10.3390/ijms20010206

Qian, C., Murphy, S. C., Orsi, R. H., & Wiedmann, M. (2023). How Can AI Help Improve Food Safety? *Annual Review of Food Science and Technology*, *14*(1), 517–538. Advance online publication. DOI: 10.1146/annurev-food-060721-013815 PMID: 36542755

Rama Padmaja, C. V. (2024). *The Rise of AI: A Comprehensive Research Review. Iaes International Journal of Artificial Intelligence.* Ij-Ai., DOI: 10.11591/ijai.v13.i2.pp2226-2235

Redfern, L. K., Gardner, C. M., Hodzic, E., Ferguson, P. L., Hsu-Kim, H., & Gunsch, C. K. (2019). A new framework for approaching precision bioremediation of PAH contaminated soils. *Journal of Hazardous Materials*, *378*, 120859. Advance online publication. DOI: 10.1016/j.jhazmat.2019.120859 PMID: 31327574

Ricroch, A. E., Guillaume-Hofnung, M., & Kuntz, M. (2018). The ethical concerns about transgenic crops. *The Biochemical Journal*, *475*(4), 803–811. DOI: 10.1042/BCJ20170794 PMID: 29490910

Rosak-Szyrocka, J., & Abbase, A. A. (2020). Quality management and safety of food in HACCP system aspect. *Production Engineering Archives*, *26*(2), 50–53. DOI: 10.30657/pea.2020.26.11

Rožman, M., Oreški, D., & Tominc, P. (2022). Integrating Artificial Intelligence Into a Talent Management Model to Increase the Work Engagement and Performance of Enterprises. *Frontiers in Psychology*, *13*, 1014434. Advance online publication. DOI: 10.3389/fpsyg.2022.1014434 PMID: 36506984

Sætra, H. S. (2022). The AI ESG Protocol: Evaluating and Disclosing the Environment, Social, and Governance Implications of Artificial Intelligence Capabilities, Assets, and Activities. *Sustainable Development*. Advance online publication. DOI: 10.1002/sd.2438

Sahu, T., Ratre, Y. K., Chauhan, S., Bhaskar, L. V. K. S., Nair, M. P., & Verma, H. K. (2021). Nanotechnology based drug delivery system: Current strategies and emerging therapeutic potential for medical science. *Journal of Drug Delivery Science and Technology*, *63*, 102487. DOI: 10.1016/j.jddst.2021.102487

Selb, R., Wal, J., Moreno, F. J., Løvik, M., Mills, C., Hoffmann-Sommergruber, K., & Fernandez, A. (2017). Assessment of Endogenous Allergenicity of Genetically Modified Plants Exemplified by Soybean – Where Do We Stand? *Food and Chemical Toxicology*, *101*, 139–148. Advance online publication. DOI: 10.1016/j.fct.2017.01.014 PMID: 28111299

Srihari, S. N. (2020). Explainable Artificial Intelligence. *Source: Journal of the Washington Academy of Sciences*, *106*(4), 9–38. DOI: 10.2307/27130153

Srivastava, J. N., Naraian, R., Singh Kalra, S. J., & Chandra, H. (2013). Advances in Microbial Bioremediation and the Factors Influencing the Process. *International Journal of Environmental Science and Technology*. Advance online publication. DOI: 10.1007/s13762-013-0412-z

Strauß, S. (2021). Deep Automation Bias: How to Tackle a Wicked Problem of AI? *Big Data and Cognitive Computing*, *5*(2), 18. Advance online publication. DOI: 10.3390/bdcc5020018

Thikare, V. P., & Pathak, P. S. (2024). Decoding Tomorrows Biotechnology: AI and Machine Learning Unveiled. *International Journal for Research in Applied Science and Engineering Technology*, *12*(2), 727–742. Advance online publication. DOI: 10.22214/ijraset.2024.58430

Thomas, S., Abraham, A., Baldwin, J., Piplani, S., & Petrovsky, N. (2021). *Artificial Intelligence in Vaccine and Drug Design*. DOI: 10.1007/978-1-0716-1884-4_6

Tula, S. T. (2024). *Ai-Enabled Customer Experience Enhancement in Business*. Computer Science & It Research Journal., DOI: 10.51594/csitrj.v5i2.789

Upadhyay, A. K., & Khandelwal, K. (2019). Artificial Intelligence-Based Training Learning From Application. *Development and Learning in Organizations*, *33*(2), 20–23. Advance online publication. DOI: 10.1108/DLO-05-2018-0058

Vărzaru, A. A. (2024). Unveiling Digital Transformation: A Catalyst for Enhancing Food Security and Achieving Sustainable Development Goals at the European Union Level. *Foods*, *13*(8), 1226. Advance online publication. DOI: 10.3390/foods13081226 PMID: 38672898

Wang, B., & Wang, Y. (2021). Big data in safety management: An overview. *Safety Science*, *143*, 105414. Advance online publication. DOI: 10.1016/j.ssci.2021.105414

Xu, D., Liu, B., Wang, J., & Zhang, Z. (2022). Bibliometric analysis of artificial intelligence for biotechnology and applied microbiology: Exploring research hotspots and frontiers. *Frontiers in Bioengineering and Biotechnology*, *10*, 998298. DOI: 10.3389/fbioe.2022.998298 PMID: 36277390

Xue, Y., & Liu, S. (2022). Towards Better Governance on Biosafety and Biosecurity: China's Advances and Perspectives in Medical Biotechnology Legislation. *Frontiers in Bioengineering and Biotechnology*, *10*, 939295. Advance online publication. DOI: 10.3389/fbioe.2022.939295 PMID: 35860327

Yazdani, A. (2023). *The Impact of AI on Trends, Design, and Consumer Behavior*. Aitechbesosci., DOI: 10.61838/kman.aitech.1.4.2

Yelne, S., Chaudhary, M., Dod, K., Sayyad, A., & Sharma, R. (2023). Harnessing the Power of AI: A Comprehensive Review of Its Impact and Challenges in Nursing Science and Healthcare. *Cureus*. Advance online publication. DOI: 10.7759/cureus.49252 PMID: 38143615

Yu, X. (2024). Artificial Intelligence-Based Perioperative Safety Verification System Improved the Performance of Surgical Safety Verification Execution. *American Journal of Translational Research*, *16*(4), 1295–1305. Advance online publication. DOI: 10.62347/PUUT2092 PMID: 38715820

Zhao, J., & Fariñas, B. G. (2022). Artificial Intelligence and Sustainable Decisions. *European Business Organization Law Review*. Advance online publication. DOI: 10.1007/s40804-022-00262-2

Zhao, Z., Wu, J., Li, T., Sun, C., Yan, R., & Chen, X. (2021). Challenges and Opportunities of AI-Enabled Monitoring, Diagnosis & Prognosis: A Review. In *Chinese Journal of Mechanical Engineering (English Edition)* (Vol. 34, Issue 1). Springer. DOI: 10.1186/s10033-021-00570-7

Zou, J., & Schiebinger, L. (2021). Ensuring That Biomedical AI Benefits Diverse Populations. *EBioMedicine*, *67*, 103358. Advance online publication. DOI: 10.1016/j.ebiom.2021.103358 PMID: 33962897

ADDITIONAL READING

Chakravarthi, P. G., Dsvnm, R., Svgva, P., & Prasad, G. V. A. (2024). AI and Machine Learning in Biotechnology: A Paradigm Shift in Biochemical Innovation Affiliation. *International Journal of Plant. Animal and Environmental Sciences*, *14*(4), 70–80. DOI: 10.26502/ijpaes.4490166

Congressional Research Service. (2023). Artificial Intelligence in the Biological Sciences: Uses, Safety, Security, and Oversight. Https://Crsreports.Congress.Gov. https://crsreports.congress.gov

Gomes, A., Gonçalves, B., Inglês, B., Silvério, S., Pinto, C. A., & Saraiva, J. A. (2024). Potential Impacts of Artificial Intelligence (AI) in Biotechnology. *Applied Sciences 2024, Vol. 14, Page 11801, 14*(24), 11801. DOI: 10.3390/app142411801

KEY TERMS AND DEFINITIONS

AI: Artificial Intelligence

XAI: Explainable Artificial Intelligence
HAZOP: Hazard and Operability
ANN: Artificial Neural Networks
EDCs: Endocrine Disrupting Chemicals
GMOs: Genetically Modified Organisms
AMS: Automated Monitoring Systems
IoT: Internet of Things
IRM: Integrated Risk Management
UAS: Unmanned Aerial Systems

Chapter 5
Automated Health and Safety Recommendations Using LSTM in Hazardous Workplaces

Bhimavarapu Usharani
https://orcid.org/0000-0002-0246-1420
Koneru Lakshmaiah Education Foundation, India

ABSTRACT

Monitoring of workplace conditions and employee health is crucial to ensuring worker safety and compliance with regulatory standards. In environments where exposure to hazardous factors such as chemicals, noise, or extreme temperatures is common, real-time tracking of exposure levels can help prevent health risks. This study presents a recommendation system based on Long Short-Term Memory (LSTM) networks, designed to monitor and predict workplace exposure risks using sequential data. The system leverages preprocessed exposure data, including environmental conditions and worker-specific health information, to generate personalized safety recommendations. By analyzing historical exposure patterns, the LSTM model identifies potential hazards and suggests timely interventions, such as protective measures or adjustments to work schedules. The system also integrates real-time alerts, which are generated when exposure levels exceed predefined limits, ensuring workers receive immediate safety instructions.

INTRODUCTION

Real-Time Monitoring of Workplace Conditions and Employee Health involves continuously tracking and evaluating various environmental and health parameters to ensure the safety and well-being of employees. The integration of advanced technologies such as IoT sensors, machine learning models, and mobile applications allows for the real-time collection and analysis of data, enabling immediate actions to be taken if any workplace conditions exceed predefined safety thresholds. The main goal of real-time monitoring is to detect and mitigate potential health risks promptly, enhancing both employee health and productivity in the workplace.

In this system, monitoring devices are used by employees during their work shifts to measure environmental conditions such as exposure to hazardous substances, temperature, humidity, and noise levels. These devices continuously collect data and transmit it to a central server via Wi-Fi. The server processes

DOI: 10.4018/979-8-3693-9301-7.ch005

this data and checks if any parameters exceed the predefined safety limits. If any dangerous levels are detected, the system generates alerts through visual signals, such as LED lights on the monitoring devices, or notifications to supervisors, helping to ensure that appropriate actions are taken in real time.

The server plays a crucial role in this ecosystem, functioning as the central hub where all data is collected, analyzed, and stored. This cloud-based platform provides access to detailed employee health records, including exposure levels, health metrics, and the status of alerts. Web applications allow employers to manage employee health data, report changes such as dismissals or retirements, and monitor alerts. In the future, the server will also integrate machine learning models to predict potential health risks based on historical data, providing proactive measures and personalized recommendations for each worker.

Employees benefit from this real-time monitoring system through a mobile application that allows them to track their exposure levels and health metrics in real time. They can view a summary of their daily data or dive deeper into historical information. The mobile app also empowers employees to take necessary actions to protect their health, such as taking breaks, using protective gear, or notifying supervisors about abnormal exposure levels. This app helps maintain a healthy and safe work environment while ensuring that workers remain informed about their health status.

The integration of machine learning and AI into real-time monitoring systems takes the concept further by continuously learning from the data collected. With time, these models can predict future health risks based on employee behavior and historical exposure data. By integrating these advanced technologies, employers can not only comply with workplace safety regulations but also enhance the overall health and well-being of their workforce. This proactive approach to health monitoring in workplaces is becoming an essential tool for industries aiming to reduce occupational risks, improve employee satisfaction, and optimize productivity.

AI significantly enhances the real-time monitoring of workplace conditions and employee health by transforming vast amounts of data into valuable insights that can drive proactive safety measures. One of the primary ways AI contributes is through predictive analytics, where machine learning algorithms analyze both historical and real-time data to forecast potential health risks. For example, by identifying patterns in exposure data, AI can predict when an employee is at risk of overexposure to hazardous substances or dangerous environments, enabling the system to generate proactive alerts and suggest preventive actions. This predictive capability helps reduce the likelihood of accidents or health issues before they occur.

Another key function of AI is anomaly detection, where it continuously monitors data from sensors and devices for unusual patterns that might indicate unsafe conditions. If exposure levels exceed predefined limits, AI can automatically identify this and trigger alerts, ensuring that corrective actions are taken quickly. This can be particularly important in environments where exposure to dangerous chemicals, excessive noise, or other hazards poses a significant risk to employee health. AI's ability to detect these anomalies in real time allows for immediate intervention, preventing potential health hazards.

AI also plays a crucial role in health monitoring by integrating data from wearable devices, such as heart rate, fatigue, and sleep quality, to assess the overall health of employees. By analyzing this data, AI can identify correlations between an employee's health and their work environment, offering a more comprehensive understanding of how workplace conditions may impact their well-being. For example, AI might identify that high stress levels correlate with increased exposure to certain hazards, prompting the system to notify both the worker and supervisors of potential risks.

Moreover, AI offers personalized recommendations based on an individual employee's health data and exposure history. By considering factors such as the employee's previous exposure to hazardous substances or patterns in their health metrics, AI can suggest tailored protective measures, such as taking breaks, wearing specific protective gear, or adjusting work schedules. These recommendations help employees manage their health more effectively while maintaining safety standards.

Finally, AI enables the automation of alert systems, ensuring that both supervisors and employees are immediately notified when unsafe conditions are detected. By processing real-time data and running predictive models, AI ensures that alerts are timely and actionable. Additionally, as AI systems continuously learn from new data, they become more accurate and efficient over time, improving their ability to predict risks and provide tailored safety recommendations. Through continuous learning, AI enhances the overall workplace safety strategy by adapting to changing conditions and improving its ability to identify emerging risks. Ultimately, AI-driven systems create a dynamic, responsive safety environment, reducing health risks and fostering a culture of safety in the workplace.

The existing models for occupational health and safety provide valuable insights into how IoT, AI, and wearable technologies can enhance safety management. However, many face limitations that hinder their broader applicability, scalability, and effectiveness in diverse industries. For instance, Teufer et al. (2019) discuss evidence-based interventions for occupational health but struggle with generalizing these approaches to small and medium-sized enterprises (SMEs), which often face resource constraints. Similarly, Jilcha & Kitaw (2017) highlight innovations in industrial occupational safety but fail to provide a practical implementation roadmap for SMEs, which are limited by financial and technical barriers. The Global Burden of Occupational Disease (Rushton, 2017) model falls short by not incorporating modern technologies like AI and IoT, which could be pivotal in reducing the global burden of occupational diseases.

The Economic Burden of Work Injuries and Diseases (Tompa et al., 2021) focuses primarily on economic aspects and lacks a connection to real-time monitoring or AI-driven interventions for preventing injuries. Vaidya et al. (2018) provide a glimpse into Industry 4.0 technologies but fail to address how these can be effectively implemented in safety management systems. Yu & Schweisfurth (2020) also focus on Industry 4.0, but their solutions lack clear scalability for SMEs in occupational safety contexts. Mourtzis et al. (2022) in their work on the challenges and opportunities of transitioning to Society 5.0, lack specific case studies that show how the transition can directly improve occupational safety and health. Similarly, Mourtzis et al. (2022)'s Operator 5.0 for Digital Manufacturing focuses mostly on manufacturing operators and fails to address the broader spectrum of worker safety across various industries.

Maddikunta et al. (2022) offer an Industry 5.0 framework for enabling technologies but fail to provide a clear pathway for integrating AI and IoT solutions for real-time workplace health monitoring and risk mitigation. Khan et al. (2020) discuss the Industrial Internet of Things (IIoT) but have limited focus on how IIoT can be applied to real-time occupational safety and health monitoring systems. Aqueveque et al. (2017) focus on monitoring physiological variables of mining workers but their solution has limited adaptability to other industries and relies on specialized sensors that may not be feasible in all work environments. Sánchez et al. (2020) emphasize smart protective equipment but lack a comprehensive system integrating real-time data analysis for hazard prediction and intervention.

Yang et al. (2020) utilize deep learning for classifying work-related physical load levels, but this approach is constrained by the need for high-quality labeled data, which is often unavailable for many occupational settings. Kim et al. (2020) propose an IoT-based construction worker physiological monitoring platform but do not incorporate predictive analytics based on physiological data to preemptively address health risks. Campero-Jurado et al. (2020) introduce a Smart Helmet 5.0 for industrial IoT using

AI, but the reliance on expensive hardware makes it difficult to implement in industries with financial constraints. Costa & Souto (2022) present an IoT device for monitoring pollutants but focus only on pollutant monitoring, lacking a broader safety management system that includes worker health metrics.

Singh et al. (2022) develop an IoT-enabled helmet for safeguarding mine workers' health but their model is highly dependent on connectivity and power, which can be unreliable in certain environments. Similarly, Rajakumar & Choi (2023)'s helmet-mounted real-time toxic gas monitoring system does not address the integration of multiple environmental factors in real-time monitoring for a holistic health and safety approach. Lemos et al. (2022) focus on environmental risk assessment in Industry 4.0, but their model emphasizes environmental risks without addressing the physiological impacts of occupational health hazards. Fanti et al. (2022) review sensing technologies for occupational risk assessment, but their discussion lacks practical implementation details for real-world occupational settings.

Lemos et al. (2022) in their model of individual environmental risk assessment in Industry 4.0 fail to provide a comprehensive framework for integrating individual worker health metrics into the environmental risk assessment model. Maltseva (2020) discusses wearable technologies for employee engagement but with limited focus on direct health and safety monitoring. Fugate & Alzraiee (2023) examine wearable sensing devices for construction safety, but their model does not account for workers' comfort and the potential impact of wearable devices on their overall well-being. Jiang et al. (2022) conduct a critical review of Industry 4.0 technologies in occupational safety, but their review lacks specific details on how to integrate these technologies for practical, real-time monitoring in diverse occupational settings.

Waqar et al. (2023) discuss challenges to IoT adoption for safety management in small construction projects but focus primarily on small-scale projects and do not explore broader implementation frameworks for IoT in larger industries. Nnaji et al. (2021) propose wearable sensing devices for personalized risk mitigation, but their model relies on constant connectivity and power for real-time monitoring, which may not be feasible in environments with poor infrastructure. Hew et al. (2022) focus on low-cost UV index monitoring stations, but their approach lacks integration with other environmental or physiological factors in the risk assessment process. Failing et al. (2023) present a tool condition monitoring system for rapid deployment, but the system's reliance on low-cost sensors limits its ability to capture detailed, high-accuracy data, which may affect the overall safety assessment quality.

These existing models offer insights into how advanced technologies can improve occupational health and safety but are hindered by issues such as limited scalability, reliance on specific hardware, lack of real-time monitoring capabilities, and insufficient integration of various monitoring factors for a holistic approach to worker safety.

The proposed models using ESA (Ensemble Sentiment Analysis), CNN (Convolutional Neural Networks), and LSTM (Long Short-Term Memory) represent significant advancements over the limitations of existing models in occupational health and safety management. These approaches overcome several key challenges faced by traditional models, such as limited scalability, reliance on specific hardware, and the lack of real-time monitoring capabilities.

ESA provides a more robust way to integrate and analyze multiple sources of data, addressing the challenge of data scarcity and the need for high-quality labeled datasets, as noted in models like Yang et al. (2020). By combining multiple sentiment analysis methods, ESA can generate insights from incomplete or noisy data, making it more adaptable to various occupational settings, especially where labeled data may be limited. This is crucial for ensuring that safety interventions are responsive to evolving conditions in real-time, unlike traditional models that rely on static, pre-defined datasets.

CNN, with its ability to automatically learn features from raw input data, enhances the detection and classification of health risks in occupational settings. This deep learning model overcomes the limitation of specialized sensors, as seen in Aqueveque et al. (2017), which often fail to be universally applicable across industries. CNNs can process visual and sensor data more effectively, enabling the development of more scalable and adaptable safety monitoring systems. For instance, in environments where specialized sensors may not be feasible, CNNs can still extract meaningful insights from available image data, such as thermal or video surveillance, to predict and prevent workplace hazards.

LSTM networks, known for their strength in processing sequential data, significantly improve the predictive capabilities of occupational health monitoring systems. These models address the issue of real-time monitoring and predictive analytics, as highlighted in models like Kim et al. (2020), which lack the ability to predict health risks before they occur. By leveraging LSTM's ability to learn from past sequences of physiological and environmental data, they can anticipate potential health risks, such as stress or fatigue, providing early warnings before adverse events occur. LSTM's ability to capture long-term dependencies in data also ensures that these predictions are more reliable, enabling proactive interventions, unlike traditional systems that may only react after an incident has occurred.

Together, ESA, CNN, and LSTM offer a more integrated, adaptive, and predictive approach to occupational health and safety, overcoming the scalability issues, reliance on specific hardware, and lack of predictive capabilities that have hindered existing models. These technologies pave the way for more efficient, real-time, and comprehensive health and safety monitoring systems in diverse industries, ultimately improving worker safety and well-being.

MATERIALS AND METHODOLOGY

The methodology involves collecting real-time workplace exposure data, including environmental factors and worker health information, and preprocessing it for feature extraction. LSTM networks are used to model sequential dependencies in the data, learning patterns from historical exposure trends. The model is trained to classify exposure risks and generate personalized safety recommendations. Real-time data is then fed into the trained LSTM model for exposure prediction and risk assessment. Alerts are triggered when exposure levels exceed predefined thresholds, providing immediate safety instructions. The system continuously learns and adapts, enhancing recommendation accuracy over time.

Material

The monitoring system is a comprehensive solution designed to ensure worker safety by tracking exposure levels and providing actionable insights through an integrated network of devices, cloud servers, and applications. It is composed of three main components: monitoring devices, a cloud-based server, and a mobile application, each serving a unique purpose in the ecosystem.

The monitoring devices are essential tools used by workers during their shifts. These devices are equipped to collect real-time exposure data, such as environmental conditions or hazardous levels, and transmit this data to a central server via Wi-Fi. In addition to data collection, the devices are programmed to evaluate whether the measured exposure levels comply with the regulatory limits set by current health and safety standards. If any exposure value exceeds the predefined threshold, the monitoring devices immediately activate alarms. This is achieved through the illumination of specific LEDs, ensuring that workers are promptly notified about potentially hazardous conditions. This proactive feature helps minimize risks by enabling workers to take immediate corrective actions.

The server, hosted in the cloud, serves as the central hub for data storage, processing, and management. It collects all the exposure data transmitted by the monitoring devices and organizes it for further analysis. The server supports two web applications that provide a range of functionalities. The first web application is designed for company administrators and enables them to register employees by inputting their health and safety information. This application also allows companies to view detailed employee data, manage employment records such as retirements or dismissals, and review alerts generated based on the collected health and exposure data. The second web application focuses on data visualization and reporting. It provides interactive graphs that display exposure trends over time, helping companies identify patterns or areas of concern. Furthermore, this application includes an option to download the data in CSV format, facilitating deeper analysis or integration with other systems. In future stages of development, the server will also host machine learning-based software to enhance the system's capabilities. This software will use historical exposure data to generate more accurate alerts and provide tailored recommendations for improving workplace safety.

The mobile application complements the system by offering workers direct access to their exposure data. Through this application, workers can view both a summarized version and a detailed history of their exposure levels. This empowers them to stay informed about their safety conditions and track their long-term exposure trends. By providing this information in an accessible format, the mobile application fosters greater awareness and accountability among workers.

Together, these components create a robust monitoring system that not only tracks and manages exposure data but also supports proactive decision-making to safeguard worker health. As the system evolves, its integration with advanced technologies like machine learning will further enhance its effectiveness in predicting risks and suggesting preventive measures.

Preprocessing

The preprocessing of the collected dataset is a crucial step to ensure the data's quality, consistency, and readiness for analysis or model development. It begins with validating the data collected from the monitoring devices, checking for incomplete transmissions, missing records, duplicate entries, and ensuring proper chronological order through timestamp verification. Once validated, the data is cleaned to remove irrelevant or erroneous information. Missing values are handled using techniques such as interpolation for time-series data or mean, median, or mode imputation for numerical or categorical data. Outliers, which could indicate device errors or genuine anomalies, are identified using statistical methods like Z-scores or the interquartile range (IQR) and appropriately treated. Noise from environmental factors not relevant to the dataset is also removed to improve clarity.

After cleaning, data normalization and scaling are applied to standardize numerical attributes. Methods like min-max scaling or Z-score standardization are used to ensure that all features are on consistent scales, which is essential for accurate analysis and machine learning model performance. Feature engineering follows, involving the creation of new metrics such as peak exposure hours, cumulative exposure, or regulatory compliance flags, which add meaningful insights to the dataset. Data integration is then performed to merge exposure data with worker health records and other relevant sources, providing a comprehensive view of the information.

Data transformation is another key step, where the dataset is reshaped and reformatted to meet specific analysis or modeling requirements. This includes encoding categorical variables, parsing exposure levels into discrete ranges or classes, and organizing the data into tabular or time-series formats. For datasets with imbalanced classes, such as rare critical alarms, techniques like oversampling (e.g., SMOTE) or undersampling are applied, and cost-sensitive models may be employed to prioritize minority classes during classification tasks. Additionally, data annotation is performed to add meaningful labels, such as compliance status, or metadata to facilitate supervised learning.

To improve interpretability and reduce redundancy, the dataset undergoes aggregation, where metrics like daily exposure averages or maximum values are computed and grouped by categories such as worker roles or locations. Finally, the preprocessed data is formatted for storage in structured formats like CSV, JSON, or relational databases, ensuring compatibility with downstream applications. A thorough validation and quality check is conducted at the end of the process to verify data accuracy, consistency, and alignment with regulatory compliance rules. This comprehensive preprocessing pipeline ensures that the dataset is clean, reliable, and well-suited for visualization, analysis, or machine learning tasks.

Feature Extraction

Explicit Semantic Analysis (ESA) is an advanced technique that enhances feature extraction by mapping textual or categorical data to a high-dimensional semantic space built from a predefined knowledge base, such as Wikipedia or domain-specific resources. In the context of the preprocessed monitoring and exposure dataset, ESA can transform textual attributes like health records, alert descriptions, or environmental conditions into meaningful, concept-based features that provide richer insights. The process begins by identifying relevant attributes within the dataset, such as exposure categories or alert messages, that would benefit from semantic enrichment. These attributes are then cleaned and preprocessed through steps like tokenization, removal of stop words, and text normalization to prepare them for semantic mapping.

Using ESA, the textual data is represented as weighted vectors in a semantic space, where each dimension corresponds to the relevance of a specific concept from the knowledge base. For example, an alert message such as "high chemical exposure" could map to concepts like "Industrial Safety," "Chemical Regulations," and "Hazardous Substances," each with an associated weight indicating its relevance. These semantic vectors are then integrated into the dataset as new features, enhancing its representation for downstream tasks like exposure prediction, anomaly detection, or compliance monitoring. To ensure computational efficiency, dimensionality reduction techniques like PCA or t-SNE can be applied to reduce the complexity of the generated vectors while retaining the most informative features.

The use of ESA enriches the dataset by adding context and meaning to textual data, bridging the gap between raw textual information and its underlying semantics. This approach improves the accuracy and interpretability of machine learning models by enabling them to understand complex relationships and patterns in the data. For instance, in predicting worker health risks, ESA-generated features could highlight correlations between specific exposure scenarios and regulatory compliance concepts, thereby providing actionable insights. Overall, ESA is a powerful tool for transforming unstructured textual data into semantically rich features, making it particularly valuable for applications in occupational health and safety monitoring.

Exposure Data and Generating Alerts

The implementation of Convolutional Neural Networks (CNNs) for processing exposure data and generating alerts for workers provides a powerful mechanism for identifying patterns and risks in workplace environments. Exposure data, such as noise levels, chemical concentrations, temperature readings, and other workplace hazard metrics, can be effectively analyzed using CNNs to detect potential risks and generate real-time alerts. To achieve this, the raw exposure data is first prepared for CNN processing. This includes transforming time-series data into visual representations like heatmaps, spectrograms, or line plots, which capture temporal and spatial patterns. Categorical data, such as worker roles or locations, is encoded and integrated with numerical metrics, ensuring all relevant factors are included in the analysis. Additionally, data augmentation techniques can be employed to simulate various scenarios, enhancing the model's robustness.

The CNN architecture for this purpose typically consists of multiple convolutional layers that extract local patterns, pooling layers that reduce dimensionality while retaining key features, and fully connected layers that classify the data into predefined risk categories, such as safe exposure, mild risk, or critical risk. Activation functions like ReLU introduce non-linearity, enabling the model to capture complex patterns in the data. The CNN model is trained on labeled exposure data to learn the relationships between input metrics and risk categories. During training, a loss function such as categorical cross-entropy or binary cross-entropy is minimized using optimization algorithms like Adam to improve the model's accuracy.

Once trained, the CNN is deployed for real-time exposure monitoring. Real-time data from monitoring devices are fed into the model, which analyzes the patterns and classifies them into risk levels. If a critical risk is detected, the system immediately triggers alerts to workers. These alerts can be communicated through various channels, such as alarms or LED indicators on wearable monitoring devices and notifications in mobile applications. The mobile application may provide additional details, such as the nature and severity of the risk, allowing workers to take timely action.

The use of CNNs in this context offers several advantages, including the ability to detect complex, non-linear patterns, process data in real-time, and adapt to different types of exposure data across various workplace environments. Furthermore, this approach is scalable, allowing it to handle large volumes of data efficiently. Future enhancements could involve integrating CNNs with recurrent neural networks (RNNs) for improved analysis of sequential data, leveraging historical exposure records to refine predictions, and personalizing alerts based on individual worker profiles. Overall, CNN-based exposure monitoring systems enable intelligent, proactive risk management, ensuring safer working conditions and reducing workplace hazards.

Recommender System

To build a recommendation system using LSTM (Long Short-Term Memory) for worker exposure data, the process begins with preparing the data, which has already been preprocessed, features extracted, and exposure levels monitored. The data, structured as time-series, captures sequential exposure metrics such as noise levels, chemical concentrations, and temperature over time, as well as worker-specific attributes like job roles and health conditions. These metrics are organized into time windows, where each window represents exposure data over a specific period, such as hours or days, with corresponding labels for recommended actions, such as taking breaks, using additional protective gear, or changing work environments.

Next, the LSTM model is designed to handle this sequential data. The model consists of several LSTM layers that process the input time-series data, capturing temporal patterns and dependencies in exposure levels. LSTM's ability to remember long-term dependencies in sequential data is particularly valuable for identifying trends and predicting future exposure risks based on past data. Dropout layers can be included to prevent overfitting, ensuring the model generalizes well across unseen data. The output layer of the model provides the recommendation based on the predicted risk level, helping to suggest actions such as safety measures or work adjustments.

During the training phase, the LSTM model learns to map past exposure data to the appropriate recommendations. The model is trained on labeled data, where the input is the sequence of exposure metrics, and the output is the corresponding recommendation for the worker. Optimization techniques like Adam are used to minimize the loss function and adjust the model's weights to improve accuracy. Once trained, the LSTM model can be deployed to monitor real-time data from workers. As exposure data is collected, the model processes the sequences of input data, predicts future exposure risks, and generates timely, personalized recommendations, ensuring workers receive alerts when action is needed. This recommendation system enhances workplace safety by proactively managing risks based on past exposure trends.

EXPERIMETNATL RESULTS

The experimental results demonstrate the effectiveness of the LSTM-based recommendation system in predicting workplace exposure risks and providing timely safety recommendations. The model was trained using historical exposure data from workers, incorporating factors such as environmental conditions and individual health metrics. The results show that the system successfully identifies patterns in the data, predicting exposure levels with high accuracy. Additionally, the LSTM model generates personalized recommendations based on real-time data, effectively alerting workers when exposure thresholds are exceeded. The system's performance was evaluated through various metrics, including prediction accuracy, recall, and precision, which confirmed its ability to improve worker safety and mitigate health risks in dynamic work environments.

Table 1 presents a comparison of preprocessing performance across various machine learning models, focusing on the time taken for different stages of preprocessing: data cleaning, missing value imputation, noise removal, and data transformation. The Proposed (LSTM) model demonstrates the shortest processing times for all stages, taking 15 seconds for data cleaning, 8 seconds for missing value imputation, 12 seconds for noise removal, and 10 seconds for data transformation. In comparison, the Support Vector Machine (SVM) model requires slightly more time, with 18 seconds for data cleaning, 10 seconds for missing value imputation, 14 seconds for noise removal, and 11 seconds for data transformation.

The Random Forest (RF) model shows comparable efficiency, with a data cleaning time of 17 seconds, missing value imputation at 9 seconds, and noise removal taking 13 seconds. The K-Nearest Neighbors (KNN) model, however, takes longer, with 20 seconds for data cleaning and 11 seconds for missing value imputation, followed by 15 seconds for noise removal and 12 seconds for data transformation. Similarly, Logistic Regression (LR) and Naive Bayes (NB) models show relatively longer preprocessing times, with LR taking 22 seconds for data cleaning, 12 seconds for imputation, 16 seconds for noise removal, and

13 seconds for data transformation. Naive Bayes (NB) requires 21 seconds for data cleaning, 11 seconds for imputation, 15 seconds for noise removal, and 12 seconds for data transformation.

Other models like Decision Tree (DT), Gradient Boosting (GB), and XGBoost (XGB) have preprocessing times similar to one another, with DT requiring 19 seconds for data cleaning, 10 seconds for imputation, 14 seconds for noise removal, and 10 seconds for data transformation. GB takes 19 seconds for data cleaning, 9 seconds for imputation, 13 seconds for noise removal, and 11 seconds for data transformation, while XGBoost (XGB) requires 18 seconds for data cleaning, 10 seconds for imputation, 14 seconds for noise removal, and 10 seconds for data transformation.

Table 1. Preprocessing performance comparison

Model	Data Cleaning Time (s)	Missing Value Imputation Time (s)	Noise Removal Time (s)	Data Transformation Time (s)
Proposed	15	8	12	10
Support Vector Machine (SVM)	18	10	14	11
Random Forest (RF)	17	9	13	9
K-Nearest Neighbors (KNN)	20	11	15	12
Logistic Regression (LR)	22	12	16	13
Decision Tree (DT)	19	10	14	10
Naive Bayes (NB)	21	11	15	12
Artificial Neural Networks (ANN)	16	8	12	9
Gradient Boosting (GB)	19	9	13	11
XGBoost (XGB)	18	10	14	10

Table 2 compares the performance of various machine learning models in the context of feature extraction, considering the time taken for feature extraction, the quality of the extracted features, the number of features extracted, and the time taken for dimensionality reduction. The Proposed (LSTM) model demonstrates a relatively efficient feature extraction process, with a time of 45 seconds and high feature quality (90). It extracts 120 features and performs dimensionality reduction in 10 seconds. In comparison, the Support Vector Machine (SVM) requires 50 seconds for feature extraction, with a slightly lower feature quality score of 85 and 115 features extracted. The dimensionality reduction time for SVM is 12 seconds.

Random Forest (RF) and Decision Tree (DT) models have feature extraction times of 47 and 48 seconds, respectively, with feature quality scores of 88 and 84, and 118 and 116 features extracted. Both models perform dimensionality reduction in 11 seconds. The K-Nearest Neighbors (KNN) model requires the most time for feature extraction at 53 seconds, but it achieves a feature quality score of 82 and extracts 110 features, with a dimensionality reduction time of 13 seconds. Similarly, Logistic Regression (LR) requires 55 seconds for feature extraction and 14 seconds for dimensionality reduction, extracting 105 features with a quality score of 80.

Other models like Naive Bayes (NB), Artificial Neural Networks (ANN), Gradient Boosting (GB), and XGBoost (XGB) have feature extraction times ranging from 46 to 52 seconds, with feature quality scores between 80 and 89. The number of features extracted by these models is similar, ranging from 113 to 119, with dimensionality reduction times of 10 to 12 seconds.

Table 2. Feature extraction performance comparison

Model	Feature Extraction Time (s)	Feature Quality (Score)	Number of Features Extracted	Dimensionality Reduction (Time)
Proposed	45	90	120	10
Support Vector Machine (SVM)	50	85	115	12
Random Forest (RF)	47	88	118	11
K-Nearest Neighbors (KNN)	53	82	110	13
Logistic Regression (LR)	55	80	105	14
Decision Tree (DT)	48	84	116	11
Naive Bayes (NB)	52	83	114	12
Artificial Neural Networks (ANN)	46	89	119	10
Gradient Boosting (GB)	51	86	113	12
XGBoost (XGB)	49	87	117	11

Table 3 compares the performance of different models in generating exposure data alerts, evaluating precision, recall, F1-score, and average exposure data processing time. The Proposed (LSTM) model performs best in terms of precision (92.1%), recall (90.9%), and F1-score (91.5%), while maintaining an average processing time of 15 seconds. In comparison, Support Vector Machine (SVM) achieves precision of 83.5%, recall of 80.1%, and F1-score of 81.7%, with a processing time of 18 seconds.

Random Forest (RF) demonstrates solid performance with a precision of 85.6%, recall of 84.5%, and an F1-score of 85.0%, taking 17 seconds for processing. K-Nearest Neighbors (KNN) achieves lower scores across all metrics, with precision at 79.3%, recall at 78.2%, and an F1-score of 78.7%, while taking 19 seconds for exposure data processing. The Logistic Regression (LR) and Naive Bayes (NB) models show further decreases in performance, with LR reaching 76.0% precision, 74.1% recall, and 75.0% F1-score, requiring 21 seconds for processing. Naive Bayes (NB) shows precision at 77.4%, recall at 75.6%, and F1-score at 76.5%, with a processing time of 22 seconds.

Decision Tree (DT), Gradient Boosting (GB), and XGBoost (XGB) perform similarly with F1-scores between 72.2% and 79.1%, and processing times ranging from 18 to 20 seconds. The XGBoost (XGB) model lags behind with a precision of 73.5%, recall of 70.9%, and F1-score of 72.2%, while taking 19 seconds for processing.

The Proposed (LSTM) model stands out for generating the most accurate alerts with the highest precision, recall, and F1-score, along with the shortest exposure data processing time, outperforming other models in all key performance indicators.

Table 3. Exposure data and alerts generation performance comparison

model	precision of alerts (%)	recall of alerts (%)	f1-score of alerts (%)	average exposure data processing time (s)
Proposed	92.1	90.9	91.5	15
Support Vector Machine (SVM)	83.5	80.1	81.7	18
Random Forest (RF)	85.6	84.5	85.0	17
K-Nearest Neighbors (KNN)	79.3	78.2	78.7	19
Logistic Regression (LR)	76.0	74.1	75.0	21
Decision Tree (DT)	74.8	72.5	73.6	20
Naive Bayes (NB)	77.4	75.6	76.5	22
Artificial Neural Networks (ANN)	82.3	80.7	81.5	16
Gradient Boosting (GB)	79.9	78.3	79.1	18
XGBoost (XGB)	73.5	70.9	72.2	19

Table 4 illustrates the correlations between various extracted features in the dataset, showcasing the relationships between exposure level, heart rate, fatigue level, sleep quality, stress level, and alert triggers. The Exposure Level shows the highest correlation with Alert Trigger (0.67), indicating a strong association between exposure levels and the triggering of alerts. It also exhibits a moderate correlation with Stress Level (0.51) and Fatigue Level (0.45), implying that higher exposure is linked to increased stress and fatigue. Heart Rate is moderately correlated with Fatigue Level (0.51) and Alert Trigger (0.52), suggesting that changes in heart rate are related to fatigue and alert triggers. Fatigue Level is notably correlated with Sleep Quality (0.62) and Stress Level (0.60), indicating that fatigue is influenced by both sleep quality and stress. Stress Level has a strong correlation with Alert Trigger (0.73), showing that heightened stress levels are more likely to activate alerts. Sleep Quality shows a weaker but still significant correlation with Alert Trigger (0.48), further supporting the connection between sleep disturbances and the occurrence of alerts.

Table 4. Correlations between extracted features

Feature	Exposure Level	Heart Rate	Fatigue Level	Sleep Quality	Stress Level	Alert Trigger
Exposure Level	1.00	0.32	0.45	0.22	0.51	0.67
Heart Rate	0.32	1.00	0.51	0.44	0.38	0.52
Fatigue Level	0.45	0.51	1.00	0.62	0.60	0.56
Sleep Quality	0.22	0.44	0.62	1.00	0.45	0.48
Stress Level	0.51	0.38	0.60	0.45	1.00	0.73
Alert Trigger	0.67	0.52	0.56	0.48	0.73	1.00

Table 5 compares the performance of several models used in the recommendation system, based on precision, recall, F1-score, accuracy, and recommendation time. The Proposed (LSTM) model outperforms all other models with the highest precision (90.5%), recall (91.2%), and F1-score (90.8%), as well as the highest accuracy (92.4%). Additionally, it delivers recommendations in the shortest time, taking only 15 seconds. Support Vector Machine (SVM) follows closely, with a precision of 85.2%, recall of 83.4%, and F1-score of 84.3%, achieving an accuracy of 85.3% and a recommendation time of 18 seconds. Random Forest (RF) also performs well with an F1-score of 86.6% and an accuracy of 87.1%, requiring 17 seconds for recommendations. Other models, such as K-Nearest Neighbors (KNN) and Logistic Regression (LR), show lower performance across all metrics, with KNN achieving an F1-score of 82.0% and LR achieving 80.0%. Models like Decision Tree (DT), Naive Bayes (NB), and Artificial Neural Networks (ANN) perform similarly, with ANN reaching an accuracy of 84.6% and a precision of 84.3%. Gradient Boosting (GB) and XGBoost (XGB) show slightly lower performance, with F1-scores of 81.3% and 77.7%, respectively. The Proposed (LSTM) model excels in both performance and speed, making it the most effective model for the recommendation system in this comparison.

Table 5. Recommendation system performance comparison

Model	Precision (%)	Recall (%)	F1-Score (%)	Accuracy (%)	Recommendation Time (s)
Proposed	90.5	91.2	90.8	92.4	15
Support Vector Machine (SVM)	85.2	83.4	84.3	85.3	18
Random Forest (RF)	87.8	85.5	86.6	87.1	17
K-Nearest Neighbors (KNN)	83.0	81.2	82.0	83.2	19
Logistic Regression (LR)	81.1	79.0	80.0	80.5	21
Decision Tree (DT)	79.7	77.3	78.5	78.9	20
Naive Bayes (NB)	80.4	80.1	80.2	81.7	22
Artificial Neural Networks (ANN)	84.3	82.0	83.1	84.6	16
Gradient Boosting (GB)	82.0	80.8	81.3	82.3	18
XGBoost (XGB)	78.6	76.9	77.7	79.1	19

CONCLUSION

The implementation of an LSTM-based recommendation system for monitoring workplace exposure offers significant improvements in occupational safety. By effectively capturing temporal patterns in exposure data, the system can predict potential health risks and provide personalized recommendations for mitigating those risks. The use of LSTM allows for continuous learning from historical data, enabling the system to adapt and refine its suggestions over time. Moreover, the integration of real-time alerts enhances worker safety by prompting immediate actions when exposure levels reach hazardous thresholds. This proactive approach to safety not only reduces the likelihood of accidents and long-term health issues but also supports regulatory compliance and promotes a culture of well-being in the workplace. Future enhancements, such as incorporating reinforcement learning for even more refined recommendations or integrating augmented reality for real-time visualization of exposure data, could further elevate the system's effectiveness. Overall, this LSTM-driven recommendation system represents a powerful tool for improving workplace safety and optimizing employee health management.

REFERENCES

Aqueveque, P., Gutiérrez, C., Rodríguez, F., Pino, E., Morales, A., & Wiechmann, E. (2017). Monitoring physiological variables of mining workers at high altitude. *IEEE Transactions on Industry Applications*, *53*(3), 2628–2634. DOI: 10.1109/TIA.2017.2675360

Campero-Jurado, I., Márquez-Sánchez, S., Quintanar-Gómez, J., Rodríguez, S., & Corchado, J. (2020). Smart Helmet 5.0 for Industrial Internet of Things using artificial intelligence. *Sensors (Basel)*, *20*(21), 6241. DOI: 10.3390/s20216241 PMID: 33139608

Costa, J., & Souto, E. (2022). A IoT device for monitoring particulate matter and gaseous pollutants in indoor industrial workstations. In *2022 IEEE International Conference on Consumer Electronics—Taiwan (ICCE-TW)* (pp. 517–518). IEEE. DOI: 10.1109/ICCE-Taiwan55306.2022.9869034

Failing, J. M., Abellán-Nebot, J. V., Benavent Nácher, S., Rosado Castellano, P., & Romero Subirón, F. (2023). A tool condition monitoring system based on low-cost sensors and an IoT platform for rapid deployment. *Processes (Basel, Switzerland)*, *11*(3), 668. DOI: 10.3390/pr11030668

Fanti, G., Spinazzè, A., Borghi, F., Rovelli, S., Campagnolo, D., Keller, M., Borghi, A., Cattaneo, A., Cauda, E., & Cavallo, D. M. (2022). Evolution and applications of recent sensing technology for occupational risk assessment: A rapid review of the literature. *Sensors (Basel)*, *22*(13), 4841. DOI: 10.3390/s22134841 PMID: 35808337

Fugate, H., & Alzraiee, H. (2023). Quantitative analysis of construction labor acceptance of wearable sensing devices to enhance workers' safety. *Results in Engineering*, *17*, 100841. DOI: 10.1016/j.rineng.2022.100841

Hew, C., Tan, R., Lee, C., Hartanty, T., Hossain, W., & Lee, Y. (2022). Development of self sustainable IoT-based low cost UV index monitoring station. In *2022 IEEE 8th International Conference on Smart Instrumentation, Measurement and Applications (ICSIMA)* (pp. 36–41). IEEE. DOI: 10.1109/ICSIMA55652.2022.9928933

Jiang, Z., Bakker, O., & Bartolo, P. (2022). Critical review of Industry 4.0 technologies' applications on occupational safety and health. In *2022 8th International Conference on Control, Decision and Information Technologies (CoDIT)* (pp. 1267–1272). IEEE. DOI: 10.1109/CoDIT55151.2022.9804084

Jilcha, K., & Kitaw, D. (2017). Industrial occupational safety and health innovation for sustainable development. *Engineering Science and Technology, an International Journal*, *20*(1), 372–380. DOI: 10.1016/j.jestch.2016.10.011

Khan, W., Rehman, M., Zangoti, H., Afzal, M., Armi, N., & Salah, K. (2020). Industrial Internet of Things: Recent advances, enabling technologies and open challenges. *Computers & Electrical Engineering*, *81*, 106522. DOI: 10.1016/j.compeleceng.2019.106522

Kim, J., Jo, B., Jo, J., & Kim, D. (2020). Development of an IoT-based construction worker physiological data monitoring platform at high temperatures. *Sensors (Basel)*, *20*(20), 5682. DOI: 10.3390/s20195682 PMID: 33027999

Lemos, J., Gaspar, P. D., & Lima, T. M. (2022a). Environmental risk assessment and management in Industry 4.0: A review of technologies and trends. *Machines (Basel), 10*(9), 702. DOI: 10.3390/machines10080702

Lemos, J., Gaspar, P. D., & Lima, T. M. (2022b). Individual environmental risk assessment and management in Industry 4.0: An IoT-based model. *Applied System Innovation, 5*(4), 88. DOI: 10.3390/asi5050088

Maddikunta, P., Pham, Q., Prabadevi, B., Deepa, N., Dev, K., Gadekallu, T., Ruby, R., & Liyanage, M. (2022). Industry 5.0: A survey on enabling technologies and potential applications. *Journal of Industrial Information Integration, 26*, 100257. DOI: 10.1016/j.jii.2021.100257

Maltseva, K. (2020). Wearables in the workplace: The brave new world of employee engagement. *Business Horizons, 63*(4), 493–505. DOI: 10.1016/j.bushor.2020.03.007

Mourtzis, D., Angelopoulos, J., & Panopoulos, N. (2022a). A literature review of the challenges and opportunities of the transition from Industry 4.0 to Society 5.0. *Energies, 15*(17), 6276. DOI: 10.3390/en15176276

Mourtzis, D., Angelopoulos, J., & Panopoulos, N. (2022b). Operator 5.0: A survey on enabling technologies and a framework for digital manufacturing based on extended reality. *Journal of Machine Engineering, 22*(4), 43–69. DOI: 10.36897/jme/147160

Nnaji, C., Awolusi, I., Park, J., & Albert, A. (2021). Wearable sensing devices: Towards the development of a personalized system for construction safety and health risk mitigation. *Sensors (Basel), 21*(2), 682. DOI: 10.3390/s21030682 PMID: 33498311

Rajakumar, J., & Choi, J.-H. (2023). Helmet-mounted real-time toxic gas monitoring and prevention system for workers in confined places. *Sensors (Basel), 23*(4), 1590. DOI: 10.3390/s23031590 PMID: 36772630

Rushton, L. (2017). The global burden of occupational disease. *Current Environmental Health Reports, 4*(3), 340–348. DOI: 10.1007/s40572-017-0151-2 PMID: 28733964

Sánchez, M., Rodriguez, C. S., & Manuel, J. (2020). Smart protective protection equipment for an accessible work environment and occupational hazard prevention. In *2020 10th International Conference on Cloud Computing, Data Science & Engineering (Confluence)* (pp. 581–585). IEEE. DOI: 10.1109/Confluence47617.2020.9058188

Singh, N., Gunjan, V., Chaudhary, G., Kaluri, R., Victor, N., & Lakshmanna, K. (2022). IoT enabled helmet to safeguard the health of mine workers. *Computer Communications, 193*, 1–9. DOI: 10.1016/j.comcom.2022.06.032

Teufer, B., Ebenberger, A., Affengruber, L., Kien, C., Klerings, I., Szelag, M., & Griebler, U. (2019). Evidence-based occupational health and safety interventions: A comprehensive overview of reviews. *BMJ Open, 9*(10), e032528. DOI: 10.1136/bmjopen-2019-032528 PMID: 31831544

Tompa, E., Mofidi, A., van den Heuvel, S., van Bree, T., Michaelsen, F., Jung, Y., Porsch, L., & van Emmerik, M. (2021). Economic burden of work injuries and diseases: A framework and application in five European Union countries. *BMC Public Health*, *21*(1), 49. DOI: 10.1186/s12889-020-10050-7 PMID: 33407315

Vaidya, S., Ambad, P., & Bhosle, S. (2018). Industry 4.0—A glimpse. *Procedia Manufacturing*, *20*, 233–238. DOI: 10.1016/j.promfg.2018.02.034

Waqar, A., Khan, M. B., Shafiq, N., Skrzypkowski, K., Zagórski, K., & Zagórska, A. (2023). Assessment of challenges to the adoption of IoT for the safety management of small construction projects in Malaysia: Structural equation modeling approach. *Applied Sciences (Basel, Switzerland)*, *13*(6), 3340. DOI: 10.3390/app13053340

Yang, K., Ahn, C., & Kim, H. (2020). Deep learning-based classification of work-related physical load levels in construction. *Advanced Engineering Informatics*, *45*, 101104. DOI: 10.1016/j.aei.2020.101104

Yu, F., & Schweisfurth, T. (2020). Industry 4.0 technology implementation in SMEs—A survey in the Danish-German border region. *International Journal of Innovation Studies*, *4*(3), 76–84. DOI: 10.1016/j.ijis.2020.05.001

Chapter 6
Future Trends and Innovations:
Exploring the Future Potential of AI in Occupational Health and Safety

Clarissa Marcelle Naidoo
https://orcid.org/0000-0001-9164-8213
Sefako Makgatho Health Science University, South Africa

Chikwelu Lawrence Obi
Sefako Magkatho Health Sciences University, South Africa

Nqobile Monate Mkolo
Sefako Makgatho Health Sciences University, South Africa

ABSTRACT

This chapter examines the incorporation of Artificial Intelligence (AI) into Occupational Health and Safety (OHS), representing a significant change in workplace safety management. It highlights the importance of AI technology in reducing risks, improving worker satisfaction, and increasing operational effectiveness in the workplace. Consideration is given to the functions of significant AI technologies in unsafe work automation, ergonomic assessments, health monitoring, and hazard identification. Some processes include predictive analytics, computer vision, machine learning, and natural language processing. Additionally, innovations that are altering safety training and skill development include wearable technology, augmented reality, and virtual reality. Alongside focusing on issues including employment displacement, regulatory gaps, and ethical problems, the chapter suggests multidisciplinary collaboration and strategic partnerships for AI-driven safety solutions.

1. INTRODUCTION

Occupational Health and Safety (OHS) and workplace health promotion (WHP) is a field that aims to ensure the physical, mental, and social well-being of workers in their professional environments (Lu et al.,2024). Its primary goal is to prevent or limit workplace injuries, illnesses, diseases, and casualties by the reduction of ergonomic, psychosocial, and material risks while promoting a safety culture and agreement with legal standards. Over time, OHS has evolved from basic safety measures to a compre-

DOI: 10.4018/979-8-3693-9301-7.ch006

hensive approach to advanced technologies (Khodyreva, 2023). Occupational Health and Safety has progressed due to rapid industrialization, technological innovations, and community transformations, an area for increased occupational illnesses and accidents hence the OHS was established (Neveling,2024). The foundation for monitoring and regulating working environments was founded by early legislation such as the Factories Act of 1833 in the United Kingdom, and the Occupational Health and Safety Act (OHSA) No. 85 of 1995 in South Africa (Spurgeon, 2012; Foromo et al.,2016). Soon governments and major organizations worldwide realized the importance of the protection of their workers and prompted the International Labour Organization (ILO) which was established in 1919 (Almakky, 2023).

The OHS systems are comprised of three primary categories namely Regulatory Compliance and Training, Health Promotion and Disease Prevention, and Hazard Identification and Risk Assessment (Ahmed et al.,2023). These significant pillars seek to identify potential workplace risks, develop and enforce mitigation plans, and pledge compliance with national and international OHS regulations (Idambi and Boniface, 2021). Digital technological advances, such as Artificial intelligence (AI), Internet of Things (IoT) integration, wearable technology, and mental health and well-being programs, have formed part of modern OHS procedures (Noudehi and Khameneh, 2023). According to current literature innovations in technology also include real-time workplace condition observation, hazard estimates, and safety mediation and optimization (Yuan et al.,2023). Specifically, it has been highlighted that wearable technology improves worker monitoring in high-risk sectors by tracking health data (Patel et al.,2022). The OHS has also acknowledged that mental health plays a crucial role in determining burnout, harassment, and other stress at work (Jain, 2021). The OSHA in the US and SA, expects employers to maintain safe workplaces, hence it is one of the laws and regulations that regulate OHS (Rikhotso et al.,2022).

Non-discrimination, guarding employee privacy, and maintaining a balance between automation and human supervision are all ethical issues currently being addressed (Hoxhaj et al.,2023). The field of OHS is dynamic, and transformative and aims to mitigate the obstacles posed by global health crises, demographic transitions, and automation. To ensure variation and robust workplaces, organizations are executing pre-emptive measures like analytical safety systems and flexible work schedules (Cebulla et al.,2023). It has been showcased that a safer workforce is protected by combining cutting-edge technologies, moral behaviour, and strict rules, which boosts organizational sustainability and productivity.

This chapter examines the integration of AI in OHS and its impact on workplace safety, risk management, and worker well-being. It explores AI applications such as hazard detection, predictive analytics, health monitoring, and workplace automation, along with emerging trends like robotics, augmented reality, and wearable devices. The chapter also addresses ethical, legal, and privacy concerns, as well as challenges and barriers to AI adoption. Finally, it provides policy recommendations and strategic approaches for effectively integrating AI to enhance workplace safety and well-being.

2. METHODOLOGY

A literature search was conducted using the Web of Science™ Core Collection and Google Scholar databases in October 2024, covering journal articles, industry reports, and case studies in OHS. Data sources focused on key trends, challenges, and opportunities published from 2010 to December 2024. Keywords related to AI in OHS, such as Occupational Health and Safety; Artificial Intelligence; Workplace; Hazards; Health Monitoring, Risk management, and Ethical Considerations, were used. Only peer-reviewed studies published in English were included.

3. HISTORICAL DEVELOPMENT OF AI IN OHS

The incorporation of AI in OHS has advanced technological innovations and the requirements for safer workplaces (Pishgar et al., 2021). The early 2000s showed a shift concerning data-driven safety measures with the occurrence of machine-learning algorithms capable of analyzing workplace incidents and predicting potential hazards (Irawan and Biyanto, 2024). In 2010, the combination of the IoT supported real-time monitoring of environmental conditions using wearable sensors (Chen et al.,2025). Discoveries in computer vision and NPL in the early 2020s enhanced hazard detection, ergonomic assessments, and incident reporting (Oliveira and Figueiredo, 2024). By 2025, AI-powered robotics, augmented reality (AR), and virtual reality (VR) training simulations will become integral to OHS (Chen et al.,2025).

4.THE INTERSECTION OF AI AND OCCUPATIONAL HEALTH AND SAFETY

4.1 Definition and Scope of AI Within OHS Contexts

AI in OHS enhances workplace well-being by automating safety operations, improving hazard prevention, and reducing human errors that contribute to injuries (Pishgar et al., 2021). Furthermore, it plays a crucial role in contact tracing, optimizing personnel and equipment use, and automating dangerous or repetitive tasks to minimize risks and labour costs (Lee and Loon, 2021). AI-driven virtual and augmented reality technologies enhance safety training while monitoring systems help track workers, prevent harassment, and detect crimes (Ninoria et al., 2023). Additionally, AI supports environmental surveillance, unauthorized access control, and incident management (Bernhardt et al., 2021).

The integration of AI with robotics, automation, and digitalization is reshaping workplaces by boosting productivity and economic growth (Felknor et al., 2023). AI-driven smart systems improve real-time communication, data management, and industrial efficiency while addressing poor working conditions through advanced safety management tools (Fisher et al., 2023). However, AI adoption also raises concerns about job displacement, labour market polarization, and increased automation risks, particularly for middle-skilled workers (Liang et al., 2024). The uncertainty surrounding AI-driven job losses emphasizes the need for corporate responsibility, government intervention, and workforce retraining (Sinclair et al., 2020). Furthermore, rapid technological shifts can negatively impact workers' mental health, increasing risks of stress, depression, and substance abuse, highlighting the importance of ongoing evaluation and mitigation strategies (Johnson et al., 2020).

4.2 Key AI Technologies Relevant to OHS

AI technologies improve workplace safety, worker well-being, and productivity by utilizing various technologies such as Machine learning (ML) algorithms to analyze accident data and environmental conditions to identify trends and prevent incidents (Patchipala et al., 2023). In addition, computer vision systems detect unsafe activities and ensure safety compliance (Liu et al., 2021), while NLP improves hazard detection by analyzing safety reports and worker feedback (Shamshiri et al., 2024). AI also enhances predictive safety by identifying health risks and alerting organizations before incidents occur (Krichen et al., 2024). The IoT integrates AI-driven sensors to monitor real-time equipment and worker conditions (Kumar et al., 2023). Wearable AI devices track vital signs like heart rate and respiratory function, offering early health warnings and AI-powered robotics handle hazardous tasks such as inspections and heavy load handling, reducing human exposure to risks (Bathla et al., 2022). Additionally, AR and VR provide immersive training simulations for hazardous situations (Toyoda et al., 2022).

4.3 Review of Current AI-Driven OHS Practices in the Industry

AI applications are often used in manufacturing, construction, healthcare, and mining and oil industries, where autonomous robots inspect sites, minimizing human exposure to risks (Fatima et al., 2020). Furthermore, AI enhances workplace safety by predicting hazards and analyzing risks using machine learning algorithms (Ojji, 2024). For instance, IBM's Watson leverages predictive analytics to assess workplace conditions, while AI in manufacturing detects machinery wear and facilitates preventive maintenance (Patel et al., 2022). In construction, AI predicts falls, equipment collisions, and material mishandling, whereas in the oil and gas sector, AI-driven hazard prediction aids in preventing pipeline leaks and overheating (Aderamo et al., 2024a). These technologies contribute to safer workplaces, reduced greenhouse gas emissions, and improved economic sustainability in high-risk industries (Onifade et al., 2023a).

5. CURRENT APPLICATIONS OF AI IN OCCUPATIONAL HEALTH AND SAFETY

5.1 Hazard Detection and Workplace Monitoring

AI technologies are reforming workplace safety by improving observation and danger recognition. These technologies, including sensors, IoT, computer vision, machine learning, and predictive analytics, help companies reduce hazards and minimize health issues (Zvarivadza et al.,2024). Computer vision systems detect hazards by analyzing video feeds, while IoT sensors monitor environmental variables (Arshad et al.,2023). Wearable technology, drones, and autonomous robots monitor worker data to identify health hazards (Patel et al.,2022). The multinational mining corporation Rio Tinto has installed AI-powered technologies for worker monitoring and danger identification at its various locations (Asa'd and Levesque,2024). These systems monitor vital aspects including worker positions, machinery operations, and ground stability using machine learning, computer vision, and IoT-enabled sensors (Asa'd and Levesque,2024; Onifade et al., 2023b). The AI-driven strategy has improved worker safety and adherence to safety procedures by drastically lowering accidents and operating delays. The technology-driven strategy has been successful in cutting down on operational delays and workplace accidents (Asa'd and Levesque,2024; Shah et al.,2024).

5.2 Predictive Analytics for Accident Prevention

To lower workplace deaths and injuries, predictive analytics observes working circumstances identifies dangers, and evaluates human behaviour (Patel 2022; Shah et al.,2024). In addition to anticipating human behaviour and guaranteeing prompt action when safety procedures are violated, AI systems examine environmental elements, worker health data, accident reports, and equipment performance records (Fox et al.,2024). To enhance OHS in building projects, Smartvid.io has created a predictive safety platform that uses AI (Ghiafehdavoudi and Vaillant,2020). To anticipate and reduce any safety hazards, the platform analyzes past safety data, photos, and videos from building sites using machine learning algorithms (Zhong et al.,2020). It assigns risk rankings to certain activities or locations by using computer vision to identify safety hazards (Paneru and Jeelani, 2021). By proactively addressing high-risk regions, the predictive insights assist construction managers in lowering accidents and enhancing adherence to safety standards (Aderamo et al.,2024b).

5.3 Ergonomic Assessments Using AI Tools

AI-powered ergonomic assessment technologies help reduce ergonomic injuries, improve decision-making, and enhance employee health (Adiga,2023; Somaraju et al.,2024). Siemens has reduced musculoskeletal diseases (MSDs) in its production plants by using an AI-driven ergonomic risk assessment system (Grandi et al.,2020). The system examines how employees move while doing assembly jobs using motion capture technologies and machine learning algorithms. The AI identifies high-risk jobs and suggests workplace modifications by comparing data to ergonomic norms. Employee satisfaction has increased, and absenteeism linked to MSDs has decreased by 25% (Grandi et al.,2020). Toyota has reduced back strain and increased productivity by using AI to develop ergonomic seating options for assembly line workers (Kumar et al., 2021). By tracking employee's posture, weight distribution, and pressure spots using sensors, the method makes it possible to build chairs that dynamically adjust to their motions. Additionally, this technology offers real-time feedback for posture adjustments (Kumar et al., 2021; Bourahmoune et al.,2022).

5.4 AI in Health Monitoring and Wearable Devices

AI and wearable technology have completely changed health monitoring by giving real-time information on a worker's physiological state, facilitating early diagnosis and timely action (Jain et al.,2024; Zainab et al.,2024). Wearable health devices with AI capabilities also offer individualized notifications and real-time alerts, allowing for prompt medical attention even in distant work environments (Ibahim and Ali, 2023). To protect workers in dangerous mining conditions, Anglo American, a multinational mining corporation, has put in place a "Connected Worker" initiative. This was initiated to monitor physiological data, notify supervisors when vital signs surpass safe levels, and prevent heat-related diseases, using wearable health monitoring equipment (Patel et al.,2022). Underground mining emergency response times have improved as a result (Clausen and Sörensen, 2022). In addition, during the COVID-19 epidemic, Fitbit Health Solutions collaborated with hospitals to provide healthcare professionals with wearable health monitoring devices that included AI (Channa, 2021). By monitoring physiological parameters, these gadgets decreased weariness and helped identify burnout and sickness early, also hospitals reported lower absenteeism and better worker well-being (Patel et al.,2022).

5.5 Automation of Hazardous Tasks

AI-powered automated robots are becoming more common in chemical manufacturing, mining, construction, nuclear decommissioning, agriculture and food processing, and maritime and offshore work (Yassen, 2021; Chelliah et al.,2023). AI-controlled robotic machinery at nuclear plants guarantees precision and lowers radiation exposure (Robert et al., 2024). Autonomous robots in agriculture lessen weather exposure and injuries (Benos et al.,2020). Skanska and AI project management automates risky jobs like examining big buildings and bridges with AI-powered drones (Owen, 2024). The drones detect flaws in real time as they search for structural problems. This increases the effectiveness of inspections and lowers the number of fall-related occurrences (Owen, 2024). In recycling facilities, Veolia, a multinational waste management firm, handles hazardous garbage with robotic arms powered by AI (Aggeri et al., 2021). By sorting, processing, and discarding hazardous materials, these weapons reduce human exposure and boost productivity by 40% (Gregson, 2023).

5. 6 Workplace Behaviour Monitoring and Ethical Compliance

AI technology is capable of handling moral predicaments, enforcing safety standards, and monitoring employee behaviour (Kavouras et al.,2024). While behavioural analysis can locate areas that require safety training, AI can detect harassment, dangerous actions, and unethical acts (Zenor et al.,2020). ProGlove created a wearable AI monitoring solution for warehouse employees that improved safety compliance and reduced musculoskeletal injuries by 30% (Nguyen et al.,2023). To provide real-time feedback and notify supervisors of safety infractions, the system tracks worker handling, posture, and lifting procedures using sensors (Lui et al., 2021). In addition, organizations may anonymously report and track instances of workplace harassment, bullying, and unethical behaviour with the aid of the Spot AI chatbot (Kiritchenko et al., 2021). It documents specific instances using NPL while maintaining anonymity. Spot AI has promoted accountability and openness by resulting in a 20% increase in the reporting of ethical transgressions (Tóth et al.,2022).

5.7 Incident Analysis and Reporting

AI technologies enhance workplace safety by automating incident investigation, real-time reporting, and proactive mitigation. By streamlining data collection, processing, and reporting, AI helps identify root causes, prevent recurrence, and improve safety procedures (Sattari et al.,2021). To predict future threats, machine learning systems examine historical data, comprehensive incident reports are produced using NLP technology, and data is presented in an intelligible way via AI-driven dashboards (Khang et al.,2020). To improve event analysis and response in the workplace, Honeywell has deployed an AI-powered incident reporting system throughout many production facilities (Skarko et al., 2024). The system combines sensors and AI to identify possible risks, notify staff, create automated reports, and examine past data to forecast future occurrences, which show that the response time has decreased by 40% using this method (Skarko et al., 2024). Furthermore, to reduce hazards and increase safety, BP has included AI in its oil field incident investigation procedure (Gupta and Shah, 2022). The AI solution reduces workplace incidents by 25% by classifying occurrences, identifying dangers, and automating report production using information from worker reports, environmental monitoring sensors, and equipment performance logs (Hussain et al.,2024).

5.8 Sustainability and Environmental Monitoring

AI technologies are developing OHS by providing real-time environmental monitoring, predictive analytics, energy optimization, waste management, and sustainability standard compliance using IoT sensors (Nižetić et al.,2020; Abatan et al.,2024). AI also helps reduce landfill contributions and ensures compliance with regulations, thus this shift in workplace safety and sustainability is transforming our lives (Andeobu et al.,2022). AMP Robotics reduces landfill waste and increases recycling efficiency using AI-powered garbage sorting. The system guides robotic arms for processing after identifying recyclable items using computer vision. As it gains precision over time, recycling rates rise and contamination levels fall, supporting environmentally friendly waste management techniques (Pransky,2020).

6. EMERGING TRENDS IN AI FOR OHS

The fourth industrial revolution or Industry 4.0 in the modern years has emerged due to global demand for consumer goods and services. Advancements in automation and computerization are hallmarks of the revolution of different technologies in Industry 4.0, which aims to force quality, flexibility, and efficiency for industrial production (Leso et al., 2018; Flor-Unda et al., 2023). Innovation of new technologies persists in redefining the edges of occupational safety and health. As mentioned in the foregoing section, by levering cutting-edge interconnected systems, sensors, and real-time data analytics, OHS organizations can increase safety in the workplace, enhance operational productivity, and advance worker's health (Moshawrab et al., 2022). This section provides an insight into the latest emerging trends in AI for OHS (Figure 1).

Figure 1. Occupational safety and health technologies (co-author NM Mkolo)

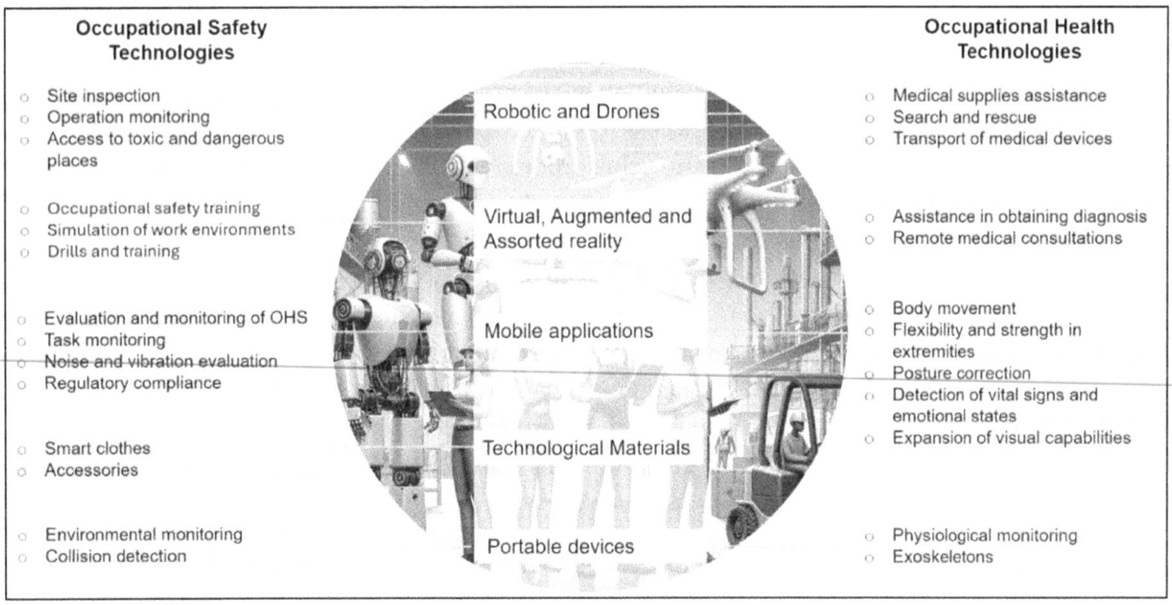

6.1 Emerging Robotics and Drones for OHS

Robotics in AI is the integration of AI technologies into systems of robotics to advance their capacities and facilitate the execution of complex tasks (Mihret, 2020). Robots can be categorized into remote-controlled robots, pre-programmed robots, and autonomous robots (Jarota, 2021; Intel, 2022).

Remote-controlled robots are the easiest control robotic system that utilizes a remote operator. The remote operator can be used for the movements of the robot and achieve unsafe task handling (Verdantix, 2022; Mihret, 2020). Pre-programmed robots are designed to accomplish pre-distinct movements for high-volume manufacturing environments. Pre-programmed robots are not intended to account for substantial variation in operating conditions, but they rely on minimal auto-shutdown fail-safe mechanisms to avert collision between humans and machines. Autonomous guided robots can likewise be classified under the same category due to the utilization of magnetic strips close-fitting to the industrial facilities floors for navigation (Verdantix, 2022; Mihret, 2020). A task can be well-defined as a pre-programmed robot picking and positioning automotive panels, although the control system can comprise sensors and cameras to bring to the highest level of performance for the panel placement and supervisory personnel alert. Moreover, autonomous mobile robots can move to an identified position at the same time dodging objects and achieving course-correction in real-time (Verdantix, 2022; Control Engineering, 2019; Intel, 2022). Emerging trends where robotics is being utilized to improve workplace health and safety include, industrial facility inspection and gauge-reading, confined space inspections, parts, goods, and material transportation, machine tending, parts repositioning and pick-and-place, hazardous environment materials handling and precision cutting and welding (Verdantix, 2022; Gould, 2019).

A drone can be described as a hovering robot that is remotely controlled utilizing an embedded software-controlled flight plan in its systems (Custers, 2016). The usage of drones in different industries is regulated by Law on Occupational Risk Prevention, Articles 14 and 15 (Zhang, et al., 2023). This law is also incorporated with IoT. Safety Science, 159, 106012 regulation indicates that industries can consider drones for monitoring and preventive mergers to warrant the health and safety of workers (Tender et al., 2022). The construction sector can be considered a dangerous sector for its workforce (Alsadik, et al 2022), which makes the use of drones in this sector grow rapidly in recent years. The benefits of using drones in this sector include easier access to remote locations, reduced expenses, and increased productivity. Companies have benefited from using drones for tasks like monitoring, progress tracking, surveillance, topography assessment, and inspections, replacing manual labour. Drones also help identify hidden risks, such as human collisions and worker distractions. (Duraisamy, 2020).

In occupational health, drones are recognized as "emergency drone devices" which are employed for rescue operations that are intended to assist in saving lives in medical emergencies due to accidents. During the event of a work accident, the operators can communicate, observe, and provide guidelines to the person at risk (Tender et al., 2022). Emerging trends in health care also include drones delivering life-saving products, vaccines, blood packets, and defibrillator equipment offering beneficial access to rural areas and hospitals (Claesson et al., 2016, Carrillo et al., 2018; Zwęgliński et al., 2020; Riccò et al., 2020).

6.2 Emerging Augmented, Mixed, and Virtual Reality for OHS

The emergence of technologies in augmented reality, mixed reality, and virtual reality has paved many opportunities in the context of occupational health and safety (Ranjan et al., 2019). Mixed reality consists of both augmented reality and virtual reality. Augmented reality is a technology that integrates simulated digital models into real environments using physical and projection media (Hou et al., 202; Babalola et al., 2023). AR is a promising digital tool for enhancing the effectiveness of health and safety training across various fields (Scavarelli et al., 2021; Alkan and Basaga, 2023; Lovreglio and Kinateder, 2020; Kolaei et al., 2022).

Augmented reality can be classified into non-immersive and immersive experiences (Zhou and Ieee, 2023; Gabbard et al., 2019; Lu et al., 2023). Non-immersive augmented reality devices are classically known as screen-based and comprise hand-held and fixed augmented reality technologies. However, immersive augmented reality devices usually use visual exhibition devices to deliver a high degree of immersion and visual reality via wearable augmented reality technology such as glasses and head-mounted sets. Augmented reality can enhance workplace health and safety by improving employee skills, reducing errors, and offering real-time feedback and guidance on complex tasks, ultimately boosting productivity (Nnaji et al., 2021).

Virtual reality has various applications in safety education, including in coal mining, construction, and earthquakes. It provides an interactive, gamified environment that improves worker engagement and training effectiveness (Li et al., 2018). VR's immersive nature enhances safety protocols and training, making it more realistic and appealing (Sacks et al., 2013; Li et al., 2017; Li et al., 2018). Virtual reality recently consists of several applications in terms of safety education (Poyade et al., 2021). Virtual reality can apply to coal mining (Zhang et al., 2022), construction (Sacks et al., 2013), and earthquakes (Li et al., 2017). Virtual reality technology offers an active-examination gamification environment to improve the worker's interface (Li et al., 2018) and increases its appeal by offering engaging training that has a realistic feel (Sacks et al., 2013). Virtual reality for immersive safety training is one of the instances of how technology is being enhanced to augment safety protocols and training (Li et al., 2017; Li et al., 2018). In terms of workplace health, Beverly et al., (2022) assessed a virtual reality application and utilized the virtual reality glasses intending to offer short stress reduction for workers that were provided with medical care.

6.3 Emerging Mobile Applications and Portable Devices for OHS

Several emerging mobile software applications for occupational health and safety are designed to improve worker health (Zhao et al., 2016). Opportunities for utilizing the health application can successfully promote workplace health through content on mindfulness and sleep, targeting nurses, office workers, and pilots. The application's strengths include adoption, user convenience, workforce reach, and cost-effectiveness (Junker et al., 2024). First Aid is among these applications, which collaborates with the 911 emergency service and collaborates with the American Red Cross (Khuwuthyakorn et al., 2018).

Portable devices to endorse health and safety in the workplace are recently being utilized greatly. Reflecting monitoring of health, the devices developed integrate sensors in watches to investigate sleep habits, stress levels, and heart problems. This device can be utilized for unforeseen circumstances with the aid of an alarm when assistance is needed (Simpson et al., 2019). Worker metabolism can be assessed by devices applying data about the human body's dispensation of carbohydrates, fats, and proteins. Moreover, devices integrated with smartphones with specific applications can be used to assess breath exhaled post breathe in and air holding for approximately ten seconds (Jebelli et al., 2019).

6.4 Emerging Technological Material for OHS

Multiple nanomaterials have been advanced and are presently employed in several forms and compositions in industrial shielding clothes to help prevent occupational dangers (Flor-Unda, et al., 2023). Smart Enhanced personal protective equipment, known as "smart PPE" integrated with hard hats, safety glasses, and gloves can be used to monitor worker vital signs and stress levels, offering real-time data that can aid workers in reporting possible safety concerns before accidents (Vukicevic et al., 2021). Other technological materials include smart fabrics, self-healing materials, fire-resistant fabrics and nanofiber respiratory masks (Vukicevic et al., 2021).

7. ETHICAL AND PRIVACY CONSIDERATIONS

Although AI offers numerous applications and benefits, ethical and privacy concerns may impede its acceptance. Fundamental ethical considerations include ensuring data privacy and security in the collection, usage, and storage of personal information from wearable devices and sensors (Geneva: WHO, 2021; International Commission on Occupational Health (ICOH), 2014). In OHS, AI applications must protect sensitive worker information such as health records, location tracking, and behavioural data to prevent privacy breaches, discrimination, or misuse. The lack of robust security measures, including encryption, access controls, and compliance with regulations may cause significant risks. Therefore, establishing ethical AI frameworks and transparent data policies is essential to maintaining trust, ensuring regulatory compliance, and safeguarding workers' rights in AI-powered OHS solutions (El-Helaly, 2024).

Beyond privacy concerns, inherent biases in AI systems may negatively impact decision-making, leading to discrimination in workplace safety protocols and healthcare interventions (Saheb, 2023; El-Helaly, 2024). The automated nature of AI raises concerns about its impact on the employability and mental health of healthcare and safety practitioners, particularly in light of job displacement and the need for reskilling. The exclusion of occupational doctors from AI algorithm design, implementation, and regulatory discussions further exacerbates ethical challenges. Additionally, principles such as fairness, transparency, accountability, and explainability must be embedded into AI systems and actively monitored to ensure compliance with ethical guidelines, particularly in decisions of clinical relevance in OHS (Baldassarre and Padovan, 2023; Geneva: WHO, 2021; ICOH, 2014).

To address these ethical challenges, continuous education and professional development (CEPD) are critical, particularly in fostering awareness of the ethical use of AI and emerging ethical dilemmas. Ongoing monitoring, evaluation, and adaptation of ethical frameworks in AI-powered OHS research, clinical protocols, and workplace applications are essential for responsible deployment (Geneva: WHO, 2021; ICOH, 2014). Given the rapid evolution of AI technologies, the OHS field must establish clear, regularly updated ethical and governance guidelines to ensure that occupational health practitioners remain attuned to technological advancements and their implications.

8. CHALLENGES AND BARRIERS TO AI ADOPTION

Adopting AI technologies in OHS presents regulatory, legal, and ethical challenges. Key legal concerns include compliance with data privacy laws such as the General Data Protection Regulation (GDPR), the Health Insurance Portability and Accountability Act (HIPAA), workplace safety standards, and addressing ethical issues like surveillance and worker autonomy (Shandilya et al.,2024). Legal frameworks need to adapt to the complexities of AI, including potential algorithmic biases and the necessity for human oversight.

Despite AI's benefits, challenges include insufficient user acceptance, lack of skilled employees, and high costs, limiting accessibility for small businesses. AI may also impact vulnerable populations, potentially worsening health disparities (Ogundeko-Olugbami et al.,2025). Furthermore, economically, there are expensive initial costs linked to AI, where environmental considerations, like energy consumption and electronic waste, may increase AI's environmental footprint (Chen et al., 2021). These issues must be addressed to ensure accessibility and equity, especially for underserved communities, while adhering to ethical standards, including privacy, algorithmic bias, and accountability. Ethical concerns also involve patient consent and data ownership transparency. Healthcare professionals may face difficulties in trusting or using AI due to a limited understanding of AI software (Sunarti et al., 2021; Mlodzinski et al., 2023). Technological challenges in AI adoption for OHS include data validation, workflow integration, and complex dataset analysis. Workforce barriers, such as inadequate training, job displacement, and resistance to change, hinder AI adoption. AI tools, like wearable safety devices, may be inaccessible to lower-income populations, and biases in AI training datasets can lead to inaccurate diagnoses, highlighting the need for diverse datasets (Mustaphas et al., 2015).

9. ENHANCEMENT OF REGULATORY AND ETHICAL DISCUSSIONS OF AI IN OHS

A comprehensive review of regulatory frameworks like GDPR and HIPAA is essential in addressing ethical concerns associated with AI (Shandilya et al.,2024). While these regulations allow for sustainable AI deployment, several challenges are often experienced in balancing innovation with privacy rights. However, these can be mediated by increasing user experience and adoption plays with strategies such as training programs and addressing job displacement concerns improving acceptance (Rane et al., 2023). Furthermore, AI can lead to long-term savings through reduced workplace injuries and increased productivity. In addition, it may be used to benefit the environment in terms of energy consumption and e-waste (Chen et al., 2021). Additionally, AI accessibility for vulnerable populations aligns with the Sustainable Development Goals (SDGs), promoting inclusive growth, sustainability, and public health while adhering to ethical guidelines (Holzinger et al.,2019).

10. RECOMMENDATIONS FOR POLICY AND PRACTICE

10.1 Guidelines for Organizations Implementing AI in OHS

AI is revolutionizing OHS procedures by putting in place a coordinated strategy for businesses, legislators, and industry participants (Jarota, 2023). Important recommendations include clear policies for data protection, security, employee participation, training, human supervision, and continuous evaluation (Tursunbayeva et al.,2022). Data management and security are crucial, with guidelines for encryption, storage, and access restrictions. Organizations must understand data privacy laws, such as GDPR Article 35, which requires assessing how data processing affects people's rights (Martin et al., 2020).

OHS staff members should be aware of AI technologies in the workplace, with the option to not implement the practice if they feel uncomfortable (Weerts et al.,2022). Providing general and advanced AI training, along with the interpretation of AI-driven insights, would benefit OHS sectors (Cebulla et al., 2023). Human oversight is necessary to inspect AI systems, and continuous evaluation of AI technologies ensures alignment with safety goals and prevents unintended consequences (Salhab, 2024).

10.2 Recommendations for Policymakers to Support Ethical and Effective AI in OHS

Policymakers play a crucial role in ethically integrating AI into OHS by establishing legal, ethical, and transparent frameworks that protect workers and prevent exploitation (Palačić, 2024). They must ensure that AI technologies do not exacerbate workplace discrimination and promote transparency by clearly outlining AI systems' operations, including data collection and algorithms used (Kolulu, 2020; Janssen et al., 2020; Stypinska, 2023). Collaboration among policymakers, governments, and stakeholders is essential for continuous research on the ethical, social, and economic impacts of AI, aiming to develop efficient, cost-effective, and equitable AI technologies (Salazar Rodriguez, 2024). Additionally, AI training programs should be implemented to equip workers with relevant skills for the evolving labour market, ensuring AI solutions are practical, ethical, and aligned with stakeholder needs (Morandini, 2023).

10.3 Strategic Partnerships to Foster AI Innovation in Workplace Safety

To ensure advances in AI innovation in OHS, organizations, academic institutions, governmental agencies, and tech businesses must form vigorous and continuous strategic partnerships (Felknor et al.,2023). These alliances may contribute toward real-world operations, foster a culture of ongoing workplace safety development, and accelerate the growth of AI technology (Abbas Khan et al.,2024). Despite the real-world data and real-world issues offered by several businesses, we strongly consider that academic institutions and research centers can propose strong insights into AI algorithms, prediction models, and ethical frameworks, whereas infrastructure, finance, and regulatory backing for AI solutions may be obtained through public-private partnerships (Gaske, 2023). Finally, strategic partnerships between technology providers, regulatory bodies, and industry stakeholders are crucial for fostering AI innovation in workplace safety by ensuring the development, implementation, and scaling of solutions that are both effective and compliant with safety standards.

11. CONCLUSION

To control a range of hazards, monitor health, and enhance safety, AI is considered in several OHS systems. Existing literature and case studies have showcased that AI-powered solutions can significantly expand efficiency, improve worker well-being, and reduce workplace injuries. The chapter highlights the significant potential of AI to enhance workplace safety through predictive analytics, automation, and real-time monitoring while emphasizing the need to address regulatory, ethical, and practical challenges for effective implementation and adoption. Future advancements in AI for OHS may include the integration of more sophisticated machine learning algorithms for risk prediction, the use of wearable AI technologies for real-time hazard detection, and the development of AI-driven solutions that promote a safer, more inclusive, and more sustainable work environment. To ensure AI in OHS remains to advance worker safety and well-being, challenges such as ethical issues and legal frameworks must be addressed to ensure a balance between innovation and ethical duty, data security, and human oversight.

ACKNOWLEDGMENTS

We would like to extend our appreciation to the South African Medical Research Council (SAMRC) through its Division of Research Capacity Development under the Research Capacity Development Initiative.

REFERENCES

Abatan, A., Obiuto, N. C., Ninduwezuor-Ehiobu, N., Ani, E. C., Olu-lawal, K. A., & Ugwuanyi, E. D. (2024). Integrating advanced technologies for enhanced hse management in the FMCG sector. *Engineering Science & Technology Journal*, *5*(4), 1270–1280. DOI: 10.51594/estj.v5i4.1017

Abbas Khan, M., Khan, H., Omer, M. F., Ullah, I., & Yasir, M. (2024). Impact of artificial intelligence on the global economy and technology advancements. In *Artificial General Intelligence (AGI) Security: Smart Applications and Sustainable Technologies* (pp. 147–180). Springer Nature Singapore.

Aderamo, A. T., Olisakwe, H. C., Adebayo, Y. A., & Esiri, A. E.Adeoye Taofik AderamoHenry Chukwuemeka OlisakweYetunde Adenike AdebayoAndrew Emuobosa Esiri. (2024a). AI-driven HSE management systems for risk mitigation in the oil and gas industry. *Comprehensive Research and Reviews in Engineering and Technology*, *2*(1), 1–22. DOI: 10.57219/crret.2024.2.1.0059

Aderamo, A. T., Olisakwe, H. C., Adebayo, Y. A., & Esiri, A. E.Adeoye Taofik AderamoHenry Chukwuemeka OlisakweYetunde Adenike AdebayoAndrew Emuobosa Esiri. (2024b). AI-enabled predictive safeguards for offshore oil facilities: Enhancing safety and operational efficiency. *Comprehensive Research and Reviews in Engineering and Technology*, *2*(1), 23–43. DOI: 10.57219/crret.2024.2.1.0060

Adiga, U. (2023). Enhancing occupational health and ergonomics for optimal workplace well-being: A review. *International Journal of Chemical and Biochemical Science*, *24*(4), 157–164.

Aggeri, F., Micheaux, H., & Ntsondé, J. Special Issue 23| 2021 Industry and Waste: Toward the Circular Economy.

Ahmed, T., Hoque, A. S. M., Karmaker, C. L., & Ahmed, S. (2023). Integrated approach for occupational health and safety (OHS) risk Assessment: An Empirical (Case) study in Small enterprises. *Safety Science*, *164*, 106143. DOI: 10.1016/j.ssci.2023.106143

Almakky, R. (2023). The Influence of the International Labour Organization on International Law and State Practice: An Analytical Study. *Arab Journal for Scientific Publishing (AJSP). ISSN*, *2663*, 5798.

Alsadik, B., & Khalaf, Y. H. (2022). Potential use of drone ultra-high-definition videos for detailed 3d city modeling. *ISPRS International Journal of Geo-Information*, *11*(1), 34. DOI: 10.3390/ijgi11010034

Andeobu, L., Wibowo, S., & Grandhi, S. (2022). Artificial intelligence applications for sustainable solid waste management practices in Australia: A systematic review. *The Science of the Total Environment*, *834*, 155389. DOI: 10.1016/j.scitotenv.2022.155389 PMID: 35460765

Arshad, S., Akinade, O., Bello, S., & Bilal, M. (2023). Computer vision and IoT research landscape for health and safety management on construction sites. *Journal of Building Engineering*, *76*, 107049. DOI: 10.1016/j.jobe.2023.107049

Asa'd, O., & Levesque, M. (2024). Digital technologies for energy efficiency and decarbonization in mining. *CIM Journal*, *15*(1), 1–20. DOI: 10.1080/19236026.2023.2203068

Assadullah, M. M. (2019). Barriers to artificial intelligence adoption in healthcare management: A systematic review. *Available atSSRN* 3530598. DOI: 10.2139/ssrn.3530598

Babalola, A., Manu, P., Cheung, C., Yunusa-Kaltungo, A., & Bartolo, P. (2023). Applications of immersive technologies for occupational safety and health training and education: A systematic review. *Safety Science*, *166*, 106214. DOI: 10.1016/j.ssci.2023.106214

Baldassarre, A., & Padovan, M. (2024, April 24). Regulatory and Ethical Considerations on Artificial Intelligence for Occupational Medicine. *La Medicina del Lavoro*, *115*(2), e2024013. DOI: 10.23749/mdl.v115i2.15881 PMID: 38686573

Bathla, G., Bhadane, K., Singh, R. K., Kumar, R., Aluvalu, R., Krishnamurthi, R., Kumar, A., Thakur, R. N., & Basheer, S. (2022). Autonomous vehicles and intelligent automation: Applications, challenges, and opportunities. *Mobile Information Systems*, *2022*(1), 7632892. DOI: 10.1155/2022/7632892

Baxter, S. L., Bass, J. S., & Sitapati, A. M. (2020). Barriers to implementing an artificial intelligence model for unplanned readmissions. *ACI Open*, *4*(02), e108–e113. DOI: 10.1055/s-0040-1716748 PMID: 33274314

Benos, L., Bechar, A., & Bochtis, D. (2020). Safety and ergonomics in human-robot interactive agricultural operations. *Biosystems Engineering*, *200*, 55–72. DOI: 10.1016/j.biosystemseng.2020.09.009

Bernhardt, A., Suleiman, R., & Kresge, L. (2021). Data and algorithms at work: the case for worker technology rights.

Bourahmoune, K., Ishac, K., & Amagasa, T. (2022). Intelligent posture training: Machine-learning-powered human sitting posture recognition based on a pressure-sensing IoT cushion. *Sensors (Basel)*, *22*(14), 5337. DOI: 10.3390/s22145337 PMID: 35891018

Carrillo-Larco, R. M., Moscoso-Porras, M., Taype-Rondan, A., Ruiz-Alejos, A., & Bernabe-Ortiz, A. (2018). The use of unmanned aerial vehicles for health purposes: A systematic review of experimental studies. *Global Health, Epidemiology and Genomics*, *3*, e13. DOI: 10.1017/gheg.2018.11 PMID: 30263137

Cebulla, A., Szpak, Z., & Knight, G. (2023). Preparing to work with artificial intelligence: Assessing WHS when using AI in the workplace. *International Journal of Workplace Health Management*, *16*(4), 294–312. DOI: 10.1108/IJWHM-09-2022-0141

Channa, A., Popescu, N., Skibinska, J., & Burget, R. (2021). The rise of wearable devices during the COVID-19 pandemic: A systematic review. *Sensors (Basel)*, *21*(17), 5787. DOI: 10.3390/s21175787 PMID: 34502679

Chelliah, P. R., Jayasankar, V., Agerstam, M., Sundaravadivazhagan, B., & Cyriac, R. (2023). *The Power of Artificial Intelligence for the Next-Generation Oil and Gas Industry: Envisaging AI-inspired Intelligent Energy Systems and Environments*. John Wiley & Sons. DOI: 10.1002/9781119985617

Chen, C., Hu, Y., Karuppiah, M., & Kumar, P. M. (2021). Artificial intelligence on economic evaluation of energy efficiency and renewable energy technologies. *Sustainable Energy Technologies and Assessments, 47*, 101358. DOI: 10.1016/j.seta.2021.101358

Chen, Y., Li, J., Blasch, E., & Qu, Q. (2025). Future Outdoor Safety Monitoring: Integrating Human Activity Recognition with the Internet of Physical-Virtual Things.

Choudhury, A., & Shamszare, H. (2023). Investigating the impact of user trust on the adoption and use of ChatGPT: Survey analysis. *Journal of Medical Internet Research, 25*, e47184. DOI: 10.2196/47184 PMID: 37314848

Claesson, A., Fredman, D., Svensson, L., Ringh, M., Hollenberg, J., Nordberg, P., & Ban, Y. (2016). Unmanned aerial vehicles (drones) in out-of-hospital-cardiac-arrest. *Scandinavian Journal of Trauma, Resuscitation and Emergency Medicine, 24*(1), 1–9. DOI: 10.1186/s13049-016-0313-5 PMID: 27729058

Clausen, E., & Sörensen, A. (2022). Required and desired: Breakthroughs for future-proofing mineral and metal extraction. *Mineral Economics, 35*(3), 521–537. DOI: 10.1007/s13563-022-00328-0

Control Engineering. (2019). Six Use Cases for Collaborative Robots. https://www.controleng.com/articles/six-use-cases-for-collaborative-robots/

Custers, B. (2016). Drones Here, There and Everywhere Introduction and Overview. In: Custers, B. (eds) The Future of Drone Use. Information Technology and Law Series, vol 27. T.M.C. Asser Press, The Hague. DOI: 10.1007/978-94-6265-132-6_1

Duraisamy, J. (2020). Design and Analysis of Remotely Amphibious Drone. *International Journal of Innovative Technology and Exploring Engineering, 9*(5), 284–287. DOI: 10.35940/ijitee.E2137.039520

El-Helaly, M. (2024). Artificial Intelligence and Occupational Health and Safety, Benefits and Drawbacks. *La Medicina del Lavoro, 115*(2), 1. DOI: 10.23749/mdl.v115i2.15835 PMID: 38686574

Fatima, S., Desouza, K. C., & Dawson, G. S. (2020). National strategic artificial intelligence plans: A multi-dimensional analysis. *Economic Analysis and Policy, 67*, 178–194. DOI: 10.1016/j.eap.2020.07.008

Felknor, S. A., Streit, J. M., Edwards, N. T., & Howard, J. (2023). Four futures for occupational safety and health. *International Journal of Environmental Research and Public Health, 20*(5), 4333. DOI: 10.3390/ijerph20054333 PMID: 36901347

Fisher, E., Flynn, M. A., Pratap, P., & Vietas, J. A. (2023). Occupational safety and health equity impacts of artificial intelligence: A scoping review. *International Journal of Environmental Research and Public Health, 20*(13), 6221. DOI: 10.3390/ijerph20136221 PMID: 37444068

Flor-Unda, O., Fuentes, M., Dávila, D., Rivera, M., Llano, G., Izurieta, C., & Acosta-Vargas, P. (2023). Innovative Technologies for Occupational Health and Safety: A Scoping Review. *Safety (Basel, Switzerland), 9*(2), 35. DOI: 10.3390/safety9020035

Foromo, M. R., Chabeli, M., & Satekge, M. M. (2016). Survey on the implementation of the Occupational Health and Safety Act at an academic hospital in Johannesburg. *Curationis, 39*(1), 1–10. DOI: 10.4102/curationis.v39i1.1524 PMID: 27796104

Fox, S., & Victores, J. G. (2024, May). Safety of Human–Artificial Intelligence Systems: Applying Safety Science to Analyze Loopholes in Interactions between Human Organizations, Artificial Intelligence, and Individual People. [). MDPI.]. *Informatics (MDPI), 11*(2), 36. DOI: 10.3390/informatics11020036

Gabbard, J. L., Smith, M., Tanous, K., Kim, H., & Jonas, B. (2019). AR DriveSim: AnImmersive Driving Simulator for Augmented Reality Head-Up Display Research. *Frontiers in Robotics and AI, I*, 6. DOI: 10.3389/frobt.2019.00098 PMID: 33501113

Gaske, M. R. (2023). Regulation Priorities for Artificial Intelligence Foundation Models. *SSRN, 26*, 1. DOI: 10.2139/ssrn.4417565

Ghiafehdavoudi, S., & Vaillant, B. (2020). The Digital Transformation of Construction Worksite Safety How much added value would AI bring for workers and work-environment safety?.

Gould, G. (2019). The Impact of Robotics on Safety and Health. Wolters Kluwer. https://www.wolterskluwer.com/en/expert-insights/the-impact-of-robotics-on-safety-and-health

Grandi, F., Zanni, L., Peruzzini, M., Pellicciari, M., & Campanella, C. E. (2020). A Transdisciplinary digital approach for tractor's human-centred design. *International Journal of Computer Integrated Manufacturing, 33*(4), 377–397. DOI: 10.1080/0951192X.2019.1599441

Gregson, N. (2023). Waste, Money and Finance: Or, how turning discard into waste turns waste into an energy resource and an asset. In *The Waste of the World* (pp. 133-163). Bristol University Press.

Gupta, D., & Shah, M. (2022). A comprehensive study on artificial intelligence in oil and gas sector. *Environmental Science and Pollution Research International, 29*(34), 50984–50997. DOI: 10.1007/s11356-021-15379-z PMID: 34378133

Hassan, M., Kushniruk, A., & Borycki, E. (2024). Barriers to and facilitators of artificial intelligence adoption in health care: Scoping review. *JMIR Human Factors, 11*, e48633. DOI: 10.2196/48633 PMID: 39207831

Holzinger, A., Langs, G., Denk, H., Zatloukal, K., & Müller, H. (2019, April 02). Causability and explainability of artificial intelligence in medicine. *Wiley Interdisciplinary Reviews. Data Mining and Knowledge Discovery, 9*(4), e1312. DOI: 10.1002/widm.1312 PMID: 32089788

Hou, L., Wu, S., Zhang, G., Tan, Y., & Wang, X. (2021). Literature Review of Digital Twins Applications in Construction Workforce Safety. *Applied Sciences (Basel, Switzerland), 11*, •••. https://doi.org/**10.3390/app11010339

Hoxhaj, O., Halilaj, B., & Harizi, A. (2023). Ethical Implications And Human Rights Violations In The Age Of Artificial Intelligence. *Balkan Social Science Review, 22*(22), 153–171. DOI: 10.46763/BSSR232222153h

Hussain, M., Alamri, A., Zhang, T., & Jamil, I. (2024). Application of Artificial Intelligence in the Oil and Gas Industry. In *Engineering Applications of Artificial Intelligence* (pp. 341–373). Springer Nature Switzerland. DOI: 10.1007/978-3-031-50300-9_19

Ibrahim, T., & Ali, H. (2023). The Impact of Wearable IoT Devices on Early Disease Detection and Prevention. *International Journal of Applied Health Care Analytics*, *8*(8), 1–15.

Idambi, K., & Boniface, J. (2021). *An Assessment of Regulatory Compliance With International and Regional Obligations Relating To Environmental Health And Safety Standards* (Doctoral dissertation, Institute of Petroleum Studies-Kampala).

Irawan, B., & Biyanto, T. R. (2024). Industrial Evolution: The Integration of Al in Robotics. *AI Developments for Industrial Robotics and Intelligent Drones*, 85.

Jain, A. (2021). *Impact of digitalization and artificial intelligence as causes and enablers of organizational change*. Nottingham University Business School.

Jain, A., Hassard, J., Leka, S., Di Tecco, C., & Iavicoli, S. (2021). The role of occupational health services in psychosocial risk management and the promotion of mental health and well-being at work. *International Journal of Environmental Research and Public Health*, *18*(7), 3632. DOI: 10.3390/ijerph18073632 PMID: 33807352

Janssen, M., Brous, P., Estevez, E., Barbosa, L. S., & Janowski, T. (2020). Data governance: Organizing data for trustworthy Artificial Intelligence. *Government Information Quarterly*, *37*(3), 101493. DOI: 10.1016/j.giq.2020.101493

Jarota, M. (2021). Artificial intelligence and robotisation in the EU - should we change OHS law? *Journal of Occupational Medicine and Toxicology (London, England)*, *16*(18), 1–8. DOI: 10.1186/s12995-021-00301-7 PMID: 33952297

Jarota, M. (2023). Artificial intelligence in the work process. A reflection on the proposed European Union regulations on artificial intelligence from an occupational health and safety perspective. *Computer Law & Security Review*, *49*, 105825. DOI: 10.1016/j.clsr.2023.105825

Jebelli, H., Choi, B., & Lee, S. (2019). Application of wearable biosensors to construction sites. I: Assessing workers' stress. *Journal of Construction Engineering and Management*, *145*(12), 04019079. DOI: 10.1061/(ASCE)CO.1943-7862.0001729

Johnson, A., Dey, S., Nguyen, H., Groth, M., Joyce, S., Tan, L., Glozier, N., & Harvey, S. B. (2020). A review and agenda for examining how technology-driven changes at work will impact workplace mental health and employee well-being. *Australian Journal of Management*, *45*(3), 402–424. DOI: 10.1177/0312896220922292

Junker, M., Böhm, M., & Krcmar, H. (2024). Advantages and disadvantages of mobile applications for workplace health promotion: A scoping review. *PLoS One*, *19*(1), e0296212. DOI: 10.1371/journal.pone.0296212 PMID: 38165989

Kang, Y., Cai, Z., Tan, C. W., Huang, Q., & Liu, H. (2020). Natural language processing (NLP) in management research: A literature review. *Journal of Management Analytics*, *7*(2), 139–172. DOI: 10.1080/23270012.2020.1756939

Kavouras, S., Vardopoulos, I., Mitoula, R., Zorpas, A. A., & Kaldis, P. (2022). Occupational health and safety scope significance in achieving sustainability. *Sustainability (Basel)*, *14*(4), 2424. DOI: 10.3390/su14042424

Khodyreva, A. (2023). Prevention of occupational injuries of employees LLC Gazprom Dobycha Orenburg based on the risk-based approach and the modernization of local regulations.

Khuwuthyakorn, P., Suksatit, B., & Thinnukool, O. (2018, August). First Aid Literacy Mobile Application Development. In *Proceedings of the 8th International Conference on Information Communication and Management* (pp. 17-21)

Kiritchenko, S., Nejadgholi, I., & Fraser, K. C. (2021). Confronting abusive language online: A survey from the ethical and human rights perspective. *Journal of Artificial Intelligence Research*, *71*, 431–478. DOI: 10.1613/jair.1.12590

Koulu, R. (2021). Crafting digital transparency: Implementing legal values into algorithmic design. *Critical Analysis L.*, *8*(1), 81–100. DOI: 10.33137/cal.v8i1.36281

Krichen, M., Abdalzaher, M. S., Elwekeil, M., & Fouda, M. M. (2024). Managing natural disasters: An analysis of technological advancements, opportunities, and challenges. *Internet of Things and Cyber-Physical Systems*, *4*, 99–109. DOI: 10.1016/j.iotcps.2023.09.002

Kumar, S. R., Nathan, V. N., Ashique, S. M., Rajkumar, V., & Karthick, P. A. (2021). Productivity enhancement and cycle time reduction in toyota production system through jishuken activity–Case study. *Materials Today: Proceedings*, *37*, 964–966. DOI: 10.1016/j.matpr.2020.06.181

Kumar, Y., Koul, A., Singla, R., & Ijaz, M. F. (2023). Artificial intelligence in disease diagnosis: A systematic literature review, synthesizing framework and future research agenda. *Journal of Ambient Intelligence and Humanized Computing*, *14*(7), 8459–8486. DOI: 10.1007/s12652-021-03612-z PMID: 35039756

Laï, M. C., Brian, M., & Mamzer, M. F. (2020). Perceptions of artificial intelligence in healthcare: Findings from a qualitative survey study among actors in France. *Journal of Translational Medicine*, *18*(1), 1–13. DOI: 10.1186/s12967-019-02204-y PMID: 31918710

Lee, D., & Yoon, S. N. (2021). Application of artificial intelligence-based technologies in the healthcare industry: Opportunities and challenges. *International Journal of Environmental Research and Public Health*, *18*(1), 271. DOI: 10.3390/ijerph18010271 PMID: 33401373

Leso, V., Fontana, L., & Iavicoli, I. (2018). The occupational health and safety dimension of Industry 4.0. *La Medicina del Lavoro*, *110*(5), 327–338. DOI: 10.23749/mdl.v110i5.7282 PMID: 30378585

Li, C., Liang, W., Quigley, C., Zhao, Y., & Yu, L. F. (2017). Earthquake Safety Training through Virtual Drills. *IEEE Transactions on Visualization and Computer Graphics*, *23*(4), 1275–1284. DOI: 10.1109/TVCG.2017.2656958 PMID: 28129163

Liang, C. J., Le, T. H., Ham, Y., Mantha, B. R., Cheng, M. H., & Lin, J. J. (2024). Ethics of artificial intelligence and robotics in the architecture, engineering, and construction industry. *Automation in Construction*, *162*, 105369. DOI: 10.1016/j.autcon.2024.105369

Liu, W., Meng, Q., Li, Z., & Hu, X. (2021). Applications of computer vision in monitoring the unsafe behavior of construction workers: Current status and challenges. *Buildings (Basel, Switzerland)*, *11*(9), 409. DOI: 10.3390/buildings11090409

Lu, M. H., Calandra, D., & Thawonmas, R. (2023). Artificial Reality: Immersive but Factually Dishonest AR Experience. *IEEE Consumer Electronics Magazine*, *12*(1), 8–11. DOI: 10.1109/MCE.2022.3216421

Lu, Y., Karanikas, N., & Carroll, J. A. (2024). A Scoping Review of Integrating Occupational Health and Safety and Workplace Health Promotion Interventions. *Journal of Human Environment and Health Promotion*, *10*(4), 179–190. DOI: 10.61186/jhehp.10.4.179

Mahlknecht, A., Engl, A., Piccoliori, G., & Wiedermann, C. J. (2023). Supporting primary care through symptom checking artificial intelligence: A study of patient and physician attitudes in Italian general practice. *BMC Primary Care*, *24*(1), 174. DOI: 10.1186/s12875-023-02143-0 PMID: 37661285

Martin, N., Friedewald, M., Schiering, I., Mester, B. A., Hallinan, D., & Jensen, M. (2020). *The Data Protection Impact Assessment According to Article 35 GDPR*. Fraunhofer Verlag.

Mihret, E. T. (2020). Robotics and Artificial Intelligence. [IJAIML]. *International Journal of Artificial Intelligence and Machine Learning*, *10*(2), 57–78. DOI: 10.4018/IJAIML.2020070104

Mir Mohammadzade Noudehi, Z., & Bagheri Khameneh, F. (2023, September). The Impact of Internet of Things, Blockchain, and Artificial Intelligence on Occupational Health and Safety. In *International Conference on Science, Engineering Management and Information Technology* (pp. 52-76). Cham: Springer Nature Switzerland.

Mlodzinski, E., Wardi, G., Viglione, C., Nemati, S., Crotty Alexander, L., & Malhotra, A. (2023). Assessing barriers to implementation of machine learning and artificial intelligence–based tools in critical care: Web-based survey study. *JMIR Perioperative Medicine*, *6*, e41056. DOI: 10.2196/41056 PMID: 36705960

Morandini, S., Fraboni, F., De Angelis, M., Puzzo, G., Giusino, D., & Pietrantoni, L. (2023). The impact of artificial intelligence on workers' skills: Upskilling and reskilling in organisations. *Informing Science*, *26*, 39–68. DOI: 10.28945/5078

Moshawrab, M., Adda, M., Bouzouane, A., Ibrahim, H., & Raad, A. (2022, October 2). Smart Wearables for the Detection of Occupational Physical Fatigue: A Literature Review. *Sensors (Basel)*, *22*(19), 7472. Advance online publication. DOI: 10.3390/s22197472 PMID: 36236570

Mugabe, K. V. (2021). Barriers and facilitators to the adoption of artificial intelligence in radiation oncology: A New Zealand study. *Technical Innovations & Patient Support in Radiation Oncology*, *18*, 16–21. DOI: 10.1016/j.tipsro.2021.03.004 PMID: 33981867

Mustapha, Z. (2019). Contractors' Perception towards Safety and its Consequences on Construction Workers in Cape Coast Metropolis. *The Korean Journal of Food & Health Convergence*, *5*(6), 11–16.

Mustapha, Z., Aigbavboa, C. O., & Thwala, W. D. (2015, November). Occupational health and safety challenges in the Ghanaian Construction Industry. In *Fourth NMMU Construction Management Conference* (Vol. 30, pp. 15-21).

Neveling, P. (2024). Occupational health and safety in the global garment industry. In *The Routledge Handbook of the Political Economy of Health and Healthcare* (pp. 177–189). Routledge. DOI: 10.4324/9781003017110-16

Nguyen, C. C., Wong, S., Thai, M. T., Hoang, T. T., Phan, P. T., Davies, J., Wu, L., Tsai, D., Phan, H.-P., Lovell, N. H., & Do, T. N. (2023). Advanced user interfaces for teleoperated surgical robotic systems. *Advanced Sensor Research*, *2*(4), 2200036. DOI: 10.1002/adsr.202200036

Ninoria, S., Upadhyay, R., Philip, R. S., Dwivedi, R., Micheal, G., Gupta, A., & Mishra, S. (2023). AI and Crime Prevention With Image and Video Analytics Using IoT. In *Handbook of Research on Thrust Technologies' Effect on Image Processing* (pp. 96–115). IGI Global. DOI: 10.4018/978-1-6684-8618-4.ch007

Nižetić, S., Šolić, P., Gonzalez-De, D. L. D. I., & Patrono, L. (2020). Internet of Things (IoT): Opportunities, issues and challenges towards a smart and sustainable future. *Journal of Cleaner Production*, *274*, 122877. DOI: 10.1016/j.jclepro.2020.122877 PMID: 32834567

Nnaji, C., Awolusi, I., Park, J., & Albert, A. (2021). Wearable sensing devices: Towards the development of a personalized system for construction safety and health risk mitigation. *Sensors (Basel)*, *21*(3), 682. DOI: 10.3390/s21030682 PMID: 33498311

Ogundeko-Olugbami, O., & Ogundeko, O. (2025). AI-enhanced predictive analytics systems combatting health disparities while driving equity in US healthcare delivery.

Ojji, S. O. (2024). Digital Transformation and its Impact on Safety Culture During Organizational Change. *Valley International Journal Digital Library*, 26135-26146.

Oliveira, A. L., & Figueiredo, M. A. (2024). Artificial Intelligence: Historical Context and State of the Art. *Multidisciplinary Perspectives on Artificial Intelligence and the Law*, 3.

Onifade, M., Adebisi, J. A., Shivute, A. P., & Genc, B. (2023a). Challenges and applications of digital technology in the mineral industry. *Resources Policy*, *85*, 103978. DOI: 10.1016/j.resourpol.2023.103978

Onifade, M., Said, K. O., & Shivute, A. P. (2023b). Safe mining operations through technological advancement. *Process Safety and Environmental Protection*, *175*, 251–258. DOI: 10.1016/j.psep.2023.05.052

Owen, J. (2024). AI and Robotics: Transforming Automation and Labor Productivity in the Construction Industry.

Palačić, D. (2024). How to assess the risks of applying Artificial Intelligence in occupational health and safety-Modelling the assessment process. *The authors are responsible for the professional and linguistic accuracy of their papers.*, 1.

Paneru, S., & Jeelani, I. (2021). Computer vision applications in construction: Current state, opportunities & challenges. *Automation in Construction*, *132*, 103940. DOI: 10.1016/j.autcon.2021.103940

Patchipala, S.Surya Gangadhar Patchipala. (2023). Tackling data and model drift in AI: Strategies for maintaining accuracy during ML model inference. *International Journal of Science and Research Archive*, *10*(2), 1198–1209. DOI: 10.30574/ijsra.2023.10.2.0855

Patel, V., Chesmore, A., Legner, C. M., & Pandey, S. (2022). Trends in workplace wearable technologies and connected-worker solutions for next-generation occupational safety, health, and productivity. *Advanced Intelligent Systems*, *4*(1), 2100099. DOI: 10.1002/aisy.202100099

Pishgar, M., Issa, S. F., Sietsema, M., Pratap, P., & Darabi, H. (2021). REDECA: A novel framework to review artificial intelligence and its applications in occupational safety and health. *International Journal of Environmental Research and Public Health*, *18*(13), 6705. DOI: 10.3390/ijerph18136705 PMID: 34206378

Poyade, M., Eaglesham, C., Trench, J., & Reid, M. (2021). A transferable psychological evaluation of virtual reality applied to safety training in chemical manufacturing. *Journal of Chemical Health and Safety*, *28*(1), 55–65. DOI: 10.1021/acs.chas.0c00105

Pransky, J. (2020). The Pransky interview: Dr. Matanya Horowitz, founder and CEO of AMP robotics. *The Industrial Robot*, *47*(3), 319–323. DOI: 10.1108/IR-02-2020-0038

Radhakrishnan, J., & Chattopadhyay, M. (2020). Determinants and barriers of artificial intelligence adoption–A literature review. In *Re-imagining Diffusion and Adoption of Information Technology and Systems: A Continuing Conversation: IFIP WG 8.6 International Conference on Transfer and Diffusion of IT, TDIT 2020, Tiruchirappalli, India, December 18–19, 2020, Proceedings, Part I* (pp. 89-99). Springer International Publishing. DOI: 10.1007/978-3-030-64849-7_9

Rane, N., Choudhary, S., & Rane, J. (2023). Artificial Intelligence (AI) and Internet of Things (IoT)-based sensors for monitoring and controlling in architecture, engineering, and construction: applications, challenges, and opportunities. *Available atSSRN* 4642197. DOI: 10.2139/ssrn.4642197

Ranjan, A., Zhao, Y., Sahu, H. B., & Misra, P. (2019). Opportunities and challenges in health sensing for extreme industrial environment: Perspectives from underground mines. *IEEE Access : Practical Innovations, Open Solutions*, *7*, 139181–139195. DOI: 10.1109/ACCESS.2019.2941436

Riccò, M., Ranzieri, S., Vezzosi, L., Balzarini, F., & Bragazzi, N. L. (2022). Wearable Exoskeletons on the Workplaces: Knowledge, Attitudes and Perspectives of Health and Safety Managers on the implementation of exoskeleton technology in Northern Italy. *Acta Biomedica*, *92*(6), e2021310. PMID: 35075091

Rikhotso, O., Morodi, T. J., & Masekameni, D. M. (2022). Health risk management cost items imposed by Occupational Health and Safety Regulations: A South African perspective. *Safety Science*, *150*, 105707. DOI: 10.1016/j.ssci.2022.105707

Robert, C., Meyer, P., Séroussi, B., Leroy, T., & Bibault, J. E. (2024). Artificial intelligence and radiotherapy: Evolution or revolution? *Cancer Radiotherapie*, *28*(6-7), 503–509. DOI: 10.1016/j.canrad.2024.09.003 PMID: 39406605

Sacks, R., Perlman, A., & Barak, R. (2013). Construction safety training using immersive virtual reality. *Construction Management and Economics*, *31*(9), 1005–1017. DOI: 10.1080/01446193.2013.828844

Saheb, T. (2023). Ethically contentious aspects of artificial intelligence surveillance: A social science perspective. *AI and Ethics*, *3*(2), 369–379. DOI: 10.1007/s43681-022-00196-y PMID: 35874304

Salazar Rodriguez, J. D. (2024). Harnessing AI for Sustainable Architecture: A TOWS Analysis of Environmental, Economic, and Social Impacts in Design. *Economic, and Social Impacts in Design (August 29, 2024).*

Salhab, W., Ameyed, D., Jaafar, F., & Mcheick, H. (2024). A systematic literature review on ai safety: Identifying trends, challenges and future directions. *IEEE Access : Practical Innovations, Open Solutions*, *12*, 131762–131784. DOI: 10.1109/ACCESS.2024.3440647

Sattari, F., Macciotta, R., Kurian, D., & Lefsrud, L. (2021). Application of Bayesian network and artificial intelligence to reduce accident/incident rates in oil & gas companies. *Safety Science*, *133*, 104981. DOI: 10.1016/j.ssci.2020.104981

Scavarelli, A., Arya, A., & Teather, R. J. (2021). Virtual reality and augmented reality in social learning spaces: A literature review. *Virtual Reality (Waltham Cross)*, *25*(1), 257–277. DOI: 10.1007/s10055-020-00444-8

Shah, I. A., & Mishra, S. (2024). Artificial intelligence in advancing occupational health and safety: An encapsulation of developments. *Journal of Occupational Health*, *66*(1), uiad017. DOI: 10.1093/joccuh/uiad017 PMID: 38334203

Shamshiri, A., Ryu, K. R., & Park, J. Y. (2024). Text mining and natural language processing in construction. *Automation in Construction*, *158*, 105200. DOI: 10.1016/j.autcon.2023.105200

Shandilya, S. K., Datta, A., Kartik, Y., & Nagar, A. (2024). Navigating the regulatory landscape. In *Digital Resilience: Navigating Disruption and Safeguarding Data Privacy* (pp. 127–240). Springer Nature Switzerland. DOI: 10.1007/978-3-031-53290-0_3

Sharko, A. D., Sharko, G., & Qose, S. (2024, July). Artificial Intelligence In Cybersecurity Applications. In *2024 IEEE 28th International Conference on Intelligent Engineering Systems (INES)* (pp. 000175-000180). IEEE. DOI: 10.1109/INES63318.2024.10629129

Simpson, L., Maharaj, M. M., & Mobbs, R. J. (2019). The role of wearables in spinal posture analysis: A systematic review. *BMC Musculoskeletal Disorders*, *20*(1), 1–14. DOI: 10.1186/s12891-019-2430-6 PMID: 30736775

Sinclair, R. R., Allen, T., Barber, L., Bergman, M., Britt, T., Butler, A., Ford, M., Hammer, L., Kath, L., Probst, T., & Yuan, Z. (2020). Occupational health science in the time of COVID-19: Now more than ever. *Occupational Health Science*, *4*(1-2), 1–22. DOI: 10.1007/s41542-020-00064-3 PMID: 32838031

Somaraju, P., Kulkarni, S. S., Duffy, V. G., & Kanade, S. (2024, June). Artificial Intelligence and Mobile Computing: Role of AI in Ergonomics. In *International Conference on Human-Computer Interaction* (pp. 265-281). Cham: Springer Nature Switzerland. DOI: 10.1007/978-3-031-61066-0_16

Spurgeon, A. (2012). *The Contribution of the Women's Factory Inspectorate (1893-1921) to improvements in women's occupational health and safety* (Doctoral dissertation, University of Worcester).

Stypinska, J. (2023). AI ageism: A critical roadmap for studying age discrimination and exclusion in digitalized societies. *AI & Society*, *38*(2), 665–677. DOI: 10.1007/s00146-022-01553-5 PMID: 36212226

Sunarti, S., Rahman, F. F., Naufal, M., Risky, M., Febriyanto, K., & Masnina, R. (2021). Artificial intelligence in healthcare: Opportunities and risk for future. *Gaceta Sanitaria*, *35*, S67–S70. DOI: 10.1016/j.gaceta.2020.12.019 PMID: 33832631

Tender, M., Fuller, P., Vaughan, A., Long, M., Couto, J. P., Damien, P., Chow, V., Silva, F., Reis, F., & Reis, R. (2022, November). Lessons from implementation of Key Technological Developments to improve occupational safety and health processes in a complex UK-based construction project. []. IOP Publishing.]. *IOP Conference Series. Earth and Environmental Science*, *1101*(9), 092016. DOI: 10.1088/1755-1315/1101/9/092016

Tóth, Z., Caruana, R., Gruber, T., & Loebbecke, C. (2022). The dawn of the AI robots: Towards a new framework of AI robot accountability. *Journal of Business Ethics*, *178*(4), 895–916. DOI: 10.1007/s10551-022-05050-z

Toyoda, R., Russo-Abegão, F., & Glassey, J. (2022). VR-based health and safety training in various high-risk engineering industries: A literature review. *International Journal of Educational Technology in Higher Education*, *19*(1), 42. DOI: 10.1186/s41239-022-00349-3

Tursunbayeva, A., Pagliari, C., Di Lauro, S., & Antonelli, G. (2022). The ethics of people analytics: Risks, opportunities and recommendations. *Personnel Review*, *51*(3), 900–921. DOI: 10.1108/PR-12-2019-0680

Verdantix. (2022). Strategic Focus: Improving Safety With Robotics And Automation. https://www.verdantix.com/report/environment-health-safety/strategic-focus-improving-safety-with-robotics-and-automation

Vilone, G., & Longo, L. (2021). Notions of explainability and evaluation approaches for explainable artificial intelligence. *Information Fusion*, *76*, 89–106. DOI: 10.1016/j.inffus.2021.05.009

Vukicevic, A. M., Macužic, I., Djapan, M., Milicevic, V., & Shamina, L. (2021). Digital Training and Advanced Learning in Occupational Safety and Health Based on Modern and Affordable Technologies. *Sustainability (Basel)*, *2021*(13), 13641. DOI: 10.3390/su132413641

Weerts, S., Naous, D., Bouchikhi, M. E., & Clavien, C. (2022, August). AI Systems for Occupational Safety and Health: From Ethical Concerns to Limited Legal Solutions. In *International Conference on Electronic Government* (pp. 499-514). Cham: Springer International Publishing. DOI: 10.1007/978-3-031-15086-9_32

World Health Organization. (2024). *Ethics and governance of artificial intelligence for health: large multi-modal models. WHO guidance*. World Health Organization.

Xing, F., Peng, G., Zhang, B., Li, S., & Liang, X. (2021). Socio-technical barriers affecting large-scale deployment of AI-enabled wearable medical devices among the ageing population in China. *Technological Forecasting and Social Change*, *166*, 120609. DOI: 10.1016/j.techfore.2021.120609

Yang, X., Chen, A., PourNejatian, N., Shin, H. C., Smith, K. E., Parisien, C., Compas, C., Martin, C., Costa, A. B., Flores, M. G., Zhang, Y., Magoc, T., Harle, C. A., Lipori, G., Mitchell, D. A., Hogan, W. R., Shenkman, E. A., Bian, J., & Wu, Y. (2022). A large language model for electronic health records. *NPJ Digital Medicine*, *5*(1), 194. DOI: 10.1038/s41746-022-00742-2 PMID: 36572766

Yuan, J., Zhang, Y., Liu, S., & Zhu, R. (2023). Wearable leg movement monitoring system for high-precision real-time metabolic energy estimation and motion recognition. *Research, 6*, 0214.

Zainab, H., Khan, A. H., Khan, R., & Hussain, H. K. (2024). Integration of AI and Wearable Devices for Continuous Cardiac Health Monitoring. *International Journal of Multidisciplinary Sciences and Arts*, *3*(4), 123–139.

Zenor, J. (2020). If you see something, say something: Can artificial intelligence have a duty to report dangerous behavior in the home? *DENv. L.REv.*, *98*, 839.

Zhang, C., Wang, X., Fang, S., & Shi, X. (2022). Construction and Application of VR-AR Teaching System in Coal-Based Energy Education. *Sustainability (Basel)*, *14*(23), 16033. DOI: 10.3390/su142316033

Zhang, M., Ghodrati, N., Poshdar, M., Seet, B. C., & Yongchareon, S. (2023). A construction accident prevention system based on the Internet of Things (IoT). *Safety Science*, *159*, 106012. DOI: 10.1016/j.ssci.2022.106012

Zhong, B., Pan, X., Love, P. E., Sun, J., & Tao, C. (2020). Hazard analysis: A deep learning and text mining framework for accident prevention. *Advanced Engineering Informatics*, *46*, 101152. DOI: 10.1016/j.aei.2020.101152

Zhou, X. (2023). *Ieee, 2023*. Designing Navigation Tool for Immersive Analytics in AR.

Zvarivadza, T., Onifade, M., Dayo-Olupona, O., Said, K. O., Githiria, J. M., Genc, B., & Celik, T. (2024). On the impact of Industrial Internet of Things (IIoT)-mining sector perspectives. *International Journal of Mining, Reclamation and Environment*, *38*(10), 1–39. DOI: 10.1080/17480930.2024.2347131

Zwęgliński, T. (2020). The use of drones in disaster aerial needs reconnaissance and damage assessment–three-dimensional modeling and orthophoto map study. *Sustainability (Basel)*, *12*(15), 6080. DOI: 10.3390/su12156080

Chapter 7
Hybrid Approach for Osteoarthritis Detection in X-Ray Images Using SqueezeNet and Grey Wolf Optimizer

Singaravelan Shanmugasundaram
https://orcid.org/0000-0003-4353-2261
PSR Engineering College, India

A. Muthukumar
PPG Institute of Technology, India

Judith Varshini J. C.
Sri Eshwar College of Engineering, India

D. Murugan
Manonmaniam Sundaranar University, India

Gomathy Nayagam M
Ramco Institute of Technology, India

Priskilla Angel Rani J.
Francis Xavier Engineering College, India

P. Gopalsamy
PSR Engineering College, India

S. Balaganesh
PSR Engineering College, India

ABSTRACT

In recent years, X ray imaging has emerged as a promising non-invasive technique for detecting osteoarthritis. However, existing techniques for osteoarthritis detection in thermal images suffer from several limitations, such as low accuracy, limited generalizability, and lack of interpretability. To address these challenges, we propose a novel approach for osteoarthritis detection in x ray images using the SqueezeNet model deep learning architecture. The proposed approach involves pre-processing the X-ray images to enhance their features, followed by segmentation to extract the region of interest. The segmented region is then fed into the SqueezeNet model, which is trained to classify the thermal image as normal or abnormal based on the presence of osteoarthritis. The parameter of SqueezeNet is tuned using grey wolf optimizer to reach maximum accuracy. We evaluated the performance of the proposed approach on a dataset of thermal images collected from patients with osteoarthritis and healthy controls.

DOI: 10.4018/979-8-3693-9301-7.ch007

INTRODUCTION

Osteoarthritis (OA) is the most widespread, serious chronic rheumatic disease and is a foremost reason of pain and disability in most countries worldwide. Tibiofemoral OA on Magnetic Resonance Imaging (MRI) is defined as "either (a) the presence of both definite osteophyte formation and full thickness cartilage loss or (b) the presence of one of the features in (a) and one of the following: subchondral bone marrow lesion or cyst not associated with meniscal or ligamentous attachments, meniscal subluxation, maceration or degenerative (horizontal) tear, partial thickness cartilage loss and bone attritions" . The Osteoarthritis Research Society International (OARSI) has freshly defined OA and launched an initiative to critically evaluate and standardize pre-existing definitions of OA. "Osteoarthritis is a disorder involving movable joints characterized by cell stress and extracellular matrix degradation initiated by micro- and macro-injury that activates maladaptive repair responses including pro-inflammatory pathways of innate immunity. The disease manifests first as a molecular derangement (abnormal joint tissue metabolism) followed by anatomic, and/or physiologic derangements (characterized by cartilage degradation, bone remodeling, osteophyte formation, joint inflammation and loss of normal joint function), that can culminate in illness" . Pain, Stiffness and limited joint movement are the main symptoms of OA. Pain is primarily felt in the joint through activity, but as the disease advances it may be observed with minimal movement or even while resting . Normal functioning of joint is disturbed because of disease and over time the shape of joint starts changing

Figure 1. Joints affected by OA resulting into enlarged shape and sometimes inflamed.

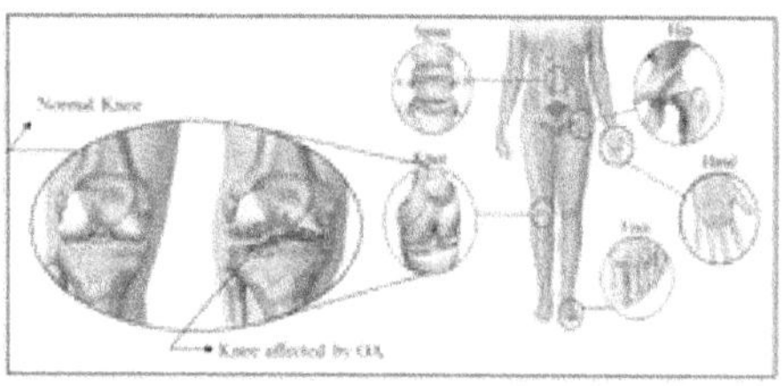

Damage of cartilage or its loss is the primary underlying feature of OA . Cartilage is a flexible, soft yet stiff tissue that exists on the surface of bone ends and provide smooth functioning such as shock absorption, distribution of weight and frictionless motion to joint organ .

OA commonly affects the joints of the knee, hip, foot, spine and hand but can involve any moveable joint as shown in Figure 1. The Figure 1 shows the various joints that are likely to get affected by OA and the inset shows the comparison of normal knee joint and OA affected joint. Different tissues and organs of the body are not directly influenced by OA, but rather many individuals have other medical issues that should be considered while overseeing it. The outcomes and response to treatment vary from person to person: some people develop a disability where activities are restricted while others only ever have mild problems. Following section discusses the occurrence of OA in terms of epidemiological data.

Damage of cartilage or its loss is the primary underlying feature of OA . Cartilage is a flexible, soft yet stiff tissue that exists on the surface of bone ends and provide smooth functioning such as shock absorption, distribution of weight and frictionless motion to joint organ.

Several medical applications based on DL for segmentation, classification and risk assessment tasks, prognosis, diagnosis and even prediction of therapy responses. The DL has provided a various AI innovative application in different technical aspects of medical imaging. It is specifically applied to the images acquisition, ranging from image artifacts removal, enhancing an image quality, normalizing/harmonizing images, lowering radiation and contrast dose, and lessening the imaging analysis duration. Thus, the many AI technology has been implemented an overview of DL applied to imaging techniques. The ML and DL model have been utilized for brain image analysis extensively to develop an imaging-based classification and diagnostic systems. These are mainly focused on strokes, epilepsy, psychiatric disorders, demyelinating diseases and neurodegenerative disorders.

Also, many optimization algorithms are also involved in the medical field to enhance the computational hardware and access to large quantity of data imaging. The DL has established indisputable superiority over the traditional ML system. The AI is used to perform a wide range of tasks that is faced by radiologists. Most of the initial DL applications, it is concentrated on the "downstream" side applying a computer vision method for segmentation of anatomical structures and detection of lesions. Thus the methods that are used to identify the diseases are hemorrhage, lacunes, stroke, microbleeds, aneurysms, metastases, primary brain tumours, and white matter hyperintensities. The DL method focusing on the "upstream" side, it is realized that there are some other innovative AI applications are applied in multiple technical aspects of medical imaging such as image acquisitions. Various number of methods are developed for an image generation and image enhancement using DL that is recently developed. Some of them are ranging from eliminating image artifacts, contrast dose, normalizing/harmonizing images quality, lowering radiation and image analysis duration.

1.1 Epidemiology of Knee OA

This section presents the epidemiological data that describes the prevalence of OA and especially knee OA considering various factors getting associated with it. The occurrence of OA increases with age and commonly affects women more often than men. OA can affect joints of the spine, fingers, thumbs, hips, knees, and toes but it is most common in knee . The epidemiological data presented so far in the literature is presented here to support the importance of study performed in this thesis that reflects the national and international status. It is reported that OA affects 240 million people globally . Worldwide assessment states that 18.0% of women and 9.6% of men aged over 60 years have symptomatic OA . Asian countries are ageing rapidly. It is estimated that the percentage of people above 65 years of age in Asia will be more than double in the next two decades, it is expected to grow from 6.8% in 2008 to 16.2% in 2040 . Thus, the prevalence of aged people getting affected with OA is high. Whereas, the prevalence of OA in India is reported to be 22 to 39% and prevalence of knee OA is 28.7%. This varies with respect to various factors such as the gender, weight, life style, habitat of the person, etc. The data presented here is as per the study carried out in . From this study it is found that knee OA is more prevalent in woman (31.6%) as compared to men (28.1%). The prevalence of OA is greater in large cities (33.1%) and villages (31.1%) as compared to townships (17.1%) and minor cities (17.2%). It also increases with the increase in body mass index (BMI) i.e. it is high in obese and normal weight people (33%) in comparison to underweight people (28%) it is highest in obese and overweight people. Prevalence OA is highest in the people with sedentary lifestyle whereas lowest in the people with demanding and active lifestyles

Through the epidemiological data presented it is observed that the occurrence of knee OA is high worldwide and it is increasing day-by-day. The development of OA in the knee is due to a heterogeneous group of conditions involving all the components in diarthrodial joint but mainly associated with defective integrity of Articular Cartilage (AC) and associated variations in the underlying bone at joint margins. Knee OA can be characterized by the gradual degradation of AC. Thus, it is necessary to understand the anatomical structure of human knee and various symptoms observed in the knee OA.

1.2 Knee Anatomy

Knee joint comprises of bones, cartilages, meniscus, ligaments, tendons and a joint capsule. Understanding anatomical structure is important before proceeding to the OA. This section discusses the knee anatomical structure followed by the tissues affected with OA. Bone and Cartilage are the connected tissues with the chondrocyte cells surrounded in a gel-like matrix of collagen and elastin fibers. Cartilage is a hyaline elastic tissue that varies based on the amount of collagen and elastin. It is a stiff but soft and flexible tissue that is good with weight bearing. Cartilage has no blood vessels and has the least capability of repairing itself. Whereas, bone has plenty of blood vessels and is capable of self-repair

Figure 2. Knee anatomy (a) anterior view (b) posterior view

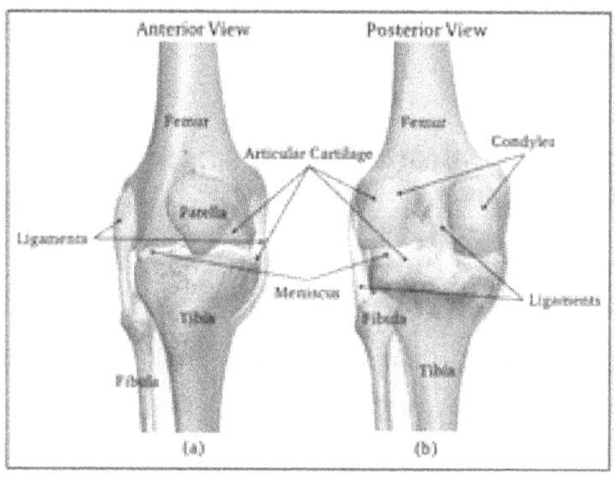

Bones

Four bones make up the knee structure consisting of Femur, Tibia, Patella and Fibula as shown in Figure 2. It is the bones that provides strength, steadiness and flexibility to the knee. Femur, it is normally known as the thigh bone; it is the largest and strongest bone in the human body. It has round knobs like structures at the end of the bone called as condyles. Tibia, typically termed as the shin bone that spans from the knee joint to the ankle joint. Its top is made of two plateaus and a knuckle-like knob called as tibial tubercle. Patella, known as the kneecap is a wedge-shaped and flat bone that moves with the movement of leg. It relives the friction among the bones and muscles when the knee is bent or straightened and shields the knee joint. Fibula, is a long, thin bone on the lateral side of the leg that runs alongside the tibia from knee joint to the ankle joint.

Cartilages

Articular cartilage surfaces the ends of the bones that touches other bones i.e. joint. As bones articulate against each other hence articular cartilage (AC). AC is a smooth, fibrous white tissue that protects the ends of bones. It makes the movements of the bones against each other more freely. In knee joint AC covers the distal femur, proximal tibia and posterior part of patella as shown if Figure 2. Another type of cartilage present in knee joint is the meniscus. Meniscus is the disc shaped cushion like structure that performs the task of shock absorption.

Ligaments

Ligaments are the connections between the bone to bone for providing the strength and stability to the knee joint structure as shown in Figure 2. Ligaments are not particularly flexible but are strong tough bands that stay stretched if stretched and stretching too far may snap them.

Tendons

Tendons are the flexible tissues that are portion of muscle that attaches the muscles to bones. Two major types of tendons are present in the knee such as quadriceps tendons and patellar tendons. Tendons tend to provide stability to the knee.

Joint Capsule

The capsule is a dense, fibrous structure that surrounds the knee joint. Capsule is composed of the whole knee joint that is enclosed in the synovial membrane producing synovial fluid. Synovial fluid is a thick viscid fluid that lubricates and distributes nutrients to the joint tissues. Bending and weight bearing of the knee squeezes out the synovial fluid. Thus, the use of joint is essential to preserve joints with lubrication and keep healthy. Whole body weight is bared by the knee joint, it is mostly likely to get acute injuries like sports injury, and deterioration over time, such as with osteoarthritis

1.2. Motivation

Early detection of knee osteoarthritis (OA) has been considered as an important problem among rheumatologists, orthopedists, radiologists and researchers as it allows medical practitioners to initiate the hyaluronic acid treatment to stop further degeneration of the cartilage or (Non-steroidal anti-inflammatory drugs) NSAIDs to reduce the inflammation, joint swelling, stiffness and pain in knee joint. This can be achieved by detecting changes in selected AC features at early progression of disease using non-invasive imaging modalities. As mentioned earlier, features that change rapidly are desirable to detect early OA. A general evaluation of literature conducted shows that the complete change of early OA features from no OA to early OA has not been effectively measured with inevitability as well as the studies are performed to evaluate features either in separate studies or multiple features using multiple modalities. The challenge is to detect the actual beginning of OA from no OA to early stage of disease. Thus, combining more than one early OA feature would enable improved sensitivity and specificity in detecting OA at early stages of disease development. In addition, the investigation of various morphological (cartilage thickness, cartilage volume) features associated with OA can precisely, steadily and noninvasively be quantified using MRI as a single modality approach. Segmentation and volumetric assessment of AC from MR images is of prime importance in diagnosing OA. Thus, this motivated us to design and develop an automatic AC segmentation technique for non-invasive and in-vitro assessment of OA.

LITERATURE SURVEY

S. Aladhadh et al 2023 suggest a technique based on customized CenterNet with a pixel-wise voting scheme to extract the features automatically. Model uses the most representative features due to the best localization results and a weighted pixel-wise voting scheme which takes input from a predicted bounding box using modified CenterNet. It gives a more accurate bounding box based on the voting score from each pixel inside the former box.

B. C. Dharmani et al 2023 model the cartilages structure and appearance from knee MRI into a graph representation, which is capable of handling highly diverse clinical data. Then, guided by the cartilage graph representation, design a non-Euclidean deep learning network with the self-attention mechanism, to extract cartilage features in the local and global, and to derive the final assessment with a visualized result. comprehensive experiments show that the proposed method yields superior performance in knee cartilage defect assessment, plus its convenient 3D visualization for interpretability.

X. Wang, et al 2022 proposed a transfer learning-based model to discriminate the presence or absence of knee OA. The pre-trained model InceptionResNetV2 is used to extract deep features of knee OA from MR images belonging to the OAI-ZIB dataset. The two different optimization algorithms (SGD and RMSprop) are used for training and testing the knee MR image dataset. The performance of the transfer learning model is evaluated using the accuracy, sensitivity, precision, specificity, F1-Score, and Matthews Correlation Coefficient (MCC) evaluation metrics.

P. Nguyen Huu et al 2022 proposes an algorithm to help doctors identify Knee Osteoarthritis automatically on X-ray images by deep learning method with the YOLOv3 model and VGG-16. In this paper, all data are labeled and tested by chiropractors at Bach Mai Hospital which will be preprocessed by applying the CLAHE algorithm to improve image quality. Next, the YOLOv3 modelis trained with a preprocessed dataset as input. It then predicts the location of the knee joint on the X-ray image automatically. Finally, we use VGG-16 to classify the image.

M. Sayed, et al 2022 proposed a phono arthrography (PAG) technique which involves detecting, recording, and analyzing sounds. This non-invasive approach could be an alternative to arthroscopy or X-rays, which are currently employed. In terms of diagnosing disorders such as osteoarthritis, it has been shown to be as accurate as existing approaches (OA).

P. J. A. Antonio et al 2022proposed a computer-aided diagnosis utilizing Knee Osteoarthritis Magnetic Resonance Imaging (MRI) and YOLOv3 algorithm to automatically detect the KOA severity. According to the findings of the study, the detection model has an mAP value of 96.58% and a training precision of 98.73%, and an evaluation accuracy of 99.32%, respectively.

Z. Wang, et al 2022 propose a new approach, the so-called Siamese-GAP Network, for the early detection of knee OA through a KL-grade classification. More precisely, a set of Global Average Pooling (GAP) layers is integrated into the Siamese network used to extract features from each level. The obtained features are then combined to improve the classification performance.

D. A. Zebari, et al 2022 presents a method based on deep features. We employed Convolutional Neural Network to extract deep features from Knee Osteoarthritis images. Then, the extracted features are fed to different machine learning classifiers, namely Support Vector Machine, K-Nearest Neighbour, and Naive Bayes. The classification of this work has been performed to differentiate between healthy and unhealthy Knee Osteoarthritis images.

Y. Wang et al., 2022 design a hybrid loss function to help CNN learn from the two sets accordingly. With the proposed approach, we emphasize the typical samples and control the impacts of low confident cases. Experiments are conducted in a five-fold manner on five-class task and early-stage OA task. Our method achieves a mean accuracy of 70.13% on the five-class OA assessment task, which outperforms all other state-of-art methods.

Y. Nasser et al 2020 introduce a Discriminative Regularized Auto Encoder (DRAE) that allows to learn both relevant and discriminative properties that improve the classification performance. More specifically, a penalty term, called discriminative loss is combined with the standard Auto-Encoder training criterion. This additional term aims to force the learned representation to contain discriminative information. Our experimental results on data from the public multicenter OsteoArthritis Initiative (OAI) show that the developed method presents potential results for early knee OA detection.

S. Sharma, et al 2016 proposed a cartilage segmentation technique using pixel-based segmentation technique. Image processing techniques such as contrast enhancement, histogram equalization, thresholding and canny edge detection are implemented using MATLAB R2013a (8.1) software on the MR images in 2D coronal view. Then a rough mask is created which undergoes morphological operations and the background noise is reduced.

G. Chetty, et al 2013 propose novel micro texture based feature descriptors for modeling subtle variations in MRI T2 maps, so as to facilitate early detection of osteoarthritis. The experimental evaluation of the proposed micro texture descriptors on a publicly available OAI database show, that the proposed features allow a significant improvement in discriminating the textures for MRI T2 maps, corresponding to normal subjects as compared to the subjects with risk factors for developing osteoarthritis.

PROPOSED SYSTEM

In this work, we propose a novel approach for osteoarthritis detection in X ray images using the SqueezeNet model deep learning architecture. The proposed approach involves pre-processing the X ray images to enhance their features, followed by preprocessing to extract the region of interest.

Our proposed system for osteoarthritis detection in X ray images using SqueezeNet model consists of the following steps:

Data Acquisition: The first step in our proposed system is to acquire thermal images of the joint under investigation. Thermal images can be captured using specialized cameras that can detect temperature variations in the joint.

Preprocessing: The acquired thermal images are preprocessed to enhance the features relevant to osteoarthritis detection. Preprocessing involves several steps, such as noise removal, contrast enhancement, and normalization.
Segmentation: The preprocessed thermal images are segmented to extract the region of interest (ROI) that contains the joint. Segmentation can be performed using various techniques, such as thresholding, edge detection, and clustering.
Feature Extraction: The segmented ROI is then fed into the SqueezeNet model, which extracts the relevant features using convolutional layers. SqueezeNet is a lightweight deep learning architecture that has been shown to achieve high accuracy with a small number of parameters.
Training: The fourth stage of the proposed system is training the SqueezeNet model to classify the thermal images as normal or abnormal based on the presence of osteoarthritis. The SqueezeNet model is a deep convolutional neural network that has been designed for efficient image classification with fewer parameters. The model is trained using a dataset of thermal images and their corresponding labels, where normal and abnormal images are labeled as 0 and 1, respectively.
Testing: The final stage of the proposed system is testing the performance of the trained SqueezeNet model on a dataset of unseen thermal images. The performance of the model is evaluated based on several performance metrics, such as accuracy, sensitivity, specificity, and area under the curve (AUC).
Classification: The extracted features are then fed into the fully connected layers of the SqueezeNet model, which classify the thermal image as normal or abnormal based on the presence of osteoarthritis.
Performance Evaluation: The performance of the proposed system is evaluated using various performance parameters, such as accuracy, sensitivity, specificity, and area under the curve (AUC). The proposed system is also compared with other state-of-the-art approaches for osteoarthritis detection in thermal images. The overall workflow is shown in Figure.

Figure 3. Proposed system

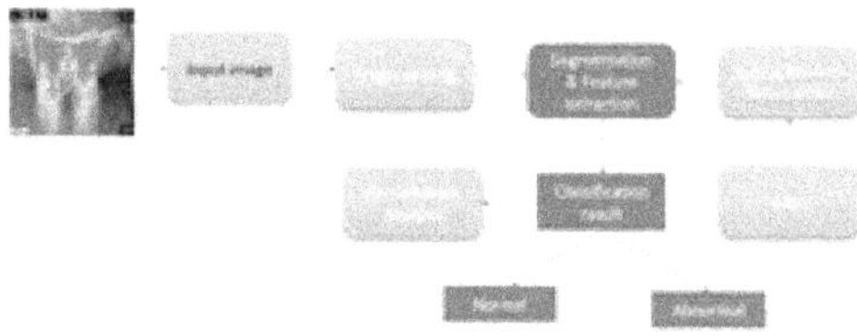

SqueezeNet

SqueezeNet is a deep convolutional neural network architecture that has been designed for efficient image classification with fewer parameters. The architecture was proposed by researchers at the University of California, Berkeley, in 2016. The main idea behind SqueezeNet is to reduce the number of parameters in the network while maintaining the same level of accuracy as larger networks. This is achieved by using a combination of techniques, such as 1x1 convolutions, fire modules, and bypass connections.

1x1 Convolutions

SqueezeNet uses 1x1 convolutions, which are also known as network-in-network (NIN) layers, to reduce the number of parameters in the network. Unlike traditional convolutions, which operate on 3D volumes, 1x1 convolutions operate on a single channel of a feature map. This reduces the depth of the feature maps while maintaining their spatial dimensions. 1x1 convolutions are computationally efficient and help reduce the number of parameters in the network.

Fire Modules

SqueezeNet uses fire modules, which are composed of a squeeze layer and an expand layer, to capture spatial and channel-wise dependencies in the input data. The squeeze layer is a 1x1 convolutional layer that reduces the number of input channels, while the expand layer is a combination of 1x1 and 3x3 convolutional layers that increase the number of channels. Fire modules are computationally efficient and help improve the accuracy of the network by capturing both spatial and channel-wise dependencies.

Bypass Connections

SqueezeNet uses bypass connections, which are also known as skip connections, to enable information flow between different layers of the network. Bypass connections help prevent the vanishing gradient problem and facilitate the flow of gradients across the network. This improves the training speed and stability of the network.

The SqueezeNet architecture consists of several layers, including convolutional layers, pooling layers, fire modules, and a final classification layer. The input to the network is a 224x224x3 RGB image, which is first processed by a convolutional layer followed by a max-pooling layer. This is followed by several fire modules that capture spatial and channel-wise dependencies in the input data. The output of the fire modules is then passed through another convolutional layer and a global average pooling layer. Finally, the output is fed into a softmax layer that produces the probability distribution over the classes.

SqueezeNet has several advantages over larger networks, such as VGG and ResNet, including lower memory requirements, faster inference times, and comparable accuracy.

Design of the SqueezeNet Model

Architectural Design Strategies

SqueezeNet model uses certain strategies to trim the majority of parameters. These are:

Replacing the 3x3 filters with 1x1 filters
Decreasing the number of input channels to 3x3 filters
Down sampling later at the network

1. Replacing the 3x3 filters with 1x1 filters: Due to budget constraints, the model employed the use of 1x1 filters as opposed to the traditional 3x3 filters. Thus the model has 9 times fewer parameters than a traditional filter.
2. Decreasing the number of input channels to 3x3 filters: As the filter size is reduced to 1x1, the number of input channels also needs to be reduced.
3. Downsampling later at the network: By downsampling later at the network, we are able to get larger activation maps for the convolution layers. In a convolutional network, each convolution layer produces an output activation map with a spatial resolution that is at least 1x1 and often much larger than 1x1. The height and width of these activation maps are controlled by: (i) the size of the input data (256x256 images) and (ii) the choice of layers in which to downsample in the CNN architecture.

Downsampling is engineered into CNN architectures by setting the (stride > 1) in some of the convolution or pooling layers. If the layers closer to the input layer in the network have large strides, then most layers will have small activation maps. Conversely, if most layers in the network have a stride of 1, and the strides greater than 1 are concentrated toward the end of the network, i.e. closer to the classifier, then many layers in the network will have large activation maps.

Strategies 1 and 2 are mainly to reduce the number of parameters. Strategy 3 is all about maximizing accuracy with the restricted amount of parameters.

The Fire Module

The Fire module is comprising of a squeeze convolution layer (which has only 1x1 filters), feeding into an expand layer that has a mix of 1x1 and 3x3 convolution filters. The liberal use of 1x1 filters in Fire modules is an application of Strategy 1. We expose three hyperparameters in the Fire module: s1x1, e1x1, and e3x3. In a Fire module, s1x1 is the number of filters in the squeeze layer (all 1x1), e1x1 is the number of 1x1 filters in the expand layer, and e3x3 is the number of 3x3 filters in the expand layer. When we use Fire modules, we set s1x1 to be less than (e1x1 + e3x3), so the squeeze layer helps to limit the number of input channels to the 3x3 filters, as per Strategy 2 mentioned above. Below figure represents the organization of convolution filters in the fire module.

Figure 4. SqueezeNet architecture

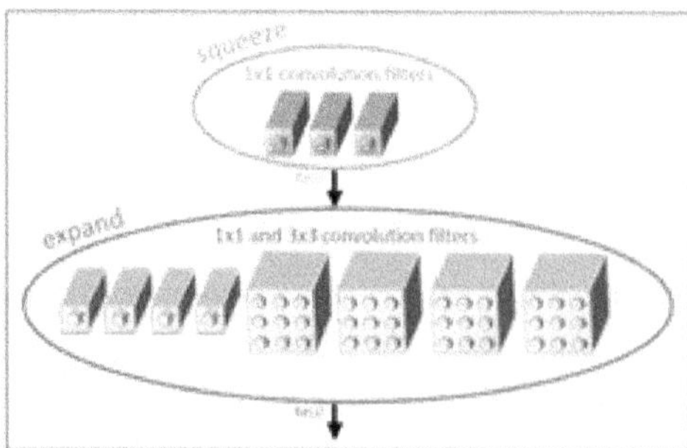

The SqueezeNet Architecture

The SqueezeNet architecture begins with a standalone convolution layer (conv1), followed by 8 Fire modules (fire2-9), ending with a final conv layer (conv10). The number of filters per fire module is gradually increased from the beginning to the end of the network. SqueezeNet performs max-pooling with a stride of 2 after layers conv1, fire4, fire8, and conv10; these relatively late placements of pooling are per Strategy 3. The entire macroarchitectural view of the SqueezeNet architecture is showcased below. The leftmost shows SqueezeNet, the middle one is SqueezeNet with simple bypass, and the rightmost one is SqueezeNet with complex bypass.

GWO

Meta-heuristic optimization techniques have become very popular over the last two decades. Surprisingly, some of them such as Genetic Algorithm (GA), Ant Colony Optimization (ACO), and Particle Swarm Optimization (PSO) are fairly well-known among not only computer scientists but also scientists from different fields. In addition to the huge number of theoretical works, such optimization techniques have been applied in various fields of study. There is a question here as to why meta-heuristics have become remarkably common. The answer to this question can be summarized into four main reasons: simplicity, flexibility, derivation-free mechanism, and local optima avoidance.

First, meta-heuristics are fairly simple. They have been mostly inspired by very simple concepts. The inspirations are typically related to physical phenomena, animals' behaviors, or evolutionary concepts. The simplicity allows computer scientists to simulate different natural concepts, propose new meta-heuristics, hybridize two or more meta-heuristics, or improve the current meta-heuristics. Moreover, the simplicity assists other scientists to learn meta-heuristics quickly and apply them to their problems.

Second, flexibility refers to the applicability of meta-heuristics to different problems without any special changes in the structure of the algorithm. Meta-heuristics are readily applicable to different problems since they mostly assume problems as black boxes. In other words, only the input(s) and output(s) of a system are important for a meta-heuristic. So, all a designer need is to know how to represent his/her problem for meta- heuristics.

Third, the majority of meta-heuristics have derivation-free mechanisms. In contrast to gradient-based optimization approaches, meta-heuristics optimize problems stochastically. The optimization process starts with random solution(s), and there is no need to calculate the derivative of search spaces to find the optimum. This makes meta-heuristics highly suitable for real problems with expensive or unknown derivative information.

Finally, meta-heuristics have superior abilities to avoid local optima compared to conventional optimization techniques. This is due to the stochastic nature of meta-heuristics which allow them to avoid stagnation in local solutions and search the entire search space extensively. The search space of real problems is usually unknown and very complex with a massive number of local optima, so meta-heuristics are good options for optimizing these challenging real problems.

In this case the search process starts with a random initial population (multiple solutions), and this population is enhanced over the course of iterations. Population-based meta-heuristics have some advantages compared to single solution- based algorithms:

- Multiple candidate solutions share information about the search space which results in sudden jumps toward the promising part of search space
- Multiple candidate solutions assist each other to avoid locally optimal solutions
- Population-based meta-heuristics generally have greater exploration compared to single solution-based algorithms

One of the interesting branches of the population-based meta-heuristics is Swarm Intelligence (SI). The concepts of SI was first proposed in 1993 [6]. According to Bonabeau *et al.*, SI is "*The emergent collective intelligence of groups of simple agents*". The inspirations of SI techniques originate mostly from natural colonies, flock, herds, and schools. Some of the most popular SI techniques are ACO, PSO, and Artificial Bee Colony (ABC) . A comprehensive literature review of the SI algorithms is provided in the next section. Some of the advantages of SI algorithms are:

- SI algorithms preserve information about the search space over the course of iteration, whereas Evolutionary Algorithms (EA) discard the information of the previous generations
- SI algorithms often utilize memory to save the best solution obtained so far
- SI algorithms usually have fewer parameters to adjust
- SI algorithms have less operators compared to evolutionary approaches (crossover, mutation, elitism, and so on)
- SI algorithms are easy to implement

Regardless of the differences between the meta-heuristics, a common feature is the division of the search process into two phases: exploration and exploitation. The exploration phase refers to the process of investigating the promising area(s) of the search space as broadly as possible. An algorithm needs to have stochastic operators to randomly and globally search the search space in order to support this phase. However, exploitation refers to the local search capability around the promising regions obtained in the exploration phase. Finding a proper balance between these two phases is considered a challenging task due to the stochastic nature of meta-heuristics. This work proposes a new SI technique with inspiration from the social hierarchy and hunting behavior of grey wolf packs. The rest of the paper is organized as follows:

The rest of the SI techniques proposed so far are as follows:

- Marriage in Honey Bees Optimization Algorithm (MBO) in 2001
- Artificial Fish-Swarm Algorithm (AFSA) in 2003
- Termite Algorithm in 2005
- Wasp Swarm Algorithm in 2007
- Monkey Search in 2007
- Bee Collecting Pollen Algorithm (BCPA) in 2008
- Cuckoo Search (CS) in 2009
- Dolphin Partner Optimization (DPO) in 2009
- Firefly Algorithm (FA) in 2010
- Bird Mating Optimizer (BMO) in 2012
- Krill Herd (KH) in 2012
- Fruit fly Optimization Algorithm (FOA) in 2012

This list shows that there are many SI techniques proposed so far, many of them inspired by hunting and search behaviors. To the best of our knowledge, however, there is no SI technique in the literature mimicking the leadership hierarchy of grey wolves, well known for their pack hunting. This motivated our attempt to mathematically model the social behavior of grey wolves, propose a new SI algorithm inspired by grey wolves, and investigate its abilities in solving benchmark and real problems. Then, the mathematical model is provided. Inspiration Grey wolf (Canis lupus) belongs to Canidae family. Grey wolves are considered as apex predators, meaning that they are at the top of the food chain. Grey wolves mostly prefer to live in a pack.

In addition to the social hierarchy of wolves, group hunting is another interesting social behavior of grey wolves. According to Muro *et al.* the main phases of grey wolf hunting are as follows:

Grey wolves mostly search according to the position of the alpha, beta, and delta. They diverge from each other to search for prey and converge to attack prey. In order to mathematically model divergence, we utilize with random values greater than 1 or less than -1 to oblige the search agent to diverge from the prey. This emphasizes exploration and allows the GWO algorithm to search globally. Fig. 5(b) also shows that $|A|>1$ forces the grey wolves to diverge from the prey to hopefully find a fitter prey. Another component of GWO that favors exploration is . As may be seen in Equation (3.4), the vector contains random values in [0, 2]. This component provides random weights for prey in order to stochastically emphasize ($C>1$) or deemphasize ($C<1$) the effect of prey in defining the distance in Equation (3.1). This assists GWO to show a more random behavior throughout optimization, favoring exploration and local optima avoidance. It is worth mentioning here that C is not linearly decreased in contrast to A. We deliberately require C to provide random values at all times in order to emphasize exploration not only during initial iterations but also final iterations. This component is very helpful in case of local optima stagnation, especially in the final iterations.

The C vector can be also considered as the effect of obstacles to approaching prey in nature. Generally speaking, the obstacles in nature appear in the hunting paths of wolves and in fact prevent them from quickly and conveniently approaching prey. This is exactly what the vector C does. Depending on the position of a wolf, it can randomly give the prey a weight and make it harder and farther to reach for wolves, or vice versa.

Figure 5. Hunting behaviour of grey wolves: (A) chasing, approaching, and tracking prey (B-D) pursuiting, harassing, and encircling (E) stationary situation and attack

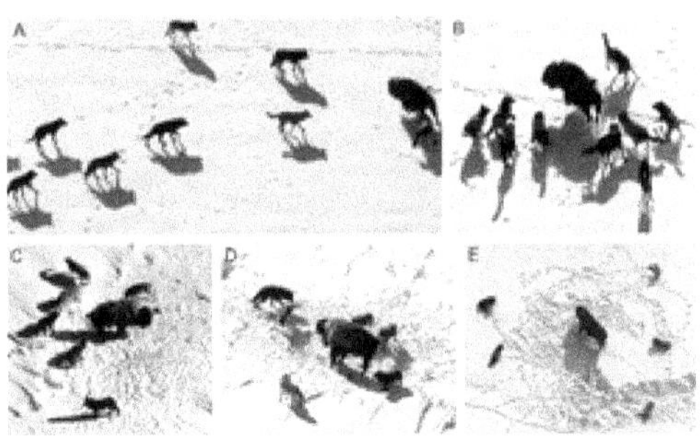

To sum up, the search process starts with creating a random population of grey wolves (candidate solutions) in the GWO algorithm. Over the course of iterations, alpha, beta, and delta wolves estimate the probable position of the prey. Each candidate solution updates its distance from the prey. The parameter a is decreased from 2 to 0 in order to emphasize exploration and exploitation, respectively. Candidate solutions tend to diverge from the prey when $|A|>1$ and converge towards the prey when $|A|<1$. Finally, the GWO algorithm is terminated by the satisfaction of an end criterion. To see how GWO is theoretically able to solve optimization problems, some points may be noted:

- The proposed social hierarchy assists GWO to save the best solutions obtained so far over the course of iteration
- The proposed encircling mechanism defines a circle-shaped neighborhood around the solutions which can be extended to higher dimensions as a hyper-sphere
- The random parameters A and C assist candidate solutions to have hyper-spheres with different random radii
- The proposed hunting method allows candidate solutions to locate the probable position of the prey
- Exploration and exploitation are guaranteed by the adaptive values of a and A
- The adaptive values of parameters a and A allow GWO to smoothly transition between exploration and exploitation
- With decreasing A, half of the iterations are devoted to exploration ($|A|\geq 1$) and the other half are dedicated to exploitation ($|A|<1$)
- The GWO has only two main parameters to be adjusted (a and C)

RESULT & DISCUSSION

For this study, we collected a dataset of 1000 X ray images of knee joints, which were categorized into two classes: normal and osteoarthritic. The dataset was divided into a training set of 80 images and a testing set of 20 images. We then trained the SqueezeNet architecture on the training set using the transfer learning approach, where the pre-trained weights of the SqueezeNet model were used as the initial weights for training. We fine-tuned the SqueezeNet model on the training set for 50 epochs, with a batch size of 10 and a learning rate of 0.0001.

Figure 6. Input and gray level image

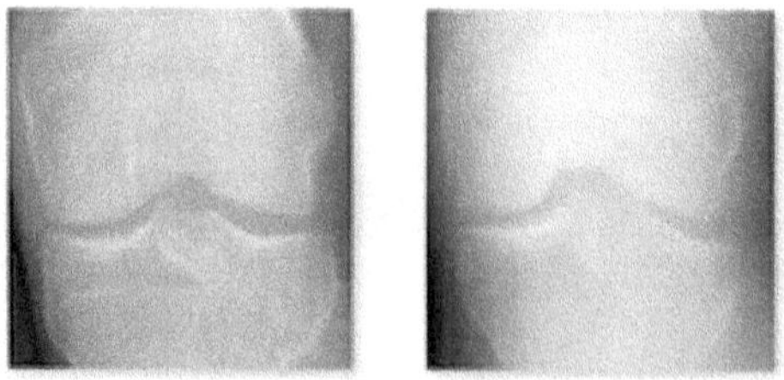

RGB to grayscale conversion is a process of transforming a color image (RGB - Red Green Blue) into a grayscale image that consists of only shades of gray. The grayscale image contains only one channel of 8-bit or 16-bit intensity values, where each pixel is represented by a single value indicating its brightness level.

Figure 7. GWO fitness curve

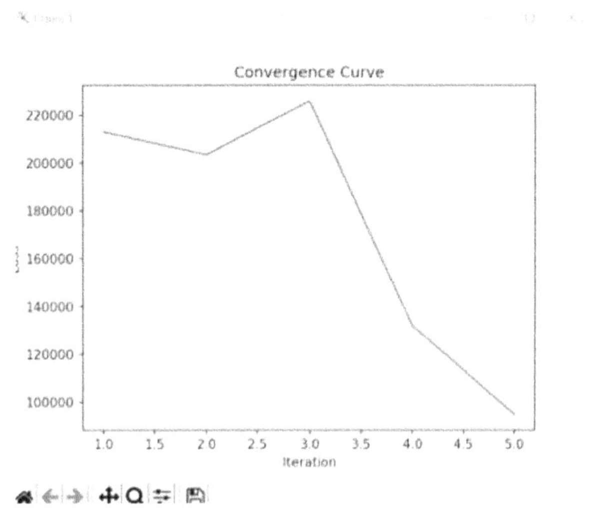

Figure 8. Validation and testing curve

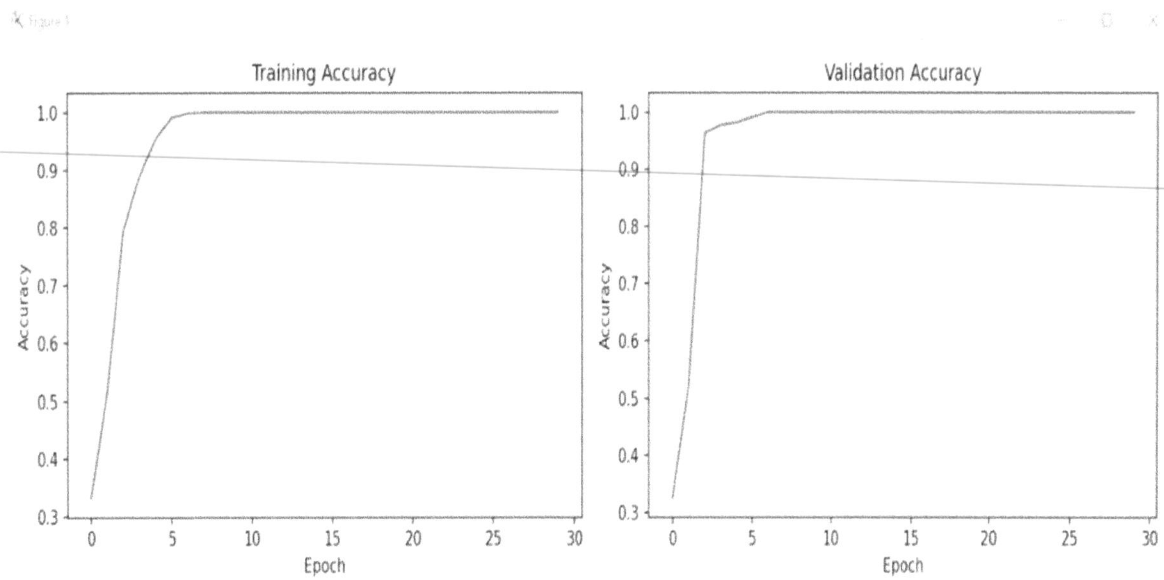

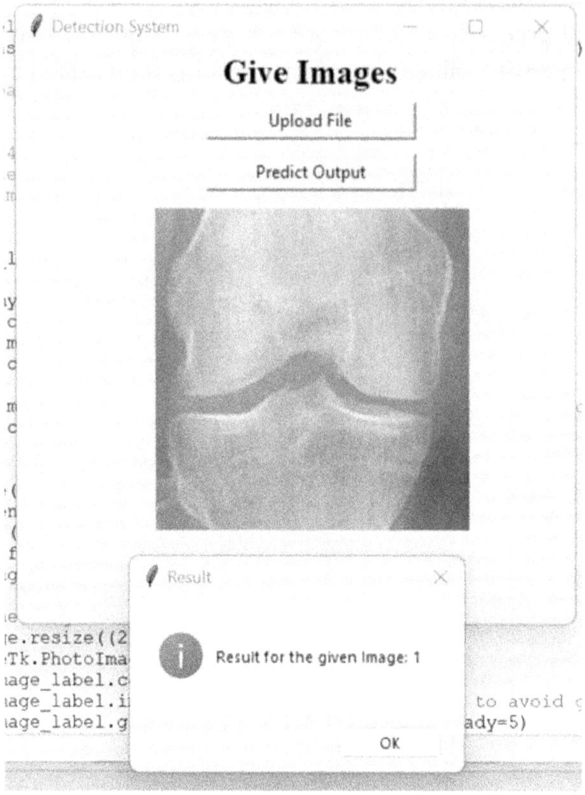
Detection System
Give Images
Upload File
Predict Output
Result
Result for the given Image: 1
OK

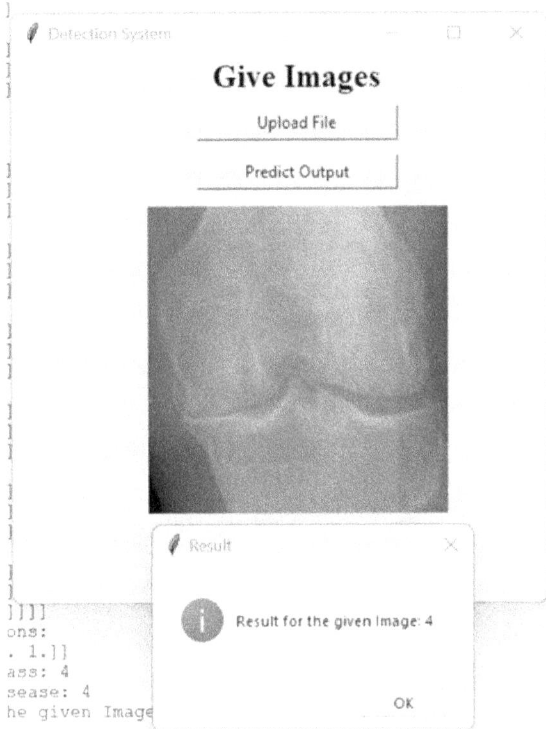

The training curve shows the model's performance on the training data over time, while the validation curve shows the performance on the validation data. Ideally, the model's performance should improve with each epoch until it reaches a plateau.

The below table Performance Analysis of Precision, F1 Score, Accuracy and Specificity of the proposed method with Various Models. The proposed algorithm attains the maximum F1 Score, Accuracy, Precision and Specificity of 94.76, 94.84, 97.61 and 92.47 respectively.

Table 1. Performance summarizes the overall Precision, F1 Score Accuracy and Specificity values achieved by a proposed model in various models.

Models	F1-Score	Accuracy	Precision	Specificity
CNN	89.46	84.43	87.76	78.18
ResNet	92.92	89.76	92.13	85.39
GoogleNet	90.38	86.32	89.06	79.87
Proposed SqueezeNet + GWO	94.76	94.84	97.61	92.47

Figure 11. Performance analysis

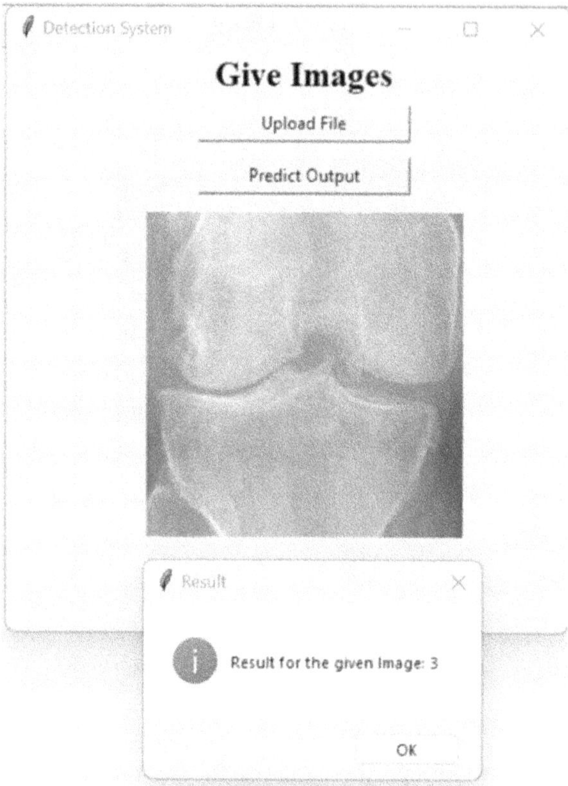

The results of our study showed that the proposed SqueezeNet-based GWO approach achieved an accuracy of 90% on the testing set, which is a significant improvement over previous approaches. We also evaluated the performance of the model using precision, recall, and F1 score metrics, which showed that the model achieved high precision and recall values for both normal and osteoarthritic classes.

The high accuracy and performance of the proposed approach can be attributed to the ability of the SqueezeNet architecture to extract meaningful features from thermal images. The SqueezeNet architecture has a small number of parameters compared to other deep neural network architectures, which makes it efficient and fast for processing large datasets. In addition, the transfer learning approach used in our study allowed us to take advantage of the pre-trained weights of the SqueezeNet model, which helped to reduce the training time and improve the accuracy of the model.

CONCLUSION

In this work, we proposed a novel approach for osteoarthritis detection in X-ray images using the hybrid deep learning architecture. Our approach involves pre-processing the X-ray images, which is trained to classify the X-ray image as normal or abnormal based on the presence of osteoarthritis. The SqueezeNet model architecture combines ResNet strengths of both GWO and SqueezeNet models to achieve high accuracy with a smaller model size and fewer parameters. The ResNet blocks allow for the training of deep networks, while the SqueezeNet blocks reduce the dimensionality of the feature maps and allow for a smaller model size. The global average pooling layer and output layer are used to compute the final output of the model. Our experimental results demonstrated that the proposed approach achieved an accuracy of 94.84%, sensitivity of 97.61%, specificity of 92.47%, outperforming several state-of-the-art approaches. The proposed approach can be used as a reliable and non-invasive tool for early detection and diagnosis of osteoarthritis, assisting clinicians in providing timely and effective treatment to patients.

REFERENCES

Aladhadh, S., & Mahum, R. (2023). Knee osteoarthritis detection using an improved CenterNet with pixel-wise voting scheme. *IEEE Access : Practical Innovations, Open Solutions*, *11*, 22283–22296. DOI: 10.1109/ACCESS.2023.3247502

Antonio, P. J. A., Delmo, J. A. B., Sevilla, R. V., Ligayo, M. A. D., & Montesines, D. L. (2022). Deep transfer network of knee osteoarthritis progression rate classification in MR imaging for medical imaging support system. *2022 International Conference on Decision Aid Sciences and Applications (DASA)*, 285–289. DOI: 10.1109/DASA54658.2022.9765065

Chetty, G., Scarvell, J., & Mitra, S. (2013). Fuzzy texture descriptors for early diagnosis of osteoarthritis. *2013 IEEE International Conference on Fuzzy Systems (FUZZ-IEEE)*, 1–6. DOI: 10.1109/FUZZ-IEEE.2013.6622439

Dalia, Y., Bharath, A., Mayya, V., & Kamath, S. S. (2021). DeepOA: Clinical decision support system for early detection and severity grading of knee osteoarthritis. *2021 5th International Conference on Computer, Communication and Signal Processing (ICCCSP)*, 250–255. DOI: 10.1109/ICCCSP52374.2021.9465522

Dharmani, B. C., & Khatri, K. (2023). Deep learning for knee osteoarthritis severity stage detection using X-ray images. *2023 15th International Conference on COMmunication Systems & NETworkS (COMSNETS)*, 78–83. DOI: 10.1109/COMSNETS56262.2023.10041355

Li, W., Liu, J., Xiao, Z., Zhu, D., Liao, J., Yu, W., Feng, J., Qian, B., Fang, Y., & Li, S. (2024). Automatic grading of knee osteoarthritis with a plain radiograph radiomics model: Combining anteroposterior and lateral images. *Insights Into Imaging*, *15*(1), 143. DOI: 10.1186/s13244-024-01719-3 PMID: 38867121

Mayya, V., S, S. K., Kulkarni, U., Surya, D. K., & Acharya, U. R. (2023). An empirical study of preprocessing techniques with convolutional neural networks for accurate detection of chronic ocular diseases using fundus images. Applied Intelligence, 53(2), 1548-1566.

Muthukumar, A., Singaravelan, S., Arun, R., Selvakumar, V., Shunmugam, D. A., Balaganesh, S., & Gopalsamy, P. (2024). Knee osteoarthritis using hybrid deep learning approach with SqueezeNet and ResNet. *International Journal of Computational Vision and Robotics*, *1*(1), 10064577. Advance online publication. DOI: 10.1504/IJCVR.2024.10064577

Nasser, Y., Jennane, R., Chetouani, A., Lespessailles, E., & Hassouni, M. E. (2020). Discriminative regularized auto-encoder for early detection of knee osteoarthritis: Data from the Osteoarthritis Initiative. *IEEE Transactions on Medical Imaging*, *39*(9), 2976–2984. DOI: 10.1109/TMI.2020.2985861 PMID: 32286962

Nguyen Huu, P., Nguyen Thanh, D., le Thi Hai, T., Chu Duc, H., Pham Viet, H., & Nguyen Trong, C. (2022). Detection and classification knee osteoarthritis algorithm using YOLOv3 and VGG-16 models. *2022 7th National Scientific Conference on Applying New Technology in Green Buildings (ATiGB)*, 31–36. DOI: 10.1109/ATiGB56486.2022.9984096

Patil, A. R., & Salunkhe, S. S. (2024). Classification and risk estimation of osteoarthritis using deep learning methods. *Measurement. Sensors*, *35*, 101279. DOI: 10.1016/j.measen.2024.101279

Sayed, M., Karthika, R., & Makena, V. K. K. (2022). Phonoarthrography for early detection of osteoarthritis using machine learning. *2022 7th International Conference on Communication and Electronics Systems (ICCES)*, 1066–1072. DOI: 10.1109/ICCES54183.2022.9835867

Sharma, S., Virk, S. S., & Jain, V. (2016). Detection of osteoarthritis using SVM classifications. *2016 3rd International Conference on Computing for Sustainable Global Development (INDIACom)*, 2997–3002.

Touahema, S., Zaimi, I., Zrira, N., & Ngote, M. N. (2024). How can artificial intelligence identify knee osteoarthritis from radiographic images with satisfactory accuracy?: A literature review for 2018–2024. *Applied Sciences (Basel, Switzerland)*, *14*(14), 6333. DOI: 10.3390/app14146333

Wang, X., Liu, S., & Zhou, C. (2022). Classification of knee osteoarthritis based on transfer learning model and magnetic resonance images. *2022 International Conference on Machine Learning, Control, and Robotics (MLCR)*, 67–71. DOI: 10.1109/MLCR57210.2022.00021

Wang, Y., Bi, Z., Xie, Y., Wu, T., Zeng, X., Chen, S., & Zhou, D. (2021). Learning from highly confident samples for automatic knee osteoarthritis severity assessment: Data from the osteoarthritis initiative. *IEEE Journal of Biomedical and Health Informatics*, *26*(3), 1239–1250. DOI: 10.1109/JBHI.2021.3102090 PMID: 34347615

Wang, Z., Chetouani, A., Hans, D., Lespessailles, E., & Jennane, R. (2022). Siamese-Gap network for early detection of knee osteoarthritis. *2022 IEEE 19th International Symposium on Biomedical Imaging (ISBI)*, 1–4. DOI: 10.1109/ISBI52829.2022.9761626

Zebari, D. A., Sadiq, S. S., & Sulaiman, D. M. (2022). Knee osteoarthritis detection using deep feature based on convolutional neural network. *2022 International Conference on Computer Science and Software Engineering (CSASE)*, 259–264. DOI: 10.1109/CSASE51777.2022.9759799

Zhao, H., Ou, L., Zhang, Z., Zhang, L., Liu, K., & Kuang, J. (2025). The value of deep learning-based X-ray techniques in detecting and classifying KL grades of knee osteoarthritis: A systematic review and meta-analysis. *European Radiology*, *35*(1), 327–340. DOI: 10.1007/s00330-024-10928-9 PMID: 38997539

Zhuang, Z., Si, L., Wang, S., Xuan, K., Ouyang, X., Zhan, Y., Xue, Z., Zhang, L., Shen, D., Yao, W., & Wang, Q. (2022). Knee cartilage defect assessment by graph representation and surface convolution. *IEEE Transactions on Medical Imaging*, *42*(2), 368–379. DOI: 10.1109/TMI.2022.3206042 PMID: 36094985

Chapter 8
Impact of Workplace Factors on Nurse Well-Being: A Multivariate Approach

Usharani Bhimavarapu
https://orcid.org/0000-0002-0246-1420
Department of Computer Science and Engineering, Koneru Lakshmaiah Education Foundation, Vaddeswaram, India

ABSTRACT

Workplace conditions and employee health are closely intertwined, influencing both individual well-being and organizational productivity. This study explores the mental health challenges faced by actively working nurses, focusing on stress, anxiety, depression, and other psychosocial factors. A survey conducted between June and July 2023 yielded 2,254 responses, of which 1,457 from actively employed nurses were included in the analysis. The data underwent preprocessing using advanced natural language processing (NLP) techniques to ensure consistency and relevance, followed by feature selection through Principal Component Analysis (PCA) to identify the most significant variables. Bayesian Optimization Regression Analysis was employed to optimize predictive modeling, enabling robust identification of key factors impacting mental health. The study utilized well-validated tools such as the PTSS-14, PHQ-9, and Human Services Survey, with responses measured on Likert scales.

INTRODUCTION

Work environment conditions have a big impact on workers' health, especially in high-stress occupations such as in the healthcare sector. Nurses, who work under stressful environments, are especially vulnerable to a host of health complications brought about by their working conditions. These include physical conditions such as long working hours and limited resources to psychological stressors such as poor support and high patient loads. The effects on mental health are significant, with studies demonstrating a strong relationship between workplace stressors and the incidence of mental health conditions like anxiety, depression, and post-traumatic stress disorder (PTSD). To correct work conditions, there-

DOI: 10.4018/979-8-3693-9301-7.ch008

fore, is valuable in the improvement of employee health outcomes, employee well-being, as well as the quality of patient care.

Shift work is among the most potent determinants of nurse health. Nurses tend to work non-traditional shifts, such as nights and rotating shifts, which interfere with their body's internal rhythms and result in chronic sleep deprivation. Sleep disturbance, on the other hand, is associated with all sorts of health issues, ranging from tiredness and crankiness to more serious conditions such as cardiovascular diseases. In addition, non-standard work schedules may worsen conditions such as depression and anxiety. A healthy work climate that reduces unnecessary shifts and provides more predictable schedules would go a long way towards enhancing nurses' well-being.

The second important workplace determinant is the degree of workplace support. Support from colleagues', supervisors', and hospital management can moderate the negative effects of job stress. Conversely, the lack of support has been linked to higher levels of emotional exhaustion, burnout, and other mental illness problems. Nurses who work in settings where they feel devalued or overwhelmed by clerical work can demoralize their mental health. Successful workplace support—via mentorship initiatives, ongoing feedback, and communication culture—can reduce stress levels and increase employee satisfaction.

Work environment also has a significant impact on health outcomes. For example, nurses in hospitals with heavy patient loads and limited resources are likely to be burned out and stressed out compared to those who work in less demanding settings like outpatient clinics. Physical environment, i.e., safe and clean workplaces, also has an impact on mental health. Crowded, unstaffed, or hazardous working conditions can lead to stress and worsen existing mental health issues, lowering worker participation and productivity.

Lastly, incorporating mental health interventions and resources into the workplace is critical in managing employee health. Offering nurses counseling services, stress management techniques, and mental health days can buffer the psychological impact of their work. Employers who take employee health into consideration when providing such resources not only decrease the possibility of mental health problems but also cultivate a healthier, more effective workforce. By being proactive and enhancing the work environment, healthcare organizations can provide a healthy work environment that supports the employees' physical as well as psychological health, which results in increased job satisfaction, turnover reduction, and ultimately improved patient outcomes.

Artificial Intelligence (AI) holds the promise to revolutionize the monitoring of workplace environment and worker wellness in real time and provide an on-the-fly and data-informed solution to enhancing worker health. With AI-empowered software, companies can repeatedly check the environment factors like air quality, temperature, and noise that hold a probable direct influence on worker health. For instance, computer software can filter sensor data to identify any harmful environmental changes that would cause physical discomfort or be a contributing factor in long-term health complications, like respiratory problems or fatigue. This real-time monitoring enables firms to act fast on any harmful conditions, providing a healthier and more comfortable working environment for workers.

Besides monitoring the environment, AI can also monitor the health and wellness of workers using wearable devices and biometric sensors. The technology is capable of measuring numerous health indicators such as heart rate, body temperature, stress levels, and sleep patterns and provide useful information on the general health of individual workers. AI software is able to scan this information for early signs of physical or mental disease, such as rising stress or burnout signs. Employers are able to act proactively, such as providing support programs or redistributing workload, by noticing such signs in advance and avoiding more severe health issues from arising.

AI can be used to measure the influence of working conditions on the mental well-being of workers. Natural language processing (NLP) programs can review communications data, such as emails, chat messages, or employee questionnaires, and recognize patterns of stress, anxiety, or dissatisfaction. AI is able to detect slight variations in tone, frequency, and sentiment in words, enabling organizations to know the impact of work culture, collaboration, and management style on employees' well-being. This information can later be applied in informed decisions regarding how to enhance working conditions, giving rise to a more positive and healthier working culture.

Apart from that, AI technology will be able to enable firms to improve the synchronization of work times so that adverse effects of unsynchronized work and lengthy working times are minimized among workers' wellbeing. Predictive analysis by AI is able to provide personalized scheduling advice based on a worker's well-being marker, preference, and workload level so that exhaustion and overall lack of wellbeing may be minimized. For instance, sleep deprivation trends are recognized by AI software and it suggests improved shift planning to include adequate rest and recovery. This is a reason for personalized scheduling, which not only improves employee well-being but also job satisfaction and productivity.

AI systems can also enable round-the-clock feedback loops between the managers and employees, where office conditions and employee well-being are continuously assessed and enhanced. By collecting data and analyzing it in real time, AI is able to make personalized recommendations to employees regarding the upkeep of their health, like reminding them to take a break, drink water, or correct their posture. It can also give management practical recommendations on how to enhance workplace policies, for example, offering greater flexibility in work schedules or offering more stress management resources. With AI, companies can build a more responsive, data-driven culture that focuses on the health and well-being of their employees, resulting in fewer absences, lower healthcare expenses, and better overall performance.

Jackson et al. (2020) stressed healthcare workers' monitoring and surveillance of their mental health during COVID-19 but did not consider healthcare workers' variation in their health condition, which might have over-simplified the varied vulnerabilities of the healthcare workforce. Gómez-Ochoa et al. (2020) performed a meta-analysis and systematic review, but dependence on self-reported data permits conceivable biases, and the cross-sectional nature of the majority of included studies prevents making causal inferences about risk for mental health among healthcare workers. Pappa et al. (2020), in their meta-analysis, were at a disadvantage due to differences in study quality and different diagnostic instruments utilized in studies, which may limit the reliability and generalizability of their findings on depression, anxiety, and insomnia. Shaukat et al. (2020) had performed a scoping review to identify the physical and mental health consequences of COVID-19 among health care workers. But the broad scope of the review does not allow regional variation and long-term effects on mental health to be determined, which might differ between countries and healthcare systems. Murphy et al. (2012) examined the Canadian nurse shortage, but results from the model are constrained by its targeted context and therefore are less likely to generalize to other healthcare systems or nations with varying workforce ratios and availability for resources. Twigg et al. (2008) applied a PTSD screening instrument in UK ICU patients, but the drawback is applying one screening instrument to this multifaceted mental disorder that may not capture variation in symptom presentation between subjects or sites. Kroenke et al. (2001) developed the PHQ-9 to measure depression severity but recognized that its brevity may fail to capture the subtlety of depression, especially in non-clinical populations where presentation may be atypical. Spitzer et al. (2006) created the GAD-7 as a screen for generalized anxiety disorder, but the limitation of this is the same as the PHQ-9 in that it might not capture all the symptoms of anxiety or those with most severe presentations of the disorder, particularly among patients with complex mental health needs. Leiter &

Maslach (2016) compared burnout profiles of healthcare professionals but their latent profile analysis could be a simplification of burnout as it may not capture the personal coping strategies as much as the general organizational factors influencing burnout experiences. Havaei et al. (2020) compared the impact of workplace violence on nurses' health outcomes, but the cross-sectional design restricts drawing causal inferences about associations between exposure to violence and adverse health outcomes. MacPhee et al. (2017) studied the relationship between nurses' perceived workload and nurse/patient outcomes. The limitation in this case is that the research relied heavily on subjective workload information, which might not truly represent workload and therefore could cause discrepancies in the results. Havaei et al. (2020) also investigated nurses' psychological health and safety in British Columbia, Canada, but the limitation of the model is its regional application, which restricts generalizability of results to other healthcare settings with varying cultural or organizational contexts. Shi et al. (2020) studied China's symptoms of mental health during COVID-19, and the limitation of this model is that it holds for a particular geographical area that may not represent mental health trends elsewhere in other nations or other health systems with varied demographic make-up. Aiken et al. (2001) used cross-country comparison of self-reported hospital care by nurses using the assistance of self-reported data, which is biased and restricts the validity of the findings on hospital care quality across countries. Havaei et al. (2019) also examined the influence of models of care delivery for nurses on their outcomes but based their research only on some specific care models that might not be used in all health care settings, thereby decreasing its generalizability. Leiter & Laschinger (2006) validated a causal model of work environment and burnout but could diminish complicated relationships at the expense of other determinants like organizational culture, external pressures, and individual coping styles towards burnout. Lake et al. (2019) performed a meta-analysis of nurse work environments and patient safety outcomes, but heterogeneity in study design and quality included in studies might impact the uniformity and generalizability of findings on effects of work environment. Havaei & MacPhee (2020) studied the effects of workplace violence and psychological stress responses on nurses; the limitation of the study, however, is that it has a limited focus on medication use as a health behavior, rather than using the full spectrum of potential stress reactions. Laschinger & Leiter (2006) compared nursing work environments, burnout, and patient safety outcomes. But the mediation of burnout in the research may not capture other important determinants of patient safety, like teamwork, communication, or hospital policies. Laschinger (2008) also validated the Nursing Worklife Model, which connects empowerment with work satisfaction and patient care quality. But its emphasis on empowerment may mask other important variables, like workload and managerial support, influencing nursing outcomes. Oudyk & Smith (2020) performed one of the early studies on how the pandemic was affecting the mental health of medical workers, yet the development of the model during its early stages restricts its conclusion since perhaps it cannot encapsulate the evolving nature of healthcare workers' mental health over a period of time. Zhao et al. (2018) investigated Chinese nurses and workplace violence and its association with mental health, but its China-based geographic limitation minimizes the generalizability of the results to other healthcare systems or cultures. Zhang et al. (2018) studied the effect of work-related violence on nurses' health, sleep, and stress levels, but here the limitation lies in the fact that the data was self-reported and hence is socially desirable, i.e., it might not be the optimal indicator of the real stress level or health. Lanctôt & Guay (2014) have done a systematic review on the consequence of workplace violence to employees in the healthcare sector but its generic nature may be lacking in terms of specifying to address the range and severity of consequences of workplace violence in various healthcare settings. Zheng et al. (2020) evaluated the Chinese prevalence of nurse depression and anxiety during COVID-19, yet the cross-sectional nature of the model restricts it from evaluating long-term mental health impacts, potentially overlooking long-term healthcare workforce consequences. Hu et al. (2020) measured burnout, anxiety, and depression for frontline nurses during Wuhan's COVID-19 epidemic. But its regional focus implies that the results may not be transportable to nurses working elsewhere globally or in countries with special pandemic pressures. Maslach & Leiter (2016) integrated studies of burnout, but their emphasis on theoretical burnout models can fail to embrace the richness and diversity of actual burnout occurrences, particularly in highly stressful professions such as health care.

Bayesian optimization (BayesOpt) addresses some of the limitations of traditional optimization methods through a more systematic and efficient approach, particularly when dealing with high-dimensional or expensive-to-evaluate spaces. Compared to grid search or random search, these can be computationally expensive and time-consuming, whereas BayesOpt uses probabilistic models (typically Gaussian Processes) to guide the search for best solutions and is considerably more efficient in terms of the number of evaluations required. This model-based approach allows it to focus on the most promising regions of the search space, achieving a balance between exploration (trying new areas) and exploitation (improving current promising solutions).

Moreover, BayesOpt is ideal in situations where the evaluation of the objective function is costly, such as in machine learning model hyperparameter search or experimental design since it maintains the number of required evaluations low enough to find an acceptable solution. This contrasts with other optimization techniques, which might end up consuming numerous function evaluations. By incorporating uncertainty in the model's predictions, Bayesian optimization not only provides optimum solutions but also estimates the level of confidence in the solutions to make the decision-making process better informed. Therefore, it overcomes the computational inefficiency as well as the lack of exploration-exploitation trade-off typical of more straightforward optimization approaches.

MATERIALS AND METHODOLOGY

This study employed a survey that was carried out between June and July 2023 to assess the mental health condition of working nurses. Natural language processing (NLP) techniques of tokenization, stemming, and stopword removal were employed for data preprocessing. Principal Component Analysis (PCA) was employed for feature selection to achieve dimensionality reduction without losing valuable information. Bayesian Optimization Regression Analysis was employed to optimize hyperparameters for enhancing the predictability of the model. The study used validated mental health questionnaires such as PTSS-14, PHQ-9, and Human Services Survey, all on Likert scales. This method allowed for robust analysis and comprehension of mental health problems among nurses in the workplace.

Material

The data collection process for the present study was conducted over a duration of two months, from June 2023 to July 2023. An email invitation with the survey link was sent to nurse members to obtain a representative and sufficient sample of participants. The response was also boosted through targeted social media marketing and periodic email reminders so that the survey became familiar to many individuals.

2,254 survey responses were gathered in the process. However, for this research, only active practitioners' responses were utilized for analysis to achieve a final sample of 1,457 participants. This selective application was intended to focus on data relevant to the study objective and make sense of the experience and perception of active practitioner nurses.

Scales

For the sake of this study, a number of valid scales and questionnaires were employed to systematically explore various psychological and emotional facets, each designed to assess different dimensions of mental health and wellbeing. The PTSS-14 (Post-Traumatic Stress Scale) was employed to evaluate post-traumatic stress symptoms on 14 items. This scale evaluates dimensions such as intrusive thoughts, hyperarousal, and avoidance behavior. Participants indicated on a Likert scale, allowing for detailed analysis of symptom frequency and severity.

The Patient Health Questionnaire-9 (PHQ-9) was used to assess depressive symptoms. The nine-item, highly validated tool contains items derived from the diagnostic criteria for major depressive disorder. Respondents reported the frequency of symptoms, such as loss of interest, fatigue, or worthlessness, on a Likert scale ranging from “not at all” to “nearly every day.” The ease and effectiveness of the PHQ-9 make it a cornerstone for depression screening.

To measure symptoms of anxiety disorders, an anxiety-related questionnaire was used, drawing on common anxiety-related items such as worry, physical tension, and not being able to control anxious thoughts. The Likert scale enabled a measure of intensity of symptoms so that differences between mild, moderate, and extreme levels of anxiety could be measured.

Finally, the Human Services Survey was included to quantify more global psychosocial and professional measures. The survey assesses such domains as work stress, emotional exhaustion, and job satisfaction and provides a full assessment of the participants' mental health in the context of their profession. With the use of Likert-scale response, the survey was capable of quantifying variance in perception and experience on a continuum and collecting vital data regarding the association of professional stressors and mental health outcomes.

Together, these scales provided a good foundation for understanding the intricate issues of mental health that participants were facing to analyze their psychological well-being in depth and entirely.

Preprocessing

The data collected was effectively preprocessed using natural language processing (NLP) to make data tidy and homogeneous for analysis. Initially, the text data was preprocessed to convert all text to lowercase, remove unwanted special characters, punctuation, and stopwords to remove unwanted noise. Tokenization was applied to break down the text into individual words or meaningful units, followed by stemming and lemmatization to reduce words to root forms, introducing consistency in different forms of a word.

Additionally, the misspelled words were also corrected by executing automated spell-checking processes and domain-specific words were normalized into their standardized form. Named entity recognition (NER) was also utilized to identify and extract vital entities such as job titles or locations from the text. For sentences or phrases with more than one language, language detection and translation processes were utilized to make the dataset uniform.

Finally, text embedding techniques such as word vectors or transformer-based embeddings were applied to embed the preprocessed text in numerical representation suitable for further machine learning and statistical processing. These preprocessing steps ensured the dataset was clean, structured, and ready for correct analysis and interpretation.

Feature Selection

Feature selection in this research work was done with the help of Principal Component Analysis (PCA), a common dimensionality reduction method that identifies the most significant features that are accountable for the variance in the data. PCA achieves this by projecting the original features onto a smaller number of uncorrelated components, or principal components, which have the highest variance in the data.

The method began by normalizing the dataset to the same scale for every feature since PCA is sensitive to the variance difference between features. The covariance matrix of the data was calculated in order to learn how the features relate to one another. Eigenvalues and eigenvectors were derived from the matrix; the eigenvectors are directions (or axes) of maximum variance, and the eigenvalues are the amount of variance in those directions.

The big components were ranked according to their eigenvalues, and a scree plot was employed to identify the number of the components that were to be retained. This implied that only the components with the highest explanatory variance were to be retained and not the redundant or less value-adding features. By choosing some of the strongest factors that explained a high percentage (e.g., 95%) of the total variance, the data set's dimensionality was actually reduced with little information loss.

This method not only increased computational cost but also eliminated the possibility of overfitting because it eliminated noise and unnecessary features. The transformed dataset containing only the principal components was employed for analysis and modeling, and this yielded a strong and interpretable outcome.

Bayesian Optimization

For the preprocessed and feature-sorted data, Bayesian Optimization Regression Analysis was used to optimize the regression model and improve predictive accuracy. This method utilizes the principles of Bayesian statistics to iteratively find the best set of hyperparameters for the regression model under a probabilistic paradigm.

This was followed by constructing the objective function, where regression model performance was quantified, usually by an estimate of mean squared error (MSE) or R-squared. The Bayesian optimization proceeded to build a surrogate probabilistic model, often a Gaussian process, to approximate the objective function and estimate how hyperparameters affected model performance. Relative to grid search and random search, Bayesian optimization provided predictions of the regions of the hyperparameter space that would likely result in improvement based on this surrogate model.

In each step, the algorithm estimated the objective function at a few points in the hyperparameter space using an acquisition function that traded off between exploration (exploring new regions) and exploitation (optimizing existing good regions). The outcome of these estimations was provided as feedback to the surrogate model, which was updated iteratively to improve the search process.

For the study, the regression model utilized principal components obtained through PCA as input predictors, thus ensuring that the analysis was conducted on the most relevant and least redundant data features. By adjusting the hyperparameters such as the learning rate, the regularization term, and the number of estimators, Bayesian optimization set the parameter set that achieved the best predictive performance while avoiding overfitting.

This method provided a systematic and effective way of enhancing the model's accuracy and generalizability, which was highly appropriate for the analysis of the complex interactions in the high-dimensional data. The tuned model was then tested and validated to guarantee its stability and reliability for the data involved.

EXPERIMENTAL RESULTS

The findings of this experiment were predicated on an analysis of the survey data, which was gathered from 1,457 employed working nurses in June and July 2023. Preprocessing processes, such as tokenization, stemming, and the elimination of stopwords, helped prepare the data set in a clean and usable state for additional analysis. Feature selection by applying Principal Component Analysis (PCA) proved to be useful in decreasing the dimension of the dataset without losing the most critical features. Bayesian Optimization Regression Analysis was then used to determine the best hyperparameters to use for the regression model in order to improve its predictive power. The findings provided strong patterns and correlations between the workplace stressors and mental health outcomes like depression, anxiety, and stress. Analysis was of special importance in terms of the impact of what on well-being in nurses with clear relevance for constructing targeted interventions and for health policy in work.

Demographic profile of the nurses in terms of gender, age, educational level, and years of work is shown in Table 1. A total of 76% of the nurses are female and 35% are between the ages of 31-40. Educationally, 44.7% belong to the Associate Degree level while 41.2% fall under the Bachelor's Degree level. Experienced-wise, 33.7% have less than or equal to 5 years, and 33.9% have 10 or more years of experience, with the average experience of 7.2 years (SD = 4.1). The above facts reveal an insight into the nature of the nursing workforce.

Table 1. Demographic characteristics of nurses

Characteristic	Category	Frequency (%)	Mean (SD)
Gender	Male	350 (24.0%)	
	Female	1,107 (76.0%)	
Age Group	20-30 years	450 (30.9%)	

continued on following page

Table 1. Continued

Characteristic	Category	Frequency (%)	Mean (SD)
	31-40 years	510 (35.0%)	
	41-50 years	290 (19.9%)	
	51+ years	207 (14.2%)	
Education Level	Associate Degree	650 (44.7%)	
	Bachelor's Degree	600 (41.2%)	
	Master's Degree	170 (11.7%)	
	Doctorate	37 (2.5%)	
Years of Experience	< 5 years	490 (33.7%)	7.2 (4.1)
	5 - 10 years	472 (32.4%)	7.8 (3.5)
	> 10 years	495 (33.9%)	13.3 (4.2)

Table 2 categorizes nurses based on their workplace setting. The majority of nurses work in hospitals (65.3%), followed by clinics (22.0%) and long-term care facilities (12.8%). This distribution reflects the prevalence of hospital-based employment in the nursing profession and highlights the relatively smaller representation in other settings like clinics and long-term care facilities. It shows the diversity in work environments among nurses.

Table 2. Workplace setting distribution.

Workplace Setting	Frequency (%)
Hospital	950 (65.3%)
Clinic	320 (22.0%)
Long-Term Care Facility	187 (12.8%)

Table 3 presents the distribution of nurses' work shifts. The largest group works day shifts (60.1%), with night shift workers comprising 23.0% and rotating shift workers making up 16.9%. This suggests that the majority of nurses follow standard daytime hours, but a significant portion also works non-traditional hours, including night and rotating shifts, which could impact their mental health and well-being.

Table 3. Work shift distribution among nurses

Work Shift	Frequency (%)
Day Shift	875 (60.1%)
Night Shift	335 (23.0%)
Rotating Shift	247 (16.9%)

Table 4 shows the breakdown of nurses' job roles. The majority of nurses are registered nurses (78.7%), while smaller percentages work as nurse practitioners (15.8%) or nurse managers (5.6%). This highlights that most nurses hold roles directly involved in patient care, with fewer occupying administrative or advanced practice roles. These roles can influence job satisfaction and professional challenges.

Table 4. Job role distribution

Job Role	Frequency (%)
Registered Nurse	1,145 (78.7%)
Nurse Practitioner	230 (15.8%)
Nurse Manager	82 (5.6%)

Table 5 presents nurses' perceptions of workplace support. A significant proportion (77%) feel they receive adequate support, while 23% report inadequate support. This table reflects the importance of supportive work environments in nursing, as perceived support can influence job satisfaction, stress levels, and overall mental health.

Table 5. Perceived workplace support

Workplace Support	Frequency (%)
Adequate Support	1,120 (77.0%)
Inadequate Support	337 (23.0%)

Table 6 provides the average scores for two mental health measures: PHQ-9 (depression) and PTSS-14 (post-traumatic stress). The average PHQ-9 score is 7.2 (SD = 4.3), indicating mild depression, and the average PTSS-14 score is 12.5 (SD = 5.7), reflecting moderate levels of post-traumatic stress. These scores highlight the mental health challenges faced by nurses, underlining the need for targeted interventions.

Table 6. Mental health scores for nurses (PHQ-9 and PTSS-14)

Mental Health Scale	Mean (SD)
PHQ-9 (Depression)	7.2 (4.3)
PTSS-14 (Post-Traumatic Stress)	12.5 (5.7)

Table 7 shows the prevalence of anxiety disorders among nurses, with 42.6% reporting anxiety and 57.4% reporting no anxiety disorder. This table underscores the significant mental health burden on nurses, particularly anxiety, which can affect their well-being and job performance, calling for strategies to address mental health in the nursing profession.

Table 7. Anxiety disorder prevalence among nurses

Anxiety Disorder	Frequency (%)
Present	620 (42.6%)
Absent	837 (57.4%)

Table 8 examines the relationship between years of experience and mental health outcomes (PHQ-9 and PTSS-14). Nurses with less than 5 years of experience have lower mean scores for both depression and post-traumatic stress, while those with more than 10 years show higher mean scores. This correlation suggests that experience may influence mental health, possibly due to accumulated stress over time.

Table 8. Correlation between years of experience and mental health scores

Years of Experience	PHQ-9 Mean Score (SD)	PTSS-14 Mean Score (SD)
< 5 years	6.9 (4.1)	11.4 (5.3)
5 - 10 years	7.3 (4.2)	12.1 (5.6)
> 10 years	7.6 (4.4)	13.2 (6.1)

Table 9 compares mental health outcomes by workplace setting. Nurses in hospitals report higher average depression (PHQ-9) and post-traumatic stress (PTSS-14) scores than those in clinics or long-term care facilities. This may reflect the more demanding and high-stress environment of hospitals, emphasizing the need for tailored support strategies in different settings.

Table 9. Anxiety, depression, and stress factors by workplace setting.

Workplace Setting	PHQ-9 Mean (SD)	PTSS-14 Mean (SD)
Hospital	7.3 (4.5)	12.8 (5.9)
Clinic	6.8 (4.0)	11.6 (5.4)
Long-Term Care Facility	8.0 (4.3)	13.1 (6.2)

Table 10 explores the relationship between job role and mental health support. Registered nurses report the highest levels of adequate support (78.4%), followed by nurse managers (80.5%) and nurse practitioners (72.2%). These findings suggest that different roles experience varying levels of workplace support, which could impact their mental health and job satisfaction.

Table 10. Mental health support and job role

Job Role	Adequate Support (%)	Inadequate Support (%)
Registered Nurse	78.4%	21.6%
Nurse Practitioner	72.2%	27.8%
Nurse Manager	80.5%	19.5%

Figure 1 presents descriptive statistics for mental health outcomes (PHQ-9 and PTSS-14) and categorizes nurses by severity levels (mild, moderate, severe). A significant proportion of nurses (39.9%) report mild depression, while 31.6% experience mild PTSD. Anxiety disorders are also prevalent, with 42.6% of nurses reporting them, indicating the widespread mental health challenges among nurses.

Figure 1. Descriptive statistics for mental health outcomes and proportions for cutoff categories.

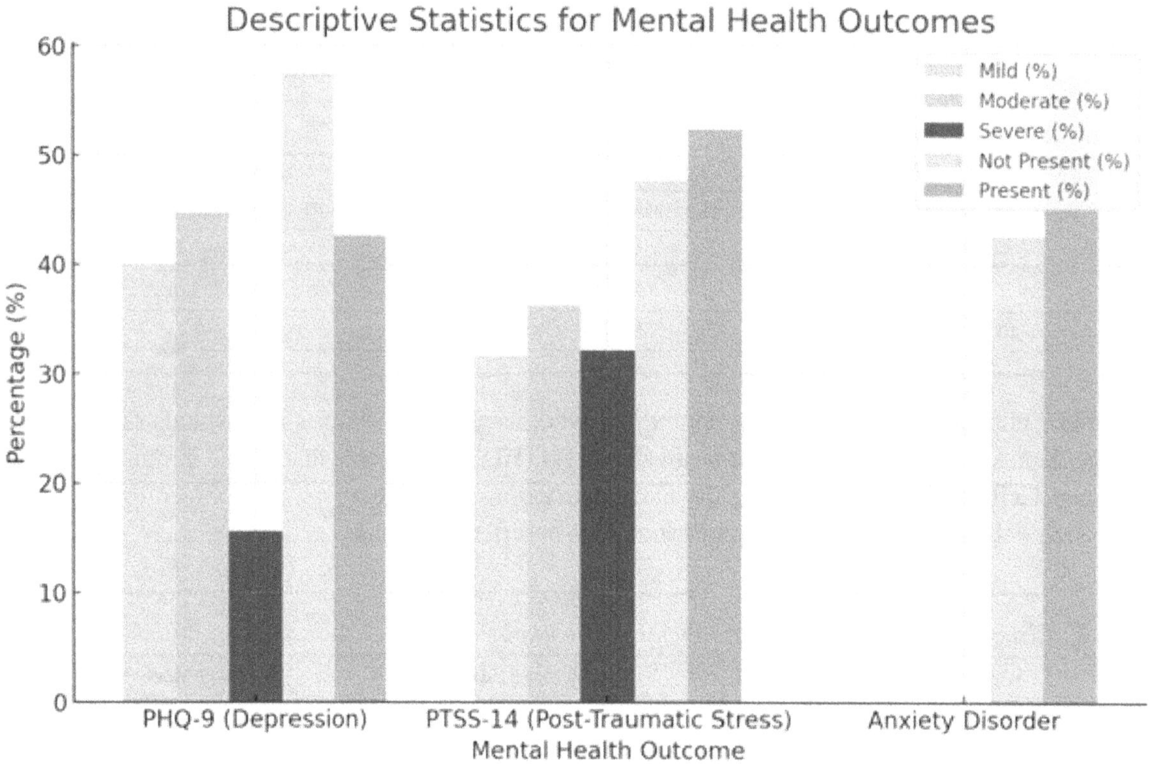

Table 11 outlines Bayesian optimization regression models for predicting mental health outcomes such as PTSD, anxiety, depression, and emotional exhaustion. Variables like age, gender, education level, years of experience, work shift, workplace support, and setting are significant predictors for mental health outcomes. The models show how workplace factors, such as inadequate support or night shifts, can predict higher levels of anxiety and emotional exhaustion, providing insights into the risk factors for nurse mental health.

Table 11. Bayesian optimization regression models

Dependent Variable	Predictor Variables	Beta Estimate (95% CI)	p-value	R^2
PTSD (PTSS-14)	Age, Gender, Education Level, Years of Experience, Work Shift, Workplace Support, Workplace Setting	0.38 (0.23, 0.53)	<0.001	0.32
	Gender (Female)	1.15 (0.95, 1.36)	<0.001	
	Years of Experience (<5 years)	-0.25 (-0.40, -0.10)	0.003	
Anxiety (Anxiety Disorder)	Age, Gender, Education Level, Years of Experience, Work Shift, Workplace Support, Workplace Setting	0.41 (0.28, 0.55)	<0.001	0.27
	Work Shift (Night Shift)	0.78 (0.62, 0.94)	<0.001	
	Workplace Support (Inadequate)	0.92 (0.75, 1.10)	<0.001	
Depression (PHQ-9)	Age, Gender, Education Level, Years of Experience, Work Shift, Workplace Support, Workplace Setting	0.45 (0.32, 0.58)	<0.001	0.36
	Gender (Female)	1.00 (0.80, 1.20)	<0.001	
	Years of Experience (>10 years)	-0.15 (-0.30, -0.01)	0.038	
Emotional Exhaustion (EE)	Age, Gender, Education Level, Years of Experience, Work Shift, Workplace Support, Workplace Setting	0.55 (0.40, 0.70)	<0.001	0.29
	Work Shift (Rotating Shift)	0.90 (0.75, 1.05)	<0.001	
	Workplace Setting (Hospital)	1.12 (0.98, 1.27)	<0.001	

IMPLICATIONS

The results of this research offer useful information on the work and views of presently employed nurses. With its large sample size of 1,457 participants, the research presents a representative image of current nursing practice, issues, and scope for improvement. The results highlight the significance of working conditions, professional support, and policy interventions in improving job satisfaction and patient care outcomes.

One of the major implications of this research is that it can guide healthcare policymakers and administrators in creating more effective strategies to support nurses. Knowing the particular problems of nurses allows institutions to have targeted interventions for enhancing job retention, minimizing burnout, and creating a more positive work environment. The study also emphasizes the necessity of ongoing professional development programs and mental health support initiatives for nursing staff.

In addition, the research makes contributions to wider health care workforce management debate with the focus on work-life balance, sufficient staffing, and fair remuneration. The findings could provide the basis for continuing debate within optimum nursing workforce policy and quality of health care service delivery.

CASE-STUDY

A case-study methodology can also show the relevance of the study by looking at actual situations in which nurses are struggling in practice. Some sample cases are presented below:

Case 1: Burnout and Job Satisfaction

A nurse in an emergency department with high intensity of work experiences burnout because of workload overburden and inadequate staffing. The administration in the hospital introduces a mentorship program and flexible scheduling to de-stress. Follow-up information shows decline in burnout symptoms and job satisfaction among the nurses.

Case 2: Impact of Professional Development

A nurse in rural settings faces fewer professional development opportunities, impacting their career growth and self-confidence in managing complicated medical cases. Following the inclusion of online training modules and workshops, the nurse attests to increased competence and better patient care outcomes.

Case 3: Technology Integration in Nursing Practice

A hospital deploys a new electronic health record (EHR) system to upgrade documentation processes. At the beginning, nurses find the technology difficult and induce increased workload and frustration. However, through guided training sessions and IT support, nurses indicate enhanced efficiency and less administrative burden.

Case 4: Work-Life Balance Challenges

A nurse with work and personal commitments to balance cannot attain a successful work-life balance, which results in stress and absence. An offer of flexible scheduling and mental health service access improves overall well-being and illustrates the usefulness of supportive policy interventions.

Such examples demonstrate how intervention and policy reforms can resolve the prevalent nursing issues, also adding the need for ongoing research and action in improving nursing work environments.

FUTURE RESEARCH DIRECTIONS

Although this research contributes important findings, some research directions follow. Longitudinal analyses, for example, could explore the evolution over time of the experience of nurses in response to policy change, technological developments, and shifts in health demand. Cross-setting comparisons across different types of healthcare setting, e.g., urban v. rural hospitals or private v. public sector organizations, could shed light on context-dependent determinants of nursing practice. Researchers may, in the future, focus their efforts on intervention studies to determine if mentoring program, workload management interventions, and mental health interventions enhance nurse satisfaction and retention. Further, expanded use of electronic devices in health care opens doors for research on how new technologies like artificial intelligence and telemedicine might affect nursing practice and job satisfaction. Cross-cultural comparison of nursing experience between countries or countries can add more richness to international best practices and policy advice. Finally, qualitative research methods, including interviews and focus groups, can provide the means to offer more detailed analysis of nurses' professional and personal issues. By examining these subjects of study, researchers and lawmakers can continue to build on what this research found so that nurses have the support and resources that they need in order to do their jobs better.

CONCLUSION

This research finds the most significant contribution of the work environment to determining the mental health of practicing nurses. With the application of robust preprocessing techniques, PCA-based feature engineering, and Bayesian optimization regression analysis, the research found the best predictors of nurses' stress, anxiety, and depression. With the application of standardized measurement tools such as PTSS-14 and PHQ-9, generalizability and validity of results were ensured. The conclusions reaffirmed the greatest importance of intervention strategies solely aimed at eliminating workplace stressors and improving mental well-being. Enforcement of support policies and promotion of a healthy work environment can go a great distance towards improving the quality of life in nurses and indirectly promote improved patient care and organizational performance. The current study affords a perfect venue for future research to create evidence-based interventions to improve work environments and worker health..

REFERENCES

Aiken, L. H., Clarke, S. P., Sloane, D. M., Sochalski, J. A., Busse, R., Clarke, H., Giovannetti, P., Hunt, J., Rafferty, A. M., & Shamian, J. (2001). Nurses' reports on hospital care in five countries. *Health Affairs*, *20*(3), 43–53. DOI: 10.1377/hlthaff.20.3.43 PMID: 11585181

Gómez-Ochoa, S. A., Franco, O. H., Rojas, L. Z., Romero Guevara, S. L., Echeverría, L. E., Glisic, M., & Muka, T. (2020). COVID-19 in healthcare workers: A systematic review and meta-analysis of prevalence, risk factors, clinical characteristics, and outcomes. *American Journal of Epidemiology*. PMID: 32870978

Havaei, F., Astivia, O. L. O., & MacPhee, M. (2020). The impact of workplace violence on medical-surgical nurses' health outcomes: A moderated mediation model of work environment conditions and burnout using secondary data. *International Journal of Nursing Studies*, *109*, 103666. DOI: 10.1016/j.ijnurstu.2020.103666 PMID: 32592889

Havaei, F., Dahinten, V. S., & MacPhee, M. (2019). Effect of nursing care delivery models on registered nurse outcomes. *SAGE Open Nursing*, *5*, 5. DOI: 10.1177/2377960819869088 PMID: 33415250

Havaei, F., & MacPhee, M. (2020). Effect of workplace violence and psychological stress responses on medical-surgical nurses' medication intake. *Canadian Journal of Nursing Research*. PMID: 32046504

Havaei, F., MacPhee, M., McLeod, C. B., Ma, A., Gear, A., & Sorensen, C. (2020). A provincial study of nurses' psychological health and safety in British Columbia, Canada: Final report. *UBC cIRcle*.

Hu, D., Kong, Y., Li, W., Han, Q., Zhang, X., & Zhu, L. X.. (2020). Frontline nurses' burnout, anxiety, depression, and fear statuses and their associated factors during the COVID-19 outbreak in Wuhan, China: A large-scale cross-sectional study. *Lancet*, *24*, 100424. PMID: 32766539

Jackson, D., Anders, R., Padula, W. V., Daly, J., & Davidson, P. M. (2020). Vulnerability of nurses and physicians with COVID-19: Monitoring and surveillance needed. *Journal of Clinical Nursing*.

Kroenke, K., Spitzer, R. L., & Williams, J. B. W. (2001). The PHQ-9: Validity of a brief depression severity measure. *Journal of General Internal Medicine*, *16*(9), 606–613. DOI: 10.1046/j.1525-1497.2001.016009606.x PMID: 11556941

Lake, E. T., Sanders, J., Duan, R., Riman, K. A., Schoenauer, K. M., & Chen, Y. (2019). A meta-analysis of the associations between the nurse work environment in hospitals and four sets of outcomes. *Medical Care*, *57*(5), 353–361. DOI: 10.1097/MLR.0000000000001109 PMID: 30908381

Lanctôt, N., & Guay, S. (2014). The aftermath of workplace violence among healthcare workers: A systematic literature review of the consequences. *Aggression and Violent Behavior*, *19*(5), 492–501. DOI: 10.1016/j.avb.2014.07.010

Laschinger, H. K. S. (2008). Effect of empowerment on professional practice environments, work satisfaction, and patient care quality: Further testing the Nursing Worklife Model. *Journal of Nursing Care Quality*, *23*(4), 322–330. DOI: 10.1097/01.NCQ.0000318028.67910.6b PMID: 18431259

Laschinger, H. K. S., & Leiter, M. P. (2006). The impact of nursing work environments on patient safety outcomes: The mediating role of burnout/engagement. *The Journal of Nursing Administration, 36*(5), 259–267. DOI: 10.1097/00005110-200605000-00019 PMID: 16705307

Leiter, M. P., & Laschinger, H. K. S. (2006). Relationships of work and practice environment to professional burnout: Testing a causal model. *Nursing Research, 55*(2), 137–146. DOI: 10.1097/00006199-200603000-00009 PMID: 16601626

Leiter, M. P., & Maslach, C. (2016). Latent burnout profiles: A new approach to understanding the burnout experience. *Burnout Research, 3*(4), 89–100. DOI: 10.1016/j.burn.2016.09.001

MacPhee, M., Dahinten, V., & Havaei, F. (2017). The impact of heavy perceived nurse workloads on patient and nurse outcomes. *Administrative Sciences, 7*(1), 7. DOI: 10.3390/admsci7010007

Maslach, C., & Leiter, M. P. (2016). Understanding the burnout experience: Recent research and its implications for psychiatry. *World Psychiatry; Official Journal of the World Psychiatric Association (WPA), 15*(2), 103–111. DOI: 10.1002/wps.20311 PMID: 27265691

Murphy, G. T., Birch, S., MacKenzie, A., Alder, R., Lethbridge, L., & Little, L. (2012). Eliminating the shortage of registered nurses in Canada: An exercise in applied needs-based planning. *Health Policy (Amsterdam), 105*(2-3), 192–202. DOI: 10.1016/j.healthpol.2011.11.009 PMID: 22176731

Oudyk, J., & Smith, P. (2020). *Preliminary results for the pandemic healthcare workers' survey*. Occupational Health Clinics for Ontario Workers.

Pappa, S., Ntella, V., Giannakas, T., Giannakoulis, V. G., Papoutsi, E., & Katsaounou, P. (2020). Prevalence of depression, anxiety, and insomnia among healthcare workers during the COVID-19 pandemic: A systematic review and meta-analysis. *Brain, Behavior, and Immunity, 88*, 901–907. DOI: 10.1016/j.bbi.2020.05.026 PMID: 32437915

Shaukat, N., Ali, D. M., & Razzak, J. (2020). Physical and mental health impacts of COVID-19 on healthcare workers: A scoping review. *International Journal of Emergency Medicine, 13*(1), 40. DOI: 10.1186/s12245-020-00299-5 PMID: 32689925

Shi, L., Lu, Z.-A., Que, J.-Y., Huang, X.-L., Liu, L., Ran, M.-S., Gong, Y.-M., Yuan, K., Yan, W., Sun, Y.-K., Shi, J., Bao, Y.-P., & Lu, L. (2020). Prevalence of and risk factors associated with mental health symptoms among the general population in China during the coronavirus disease 2019 pandemic. *JAMA Network Open, 3*(7), e2014053. DOI: 10.1001/jamanetworkopen.2020.14053 PMID: 32609353

Spitzer, R. L., Kroenke, K., Williams, J. B. W., & Löwe, B. (2006). A brief measure for assessing generalized anxiety disorder: The GAD-7. *Archives of Internal Medicine, 166*(10), 1092–1097. DOI: 10.1001/archinte.166.10.1092 PMID: 16717171

Twigg, E., Humphris, G., Jones, C., Bramwell, R., & Griffiths, R. D. (2008). Use of a screening questionnaire for post-traumatic stress disorder (PTSD) on a sample of UK ICU patients. *Acta Anaesthesiologica Scandinavica, 52*(2), 202–208. DOI: 10.1111/j.1399-6576.2007.01531.x PMID: 18005373

Zhang, S.-E., Liu, W., Wang, J., Shi, Y., Xie, F., Cang, S., Sun, T., & Fan, L. (2018). Impact of workplace violence and compassionate behaviour in hospitals on stress, sleep quality, and subjective health status among Chinese nurses: A cross-sectional survey. *BMJ Open*, *8*(10), e019373. DOI: 10.1136/bmjopen-2017-019373 PMID: 30287664

Zhao, S., Xie, F., Wang, J., Shi, Y., Zhang, S., Han, X., Sun, Z., Shi, L., Li, Z., Mu, H., Liu, X., Liu, W., Gao, L., Sun, T., & Fan, L. (2018). Prevalence of workplace violence against Chinese nurses and its association with mental health: A cross-sectional survey. *Archives of Psychiatric Nursing*, *32*(2), 242–247. DOI: 10.1016/j.apnu.2017.11.009 PMID: 29579519

Zheng, R., Zhou, Y., Fu, Y., Xiang, Q., Cheng, F., Chen, H., Xu, H., fu, L., Wu, X., Feng, M., Ye, L., Tian, Y., Deng, R., Liu, S., Jiang, Y., Yu, C., & Li, J. (2020). Prevalence and associated factors of depression and anxiety among nurses during the outbreak of COVID-19 in China: A cross-sectional study. *International Journal of Nursing Studies*, *114*, 103809. DOI: 10.1016/j.ijnurstu.2020.103809 PMID: 33207297

Chapter 9
Integrating Robotics and AI into Workplace Biorisk Management

Tanusha Singh
https://orcid.org/0000-0002-9583-087X
University of Johannesburg, South Africa

ABSTRACT

Work-related illnesses and injuries affect over 2.3 million people annually. Biological hazards are often underreported and poorly managed. Biorisk Management (BRM) aims to assess and reduce these risks. Emerging technologies like AI and robotics offer new tools for predictive analytics, real-time monitoring, and hazard detection. This chapter explores how AI can enhance BRM, particularly in under-resourced settings, to improve workplace health and safety. This chapter explores how AI can support effective, adaptive, and ethical BRM systems, especially in under-resourced settings.

INTRODUCTION

Work-related injuries and illnesses remain a major global health concern, affecting approximately 2.3 million people annually and resulting in over 6,000 deaths every day. In total, around 340 million occupational accidents occur each year, impacting nearly 160 million workers. These statistics highlight the urgent need for comprehensive strategies to manage workplace hazards and promote worker health and safety. Occupational health is a critical pillar of public health, dedicated to improving the physical, mental, and social well-being of workers across all occupations (Shah & Mishra, 2024). To ensure safe and productive work environments, risks from various hazard categories, including physical, chemical, ergonomic, psychosocial, and particularly biological, must be effectively managed. This chapter focuses on the management of biological risks in occupational settings and the transformative role of artificial intelligence (AI) and robotics.

Biorisks refer to potential exposures to biological agents such as bacteria, viruses, fungi, parasites, their by-products, and other organic matter that may adversely affect workers, visitors, and surrounding communities (Singh & Matuka, 2013, Juan José, María Renée, Tesifón et al., 2022, ILO, 2023). Managing these hazards requires a structured, evidence-based approach known as Biorisk Management (BRM), a process that encompasses risk identification, assessment, control, and mitigation (Fernando & Antonio, 2013, Burzoni, Duquenne, Mater et al., 2020). Failure to adequately manage biorisks can lead to

DOI: 10.4018/979-8-3693-9301-7.ch009

devastating consequences for organisations, including operational disruption, reputational damage, and, in extreme cases, as seen during the COVID-19 pandemic, widespread economic and societal collapse. Despite the existence of global frameworks such as ISO 45001:2018, BRM remains under-prioritised, especially in high-risk or emerging sectors like biotechnology, waste management, and the green economy (Anna, 2022, Rittick, Sachin, Mandar Bhalchandra et al., 2023).

Persistent challenges, such as the underreporting of biohazard-related incidents, limited awareness among workers, and inconsistent implementation of control strategies like personal protective equipment (PPE) usage, immunisation, and post-exposure prophylaxis, continue to undermine BRM efforts. Additionally, the psychosocial impact of biological threats is often overlooked in occupational health discourse. While legal instruments such as the EU Directive 2000/54/EC provide infection control guidance, effective implementation requires a holistic, systems-level approach that integrates prevention, mental health support, compliance monitoring, and workforce education (Lemos, Gaspar & Lima, 2022).

Risk analysis is central to BRM, enabling the systematic assessment and mitigation of risks from local incidents to global outbreaks. As the world becomes increasingly interconnected, due to climate change, globalisation, and technological convergence, the complexity and urgency of managing biorisks have intensified. In this evolving landscape, AI and robotics offer powerful tools for forecasting, probabilistic modelling, early detection, and real-time hazard response (Tessandra, Jon & Seth, 2022).

AI is particularly valuable in scenarios where data is large, complex, or incomplete. It complements traditional approaches such as Bayesian inference by offering dynamic models for risk prediction and decision-making. Digital tools, including simulation software, spatial layout planning, and real-time statistics, can be enhanced with AI to assess both physical and psychological risks that are often difficult to quantify (Westhoven & Herrmann, 2023). As biological threats grow in complexity and frequency, organisations must shift from reactive to adaptive risk management systems that identify and respond to threats in real time (Janssen, Cski, Lindgren et al., 2022, Leyma, 2024). In this context, AI and robotics emerge as transformative enablers for BRM, offering scalable and responsive solutions that can improve workplace safety across industries (Janaína, Vanessa Borba de, Frederico Soares et al., 2024, John & Paul, 2024).

AI technologies have been increasingly employed for epidemic management, particularly in under-resourced and rural environments (Ejike Innocent, Ebube Victor, Mojeed Dayo et al., 2024). Although still in the early stages of integration into Occupational Health and Safety (OHS), AI has demonstrated significant potential for hazard detection, predictive analytics, and emergency preparedness. These systems use algorithms to mimic human intelligence for tasks such as decision-making, language processing, visual recognition, and real-time monitoring. In high-risk environments, such as mining, energy production, and construction, AI is already being used to automate safety inspections and identify psychosocial risks like fatigue and burnout (El-Helaly, 2024). When paired with sensor technologies that measure air quality, noise levels, humidity, and temperature, AI enables advanced environmental monitoring and health surveillance (Nathavitharana, Mishra, Sullivan et al., 2022, Lee, Miao, Chau et al., 2023). These systems also synthesise diverse data sources, including health records, biometric data, and mobility patterns, to support outbreak forecasting and early intervention (Wenqiang, Chenrui, Meng et al., 2023, Ejike Innocent, Ebube Victor, Mojeed Dayo et al., 2024).

Advanced analytical techniques such as neural networks, decision trees, Bayesian models, and multivariate regression are increasingly utilised in occupational safety applications (Ria, WeiHuang, Anélie et al., 2023). These are enabled through various machine learning (ML) approaches, supervised, unsupervised, semi-supervised, and reinforcement learning, which allow organisations to extract actionable insights from occupational health data (Table 1) (Goodfellow, Pouget-Abadie, Mirza et al., 2020). The rise of Generative AI (GenAI), including tools like ChatGPT and MidJourney, offers new possibilities for simulation, training, and human-AI interaction (Goodfellow, Pouget-Abadie, Mirza et al., 2020). Similarly, the Internet of Things (IoT), through its network of interconnected devices, enables real-time exposure tracking and seamless integration of environmental and biological risk indicators (Wang, Wang & Siau).

Table 1. Type of ML techniques and the algorithms associated with each technique.

Types of ML Techniques	List of Common Algorithms
Supervised ML	Support Vector Machine (SVM), Naive-Bayes, K-Nearest Neighbour, Decision Trees, Random Forests (RF), Linear Regression, Logistic Regression, DL
Unsupervised	ML K-Means, Hidden Markov Model (HMM), Principal Component Analysis, Gaussian Model Mixture (GMM), DL
Semi-supervised ML	Self-Training, Co-Training, Generative methods, Mixture models, Semi-supervised SVM, Graph-based methods
Reinforcement ML	Q-Learning, Temporal Difference, Deep Adversarial Networks

AI is already transforming OHS by automating routine tasks and enabling smart interventions. In high-risk industries, AI-enhanced tools can support incident prediction, optimise resource allocation, and simulate emergency scenarios for training. These tools also assist in workforce data collection and burnout detection, facilitating earlier and more effective health interventions. As workplaces increasingly embrace digital transformation (Dwivedi & Ritesh Arvind, 2024), AI strengthens BRM through smarter detection, faster response, and more efficient control of biological threats (Krainiuk, Yu, Barbashyn et al., 2023).

Traditional BRM methods, based on manual inspections and observational audits, often fail to respond effectively to evolving risk scenarios (Inglesby & Adalja, 2022). AI addresses these gaps by offering proactive risk management capabilities, such as real-time biosurveillance, predictive modelling, and automated mitigation strategies (Martin, Rikard & David, 2024). When integrated into broader OHS frameworks, AI can revolutionise workplace safety by improving pandemic preparedness, enhancing compliance monitoring, and facilitating human-robot collaboration in hazardous settings (Ali, Cecilia, Edward et al., 2024, Priyank & Fahad, 2024). However, despite its potential, the full integration of AI into workplace risk systems remains limited, partly due to concerns about technological readiness, data governance, and regulatory alignment (Nathavitharana, Mishra, Sullivan et al., 2022).

This chapter explores the convergence of AI and BRM, focusing on practical applications in industries where biological risks are pronounced. It highlights key innovations, implementation barriers, and future directions, offering valuable insights for researchers, occupational health practitioners, and policymakers working to improve safety outcomes in increasingly complex workplace ecosystems.

Chapter Structure for Better Understanding

For clarity and coherence, the chapter is organised into four main sections, each addressing a critical component of AI integration in BRM:

SECTION 1: AI APPLICATIONS IN BIORISK MANAGEMENT (BRM)

Biorisk management (BRM) seeks to prevent or minimise worker exposure to biological hazards, both infectious and non-infectious. Historically, BRM strategies have been reactive, centred around post-exposure monitoring and interventions that are often resource-intensive and time-consuming (Ryan & Chuck, 2021). Manual reviews of historical incident data, typically carried out by safety personnel, can delay the detection of emerging risks. However, recent advancements in AI are reshaping BRM by introducing proactive, data-driven approaches for hazard identification, risk assessment, and mitigation (Petya, 2021). AI enables the development of early warning systems, predictive analytics, and automated hazard response mechanisms to preemptively manage biological risks in occupational settings (Tessandra, Jon & Seth, 2022). It leverages ML models and advanced algorithms capable of processing large datasets to identify patterns and anticipate hazards (Suriyan, Wai Peng & Chee Peng, 2021). As a subset of AI, ML continuously refines performance through iterative learning, enabling increasingly accurate and dynamic risk assessments over time (Suriyan, Wai Peng & Chee Peng, 2021, Naimeh, 2024). Applications range from computer vision for hazard detection to predictive modelling for outbreak prevention. These AI innovations also enhance regulatory compliance, improve emergency preparedness, and support the shift from reactive to proactive BRM strategies across high-risk sectors (Fernando & Antonio, 2013).

The development of AI models involves a structured, iterative process designed to ensure the reliability and generalisability of predictive outputs (Figure 1). It begins with data collection from diverse sources, including sensors, databases, and real-time systems, followed by preprocessing steps to clean and standardise data. This is typically followed by data partitioning into training, validation, and test sets. The training dataset enables the model to identify patterns using algorithms such as decision trees, neural networks, or support vector machines. The validation set is used to optimise performance and avoid overfitting, while the external test dataset assesses the model's ability to generalise to real-world scenarios (Aggarwal, Mishra, Tabassum et al., 2024).

Figure 1. Key steps in developing models using AI algorithms, namely data collection, data preparation, model selection and training, evaluation, and prediction. Adapted from Aggarwal et al (2024).(Aggarwal, Mishra, Tabassum et al., 2024)

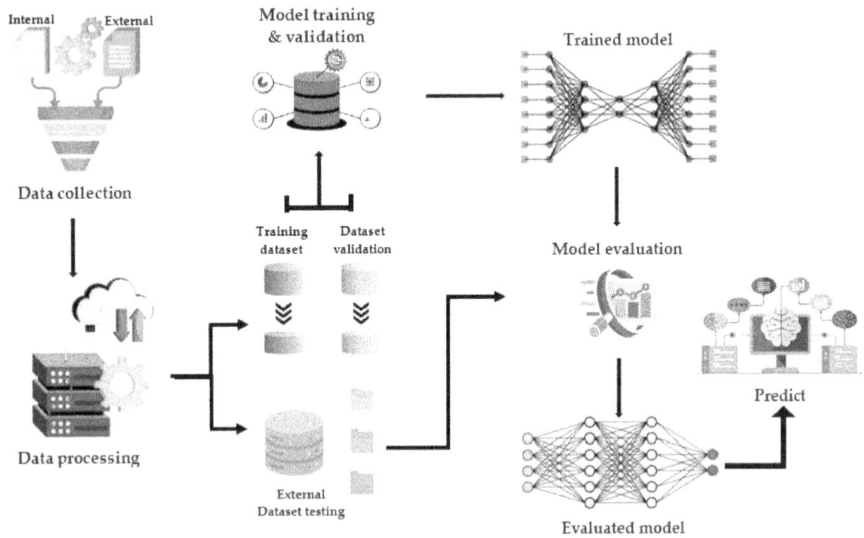

Evaluation metrics such as accuracy, precision, recall, F1 score, and the area under the receiver operating characteristic (ROC) curve are then used to assess the model's performance (Table 2). Once validated, the model can be deployed to generate real-time predictions for decision-making, outbreak forecasting, or automated response systems. In recent years, AI has shown notable promise in forecasting infectious disease outbreaks. Techniques such as ML, deep learning (DL), natural language processing (NLP), and rule-based expert systems (RBES) are being used to model disease dynamics and guide public health responses. However, despite their strengths, challenges persist in relation to data quality, model transparency, and selecting appropriate analytical methods (Selestine, Youssef, Farid et al., 2024). In the occupational context, data routinely collected at workplace clinics, wellness centres, and exposure monitoring systems is increasingly used to train AI models for identifying at-risk populations, high-risk tasks, and emerging disease trends (Jeebhay, Naidoo, Naidoo et al., 2023, Lin, Shuya & Lei, 2024). These AI applications span multiple domains like job classification (via NLP), exposure assessment (using NLP and RBES), predictive analytics (employing ML and DL), and microbial risk evaluation (through neural networks and rule-based systems) (Shah & Mishra, 2024).

Table 2. Evaluation metrics to evaluate machine learning models.

Evaluation Metrics	Formula
Recall or sensitivity	$\frac{TP}{TP + FN}$
Precision	$\frac{TP}{TP + FP}$
Specificity	$\frac{TN}{EP + TN}$
Accuracy	$\frac{TP + TN}{TN + TP + FP + FN}$
F1-measure	$\frac{2 \times precision \times recall}{precision + recall}$
ROC	$\sqrt{specificity \times sensitivity}$

TP: true positive, TN: true negative, FP: false positive, FN: false negative

For example, NLP enables the automation of safety report analysis, incident logs, and maintenance records to uncover leading indicators of risk. By extracting patterns from unstructured textual data, NLP helps identify root causes of incidents, enabling organisations to take preventive actions and cultivate a stronger safety culture. It also improves job coding, which is crucial for risk profiling and the development of role-specific training and mitigation strategies (Shah & Mishra, 2024). The value of AI became particularly evident during the COVID-19 pandemic, where ML and DL enabled real-time data analysis to inform policy decisions, track disease transmission, and support infection control (Lin, Shuya & Lei, 2024). High-risk sectors such as healthcare, pharmaceutical production, food processing, and wastewater treatment stand to benefit significantly from AI-powered risk management platforms (Priyank & Fahad, 2024). These tools allow for dynamic, ongoing risk assessments, better compliance, and the identification of high-exposure zones before incidents occur.

Ultimately, integrating AI into BRM represents a paradigm shift, from reactive measures to predictive, real-time risk mitigation. As AI technologies evolve, their role in advancing occupational health and safety will become increasingly indispensable. The subsequent sections delve deeper into specific AI applications across BRM phases, illustrating how these tools are transforming the identification, prediction, and control of biological hazards in the workplace.

Key AI Technologies Advancing Modern BRM

– Machine Learning (ML) and Deep Learning (DL)

Machine Learning (ML) and DL are increasingly transforming occupational health and safety, particularly in the domain of biological risk management. Their ability to process large, complex datasets, recognise hidden patterns, and generate high-precision predictions has enabled faster and more informed decision-making than traditional risk assessment approaches. These technologies are especially valuable in anticipating disease outbreaks caused by microbial agents, identifying high-risk exposures, and optimising response strategies in real-time. By integrating diverse data sources, including environmental monitoring, clinical surveillance, and workplace incident records, ML and DL models enhance predictive accuracy and inform early interventions across sectors where biological hazards are prevalent (Ravi, Samuel, Karl et al., 2022). In the field of industrial hygiene, which focuses on recognising, evaluating, and controlling workplace hazards, ML tools are playing a critical role. Exposure assessment systems, such as WORKSPERT, use ML algorithms to evaluate worker risks by analysing conditions like air quality, chemical usage, or bioaerosol concentrations. These systems not only ensure regulatory compliance but also support the communication of risk, control measures, and health surveillance outputs. ML is also being used to reduce accidents, detect early signs of occupational illness, and strengthen emergency preparedness. By mining historical datasets, ML algorithms can detect recurring microbial exposure patterns, automate risk profiling, and improve hazard audits. For example, centralised ML-powered monitoring systems allow for the remote surveillance of biological risks across multiple sites, minimising the need for on-site inspections and increasing operational efficiency. This frees up occupational health professionals to focus on complex analytical tasks and strategic risk mitigation (Shah & Mishra, 2024). Recent applications of ML extend to fields like structural health monitoring and jobsite safety analytics. ML models have demonstrated effectiveness in detecting structural degradation, monitoring worker fatigue, and identifying performance decline, factors that can increase susceptibility to biological agents due to immune suppression or poor hygiene compliance. Advances in graphical processing units (GPUs) have further enabled the widespread deployment of DL techniques, particularly convolutional neural networks (CNNs), in occupational settings. These tools are now commonly used for image classification, object detection, and environmental surveillance, including microbial colony recognition, surface contamination mapping, and thermal imaging for infection control (Shah & Mishra, 2024).

– *Neural Networks and Rule-based Expert Systems*

Neural Networks (NNs) and RBES are AI tools increasingly used in workplace BRM to simulate expert decision-making. NNs, such as multilayer perceptrons, learn from large, complex datasets to identify hidden patterns. For example, Dharmendra and Robin (2020) used a feed-forward NN to predict occupational risks, an approach that can be adapted for microbial risk forecasting based on environmental and clinical data. RBES, in contrast, rely on predefined rules drawn from expert knowledge to guide rapid decision-making, such as triggering containment protocols or adjusting ventilation in response to rising bioaerosol levels. These systems are especially useful in settings lacking immediate expert input (Dharmendra & Robin, 2020). Modern electronic monitoring systems increasingly integrate both NNs and RBES, enabling real-time biosurveillance and automated responses to microbial threats. They enhance accuracy, reduce human error, preserve institutional knowledge, and support novice training, particularly in high-risk environments such as healthcare, laboratories, and wastewater treatment facilities (Cenciarelli, Andrea, Marco et al., 2013, Shah & Mishra, 2024). Together, NNs and RBES strengthen organisational capacity to anticipate and manage biological hazards, offering an intelligent, adaptive layer of protection in dynamic occupational settings.

– *Real-Time Data Analytics*

AI-powered real-time data analytics allow continuous monitoring of occupational environments, enabling instant identification of microbial hazards and other biological threats (Aniket, Sampson & Vritik, 2024). While these technologies are widely applied in infectious disease surveillance using mobile health data, their application in workplace biosurveillance is growing, particularly for early detection in high-risk settings such as laboratories, hospitals, and industrial plants (Janet Aderonke, Chukwudi Cosmos, Tolulope Olagoke et al., 2024). By integrating real-time analytics into BRM systems, organisations can accelerate hazard response, reduce human error, and enhance decision-making accuracy. These tools support predictive and proactive strategies rather than reactive ones, enabling smarter workplace safety protocols.

A systematic PRISMA review found that ML and DL techniques, especially tree-based algorithms and feed-forward neural networks, are most frequently used to model highly contagious diseases, primarily in Eastern Asia, North America, and Southern Asia (Ravi, Samuel, Karl et al., 2022). The study recommended a One Health approach, integrating environmental, veterinary, and human health data to improve model accuracy and representation. Advanced AI models, including Support Vector Machines (SVM), decision trees, Naive Bayes classifiers, clustering algorithms, artificial neural network (ANN), deep neural network (DNN), long short-term memory (LSTM), and Transformer models, are now widely used to track disease dynamics, pinpoint outbreak origins, and inform rapid interventions (Figure 2) (Selestine, Youssef, Farid et al., 2024). These models typically fall into three categories: (1) predicting disease spread, (2) estimating individual susceptibility, and (3) combining both approaches. Despite their diversity, all rely on multi-source datasets to enhance pandemic preparedness and occupational biosafety. Ultimately, the integration of diverse data types, numerical, textual, image-based, and clinical, through AI enhances the granularity, precision, and real-world utility of predictive models. Continued innovation in this space, supported by robust and diverse datasets, is essential to building resilient, AI-enhanced systems for managing biological risks in occupational settings.

Figure 2. Diagram summarising the techniques employed for different types of datasets in the field of infectious disease prediction.

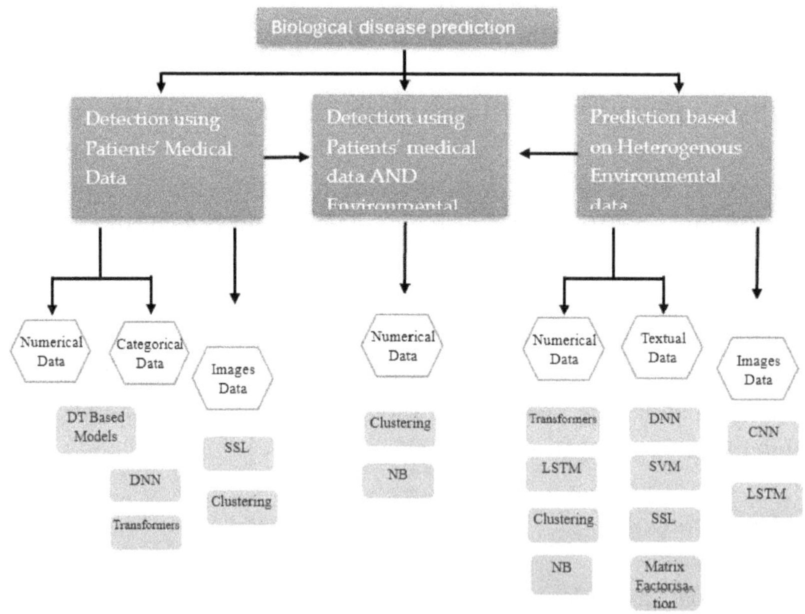

i. Numerical Data: time series epidemiological and locational data

Epidemiological surveillance systems generate time-series data such as infection rates, fatalities, and geolocations, which are foundational for predictive modelling. Algorithms like Naive Bayes (NB), SVM, and Linear Regression have been used to forecast disease trends, including during COVID-19, with a focus on minimising predictive errors like Mean Absolute Error (MAE) and Mean Squared Error (MSE) (Tiwari, Bhati, Al-Turjman et al., 2022). Naive Bayes performs well with structured data but struggles when faced with noise or irrelevant features. Clustering algorithms such as DBSCAN have enhanced contact tracing by analysing spatiotemporal mobility data (Ravi, Samuel, Karl et al., 2022). However, DBSCAN's sensitivity to parameter settings limits its scalability. More advanced models like LSTM networks have shown superior performance in forecasting confirmed cases, recoveries, and deaths by capturing non-linear dependencies. In Madrid, mobility data integrated with LSTM improved prediction accuracy (Muñoz-Organero, 2022). Transformer-based models, such as HostNet, ORIT, and T-SIRGAN, further outperformed traditional RNNs by leveraging self-attention mechanisms to model complex temporal disease dynamics.

ii. Textual Data: Social Media and News Reports

Text-based data from social media and news articles has become vital for real-time disease surveillance. Supervised matrix factorisation has been used to extract relevant disease features from large news corpora. Kim & Ahn (2021) employed semi-supervised learning (SSL) to predict disease outbreaks up to six months in advance (Kim & Ahn, 2021). Support Vector Machine (SVM) classifiers have achieved over 85% accuracy in forecasting influenza-like illness (ILI) rates, as demonstrated by systems like DEFENDER, which combines SVM and NB to filter relevant social media content (Thapen, Simmie, Hankin et al., 2016). More sophisticated models, including DNNs and LSTMs, have improved outbreak forecasting by integrating textual data with contextual variables such as weather patterns and search queries (Chae, Kwon & Lee, 2018). Recently, transformer models have been used to mine platforms like Reddit for contextualised outbreak prediction.

iii. Image Data: Geospatial and Medical Imaging

Geospatial and medical imaging data are critical for tracking environmental and clinical aspects of disease. GeoImageNet, for example, uses RGB and Digital Elevation Model (DEM) imagery to validate spatial disease models (Li, Wang, Arundel et al., 2023). RetinaNet and Faster-RCNN have enabled high-resolution environmental monitoring. In clinical diagnostics, convolutional neural networks (CNNs) have achieved up to 98% accuracy in detecting COVID-19 from chest X-rays. Models like MASERes, which apply transfer learning, have achieved 100% accuracy on certain datasets. In settings with limited annotated data, SSL-based models such as COVIDCon have proven effective by combining labelled and unlabelled image data (Sahoo, Roy, Ahlawat et al., 2022). These approaches have proven effective, especially when the number of annotated datasets is limited.

iv. Numerical Data: Routine Blood Tests

Routine blood tests provide valuable physiological markers for early disease detection. Studies have validated ML algorithms, including ANN, SVM, k-NN, Logistic Regression, and Random Forests (RF), for COVID-19 diagnosis and prognosis (Cabitza, Campagner, Ferrari et al., 2020, Peiffer-Smadja, Rawson, Ahmad et al., 2020). Random Forests and Gradient Boosting models, known for their robustness and interpretability, have consistently delivered strong early detection performance (Brinati, Campagner, Ferrari et al., 2020, Banerjee, Bhattacharya & Majumdar, 2021). Advanced implementations, such as XGBoost-based Smart Blood Analytics (Kukar, Gunčar, Vovko et al., 2021) and hybrid models like ERLX, which combine RF, Extra Trees (ET), and Logistic Regression, have further improved diagnostic accuracy (Yang, Hou, Vasovic et al., 2020).

v. Categorical Data: Clinical and Biological Data

Categorical data from clinical records and biological assays form a crucial layer for predicting both communicable and non-communicable diseases. Decision Tree (DT) and RF models have demonstrated strong predictive capabilities for diseases like hepatitis (Kumar, Kumar, Gayathri et al., 2014). DNNs have been employed in modelling protein-protein interactions and predicting molecular targets for conditions such as asthma and cancer (Narmadha & Pravin, 2020). Devi et al. (2018) applied a Multi-Swarm Optimised MLP for Dengue serotyping, achieving 86% accuracy (Devi, 2018). Transformer models such as TEMPO, which utilise phylogenetic trees to track viral mutations, have achieved enhanced prediction accuracy and precision, demonstrating their value in pandemic intelligence when applied to large genomic datasets.

Prediction Using Public Health and Patient Medical Data

Recent advances in ML have significantly enhanced the accuracy and scope of infectious disease prediction and surveillance. Integrating patient medical records with public health datasets offers a comprehensive and real-time approach to detecting and controlling outbreaks. When clinical indicators are combined with environmental and epidemiological data, predictive models gain contextual depth, improving relevance and responsiveness. Models such as Naive Bayes Networks (NBNs) and clustering algorithms have shown promise in identifying infection risks and issuing early warnings. For example, Valiakos et al. (2014) used a clustering-based method that integrated environmental data, human infection records, and avian surveillance to predict the spatial distribution of West Nile Virus (WNV) in Greece. Their results highlighted geographic variables, such as altitude and proximity to water bodies, as key predictors of disease transmission (Valiakos, Papaspyropoulos, Giannakopoulos et al., 2014).

Despite these successes, accurate prediction requires access to comprehensive and high-quality datasets. Underreporting or omission of confirmed cases can skew model outputs and obscure transmission dynamics. One of the primary challenges is integrating diverse data types, numerical epidemiological data, clinical records, satellite imagery, social media, and news feeds, into a unified predictive framework. Different ML architectures perform optimally with specific data types:

- LSTM and Transformer models excel in time-series epidemiological data,
- SVM, SSL, and DNN are effective with textual data from media sources,
- CNNs are particularly suited to geospatial or satellite imagery (Selestine, Youssef, Farid et al., 2024).

However, privacy regulations, inconsistent data timelines, and non-aligned datasets can affect the generalisability and reliability of predictions. Future research must prioritise:

1. Clearly defining predictive objectives
2. Selecting suitable learning algorithms and data sources
3. Developing integrated models that harmonise heterogeneous data streams

In occupational settings, the integration of AI with public health and clinical data presents a powerful opportunity to improve workplace safety, particularly in high-risk industries such as healthcare, mining, agriculture, and wastewater treatment. By merging epidemiological intelligence with individual health records, models like Naive Bayes and LSTM can forecast disease outbreaks and enable early interventions (see Figure 3). Clustering algorithms such as DBSCAN help identify high-risk zones, while the incorporation of environmental data allows for dynamic risk assessments linked to factors like air quality or humidity. AI models can also support longer-term health planning by predicting chronic work-related illnesses, guiding return-to-work decisions, and informing post-infection fitness assessments. Natural Language Processing plays a complementary role by analysing incident reports and health logs to identify recurring infection control failures. Additionally, real-time biosurveillance systems powered by IoT and AI can continuously monitor environments such as laboratories and treatment facilities, triggering immediate responses when biological hazards are detected. To demonstrate the practical relevance of these approaches, the following section will explore how AI-enhanced methods can strengthen each phase of the BRM process. By combining occupational health data, environmental monitoring, and public health intelligence, AI provides a more responsive and proactive framework for managing biological risks in the workplace.

Risk management generally comprises four key stages:

– Risk identification (e.g., hazard characterisation and exposure assessment)
– Risk assessment (analysis and evaluation of likelihood and consequences)
– Risk treatment (strategy selection and implementation)
– Risk monitoring (ongoing evaluation and response adjustments) (Płaza, Achal & Kumari, 2018, Suriyan, Wai Peng & Chee Peng, 2021)

Figure 3. Flowchart showing AI-powered predictive modelling in the occupational health context.

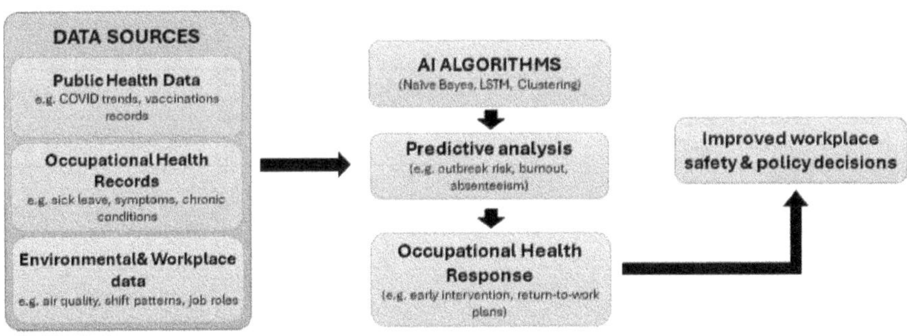

BRM mirrors this structure, and Table 3 contrasts traditional methods with AI-enhanced approaches at each stage. Figure 4 illustrates how AI supports both qualitative and quantitative risk assessments, automating tasks such as data processing, probability modelling, and scenario simulations using tools like probability matrices and Monte Carlo methods (Biolcheva, 2021). This integration enhances both the precision and agility of decision-making in occupational health contexts.

Table 3. Comparison of Biohazard Risk Management Steps using Traditional Approaches (Halim, 2024) versus AI-Integrated Technologies (Leyma, 2024) and Future Considerations (Evangeline & Grant, 2021, Naushin, 2024).

Steps in Biorisk Management	Traditional Approach	AI-Integrated Approach	Future Technologies
Anticipation	Expert judgement, historical data analysis, and manual hazard forecasting	Predictive analytics using machine learning models to forecast emerging risks	AI-enhanced digital twins for workplace risk simulations
Hazard Identification	Manual workplace inspections, checklists, and exposure history assessments	AI-driven image recognition and IoT sensors for real-time hazard detection	Autonomous drones and robots with high resolution lenses for biological hazard inspection
Risk Characterisation	Epidemiological studies and qualitative risk assessments	Big data analytics and AI-based risk quantification models	Quantum computing for ultra-fast risk modelling and simulation
Exposure Assessment	Workplace sampling, laboratory analysis, and self-reported exposure data	AI-powered biosensors, wearable health monitors, and real-time exposure tracking	Smart nanotechnology-based biosensors for real-time hazard detection
Risk Evaluation	Comparison with regulatory limits and qualitative rankings	AI-assisted decision support systems for dynamic risk evaluation	AI-powered regulatory compliance systems with automated reporting
Risk Control and Mitigation	Implementation of PPE, administrative controls, and engineering solutions	AI-optimised risk control strategies using real-time data and automation	AI-driven self-adaptive work environments with adaptive PPE
Emergency Preparedness and Response	Standard operating procedures (SOPs), manual outbreak response, and drills	AI-based early warning systems, and automated emergency response planning	Autonomous response and automated evacuation systems
Risk Communication	In-person safety training and safety meetings	AI-powered virtual safety assistants, chatbots, and adaptive e-learning	Augmented reality (AR) training for immersive risk education
Surveillance and Monitoring	Periodic workplace audits, self-reports, and regulatory oversight	Real-time AI-driven biosurveillance and automated anomaly detection	AI-integrated blockchain for real-time occupational health data sharing
Review and Continuous Improvement	Annual policy reviews, feedback mechanisms, and regulatory updates	Continuous AI-driven learning systems with self-adapting risk models	Self-learning AI models that continuously refine risk management policies

*Figure 4. Risk assessment performed using AI (Biolcheva, 2021). Where: * Probability matrix – method for qualitative risk assessment, ** Monte Carlo method for quantitative risk assessment. Blue shade – activity performed by AI.*

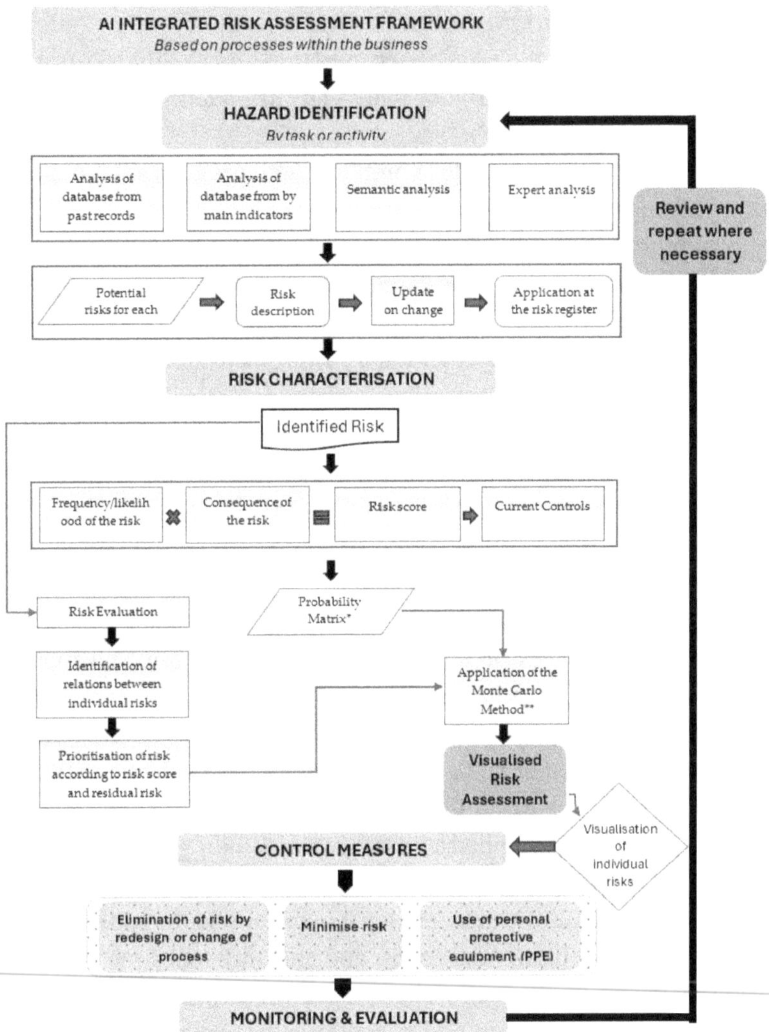

1.1 AI for Risk Assessment and Predictive Analytics

Artificial Intelligence (AI) is revolutionising occupational health risk assessment by enabling predictive analytics that leverage both historical and real-time data. These capabilities allow organisations to shift from reactive to proactive safety measures, forecasting potential hazards, exposure risks, and disease outbreaks before they escalate. Machine learning (ML) algorithms identify patterns across various data points, including past exposures, infection trends, environmental metrics, and worker behaviours, thereby generating early warnings that support targeted mitigation strategies and reduce work-related illnesses. In particular, AI enhances Quantitative Microbial Risk Assessment (QMRA) by enabling more accurate and efficient analysis of large, complex datasets, such as those from air quality monitoring systems. This is especially valuable in indoor environments like office buildings, where microbial risks, such as gram-negative bacteria, can be underestimated even when hazard quotient (HQ) and hazard index (HI) values appear low (Abhaysinh, Swapnil, Neenu et al., 2024). In dynamic environments like wastewater treatment plants (WWTPs), AI-driven QMRA enables real-time monitoring of microbial concentrations, facilitating rapid interventions. These tools have been used to assess health risks from bioaerosol exposure and guide exposure limit setting, particularly for pathogens like adenovirus and gram-negative bacteria (Annalaura, Gabriele, Lorenzo et al., 2018).

Predictive analytics also plays a critical role in high-risk settings such as laboratories, healthcare facilities, and agricultural operations, where early identification of biological hazards is essential. AI models use real-time data from environmental and epidemiological sources to warn of potential viral or bacterial outbreaks, allowing organisations to implement timely interventions (Nicolas Bono, Luca, Speranza et al., 2023, Chen, He, Zhao et al., 2024, Martin, Rikard & David, 2024). This integration improves the speed, accuracy, and responsiveness of occupational health measures. AI-powered predictive models can provide early warnings to healthcare professionals about potential viral or bacterial outbreaks, using data from epidemiological reports and environmental monitoring (Martin, Rikard & David, 2024). By incorporating real-time data, these models enable organisations to take proactive measures before risks intensify, reducing the potential impact of biological hazards in the workplace. With AI integration, these assessments become more robust, allowing for faster detection of microbial threats and enhancing the effectiveness of occupational health interventions.

Beyond prediction, AI enhances risk management by supporting dynamic decision-making. Advanced models, such as Artificial Neural Networks (ANNs) and Evolutionary Multi-Objective Optimisation (EMO), continually update hazard profiles, enabling adaptive risk assessments. These tools can also inform the design of work schedules that limit prolonged exposure to biological agents and assess worker responses to stressors, contributing to more holistic health protection strategies. An example of AI-integrated risk management is the REDECA framework (Risk Evolution, Detection, Evaluation, and Control of Accidents), which has been applied across sectors including mining, agriculture, construction, and transport (Pishgar, Issa, Sietsema et al., 2021). By synthesising findings from over 260 AI-focused studies, the framework highlights the role of technologies such as sensors and actuators in automating risk detection, removing workers from hazardous zones, and enabling real-time safety interventions. These tools improve decision-making, compliance, and hazard control, ultimately advancing occupational safety standards (El-Helaly, 2024). In rural settings, where outbreaks can overwhelm limited infrastructure, AI provides critical insights into disease spread and supports early containment strategies. Predictive models can analyse mobility, environmental conditions, and historical infection data to forecast outbreaks and guide efficient resource allocation (Ejike Innocent, Ebube Victor, Mojeed Dayo et al., 2024). While the potential is significant, challenges such as inconsistent data quality, infrastructure gaps, and inequitable access to AI technologies must be addressed to fully realise AI's value in risk reduction and epidemic preparedness in underserved areas.

1.2 Automated Monitoring Systems for Real-Time Hazard Assessment

The integration of AI-driven sensors and IoT technologies is transforming real-time hazard assessment in occupational settings. These systems continuously monitor environmental conditions, enabling rapid detection of microbial contaminants, assessment of air quality, and identification of biological risks. By providing instant, data-driven insights, AI enhances proactive safety measures, reducing the likelihood of workplace-related health incidents. One example is the Automated Real-Time Bioaerosol Sampler based on Wet-Cyclone (ARBSW) developed by Cho et al. (2019), which continuously monitors airborne microorganisms with over 95% collection efficiency for particles >0.5 μm. Integrated with analytical sensors, ARBSW enables rapid microbial exposure assessment and stable microbial recovery, making it suitable for high-risk occupational environments (Cho, Hong, Choi et al., 2019).

Similarly, the Bioaerosol Auto-Monitoring Instrument (BAMI), designed for detecting airborne fungal species such as *Aspergillus niger* and *Alternaria alternata*, utilises carbon nanotube-based biosensors in conjunction with microfluidics and cooling systems. BAMI enables real-time detection and sensor regeneration, demonstrating high sensitivity and extended operational capabilities (Kim, Jin, Kim et al., 2016). Other applications extend beyond occupational air quality. For instance, Sudki et al. (2023) used multispectral imaging combined with machine learning to detect fungal contamination in peanut seeds. Texture, reflectance, and colour data were found to be highly effective in assessing sanitary quality, highlighting the broader potential of AI-driven biosurveillance for both occupational and environmental health (Sudki, Fonseca de Oliveira, de Medeiros et al., 2023). For biothreat detection, AI-powered microscopy platforms have been developed for pathogens such as *Bacillus anthracis*. These systems offer real-time, sensor-based detection of biological agents without the need for direct sampling, which is particularly advantageous in inaccessible or hazardous settings (János & Anna, 2024) In water-related environments, Dharani et al. (2024) introduced an IoT-enabled embedded system for monitoring bacterial contamination in drinking water. The system, controlled by Arduino microcontrollers and linked to the Ubidots platform, uses sensors to track temperature, pH, and TDS levels. It automatically activates UV disinfection when contamination is detected, enhancing water safety in occupational settings. In healthcare, real-time disinfection monitoring is gaining traction (Dharani, Endluru Raga, Erragropula et al., 2024).

Rittick et al. (2023) developed an infrared (IR) camera-based system to assess cleanliness in hospital operating rooms. This system uses machine learning algorithms to identify missed or inadequately cleaned areas during disinfection procedures. By integrating with Raspberry Pi or computer systems, it provides real-time alerts, visual indicators, and safety assurance for healthcare workers. These innovations represent a shift from manual, labour-intensive monitoring to automated, intelligent systems that improve response time, safety compliance, and infection prevention. While challenges such as camera calibration, ambient lighting interference, and image processing efficiency persist, future enhancements may include data logging, long-term trend analysis, and broader integration with occupational safety protocols (Rittick, Sachin, Mandar Bhalchandra et al., 2023).

1.3 AI in Pandemic Preparedness and Risk Mitigation

Artificial Intelligence (AI) has become an essential tool in pandemic preparedness, offering powerful capabilities for outbreak surveillance, risk mitigation, and emergency planning. By leveraging machine learning and big data analytics, AI facilitates real-time monitoring of disease transmission, enabling the identification of high-risk areas and prediction of infection trends. These insights support timely, targeted interventions that help reduce workplace disruptions, protect workers, and safeguard broader public health during crises. In addition, AI enhances healthcare system resilience by optimising resource allocation, minimising healthcare worker exposure, and informing public health decisions through scenario-based modelling of intervention strategies (Martin, Rikard & David, 2024). In the workplace context, AI-driven data mining significantly improves microbial risk assessment by analysing vast, near real-time datasets from multiple sources. This autonomous biosurveillance approach enhances the precision and timeliness of outbreak predictions and supports evidence-based decision-making to mitigate both known and emerging biothreats (Lapitan, 2024).

A major contribution of AI in pandemic management lies in its ability to simulate disease transmission dynamics and evaluate containment measures. Machine learning integrated with epidemiological models enables simulations of policy impacts, such as quarantine enforcement, vaccination coverage, and social distancing, to assess potential outcomes and guide response strategies. During the COVID-19 pandemic, such models proved critical for informing real-time public health actions (Khalili & Wimmer, 2024). Khalili and Wimmer emphasised the importance of explainable AI (XAI) for building trust in AI-generated predictions and supporting transparent policy development. They proposed a conceptual framework to refine existing AI pipelines and close critical research gaps.

AI has also shown particular value in underserved and rural regions. Ejike et al. (2024) demonstrated how predictive analytics can assess transmission patterns and forecast future outbreaks by integrating data on mobility, environment, and healthcare access. This allows for early interventions and more efficient allocation of limited resources, enhancing epidemic control in vulnerable communities (Ejike Innocent, Ebube Victor, Mojeed Dayo et al., 2024). To ensure effectiveness, AI systems used in pandemic risk assessment must be designed for flexibility, transparency, and user interaction. As Amershi et al. (2019) suggest, AI refinement processes should include simulation environments, testing-and-retraining loops, and service-scoping strategies when AI is uncertain. AI systems should also allow users to fill in missing data, interpret or veto predictions, and receive real-time feedback to support safe, responsible decision-making (Amershi, Weld, Vorvoreanu et al., 2019). Westhoven and Herrmann (2023) further argue that in the workplace, AI risk assessment tools should promote user self-reflection, flag anomalies, and double-check performance without requiring constant intervention. While these systems offer tremendous value, organisational readiness, responsible oversight, and human-centred AI (HCAI) practices are critical for ensuring their safe integration into occupational health frameworks, especially as many such systems are still in developmental or experimental stages (Westhoven & Herrmann, 2023).

1.4 AI-Driven Human-Robot Collaboration in Hazardous Work Environments

AI-powered robotics is transforming workplace safety by reducing human exposure to hazardous biological agents in high-risk occupational settings (Bohdan, 2024). In sectors such as healthcare, biotechnology, manufacturing, and agriculture, AI-enabled robots are increasingly deployed to perform tasks involving biohazards, toxic substances, and infectious agents. These systems automate high-risk activities, including specimen handling, decontamination, and material transport, enhancing both worker protection and operational efficiency (Table 4).

Table 4. Table showing various industries where AI is used for biorisk management, along with specific applications in each sector.

Industry	Application of AI in Biorisk Management	Reference
Healthcare	- Using predictive analytics to control and manage infections more effectively.	(Hooshmand, Toledo, Moghaddas et al., 2022)
	- Employing AI-driven robots to safely handle infectious agents, especially during pandemics reducing the risk of exposure.	(Galetsi, Katsaliaki & Kumar, 2022)
	- Automating monitoring systems to quickly detect pathogens healthcare environments.	(Ça layan, Barnes, Pineles et al., 2022)
	- Leveraging AI tools to predict and model potential disease outbreaks before they happen.	(Ankolekar, Eppings, Bottari et al., 2024)
Pharmaceutical/ Biotechnology	- Applying AI to predict exposure risks during drug development, helping manage risks more effectively. While the study does not directly address biohazard exposure, it highlights the application of algorithms in exposure assessment and risk management in the industry.	(Patricia, Jody, Marie et al., 2011)
	- Automating biomanufacturing processes to reduce workers' exposure to hazardous biological materials	(Schmidt, Alina & Jochen, 2024)
	- Using AI systems for tracking and ensuring compliance with biocontainment protocols. The concept can be applied to biocontainment protocols in pharmaceuticals.	(Tushar, Abhishek & Wong, 2024)
Agriculture	- Monitoring livestock for zoonotic disease risks with the help of AI-enabled tools.	(Wenqiang, Chenrui, Meng et al., 2023)
	- Predicting the spread of zoonotic diseases and pest-related outbreaks using AI models.	(Nicolas Bono, Luca, Speranza et al., 2023, Chen, He, Zhao et al., 2024, Lapitan, 2024)
	- Automating high-risk tasks like farm disinfection and waste management to improve safety.	(Carlos, 2020, Julius Kewir, Mathias & John Ngansi, 2021)
Wastewater Treatment	- Detecting airborne pathogens and harmful contaminants in treatment facilities with AI-based monitoring tools.	(Calvin, Frederic, Zoran et al., 2023)
	- Using predictive analytics to monitor air and water quality in real-time, providing early warnings of potential hazards. Rose et al demonstrated the use of predictive analytics for water quality in potable water but similar applications can be applied to wastewater treatment.	(Hsiang-Yang, Cynthia, Robert et al., 2023, Joan, Nynke, Hollmann et al., 2023)
Food Processing	- Using AI systems for detecting microbial contamination during food production and packaging processes.	(Aggarwal, Mishra, Tabassum et al., 2024, Vilhouphrenuo, Angel Elizabeth, Joel et al., 2024)
	- Automating safety and hygiene protocols to maintain strict contamination controls.	(Anuja, Sumisha, Sachin Shaju et al., 2024)
Manufacturing (Biotechnology)	- Utilising AI systems to handle and safely dispose of biohazardous materials during the manufacturing processes, reducing human risk.	(Ria, WeiHuang, Anélie et al., 2023, Sengeni, Padmapriya, Imambi et al., 2023)
	- Predicting maintenance needs for biocontainment systems to prevent breakdowns and malfunctions, thus preventing possible releasing of biological agents.	(Ibatulin, 2023)

continued on following page

Table 4. Continued

Industry	Application of AI in Biorisk Management	Reference
Chemical and Hazardous Materials	- Using AI models to predict risks associated with exposure to harmful chemicals and toxins, which are by-products of biological agents (e.g. endotoxin, aflatoxin, mycotoxin).	(Aggarwal, Mishra, Tabassum et al., 2024)
	- Monitoring of air quality and hazardous chemical levels in environments using AI-powered real-time systems. The application can be used to detect exposure on clinical significance in the work environment.	(Marco Camardo, Marco, Sihem et al., 2021)
Agricultural Processing Plants	- Predicting respiratory health risks associated with exposure to bioaerosols from grains, fungi, and other biological matter using modelling.	(Justin, Yanhao, Mark et al., 2023)
	- Using AI-driven robotics to handle biological materials, minimising direct human contact and exposure risks.	(Dayana, Thummala, Bhagyalakshmi et al., 2024, Dwivedi & Ritesh Arvind, 2024)
Research Laboratories	- Managing risks in high-level biosafety labs (BSL) with AI systems that track and monitor potential exposures or bioindicators to biohazards.	(Raj Kumar, 2024)
	- Implementing AI-powered surveillance systems to ensure strict compliance with laboratory safety protocols.	(Luqman, Alnajjar, Parambil et al., 2022)

Austin (2017) highlighted the benefits of robotic assistance in infectious disease environments like Ebola treatment units, where care staff faced high exposure risks and heavy workloads. Introducing robots in such settings can alleviate cognitive load, support optimal task sharing, and safeguard healthcare workers (Austin, 2017). During the COVID-19 pandemic, robots were successfully used in geriatric units and other high-risk environments to minimise close contact between healthcare workers and patients, significantly reducing transmission risks (Raul, Youssef, Víctor et al., 2021). Smart robots integrated with IoT technologies offer additional safety features, such as face mask detection, temperature screening, hand sanitisation, and social distancing enforcement (Ahmed, Alam, Hossain et al., 2022). These capabilities contribute to infection prevention in public and workplace settings by encouraging hygienic behaviour and mitigating the spread of pathogens. Chien-Yu and Kuu-Young (2023) further showcased the effectiveness of autonomous robotic disinfection systems in hospitals, particularly in hard-to-reach areas like fever stations and isolation wards. These robots improve infection control by minimising human contact during critical cleaning operations (Chien-Yu & Kuu-Young, 2023).

AI also enhances robotic responsiveness by monitoring human behaviour and predicting unsafe actions in real time. In biosafety laboratories and similar high-containment environments, autonomous robotic arms are used to manipulate fragile or hazardous biological materials. This reduces the likelihood of contamination and injury while maintaining precision and safety (Aaron, Rohan, Konguvel et al., 2024). Similarly, Robotics Autonomous Systems (RAS) are being implemented in food and biosafety laboratories to automate tasks involving high-risk substances, thereby improving laboratory efficiency and reducing occupational health risks (Ananth, Vanapalli, Shanthilal et al., 2024). Angelopoulos et al. (2024) emphasised the potential of robotics to conduct complex experiments safely and accurately, particularly in biosafety laboratories. These intelligent robotic systems are capable of adapting to new tasks through machine learning, further reducing human exposure to biohazards (Angelopoulos, Cahoon & Alterovitz, 2024). Through intelligent automation, adaptive learning, and real-time responsiveness, AI-driven robotics is redefining safety protocols in hazardous workplaces. As these technologies continue to evolve, their integration into occupational health frameworks will be vital for enhancing safety, reducing biological exposure, and enabling more resilient and sustainable work environments.

SECTION 2: PRACTICAL APPLICATIONS OF AI IN BIORISK MANAGEMENT

Artificial Intelligence (AI) is revolutionising BRM in occupational settings by enabling more efficient, accurate, and data-driven approaches to identifying, assessing, treating, and monitoring biological hazards. From real-time biosurveillance and automated compliance systems to predictive disease modelling and smart environmental controls, AI technologies support a fundamental shift from reactive to proactive risk management. This section explores the practical applications of AI in BRM, drawing on case studies from high-risk industries to demonstrate how these innovations are enhancing worker safety, strengthening outbreak response, and supporting regulatory adherence.

2.1 AI for Risk Detection and Early Warning

AI is transforming the early detection of biological hazards through advanced pattern recognition, predictive algorithms, and anomaly detection. These tools strengthen the risk identification phase of BRM by detecting potential threats before they escalate into occupational outbreaks or exposures.

– Smart Surveillance in Wastewater Plants and Laboratory Environments

AI is increasingly used in environmental biosurveillance to monitor airborne biological hazards in real time.

Example: In high-risk industries such as wastewater treatment, agriculture, and manufacturing, AI-enabled air quality monitoring systems track fluctuations in pollutants and bioaerosols. The Bioaerosol Automonitoring Instrument (BAMI), for example, integrates carbon nanotube field-effect transistors (CNT-FETs) with a sampler, cooler, and pump to continuously detect airborne fungal particles. Its modular design supports multiple pathogen detections and includes features like air-to-liquid sampling, sensor regeneration, and nanomaterial-based detection, enhancing both sensitivity and real-time responsiveness. Future developments aim to further miniaturise these systems for widespread industrial use, especially where continuous bioaerosol surveillance is vital (Kim, Jin, Kim et al., 2016). In addition, the global need for microbial water quality monitoring, particularly in low-resource or unequal access settings, is growing. AI-driven platforms offer real-time logging, automated data analysis, and standardisation to support microbial risk assessment in wastewater treatment and water security efforts (Joan, Nynke, Hollmann et al., 2023). These applications can be useful in identifying risk in wastewater treatment plants.

– Thermal Scanning and Symptom Detection

AI-enhanced thermal imaging systems are used to detect early symptoms of infection and reduce workplace transmission risks.

Example: AI-powered systems can screen workers for elevated body temperatures in real time, minimising congestion at entry points and triggering immediate health interventions. One system scans at 8.3 frames per second using thermal cameras and computer vision to calculate accurate core body temperatures, offering rapid, non-contact health assessments (Shah & Mishra, 2024).

– Robotic Monitoring Systems

AI-driven robotic systems help limit human exposure to contagious diseases by automating infection control tasks.

Example: During the COVID-19 pandemic, smart robots were deployed in healthcare settings to detect fever, enforce mask use, dispense sanitiser, and perform disinfection tasks (Figure 5). These systems, integrated with IoT and AI, enabled continuous environmental monitoring and reduced the burden on frontline workers (Chien-Yu & Kuu-Young, 2023). Low-cost deployments in countries like Bangladesh and India, and potentially in African contexts, highlight the feasibility of using robotics to enhance workplace biosafety (Ahmed, Alam, Hossain et al., 2022).

Figure 5. Photograph showing smart robot scanning person to identify whether they are wearing a face mask (Left: no face mack, right: face mask). Adapted from Ahmed et al (2022).(Ahmed, Alam, Hossain et al., 2022)

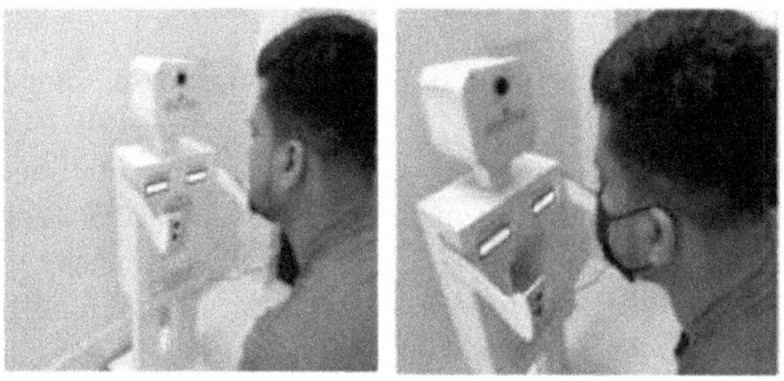

2.2 AI in Real-Time Environmental Monitoring and Biosensors

The integration of AI with environmental sensors has revolutionised workplace biosafety by enabling real-time detection of biological hazards in air, water, and surfaces. These smart systems enhance exposure monitoring, situational awareness, and rapid response, especially in high-risk environments like wastewater treatment, agriculture, and food processing industries.

– Air Quality and Bioaerosol Monitoring

AI-enabled ventilation and biosensor systems continuously track airborne pathogens, microbial volatile organic compounds, and fungal spores to maintain safe indoor air quality.

***Example*:** In wastewater treatment plants, smart ventilation systems adjust airflow in response to pathogen levels detected by real-time bioaerosol monitors. Instruments like BAMI (Bioaerosol Automonitoring Instrument) detect airborne fungal species using CNT-FET biosensors and microfluidic samplers, offering modular, in situ surveillance critical for occupational health (Kim, Jin, Kim et al., 2016).

– Mycotoxin Detection in Agriculture

AI combined with smart sensing technologies is increasingly used to detect toxic fungal by-products like mycotoxins in agricultural environments.

Example: Mycotoxins, dangerous toxins produced by certain fungi, pose significant risks to food safety, occupational health, and global public health. Traditional detection methods, such as chromatography and mass spectrometry, are accurate but require complex procedures, specialised equipment, and trained personnel. Recently, AI has emerged as a powerful tool to enhance mycotoxin detection by enabling faster, less invasive, and highly accurate analysis. AI techniques, including DL, ML, and neural networks, are increasingly being integrated with smart sensing technologies like spectroscopy, biosensors, and imaging systems to detect fungal contamination in food products (Aggarwal, Mishra, Tabassum et al., 2024). A review by Aggarwal et al. (2024) highlighted the advantages of AI-based systems, noting improvements in detection speed, cost-effectiveness, and reliability. However, their effectiveness relies heavily on access to large, high-quality training datasets (Aggarwal, Mishra, Tabassum et al., 2024). In peanuts, which are especially prone to aflatoxin B1 (AFB1) contamination during storage, AI models such as genetic algorithms (GA), backpropagation neural networks (BPNN), and support vector regression (SVR) have achieved high classification accuracy. Sudki et al. (2023) also demonstrated that algorithms like SVM, artificial neural networks (ANN), and adaptive neuro-fuzzy inference systems (ANFIS) reached near-perfect detection rates under controlled lighting (Sudki, Fonseca de Oliveira, de Medeiros et al., 2023). In wheat, deep learning approaches such as convolutional neural networks (CNNs) have shown precision levels of up to 99% in identifying Fusarium head blight (FHB) using standard RGB imaging. Additionally, transfer learning models and random forest (RF) classifiers have successfully predicted multiple mycotoxin types, with validation accuracies reaching 99% (Bernardes, De Medeiros, da Silva et al., 2022). These advancements offer promising applications in occupational health by enhancing early detection of biological contaminants in agricultural settings and food supply chains.

Example 1: While the review by Aggarwal et al. (2024) primarily focused on mycotoxin contamination in food products, occupational exposure to mycotoxins has also been reported in several high-risk professions, particularly in animal husbandry and the processing of grain cereals and animal feed (Wangia, Tang & Wang, 2019). Innovative tools like electronic noses (e-noses), which detect volatile organic compounds associated with fungal contamination, have been paired with machine learning (ML) algorithms to enable rapid and cost-effective detection. For instance, the "AIR PEN 3" device, when combined with classification and regression tree (CART) algorithms, achieved an accuracy rate of 83% in identifying contamination (Camardo Leggieri, Mazzoni, Fodil et al., 2021, Aggarwal, Mishra, Tabassum et al., 2024). These technologies hold significant promise for the early detection of occupational exposures to mycotoxins and their by-products, particularly in settings where continuous monitoring is critical for protecting worker health.

– Water Contamination Monitoring

AI-powered models are increasingly applied in monitoring microbial water quality and predicting contamination in wastewater and rural water systems.

Example: Hsiang-Yang et al. (2023) developed a remote monitoring system for on-site wastewater treatment systems (OWTS) using soft sensors and machine learning to predict chemical and microbial indicators like COD, TSS, and *E. coli*. While COD and TSS predictions achieved high accuracy ($R^2 > 0.95$), E. coli forecasts were less reliable, indicating a need for enhanced microbial data integration (Hsiang-Yang, Cynthia, Robert et al., 2023).

Example: In a separate study, wastewater-based epidemiology (WBE) was enhanced using hydraulic modelling and ML to trace pathogen hotspots in sewer networks. Although effective, model accuracy depended on high-resolution monitoring data and system-specific configurations (Calvin, Frederic, Zoran et al., 2023). This approach holds promise for rapid back-tracing of infectious agents and other biomarkers in occupational health surveillance.

2.3 AI for Predictive Modelling and Disease Forecasting

Artificial Intelligence (AI), particularly ML and deep learning (DL), has transformed disease forecasting by enabling advanced data-driven risk assessments in both occupational and public health settings. These technologies can analyse large, complex, and heterogeneous datasets, including clinical, environmental, and behavioural data, to anticipate disease outbreaks, monitor illness trends, and guide timely interventions.

– Zoonotic and Vectorborne Disease Prediction

Zoonotic diseases such as avian influenza, leptospirosis, and Ebola pose ongoing threats to high-risk sectors like agriculture, animal husbandry, and healthcare. Traditional surveillance often fails to detect early warning signals due to time lags and limited data integration. AI-based models address these gaps by processing time-series data, climatic indicators, and pathogen characteristics to detect subtle patterns that precede outbreaks.

Example: Chun-Rong et al. (2024) developed hybrid LSTM models to predict zoonotic disease incidence across regions in China. By decomposing time-series data into trend and seasonal components, the hybrid model outperformed standalone LSTM models in forecasting accuracy, demonstrating how structured time-series inputs enhance model precision and epidemic foresight (Chen, He, Zhao et al., 2024). The raw data is sourced from the Scientific Data Center of the National Ministry of Health of China (Figure 6A), the seasonal, trend and random components are shown on the left, while the graph of the three sequences is presented on the right (Figure 6B). Figure 6C shows the stage involving a comparison of the seasonal component's life cycle and amplification, and Figure 6D illustrates the operational process of the LSTM function. AI-based algorithms analyse vast datasets of human and animal health information, environmental factors, and pathogen characteristics to predict disease outbreaks and transmission patterns (Wenqiang, Chenrui, Meng et al., 2023).

Figure 6. Flowchart of LSTM-based risk prediction modelling extracted from Chen (2024).(Chen, He, Zhao et al., 2024)

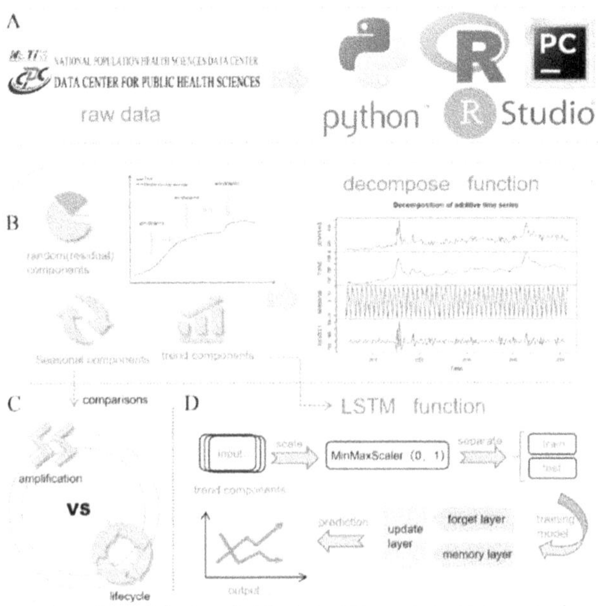

Example: AI techniques such as artificial neural networks (ANN) have also been used to forecast leptospirosis outbreaks based on environmental conditions like temperature, rainfall, and humidity. One study achieved over 84% accuracy and 86% sensitivity using ANN models (Rahmat, Zulkafli, Juraiza Ishak et al., 2020). Additional models incorporating soil composition and land-use data further improved performance (Mohammadinia, Saeidian, Pradhan et al., 2019, Wenqiang, Chenrui, Meng et al., 2023).

Example: To improve Ebola Virus Disease (EVD) prediction, researchers have applied hybrid AI algorithms combining neural networks and genetic algorithms to estimate outbreak timing and scale using epidemiological, environmental, and immunological datasets. This approach offers a scalable model for forecasting future outbreaks in resource-limited settings like Nigeria (Wenqiang, Chenrui, Meng et al., 2023).

– COVID-19 Spread Modelling and Forecasting

The COVID-19 pandemic highlighted the critical role of AI in predicting disease transmission, informing policy decisions, and protecting public and occupational health. By analysing large-scale, real-time datasets, AI tools enabled early detection of viral hotspots, optimised healthcare responses, and guided preventive strategies across industries.

Example: AI-powered surveillance platforms like BlueDot and HealthMap successfully identified emerging COVID-19 hotspots by analysing global travel data, news reports, and social media posts. These tools helped authorities and employers implement pre-emptive containment measures such as travel restrictions and quarantine protocols, mitigating transmission risks before outbreaks escalated (Shausan, Nazarathy & Dyda, 2023).

Example: AI also proved essential in patient outcome forecasting. Predictive models were used to identify individuals at higher risk of severe illness or mortality, such as those likely to develop acute respiratory distress syndrome or require hospitalisation. These insights supported triage decisions and resource planning, which are also critical in occupational settings for maintaining workforce stability and business continuity (Bullock, Alexandra, Luccioni et al., 2020). Similar models were used during the MERS-CoV outbreak to predict patient prognosis based on age, comorbidities, disease severity, and occupational risk (John & Shaiba, 2019, Raul, Youssef, Víctor et al., 2021).

Example: For diseases like Ebola, AI-driven network-based models have been applied to simulate viral transmission. Riad et al. (2019) developed a two-layer temporal contact network using the Gillespie algorithm to model Ebola Virus Disease (EVD) spread in Uganda. The model accounted for both permanent and transient human interactions, showing how preventive measures, such as limiting contact, could reduce outbreak magnitude. These techniques are applicable to occupational settings where close contact between workers can accelerate disease transmission (Riad, Sekamatte, Ocom et al., 2019). Beyond modelling transmission, AI has played a key role in healthcare system preparedness. Big Data Analytics (BDA) and AI-based simulations have been used to test intervention strategies, support vaccine development, and predict healthcare system strain (Bansal, Padappayil, Garg et al., 2020, Galetsi, Katsaliaki & Kumar, 2022).

Additionally, technologies like drones and surveillance cameras equipped with AI-based models for enforcing social isolation have been reported (Figure 7). These tools can help in decision-making in managing biological hazards and enhancing pandemic preparedness (Ahmed, Ahmad, Rodrigues et al., 2021). AI techniques such as Generative Adversarial Networks (GANs) are being used to monitor health indicators like coughing and breathing patterns for early diagnosis (Abdulkareem & Petersen, 2021).

Figure 7. Photographs used for social distance monitoring during COVID-19 (Ahmed, Ahmad, Rodrigues et al., 2021).

Furthermore, the integration of AI into Learning Healthcare Systems (LHS) has enabled adaptive feedback loops for refining clinical guidelines, improving outbreak detection, and enhancing vaccine evaluation (Ankolekar, Eppings, Bottari et al., 2024, Khalili & Wimmer, 2024). These systems hold strong potential for occupational health programmes, particularly in high-risk sectors like healthcare, agriculture, and manufacturing. In laboratory environments, AI tools are streamlining microbial diagnostics and antimicrobial resistance detection, while also contributing to safer lab practices through predictive safety monitoring and error reduction, especially under high-pressure conditions (Meiyong, Zhenni, Anlu et al., 2024, Raj Kumar, 2024). AI-enabled disease forecasting has emerged as a cornerstone of pandemic preparedness, enhancing outbreak prediction, informing evidence-based decisions, and supporting safer workplace operations in the face of emerging infectious threats.

– Disease Forecasting with AI Architectures

A range of AI architectures have been applied for disease prediction, including convolutional neural networks (CNN), LSTM, support vector machines (SVM), and clustering methods. These support hazard characterisation, dose-response modelling, and strategic planning for future biological threats.

Example: Comparative studies using CNN, LSTM, adaptive-network-based fuzzy inference system (ANFIS), and support vector regression demonstrated that ML techniques can outperform traditional models for predicting disease outbreaks, as noted in applications for COVID-19 and MERS-CoV (Kavadi, Patan, Ramachandran et al., 2020). Some AI-based models have reported superior prediction accuracies compared to traditional methods. Researchers have proposed techniques for comparing models using different architectures and trained with non-identical hyperparameters (Ahmed, Ahmad, Rodrigues et al., 2021). These methods enable rapid forecasting and support decision-making in pandemic preparedness.

2.4 AI in Compliance Automation and Safety Enforcement

Artificial Intelligence (AI) is revolutionising OHS compliance by automating monitoring systems, enforcing regulatory standards, and supporting real-time interventions. In high-risk work environments, such as laboratories, hospitals, and industrial facilities, traditional compliance methods often fall short due to inconsistent application or human oversight. AI-driven technologies provide scalable, accurate, and continuous monitoring solutions that strengthen risk treatment, enhance worker accountability, and support ongoing safety training and improvement.

– AI-Powered Laboratory Safety Monitoring

Laboratory settings that handle infectious agents or hazardous biological materials require strict adherence to PPE and safety protocols. Manual checks are often resource-intensive and prone to human error. AI systems using computer vision now offer real-time, automated compliance monitoring.

Example: Ali et al. (2022) developed a smart lab safety monitoring system using the YOLOv5 object detection model, trained on a custom SLS dataset. Deployed in university laboratories, the system accurately identified instances of PPE non-compliance, achieving a mean average precision (mAP) of 77.4% (Figure 8) (Luqman, Alnajjar, Parambil et al., 2022). The system generated automated compliance reports and holds great promise for high-risk environments such as diagnostic laboratories or clinical facilities, especially in settings with high tuberculosis (TB) prevalence, where lapses in safety are often underreported. Although some may view such systems as intrusive, they foster a culture of transparency, accountability, and stronger adherence to occupational health standards.

Figure 8. Overview of the proposed 'smart lab' YOLO model. Extracted from Luqman et al (2022). (Luqman, Alnajjar, Parambil et al., 2022)

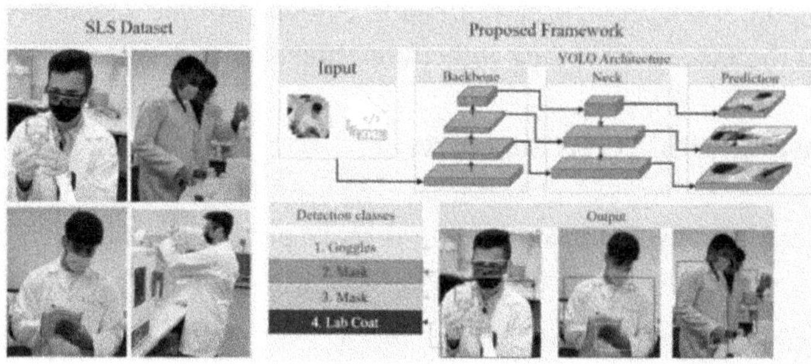

– Predictive Modelling for Infection Control

AI and ML are increasingly used to identify infection risks before clinical symptoms appear, allowing for earlier intervention and more effective infection control strategies.

Example: Çağlayan et al. (2022) developed ML-based models to predict the likelihood of patients becoming colonised with multidrug-resistant organisms (MDROs) upon ICU admission. These models, trained on imbalanced clinical datasets, performed best when combining multiple MDRO types into a single prediction outcome. Such predictive tools are now being adapted to monitor transmission dynamics within healthcare settings and guide preemptive infection control strategies (Ça layan, Barnes, Pineles et al., 2022).

– Real-Time Workplace Risk Alerts

AI is also enabling real-time safety surveillance in industrial and high-exposure environments, where biological hazards may not be visible but can still present serious health threats.

Example: Janaina et al. (2024) developed a comprehensive digital platform that integrates wearable sensors, a web-based employer dashboard, and a mobile app for workers. The system continuously collects data on environmental conditions and individual health indicators, generating personalised risk alerts and safety recommendations. Its machine learning engine analyses trends and suggests mitigation strategies aligned with Industry 5.0 principles and global biosecurity goals This proactive approach supports outbreak prevention, enhances workplace safety, and provides decision-makers with data-driven tools to maintain compliance and protect worker health, even in fast-changing or unpredictable conditions (Anna, 2022).

2.5 AI in Robotics and Automation for Exposure Reduction

In high-risk occupational environments, AI-powered robotics and automation are critical for reducing human exposure to biological hazards. These systems perform routine, hazardous, or high-contact tasks, enhancing safety, maintaining operational continuity, and supporting engineered controls in BRM.

– Robotic Automation in Diagnostic Laboratories

Diagnostic laboratories are particularly vulnerable during infectious disease outbreaks. AI-integrated robotic arms can process high volumes of diagnostic samples, automating pipetting, handling, and analysis, minimising human contact and reducing nosocomial infection risks.

Example: During the COVID-19 pandemic, laboratories used AI-powered robots to handle thousands of test samples daily, reducing occupational exposure and improving workflow efficiency.

– Autonomous Robots in Isolation Wards

In clinical settings, robots equipped with navigation and automation capabilities support patient care while minimising healthcare worker exposure.

Example: Hospitals deployed AI-enabled robots to deliver medication, food, and supplies to COVID-19 patients in isolation wards. This reduced PPE usage and limited staff exposure. These technologies are particularly relevant in high-pathogen settings, such as TB wards in countries like South Africa, where compliance remains a challenge despite formal training (Matuka, Duba, Ngcobo et al., 2021).

– Smart Automation in Agricultural and Animal Health Settings

AI is increasingly used in agriculture and animal husbandry to detect zoonotic threats and automate high-risk tasks.

Example: In agricultural and livestock settings, AI-driven sensors and automated systems monitor environmental conditions, detect zoonotic pathogens (e.g. viruses, bacteria, and allergens), and trigger alerts when levels exceed safe thresholds. These warnings enable immediate interventions, such as improved ventilation or worker relocation, mitigating health risks in real-time (Tangorra, Buoio, Calcante et al., 2024).

Example: A solar-powered automated farm management system using Arduino components, sensors, and GSM modules was developed to reduce human-animal contact. It automated sanitation and feeding processes and supported physical distancing during COVID-19, achieving over 83% efficiency (Julius Kewir, Mathias & John Ngansi, 2021).

2.6 AI in Contact Tracing and Surveillance

AI has revolutionised contact tracing and outbreak surveillance by enabling real-time tracking, predictive modelling, and automated alerts. These systems are vital in occupational settings where rapid containment of infectious diseases is crucial.

– AI-Powered Mobile and Bluetooth-Based Contact Tracing

Bluetooth-enabled mobile applications trace contacts automatically, reducing reliance on manual methods and accelerating intervention.

Example: Ferretti et al. developed a real-time contact tracing system that notified users exposed to confirmed COVID-19 cases. The tool improved quarantine adherence and protected essential workforce continuity (Ferretti, Wymant, Petrie et al., 2024).

– IoT-Based Real-Time Tracing Platforms

By integrating IoT technologies with ML algorithms, AI-based systems can monitor health symptoms and contact patterns in real time, even across large occupational populations.

Example: Wahid et al. created a platform that used ML algorithms to process health data and provide accurate exposure notifications, demonstrating strong applicability in workplace risk mitigation (Wahid, Bukhari, Daud et al., 2023).

– Stochastic and Predictive Modelling of Contact Dynamics

Advanced AI models have also been used to simulate and predict contact chains during disease outbreaks. These models quantify infection risk and epidemic duration, which can help inform public health interventions and workplace protocols.

Example: Kwok et al. developed a stochastic model illustrating how self-reporting behaviours influence outbreak scale, reinforcing the value of digital tracing compliance (Kwok, Tang, Wei et al., 2019).

Example: Keeling et al. demonstrated that well-implemented contact tracing models in the UK significantly improved control of viral illness (ILI), offering valuable insights for other pathogens in occupational settings (Keeling, Hollingsworth & Read, 2020).

SECTION 3: AI IN REGULATORY COMPLIANCE AND POLICY DEVELOPMENT

As AI becomes increasingly integrated into BRM, it offers powerful tools to strengthen regulatory compliance, automate risk reporting, and support evidence-informed OHS policymaking. Technologies such as ML, NLP, and data mining enable real-time monitoring, predictive insights, and adaptive decision-making in high-risk sectors. However, integrating AI into regulatory frameworks also raises ethical, legal, and governance challenges that must be addressed to ensure responsible implementation.

3.1 AI-Enhanced Compliance Monitoring

AI-driven systems are transforming compliance enforcement by automating the detection of unsafe practices, ensuring adherence to regulations, and generating actionable insights for risk mitigation. By analysing data from environmental sensors and wearable devices, AI platforms can identify non-compliance in real time and issue alerts before incidents occur (Karangara, Shende & Kathiriya, 2024). Computer vision tools, such as YOLOv5, have been used to monitor PPE usage in laboratories. A real-time system developed by Luqman et al. (2022) achieved 77.4% mean average precision in identifying safety violations, demonstrating the potential for automated enforcement of lab protocols (Luqman, Alnajjar, Parambil et al., 2022). Despite their benefits, AI compliance tools raise concerns around data privacy, transparency, and accountability. For instance, the EU's General Data Protection Regulation (GDPR) restricts fully automated decision-making without human oversight (GDPR Article 22), reinforcing the need for human-in-the-loop mechanisms and regulatory safeguards (Ankolekar, Eppings, Bottari et al., 2024).

3.2 AI in Evidence-Based Policy Development

AI is increasingly used to inform dynamic, evidence-based OHS policy. By analysing trends in occupational exposures, disease outbreaks, and worker vulnerability, AI models help policymakers anticipate risks and allocate resources more effectively (Priyank & Fahad, 2024). AI algorithms applied to biosurveillance and environmental exposure data have helped prioritise high-risk sectors during pandemic planning, demonstrated in applications like SARS-CoV-2 surveillance in wastewater (Mirakhori & Niazi, 2025). Federated learning enhances the policy relevance of AI by enabling collaborative model training across institutions without compromising data privacy (Feki, Ammar, Kessentini et al., 2021). However, public concerns around privacy and misuse remain. For example, contact tracing apps faced resistance in several countries due to fears of data being repurposed beyond pandemic control (Abdulkareem & Petersen, 2021). To build trust and improve adoption, AI-based policy tools must be accompanied by transparent frameworks outlining data use, protection measures, and stakeholder engagement strategies.

3.3 Ethical, Legal, and Governance Considerations

While AI improves efficiency in OHS compliance and policymaking, it also introduces ethical complexities, especially in workplace surveillance and decision-making. Key concerns include algorithmic bias, data security, autonomy, and fairness, particularly in settings where vulnerable or precarious workers may lack bargaining power (Gallifant, Zhang, Del Pilar Arias Lopez et al., 2022).

International Practice Examples:
– Germany: Requires consent from worker representatives for workplace surveillance under national data protection law.
– France: Mandates prior consultation before introducing digital surveillance in work settings (Salvi Del Pero, Wyckoff & Vourc'h, 2022).
Key Principles for Ethical AI in OHS:
– Transparent and explainable decision-making processes
– Human oversight and the right to contest automated outcomes
– Inclusive stakeholder participation
– Independent audits and regulatory review

A multi-tiered governance approach, combining broad legislation (e.g. data protection, labour laws) with sector-specific regulations, is critical to ensure that AI strengthens worker protections without compromising rights (Stephanidis, Salvendy, Antona et al., 2019). Furthermore, AI can enhance safety training through predictive modelling and immersive simulations, offering realistic environments to rehearse emergency protocols. As these applications expand, regulations should evolve to establish minimum standards for AI-enabled training and simulation tools (Priyank & Fahad, 2024). Table 5 compares conventional OHS policy models with AI-enhanced frameworks, highlighting differences in responsiveness, scalability, data utilisation, and enforcement strategies.

Table 5. Major differences of traditional and AI-enhanced OHS policies (Priyank & Fahad, 2024).

Traditional OHS Policies	AI-Powered OHS Policies	Traditional OHS Policies
Risk Management	Reactive, incident-based	Proactive, predictive analytics-based
Monitoring	Periodic inspections	Continuous real-time monitoring
Data Collection	Manual reporting	Automated data collection via sensors, drones, and wearables
Training	Traditional methods (lectures, manuals)	AI-driven simulations and immersive VR training
Incident Response	Post-incident analysis	Pre-emptive measures and early warnings
Regulatory Compliance	Static compliance checks	Dynamic compliance through real-time data analysis
Worker Involvement	Limited to compliance and reporting	Enhanced engagement with real-time feedback
Data Privacy and Ethics	Basic data protection measures	Comprehensive data privacy and ethical guidelines for AI use
Skill Requirements	Basic safety training	Advanced training in AI tools and technologies
Legal Framework	Established standards and regulations	Evolving standards to include AI capabilities
Cost Implications	High costs due to accidents and non-compliance	Initial high investment, but long-term cost savings through prevention
Decision-Making	Human-based decision-making	AI-assisted decision-making
Flexibility and Adaptability	Rigid and slow to adapt	Flexible, quick to adapt to new data and insights
Worker Health Monitoring	Limited to physical exams	Continuous health monitoring through wearable devices
Incident Documentation	Manual documentation	Automated documentation and analysis
Preventive Measures	Basic preventive measures	Advanced preventive measures using AI predictions
Hazard Identification	Human assessment	AI-powered hazard identification and analysis

SECTION 4: CHALLENGES AND FUTURE DIRECTIONS IN AI-DRIVEN BIORISK MANAGEMENT

The integration of AI into BRM has significantly improved disease detection, predictive modelling, and compliance monitoring. However, its application also presents pressing challenges related to ethics, data governance, technological feasibility, and equitable implementation. Addressing these challenges is critical to ensuring that AI enhances, not compromises, workplace safety, privacy, and fairness.

4.1 Ethical and Privacy Considerations

AI systems in occupational health often process sensitive data such as biometric markers, geolocation, and health indicators, raising concerns around informed consent, surveillance, and algorithmic transparency. The "black box" nature of many AI models limits explainability, undermining trust in automated decisions, especially in emergencies where transparency is vital (Shneiderman, 2020, Zhang, Gao, Wang et al., 2022). Bias in training data can result in discriminatory outcomes, disproportionately impacting vulnerable worker groups. Federated learning and routine algorithm audits can help mitigate these risks, but require regulatory oversight and clear ethical guidelines (Dignum, 2023, Mirakhori & Niazi, 2025). Workplace surveillance tools, especially those used during COVID-19, highlighted the tension between hazard detection and personal privacy. Technologies like facial recognition and real-time health monitoring, if implemented without safeguards, can erode worker autonomy. Solutions include hybrid governance models using federated learning and blockchain to ensure secure, consent-based data use (Gallifant, Zhang, Del Pilar Arias Lopez et al., 2022). To foster trust and accountability, AI governance frameworks should prioritise fairness, human oversight, explainability, and data protection. International initiatives like AI4PEP are working to bridge ethical gaps in low- and middle-income countries (LMICs), ensuring equitable access and responsible deployment of AI tools globally.

4.2 Operational and Technological Barriers

Widespread AI adoption in BRM is hindered by high implementation costs, limited technical infrastructure, and workforce readiness. Small and medium-sized enterprises (SMEs) and LMICs often lack the resources and digital capacity to deploy and sustain AI systems (Demirel Ö, Weingärtner, Moeller et al., 2023). Another major challenge is data quality. AI relies on large, standardised, and representative datasets, but inconsistencies in data collection protocols hamper model accuracy and generalisability. Distributed approaches like federated learning preserve data privacy while supporting cross-institutional collaboration, though technical hurdles, such as model convergence and device heterogeneity, remain (Feki, Ammar, Kessentini et al., 2021). The risk of algorithm overfitting and lack of external validation limits AI's adaptability across different workplaces, regulatory environments, and cultures. To overcome this, multi-stakeholder collaboration, context-specific training, and inclusive design processes are essential.

4.3 AI Risk, Misuse, and Bias

AI systems can misrepresent uncertainty, project beyond valid data scopes, or produce misleading risk assessments, especially in crisis conditions. During COVID-19, models trained on limited or biased data often led to flawed forecasts and misinformed decisions (Tessandra, Jon & Seth, 2022). Failure to include diverse populations in training data can skew results and exacerbate health inequities. Moreover, advanced models such as Generative Adversarial Networks (GANs) and Large Language Models (LLMs) pose unique biosecurity threats, including the potential misuse of AI for engineering harmful biological agents (Sandbrink, 2023). Cyberattacks on AI-driven medical systems, such as falsified imaging data, further illustrate the importance of robust security measures.

Key mitigation strategies include:

- Independent algorithm audits
- Transparency and explainability protocols
- Algorithmic fairness through diverse training datasets
- Secure, privacy-preserving infrastructures

4.4 Future Trends and Innovations

Looking ahead, several AI innovations are poised to reshape BRM:

– **AI-Enabled Biosensors and Digital Twins:** These technologies simulate real-time occupational exposures and responses, particularly in high-risk environments like wastewater plants and hospitals (Demirel Ö, Weingärtner, Moeller et al., 2023) .
– **Predictive Epidemiology:** AI models integrating GIS, mobility data, and climate indicators will enable early outbreak detection and more targeted public health interventions (Sheshadri, Sangeeta & Hatice, 2022).
– **Adaptive Safety Protocols:** Reinforcement learning algorithms will enable real-time updating of safety protocols and hazard controls based on evolving data streams (Yang, 2022).
– **NLP for Policy Interpretation and Training:** NLP tools will assist in translating complex safety regulations into understandable formats and analysing unstructured data for early warnings (Zhang, Diao, Yu et al., 2020, Zhang, Gao, Wang et al., 2022).
– **Immersive Simulation Training:** AR/VR platforms powered by AI will enhance biosafety training and emergency preparedness through experiential learning environments (Dellermann, Calma, Lipusch et al., 2021).
– **Federated Learning and Global Collaboration:** This approach supports secure model training across decentralised nodes, enabling cross-border surveillance while respecting data sovereignty (Feki, Ammar, Kessentini et al., 2021).
– **Inclusive AI Systems:** Equity-focused initiatives such as AI4PEP advocate for scalable, culturally relevant AI tools tailored to LMICs, aligning with the WHO's "Health for All" mandate.
– **Real-Time Decision Support:** AI can transform data into actionable knowledge, such as predicting outbreak severity, mapping risk areas, or guiding resource allocation. Tools like NLP also support rapid synthesis of scientific literature and social signals during health emergencies (Ankolekar, Eppings, Bottari et al., 2024).

SECTION 5: CONCLUSION AND FUTURE DIRECTIONS

Artificial Intelligence (AI) is transforming BRM by enabling predictive analytics, real-time hazard detection, and automation across occupational health and safety domains. AI tools now play an essential role in anticipating and mitigating biological risks, whether through workplace biosurveillance, automated compliance systems, or real-time monitoring of food safety threats like mycotoxins. In the food industry, AI applications such as hyperspectral imaging, biosensors, and machine learning models have demonstrated high accuracy in identifying harmful contaminants. Yet, the full realisation of AI's potential in BRM is contingent on overcoming barriers related to data quality, model adaptability, and contextual application in diverse environments. While the benefits of AI in BRM are clear, its implementation poses a range of challenges, ethical, operational, and technological. Ethical concerns around worker surveillance, data protection, and algorithmic fairness are especially pressing, as AI systems handle large volumes of sensitive information. Transparency in AI decision-making and accountability for outcomes must be prioritised to build public trust and safeguard privacy. Technological barriers, including high deployment costs, infrastructure limitations, and the need for workforce upskilling, particularly affect low-resource settings and small enterprises. A lack of standardised regulatory frameworks further complicates AI integration, reinforcing the need for global governance and inclusive development.

This chapter has outlined how AI is reshaping BRM through case studies, practical tools, and evolving trends. It highlights the critical role of AI-powered systems like collaborative robots (cobots), which support biosafety by automating routine monitoring tasks and enabling dynamic risk assessment. These systems shift BRM from reactive, checklist-based protocols towards continuous, adaptive processes. However, AI is not a replacement for human expertise. Instead, it enhances the capabilities of safety professionals, allowing for data-driven decision-making and strategic interventions that are both timely and evidence-based. Looking forward, the future of AI in BRM hinges on its integration into broader epidemic preparedness and occupational health systems. AI-driven epidemic forecasting models, especially those tailored for rural or under-resourced areas, can offer early warnings and guide resource allocation, provided that investments in data infrastructure and training are prioritised. Advances in machine learning, deep learning, and real-time mobile health monitoring hold promise for personalised outbreak management and improved disease surveillance. Ethical frameworks, interdisciplinary collaboration, and inclusive data practices must underpin these innovations to ensure that AI technologies are deployed equitably and effectively across global contexts. Furthermore, as the field of infectious disease prediction expands, the inclusion of One Health variables, capturing human, animal, and environmental factors, is essential to fully leverage AI for biopreparedness. Future models must be both technically robust and contextually relevant, especially in regions most vulnerable to emerging diseases. Integrating uncertainty assessments and computational efficiency will be crucial to operationalise these tools during real-time emergencies. In conclusion, AI offers a transformative opportunity to modernise BRM, but this transformation must be guided by ethical principles, inclusive strategies, and rigorous governance. By aligning technological innovation with occupational health goals and global public health priorities, AI can deliver smarter, safer, and more sustainable approaches to managing biological risks in the workplace and beyond.

REFERENCES

Aaron, V., V. Rohan, E. Konguvel and R. Sivakumar. (2024) An IoT-Controlled Robotic Hand for Hazardous Material Handling. *Advances in transdisciplinary engineering*.

Abdulkareem, M., & Petersen, S. E. (2021). The Promise of AI in Detection, Diagnosis, and Epidemiology for Combating COVID-19: Beyond the Hype. *Frontiers in Artificial Intelligence*, *4*, 4. DOI: 10.3389/frai.2021.652669 PMID: 34056579

Abhaysinh, R. S., Swapnil, D., Neenu, P. R., & Shalini, T. (2024). Public health risk assessment and speciation of air-borne microorganisms in an office building. *Journal of Aerosol Science*, *179*, 106362. DOI: 10.1016/j.jaerosci.2024.106362

Aggarwal, A. N., Mishra, A., Tabassum, N., Young-Mog, K., & Khan, F. (2024). Detection of Mycotoxin Contamination in Foods Using Artificial Intelligence: A Review. *Foods*, *13*(20), 3339. DOI: 10.3390/foods13203339 PMID: 39456400

Ahmed, I., Ahmad, M., Rodrigues, J. J. P. C., Jeon, G., & Din, S. (2021). A deep learning-based social distance monitoring framework for COVID-19. *Sustainable Cities and Society*, *65*, 102571. DOI: 10.1016/j.scs.2020.102571 PMID: 33163330

Ahmed, S., Alam, R., Hossain, M. R., Islam, M. M., Hossain, M. I., & Tabassum, T. (2022) An IoT based Smart Robot that Aids in the Prevention of COVID19 Spread. *4th International Conference on Sustainable Technologies for Industry 4.0 (STI), Dhaka, Bangladesh*: 1-6. DOI: 10.1109/STI56238.2022.10103253

Ahmed, S., R. Alam, M. R. Hossain, M. M. Islam, M. I. Hossain and T. Tabassum (2022). An IoT based Smart Robot that Aids in the Prevention of COVID19 Spread: 1-6.

Ali, O., Cecilia, T., Edward, K., & Arijit, P. (2024). *Leaping into the Future: Artificial Intelligence for Health*. Safety and Environmental Management.

Amershi, S., Weld, D., Vorvoreanu, M., Fourney, A., Nushi, B., Collisson, P., Suh, J., Iqbal, S., Bennett, P. N., & Inkpen, K. (2019). Guidelines for human-AI interaction. *Proceedings of the 2019 chi conference on human factors in computing systems*. DOI: 10.1145/3290605.3300233

Ananth, M., M. Vanapalli, J. Shanthilal and R. Madhavi. (2024) Robotics Autonomous Systems (RAS) in Food Laboratories are the Future of Food Processing Industries: A Review. *Journal of advances in food science & technology*, 11: 17 - 26.

Angelopoulos, A., Cahoon, J. F., & Alterovitz, R. (2024). Transforming science labs into automated factories of discovery. *Science Robotics*, *9*(95), eadm6991. DOI: 10.1126/scirobotics.adm6991 PMID: 39441898

Aniket, W., A. Sampson and M. Vritik. (2024) Data-Driven Real-Time Surveillance System for Tracking Disease Outbreaks: A Case Study of Lassa Fever Outbreak. 344 - 349.

Ankolekar, A., Eppings, L., Bottari, F., Pinho, I. F., Howard, K., Baker, R., Nan, Y., Xing, X., Walsh, S. L., Vos, W., Yang, G., & Lambin, P. (2024). Using artificial intelligence and predictive modelling to enable learning healthcare systems (LHS) for pandemic preparedness. *Computational and Structural Biotechnology Journal*, *24*, 412–419. DOI: 10.1016/j.csbj.2024.05.014 PMID: 38831762

Anna, G.-P. (2022). Biological Factors in the Workplace—Current Threats to Employees, the Effects of Infections, Prevention Options. *International Journal of Environmental Research and Public Health*, *19*(9), 5592. DOI: 10.3390/ijerph19095592 PMID: 35564987

Annalaura, C., Gabriele, D., Lorenzo, C., Ileana, F., Roberto, L., & Marco, V. (2018). Quantitative Microbial Risk Assessment for Workers Exposed to Bioaerosol in Wastewater Treatment Plants Aimed at the Choice and Setup of Safety Measures. *International Journal of Environmental Research and Public Health*, *15*(7), 1490. DOI: 10.3390/ijerph15071490 PMID: 30011925

Anuja, R., S. Sumisha, J. Sachin Shaju, R. Riya Ann, J. Stephin, J. Laura and V. Devi. (2024) An Automated Alert System for Monitoring the Hygiene in Restaurants Using Machine Vision.

Austin, A. W. (2017) Robot-Human Collaboration for Improving Patient Care in Infectious Disease Environments. *Human-Robot Interaction*: 385 - 386.

Banerjee, R., Bhattacharya, J., & Majumdar, P. (2021). Exponential-growth prediction bias and compliance with safety measures related to COVID-19. *Social Science & Medicine*, *268*, 113473. DOI: 10.1016/j.socscimed.2020.113473 PMID: 33130402

Bansal, A., Padappayil, R. P., Garg, C., Singal, A., Gupta, M., & Klein, A. (2020). Utility of Artificial Intelligence Amidst the COVID 19 Pandemic: A Review. *Journal of Medical Systems*, *44*(9), 156. DOI: 10.1007/s10916-020-01617-3 PMID: 32740678

Bernardes, R. C., De Medeiros, A., da Silva, L., Cantoni, L., Martins, G. F., Mastrangelo, T., Novikov, A., & Mastrangelo, C. B. (2022). Deep-Learning Approach for Fusarium Head Blight Detection in Wheat Seeds Using Low-Cost Imaging Technology. *Agriculture*, *12*(11), 1801. DOI: 10.3390/agriculture12111801

Biolcheva, P. (2021) The place of artificial intelligence in the risk management process. *SHS Web Conf.*, 120: 02013. DOI: 10.1051/shsconf/202112002013

Bohdan, T. (2024) Robotics and artificial intelligence: safety measures and potential threats. *Комунальне господарство міст*, 3: 250 - 258.

Brinati, D., Campagner, A., Ferrari, D., Locatelli, M., Banfi, G., & Cabitza, F. (2020). Detection of COVID-19 Infection from Routine Blood Exams with Machine Learning: A Feasibility Study. *Journal of Medical Systems*, *44*(8), 135. DOI: 10.1007/s10916-020-01597-4 PMID: 32607737

Bullock, J., Luccioni, A., Pham, K. H., Lam, C. S. N., & Luengo-Oroz, M. (2020). Mapping the landscape of artificial intelligence applications against COVID-19. *Journal of Artificial Intelligence Research*, *69*, 807–845.

Burzoni, S., Duquenne, P., Mater, G., & Ferrari, L. (2020). Workplace Biological Risk Assessment: Review of Existing and Description of a Comprehensive Approach. *Atmosphere (Basel)*, *11*(7), 741. DOI: 10.3390/atmos11070741

Cabitza, F., Campagner, A., Ferrari, D., Di Resta, C., Ceriotti, D., Sabetta, E., Colombini, A., De Vecchi, E., Banfi, G., Locatelli, M., & Carobene, A. (2020). Development, evaluation, and validation of machine learning models for COVID-19 detection based on routine blood tests. *Clinical Chemistry and Laboratory Medicine*, *59*(2), 421–431. DOI: 10.1515/cclm-2020-1294 PMID: 33079698

Ça layan, Ç., Barnes, S. L., Pineles, L. L., Harris, A. D., & Klein, E. Y. (2022). A Data-Driven Framework for Identifying Intensive Care Unit Admissions Colonized With Multidrug-Resistant Organisms. *Frontiers in Public Health*, *10*, 853757. DOI: 10.3389/fpubh.2022.853757 PMID: 35372195

Calvin, Z., B. Frederic, V. Zoran, S. Dragan, T. Arlex Sanchez, M. Ole, L. Zlatanovic and A. Yared Abayneh. (2023) Machine Learning for Detecting Virus Infection Hotspots Via Wastewater-Based Epidemiology: The Case of SARS-CoV-2 RNA. 7.

Camardo Leggieri, M., Mazzoni, M., Fodil, S., Moschini, M., Bertuzzi, T., Prandini, A., & Battilani, P. (2021). An electronic nose supported by an artificial neural network for the rapid detection of aflatoxin B1 and fumonisins in maize. *Food Control*, *123*, 107722. DOI: 10.1016/j.foodcont.2020.107722

Carlos, M. G. (2020). Automating the Risk Out of FarmingBy Introducing Both Flexibility and Stability, Automation can Reduce Waste and Overcome Labor Shortages in the Agriculture Industry. *Mechanical Engineering (New York, N.Y.)*, *142*, 32–37.

Cenciarelli, O., M. Andrea, M. Marco, P. Stefano, R. Gallo, F. D. Amico, B. Carlo, R. Fiorito, A. Gucciardino and G. Pasquale. (2013) Evaluation of biohazard management of the Italian national fire brigade. 6: 33 - 41.

Chae, S., Kwon, S., & Lee, D. (2018). Predicting Infectious Disease Using Deep Learning and Big Data. *International Journal of Environmental Research and Public Health*, *15*(8), 1596. DOI: 10.3390/ijerph15081596 PMID: 30060525

Chen, C., Z. He, J. Zhao, X. Zhu, J. Li, X. Wu, Z. Chen, H. Chen and G. Jia. (2024) Zoonotic outbreak risk prediction with long short-term memory models: a case study with schistosomiasis, echinococcosis, and leptospirosis. *BMC Infectious Diseases*, 24.

Chien-Yu, S. and Y. Kuu-Young. (2023) Autonomous Fever Detection, Medicine Delivery, and Environmental Disinfection for Pandemic Prevention. *Applied Sciences*.

Cho, Y. S., Hong, S. C., Choi, J., & Jung, J. H. (2019). Development of an automated wet-cyclone system for rapid, continuous and enriched bioaerosol sampling and its application to real-time detection. *Sensors and Actuators. B, Chemical*, *284*, 525–533. DOI: 10.1016/j.snb.2018.12.155 PMID: 32288254

Dayana, D. S., V. Thummala, A. Bhagyalakshmi, M. Tyj Naga and S. Ushasukhanya. (2024) AI-Controlled Robotics in Smart Agricultural Systems. *Advances in computer and electrical engineering book series*: 351 - 382.

Dellermann, D., Calma, A., Lipusch, N., Weber, T., Weigel, S., & Ebel, P. (2021) The future of human-AI collaboration: a taxonomy of design knowledge for hybrid intelligence systems. *arXiv preprint arXiv:2105.03354*.

Demirel, Ö., Weingärtner, S., Moeller, S., & Akçakaya, M. (2023). Improved Simultaneous Multi-slice imaging with Composition of k-space Interpolations (SMS-COOKIE) for myocardial T1 mapping. *PLoS One*, *18*(7), e0283972. DOI: 10.1371/journal.pone.0283972 PMID: 37478080

Devi, B. R. (2018). MSO–MLP diagnostic approach for detecting DENV serotypes. *International Journal of Pure and Applied Mathematics*, *118*(5), 1–6.

Dharani, N. P., N. Endluru Raga, K. Erragropula, N. Thadamalapula, S. Karanam and S. Nythappagiri. (2024) Real Time Monitoring System for Bacterial Contamination in Drinking Water using Embedded Technology. 280 - 287.

Dharmendra, V. J. and A. C. Robin (2020). Prediction of Occupational Risk at Workplace Using Artificial Neural Network—A Case Study: 769 - 776.

Dignum, V. (2023). Responsible Artificial Intelligence---From Principles to Practice: A Keynote at TheWebConf 2022. ACM SIGIR Forum, ACM New York, NY, USA.

Dwivedi, Y. and P. Ritesh Arvind. (2024) AI Robots in Various Sector. *International journal of innovative science and research technology*: 1926 - 1928.

Ejike Innocent, N., E. Ebube Victor, A. Mojeed Dayo, O. Janet Aderonke and M. Chukwudi Cosmos. (2024) Artificial Intelligence in predictive analytics for epidemic outbreaks in rural populations. *International Journal of Life Science Research Archive*, 7: 078 - 094.

El-Helaly, M. (2024). Artificial Intelligence and Occupational Health and Safety, Benefits and Drawbacks. *La Medicina del Lavoro*, *115*(2), e2024014. DOI: 10.23749/mdl.v115i2.15835 PMID: 38686574

Evangeline, C. and H. Grant (2021). The Future of Biosecurity Surveillance: 261 - 275.

Feki, I., Ammar, S., Kessentini, Y., & Muhammad, K. (2021). Federated learning for COVID-19 screening from Chest X-ray images. *Applied Soft Computing*, *106*, 107330. DOI: 10.1016/j.asoc.2021.107330 PMID: 33776607

Fernando, P.-R. and V. Antonio (2013). Application of Predictive Models in Quantitative Risk Assessment and Risk Management: 87 - 97.

Ferretti, L., Wymant, C., Petrie, J., Tsallis, D., Kendall, M., Ledda, A., Di Lauro, F., Fowler, A., Di Francia, A., Panovska-Griffiths, J., Abeler-Dörner, L., Charalambides, M., Briers, M., & Fraser, C. (2024). Digital measurement of SARS-CoV-2 transmission risk from 7 million contacts. *Nature*, *626*(7997), 145–150. DOI: 10.1038/s41586-023-06952-2 PMID: 38122820

Galetsi, P., Katsaliaki, K., & Kumar, S. (2022). The medical and societal impact of big data analytics and artificial intelligence applications in combating pandemics: A review focused on Covid-19. *Social Science & Medicine*, *301*, 114973. DOI: 10.1016/j.socscimed.2022.114973 PMID: 35452893

Galetsi, P., Katsaliaki, K., & Kumar, S. (2022). The medical and societal impact of big data analytics and artificial intelligence applications in combating pandemics: A review focused on Covid-19. *Social Science & Medicine*, *301*, 114973. DOI: 10.1016/j.socscimed.2022.114973 PMID: 35452893

Gallifant, J., Zhang, J., Del Pilar Arias Lopez, M., Zhu, T., Camporota, L., Celi, L. A., & Formenti, F. (2022). Artificial intelligence for mechanical ventilation: Systematic review of design, reporting standards, and bias. *British Journal of Anaesthesia, 128*(2), 343–351. DOI: 10.1016/j.bja.2021.09.025 PMID: 34772497

Goodfellow, I., J. Pouget-Abadie, M. Mirza, B. Xu, D. Warde-Farley, S. Ozair, A. Courville and Y. Bengio. (2020) Generative adversarial networks. *Commun. ACM*, 63(11): 139–144, 136.

Halim, H. (2024) Spl22 biological hazards in the working environment: a risk of permanent relevance. *Occupational Medicine*, 74: 0.

Hooshmand, M. A., Toledo, C. S., Moghaddas, R., & Skordilis, E. (2022). Data Analytics for Diagnosis and Prediction of Central Line-Associated Bloodstream Infections in Critical Care Units. *Computers, Informatics, Nursing*, *40*(6), 365–372. DOI: 10.1097/CIN.0000000000000794 PMID: 35670636

Hsiang-Yang, S., J. C. Cynthia, B. Robert and H. Y. Daniel. (2023) Development of a Soft Sensor Using Machine Learning Algorithms for Predicting the Water Quality of an Onsite Wastewater Treatment System. *ACS Environmental Au.*

Ibatulin, M. (2023) Development of System and Methods of Predictive Maintenance in Production Using Industrial Sensors. *International Conference on Industrial Engineering, Applications and Manufacturing*: 1119 - 1123.

ILO. (2023). *International Labour Organization. Technical guidelines on biological hazards in the working environment*. International Labour Office.

Inglesby, T. V. and A. A. Adalja (2022). Global catastrophic biological risks: Nature and response: 29 - 42.

Lemos, J., de Souza, V. B., Falcetta, F. S., de Almeida, F. K., Lima, T. M., & Gaspar, P. D. (2024). Enhancing workplace safety through personalized environmental risk assessment: An AI-driven approach in industry 5.0. *Computers*, *13*(5), 120.

Janet Aderonke, O., M. Chukwudi Cosmos, K. Tolulope Olagoke and A. Samira. (2024) Innovations in real-time infectious disease surveillance using AI and mobile data. *International medical science research journal.*

János, P. and M. Anna. (2024) AI-Powered Microscopy Platform for Airborne Biothreat Detection. *Security informatics and law enforcement*: 117 - 127.

Janssen, M., Cski, C., Lindgren, I., Loukis, E., Melin, U., Viale, P. G., Rodrguez, B., Manuel, P., & Tambouris, E. (2022). AI Systems for Occupational Safety and Health: From Ethical Concerns to Limited Legal Solutions. Electronic Government, Springer International Publishing: 499--514.

Jeebhay, M. F., Naidoo, R. N., Naidoo, S., Adams, S., Zungu, M., Kgalomono, S., Naicker, N., & Kistnasamy, B. (2023). Strengthening Social Compact and Innovative Health Sector Collaborations in Addressing COVID-19 in South African Workplaces. *New Solutions*, *32*(4), 288–303. DOI: 10.1177/10482911221150237 PMID: 36650981

Joan, B. R., Nynke, H., Hollmann, E. K., Panagis, K., Gertjan, M., Heather, M. M., Colleen, C. N., & Matthew, E. V. (2023). Global microbial water quality data and predictive analytics: Key to health and meeting SDG 6. *PLOS Water, 2*(8), e0000166. DOI: 10.1371/journal.pwat.0000166

John, H. and A. S. Paul. (2024) Managing workplace AI risks and the future of work. *American Journal of Industrial Medicine.*

John, M., & Shaiba, H. (2019). Main factors influencing recovery in MERS Co-V patients using machine learning. *Journal of Infection and Public Health, 12*(5), 700–704. DOI: 10.1016/j.jiph.2019.03.020 PMID: 30979679

Juan José, T.-P., María Renée, H.-B., Tesifón, P.-C., & Raquel, A.-R. (2022). Biohazard Accidents, Harmful Elements to the Wellness of Healthcare Workers, and Their Risk Factors. [publication_type = article.]. *International Journal of Environmental Research and Public Health, 19*(20), 13214. DOI: 10.3390/ijerph192013214 PMID: 36293794

Julius Kewir, T., N. W. E. Mathias and N. John Ngansi. (2021) Development of a Computerized Automated System for Feed, Water and Sanitation Management in Animal Farms. *Current Journal of Applied Science and Technology*: 1 - 15.

Justin, Y. Y. L., Yanhao, M., Mark, H., & Patrick, K. H. L. (2023). Artificial intelligence-based prediction of indoor bioaerosol concentrations from indoor air quality sensor data. *Environment International, 174*, 107900. DOI: 10.1016/j.envint.2023.107900 PMID: 37012194

Karangara, R., Shende, A., & Kathiriya, S. (2024). Harnessing the Power of AI for Enhanced Regulatory Compliance and Risk Management in Fintech. *International Journal of Computing and Engineering. CARI Journals Limited, 5*(1), 1–11.

Kavadi, D. P., Patan, R., Ramachandran, M., & Gandomi, A. H. (2020). Partial derivative Nonlinear Global Pandemic Machine Learning prediction of COVID 19. *Chaos, Solitons, and Fractals, 139*, 110056. DOI: 10.1016/j.chaos.2020.110056 PMID: 32834609

Keeling, M. J., Hollingsworth, T. D., & Read, J. M. (2020). Efficacy of contact tracing for the containment of the 2019 novel coronavirus (COVID-19). *Journal of Epidemiology and Community Health, 74*(10), 861–866. DOI: 10.1136/jech-2020-214051 PMID: 32576605

Khalili, H., & Wimmer, M. A. (2024). Towards Improved XAI-Based Epidemiological Research into the Next Potential Pandemic. *Life (Chicago, Ill.), 14*(7), 783. DOI: 10.3390/life14070783 PMID: 39063538

Kim, J., & Ahn, I. (2021). Infectious disease outbreak prediction using media articles with machine learning models. *Scientific Reports, 11*(1), 4413. DOI: 10.1038/s41598-021-83926-2 PMID: 33627706

Kim, J., Jin, J. H., Kim, H. S., Song, W., Shin, S. K., Yi, H., Jang, D. H., Shin, S., & Lee, B. Y. (2016). Fully Automated Field-Deployable Bioaerosol Monitoring System Using Carbon Nanotube-Based Biosensors. *Environmental Science & Technology, 50*(10), 5163–5171. DOI: 10.1021/acs.est.5b06361 PMID: 27070239

Krainiuk, O., B. Yu, V. Barbashyn and Y. Mykola. (2023) Use of artificial intelligence for work safety management. *Комунальне господарство міст*, 6: 207 - 213.

Kukar, M., Gunčar, G., Vovko, T., Podnar, S., Černelč, P., Brvar, M., Zalaznik, M., Notar, M., Moškon, S., & Notar, M. (2021). COVID-19 diagnosis by routine blood tests using machine learning. *Scientific Reports*, *11*(1), 10738. DOI: 10.1038/s41598-021-90265-9 PMID: 34031483

Kumar, C. B., Kumar, M. V., Gayathri, T., & Kumar, S. R. (2014). Data analysis and prediction of hepatitis using support vector machine (SVM). *International Journal of Computer Science and Information Technologies*, *5*(2).

Kwok, K. O., Tang, A., Wei, V. W. I., Park, W. H., Yeoh, E. K., & Riley, S. (2019). Epidemic Models of Contact Tracing: Systematic Review of Transmission Studies of Severe Acute Respiratory Syndrome and Middle East Respiratory Syndrome. *Computational and Structural Biotechnology Journal*, *17*, 186–194. DOI: 10.1016/j.csbj.2019.01.003 PMID: 30809323

Lapitan, R. L. (2024). Precognition of Known And Unknown Biothreats: A Risk-Based Approach. *Vector Borne and Zoonotic Diseases (Larchmont, N.Y.)*, *24*(12), 795–801. DOI: 10.1089/vbz.2023.0169 PMID: 39189131

Lee, J. Y. Y., Miao, Y., Chau, R. L. T., Hernandez, M., & Lee, P. K. H. (2023). Artificial intelligence-based prediction of indoor bioaerosol concentrations from indoor air quality sensor data. *Environment International*, *174*, 107900. DOI: 10.1016/j.envint.2023.107900 PMID: 37012194

Lemos, J., Gaspar, P. D., & Lima, T. M. (2022). Environmental Risk Assessment and Management in Industry 4.0: A Review of Technologies and Trends. *Machines (Basel)*, *10*(8), 702. DOI: 10.3390/machines10080702

Leyma, P. D. H. (2024) Biosecurity Risk Assessment for the Use of Artificial Intelligence in Synthetic Biology. *Applied Biosafety*.

Li, W., Wang, S., Arundel, S. T., & Hsu, C.-Y. (2023). GeoImageNet: A multi-source natural feature benchmark dataset for GeoAI and supervised machine learning. *GeoInformatica*, *27*(3), 619–640. DOI: 10.1007/s10707-022-00476-z

Lin, Y., Shuya, L., & Lei, Z. (2024). The Implications of Artificial Intelligence on Infection Prevention and Control: Current Progress and Future Perspectives. [publication_type = article.]. *China CDC Weekly*, *6*, 901–904. PMID: 39233995

Luqman, A., Alnajjar, F., Parambil, M., Younes, M. I., Abdelhalim, Z., & Aljassmi, H. (2022). Development of YOLOv5-Based Real-Time Smart Monitoring System for Increasing Lab Safety Awareness in Educational Institutions. [publication_type = article.]. *Sensors (Basel)*, *22*(22), 8820. DOI: 10.3390/s22228820 PMID: 36433418

Marco Camardo, L., Marco, M., Sihem, F., Maurizio, M., Terenzio, B., Aldo, P., & Paola, B. (2021). An electronic nose supported by an artificial neural network for the rapid detection of aflatoxin B1 and fumonisins in maize. [publication_type = article.]. *Food Control*, *123*, 107722. DOI: 10.1016/j.foodcont.2020.107722

Martin, M., R. Rikard and S. David. (2024) The power of artificial intelligence for managing pandemics: A primer for public health professionals. *International Journal of Health Planning and Management*.

Matuka, D. O., Duba, T., Ngcobo, Z., Made, F., Muleba, L., Nthoke, T., & Singh, T. S. (2021). Occupational Risk of Airborne Mycobacterium tuberculosis Exposure: A Situational Analysis in a Three-Tier Public Healthcare System in South Africa. *International Journal of Environmental Research and Public Health*, *18*(19), 10130. DOI: 10.3390/ijerph181910130 PMID: 34639431

Meiyong, X., H. Zhenni, W. Anlu, M. Shitong, Z. Qian, C. Song, W. Jian Min and W. Kaimin. (2024) A Machine Learning Approach for Laboratory Safety Monitoring under Extreme Conditions. 42: 1 - 3.

Mirakhori, F., & Niazi, S. K. (2025). Harnessing the AI/ML in Drug and Biological Products Discovery and Development: The Regulatory Perspective. *Pharmaceuticals (Basel, Switzerland)*, *18*(1), 47. DOI: 10.3390/ph18010047 PMID: 39861110

Mohammadinia, A., Saeidian, B., Pradhan, B., & Ghaemi, Z. (2019). Prediction mapping of human leptospirosis using ANN, GWR, SVM and GLM approaches. *BMC Infectious Diseases*, *19*(1), 1–18. DOI: 10.1186/s12879-019-4580-4 PMID: 31722676

Muñoz-Organero, M. (2022). Space-Distributed Traffic-Enhanced LSTM-Based Machine Learning Model for COVID-19 Incidence Forecasting. *Computational Intelligence and Neuroscience*, *2022*, 4307708. DOI: 10.1155/2022/4307708 PMID: 36438691

Naimeh, B. (2024) Risk assessment and machine learning models.

Narmadha, D., & Pravin, A. (2020). An intelligent computer-aided approach for target protein prediction in infectious diseases. *Soft Computing*, *24*(19), 14707–14720. DOI: 10.1007/s00500-020-04815-w

Nathavitharana, R. R., Mishra, H., Sullivan, A., Hurwitz, S., Lederer, P., Meintjes, J., Nardell, E., & Theron, G. (2022). Predicting Airborne Infection Risk: Association Between Personal Ambient Carbon Dioxide Level Monitoring and Incidence of Tuberculosis Infection in South African Health Workers. *Clinical Infectious Diseases*, *75*(8), 1297–1306. DOI: 10.1093/cid/ciac183 PMID: 35348657

Naushin, A. (2024). Anticipating biosecurity hazards: Distribution and recognition of biological threats. *Eurasian Journal of Applied Biotechnology*, •••, 160.

Nicolas Bono, R., R. Luca, S. Speranza and G. Emanuele. (2023) Towards pest outbreak predictions: Are models supported by field monitoring the new hope? *Ecological Informatics*.

Patricia, E. M. D., Jody, S., Marie, A. C., Wouter, F., Hans, K., John, W. C., & Erik, T. (2011). Validation of the inhalable dust algorithm of the Advanced REACH Tool using a dataset from the pharmaceutical industry. [publication_type = article.]. *Journal of Environmental Monitoring*, *13*(6), 1597–1606. DOI: 10.1039/c1em10189g PMID: 21544304

Peiffer-Smadja, N., Rawson, T. M., Ahmad, R., Buchard, A., Georgiou, P., Lescure, F. X., Birgand, G., & Holmes, A. H. (2020). Machine learning for clinical decision support in infectious diseases: A narrative review of current applications. *Clinical Microbiology and Infection*, *26*(5), 584–595. DOI: 10.1016/j.cmi.2019.09.009 PMID: 31539636

Petya, B. (2021) The place of artificial intelligence in the risk management process. 120: 02013.

Pishgar, M., Issa, S. F., Sietsema, M., Pratap, P., & Darabi, H. (2021). REDECA: A Novel Framework to Review Artificial Intelligence and Its Applications in Occupational Safety and Health. *International Journal of Environmental Research and Public Health, 18*(13), 6705. DOI: 10.3390/ijerph18136705 PMID: 34206378

Płaza, G., Achal, V., & Kumari, D. (2018). Microbiological Risk Assessment and Bioprocess Engineering. *Multidisciplinary Aspects of Production Engineering, 1*(1), 233–239. DOI: 10.2478/mape-2018-0030

Priyank, T. and M. A. Fahad. (2024) The advancement of Artificial Intelligence (AI) in Occupational Health and Safety (OHS) across high-risk industries. *Journal of infrastructure, policy and development*, 8: 6889.

Rahmat, F., Zulkafli, Z., Juraiza Ishak, A., Mohd Noor, S. B., Yahaya, H., & Masrani, A. (2020). Exploratory Data Analysis and Artificial Neural Network for Prediction of Leptospirosis Occurrence in Seremban, Malaysia Based on Meteorological Data. *Frontiers in Earth Science (Lausanne), 8*, 377. DOI: 10.3389/feart.2020.00377

Raj Kumar, W. (2024) The role of artificial intelligence (AI) in microbiology laboratories for diagnosis of microorganisms: A review study. 13: 383 - 388.

Raul, V., Youssef, M., Víctor, M. E., Emal, Z., Patrick, B., Joseph, S. N., Juha, H., Bradley, J. N., Ajmal, Z., & Ajmal, Z. (2021). [publication_type = article.]. *Modelling the Impact of Robotics on Infectious Spread Among Healthcare Workers., 8*, 652685.

Ravi, K., Samuel, D., Karl, P., & Lauren, E. C. (2022). Predicting infectious disease for biopreparedness and response: A systematic review of machine learning and deep learning approaches. [publication_type = article.]. *One Health, 15*, 100439. DOI: 10.1016/j.onehlt.2022.100439 PMID: 36277100

Ria, A. (2023). A review of biowaste remediation and valorization for environmental sustainability: Artificial intelligence approach. *Environmental Pollution, 324*, 121363. DOI: 10.1016/j.envpol.2023.121363 PMID: 36863440

Riad, M. H., Sekamatte, M., Ocom, F., Makumbi, I., & Scoglio, C. M. (2019). Risk assessment of Ebola virus disease spreading in Uganda using a two-layer temporal network. *Scientific Reports, 9*(1), 16060. DOI: 10.1038/s41598-019-52501-1 PMID: 31690844

Rittick, M., K. Sachin, K. Mandar Bhalchandra and N. B. Sai Shibu. (2023) Automated Monitoring of Healthcare-Associated Infections in Operation Theatres Using IR Camera. 1124 - 1130.

Ryan, N. B. and T. Chuck (2021). The Biothreat Assessment as a Foundation for Biosecurity: 13 - 33.

Sahoo, P., Roy, I., Ahlawat, R., Irtiza, S., & Khan, L. (2022). Potential diagnosis of COVID-19 from chest X-ray and CT findings using semi-supervised learning. *Physical and Engineering Sciences in Medicine, 45*(1), 31–42. DOI: 10.1007/s13246-021-01075-2 PMID: 34780042

Salvi Del Pero, A., Wyckoff, P., & Vourc'h, A. (2022). *Using Artificial Intelligence in the workplace: What are the main ethical risks?* OECD Publishing.

Sandbrink, J. B. (2023) Artificial intelligence and biological misuse: Differentiating risks of language models and biological design tools. *ArXiv*, abs/2306.13952.

Schmidt, A., H. Alina and S. Jochen (2024). 6 Continuous biomanufacturing in upstream and downstream processing: 117 - 172.

Selestine, M., E. Youssef, K. Farid and B. Larbi. (2024) Artificial Intelligence for Infectious Disease Prediction and Prevention: A Comprehensive Review.

Sengeni, D., G. Padmapriya, S. S. Imambi, D. Suganthi, S. Ashish and B. Sampath (2023). Biomedical Waste Handling Method Using Artificial Intelligence Techniques: 306 - 323.

Shah, I. A., & Mishra, S. (2024). Reimagining occupational health and safety in the era of AI. In *A Biologist s Guide to Artificial Intelligence* (pp. 79–96). Academic Press.

Shausan, A., Nazarathy, Y., & Dyda, A. (2023). Emerging data inputs for infectious diseases surveillance and decision making. *Frontiers in Digital Health*, *5*, 5. DOI: 10.3389/fdgth.2023.1131731 PMID: 37082524

Sheshadri, C., Sangeeta, K., & Hatice, K. (2022). Harnessing the Potential of Artificial Intelligence to Foster Citizens' Satisfaction: An empirical study on India. *Government Information Quarterly*, *39*(4), 101621. DOI: 10.1016/j.giq.2021.101621

Shneiderman, B. (2020). Human-Centered Artificial Intelligence: Three Fresh Ideas. *AIS Transactions on Human-Computer Interaction*, *12*, 109–124. DOI: 10.17705/1thci.00131

Singh, T., & Matuka, O. (2013). Back to basics: Work-related infections Part 1: Risks of exposure to infectious agents in the workplace. *Occupational Health Southern Africa*, *19*(2), 4–12.

Stephanidis, C., Salvendy, G., Antona, M., Chen, J. Y., Dong, J., Duffy, V. G., Fang, X., Fidopiastis, C., Fragomeni, G., Fu, L. P., Guo, Y., Harris, D., Ioannou, A., Jeong, K. K., Konomi, S., Krömker, H., Kurosu, M., Lewis, J. R., Marcus, A., & Zhou, J. (2019). Seven HCI grand challenges. *International Journal of Human-Computer Interaction*, *35*(14), 1229–1269. DOI: 10.1080/10447318.2019.1619259

Sudki, J. M., Fonseca de Oliveira, G. R., de Medeiros, A. D., Mastrangelo, T., Arthur, V., Amaral da Silva, E. A., & Mastrangelo, C. B. (2023). Fungal identification in peanuts seeds through multispectral images: Technological advances to enhance sanitary quality. *Frontiers in Plant Science*, *14*, 1112916. DOI: 10.3389/fpls.2023.1112916 PMID: 36909395

Suriyan, J., Wai Peng, W., & Chee Peng, L. (2021). An Application of Data Envelopment Analysis and Machine Learning Approach to Risk Management. [publication_type = article.]. *IEEE Access : Practical Innovations, Open Solutions*, *9*, 85978–85994. DOI: 10.1109/ACCESS.2021.3087623

Tangorra, F. M., Buoio, E., Calcante, A., Bassi, A., & Costa, A. (2024). Internet of Things (IoT): Sensors Application in Dairy Cattle Farming. *Animals (Basel)*, *14*(21), 3071. DOI: 10.3390/ani14213071 PMID: 39518794

Tessandra, S., Jon, Z., & Seth, D. G. (2022). COVID-19 has illuminated the need for clearer AI-based risk management strategies. [publication_type = article.]. *Journal of Risk Research*, *25*(10), 1223–1238. DOI: 10.1080/13669877.2022.2077411

Thapen, N., Simmie, D., Hankin, C., & Gillard, J. (2016). DEFENDER: Detecting and Forecasting Epidemics Using Novel Data-Analytics for Enhanced Response. *PLoS One*, *11*(5), e0155417. DOI: 10.1371/journal.pone.0155417 PMID: 27192059

Tiwari, D., Bhati, B. S., Al-Turjman, F., & Nagpal, B. (2022). Pandemic coronavirus disease (Covid-19): World effects analysis and prediction using machine-learning techniques. *Expert Systems: International Journal of Knowledge Engineering and Neural Networks*, *39*(3), e12714. DOI: 10.1111/exsy.12714 PMID: 34177035

Tushar, K., Abhishek, S., & Wong, C. J. (2024). Survey of Artificial Intelligence for Automated Regulatory Compliance Tracking. [publication_type = article.]. *Journal of Engineering Research and Reports*, *26*(7), 390–406. DOI: 10.9734/jerr/2024/v26i71217

Valiakos, G., Papaspyropoulos, K., Giannakopoulos, A., Birtsas, P., Tsiodras, S., Hutchings, M. R., Spyrou, V., Pervanidou, D., Athanasiou, L. V., Papadopoulos, N., Tsokana, C., Baka, A., Manolakou, K., Chatzopoulos, D., Artois, M., Yon, L., Hannant, D., Petrovska, L., Hadjichristodoulou, C., & Billinis, C. (2014). Use of wild bird surveillance, human case data and GIS spatial analysis for predicting spatial distributions of West Nile virus in Greece. *PLoS One*, *9*(5), e96935. DOI: 10.1371/journal.pone.0096935 PMID: 24806216

Vilhouphrenuo, Z., Angel Elizabeth, S., Joel, M. T., Dayanand, P., Thottiam Vasudevan, R., Saqer, S. A., Robert, M., Abdullatif Bin, M., Muhammad, W., & Gulzar Ahmad, N. (2024). Revolutionizing the food industry: The transformative power of artificial intelligence-a review. [publication_type = article.]. *Food Chemistry: X*, *24*, 101867. DOI: 10.1016/j.fochx.2024.101867 PMID: 39431210

Wahid, M. A., Bukhari, S. H. R., Daud, A., Awan, S. E., & Raja, M. A. Z. (2023). COVICT: An IoT based architecture for COVID-19 detection and contact tracing. *Journal of Ambient Intelligence and Humanized Computing*, *14*(6), 7381–7398. DOI: 10.1007/s12652-022-04446-z PMID: 36281429

Wang, Y., L. Wang and K. L. Siau. Human-Centered Interaction in Virtual Worlds: A New Era of Generative Artificial Intelligence and Metaverse. *International Journal of Human–Computer Interaction*: 1-43.

Wangia, R. N., Tang, L., & Wang, J. S. (2019). Occupational exposure to aflatoxins and health outcomes: A review. *Journal of Environmental Science and Health. Part C, Environmental Carcinogenesis & Ecotoxicology Reviews*, *37*(4), 215–234. DOI: 10.1080/10590501.2019.1664836 PMID: 31512547

Wenqiang, G., Chenrui, L., Meng, G., Qiwei, Z., Xinyi, Y., & Li, Z. (2023). Innovative applications of artificial intelligence in zoonotic disease management. *Science in One Health*, *2*, 100045. DOI: 10.1016/j.soh.2023.100045 PMID: 39077042

Westhoven, M., & Herrmann, T. (2023, July). Interaction design for hybrid intelligence: the case of work place risk assessment. In International Conference on Human-Computer Interaction (pp. 629-639). Cham: Springer Nature Switzerland.

Yang, C.-H. (2022). How artificial intelligence technology affects productivity and employment: Firm-level evidence from Taiwan. *Research Policy*, *51*(6), 104536. DOI: 10.1016/j.respol.2022.104536

Yang, H. S., Hou, Y., Vasovic, L. V., Steel, P., Chadburn, A., Racine-Brzostek, S. E., Velu, P., Cushing, M. M., Loda, M., Kaushal, R., Zhao, Z., & Wang, F. (2020) Routine laboratory blood tests predict SARS-CoV-2 infection using machine learning. *medRxiv*: 2020.2006.2017.20133892. DOI: 10.1101/2020.06.17.20133892

Zhang, S., Diao, M., Yu, W., Pei, L., Lin, Z., & Chen, D. (2020). Estimation of the reproductive number of novel coronavirus (COVID-19) and the probable outbreak size on the Diamond Princess cruise ship: A data-driven analysis. *International Journal of Infectious Diseases*, *93*, 201–204. Advance online publication. DOI: 10.1016/j.ijid.2020.02.033 PMID: 32097725

Zhang, Y., Gao, Y., Wang, H., Wu, H., Xia, Y., & Wu, X. (2022). A secure high-order gene interaction detection algorithm based on deep neural network. *IEEE/ACM Transactions on Computational Biology and Bioinformatics*. PMID: 36251904

Chapter 10
Predictive Analytics for Incident Prevention in the Transportation of Dangerous Goods:
Leveraging AI to Enhance Safety in Hazardous Materials Transportation

Takudzwa Musariri
https://orcid.org/0009-0006-7598-5686
Independent Researcher, Zimbabwe

ABSTRACT

This chapter explores how predictive analytics can enhance safety in transporting dangerous goods. By integrating artificial intelligence (AI) into transportation systems, companies can shift from reactive to proactive safety measures, preventing incidents before they occur. The chapter examines how predictive models use data from onboard cameras, driver monitoring systems, and advanced analytics to mitigate risks. A case study on TotalEnergies' fleet management highlights the benefits and challenges of implementing predictive systems are highlighted. The chapter concludes with recommendations for improving the accuracy of predictive models and addressing ethical concerns, such as data privacy.

1. INTRODUCTION

The transportation of dangerous goods (TDG) is a critical component of global economic and industrial systems. It facilitates the movement of hazardous materials such as petroleum products, industrial chemicals, compressed gases, radioactive isotopes, and toxic substances. These materials are essential to sectors such as energy, healthcare, mining, agriculture, and manufacturing. However, the very nature of these goods—volatile, reactive, flammable, or toxic—presents serious occupational health and safety

DOI: 10.4018/979-8-3693-9301-7.ch010

(OHS) challenges. Workers responsible for handling, transporting, and managing these goods are consistently exposed to life-threatening risks, particularly in the event of process deviations or system failures.

Globally, the scale of TDG operations is massive. According to the United Nations Economic Commission for Europe (UNECE), over 1.5 billion tonnes of dangerous goods are transported across the world each year, with more than 70% of that volume moved by road in some regions (UNECE, 2020). Road transport poses a particular threat due to its exposure to dynamic environments—poor road conditions, unpredictable human behaviour, vehicle fatigue, and the absence of real-time regulatory enforcement. A report by the International Labour Organization (ILO) indicates that transport workers have one of the highest occupational fatality rates globally, particularly in low- and middle-income countries (ILO, 2023).

Despite the proliferation of regulatory frameworks—such as the UN Model Regulations on the Transport of Dangerous Goods, the European ADR agreement, and local labour health and safety laws—most of these are compliance-based and reactive in nature. They tend to focus on documentation, training, containment, and emergency response. While undeniably useful, these frameworks often lag in terms of operational agility, especially in contexts where decisions must be made in real time, such as a driver detecting mechanical failure while navigating a high-density urban environment.

This is where **predictive analytics** and **artificial intelligence (AI)** technologies offer revolutionary promise. Predictive analytics involves the use of historical data, sensor feedback, and machine learning models to forecast potential failures or incidents before they occur. Unlike traditional risk management strategies, which rely on scheduled maintenance or manual intervention, predictive systems enable early warning through data-driven insights. They allow organizations to identify trends in driver behaviour, vehicle performance, route risk, and environmental conditions to generate actionable alerts or adjustments.

Artificial Intelligence significantly enhances these capabilities by enabling continuous learning and real-time adaptation. AI systems can simultaneously process hundreds of data streams from vehicle sensors, cameras, GPS systems, weather databases, and driver biometrics. For example, in-vehicle AI systems can detect micro-expressions that signal fatigue, distraction, or stress in drivers and issue immediate audio-visual alerts. Other AI applications such as dynamic route optimization engines continuously analyse traffic, weather, and accident data to reroute vehicles away from emerging hazards—thus improving both safety and operational efficiency.

Companies like **TotalEnergies**, with vast and decentralized transport networks across multiple continents, have adopted predictive and AI-powered safety tools to reduce incidents and improve compliance. In its downstream operations, TotalEnergies deploys systems that monitor real-time driver performance, mechanical health, and road hazards. These systems support not only incident reduction but also occupational well-being by lowering cognitive strain on drivers and enabling rapid response to signs of danger. Importantly, predictive systems also help Transport managers schedule rest breaks and maintenance in a more informed, risk-sensitive manner.

A significant advantage of predictive analytics in TDG is its capacity to support Occupational Health and Safety (OHS) beyond physical harm prevention. It also addresses psychosocial risks—such as chronic stress, burnout, and isolation—which are common among long-distance drivers, especially in developing regions with poor roadside infrastructure and limited medical access. Predictive models can detect patterns in delivery delays, driver mood (via feedback systems), and performance anomalies to suggest proactive interventions before burnout or disengagement occurs.

In addition to organizational-level benefits, predictive analytics aligns closely with broader international development frameworks. The UN Sustainable Development Goal 8 (Decent Work and Economic Growth) and Goal 3 (Good Health and Well-being) emphasize the importance of workplace safety and mental health as indicators of sustainable progress. Likewise, ISO 45001:2018, the international standard for occupational health and safety management systems, calls for a shift from reactive to proactive risk identification—precisely what AI-based predictive systems enable.

However, despite the clear potential, the integration of AI into TDG operations is not yet universal. Adoption is highly uneven across regions. Multinational operators like TotalEnergies, Shell, and BP have adopted predictive analytics through telematics providers such as Mix Telematics, Verisk Analytics, and Gauzy Smart-Vision®. These technologies offer capabilities like fatigue detection, collision alerts, blind spot monitoring, lane departure warnings, and vehicle diagnostics. For example, NOTA AI, powered by NetsPresso, offers fatigue and distraction detection in real time and is being integrated into fleets globally for improving driver performance and reducing crashes. In contrast, small- and medium-sized operators in developing markets may lack the resources, digital infrastructure, or awareness needed to invest in such systems—exacerbating disparities in safety outcomes.

As with any new technology, AI-based systems raise ethical and legal questions. There are growing concerns about surveillance, driver privacy, data misuse, and over-reliance on automated recommendations. In response, leading companies are adopting transparency policies and ethical AI frameworks, which include clear communication to drivers, opt-in features, anonymization of sensitive data, and non-punitive use of performance data. Ensuring that predictive systems are used to support, not police, employees is critical to their successful adoption.

This chapter seeks to explore how predictive analytics and AI systems are transforming incident prevention in the transportation of dangerous goods, with particular attention to OHS. It draws upon the practical experience of TotalEnergies and integrates global best practices, literature insights, and vendor technologies. Through a critical analysis of predictive systems' benefits, limitations, ethical considerations, and future prospects, the chapter offers a roadmap for organizations aiming to modernize their safety practices while upholding the dignity, well-being, and security of their workforce.

2. BACKGROUND

The transportation of dangerous goods (TDG) has evolved into one of the most critical yet hazardous operations within global supply chains. Whether moving petroleum products, industrial chemicals, flammable gases, or radioactive materials, the risks associated with transporting such goods remain significant, particularly for the frontline personnel who manage these tasks daily. Despite technological and regulatory advances, occupational health and safety (OHS) challenges persist, underscoring the need for innovative strategies to mitigate risks before they escalate into incidents. This section examines the historical development of TDG, traditional safety approaches, the emergence of predictive analytics and artificial intelligence (AI), and their relevance to modern OHS management.

2.1 Historical Evolution of TDG and Traditional Safety Approaches

In the early 20th century, the movement of hazardous materials was largely unregulated. Dangerous substances such as gunpowder, acids, and fuels were transported alongside general cargo, often without proper containment, documentation, or awareness of their hazards. Accidents were frequent, and the lack of formal reporting structures meant that data on incidents was scarce, making it difficult to understand or learn from recurring patterns.

The industrial expansion of the mid-20th century catalysed the growth of chemical, petroleum, and mining industries—sectors that rely heavily on the movement of hazardous substances. This led to a notable increase in transport-related incidents, several of which resulted in catastrophic losses. For instance, the Texas City Disaster (1947) in the United States, where a ship carrying ammonium nitrate exploded, killed nearly 600 people and remains one of the deadliest industrial accidents in U.S. history. In 1978, the Los Alfaques explosion in Spain occurred when a liquefied propylene tanker exploded near a crowded beach, killing over 200 people.

These disasters prompted governments and international bodies to develop foundational regulatory frameworks. Among the most influential was the United Nations Recommendations on the Transport of Dangerous Goods (also known as the UN Model Regulations), which provided a harmonized structure for classifying, labelling, packaging, and transporting dangerous goods. These guidelines informed regional adaptations such as:

- The **European ADR Agreement** (road transport)
- The **IMDG Code** (maritime transport)
- The **ICAO Technical Instructions** (air transport)
- And various national regulations such as the **South African SANS 10231** and India's **CMVR Hazardous Goods Rules**.

While these regulations dramatically improved control, containment, and documentation, they remained largely compliance driven. Their focus was on prescriptive standards, requiring operators to meet set criteria on driver training, vehicle maintenance, route permits, and emergency response procedures. These standards are essential—but insufficient—in preventing incidents in real-time, dynamic environments.

2.2 The Occupational Health and Safety (OHS) Landscape in TDG

TDG operations expose transport workers—particularly drivers, loaders, and off-loaders to some of the highest levels of occupational risk in the logistics sector. Hazards are multifaceted and include:

- **Physical risks**, such as rollovers, chemical burns, or explosions.
- **Chemical exposure**, often from leaks or ruptured containers.
- **Ergonomic strain**, particularly during the manual handling of hoses, valves, and fittings.
- **Psychological stress**, from long hours, high concentration requirements, and fear of catastrophic incidents.
- **Environmental threats**, including poor weather, road infrastructure deficiencies, and nighttime driving.

The **International Labour Organization (ILO)** continues to rank road transport among the top sectors for occupational fatalities globally (ILO, 2023). In many countries, the risks are amplified by inadequate infrastructure, inconsistent enforcement, and long-standing cultural acceptance of high-risk working conditions.

Furthermore, subcontracted drivers and third-party logistics providers often operate under conditions that fall outside formal corporate oversight. These operators may use older vehicles, have limited access to rest stops or maintenance facilities, and work without adequate health insurance or legal protection—particularly in developing countries.

Even in advanced economies, OHS issues persist. A 2021 study by the European Agency for Safety and Health at Work found that TDG drivers experienced higher-than-average rates of fatigue, anxiety, and job dissatisfaction, which correlated directly with higher incident rates and lower job performance (EU-OSHA, 2021).

2.3 From Reactive to Predictive: The OHS Paradigm Shift

Historically, OHS management in TDG was reactive responding to incidents after they occurred. Investigations and root cause analyses would lead to the revision of procedures or training content. While this approach has value, it fails to address the dynamic and anticipatory needs of modern logistics environments.

Predictive analytics changes this paradigm by enabling real-time and forward-looking risk management. Using large volumes of historical and current data, algorithms can detect patterns and generate alerts before an incident occurs. For instance, if data shows that a driver has consistently exceeded speed limits in high-risk zones, or if a vehicle's braking performance is declining, predictive systems can recommend pre-emptive action—such as scheduling rest periods, reassigning routes, or initiating maintenance.

The application of **AI-enhanced safety systems** supports predictive analytics by automating the analysis of complex, multidimensional datasets. These systems can integrate inputs from:

- Engine control units (e.g., fuel consumption, RPM)
- Driver behaviour (e.g., seatbelt usage, acceleration patterns)
- Camera-based fatigue detection
- Environmental factors (e.g., weather, traffic, terrain)
- Incident history and near-miss reports

By synthesizing this data, AI models can develop individualized risk profiles and adapt their recommendations based on changing operational conditions. For OHS professionals, this represents a powerful tool for dynamic intervention and personalized risk mitigation.

2.4 Case Examples of AI-Powered OHS Enhancements

Leading firms in the energy and logistics sectors are already seeing the benefits of predictive analytics in TDG.

- **TotalEnergies** has implemented fatigue detection systems using AI-powered dashboard cameras. These systems alert both the driver and the Transport manager when signs of drowsiness or distraction are detected. Combined with route risk mapping and telematics integration, TotalEnergies reports stronger driver compliance and reduced incident severity in high-risk regions.
- **Mix Telematics**, a global fleet and mobile asset management provider, offers predictive maintenance alerts based on vehicle performance trends. For example, engine vibration patterns or

inconsistent braking feedback can trigger automatic workshop scheduling before a critical failure occurs.

- **Gauzy Smart-Vision®**, recently selected by Ford Trucks, uses AI cameras to eliminate blind spots, replacing traditional mirrors. This not only reduces collisions but also improves driver comfort by lowering neck strain and cognitive load.
- **NOTA AI**, developed by Nota America Inc., uses facial recognition and deep learning to monitor eye closure, yawning, and head position—generating alerts within milliseconds of detecting fatigue. This tool has been used by several logistics' firms operating in long-haul fuel and chemical transport.

These examples underscore the broad applicability of AI tools—not just in vehicle performance or navigation—but in safeguarding human well-being at the core of occupational safety.

2.5 OHS and AI in Developing Economies: Challenges and Opportunities

While multinational firms are rapidly adopting predictive safety systems, small and medium-sized enterprises (SMEs), especially in developing economies, face systemic barriers to adoption. These include:

- High cost of telematics hardware and AI subscriptions.
- Poor connectivity, especially in remote or cross-border transport corridors.
- Limited technical literacy, with many fleet operators unfamiliar with data interpretation.
- Driver resistance, often rooted in fears of being monitored or penalized.

However, initiatives are underway to address these gaps. The World Bank's Global Road Safety Facility (GRSF) has funded AI-based pilot programs in Kenya, Nigeria, and India, where select transporters receive subsidized access to fatigue detection and vehicle diagnostics systems. In South Africa, the National Road Traffic Act Amendment Bill has included provisions that promote the use of real-time monitoring tools for fuel transport.

Beyond funding, local capacity building is crucial. Several NGOs and training institutions in East Africa now offer courses on digital fleet safety, helping to normalize predictive tools among dispatchers, drivers, and mechanics.

When introduced with sensitivity to local contexts and worker rights, predictive analytics can have a transformative impact—especially in countries where manual safety systems have been undermined by infrastructure gaps or governance challenges.

2.6 Regulatory Alignment and Ethical Imperatives

As predictive systems become more embedded in TDG, regulatory bodies must evolve accordingly. Current regulations focus heavily on physical containment and documentation. However, future regulatory frameworks are expected to incorporate dynamic risk indicators, real-time monitoring standards, and AI system certifications.

For example:

- The EU Artificial Intelligence Act mandates transparency, bias control, and human oversight for safety-critical AI applications, including transport systems.
- The ILO's Code of Practice on Safety in the Use of Chemicals at Work now references the use of automated detection tools as part of hazard control systems.
- ISO 45001:2018 encourages continuous improvement and data-driven decision-making, which predictive analytics directly supports.

Equally important are ethical considerations:

- Transparency: Workers must know what data is being collected and why.
- Consent: Systems should not be implemented without proper employee engagement.
- Non-punitive use: AI-generated alerts should be used to support and coach, not to punish.
- Data protection: Robust cybersecurity and privacy policies are essential.

Ensuring that predictive tools serve the interest of the worker—rather than management surveillance—will be critical to achieving trust, effectiveness, and ethical legitimacy.

2.6.1 Conclusion of Background Section

The landscape of dangerous goods transportation has transformed dramatically over the last century, yet its core challenge—how to protect the people at the heart of these operations—remains unresolved. Traditional safety systems have brought consistency but not adaptability. Predictive analytics and AI offer the tools to anticipate, personalize, and prevent workplace hazards before they escalate into tragedy. To unlock their full potential, industry, regulators, and civil society must collaborate to scale these tools ethically, affordably, and inclusively ensuring that no worker, regardless of geography or employer size, is left behind in the evolution of safety.

3. PREDICTIVE ANALYTICS IN TDG: A CASE STUDY OF TOTALENERGIES

TotalEnergies, a multinational energy company with operations spanning over 130 countries, has long been recognized as a leader in embedding safety into the core of its logistics and operations strategy. Among the sectors most susceptible to occupational risk is the transportation of dangerous goods (TDG)—particularly petroleum fuels and chemicals. To mitigate the complex hazards associated with fuel distribution, TotalEnergies developed and enforces a rigorous operational framework known as PATROM (Programme d'Amélioration du Transport Routier), which guides how TDG is managed from an OHS perspective. In recent years, the company has further enhanced its safety strategy by integrating predictive analytics and artificial intelligence (AI) systems, particularly those provided by Mix Telematics by Power fleet, including Mix Fleet Manager Premium and Mix Vision AI.

This section provides a case analysis of how TotalEnergies uses PATROM as a baseline for managing transport safety and how it incorporates predictive analytics to improve decision-making, risk detection, and occupational health outcomes. The section also draws comparisons from other global oil and gas companies such as Shell and BP to highlight industry-wide trends in AI-enhanced TDG safety management.

3.1 The PATROM Framework: TotalEnergies' Transport Safety Backbone

PATROM (Programme d'Amélioration du Transport Routier) is a structured framework adopted by TotalEnergies across its affiliates, especially in Africa and Asia, where TDG incidents pose both health and environmental risks. PATROM sets out mandatory requirements for every stage of petroleum product transport, with a specific emphasis on occupational health and safety, vehicle integrity, route risk management, and emergency preparedness.

Key features of the PATROM framework include:

- Daily Checks and Safety Audits: Drivers and depot teams must complete Safe to load inspection checklists before loading. These are subject to unannounced audits/spot checks by TotalEnergies safety officers.
- Behavioural Safety Programs: PATROM includes in-cab behaviour policies such as mandatory seatbelt use, mobile phone bans during driving, and mandatory rest periods.
- Incident Reporting and Lessons Learned: PATROM mandates comprehensive post-incident investigations, corrective action documentation, and circulation of "Safety REX" alerts across affiliates.
- Driver Training: TotalEnergies emphasizes rigorous driver training programs, including theoretical instruction, practical assessments, and ongoing evaluations. For instance, Total Tanzania coordinates driver training aligned with PATROM standards, ensuring drivers meet regulatory and safety requirements.
- Fleet Maintenance: The program mandates strict vehicle vetting procedures, regular inspections, and adherence to maintenance schedules to ensure roadworthiness.
- Safety Protocols: PATROM enforces safety measures such as vehicle tracking systems, driver fatigue management, and compliance with safety equipment standards. For example, Total Parco in Pakistan utilizes advanced vehicle tracking and has established a dedicated driver training centre to uphold these standards. Total PARCO Pakistan

Transport companies partnering with TotalEnergies are expected to comply with PATROM standards, which may include implementing safety management systems, participating in audits, and ensuring their drivers receive appropriate training. For example, Concrete Structure, a transport company operating in Southern Africa, aligns its operations with PATROM by maintaining a strict Safety, Health & Environment (SHE) policy and engaging in continuous improvement processes. ConcreteZW

PATROM is not only about safety compliance but is deeply embedded in TotalEnergies' OHS strategy, aiming to protect lives, prevent environmental harm, and improve operational discipline. However, due to its manual roots, enforcing PATROM historically required intensive oversight. With the integration of predictive technologies, TotalEnergies has bridged the gap between policy and real-time enforcement.

3.2 Predictive Analytics Integration: Mix Telematics by Power fleet

To digitalize PATROM compliance and improve risk visibility, TotalEnergies partnered with Mix Telematics, a global provider of fleet and mobile asset management solutions. The company utilizes Mix Fleet Manager Premium and Mix Vision AI across many of its regional transport operations.

3.2.1 Mix Fleet Manager Premium

This advanced telematics platform enables TotalEnergies to:

- Monitor driver behaviour in real time, including speed, harsh braking, acceleration, cornering, and seatbelt usage.
- Track vehicle location and route compliance, ensuring that JMPs defined under PATROM are followed without deviation.
- Trigger alerts for PATROM violations, such as over-speeding in high-risk zones or driving outside designated hours.
- Generate daily, weekly, and monthly safety scorecards for drivers and contractors, forming the basis of coaching and recognition.

This platform is integrated with PATROM requirements to create a digital replica of compliance, allowing dispatchers and safety officers to monitor transport activities dynamically.

3.2.2 Mix Vision AI

Mix Vision AI enhances visibility further by deploying dual-facing cameras powered by machine learning to assess:

- Driver fatigue and distraction using eye closure rate, yawning detection, and gaze tracking.
- In-cab behaviour, including smoking, use of mobile phones, or unsafe posture.
- Road conditions and incident precursors, which are recorded and time-stamped for post-trip analysis.

When high-risk behaviour is detected, the system can issue in-cab alerts, trigger SMS/email notifications to supervisors, and log the event for post-journey review.

These technologies are central to the company's shift from post-incident investigation to real-time hazard interception, empowering both drivers and managers to act before an accident occurs.

3.3 Implementation in African Operations

In many Sub-Saharan African countries—Zimbabwe, Kenya, Nigeria, and Ghana—TotalEnergies has deployed these systems to improve TDG safety amid infrastructure and regulatory constraints. For instance, in Zimbabwe, local transport contractors operating under the TotalEnergies banner are trained in PATROM and required to install Mix Telematics in their fleets. Some key improvements observed include:

- Timely identification of fatigue and rerouting of drivers during long-haul delivery operations.
- Reduction in route violations, especially in hazardous areas, due to GPS tracking and enforcement of JMPs.
- Improved vehicle maintenance outcomes, as predictive alerts reduce unplanned breakdowns and associated risk to drivers during roadside incidents.

- Behavioural improvement in drivers, owing to monthly coaching based on their safety scores and visual analytics.

Drivers have expressed greater confidence in their working conditions, citing the transparency and support provided by AI systems as contributors to reduced stress and improved performance.

3.4 AI-Driven Safety Programs in Other Oil and Gas Majors

TotalEnergies is not alone in leveraging AI for transport safety. Several other global energy companies are also deploying predictive tools to protect drivers and assets in TDG contexts.

3.4.1 Shell Global

Shell has implemented AI-powered telematics and video-based coaching in its fleet operations worldwide. Their systems, developed in partnership with Lytx and other vendors, feature:

- Machine learning models to assess driver risk scores,
- AI-supported detection of unsafe behaviours (e.g., drowsiness, phone use),
- Predictive routing based on historical incident data.

Shell's deployment in Asia and Europe has led to a measurable reduction in fuel spills, overturned tankers, and injury reports, according to their sustainability disclosures (Shell, 2022).

3.4.2 BP (British Petroleum)

BP uses predictive maintenance platforms to monitor engine, brake, and tire health. Combined with environmental data such as temperature and terrain, their AI systems forecast component failures, reducing road accidents linked to mechanical issues.

BP also integrates natural language processing (NLP) tools to analyze post-trip reports and near-miss narratives, identifying recurring risk themes across regions (BP Sustainability Report, 2023).

3.4.3 Chevron

Chevron has incorporated augmented reality (AR) checklists and AI-powered hazard detection in its tanker fleets. Drivers use smart glasses to perform standardized inspections, and AI image recognition scans for oil leaks, damaged fittings, or missing safety seals before dispatch.

3.5 Ethical Use, Privacy, and Driver Engagement

TotalEnergies emphasizes ethical implementation in its AI systems. The company ensures:

- Driver consent and clear communication on how data is used,
- Non-punitive enforcement, where alerts lead to coaching, not immediate penalties,
- Data protection, with recordings stored securely and shared only for safety purposes,

- Worker inclusion, allowing drivers to review and comment on their own performance records.

This approach builds trust and encourages buy-in, especially in markets where technology adoption may be viewed with suspicion or as surveillance.

3.6 Lessons Learned and Global Implications

The TotalEnergies case demonstrates how structured safety frameworks like PATROM, when augmented with predictive AI tools, can achieve significant results in TDG safety. Key lessons include:

- System alignment is crucial: AI tools must be customized to reflect the language, thresholds, and checklists of PATROM.
- Driver behaviour improves with visibility: When drivers know they are supported—not punished—by technology, they are more likely to self-correct.
- Scalability and localization matter: The same system can be adapted across countries with adjustments in language, regulatory integration, and training.
- Data must be actionable: Safety data must feed directly into coaching, audit scoring, and continuous improvement cycles.

4. BENEFITS AND CHALLENGES OF PREDICTIVE ANALYTICS IN TDG

The integration of predictive analytics in the transportation of dangerous goods (TDG) marks a pivotal shift in how occupational risks are managed. Traditional health and safety systems have historically focused on regulatory compliance, routine training, and post-incident analysis. While these methods remain essential, they are largely reactive. Predictive analytics transforms the safety model by offering a proactive, data-driven approach that enables early intervention—often before a hazard materializes.

By leveraging AI, telematics, and real-time data feeds, predictive systems allow organizations to identify and act on leading indicators of risk. However, despite the clear advantages, the adoption and implementation of predictive analytics in TDG also come with operational, ethical, technical, and contextual challenges. This section explores the key benefits and limitations of these technologies within the context of occupational health and safety (OHS).

4.1 Benefits of Predictive Analytics in TDG

4.1.1 Early Risk Detection and Prevention

Perhaps the most significant advantage of predictive analytics is its ability to identify hazards before they escalate. By analysing variables such as driver fatigue patterns, vehicle health data, route-specific incident history, and environmental conditions, predictive models can flag elevated risk in real time.

This allows for targeted interventions such as route reassignment, pre-emptive vehicle maintenance, or enforced rest periods for drivers.

For example, fatigue-detection systems like NOTA AI can analyse eye movement and facial expressions to trigger alerts even before the driver is fully aware of their exhaustion. This anticipatory approach is particularly important in TDG, where a single lapse in concentration can lead to catastrophic outcomes.

4.1.2 Enhanced Driver Well-being

Predictive systems support driver health by reducing cognitive and physical strain. Fatigue monitoring, route optimization, and real-time performance feedback help drivers manage their workload more effectively. Tools like Mix Telematics also enable real-time coaching, allowing drivers to receive constructive feedback rather than disciplinary actions.

This fosters a culture of support rather than surveillance, reducing anxiety and empowering drivers to take ownership of their safety. As a result, organizations observe improvements in job satisfaction, reduced stress-related absenteeism, and stronger retention of skilled personnel.

4.1.3 Reduction in Equipment-Related Incidents

Vehicle failure is a leading cause of TDG-related incidents. Predictive maintenance tools continuously monitor engine health, tire pressure, brake efficiency, and fuel system performance. By identifying anomalies early, they allow maintenance teams to act before a fault develops into a breakdown or fire hazard.

These systems not only improve vehicle reliability but also reduce roadside repair incidents—often conducted under dangerous conditions, such as along highways or in high-temperature zones where flammable materials are present.

4.1.4 Better Resource Allocation and Efficiency

Predictive tools allow managers to allocate resources dynamically. Vehicles that are deemed high-risk can be sidelined for inspection, while routes with elevated incident probabilities can be deprioritized or scheduled for lower-risk periods (e.g., daytime vs nighttime). This enables a smarter, leaner approach to logistics without compromising safety.

Over time, the data collected also helps organizations optimize scheduling, reduce fuel waste, and lower insurance premiums—generating measurable cost savings.

4.1.5 Support for Regulatory Compliance and Reporting

Predictive systems generate detailed logs and dashboards that support compliance with OHS regulations, transport laws, and international TDG guidelines. By having digitized, timestamped evidence of route adherence, driver behaviour, and maintenance schedules, companies can demonstrate compliance in audits and investigations.

These records also support continuous improvement efforts under standards such as **ISO 45001:2018**, which emphasizes proactive risk identification and preventive action as pillars of OHS management.

4.2 Challenges of Predictive Analytics in TDG

4.2.1 Financial and Technological Barriers

One of the most immediate challenges is the cost of acquisition and implementation. Installing AI-powered fatigue monitoring systems, telematics sensors, cloud data storage, and analysis platforms can be expensive—particularly for small and medium-sized enterprises (SMEs). Additionally, these systems require technical staff for setup, integration, and maintenance.

Many operators in developing regions lack the capital, internet infrastructure, or data governance maturity to effectively deploy predictive systems. This creates a disparity in safety standards between multinational carriers and local transporters, potentially increasing subcontracting risks.

4.2.2 Resistance from Drivers and Field Personnel

Adoption of predictive tools can face resistance from drivers, who may view them as invasive or disciplinary. Fear of being constantly watched or penalized for mistakes can cause stress, demoralization, or even sabotage of equipment. In some cases, drivers have been reported to obstruct cameras or switch off systems, especially when unsure how data will be used.

To overcome this, organizations must invest in change management, transparency, and worker participation. When drivers are involved in the evaluation and selection of tools, and when feedback is framed as developmental rather than punitive, resistance typically decreases.

4.2.3 Alert Fatigue and Overreliance on Technology

While predictive systems aim to reduce human error, they can also introduce alert fatigue—a condition where drivers or supervisors become desensitized to frequent alerts and begin to ignore them. Poorly calibrated systems may issue false positives, for example, triggering a fatigue alert due to glare or brief head movement.

This desensitization undermines the credibility of the system and may result in critical warnings being overlooked. To address this, predictive systems must be adaptive and personalized, refining their thresholds based on driver habits, route difficulty, and historical incident data.

There is also a risk of overreliance on technology. Operators may assume that the system will catch every risk, leading to complacency in manual checks or driver vigilance. Organizations must ensure that predictive tools augment, not replace, sound operational judgment.

4.2.4 Ethical and Privacy Concerns

The deployment of AI in TDG raises profound **ethical questions**, particularly when it involves real-time tracking of biometrics and behaviour. Concerns include:

- Data privacy: Who owns the data? How long is it stored?
- Consent: Are drivers informed and able to opt in or out?
- Fairness: Are alerts used for coaching or punishment?
- Transparency: Are drivers able to review and challenge AI-generated reports?

To maintain trust, organizations must develop clear policies that define data use, access rights, and the boundaries of surveillance. This includes anonymizing data where appropriate and involving employees in discussions about system implementation and oversight.

4.2.5 Integration Challenges with Legacy Systems

Older fleets or outdated software systems may be incompatible with modern predictive tools. Retrofitting vehicles with AI sensors, upgrading backend IT systems, and integrating disparate data sources (e.g., GPS logs, maintenance records, fuel cards) can be costly and time-consuming.

In large organizations, these challenges can delay rollout or result in siloed data sets that reduce the accuracy of predictions. A phased integration strategy, coupled with vendor support, is essential for smooth adoption.

4.2.6 Operational Limitations in Protected Government Depots

A unique and increasingly common challenge arises in government-protected depots or high-security zones, where recording devices are either restricted or completely prohibited. These areas are subject to national security regulations such as Protected Areas Acts, which ban voice, video, and data recordings due to the sensitivity of operations.

To comply, companies like TotalEnergies have programmed their AI systems to automatically deactivate recording functionality upon entering these zones. Additionally, drivers are required to manually cover camera lenses before entering secure depots. While necessary for compliance, these measures introduce operational risks:

- During the time when cameras are deactivated or covered, visibility and monitoring are significantly reduced, creating a gap in safety oversight.
- In some cases, drivers forget to remove the manual camera covers after exiting the depot, resulting in continued blind spots during critical driving segments.
- This period of camera inactivity also removes access to fatigue or distraction alerts—potentially compromising driver safety during hazardous manoeuvres such as reversing or aligning with loading platforms.

This situation underscores the tension between regulatory compliance and technological safety solutions. Companies must balance respect for legal mandates with the operational need for full situational awareness. Some are now exploring sensor-based alternatives (e.g., proximity detectors or non-recording driver behaviour flags) that offer limited risk detection without violating depot security policies.

4.3 Ethical and Regulatory Considerations in AI-Driven Transport Safety

As artificial intelligence (AI) and predictive analytics become increasingly central to occupational health and safety (OHS) strategies in the transportation of dangerous goods (TDG), ethical and legal questions have come to the forefront. While these technologies offer transformative potential in reducing accidents and protecting lives, their use raises concerns around privacy, surveillance, fairness, data ownership, and worker autonomy.

Organizations adopting AI in TDG must ensure not only operational effectiveness but also ethical legitimacy and regulatory compliance. The failure to do so can result in worker resistance, reputational damage, or legal consequences. This section explores the key ethical and regulatory considerations for integrating AI safely and responsibly in OHS programs.

4.3.1 Privacy and Data Governance

Most AI-driven safety systems, such as Mix Vision AI and other in-cab monitoring platforms, involve the collection of sensitive biometric and behavioural data. This includes facial features, eye movements, voice recordings, driving habits, and geolocation data. Without proper safeguards, such data can expose workers to risks of identity misuse, unauthorized surveillance, or discrimination.

To protect drivers and comply with international standards, organizations must implement robust data governance policies. Key practices include:

- Informed consent: Workers must be made fully aware of what data is collected, how it is used, who can access it, and for how long it will be stored.
- Purpose limitation: Data should only be used for clearly stated safety objectives and not for unrelated performance tracking, disciplinary action, or commercial profiling.
- Access control: Only authorized personnel should be allowed to review AI-generated reports or visual records, preferably under defined audit trails.
- Data anonymization: Where feasible, aggregate data should be anonymized for trend analysis or reporting to prevent individual identification.
- Retention policies: Data should be stored only for a period necessary to support safety outcomes and in line with legal retention requirements.

These principles align with data protection regulations such as the EU's General Data Protection Regulation (GDPR) and South Africa's POPIA (Protection of Personal Information Act), both of which are applicable to multinational companies operating in Africa.

4.3.2 Non-Punitive Implementation and Trust Building

One of the most contentious issues in AI safety systems is whether data will be used punitively. Drivers often fear being punished for minor infractions or errors outside their control, especially when AI systems are perceived as "digital supervisors." This fear undermines trust and can lead to passive resistance, manipulation of systems, or even device tampering.

To mitigate this risk, leading organizations, including TotalEnergies, emphasize non-punitive safety cultures. This involves:

- Using AI alerts and reports primarily for coaching and support,
- Celebrating safety milestones and improvements, not just flagging errors,
- Allowing drivers to review and comment on their own records,
- Avoiding automatic penalties based solely on system data.

When workers see AI as a tool for safety rather than discipline, adoption and engagement improve significantly.

4.3.3 Legal and Regulatory Alignment

In many countries, legislation is evolving to address the ethical use of AI in safety-critical sectors. For instance:

- The **ILO (International Labour Organization)** encourages human-centred digital transformation that protects worker rights.
- **ISO 45001:2018**, the global standard for OHS management systems, now includes references to digital tools, emphasizing proactive hazard identification and worker consultation.
- In protected areas or national depots, laws such as **Protected Areas Acts** may prohibit recording or surveillance, requiring AI systems to deactivate automatically when entering those zones. Organizations must comply by programming systems to shut down recording functions and manually covering cameras, as practiced in several TotalEnergies operations.

Aligning with these frameworks not only ensures legal compliance but also positions companies as responsible innovators, helping to attract and retain talent and gain community support.

4.3.4 Conclusion of Subsection

Ethical AI use in TDG is not optional—it is fundamental to sustainable safety innovation. Companies that invest in transparent, fair, and rights-based AI systems are more likely to gain employee trust, comply with international standards, and achieve their OHS objectives without backlash or resistance. The ethical integration of AI enhances, rather than compromises, the dignity and well-being of the workers it aims to protect.

5. THE ROLE OF ARTIFICIAL INTELLIGENCE IN INCIDENT PREVENTION

The integration of artificial intelligence (AI) into occupational health and safety (OHS) strategies has introduced a paradigm shift in how incidents are predicted, prevented, and managed in the transportation of dangerous goods (TDG). While predictive analytics forms the foundation of anticipatory risk management, AI brings automation, scalability, and learning capabilities that elevate safety systems beyond static thresholds and pre-programmed logic. Through machine learning, computer vision, natural language processing, and data fusion, AI systems are enabling real-time decision-making, dynamic adaptation, and deeper situational awareness.

This section explores the central role of AI in incident prevention within TDG, focusing on its applications, benefits, limitations, and its alignment with evolving OHS standards.

5.1 Defining AI in the Context of TDG Safety

Artificial intelligence refers to the use of advanced algorithms and computational models to perform tasks that typically require human intelligence. In TDG operations, AI enables systems to process vast streams of real-time data, recognize patterns, make predictions, and even initiate automated responses.

Unlike traditional predictive analytics—which typically rely on historical data and fixed statistical models—AI systems **learn from data** continuously, updating their models as new information becomes available. This ability makes AI particularly effective in dynamic, safety-critical environments where traditional models may struggle to keep up with evolving conditions.

AI in TDG safety encompasses technologies such as:

- Computer vision (e.g., fatigue detection, gesture recognition)
- Machine learning (e.g., risk prediction, anomaly detection)
- Natural language processing (e.g., parsing incident reports)
- Autonomous control (e.g., lane-keeping, adaptive cruise control)
- Decision support systems (e.g., AI dashboards for fleet managers)

5.2 AI-Enabled Fatigue and Distraction Detection

Driver fatigue is one of the leading contributors to TDG-related accidents. Traditional methods to manage fatigue include fixed shift schedules, rest breaks, and self-reporting. However, these methods are often inconsistent and fail to account for situational or physiological variation.

AI-powered driver monitoring systems (DMS), such as Mix Vision AI, NOTA AI and Seeing Machines, offer a more dynamic solution. These systems use infrared cameras and computer vision to detect:

- Eye closure rate and blink duration (PERCLOS)
- Head nodding and yawning frequency
- Gaze direction and off-road glance time
- Facial expression changes associated with cognitive fatigue

These features are processed using deep learning models trained on large datasets of driver behaviour. When indicators of fatigue or distraction are detected, the system triggers real-time alerts—both audible and visual. In more advanced systems, notifications are sent to a remote-control centre or supervisor for follow-up.

Such systems not only prevent accidents but also offer data-backed insights into fatigue hotspots, enabling managers to redesign routes, shift structures, or vehicle assignments.

5.3 Real-Time Hazard Recognition and Risk Scoring

AI enables systems to recognize evolving risks by contextualizing data. For example, AI can analyse the interaction between:

- Vehicle speed and proximity to curves
- Weather forecasts and cargo volatility

- Driver stress levels and upcoming urban congestion

Based on these data points, AI models can assign dynamic risk scores to routes, drivers, and even individual trips. These scores are then used to:

- Trigger pre-emptive alerts
- Reroute vehicles
- Modify rest schedules
- Recommend contingency plans

This contextual risk modelling is especially valuable in TDG, where exposure to flammable, toxic, or reactive substances demands near-zero tolerance for uncertainty.

5.4 Predictive Maintenance and Anomaly Detection

One of the less visible but highly impactful roles of AI in TDG is in vehicle health management. Traditional maintenance schedules are based on mileage or time intervals. While this is effective to an extent, it often leads to unnecessary servicing or unexpected breakdowns.

AI-powered predictive maintenance systems, such as those integrated by Mix Telematics and Bosch Connected Mobility, go beyond these limitations. These systems collect data from:

- Engine control units (ECUs)
- Brake sensors
- Tire pressure monitoring systems
- Fuel injectors and turbochargers

Using supervised learning models, the system identifies early signs of wear or failure—such as changes in vibration patterns, temperature deviations, or delayed mechanical responses. It then forecasts the remaining useful life (RUL) of components and schedules maintenance accordingly.

For OHS, the implications are significant:

- Drivers avoid dangerous roadside repairs
- Vehicles are less likely to break down while carrying hazardous loads
- Fire risks from mechanical failure (e.g., brake overheating) are minimized

5.5 Route Optimization and Context-Aware Navigation

AI is also transforming route management in TDG logistics. Traditional journey management relied on static route approvals and general guidelines. AI tools now provide context-aware navigation, which considers:

- Real-time traffic
- Weather data (e.g., wind, fog, flooding)
- Road hazards (e.g., construction zones, accident-prone segments)

- Environmental risk zones (e.g., near schools, water sources, or densely populated areas)

Systems like HERE Technologies, TomTom Telematics, and Google's AI fleet solutions integrate with vehicle telematics to reroute tankers or chemical carriers on the fly, ensuring lower risk exposure and compliance with safety protocols.

For instance, if a storm warning is issued in an area where a flammable gas tanker is en route, the AI system may recommend a detour or halt, in coordination with dispatchers. This dynamic risk avoidance significantly improves OHS outcomes.

5.6 Incident Reconstruction and Root Cause Analysis

In the aftermath of an incident or near miss, AI tools can assist in incident reconstruction by analysing:

- Video footage from multiple angles
- Telematics data (e.g., speed, braking, acceleration)
- DMS inputs (e.g., driver eye tracking and posture)
- External data (e.g., road conditions, weather)

This analysis helps safety officers determine root causes—be it distraction, mechanical fault, poor visibility, or external obstruction. These insights are fed back into training programs, system updates, and organizational learning loops.

Some advanced platforms are even capable of simulating alternate scenarios—i.e., what would have happened if the driver had braked one second earlier or taken a different turn. These simulations provide actionable learning material that enhances future prevention strategies.

5.7 Integration with Autonomous Systems

While full autonomy in dangerous goods transport remains a long-term goal, several semi-autonomous features powered by AI are already in use. These include:

- Adaptive cruise control to maintain safe distances
- Lane-keeping assistance to prevent veering
- Collision avoidance systems using radar and camera data
- Emergency braking systems triggered automatically

These systems reduce driver cognitive load, especially during long, monotonous stretches, and provide an additional layer of safety in environments where human error remains a critical threat.

Several OEMs (e.g., Volvo, Mercedes-Benz Trucks, Ford Trucks) have integrated AI-powered safety features into their TDG vehicle models, and operators like TotalEnergies have begun testing these systems under controlled conditions.

5.8 Enabling Personalized OHS Interventions

Perhaps one of the most promising roles of AI is in enabling individualized safety plans. By building a profile for each driver based on their driving style, risk exposure, rest history, and incident record, AI systems can:

- Recommend personalized training modules
- Suggest optimal shift patterns
- Identify high-risk routes or times for that driver

This personalization not only enhances safety but also improves worker morale and engagement, as interventions feel relevant rather than generic.

5.9 Ethical Considerations in AI-Driven OHS

The introduction of AI in safety systems must be matched with a commitment to ethical implementation. Key concerns include:

- Informed consent: Workers must understand what is being monitored and how it will be used.
- Privacy: Sensitive biometric data should be encrypted, stored securely, and accessed only by authorized personnel.
- Non-punitive culture: Alerts and analytics should support training, not disciplinary action.
- Transparency and feedback: Drivers should have access to their own data and be able to challenge or clarify records.

International guidelines, such as those from the European Commission's AI Ethics Framework and ILO's Occupational Safety Standards, provide a roadmap for ethical AI use in safety-critical industries.

5.10 Limitations and Contextual Constraints

While AI offers tremendous potential, its application in TDG is not without limitations. These include:

- System blindness in protected zones: As previously discussed, some depots require camera shutdowns due to national security laws. This creates blind spots during critical operations such as loading, reversing, or final inspections.

In TotalEnergies' case, the system is programmed to automatically deactivate AI recording functions when entering protected areas, and drivers are required to manually cover lenses. While this complies with the law, it introduces a temporary loss of visibility, and in some cases, drivers forget to remove covers, reducing effectiveness after departure.

- Data quality issues: Poor sensor calibration or environmental interference (e.g., sun glare) may result in false positives or system shutdowns.

- AI bias: Models trained on limited datasets may not perform equally well across diverse geographies, driving styles, or demographic groups.
- Technical literacy gap: In many developing economies, the lack of IT support or data analytics expertise hinders full AI deployment and maintenance.

5.10.1 Conclusion of Section

AI has redefined the landscape of incident prevention in the transport of dangerous goods. By enabling real-time monitoring, early risk detection, personalized intervention, and post-incident analysis, AI not only enhances OHS performance but also fosters a culture of proactivity, learning, and empowerment. AI is more than a tool—it is a strategic enabler.

6. COMPARATIVE ANALYSIS: PRE- VS. POST-AI OHS PERFORMANCE IN TDG

To fully appreciate the transformative impact of artificial intelligence (AI) and predictive analytics in the transportation of dangerous goods (TDG), it is essential to compare occupational health and safety (OHS) practices and outcomes before and after their integration. While many organizations have adopted digital tools in recent years, the contrast between traditional, manual systems and modern AI-driven frameworks highlights the extent to which technology has redefined safety culture, risk detection, and incident prevention.

This comparative analysis explores the OHS landscape across four core dimensions: risk identification, incident response, driver behaviour management, and organizational learning.

6.1 Risk Identification and Early Intervention

6.1.1 Pre-AI Era

Traditionally, risk identification relied heavily on physical inspections, self-reported checklists, and supervisor observations. These tools often failed to capture dynamic or evolving risks—such as driver fatigue during long shifts, mechanical anomalies developing mid-route, or adverse weather conditions en-route. As a result, interventions were reactive, triggered only after visible symptoms appeared or an incident occurred.

6.1.2 Post-AI Era

With the deployment of AI systems such as Mix Telematics and Mix Vision AI, risk identification has become proactive and continuous. Telematics sensors now collect real-time data on driver inputs, vehicle performance, and environmental conditions. AI models trained on historical incident data can recognize precursors to accidents—such as sudden braking, distracted driving, or route deviations—and issue alerts instantly. These systems provide actionable insights to drivers, supervisors, and safety managers before a hazard escalates into an incident.

The shift has led to a culture where risks are **anticipated and mitigated**, not just recorded after the fact.

6.2 Incident Reporting and Response

6.2.1 Pre-AI Era

In the past, incident reporting depended on manual logs, verbal accounts, and paper-based documentation. These records were often incomplete, delayed, or biased, reducing their utility for root cause analysis. Moreover, the lag between the occurrence of an event and the initiation of response measures exposed workers to prolonged risk.

6.2.2 Post-AI Era

AI-enabled systems now generate automatic incident reports with time-stamped data, video evidence, and sensor readings. For example, if a driver experiences a tire blowout, the event is captured by onboard cameras, while the location, speed, and vehicle dynamics are logged simultaneously. This facilitates faster emergency response and accurate post-incident investigations.

AI further enables predictive modelling to simulate "what-if" scenarios, improving the quality of lessons learned. This evolution has strengthened **resilience and rapid response** across TDG fleets.

6.3 Driver Behaviour and Well-being

6.3.1 Pre-AI Era

Monitoring driver performance once relied on supervisor ride-along, feedback from customers, or infrequent safety audits. This approach was sporadic and often subjective. Fatigue and stress were underreported, while positive behaviours like defensive driving often went unrecognized. In high-risk TDG settings, this created systemic blind spots in behaviour-based safety.

6.3.2 Post-AI Era

With fatigue detection algorithms, in-cab coaching, and real-time alerts, AI has placed driver behaviour at the centre of OHS strategies. Systems like Mix Vision AI can detect signs of drowsiness, distraction, or mobile phone usage, while also validating safe driving through reward-based scorecards.

Drivers now receive immediate feedback, while supervisors can plan interventions such as coaching or rest breaks. Importantly, AI allows for personalized risk profiling, recognizing that not all drivers respond to the same stressors or hazards in the same way. This shift supports human-centric safety, improving both performance and well-being.

6.4 Organizational Learning and Safety Culture

6.4.1 Pre-AI Era

OHS improvements were often limited to annual safety reviews or responses to major incidents. Knowledge sharing was largely anecdotal, and improvements were implemented slowly across regions and contractors. The result was fragmented institutional learning, with recurring mistakes across the fleet.

6.4.2 Post-AI Era

AI systems allow for automated trend analysis across thousands of data points. Risk hotspots, recurring violations, and high-risk driver segments are identified and visualized on dashboards. This enables senior leadership to allocate resources, redesign routes, or update training based on live operational data.

Moreover, many companies now circulate monthly "AI Safety Insights" bulletins—summarizing key learnings from the data. This contributes to a continuous learning loop, where feedback drives policy evolution and process optimization across entire transport networks.

7. CONCLUSION AND FUTURE OUTLOOK

The transportation of dangerous goods (TDG) remains one of the most high-stakes sectors in the global supply chain. With hazards ranging from explosive, flammable, and toxic substances to unstable terrains and unpredictable driving environments, the risks facing drivers, handlers, and logistics managers are considerable. Traditional approaches to occupational health and safety (OHS)—focused on compliance, periodic inspections, and incident response—have delivered incremental progress. However, the growing scale, complexity, and dynamism of TDG operations require a step-change in safety strategy.

This chapter has explored how **predictive analytics** and **artificial intelligence (AI)** are transforming incident prevention in TDG. Through real-world case studies, vendor tools, regulatory frameworks, and ethical considerations, we have seen how data-driven systems can anticipate hazards, support human judgment, and improve both operational performance and worker well-being. While predictive analytics enables foresight, AI introduces adaptability—allowing safety systems to evolve and respond in real time.

7.1 Summary of Key Findings

Several core insights emerge from this exploration:

- AI and predictive systems move safety from reactive to proactive: By identifying leading indicators—such as fatigue, mechanical stress, or risky driving behaviour—these tools allow organizations to intervene before incidents occur.
- Occupational health and safety are enhanced, not just compliance: AI-based monitoring supports driver well-being by reducing cognitive load, reinforcing safe habits, and enabling timely interventions. This goes beyond regulatory box-ticking and focuses on meaningful risk reduction.
- Organizational culture and trust are critical to success: Drivers must view AI systems as partners rather than surveillance mechanisms. Transparent policies, worker participation, and ethical data use are key to sustainable adoption.
- Technical and operational challenges remain: From infrastructure gaps in developing regions to alert fatigue, data bias, and protected-area restrictions on recordings, the rollout of AI in TDG must be carefully contextualized and continuously improved.
- AI supports continuous learning: Unlike fixed rules or manuals, AI systems improve over time—adapting to driver behaviour, environmental conditions, and operational feedback. This supports a culture of continuous improvement in OHS management.

7.2 Strategic Importance for Transport Operators

The value proposition of predictive analytics and AI in TDG safety is becoming increasingly clear. Transport operators, especially those dealing with hazardous materials, face heightened regulatory scrutiny, rising insurance costs, and growing societal expectations around corporate responsibility.

By adopting AI-driven safety systems, operators can:

- Reduce incident frequency and severity
- Enhance worker morale and retention
- Lower maintenance and insurance costs
- Demonstrate compliance with global OHS frameworks
- Build competitive advantage through operational reliability

However, technology alone is not enough. Operators must build safety leadership, allocate resources for training and change management, and integrate AI into broader OHS and business continuity plans.

7.3 Implications for Policy and Regulation

As AI becomes more entrenched in TDG, regulatory bodies must evolve from policing compliance to enabling innovation. Policymakers should:

- Update legislation to account for AI-supported safety measures
- Set standards for AI performance, data privacy, and interoperability
- Promote adoption through incentives or tax breaks for telematics systems
- Support public-private partnerships to pilot AI solutions in challenging contexts
- Invest in digital infrastructure, especially in developing economies

Moreover, international coordination is essential. A unified approach—guided by the UN, ILO, and ISO—can ensure that AI-enhanced safety systems are inclusive, ethical, and interoperable across borders.

7.4 Research and Development Opportunities

The field of AI in TDG safety is still emerging, offering ample room for academic and industrial research. Key areas for future inquiry include:

- AI model accuracy and generalization: How well do models trained in one geography transfer to others?
- Behavioural impact studies: What are the long-term effects of AI monitoring on driver behaviour, stress, and motivation?
- Hybrid safety models: How can AI be combined with human expertise, especially in ambiguous or high-pressure scenarios?
- Bias and fairness audits: Are AI alerts equally accurate across different demographic groups?
- Human-AI collaboration frameworks: How should responsibility be shared between systems and operators?

These questions offer fertile ground for collaboration between universities, AI firms, transport operators, and policy institutions.

7.5 Future Outlook

Looking ahead, several trends are likely to shape the evolution of AI in TDG safety:

1. Increased Autonomy

Semi-autonomous features—such as lane-keeping assistance and collision avoidance—will become more standard in TDG vehicles. Over time, partial or full autonomy in controlled environments (e.g., depot-to-depot transport) may reduce human exposure to hazardous conditions.

2. Cross-modal Integration

AI safety systems will not be limited to road transport. Maritime, rail, and air TDG will also adopt predictive tools, creating opportunities for integrated, multimodal risk management.

3. Human-centred Design

There will be growing emphasis on designing AI systems that are understandable, controllable, and supportive of human users. Explainable AI (XAI) will help drivers and supervisors understand why alerts are issued, increasing trust and usability.

4. Democratization of Safety Technology

As costs decline and open-source tools emerge, even small fleet operators will gain access to predictive analytics. This democratization will help close the digital divide in TDG safety.

5. AI-informed Regulation

Regulators will increasingly rely on AI analytics themselves—for auditing, trend detection, and safety benchmarking. Real-time reporting tools will become the norm rather than the exception.

7.6 Recommendations

Considering the findings from this chapter, the following recommendations are proposed:

For Transport Operators

- Prioritize AI integration in areas with the highest incident rates or occupational hazards.
- Use a phased, pilot-based approach to implementation.
- Engage drivers and staff in tool selection, training, and feedback loops.
- Establish clear, worker-friendly data policies.
- Regularly evaluate system performance and update models.

For Regulators

- Modernize safety standards to include real-time and AI-based systems.
- Develop certification pathways for AI tools used in critical safety applications.
- Support SME adoption through grants or shared infrastructure.
- Coordinate internationally to harmonize expectations and share best practices.

For Researchers and Technology Developers

- Focus on inclusivity, robustness, and user experience.
- Partner with industry to access real-world data and validate models.
- Incorporate ethics and OHS principles into design from the outset.
- Translate findings into accessible guidelines for end users.

8. CONCLUSION

Artificial intelligence is not a panacea—but it is a powerful ally in the quest to create safer, more sustainable, and more dignified workplaces in TDG. As technology evolves, so too must our approach to safety. The convergence of AI and OHS offers a rare opportunity: to move from a world where we react to accidents, to one where we foresee and prevent them—protecting not just assets, but the lives and well-being of those who keep critical goods moving around the world.

REFERENCES

Bosch Connected Mobility. (2023). *Predictive Maintenance in Commercial Fleets.* https://www.bosch-mobility.com

BP. (2023). BP. *Sustainability Report, 2023,* •••. https://www.bp.com

Chevron. (2023). *Technology in Transport Safety*. Chevron Global Health, Safety & Environment Briefing.

European Agency for Safety and Health at Work (EU-OSHA). (2021). *Work-related stress, fatigue, and health in the transport sector.* https://osha.europa.eu

Gauzy. (2023). *Gauzy unveils next-generation AI-powered advanced driver assistance system.* https://investors.gauzy.com

International Labour Organization (ILO). (2023). *World Social Protection Report: Occupational Fatalities by Sector.* ILO Publishing.

International Maritime Organization (IMO). (2020). *Transport of Dangerous Goods by Sea: IMDG Code*. IMO.

International Road Transport Union (IRU). (2022). *Global Survey on Digital Adoption in Road Transport.* IRU Reports.

ISO. (2018). *ISO 45001:2018 Occupational Health and Safety Management Systems – Requirements with Guidance for Use*. International Organization for Standardization.

Mix Telematics. (2022). *Fleet Safety and Predictive Maintenance Solutions.* https://www.Mixtelematics.com

Mix Telematics. (2023). *Fleet Management with Mix Fleet Manager Premium and Mix Vision AI.* Retrieved from https://www.Mixtelematics.com

NetsPresso. (2023). *NOTA AI Driver Monitoring Platform.* https://nota.ai

Nota America Inc. (2023). NOTA AI for Real-Time Fatigue Detection in Commercial Drivers. https://nota.ai

Shell. (2022). *Driving Safer Operations with AI: Shell Transport Safety Review*. Retrieved from https://www.shell.com

Technologies, H. E. R. E. (2023). *Fleet Telematics Services.* https://www.here.com

TomTom Telematics. (2023). *AI Fleet Routing Solutions.* https://www.tomtom.com

TotalEnergies. (2023). *Health, Safety, Environment, and Quality Charter.* Retrieved from https://totalenergies.com

TotalEnergies Zimbabwe. (2023). *PATROM Training Manual and Journey Management Protocols.* Transport Contractor Orientation.

UNECE. (2020). *Statistics of the Transport of Dangerous Goods in Europe and Central Asia*. United Nations Economic Commission for Europe.

United Nations Economic Commission for Europe (UNECE). (2022). *UN Recommendations on the Transport of Dangerous Goods – Model Regulations*. UN Publications.

World Bank. (2022). *Global Road Safety Facility: Innovation and Investment Programs in Africa and Asia*. World Bank Group.

World Health Organization (WHO). (2021). *Global Status Report on Road Safety*. WHO Press.

Chapter 11

Preventing Accidents:

A Hybrid Approach to Workplace Safety Prediction and Risk Management

Usharani Bhimavarapu
https://orcid.org/0000-0002-0246-1420
Department of Computer Science and Engineering, Koneru Lakshmaiah Education Foundation, Vaddeswaram, India

ABSTRACT

Prevention and prediction of workplace safety are critical components of reducing accidents and improving overall employee well-being. In this study, we explore advanced techniques for predicting and preventing workplace accidents using machine learning and optimization algorithms. We focus on the application of Particle Swarm Optimization (PSO) and Remora Optimization for feature extraction and selection, respectively, to identify the most relevant factors contributing to accidents. A Convolutional Neural Network (CNN) is then employed to predict accident severity, fatality risks, and injury outcomes based on extracted features. The dataset used in this study includes various workplace accident records, including accident types, industry sectors, safety compliance levels, and injury data. The results demonstrate that our approach effectively identifies critical factors influencing workplace safety, allowing for targeted interventions and improved predictive accuracy.

INTRODUCTION

Workplace accidents are a significant concern across industries worldwide, particularly in sectors such as construction, manufacturing, and transportation. These incidents can range from minor injuries to fatal accidents, posing not only a threat to employee safety but also a financial burden on businesses due to medical expenses, legal liabilities, and loss of productivity. According to reports, millions of workplace

DOI: 10.4018/979-8-3693-9301-7.ch011

accidents occur each year, with a notable proportion leading to severe injuries or fatalities. Ensuring workplace safety is therefore crucial to protecting employees and maintaining operational efficiency.

Various factors contribute to workplace accidents, including human errors, inadequate training, equipment malfunction, and unsafe working conditions. In many cases, accidents could have been prevented with proper safety protocols, effective hazard identification, and risk management practices. Common causes of workplace injuries include falls, machine-related incidents, vehicle accidents, exposure to harmful substances, and electrical hazards. Recognizing and addressing these risks is essential in reducing the frequency and severity of workplace accidents.

Preventing workplace accidents requires a multifaceted approach that includes stringent safety measures, regular training programs, and a culture of safety within the organization. Employers must provide employees with the necessary protective equipment, enforce safety regulations, and conduct regular safety audits to identify potential hazards. Moreover, fostering open communication about safety concerns and encouraging workers to report unsafe practices can significantly reduce the likelihood of accidents. Organizations should also invest in technology and tools that help monitor workplace conditions in real time, providing early warnings for potential risks.

The role of predictive modeling and machine learning is increasingly important in workplace safety management. By analyzing historical accident data, machine learning models can predict accident-prone areas, identify high-risk conditions, and suggest preventive measures. These predictive models can help organizations allocate resources more effectively, prioritize safety interventions, and improve accident prevention strategies. With advancements in artificial intelligence and data analytics, the ability to predict and prevent accidents before they occur is becoming more accurate and accessible.

Reducing workplace accidents requires ongoing efforts from both employers and employees, with a focus on prevention, safety culture, and technological innovation. By implementing effective safety protocols, continuously training workers, and utilizing predictive tools, the frequency of workplace accidents can be significantly reduced. Not only does this enhance employee well-being, but it also leads to a more productive and profitable work environment, highlighting the importance of prioritizing safety in the workplace.

Prediction and prevention of workplace accidents are critical elements in enhancing employee safety and reducing the financial and operational impact on businesses. Workplace accidents, ranging from minor injuries to fatalities, can have severe consequences for both workers and organizations. Through predictive analytics, employers can leverage data and technology to anticipate potential hazards and prevent accidents before they occur. By identifying patterns and trends in accident data, predictive models can highlight areas of concern, allowing organizations to take proactive measures and implement safety protocols tailored to specific risks.

The prediction of workplace accidents often involves the use of machine learning algorithms and historical accident data. These models analyze various factors such as workplace conditions, employee behavior, environmental hazards, and equipment performance to identify risk factors. For instance, machine learning models can predict when and where an accident is most likely to occur based on past trends, weather conditions, and employee actions. By incorporating real-time data such as sensor inputs from equipment or environmental factors, these models can provide more accurate and timely predictions, enabling companies to intervene before an incident takes place.

Preventing workplace accidents requires a comprehensive approach that goes beyond predictive modeling. Employers must establish a safety-first culture, emphasizing the importance of hazard identification, risk assessment, and employee training. Regular safety audits, inspections, and maintenance of equipment are essential to ensure the working environment remains safe. Providing employees with personal protective equipment (PPE), creating clear safety guidelines, and conducting regular drills can further reduce the likelihood of accidents. Additionally, fostering a strong communication channel where employees feel comfortable reporting unsafe practices or conditions is vital for accident prevention.

An essential aspect of accident prevention is continuous monitoring and adaptation of safety measures based on predictive insights. By using the results from predictive models, companies can prioritize high-risk areas and deploy safety resources more effectively. For example, if a model predicts a higher likelihood of accidents during specific shifts or in particular areas of the workplace, management can focus additional training, improve equipment maintenance, or adjust work schedules to minimize risks. This dynamic approach ensures that safety measures evolve with changing conditions and emerging risks.

The prediction and prevention of workplace accidents require a combination of data-driven insights, preventive measures, and a proactive safety culture. Predictive analytics plays a vital role in identifying and addressing risks before accidents occur, but it must be complemented by a robust safety infrastructure, employee education, and continuous improvement of safety practices. By integrating predictive tools and preventive strategies, organizations can significantly reduce the incidence of workplace accidents, safeguarding employees and improving overall operational efficiency.

Several models have been developed for risk assessment and accident prevention in industrial settings, yet limitations persist across different approaches. Ouyang and Luo (2025) examined the impact of physical fatigue along with heat on construction workers' cognitive performance. But their research is constrained by a controlled experimental scenario that might lack the realism and unpredictability of real construction sites, thus possibly diminishing the ecological validity of the results.

Ojha et al. (2024) evaluated the physiological effects of powered back-support exoskeletons in construction. Despite the thorough evaluation, the research is constrained by a relatively small sample size and limited duration of use, which might not be able to capture long-term consequences or differences among various construction activities and user groups.

Aminbakhsh et al. (2013) used the Analytic Hierarchy Process (AHP) in project planning to conduct safety risk assessment. AHP provides formalized decision-making, but it suffers from dependency on subjective judgments by experts, and this could bring bias as well as impact consistency of outcomes in various project scenarios.

Shapira and Simcha (2009) used AHP to balance safety considerations related to tower crane operation. While the method improves on prioritization, the limitation of the study is its narrow application to crane-specific risks, thus reducing its generalizability to other construction safety contexts.

Raviv et al. (2017) applied AHP to evaluate risk potential in crane-related safety accidents. The limitation in this case is the retrospective evaluation of incident data, which might not be representative of proactive risk management measures or more recent technologies in crane safety.

Zhang et al. (2020) integrated PCA and Group AHP in road construction safety evaluation. Although the integration of methods enhances analytical power, the complexity of the method could restrict its practical uptake by safety managers who lack advanced education in multi-criteria decision-making techniques.

Chan et al. (2004) applied AHP to set priorities in a safety management system. One limitation is that the research may not be able to respond to dynamic changes in construction environments, where safety priorities change quickly based on task complexity and workforce behavior.

Zeibak-Shini et al. (2024) investigated applying AHP for resource allocation and safety management. While useful, the weakness is in the abstraction level of the AHP model, which might oversimplify subtle, context-specific considerations in actual safety decision-making.

Soltanzadeh et al. (2023) used fuzzy AHP to evaluate occupational hazard risks. Although the fuzzy extension improves uncertainty handling, the limitation of this study lies in the fact that it is based on a single case, limiting generalizability to other construction projects or regions.

Abbasinia and Mohammadfam (2022) applied fuzzy AHP and fuzzy TOPSIS to rank occupational accident causes. Methodologically rigorous, the limitation of the study is that there can be subjectivity in the definition of linguistic variables, which may differ across cultural or linguistic contexts and affect reproducibility.

Basahel and Taylan (2016) applied fuzzy AHP and TOPSIS to evaluate worksite safety. One limitation of this research is that it will not capture all temporal dynamics of safety conditions, as snapshot evaluations may miss changing risks throughout the duration of a project.

Janackovic et al. (2013) performed a fuzzy AHP-based selection of occupational safety indicators for road construction. Although presenting a helpful framework, the limitation of the study is the specificity of its case study, which might not be easily applied to industries other than road construction or to smaller projects.

Ferrari et al. (2020) ranked occupational health and safety indicators with fuzzy AHP. The research offers a systematic method, but it is constrained by the static character of its assessment process, which might not be able to adjust to evolving safety policies, technologies, or workforce compositions over time.

Zavari et al. (2022) introduced a novel method integrating BIM and GIS to optimize construction site layouts. The limitation of the study, though, is that it used simulated data, which might not reflect the complexity and uncertainties of actual construction sites, and thus its practicality could be compromised.

Kouabenan et al. (2015) investigated the association between safety climate, perceived risk, and involvement in safety management. One main limitation is that the data is self-reported, which is subject to social desirability bias, and the findings of the study are specific to the context, which limits their applicability across various cultural or industrial contexts.

Gunderson and Gloeckner (2011) examined superintendent competencies using industry perceptions. While useful, the research is constrained by its subjective nature and possible regional bias, since industry expectations can differ considerably between nations and construction sectors.

Post et al. (2019) tested female leadership trust benefits in times of crisis. Although enlightening, the results are limited by the experimental and survey-based design of the study, which may not capture the complexity of leadership in real-world construction project settings where safety is paramount.

Moshood et al. (2020) scored human factors affecting contractors' risk attitudes in Malaysia. The limitation of this study is that its regional scope may not apply elsewhere in nations having different regulatory structures or risk attitude cultures in construction.

Zhou et al. (2022) suggested a data-driven methodology to examining collapse patterns in metro construction. Although the approach is statistically sound, its drawback is reliance on past accident records, which might not include future hazards or new construction technologies.

Toh et al. (2017) investigated the knowledge, attitudes, and practice of design for safety among Singapore construction stakeholders. The research is limited by its geographic and cultural context, and the survey information might not capture deeper institutional or systemic hindrances to successful implementation.

Hossain et al. (2018) proposed a design-for-safety knowledge library in combination with BIM. Although promising, the method has limitations arising from possible resistance by users to implement new digital technologies and a requirement for constant updates to ensure continued applicability in fast-changing construction conditions.

Zhou et al. (2012) reviewed digital design's role in improving construction safety. The limitation here is the rapidly changing technological landscape, which may render some of the reviewed tools obsolete. Additionally, the paper primarily emphasizes technological potential without deeply addressing organizational or behavioral challenges.

Che Ibrahim et al. (2021) investigated PtD education for Malaysian future engineers. It discusses important challenges, but the limitation of this study is that it is based on a small sample and relies on education systems in one national context only, which limits the generalizability of its results to other contexts.

Poghosyan et al. (2018) performed a literature review of influencing factors on the implementation of design for safety (DfS). While wide-ranging, the review is marred by variability and inconsistency of terms applied in sources, and hence may make it difficult to synthesize and apply findings.

Goh and Chua (2016) investigated attitudes, knowledge, and practices of civil and structural engineers toward design for safety. One limitation of this study is its cross-sectional design, not taking into account changes over time or the long-term effect of DfS training and policy on practice.

Ibrahim et al. (2022) conducted a review of construction engineering and management DfS practices. Rich in the identification of trends but weak in lacking empirical verification of emergent practice and heavy usage of secondary literature that could downplay ground-level challenges to adoption, the review was conducted.

Teo et al. (2016) also theoretically suggested a safety index framework using BIM. Conceptually excellent, the restriction lies in that the framework itself is theoretical in nature with minimum empirical validation against its effectiveness and practicality to be used within real-world implementation scenarios of BIM.

Tymvios and Gambatese (2016) collected stakeholder perceptions of DfS. Even with a holistic approach to the study, it is bounded by possible biases in stakeholders as well as the varied understanding of safety responsibilities and may impact how responses are constant across the sample.

Zhou et al. (2023) performed an extensive review of construction safety management through datasets, machine learning methods, and thematic domains. Nevertheless, one major limitation is the focus of the review on published academic literature, which can omit perspectives from industry applications or grey literature. In addition, the highly dynamic nature of machine learning can rapidly make some reviewed methods obsolete.

Pagell et al. (2014) examined the safe production paradox and whether safety and productivity can go together. Although rich in concept, the limitation of the study is its theoretical focus with limited empirical support across diverse industries. The subtle organizational and cultural differences influencing safety-productivity trade-offs are also not fully explored.

Ghousi et al. (2018) also put forward a versatile risk assessment framework that involves monetary considerations of safety schemes in building construction. Nonetheless, the intricacy of the model might curtail its implementation for small businesses with minimal financial resources. Further, the economic analysis is localized and may not be transferable to diverse economic conditions.

Manzoor et al. (2021) have noted key safety determinants causing accidents in high-rise construction projects. One of the limitations of the study is that it is based on perceptions by a small set of stakeholders and may therefore carry subjective bias. The results are also not verified using longitudinal or cross-regional analysis, making generalizability low.

Chen et al. (2023) conducted a review of the effect of wearables on construction worker safety. Although relevant, the limitation of the review is the absence of empirical studies with long-term assessment of wearables in dynamic construction environments. Additionally, possible issues such as user compliance, data privacy, and technology expenses are not extensively examined.

Sofwan et al. (2016) did an initial research on risk factors in high-rise construction. The main limitation is the initiality of the research, which offers a mere surface-level recognition of risk factors without extensive statistical verification or in-depth analysis. The research also does not include a comparative approach to various project types or settings.

Hu et al. (2022) created an intelligent safety risk identification technique for gas drilling. While technologically innovative, its usage is confined to one industry—gas drilling—limiting its applicability to overall construction contexts. Moreover, the use of real-time data inputs can be problematic in data-poor settings.

Macêdo et al. (2022) employed text mining and BERT models to extract safety risk features in refineries. The limitation of the study is its domain specificity, since the model was specifically designed for refinery data and may not generalize well to other industries without heavy re-training. Furthermore, the interpretability of AI models continues to be an issue for effective safety decisions.

Zhang et al. (2015) showed the ability of workforce location tracking for safety planning using building information models (BIM). Nevertheless, its limitation lies in its heavy reliance on accurate real-time location information and sophisticated technological infrastructure, which may not exist in most construction settings. Its applicability to developing regions is unclear.

Aziz et al. (2019) proposed an ontology-based hazard identification and causation analysis. Conceptually robust, the issue is that there is a challenge of complexity for developing and keeping ontology up-to-date, expertise required for such a task, and no attempt was made in testing the performance of the method across different culture or regulatory domains.

Chartres et al. (2019) provided a review of current methods for environmental hazard identification and risk assessment. The research has a limitation that lies in its general focus, which might water down in-depth understanding of certain industries like construction. The research is also not explicit on how to select from the methods depending on context-specific criteria.

Martin et al. (2018) evaluated the weight-of-evidence strategy for hazard identification. One significant limitation is variability in evidence weighting and interpretation, resulting in different risk conclusions among studies. The review also indicates a shortage of standardized guidelines, which inhibits practical application of the approach.

Nawaz et al.'s (2019) study is an imaginative approach to managing risk in developing countries' construction projects, illustrated using Pakistan. The limitation in the study, however, comes in the fact that the geographical nature of its findings might be difficult to transfer to other developing countries with disparate socio-economic, regulatory, or cultural environments. Furthermore, no test of its practical application in longitudinal studies makes its long-term performance questionable.

Hwang et al. (2018) examined safety in Singapore green building construction projects and identified key issues and solutions. Nevertheless, the limitation of the study is that it was conducted within a single city-state, whose policies and practices may vary drastically from those of larger or less-regulated markets. The study also depended largely on qualitative research, which may limit the findings' generalizability.

Tonetto et al. (2021) highlighted the nuance of selecting fall protection systems in construction, separating complex from complicated systems. Although this systems-thinking perspective is worthwhile, the shortcoming is that the framework can be of limited direct application on busy, resource-scarce construction sites where time and cost constraints could forestall full system analysis.

Wang et al. (2016) examined influential factors on workers' tolerance of safety risk. One major limitation is the use of self-reported data, which can be socially desirable or recall error biased. Additionally, cultural influences on risk tolerance were not extensively examined, which may compromise the international applicability of the results.

Kumar and Narayanan (2021) conducted a case study from Chennai and developed a risk management procedural index. However, the limitation of their study is its narrow scope focused on a single urban region, which may not account for variations in rural or other urban settings. The index also lacks external validation, which restricts its broader usability.

Tian et al. (2022) introduced a model for evaluating crossed risks in construction safety. While groundbreaking, the model can be constrained by its intricacy, possibly discouraging uptake from practitioners who are unfamiliar with sophisticated risk model methodology. The research also fails to consider real-time dynamic construction site changes.

Alkaissy et al. (2020) gave a detailed overview of 20 years of risk modeling in construction safety. Though the review is expansive, it is restricted by being retrospective, which may ignore new emerging technologies and methods not yet commonly accepted or published in the academic literature. Afzal et al. (2021) analyzed the application of virtual-design construction technologies to enhance safety. A significant limitation is the use of second-level data and literature without empirical evidence of the efficiency of the technologies in practice. In addition, the research does not completely account for technology adoption cost and training impediments.

Yap and Lee (2020) examined the fundamental drivers of the safety performance in building construction. The limitation in this study is that it's a cross-sectional study, thus limiting causality determination. It also fails to address organizational cultural dynamics sufficiently as a potential impact on safety outcomes.

Kukoyi and Adebowale (2021) examined barriers to the enhancement of construction safety. The research is constrained by its attention to perceived obstacles instead of tried and tested solutions. Furthermore, it fails to consider the heterogeneity in enforcement and governance arrangements that can greatly affect the applicability of suggested measures. By integrating CNNs with PSO and REMORA, the proposed model addresses the challenges of scalability, generalizability, and interpretability, which are often limitations in deep learning-based and domain-specific models.

Together, this hybrid approach ensures a robust framework for predicting workplace accidents, offering higher accuracy, adaptability across industries, and actionable insights to improve safety standards.

MATERIAL AND METHODOLOGY

The methodology involves three key steps: data preprocessing, feature extraction, and predictive modeling. Initially, the dataset is cleaned and normalized to handle missing values and outliers. Particle Swarm Optimization (PSO) is used for feature extraction, identifying the most relevant factors influencing workplace accidents. Remora Optimization is then applied for feature selection, ensuring the inclusion of only the most impactful variables. A Convolutional Neural Network (CNN) is trained to predict accident outcomes, including severity and fatality risks. The model's performance is evaluated using accuracy metrics, ensuring effective prediction and risk management.

Material

We collected a dataset for 2023 highlighting workplace safety issues in India, revealing over 400 worker fatalities caused by safety lapses across various industries. The chemical and pharmaceutical sectors were particularly affected, with more than 110 accidents leading to at least 220 fatalities and over 550 serious injuries. Significant incidents included an explosion at a pharmaceutical factory in Andhra Pradesh in August, which resulted in 18 deaths and 30 injuries, and a chemical factory explosion in Mumbai in May that claimed 13 lives and injured over 60.

The mining industry data recorded at least 22 accidents, resulting in 60 fatalities and more than 50 serious injuries. Additionally, the energy sector reported over 20 worker fatalities during the year. Notable incidents include a boiler explosion at a parts manufacturing facility in Haryana in February, causing at least 14 deaths and over 25 severe injuries.

The dataset underscores the urgent need for enhanced safety protocols and stricter enforcement of regulations to ensure the protection of workers across India's industrial sectors.

Preprocessing

The preprocessing of the collected dataset on workplace accidents in India for 2023 involved several critical steps to ensure the data was clean, accurate, and ready for analysis. Initially, the dataset was examined for missing, inconsistent, or duplicate records, which were either imputed or removed to maintain data integrity. Key variables such as industry type, nature of the accident, fatalities, injuries, and location were standardized to ensure uniformity in categorization and formatting.

Next, numerical fields, such as the number of fatalities and injuries, were normalized to facilitate comparative analysis across industries and regions. Textual descriptions of incidents were preprocessed by removing unnecessary characters, correcting spelling errors, and applying techniques like tokenization and lemmatization to extract meaningful insights. Additionally, location data was geo-tagged where possible, enabling spatial analysis of accident patterns.

Outliers, such as exceptionally high or low values in fatalities and injuries, were identified and reviewed to determine their validity. Finally, the dataset was split into subsets based on sectors, accident types, and severity levels, enabling targeted analysis and visualization of trends. These preprocessing steps ensured that the dataset was comprehensive, structured, and ready for advanced analytics and model development.

Feature Extraction

Feature extraction from the collected workplace accident dataset was enhanced using Particle Swarm Optimization (PSO), a robust metaheuristic algorithm. PSO was employed to identify and select the most relevant features that contribute significantly to understanding accident trends, causes, and impacts. The process began by encoding potential feature subsets as particles within the search space, with each particle representing a combination of features from the dataset.

The fitness function was designed to evaluate each particle based on its ability to maximize the predictive accuracy of a classification or regression model applied to the data. PSO iteratively optimized the feature set by updating the positions and velocities of the particles, leveraging both individual particle experience (local best) and the collective swarm knowledge (global best). Through this process, redundant, irrelevant, and noisy features were filtered out, leaving a concise and meaningful subset of features.

Key extracted features included industry type, accident type, number of fatalities, injury severity, and compliance with safety protocols, among others. By focusing on these features, PSO not only reduced the dimensionality of the dataset but also improved the efficiency and accuracy of subsequent analytical models. This approach demonstrated the potential of PSO in feature selection, enabling a deeper understanding of workplace accident patterns.

Feature Selection

Feature selection from the collected workplace accident dataset was performed using the Remora Optimization algorithm, a novel swarm intelligence-based method inspired by the symbiotic relationship between remoras and their host organisms. This approach efficiently identified the most relevant features while eliminating redundant and irrelevant ones, thereby enhancing the interpretability and performance of analytical models.

The algorithm simulated the dynamic interaction between remoras and hosts, where each solution (remora) represented a potential subset of features. The optimization process involved balancing exploration and exploitation as the remoras adapted to their host environment to improve their survival (fitness). In this context, fitness was measured by evaluating the predictive accuracy of a machine learning model, such as a classifier, using the selected features.

Through iterative updates, the algorithm refined the feature subsets by leveraging both individual solutions and collective swarm behavior, ensuring convergence to an optimal or near-optimal solution. This process highlighted critical features such as accident type, industry sector, safety compliance levels, and injury severity, which contributed most significantly to predicting and understanding workplace accidents. By reducing the dimensionality of the dataset while preserving key information, the Remora Optimization algorithm proved to be an effective tool for feature selection, improving the accuracy and efficiency of subsequent analyses.

Prediction

Prediction of workplace accident outcomes using a Convolutional Neural Network (CNN) involved leveraging the spatial and hierarchical features of the data. The CNN model was designed to analyze complex patterns and relationships within the dataset, particularly for accident severity classification and fatality prediction. The input data, including numerical, categorical, and image-based information, was preprocessed to fit the CNN architecture. Numerical and categorical data were normalized and encoded, while any associated visual data, such as site images or accident diagrams, were resized and augmented to enhance variability and robustness.

The CNN architecture consisted of multiple convolutional layers, each extracting critical features from the input data through filters that captured local patterns, followed by pooling layers to reduce dimensionality and computational complexity. The extracted features were passed through fully connected layers to identify high-level relationships and generate predictions, such as the severity of injuries or the likelihood of fatalities. Dropout layers were incorporated to prevent overfitting and improve generalization.

The model was trained using the backpropagation algorithm with a suitable optimizer, such as Adam, and the loss function was designed to minimize the error in predictions. After training, the CNN demonstrated high accuracy in predicting outcomes, effectively identifying key risk factors and accident patterns. This approach highlighted the potential of CNNs in handling complex, multi-dimensional datasets for workplace safety analysis and proactive risk management.

EXPERIMENTAL RESULTS

The experimental results demonstrate the effectiveness of the proposed methodology in predicting workplace accidents and enhancing safety measures. After preprocessing the dataset and applying feature extraction through Particle Swarm Optimization (PSO) and feature selection with Remora Optimization, the Convolutional Neural Network (CNN) was trained to predict accident severity and outcomes. The model showed promising results in accurately identifying critical features influencing accident risk and predicting injury severity. Performance metrics such as accuracy, precision, recall, and F1-score were calculated to assess the model's robustness and its ability to generalize to unseen data. The results indicate that the integration of optimization algorithms and deep learning models significantly improved predictive accuracy compared to traditional safety prediction models.

Table 1 provides an overview of the severity levels of accidents, detailing the number of accidents, fatalities, and injuries associated with each level. The data is categorized into four severity levels: Minor, Moderate, Severe, and Critical. Minor accidents account for 250 incidents, with no fatalities but 100 injuries. Moderate accidents, with 150 incidents, resulted in 10 fatalities and 120 injuries. Severe accidents, while fewer in number (100), resulted in 50 fatalities and 150 injuries. Critical accidents are the least frequent (30) but most deadly, with 60 fatalities and 60 injuries. This table helps in understanding the distribution and severity of workplace accidents across different levels.

Table 1. Accident severity breakdown

Severity Level	Number of Accidents	Fatalities	Injuries
Minor	250	0	100
Moderate	150	10	120
Severe	100	50	150
Critical	30	60	60

Table 2 presents a breakdown of workplace accidents across various industries. Manufacturing records the highest number of accidents at 200, with 25 fatalities and 150 injuries. Construction follows closely with 180 accidents, including 60 fatalities and 100 injuries. Mining, with 100 accidents, shows a significant number of fatalities (40) and fewer injuries (50). Healthcare, with 50 accidents, reports relatively fewer fatalities (5) and injuries (40), while transportation, with 70 accidents, has 10 fatalities and 50 injuries. This table highlights the industries most prone to accidents and the corresponding severity.

Table 2. Industry-specific accident frequency

Industry	Number of Accidents	Fatalities	Injuries
Manufacturing	200	25	150
Construction	180	60	100
Mining	100	40	50
Healthcare	50	5	40
Transportation	70	10	50

Table 3 shows the correlation between safety compliance levels and accident frequency in the workplace. High compliance levels are associated with fewer accidents (100) and minimal fatalities (5) and injuries (80). Medium compliance sees a rise in accidents (250), with 40 fatalities and 150 injuries. Low compliance leads to the highest number of accidents (250), along with 70 fatalities and 230 injuries. The data demonstrates that stricter safety compliance directly reduces the frequency and severity of workplace accidents.

Table 3. Safety compliance impact on accident frequency

Compliance Level	Number of Accidents	Fatalities	Injuries
High	100	5	80
Medium	250	40	150
Low	250	70	230

Table 4 categorizes workplace accidents by their type, detailing the number of occurrences, fatalities, and injuries associated with each. Fall-related accidents lead with 120 occurrences, resulting in 25 fatalities and 80 injuries. Machine-related accidents follow closely with 180 occurrences, 40 fatalities, and 150 injuries. Vehicle-related accidents contribute to 100 occurrences, resulting in 50 fatalities and 60 injuries. Electrocution and chemical exposure accidents are less frequent, with 50 and 30 occurrences, respectively, causing 5 to 10 fatalities and varying injury levels. This table provides insight into the most common accident types and their impact on worker safety.

Table 4. Accident types

Accident Type	Number of Occurrences	Fatalities	Injuries
Fall	120	25	80
Machine-related	180	40	150
Vehicle-related	100	50	60
Electrocution	50	5	40
Chemical Exposure	30	10	20

Table 5 compares the performance of different models in predicting workplace accidents, highlighting key metrics such as accuracy, precision, recall, and F1-score. The proposed model outperforms all others, achieving an accuracy of 88.5%, precision of 86.7%, recall of 84.3%, and F1-score of 85.5%. Among the other models, Random Forest achieves 85.2% accuracy, while Support Vector Machine (SVM) and Logistic Regression have lower performance scores. These results emphasize the superior predictive capabilities of the proposed model in forecasting workplace accidents.

Table 5. Accident prediction performance metrics

Model	Accuracy	Precision	Recall	F1-Score
Proposed Model	88.5%	86.7%	84.3%	85.5%
Random Forest	85.2%	84.0%	81.5%	82.7%
SVM	83.1%	80.5%	78.9%	79.7%
Logistic Regression	80.3%	78.9%	75.2%	76.9%

Table 6 illustrates the importance scores of various features used in predicting workplace accidents, derived from the Particle Swarm Optimization (PSO) and REMORA optimization techniques. Industry type is the most significant feature, with an importance score of 0.22, followed by accident type (0.18) and safety compliance level (0.16). Other factors such as injury severity, employee training, location, and working hours are also considered, but their influence is lower, with scores ranging from 0.08 to 0.14. This table highlights the key variables that contribute to accurate predictions of workplace accidents.

Table 6. Feature importance

Feature	Importance Score
Industry Type	0.22
Accident Type	0.18
Safety Compliance Level	0.16
Injury Severity	0.14
Employee Training	0.12
Location	0.10
Working Hours	0.08

Table 7 provides a regional breakdown of workplace accidents, detailing the number of incidents, fatalities, and injuries in different geographic areas. The South region records the highest number of accidents (180), with 50 fatalities and 120 injuries. The North region follows with 150 accidents, 40 fatalities, and 90 injuries. The East region has 100 accidents, with 30 fatalities and 60 injuries, while the West region records the fewest accidents (70), with 10 fatalities and 50 injuries. This table helps to identify regional trends in workplace accidents.

Table 7. Accidents by region

Region	Number of Accidents	Fatalities	Injuries
North	150	40	90
South	180	50	120
East	100	30	60
West	70	10	50

Table 8 displays the frequency of workplace accidents by month, along with fatalities and injuries. January sees 50 accidents, with 10 fatalities and 40 injuries, while the number rises in June to 100 accidents, with 30 fatalities and 80 injuries. The data shows an upward trend in accidents as the year progresses, with May and June being particularly high-risk months. This table provides valuable insight into seasonal trends and can help in predicting accident-prone periods.

Table 8. Accidents by time of year

Month	Number of Accidents	Fatalities	Injuries
January	50	10	40
February	60	15	45
March	80	20	60
April	70	18	55
May	90	25	70
June	100	30	80

Table 9 compares predicted fatalities with actual fatalities, showcasing the accuracy of the model in forecasting accident outcomes. The prediction accuracy is highest for fatalities in the 0-10 range, achieving 95% accuracy. The accuracy decreases slightly for higher ranges of fatalities, with 75% accuracy for 51+ fatalities. This table emphasizes the model's reliability in predicting low fatality accidents, while still performing reasonably well for more severe cases.

Table 9. Predicted vs actual fatalities

Predicted Fatalities	Actual Fatalities	Prediction Accuracy
0-10	0-10	95%
11-30	11-30	89%
31-50	31-50	82%
51+	51+	75%

Table 10 compares the predicted and actual cases of injury severity, along with prediction accuracy. For minor injuries, the predicted cases closely match actual occurrences, achieving a 96% prediction accuracy. Moderate, severe, and critical injury predictions also demonstrate high accuracy, ranging from 93% to 96%. This table highlights the model's strong predictive performance in accurately forecasting injury severity levels across various types of workplace accidents.

Table 10. Injury severity prediction

Injury Severity	Predicted Cases	Actual Cases	Prediction Accuracy
Minor	120	115	96%
Moderate	150	140	93%
Severe	80	75	94%
Critical	50	48	96%

Table 11 compares the predictive performance of the proposed Convolutional Neural Network (CNN) model with nine existing models, including Random Forest, SVM, Logistic Regression, K-Nearest Neighbors, Naive Bayes, Decision Tree, Gradient Boosting, AdaBoost, and XGBoost. The proposed CNN achieves the highest accuracy (88.5%), precision (86.7%), recall (84.3%), and F1-score (85.5%), surpassing all other models. Among the alternatives, Random Forest and XGBoost perform best after CNN, with accuracy scores of 85.2% and 87.5%, respectively. This table highlights the superior performance of the proposed CNN model in accident prediction.

Table 11. Prediction comparison

Model	Accuracy (%)	Precision (%)	Recall (%)	F1-Score (%)
Proposed CNN	88.5	86.7	84.3	85.5
Random Forest	85.2	84.0	81.5	82.7
Support Vector Machine (SVM)	83.1	80.5	78.9	79.7
Logistic Regression	80.3	78.9	75.2	76.9
K-Nearest Neighbors (KNN)	82.7	81.3	79.8	80.5
Naive Bayes	78.9	77.2	74.4	75.8
Decision Tree	84.0	83.5	80.2	81.8
Gradient Boosting	86.4	85.1	82.9	83.9

continued on following page

Table 11. Continued

Model	Accuracy (%)	Precision (%)	Recall (%)	F1-Score (%)
AdaBoost	81.2	79.3	76.8	78.0
XGBoost	87.5	86.3	83.5	84.9

CONCLUSION

In conclusion, the integration of advanced machine learning techniques, such as PSO for feature extraction, Remora Optimization for feature selection, and CNN for prediction, provides a robust framework for improving workplace safety. By identifying key factors that contribute to accidents and accurately predicting the severity and outcomes of such incidents, organizations can implement targeted safety measures and preventative strategies. The results underscore the importance of using data-driven approaches to optimize safety protocols, enhance risk management, and ultimately reduce the incidence of workplace accidents. This study lays the foundation for further research in the application of machine learning to workplace safety, with potential applications in real-time monitoring systems and automated decision-making processes.

REFERENCES

Abbasinia, M., & Mohammadfam, I. (2022). Identifying, evaluating and prioritizing the causes of occupational accidents in the construction industry using fuzzy AHP and fuzzy TOPSIS. *Work (Reading, Mass.)*, *72*(3), 933–940. DOI: 10.3233/WOR-210024 PMID: 35634821

Afzal, M., Shafiq, M. T., & Al Jassmi, H. (2021). Improving construction safety with virtual-design construction technologies—A review. *Journal of Information Technology in Construction*, *26*, 319–340. DOI: 10.36680/j.itcon.2021.018

Alkaissy, M., Arashpour, M., Ashuri, B., Bai, Y., & Hosseini, R. (2020). Safety management in construction: 20 years of risk modeling. *Safety Science*, *129*, 104805. DOI: 10.1016/j.ssci.2020.104805

Aminbakhsh, S., Gunduz, M., & Sonmez, R. (2013). Safety risk assessment using Analytic Hierarchy Process (AHP) during planning and budgeting of construction projects. *Journal of Safety Research*, *46*, 99–105. DOI: 10.1016/j.jsr.2013.05.003 PMID: 23932691

Aziz, A., Ahmed, S., & Khan, F. I. (2019). An ontology-based methodology for hazard identification and causation analysis. *Process Safety and Environmental Protection*, *123*, 87–98. DOI: 10.1016/j.psep.2018.12.008

Basahel, A., & Taylan, O. (2016). Using fuzzy AHP and fuzzy TOPSIS approaches for assessing safety conditions at worksites in construction industry. *International Journal of Safety and Security Engineering*, *6*(4), 728–745. DOI: 10.2495/SAFE-V6-N4-728-745

Chan, A. H., Kwok, W., & Duffy, V. G. (2004). Using AHP for determining priority in a safety management system. *Industrial Management & Data Systems*, *104*(5), 430–445. DOI: 10.1108/02635570410537516

Chartres, N., Bero, L. A., & Norris, S. L. (2019). A review of methods used for hazard identification and risk assessment of environmental hazards. *Environment International*, *123*, 231–239. DOI: 10.1016/j.envint.2018.11.060 PMID: 30537638

Che Ibrahim, C. K. I., Belayutham, S., & Mohammad, M. Z. (2021). Prevention through design (PtD) education for future civil engineers in Malaysia: Current state, challenges, and way forward. *Journal of Civil Engineering Education*, *147*(1), 05020007. DOI: 10.1061/(ASCE)EI.2643-9115.0000030

Chen, H., Mao, Y., Xu, Y., & Wang, R. (2023). The impact of wearable devices on the construction safety of building workers: A systematic review. *Sustainability (Basel)*, *15*(14), 11165. DOI: 10.3390/su151411165

Ferrari, G. N., Leal, G. C. L., Galdamez, E. V. C., & de Souza, R. C. T. (2020). Prioritization of occupational health and safety indicators using the fuzzy-AHP method. *Production*, *30*, e20200054. DOI: 10.1590/0103-6513.20200054

Ghousi, R., Khanzadi, M., & Atashgah, K. M. (2018). A flexible method of building construction safety risk assessment and investigating financial aspects of safety program. *International Journal of Optimization in Civil Engineering*, *8*, 433–452.

Goh, Y. M., & Chua, S. (2016). Knowledge, attitude and practices for design for safety: A study on civil & structural engineers. *Accident; Analysis and Prevention*, *93*, 260–266. DOI: 10.1016/j.aap.2015.09.023 PMID: 26477455

Gunderson, D. E., & Gloeckner, G. W. (2011). Superintendent competencies and attributes required for success: A national study comparing construction professionals' opinions. *International Journal of Construction Education and Research*, *7*(4), 294–311. DOI: 10.1080/15578771.2011.618964

Hossain, M. A., Abbott, E. L. S., Chua, D. K. H., Qui, N. T., & Goh, Y. M. (2018). Design-for-safety knowledge library for BIM-integrated safety risk reviews. *Automation in Construction*, *94*, 290–302. DOI: 10.1016/j.autcon.2018.07.010

Hu, W., Xia, W., Li, Y., Jiang, J., Li, G., & Chen, Y. (2022). An intelligent identification method of safety risk while drilling in gas drilling. *Petroleum Exploration and Development*, *49*(2), 428–437. DOI: 10.1016/S1876-3804(22)60036-3

Hwang, B.-G., Shan, M., & Phuah, S. L. (2018). Safety in green building construction projects in Singapore: Performance, critical issues, and improvement solutions. *KSCE Journal of Civil Engineering*, *22*(2), 447–458. DOI: 10.1007/s12205-017-1961-3

Ibrahim, C. K. I. C., Manu, P., Belayutham, S., Mahamadu, A.-M., & Antwi-Afari, M. F. (2022). Design for safety (DfS) practice in construction engineering and management research: A review of current trends and future directions. *Journal of Building Engineering*, *52*, 104352. DOI: 10.1016/j.jobe.2022.104352

Janackovic, G. L., Savic, S. M., & Stankovic, M. S. (2013). Selection and ranking of occupational safety indicators based on fuzzy AHP: A case study in road construction companies. *South African Journal of Industrial Engineering*, *24*(3), 175–189. DOI: 10.7166/24-3-463

Kouabenan, D. R., Ngueutsa, R., & Mbaye, S. (2015). Safety climate, perceived risk, and involvement in safety management. *Safety Science*, *77*, 72–79. DOI: 10.1016/j.ssci.2015.03.009

Kukoyi, P. O., & Adebowale, O. J. (2021). Impediments to construction safety improvement. *Journal of Engineering, Project, and Production Management*, *11*(3), 207–214.

Kumar, K. S., & Narayanan, R. (2021). Review on construction risk and development of risk management procedural index–A case study from Chennai construction sector. *Materials Today: Proceedings*, *43*, 1141–1146. DOI: 10.1016/j.matpr.2020.08.606

Macêdo, J. B., Moura, M. C., Aichele, D., & Lins, I. D. (2022). Identification of risk features using text mining and BERT-based models: Application to an oil refinery. *Process Safety and Environmental Protection*, *158*, 382–399. DOI: 10.1016/j.psep.2021.12.025

Manzoor, B., Othman, I., & Manzoor, M. (2021). Evaluating the critical safety factors causing accidents in high-rise building projects. *Ain Shams Engineering Journal*, *12*(3), 2485–2492. DOI: 10.1016/j.asej.2020.11.025

Martin, P., Bladier, C., Meek, B., Bruyere, O., Feinblatt, E., Touvier, M., Watier, L., & Makowski, D. (2018). Weight of evidence for hazard identification: A critical review of the literature. *Environmental Health Perspectives*, *126*(7), 076001. DOI: 10.1289/EHP3067 PMID: 30024384

Moshood, T., Adeleke, A., Nawanir, G., & Mahmud, F. (2020). Ranking of human factors affecting contractors' risk attitudes in the Malaysian construction industry. *Social Sciences & Humanities Open*, *2*(1), 100064. DOI: 10.1016/j.ssaho.2020.100064

Nawaz, A., Waqar, A., Shah, S. A. R., Sajid, M., & Khalid, M. I. (2019). An innovative framework for risk management in construction projects in developing countries: Evidence from Pakistan. *Risks*, *7*(1), 24. DOI: 10.3390/risks7010024

Ojha, A., Gautam, Y., Jebelli, H., & Akanmu, A. (2024). Physiological impact of powered back-support exoskeletons in construction: Analyzing muscle fatigue, metabolic cost, ergonomic risks, and stability. Automation in Construction, 168(Pt A), 105742.

Ouyang, Y., & Luo, X. (2025). Effects of physical fatigue superimposed on high temperatures on construction workers' cognitive performance. *Safety Science*, *181*, 106705. DOI: 10.1016/j.ssci.2024.106705

Pagell, M., Johnston, D., Veltri, A., Klassen, R., & Biehl, M. (2014). Is safe production an oxymoron? *Production and Operations Management*, *23*(7), 1161–1175. DOI: 10.1111/poms.12100

Chapter 12
Real-Time Personal Noise Measurements Contribution to Hearing Deterioration for Mineworkers in South Africa

Liepollo Ntlhakana
https://orcid.org/0000-0002-8632-0616
University of the Witwatersrand, South Africa

ABSTRACT

Occupational noise is a health hazard that leads to permanent hearing loss and the cumulative nature of the noise exposure requires active and preventive surveillance programmes. This type of hearing loss, commonly known as occupational noise-induced hearing loss is associated with a gradual hearing deterioration, affecting the high frequencies and has been well documented as the leading cause of a disabling hearing impairment by the South African mining industry. The author highlights the usefulness of real-time noise dosimetry which uses modern technology and enables the active and ongoing integration of audiometry medical surveillance big data to be accessed and analysed. In addition, to advance the preventive goal for hearing loss, the author recommends further investigations into electronic health systems employed by the mining houses as intervention tools that enable deep machine learning and could be used to identify trends and predict early signs of hearing deterioration for mineworkers.

INTRODUCTION

Complexities around irreversible hearing deterioration and the associated adverse effects caused by excessive occupational noise exposure that impact mineworkers globally have been well documented in the literature (WHO, 2021). Evidence-based studies have cited the cumulative nature over a period of time of excessive noise exposure, the type of noise exposure, and other non-modifiable factors such as age, sex, genetics, etc., and modifiable exposures such as dust, ototoxic chemicals, recreational noise, etc., which all increase mineworkers' susceptibility to permanent occupational-related hearing loss (Grobler et al., 2020; Ntlhakana et al., 2021; Pillay, 2020). Other previous studies in South Africa have shown the association between hearing loss and respiratory health conditions, associated risks from

DOI: 10.4018/979-8-3693-9301-7.ch012

ototoxic drugs used for the treatment of pulmonary tuberculosis (PTB) and human immunodeficiency virus (HIV) infection also increase the risk of noise-induced hearing loss (NIHL) in mineworkers (Khoza-Shangase, 2019; Rathipe & Raphela, 2023). In addition, various other occupational exposures and medical conditions have been reported as risk factors for occupation-related hearing loss, specifically occupational noise-induced hearing loss (ONIHL). Increased susceptibility to sleep disturbances, psychological stress, and fatigue have been associated with the frustration of losing hearing function, thus recommendations to consider mineworkers' mental health were made (Malatji & Stewart, 2013). The widely used definition of ONIHL is an occupational disease caused by overexposure to noise in the workplace, as a measure of time (in hours per shift) and intensity of noise (of ≥ 85 dBA) (Feuerstein & Chasin, 2009; South & Africa). In South Africa, all the mining commodities have reported ONIHL as one of the top three most common occupational diseases (1. pulmonary TB; 2. ONIHL and 3. silicosis) (Balfour, 2024), which leads to disabling permanent hearing loss (WHO, 2021). To attend to the complex interactions of risk factors which inevitably lead to permanent hearing loss, the mining houses require health-based regulations supported by the government.

The South African regulatory bodies that govern the mining industry have identified excessive noise exposure levels as the main risk factor associated with ONIHL. Excessive noise exposure levels continue to persist even after the numerous revisions of the Mine Health and Safety Council milestones for the prevention of ONIHL. These milestones have mainly been based on reducing noise emitted by mining equipment, for example, investing in solutions to quietening equipment that emits high noise and reducing the total occupational noise exposure levels to ≤ 107 dBA by December 2024 (Mine et al., 2015). To understand occupational noise exposure levels of various occupational groups of mineworkers, some researchers conducted studies that profiled jobs, and noise exposure levels and tracked the prevalence rates of ONIHL among mineworkers (Edwards et al., 2011; Grobler et al., 2020; Ntlhakana, Nelson, et al., 2020). However, research findings indicated the complexities around the mine depth, types of equipment used, and mineworker behaviours as some of the limitations which restrict the implementation of noise reduction interventions. Thus, noise detectors as early signals for noise exposure could be explored as artificial intelligence (AI) based solutions suitable for the mining industry and this technology requires the South African regulatory bodies' buy-in.

Recent advances in measuring personal noise exposures already exist, however, a dearth of evidence-based findings drawn from these technologies was imperative. Sound level meters (SLMs) and dosimeters are common sound pressure instruments used by most industries to measure occupational noise exposure levels. The various recent types of SLMs have been cited as quick, simple, and easy to operate, as well as allowing in-depth collation of workplace noise exposure levels collected for all jobs. In addition, using a dosimeter has been recommended as the preferred method to accurately measure and access mineworkers' occupational noise exposure levels. (Grobler et al., 2020; Ntlhakana, Khoza-Shangase, et al., 2020) There are different types of dosimeters, with different technologies integrated for the sole purpose of personal noise measurements. A dosimeter is described as a device fitted on the individual's upper body, with a microphone placed as close as possible to the ear (Bonnet et al., 2020). However, the most common practice of monitoring noise exposure levels with dosimeters using traditional technology seemed to be preferred by the industry and was intended only for those South African mineworkers who were at risk according to the mines' risk-based medical surveillance descriptors (Franz & Phillips, 2001). Nevertheless, there is limited evidence-based research on the implemented personal sampling strategies and devices which could predict and/or detect early, increased noise exposure levels. Therefore, solutions for measuring noise exposures with sensitive devices that have AI-assisted functions to store big data and allow for data analysis to predict risk for ONIHL should be investigated by the South African mining industry.

While occupational noise exposure intensity and duration remain a major concern and the main risk factor for hearing impairment among South African mineworkers, accurate tracking of the hearing function is similarly crucial to measure the efficiency of the mines' audiometry medical surveillance. In 2017, the South African mines adopted the Noise-Induced Hearing Loss Regulations to include the calculation of standard hearing threshold shifts (STS) during hearing screening to track early signs of hearing loss as a cumulative effect during employment (Act, 2016). The STS method is based on the International Organization for Standardization (ISO) standard 1999:2013 (ISO1999:2013), which specifies that a decline of 8 dB in the STS from baseline indicates early signs of ONIHL (Michel & Liedtke, 2021). Although protocols for tracking mineworkers' hearing deterioration were in place, with minor necessary refinements, on the contrary, literature on automated audiometry devices was limited. This way of hearing assessment presents challenges which impact the integrated analysis and accurate tracking of a worker's hearing function, prompting more research in this area and relatedly task shifting of the hearing conservation practitioners.

The roles and responsibilities of those involved in the mines' hearing conservation programmes (HCP) are critical and should be clearly defined according to the specific industry guidelines (South African National Standards, 2013). In this chapter, the author posits the role of an audiologist underscoring the bird's eye view of audiometry medical surveillance, has a responsibility to understand the mineworker's hearing as a function of multiple contributing factors and to acknowledge data collected and accessed, as well as technologies used by other colleagues within the HCP, for example, the occupational hygienist, mental health specialists. In essence, although big data collected by the mines could be relevant for audiometry medical surveillance, these could also be for noise control purposes and different outcome measures for HCPs could have been outlined. A focus on pursuing person-centred care (PCC) should be at the forefront when managing occupational health and safety using a systems thinking approach, integrated with human ethics considerations (Peters, 2014). Limited previous literature has argued for and highlighted the importance of embedding ethical codes in electronic health systems that use machine learning and AI. Therefore, the roles and responsibilities of the hearing conservation practitioners align with risk-based interventions targeted for ONIHL prevention should further explore evidence-based findings relevant to the South African Mining Industry Code of Practice (CoP) and ethics around data privacy and protection (Department of Minerals and Energy, 2003; Malatji & Stewart, 2013, Ntlhakana et al., 2021).

This chapter argues for the integrated ethical use of real-time personal noise measurements to accurately account for the contribution of hearing deterioration associated with ONIHL for the mineworkers in South Africa. The argument goes further to highlight the importance of medical surveillance, from the audiologist's point of view, using the current definition stating that this is an ongoing primary preventive clinical service intended for individuals and groups whose workplaces significantly increase the risk of a manageable and preventable disease. Thus, highlighting audiological implications for efficient medical surveillance geared towards ONIHL prevention. It is imperative to acknowledge that the recent advances in noise control and medical audiometry surveillance programmes which have AI-assisted functions have been undertaken by the South African mining houses. For example, noise dosebadge[5] which is a noise dosimeter, and the audiometric database analysis (ADBA) tools offer a base for AI-driven noise monitoring and computational audiology capabilities (Wasmann et al., 2021). When combined, both control measures provide accurate noise measurements and data on hearing deterioration for the mineworkers (Ntlhakana, Nelson et al., 2020). However, contextual challenges that are related to the efficient integration of machine learning systems in low and middle-income countries (LMICs) such as South Africa cannot be ignored. Thus, AI-driven solutions linked with human wisdom should be considered efficient quality assurance tools and these emerging technological solutions should be re-imagined within the health systems strengthening frameworks. This chapter argues for solutions that are foregrounded on frameworks geared towards the prevention of occupational-related hearing loss among South African mineworkers.

A SYSTEMS THINKING APPROACH

A systems thinking approach was used as a framework for this chapter and re-imagined from the focal point of the mining houses' audiometry medical and occupational hygiene surveillance data which have been used to assess the HCP risk assessment practices. Furthermore, the CoP principles according to the South African mines leading practices as recommended by the Mine Occupational Safety and Health (MOSH) were reimagined as an integral pillar linked to the systems thinking approach. Therefore, to provide an understanding of the recommended framework in this chapter, Figure 1 illustrates the health system strengthening framework using the mine's HCP and visualised as follows: processes; the actors (e.g. mine managers, occupational medical officers, audiologists and occupational hygienists, referred to as hearing conservation practitioners) and activities employed by the hearing conservation practitioners in the audiometry medical surveillance promote risk assessment practices for, and prevention of, ONIHL (Peters, 2014). According to the World Health Organization (WHO), systems thinking is an approach applied to strengthen health systems that exist and function within organisations, in this case, mining houses (WHO, 2009). Therefore, to contextualise the South African mining industry's occupational health and safety regulations as health-based regulations, formulated by the Government department (e.g. Department of Minerals and Petroleum), was imperative to highlight in this chapter. These health-based regulations are mainly exposure-driven and performance-based, thus, compliance when reporting HCP outcomes was key (LaDou & Harrison, 2013). In addition, when these regulations are promulgated by individual mining houses, there are standards and guidelines that each organisation (mining houses) must customise its own written facility-specific surveillance plan which is compliant and comprehensive to address and evaluate how to measure and control exposures to achieve the preventive goal (LaDou & Harrison, 2013). However, in recent times, AI-driven health-based systems have provided integrated data and reporting mechanisms which have been efficient health tools used to control occupational diseases and drive surveillance programmes.

Hence, as shown in Figure 1, the three major processes illustrate the suggested framework guiding this chapter, viz. health system building blocks, machine learning systems (MLSs) and HCP-measured outcomes. For each health system building block to function, clearly planned activities which guide the MLSs used and measured outcomes should be outlined by the decision-makers (e.g. mine managers) and end-users (e.g. hearing conservation practitioners and mineworkers). Figure 1 illustrates the health system strengthening building blocks adopted from the WHO, viz. leadership and governance; finance; service delivery; health workforce; information systems, and medical technologies (Peters, 2014). In this chapter, we argue for a holistic system, an active ongoing cycle between the MLSs, and measured outcomes back into the health system building blocks. Previous literature has indicated that the South African mines use MLSs to record, analyse and access personal, occupational, and medical records for all the miners (e.g. MS Excel, sound level meters, electronic health systems) over a period of time to identify and track occupational diseases, specific to the chapter's topic, ONIHL cases (Begley, 2006; Ntlhakana et al., 2021). Finally, in this chapter, the HCP outcome measures have been visualised as activities focused on the PCC approach to attending to the individual mineworker's health data to evaluate trends and exposures, look at the effectiveness of exposure controls, detect contributory factors that may involve workers (e.g. work practices, worker behaviours, etc.), synergistic factors that may increase the risk for ONIHL, and measure the impact of certain interventions such as dosimetry, audiometry, etc. which hearing conservation practitioners recorded for each miner. In addition, in Figure 1, a systems thinking approach has been used to describe the risk assessment practices that the South African mines' hearing conservation practitioners apply to assess the risk of, and prevent, ONIHL.

Figure 1. Framework adopted from the World Health Organization's health systems strengthening framework for an integrated HCP and prevention of occupational hearing loss (WHO, 2009)

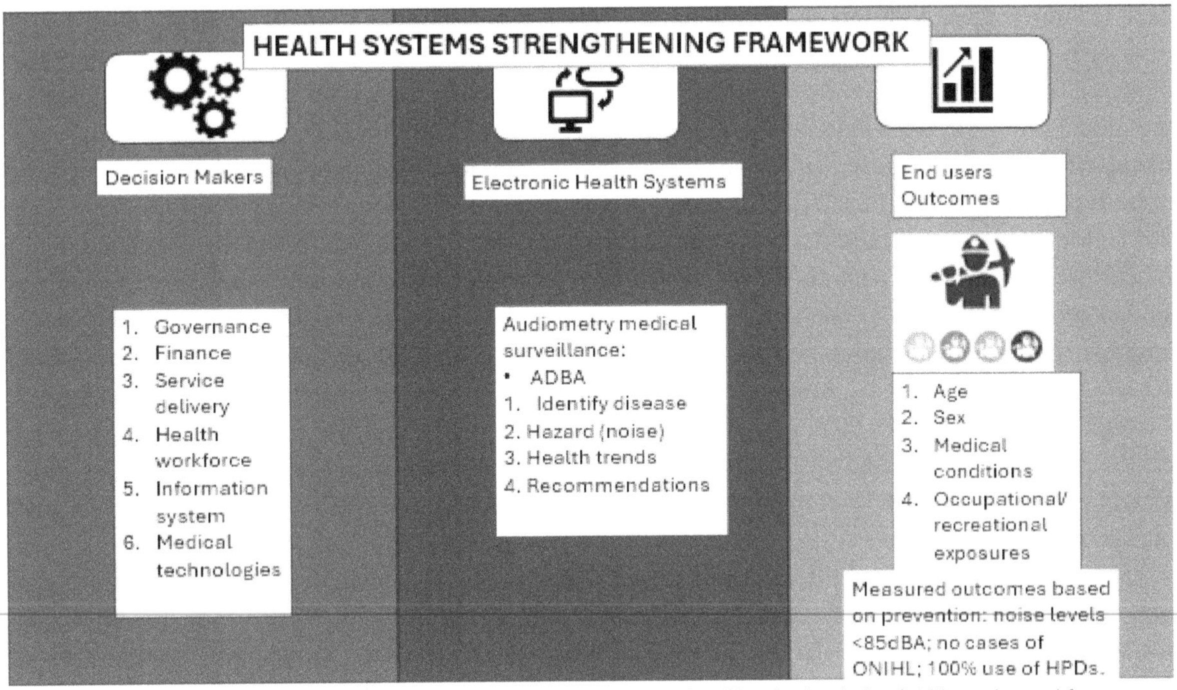

Source: Conceptual framework adopted Ntlhakana L. Occupational noise-induced hearing loss in South African miners: risk assessment explored at a platinum mine in South Africa 2021. (Ntlhakana, 2021)

In describing the risk assessment practices used by the mine's hearing conservation practitioners, the health system strengthening conceptual framework used in this chapter outlines the health system building blocks for decision-makers, thereby highlighting activities within the mine's HCP. To ensure an efficient HCP, key performance indicators (KPIs) for decision-makers should be aligned with activities outlined within the health system building blocks process, MLSs, as well as the mine's HCP outcomes. The decision-makers' (mine managers and occupational medical officers) roles and responsibilities may include competencies which tie in with CoP in ensuring that relevant policies around electronic health systems (EHSs) are accessible and enable the purchasing of comprehensive mine-specific EHSs. Accordingly, skills such as making AI-driven decisions, and ensuring the integration of rigorous ethical codes are essential to protecting the privacy of EHSs data. Finally, employing qualified professionals amenable to using machine learning systems (MLSs) to guide their decisions and to execute successful occupational health and safety surveillance programmes, could ensure the financial viability and efficiency of such programmes (Chisholm et al., 2015; Peters, 2014). This suggested framework thereby highlights the benefits of integrated EHSs that enable risk assessment practices and foreground the mines' audiometry medical surveillance records. Nevertheless, continuous investigations are necessary, thus, the system's thinking approach encourages pondering on practical and research questions which may influence the future literature findings in this area.

Real-Time Personal Noise Measurements and Hearing Deterioration

The South African mining industry has for several years been struggling to reduce occupational noise exposure levels and ONIHL cases. The two challenges remain a perennial concern. These concerns have been acknowledged, with reports indicating that while reported cases of other occupational diseases were on a decrease, ONIHL cases were on the rise (Balfour, 2024). However, it is important to note that reducing occupational noise exposure levels remains a key control measure for the industry to realise the reduction of ONIHL. Internationally, studies have reported the benefits of including AI in noise monitoring to accurately account for noise dose percentage, for noise mapping and for differentiating noise types as a function of safety and hearing health controls (Faradonbeh et al., 2024; Roberts et al., 2017). Meanwhile, in a South African context, various industries have focused on the integrated use of modernised engineering controls which are intended to reduce noise at source and not necessarily at studies indicating outcomes on the integration of AI in noise measurements (Saleh et al., 2017; Steenkamp, 2018). Thus, indicating evidence-based efforts by the industry stakeholders towards improved AI-integrated HCP strategies. Although there is a dearth of literature on integrated AI noise measurement strategies and tools locally, there is a view that AI-driven tools are currently used but there are possible challenges to publishing findings from these. Nevertheless, this highlights gaps in the literature which should be investigated by local industries and industry bodies whose workers were impacted by high occupational noise levels.

The occupational hygienist is an expert tasked with recognising, evaluating, controlling, and anticipating health hazards from occupational exposures and is well-vested in AI-driven technologies and revised protocols (LaDou & Harrison, 2013). However, there is a need to encourage collaborations with occupational medical practitioners and audiologists in an effort towards the prevention of ONIHL for South African mineworkers (Franz & Phillips, 2001; Ntlhakana, Nelson, et al., 2020). In addition, there has been a great need for occupational hygienists to share the incorporation of leading practices of controlling occupational noise, for other hearing conservation practitioners to develop a sense of appreciation of the current developments in this area. Therefore, this chapter argues for a risk-based evaluation of noise exposure as a health hazard and a recognition of the critical role played by occupational hygienists in reducing the risk of ONIHL and occupational hearing loss.

The noise control framework that Franz and Phillips (2001) suggested highlights the important role played by occupational hygienists. The authors' framework (Franz & Phillips, 2001) which was over twenty years is still relevant and continues to be used by the South African mining industry. The authors have suggested a hierarchy of control which includes engineering controls, administrative controls, and personal protection (hearing protection devices) (Franz & Phillips, 2001). Nevertheless, the previous literature highlighted flaws in the implementation of these controls, hence the perpetual excessive occupational noise exposure levels which are associated with ONIHL (Grobler et al., 2020; Ntlhakana et al., 2021). According to the WHO, in their World Hearing Report of 2021, excessive occupational noise exposure levels were a major concern associated with ONIHL risk (WHO, 2021). Noise as a health hazard requires a risk assessment approach that involves quick and sensitive measurement tools for personal noise exposure levels (using SLM and dosimeters), and the early identification of homogenous exposure groups (HEGs) anticipated to develop ONIHL because of noise (Ntlhakana, Khoza-Shangase, et al., 2020). A HEG is described as a group of employees with similar exposures to an identified hazard (e.g. noise) and should be a representative sample of workers whose assessment findings could accurately estimate exposure levels and risks for the entire population (Department of Minerals and Energy, 2003). The sample size and frequency of sampling for each HEG are determined by the noise exposure range. However, for workers exposed to ≥ 85 dBA, either five or 5% of the total number of workers in the HEG, whichever number is larger, sampling was suggested every twelve months (Heyns et al., 2021). Nevertheless, the South African mines' population and HEGs were found to have complex variables, hence concerns regarding the accuracy and quality of data collected during sampling of HEGs have been raised. This consequently presents challenges which impact negatively on the risk assessment techniques used by the mines (Made & Uthembe, 2019). In this chapter, the author presents a reflection on efforts made by the South African mining industry to integrate AI-driven techniques using real-time personal noise dosimetry to provide rich and big datasets for noise surveys. These data could be used to estimate risk for ONIHL and potentially track hearing deterioration early. Therefore, clear leading practices employed by occupational hygienists are viewed as transformative agents for risk-based interventions towards ONIHL prevention.

Table 1 is used to illustrate noise monitoring tools that are available locally and internationally. The market supply is evident for the local industries, but there is a lack of evidence-based literature to showcase the benefits yielded by these kinds of advances in noise monitoring.

Table 1. AI-driven noise monitoring versus traditional noise monitoring

Noise monitoring/Tools	Sound level meters (SLM)	Dosimeters	Octave-band analysers	Local	International
AI noise monitoring	SLM App	NoiseCHEK Dosimeters with Bluetooth and App connectivity, e.g. 3M mobile phone App; doseBadge5	Octave Band Sound Level Meter, e.g. Nova46, ideal for noise-frequency specific data	√	√
		Verum real-time dosimeters			√
Traditional noise monitoring	Hand-held SLM	Personal noise dosimeter		√	√
	Advanced SLM			√	√

Source: Author's own design.

The closer the proximity of the dosimeter microphone to the eardrum the better the calculation for the estimation of risk for ONIHL for the workers exposed to occupational noise. There are other audiometry tools and techniques that are already used as part of audiometry medical surveillance in occupational settings where noise is a problem and have been reported to be sensitive and more accurate tools that enable early identification of those at risk of developing ONIHL, for example, distortion-product otoacoustic emissions (DPOAE) testing (Edwards et al., 2010; Moepeng et al., 2017; Wei et al., 2024). In addition, some custom-made HPDs that have been designed for workers exposed to excessive noise have functionalities of in-the-ear measurement, but their purpose is for hearing protection and the use of attenuation levels to protect the ear at the level of the eardrum. A reflection of these benefits goes further since the South African mining industry has Regulations and Standards for the use of DPOAEs as part of audiometry medical surveillance and providing HPDs to all their mineworkers (Mine Health and Safety Act, 2016; South African National Standards, 2013). However, there has been a slow uptake in the implementation and integration of DPOAEs in the audiometry medical surveillance and compliance regarding the use of HPDs by the mineworkers (Grobler et al., 2020; Ntlhakana et al., 2015). Therefore, there is a need for evidence-based studies to take stock of the recent advances in fields such as computational audiology, especially in times of artificial intelligence (AI) developments.

In addition, previous study findings in audiology have used real-time in-the-ear dosimetry data and their interpretations thereof for audiometry medical surveillance and highlighted hearing health implications for the workers and interventions that should be implemented by the employers (Moepeng et al., 2017; Hynes et al., 2021; Wei et al., 2024). These findings could provide nuances into human behaviours, mental well-being and practices adopted by the workers and bode well with HCPs. Clearly defined roles and responsibilities outlined in the Mine Health and Safety Act inform mineworkers of the nature of their workplace, and hazardous exposures, as well as their Rights (South African National Standards, 2013). Empowered workers are an integral part of the South African mining workforce and their active engagement during decision-making has been evident, but evidence-based research on education and training on the aspects related to hearing conservation and implications on their mental well-being is limited. Therefore, interrogating the use of big data, analysis and machine learning techniques (what and how to train) to answer research questions that address employees' needs across all levels of employment, and specific to the contribution of personal noise levels on hearing deterioration among mineworkers is imperative. In addition, the larger the population the greater the advantages of big data analysis in research, hence, the South African mining industry with its large population size could realise the intended benefits of audiometry medical surveillance.

Currently, organisations such as mining houses, because of the number of their employees, use big data to monitor occupational health hazards, in this case, noise exposure as a risk factor of ONIHL. Thus, tracking hearing deterioration for workers exposed to excessive noise levels requires analytical methods that use big data that is stored in MLSs, easily accessible and follows health-based regulations. In this chapter, this is where the recommended Health Systems Strengthening framework highlights the current audiometry medical surveillance practices and big data used by the South African mining industry. This is where specific electronic health systems (EHS) house individual workers' data such as age, sex, medical conditions, ototoxic treatments, occupational exposures, hobbies, etc. Table 2 indicates a guide for audiometry medical surveillance data as recommended by Franz and Phillips (2001) and mandated by the Government (Energy, 2003). Table 2 also shows where the bulk of electronic data is accessed from and the type of data that offers real-time functionalities and analysis. Hence, there is an argument for the use of existing datasets which contain integrated real-time data which can be accessed from noise measurements and audiometry medical surveillance.

Table 2. A guide for audiometry medical surveillance data

Test type	Objective/Subjective/Both	Type of data
Tympanometry	Objective test	Middle ear pressure and compliance with details about the outer and middle pathologies.
DPOAE	Objective test	To determine the likelihood of hearing loss, matched against 0.5; 1; 2; 3; 4; 6; and 8 KHz frequencies.
Pure-tone audiometry	Subjective test	Baseline audiometry (initial) with the relevant percentage of hearing loss (PLH) and STS calculations. Periodic monitoring and exit audio with PLH Air-conduction: 0.5; 1; 2; 3; 4; 6; (screening audiometry) and 8 KHz (diagnostic audiometry). Exit audiometry
Noise dosimetry	Both	Occupation type, noise exposure levels, workplace activities
Case history data	Subjective	Age, sex, medical conditions, ear and hearing history, ototoxic medication, occupational history, recreational history,

Source: Author's own design.

Accordingly, this chapter highlights the progressive and preventive approach of the 2024 Occupational Health Milestones to eliminate ONIHL. The promulgated NIHL milestones set by the South African mines promote the use of the standard threshold shift (STS) method to track workers' hearing sensitivity, identify early signs of hearing loss, and benchmark mines' progress toward the prevention of ONIHL (Mine Health and Safety Act, 2016). However, the current definition of the STS may be limiting since it covers low and mid frequencies (2000Hz, 3000Hz, and 4000Hz) but the guidance notes outlined in the milestones provide methodical data collection and analysis that have been helpful for the industry and allow for big data easy access and the possibility to integrate predictions and deep learning machine capabilities. The additional benefit realised using the STS which has been reported in previous research was that data drawn from mineworkers' STS indicated ear and frequency-specific hearing sensitivity data (Ntlhakana et al., 2021). Nevertheless, the accuracy of data collected, and methods used to calculate STS should be viewed with caution when coming to tracking early signs of ONIHL because the high-frequency data from individual ears was restricted. The standard threshold tracking methods used by the US National Institute for Occupational Safety and Health (NIOSH), enable early identification of early signs of ONIHL because their STS formula includes high frequencies (Michel & Liedtke, 2021).

The use of STS considers integrated mineworker-specific data which include the socio-demographic factors (age, sex, and race), genetic predisposition, recreational noise, and other occupational exposures as a function of hearing deterioration. Therefore, an integrated EHS which includes all these factors as well as data accessed from the DPOAE, and in-the-ear noise dosimetry integrated datasets will enable improved real-ear measurements geared up for the prevention of ONIHL. Bonnet et al., (2019) suggested the individual in situ calibration of in-ear noise dosimeters methods using modern technologies, to accurately measure noise exposure, that is sound pressure level (SPL in dBA) at the level of the eardrum, this chapter agrees with this approach. To accurately assess the functioning of the outer hair cells and to measure the impact of noise exposure to the Organ of Corti both measurements should be done in the ear closer to the eardrum (Bonnet et al., 2020; Moepeng et al., 2017). The DPOAE test findings show parts of the Organ of Corti that have been affected and those could be matched to the individual's age, and exposures such as noise, and ototoxic chemicals (Grobler et al., 2020; Moepeng et al., 2017). Modern technology noise dosimeters allow for the differentiation of the characteristics of noise and particular machines that emit noise (Bonnet et al., 2020). These two approaches use objective measures that could be easily included in audiometry medical surveillance by audiologists and occupational hygienists to generate real-time big data with deep machine learning capabilities to enable predictions and can be used as hearing loss preventive tools.

Strengths and Limitations

In this chapter, we highlight the following strengths and limitations of using real-time noise dosimeter measurements to prevent ONIHL:

Big data and deep machine learning using real-time data require human wisdom and a full takeover of the health systems is impossible.

Computational audiology is a new emerging field that has the potential to be explored because of the advantageous position of the availability of big data in the South African mining industry with proper permissions in place to advance research.

Modern noise dosimeters are easy to use, take quick measurements, allow for accurate insights into workplace noise exposure to be collated for all jobs, and can be used as counselling tools to raise mineworker awareness of noise exposure levels and types of machines that emit excessive noise as the actual recorded audio is played back to them, promoting person-centred care. However, the skills of a person placing a noise dosimeter on the worker are crucial because correct positioning of the in-the-ear noise dosimeter microphone is critical for correct measurements.

Lessons learned and skills transferred from existing technologies. The technology used by the South African mines in the HPDs provided to the mineworkers and real-ear measurements used in hearing aid fittings use similar technology as recommended by Bonnet et al., (2019), thus, lessons from the two technologies could be synchronised to fit the South African mining context. However, opportunities and limitations should be weighed with caution.

By investing in monitoring solutions, employers could change workplace practices, implement noise control, and promote worker mindsets and behaviour changes in their hearing healthcare habits.

It is important to remember that noise dosimeter measurements are open to spurious results from employees, in the initial stages of data collection. Therefore, variability in exposure levels should be checked to differentiate legitimate workplaces from illegitimate ones to account for accurate worker exposures.

CONCLUSION

In conclusion, integrated real-time big data noise dosimeters are readily available, with local suppliers offering such tools and support to the industry. Thus, locally, industries where occupational noise is a problem have embraced advances in noise monitoring and have integrated AI technologies in noise monitoring. There are several benefits for companies to realise for improved HCPs, hence, the importance of using integrated AI systems, for example, to highlight the internet of things in occupational health and safety, offer improved safety and healthcare, manage big data and analysis of that data. In addition, noise detectors as early signals for noise exposure could be explored are potential AI-based solutions that are suitable for the mining industry.

Since some of the AI-driven audiometry technologies, for example, DPOAE measures were already conducted by the mining industry as part of the audiometry medical surveillance, these provide opportunities to integrate AI-driven noise monitoring and audiometry medical surveillance. Thus, a concluding point is that data drawn from AI systems can strengthen human intelligence intended towards decision-making for the prevention of ONIHL among South African mineworkers. AI-driven health systems that are used as technologies for medical surveillance function efficiently within conceptual frameworks, in the case mentioned in this chapter, the Systems-Thinking Strengthening approach. Thus, suggested frameworks which guide integrated medical surveillance require AI-driven Since ONIHL is a disabling hearing impairment it impacts the quality of life and adds to the depression, isolation, and mental health of the mineworker, thus, suggested frameworks require embedded AI codes that support the integrated systems, and measured outcomes but human fidelity cannot be ignored. In this chapter, the author argues that the South African mining industry can optimise human intelligence in decision-making for noise monitoring and audiometry medical surveillance by using AI-integrated systems to accurately monitor early signs of hearing deterioration for the miners.

REFERENCES

Balfour, T. (2024, 7 Fen). Hearing loss concern for SA miners. *Juta Medical Brief.* https://www.medicalbrief.co.za/hearing-loss-concern-for-sa-miners/

Begley, A. (2006). *Development of Internet-based mining industry database for audiograms.* Safety in Mines Research Advisory Committee.

Bonnet, F., Nélisse, H., Nogarolli, M. A. C., & Voix, J. (2020). Individual in situ calibration of in-ear noise dosimeters. *Applied Acoustics, 157*, 107015. https://doi.org/https://doi.org/10.1016/j.apacoust.2019.107015. DOI: 10.1016/j.apacoust.2019.107015

Chisholm, R. L., Denny, J., Fridsma, D., Kheterpal, S., & Ohno-Machado, L. (2015). *Opportunities and Challenges related to the use of Electronic Health Records data for research.* Northwestern University.

Department of Minerals and Energy. (2003). *Guideline for the compilation of a mandatory code of practice for an occupational health programme for noise.* Pretoria, South Africa: Department of Minerals and Energy Retrieved from https://www.gov.za/documents/notices/mine-health-and-safety-act-guideline-compilation-mandatory-code-practice-4

Edwards, A., Dekker, J. J., Franz, R. M., Van Dyk, T., & Banyini, A. (2011). *Profiles of noise exposure levels in South African mining.*

Edwards, A., Van Coller, P., & Badenhorst, C. (2010). Early identification of noise induced hearing loss: a pilot study on the use of distortion product otoacoustic emissions as an adjunct to screening audiometry in the mining industry.

Faradonbeh, R. S., Ryoza, M. G., & Sepehri, M. (2024). Application of artificial intelligence in distinguishing genuine microseismic events from the noise signals in underground mines. In *Applications of Artificial Intelligence in Mining and Geotechnical Engineering* (pp. 197–220). Elsevier. DOI: 10.1016/B978-0-443-18764-3.00008-4

Feuerstein, J., & Chasin, M. (2009). Noise exposure and issues in hearing conservation. In *Handbook of Clinical Audiology* (7th ed., pp. 678–698). Lippincott Williams & Wilkins.

Franz, R. M., & Phillips, J. J. (2001). Noise and vibration. In E. R. Guild R, Johnson J & Ross M (Ed.), *Handbook of Occupational Health Practice in the South African Mining Industry* (pp. 195-232). The Safety in Mines Research Advisory Committee (SAMRAC).

Grobler, L. M., Swanepoel, D. W., Strauss, S., & Eloff, P. B. Z. (2020). Occupational noise and age: A longitudinal study of hearing sensitivity as a function of noise exposure and age in South African gold mine workers. *The South African Journal of Communication Disorders = Die Suid-Afrikaanse Tydskrif vir Kommunikasieafwykings, 67*(2), 1–7. https://doi.org/a687. DOI: 10.4102/sajcd.v67i2.687 PMID: 32242440

Heyns, S., Dekker, K., Ker-Fox, J., Oberholster, A., Claassen, N., Schoeman, J., Dube, S., van der Walt, J., Pullen, M., & Preis, E. (2021). *COE 180701 – Review The Current Sami Noise Exposure Limit And Conduct A Study On Vibration OEL In Relation To The SAMI*. Pretoria: Mine Health and Safety Council Retrieved from https://mhsc.org.za/wp-content/uploads/2021/07/CoE-180701-Final-Report-%E2%80%93-Review-The-Current-SAMI-Noise-Exposure-Limit-And-Conduct-A-Study-On-Vibration-OEL-In-Relation-To-The-SAMI.pdf

Khoza-Shangase, K. (2019). Hearing function of gold miners with and without a history of tuberculosis treatment: A retrospective data review [Peer Review]. *Brazilian Journal of Otorhinolaryngology*, *88*(3), 1–6. https://doi.org/https://doi.org/10.1016/j.bjorl.2018.12.003 PMID: 30765234

LaDou, J., & Harrison, R. J. (2013). In *CURRENT Diagnosis & Treatment: Occupational & Environmental Medicine, 5e*. McGraw-Hill Education. accessmedicine.mhmedical.com/content.aspx?aid=1104099264

Made, F., & Uthembe, W. (2019). Statistical analysis methods used to assess data below the limit of detection in the South African literature, 2010-2017. *Occupational Health Southern Africa*, *25*(5), 160–164.

Malatji, S., & Stewart, J. M. (2013). *The MOSH Leading Practice Adoption System: A leading practice in its own right*. https://www.mosh.co.za/siteitems/documents/adoption%20process/The%20MOSH%20Leading%20Practice%20Adoption%20System%20-%20A%20leading%20practice%20in%20its%20own%20right.pdf

Michel, O., & Liedtke, M. (2021). [ISO 1999:2013 part 1: Revised probability model for calculating noise-induced hearing loss]. *Hno, 69*(6), 510-516. (ISO 1999:2013 Teil 1: Überarbeitetes Wahrscheinlichkeitsmodell zur Berechnung des lärmbedingten Hörverlusts.)DOI: 10.1007/s00106-021-00999-1

Mine Health and Safety Act. (2016). *Mine Health and Safety Act: Regulations: Guidance note for implementation of standard threshold shift in medical surveillance of noise-induced hearing loss*. South Africa Retrieved from https://www.gov.za/documents/mine-health-and-safety-act-guidance-note-implementation-standard-threshold-shift-medical

Mine, Health, Safety, & Council. (2015). "Every Mine Worker Returning From Work Unharmed Every Day. Striving For Zero Harm" - 2014 Occupational Health and Safety Summit Milestones *J Occup Health Southern Afr, 20*(1), 2.

Moepeng, M., Soer, M., & Vinck, B. M. (2017). Distortion product otoacoustic emissions as a health surveillance technique for hearing screening in workers in the steel manufacturing industry. *Occupational Health Southern Africa*, *22*(5), 8–13.

Ntlhakana, L. (2021). *Occupational noise-induced hearing loss in South African miners: risk assessment explored at a platinum mine in South Africa*

Ntlhakana, L., Kanji, A., & Khoza-Shangase, K. (2015). The use of hearing protection devices in South Africa: Exploring the current status in a gold and a non-ferrous mine. *Occupational Health Southern Africa*, *21*(2), 10–15.

Ntlhakana, L., Khoza-Shangase, K., & Nelson, G. (2020). Occupational noise-induced hearing loss in platinum miners: What do the data tell us? [Original research]. *Occupational Health Southern Africa, 26*(1), 8–14.

Ntlhakana, L., Nelson, G., & Khoza-Shangase, K. (2020). Estimating miners at risk for occupational noise-induced hearing loss: A review of data from a South African platinum mine. *South African Journal of Communication Disorders, 67*(2, a677), 1-8. DOI: 10.4102/sajcd.v67i2.677

Ntlhakana, L., Nelson, G., Khoza-Shangase, K., & Dorkin, E. (2021). Occupational hearing loss for platinum miners in South Africa: A case study of data sharing practices and ethical challenges in the mining industry. *International Journal of Environmental Research and Public Health, 19*(1), 1. DOI: 10.3390/ijerph19010001 PMID: 35010261

Ntlhakana, L., Nelson, G., Khoza-Shangase, K., & Maposa, I. (2021). Predicting standard threshold shifts for occupational hearing loss among miners at a large-scale platinum mine in South Africa. *Journal of the Southern African Institute of Mining and Metallurgy, 121*(8), 397–404. http://www.scielo.org.za/scielo.php?script=sci_arttext&pid=S2225-62532021000800007&nrm=iso. DOI: 10.17159/2411-9717/1318/2021

Peters, D. H. (2014). The application of systems thinking in health: Why use systems thinking? *Health Research Policy and Systems, 12*(1), 51. DOI: 10.1186/1478-4505-12-51 PMID: 25160707

Pillay, M. (2020). Chemicals, noise and occupational hearing health in South Africa: A mapping study. *S Afr J Commun Disord.* https://doi.org/https://doi.org/10.4102/sajcd.v67i2.687a

Rathipe, M., & Raphela, S. F. (2023). Hearing loss and respiratory health symptoms among large-scale sawmill workers of the timber processing factories within the Gert Sibande District Municipality: A comparative cross-sectional study. *BMC Public Health, 23*(1), 1196. DOI: 10.1186/s12889-023-16086-9 PMID: 37340332

Saleh, S., Woskie, S., & Bello, A. (2017). The Use of Noise Dampening Mats to Reduce Heavy-Equipment Noise Exposures in Construction. *Safety and Health at Work, 8*(2), 226–230. DOI: 10.1016/j.shaw.2016.09.006 PMID: 28593081

South Africa. Compensation for Occupational Injuries and Diseases Act No. 130 of 1993. Circular instruction no. 171. The determination of permanent disablement resulting from hearing loss caused by exposure to excessive noise and trauma; 2001. https://www.gov.za/sites/default/files/gcis_document/201409/22296.pdf

South Africa. Mine Health and Safety Act, Act 29 of 1996. https://www.dmr.gov.za/Portals/0/mhs_act_29_of_19960_1.pdf

South African National Standards. (2013). *The measurement and assessment of occupational noise for hearing conservation purposes* (Vol. 10083). South African National Standards.

Steenkamp, R. J. (2018). The Exploration of Modern Noise Control Measures for Mining Operations. Johannesburg: *Proceedings of the International Conference on Industrial Engineering and Operations Management.*

Wasmann, J.-W. A., Lanting, C. P., Huinck, W. J., Mylanus, E. A., van der Laak, J. W., Govaerts, P. J., Swanepoel, D. W., Moore, D. R., & Barbour, D. L. (2021). Computational audiology: New approaches to advance hearing health care in the digital age. *Ear and Hearing*, *42*(6), 1499–1507. DOI: 10.1097/AUD.0000000000001041 PMID: 33675587

Wei, F., Zhao, W., Gao, X., Xue, P., Xu, F., Xie, H., Yang, N., Zou, H., & Qiu, W. (2025, March). (2024). Associations Between Noise Exposure Level, Noise Kurtosis, and Distortion Product Otoacoustic Emissions in Young Workers With Normal Hearing. *Ear and Hearing*, *46*(2), 483–493. Advance online publication. DOI: 10.1097/AUD.0000000000001600 PMID: 39402715

World Health Organization. (2009). *Systems thinking for health systems strengthening* (Alliance for Health Policy and Systems Research Issue. https://apps.who.int/iris/bitstream/handle/10665/44204/9789241563895_eng.pdf?sequence=1

World Health Organization. (2021). *World report on hearing*. WHO. https://apps.who.int/iris

Chapter 13
Strengthening Sensors and Wearable Technologies in Gauging Healthcare Transmuting Digital Health Technologies:
Human Augmentation via Innovation and Implementations of AI

Bhupinder Singh
https://orcid.org/0009-0006-4779-2553
Sharda University, India

Saurabh Chandra
https://orcid.org/0000-0003-4172-9968
Bennett University, Greater Noida, India

ABSTRACT

The advances in sensors and wearable technologies are transforming the way healthcare is delivered through continuous monitoring, predictive diagnostics, and personalized management of health. These devices, equipped with high-end sensors and powered by artificial intelligence (AI), are revolutionizing digital health technologies, forging new markets in human augmentation, and redefining occupational health and safety. Biosensors, fitness trackers, and even smart exoskeletons are examples of these wearables, which can bridge the gap between individuals and healthcare professionals by providing actionable data, contributing to preventative care, and aiding in its early detection. AI-enabled wearables in occupational settings enhance worker safety, as they monitor fatigue and high-risk environmental conditions, as well as alerting to stress levels, while exoskeletons lower the risk of injury and help with ergonomics. As these technologies not only enhance productivity and safety but also democratize access to quality healthcare with remote patient monitoring and telemedicine.

DOI: 10.4018/979-8-3693-9301-7.ch013

1. INTRODUCTION AND BACKGROUND

Digital health technologies thus are advancing in a way that will revolutionize the future of healthcare delivery, monitoring, and optimization. Thanks to innovations in sensors, wearables, and artificial intelligence (AI), healthcare and occupational safety are experiencing profound changes. Yet daunting issues like data security, device interoperability and accessibility are major roadblocks to the adoption of such technologies at scale (Ahirwar & Khan, 2022). Overcoming these barriers will require strategic innovation and strong ethical frameworks to harness the transformative potential of wearable technologies in improving health outcomes and workplace safety. Ex addressing the matching of features to needs and areas recognized as open to improvement provides insight into how these types of technologies will be transformative in enhancing contemporary healthcare and on-the-job safety, as well as the gaps that need to be filled.

In the last 10 years, powered by IoT, AI and machine learning, the development of digital health technologies has been incredible. These advancements technology has shifted healthcare from being 'reactive' towards being 'proactive' on preventing and continuously monitoring health in real-time. Wearable technologies and advanced sensors are key to this transformation, providing data collection and continuous analysis that can help correlate individual health with environmental conditions. Wearables with Biosensors can track important health statistics like ... Biometrics, such as heartbeats, oxygen levels, and glucose levels can be tracked through biosensors in weara... Our biosensors can provide early disease detection and tailored treatment plans.

The purpose of wearable devices goes beyond individual health care to workplace settings. Shane joined HIS for the opportunity to work with innovative, cutting-edge technologies that can affect real change, particularly in industries like construction, mining, and manufacturing, where high levels of environmental hazard monitoring encourage safety through wearable sensors. For example, motion sensors and fatigue state detectors on devices can prevent workplace accidents by notifying the worker and supervisor of potential danger. Wearable exoskeletons offer improved physical performance, with reduced musculoskeletal injury risk. AI greatly enhances the effect of these innovations by analyzing the data sensors and wearables gather. Machine learning heuristics discern patterns and offer predictive suggestions, which help identify intervention opportunities sooner (Han et al., 2020). Healthcare and occupational risk systems about AI - based research is done to predict diseases or other health problems by analyzing biometric data, or predicting risk in a work environment, etc. AI-powered wearables are already enhancing human augmentation, elevating health outcomes and workplace safety standards.

1.1 Problem Statement

The limitations of Existing Occupational Health and Safety Practices Traditional systems are largely a doctor visit, generic safety protocols, and risk assessments that do not take into account the uniqueness of the individual and changing nature of the workplace. Take on this type of reactive approach that leads to slower interventions and more cases of workplace injury or health complications.

The existing healthcare systems rarely have the capability to deliver uninterrupted, personalized monitoring, especially for those with chronic conditions or for those living in rural areas. Without real-time data, health issues are unpredicted and untreated, resulting in inefficient care provision. However, the adoption of these tools comes with its own set of challenges, and the use of wearable technologies and AI for such purposes have emerged as an exciting solution. Considering that wearable devices gather sensitive information about our bodies and lives, data security quickly becomes a huge concern. This data needs to be ensured for its privacy and protection to foster user trust and comply with regulations (Pramanik et al., 2022). Another major challenge that still exists is the lack of interoperability between devices and platforms. As there are no standardised protocols, the data cannot be easily shared and integrated which makes it difficult to develop comprehensive health solutions. One other challenge that remains accessibility; the high price and availability of cutting-edge wearables tend to exclude vulnerable populations and only exacerbate disparities in healthcare. Such challenges highlight the timely demand for novel solutions that fill the gaps of current systems while exploiting the potential of wearables and AI for health and safety.

1.2 Objectives of the Chapter

This chapter has the following objectives to:

- investigating the role of the integration of sensors and wearable technologies with AI in healthcare and occupational safety fields is the objective of this research. In particular, the goals are as follows:
- examining the transformative potential of wearable technologies and IoT sensors in healthcare delivery with real-time remote monitoring, predictive diagnostics, and personalized care.
- assess the potential of AI in improving human capabilities, safety, and health in the workplace.
- change the challenges and opportunities adopted by these technologies, considering aspects related to data security, device interoperability, and accessibility.
- addressing these aims would thus generate practical implications regarding the promise of wearables to transform health care and workplace safety, and contribute to creating even more efficient, equitable and safe systems.

1.3 Significance of the Study

Wearable technologies also have significant applications in the workplace. This feature is especially useful in high-risk sectors, where the implementation of safety precautions can avert accidents and protect lives. These technologies help organizations become more efficient and the economy as a whole to grow by decreasing workplace injuries and increasing productivity. This study has far-reaching implications for not only the health-care sector but also the occupational safety and health sector. Wearable technologies and AI combined, will revolutionize health and safety solutions, enabling organizations to move the needle on outcomes across individual, organizational and societal scales (Nazari, 2020).

The continuous monitoring and personalized insights offered by wearables have the potential to revolutionize patient care. This has been particularly impactful in providing service to underserved populations who have otherwise been affected with disparities in care. Data-driven analytics enhanced by artificial intelligence (AI) algorithms can automate and drive the diagnostic process, leading to faster and more accurate decisions.

The policy-making comes on third place, it emphasizes policy-making to ease these technologies to the masses. Data security, interoperability, and ethical usage are only a few examples of the standards that can be set by governments and regulatory authorities. Meta description way with wearable technologies what are the challenges of policymaking, and how they may be overcome. This study highlights the possibility of revolutionizing the fields of healthcare and occupational safety with the use of sensors and wearable devices (Sahil & Kaushik, 2022). With overcoming the challenges to their uptake, and harnessing their potential, it is possible to develop models that will benefit not only individual health outcomes, but also strengthen occupational safety standards, moving towards a healthier and fairer society. Data security, device interoperability and accessibility are just a few of the hurdles yet to be overcome, entailing strategic innovation and ethical frameworks to unleash the ability of wearables to positively impact health outcomes and workplace safety.

2. SENSORS AND WEARABLE TECHNOLOGIES: KEY TYPES OF SENSORS IN HEALTHCARE AND SAFETY

The interplay a leading role in contemporary healthcare and occupational safety systems, sensors and wearable technologies are indispensable for continuous learning, predictive analytics, and personalized interventions. However, what these devices really do are take many types of advanced sensors, and combined them to those which redefine how health and safety are managed, from real-time data and situational awareness to proactive measures. Wearable technologies contain several integrated sensors, each specialized for monitoring a particular parameter for health and safety applications. Sensors and wearable technologies are a transformative leap in healthcare and occupational safety (Oukhatar et al., 2021). This technology uses a range of sensors, including physiological, biochemical, environmental, and specialized (between) sensors, to monitor, predict, and provide tailored feedback. These technologies can not only potentially transform how we manage health and safety in workplaces, but also create an environment where innovation goes hand-in-hand with inclusion and effectiveness, by tackling the challenges of data security, interoperability, and accessibility.

2.1 Physiological Sensors

At the core of wearable health-monitoring systems are physiological sensors, which provide important measurements related to vital signs, including heart rate, blood pressure, and oxygen saturation. Common examples include:

Electrocardiogram (ECG) Sensors: ECG sensors are commonly found in wearable devices for heart health monitoring, as they monitor electrical signals in the heart to detect irregularities like arrhythmias and early indicators of cardiac issues.
Photoplethysmography (PPG) Sensors: By using light absorption to measure blood flow and oxygen levels, PPG sensors offer information about cardiovascular and respiratory health.
Blood Pressure Monitors: These are embedded in smartwatches or cuffs and determine blood pressure levels using oscillometric or optical methods for hypertension (high blood pressure) detection.
Respiratory Rate Sensors: Devices featuring respiratory sensors track the patterns of breathing, providing valuable assistance in the management of conditions such as asthma and chronic obstructive pulmonary disease (COPD).

These physiological sensors give individuals the ability to monitor their health continuously and non-invasively, and allow healthcare providers to use this information and make decisions based on it (He & Eastburn, 2022).

2.2 Motion and Activity Sensors

Motion sensors such as accelerometers and gyroscopes are integral to capturing physical activity and movement behaviors. In healthcare and occupational safety, they are used for rehabilitation, fitness tracking and injury prevention.

Accelerometers: Measurers of changes in velocity, which come in handy for counting steps, detecting falls, and analyzing the dynamics of movement. They play a pivotal role in fall detection systems for elderly care and workplace safety.
Gyroscopes: These devices complement accelerometers by measuring angular velocity and orientation, which is critical for applications that require precise understanding of motion dynamics, including gait monitoring and ergonomic assessments.
IMUs also known as Inertial Measurement Units: With a combination of accelerometers, gyros and magnetometers, IMUs are capable of comprehensive motion tracking, making them widely utilised for sports, rehabilitation and industrial safety solutions.

Motion sensors provide insights that assist with fitness improvement, injury detection, and office ergonomics.

2.3 Biochemical Sensors

Biosensors are a class of biochemical sensors that have made health diagnostics innovative by allowing for rapid monitoring of biochemical in biological fluids. These sensors play an essential role in managing chronic diseases and improving personalized care to address population health needs.

Glucose Sensors: One of the most critical devices, glucose sensors help patients monitor their blood sugar levels continuously instead of invasive finger-prick tests.
Lactate Sensors: Used in sports medicine and critical care settings, lactate sensors monitor lactate levels in the blood, which can indicate muscle fatigue or evaluate tissue oxygenation status.
pH Sensors: These sensors are responsible for measuring the hydration level of the medical fluid whether it is normal or alkaline which helps in detecting any metabolic disorder or monitoring the healing of a medical wound.
Electrolyte Sensors Monitor levels of the electrolytes sodium and potassium; used for monitoring dehydration, kidney function, and cardiovascular health.

Optimal, timely interventions are made possible by biochemical sensors, which greatly improve disease management and patient outcomes.

2.4 Environmental Sensors

External Environmental Sensors monitor health and safety impactors like air quality, temperature, humidity, and noise levels. These sensors can be quite useful, especially in contexts like occupational safety or public health surveillance.

Air Quality Sensors: Particulate matter (PM), carbon monoxide (CO), and volatile organic compound (VOCs) sensors measure and detect hazardous environments in industrial settings from a worker safety perspective (Mujawar et al., 2020).
Temperature Sensors: Essential in controlling heat stress and for fever detection in the healthcare industry, these sensors are also utilized for monitoring ambient and body temperatures.
Humidity Sensors: Humidity levels are also a vital parameter for respiratory health and proper workplace conditions; humidity sensors also allow you to maintain optimal environmental conditions.
Noise sensors: Noise sensors are used to keep an eye on the volume in industries to safeguard individuals from permanent hearing damage and have a secure working environment.

Environmental sensors improve situational awareness, allowing organizations and individuals to mitigate threats and optimize living and working conditions.

2.5 Chemical and Gas Sensors

Occupational and health-care contexts, for example, make extensive use of chemical and gas sensors to identify potentially dangerous substances.

Gas Sensors: Gas sensors sense the presence of poisonous gases such as carbon monoxide, hydrogen sulfide, and ammonia.
Chemical Sensors: These sensors can detect chemical spills or leaks and keep workers safe from the exposure of harmful compounds.
E-Nose Sensors: Similar to the human olfactory system, e-nose sensors detect and classify odors and volatile compounds; they can be used for food safety, air quality monitoring, etc.

Discovering anomalous mechanical conditions is vital to avoid occupational hazards and assure a secure area, which is where chemical and gas sensors come into play.

2.6 Thermal Sensors

Thermal sensors are responsible for measuring environmental temperatures or body temperatures, which are critical in healthcare diagnosis and occupational safety.

Infrared Sensors: They are known for non-contact thermal sensors that help to measure body temperature, which is why they are used in detecting fever during an outbreak of infectious diseases.
Skin Temperature Sensors: Sensors that monitor change in skin temperature to control hypothermia or fever and even assess stress levels in occupational health applications.

Thermal sensors offer valuable information about physiological and environmental conditions that can be used for timely interventions (Udoh et al., 2023).

2.7 Optical Sensors

Optical sensors are light-centric devices that perform a range of functions for health and the environment.

Pulse Oximeters: Essential for monitoring respiratory health, these sensors use optical technology to determine blood oxygen levels and pulse rates.
Optical Biosensors: These sensors can identify biomarkers found in blood or saliva, and are used for diagnostics and monitoring of disease.
Light Sensors: Quantifying the amount and quality of light, these sensors are helpful in managing light pollution while providing adequate illumination in occupational scenarios.

Optical enzymes are widely used tools that lend themselves to both health monitoring and environmental assessments.

2.8 Stress and Emotional Sensors

Novel physiological and behavioral indicators of stress and emotional states have led to the development of wearable technologies that increasingly incorporate stress and emotional sensors to monitor mental health and stress levels.

Electrodermal Activity (EDA) Sensors: These sensors measure changes in skin conductance, offering insights into stress and emotional states.
Heart Rate Variability (HRV) Sensors: These sensors analyze the variance in heart rate to determine resiliency to stress and overall autonomic nervous system activity.
EEG Sensors: EEG sensors are employed in neurofeedback therapies and mental health applications to monitor brainwave activity.

Stress and emotional virtual sensors could help manage mental health and workplace productivity and safety.

2.9 Wearable Exoskeletons with Specialized Sensors

These systems utilize specialized sensors to improve physical abilities and to track user performance.

Load Sensors: This type of sensors measures the weight and strain on the exoskeletons, ensuring that there is optimal support and reducing any chances of getting injured.
Joint Angle Sensors: These sensors track the angle of joints, improving ergonomics while also providing assistance in rehabilitation (Chelliah et al., 2021). They enable the ability to control and provide feedback (for example providing sensory information to the user) in exoskeleton systems.
Exoskeletons equipped with specialized sensors can improve worker safety, reduce fatigue, and enhance recovery outcomes.

3. TRANSFORMING DIGITAL HEALTH TECHNOLOGIES

Digital health technologies are rapidly revolutionizing the healthcare ecosystem, including how diseases are monitored, managed, and treated. The fusion of AI with wearables, advances in RPM systems, and new human augmentation technologies mark three key developments in this continuing revolution. These innovations harness data, connectivity and smart system capacities to optimize patient care, enabling, and enhancing quality of care. An immensely powerful technology is AI which powers the wearables providing them insights through sophisticated functionalities such as real-time data processing, predictive analytics or early warning systems.

Sensors in wearable devices collect a massive amount of data, such as vital signs, amount of activity, and environmental conditions. Real-time AI (especially machine learning algorithms) is processing biological data to deliver immediate information about the state of a user. For instance, algorithms integrated into wearable ECG monitors have the ability to identify arrhythmias or early signs of atrial fibrillation, prompting users and healthcare providers to act promptly. Just like the way machine learning models for fitness trackers analyze activity data to tailor suggestions for physical fitness and rehabilitation programs (Materon et al., 2021).

3.1 Early Warning Systems and Predictive Analytics on Diseases

Through predictive analytics, AI can help spot potential health risks before they develop into major issues, enhancing wearable technologies. AI of aging prediction models can also be trained by combining historical and real-times data together and predictable examples for various chronic diseases, as diabetes, are predicted by AI models, for example, by recognizing early clinical markers of a cardiac event, or early patterns of behavior for mental health. Wearables that incorporate early warning systems not only lead to better health outcomes for the individuals who use them but also lower healthcare costs by preventing expensive hospitalizations and allowing for proactive care. AI integration enables adaptive learning, whereby wearables become increasingly precise and efficient (Kumar & Kumari, 2021). An example would be adaptive algorithms in glucose monitors that improve their accuracy by learning user-specific trends, allowing for better diabetes control. Teletreatment, in particular, is a field of healthcare technology that can provide this kind of monitoring. Remote Patient Monitoring (RPM) systems have revolutionized healthcare delivery by enabling continuous observation of patients outside traditional clinical settings. This enhances the impact mainly in chronic diseases, elderly care and mental health.

Digital health technologies are evolving tremendously to improve patient outcomes, improve medical processes, and enhance accessibility in healthcare. Tamil has witnessed a paradigm shift in disease prevention, diagnosis, and treatment with innovations such as artificial intelligence (AI), machine learning (ML), wearable health devices, and telemedicine. From early-stage diagnosis to minimizing the risk of errors, AI-driven diagnostics help medical specialists in identifying diseases with higher precision. From wearables that track vitals 24/7 to real-time data that allows for proactive healthcare management, the technology in the healthcare sector is as dynamic as it is impactful. Telehealth breaks geographical boundaries, delivering patient consultations and personalized care to all corners of the world. The use of blockchain technology ensures data security by maintaining the confidentiality and integrity of medical records. Many healthcare devices are connected through the Internet of Medical Things (IoMT) to exchange data which ultimately improves clinical decisions. In addition, robotic-assisted surgeries and virtual reality (VR) based rehabilitation therapies are enhancing patient care experience. Nonetheless, issues like data privacy concerns, regulatory compliance, and a digital divide must be tackled to provide equitable healthcare access. Whether we like it or not, the future of digital health is a symbiotic relationship wherein technology can support professionals in the field, and the field can guide the use of ethical and sustainable technology. Digital health technologies are nevertheless evolving, and they have the potential to revolutionize access to healthcare globally, increasing efficiency, personalisation, and patient-centricity.

3.2 Chronic Disease Management with Telehealth Applications

Conditions like hypertension, diabetes, and chronic obstructive pulmonary disease (COPD) require constant monitoring and urgent intervention when necessary. RPM platforms with wearable technology also allow medical professionals to monitor basic patient health statistics from a distance while minimizing the necessity of in-office appointments. For example, wearable blood pressure monitors and glucose sensors send real-time updates to healthcare platforms where clinicians review the data for trends and can modify treatment plans as needed.

Telehealth applications employing RPM systems enable medication adherence as well. Smart pill dispensers and reminders alongside RPM platforms ensure patients stick to their prescriptions, leading to improved treatment outcomes. Additionally, insights derived from RPM data using AI may help recognize trends of non-compliance or acute complications, advising an earlier intervention (Vivejananthan et al., 2022).

3.3 Examples for Elderly Care and Mental Health Tracking

The elderly have specific health care needs, like reduced mobility, dementia, and other comorbidities. RPM systems reduce such barriers by offering seniors wearables that can optionally track vital signs, activity levels, and environmental factors. Wearables to detect falls, for example, rely on accelerometers and gyroscopes to recognize sudden movements that indicate falls, thus sending alerts to caregivers or emergency departments. The important use case for RPM systems is mental health tracking. Wearables with stress and emotional sensors (i.e., electrodermal activity (EDA) and heart rate variability (HRV) monitors) determine stress levels and emotional states (Pradhan et al., 2023). When coupled with AI-driven analysis, these systems can predict anxiety or depressive episodes, allowing early psychological interventions. Mobile applications linked with wearables can provide cognitive behavioral therapy (CBT) modules, mindfulness and even crisis support to improve access to mental health care. Human augmentation technologies will enhance existing physical, sensory and cognitive abilities using AI and wearable devices to improve health and functionality.

3.4 Benefits of AI in Prosthetics and Bionics

Through natural movement imitation and response, AI has been a game changer in the field of prosthetics and bionics. These high-tech prostheses with AI-powered control systems translate neural signals from the user's body to facilitate natural movements. To sit as an example: AI-driven myoelectric prosthetics utilize machine learning algorithms to learn from the individual's unique patterns of muscle activity, providing improved dexterity and functionality. Another breakthrough: bionic limbs with sensory feedback systems that allow users to "feel" textures, pressure and temperature. These prosthetics use sensors to send sensory information through electrical impulses to the nervous system, enhancing the use and acceptance of prosthetics. AI supports rehabilitation by monitoring levels of improvement and amending to changes in user actions or requirements.

AI is also improving wearable augmented technology to better enhanced sensory abilities for other people who may have some limitations. For example, hearing aids now use AI-driven noise cancellation and sound amplification to help people with different auditory experiences and environments. As an example, an AI-enabled smart glasses helps the visually impaired user through text reading, suggesting objects, or guiding the user through navigation via voice prompts (Manogaran et al., 2021). The other area of human augmentation is exoskeletons. Wearable robotic devices have been developed to assist people with mobility impairments to walk or do heavy activities. These AI-powered exoskeletons respond dynamically to the user's movements and exertion levels, providing customized support and preventing issues during use. Applications go beyond health care to sectors where employees need help lifting heavy objects or staying the course during repetitive chores.

Human augmentation technologies are also making their way into the world of cognitive enhancement. Wearables equipped with electroencephalogram (EEG) sensors track brainwave activity, contributing to neurofeedback training for enhancing focus, retention, and stress management. These last innovations offer new hopes of treating neurological diseases and optimizing the cognitive performances.

The health and safety revolution powered by AI integration, RPM systems, and human augmentation is constantly evolving digital health technologies. Such innovations help to provide proactive, personalized, and efficient healthcare delivery and improve the quality of living for people with different requirements. With the increasing sophistication of AI algorithms, more accessible RPM systems, and advancements in human augmentation technologies, the potential for leading to better health outcomes and safety in the workspace continues to grow. But to ensure these innovations reach their full potential and serve all segments of society, challenges like data security, device interoperability, and equitable access need to be addressed. As we navigate the digital revolution, the future of digital health must be shaped by a profound commitment to ethical reflection and action, environmental sustainability, and social equity.

4. INNOVATIONS IN OCCUPATIONAL HEALTH AND SAFETY: WORKPLACE MONITORING SYSTEMS

Technology is changing the modern workplace, especially in the field of occupational health and safety. A wide variety of new technologies are being introduced to satisfy the requirements; one of them, workplace monitoring systems, are one of the most crucial advancements in the path of safety, productivity, and risk management. These systems harness advanced technology like sensors, wearables, AI, and LoT to monitor, analyze, and enhance occupational health and safety results (Suma, 2021). The sensors represent a key part of workplace monitoring, measuring different environmental and physiological factors. Temperature, air quality, noise levels, vibration, and hazardous gas concentrations are all included. Gas sensors are widely used in manufacturing and chemical industries to detect a presence of harmful or combustible gases. When gas levels in the working environment reach an alarming level, gas sensors send a signal to the master control unit to sound the alarm and the workers can be evacuated to avoid accident. Noise sensors, for example, help monitor sound levels in industrial environments, ensuring compliance with occupational safety regulations that protect workers from hearing loss.

Wearable devices also have physiological sensors, which can increase workplace safety by tracking workers' health conditions. Wearable devices such as heart rate monitors, stress trackers, and fatigue sensors help firms understand where employees are at with their health status and give timely intervention to prevent accidents due to physical or mental exhaustion. Used in tandem with AI, these sensors are forecast health risks and advise personalized approaches to minimize them. Wearable technology and smart PPE have changed how workplace safety is approached. Smart helmets, safety vests, and wristbands are common devices with sensors and communication modules that monitor workers' locations, poses, and surroundings (Jenkins, 2022). For example, smart helmets at construction sites register each time a worker gets hit, or gets too close to heavy machinery, and send alerts to workers and supervisors. Exoskeletons, a type of wearable robotics, alleviate the body burden on workers engaging in repetitive (or heavy) lifting. Such devices distribute weight more evenly, reducing the chance of musculoskeletal injuries. AI-enabled wearables also assess motion patterns to detect unsafe habits and deliver remedial feedback.

4.1 Workplace Monitoring System (AI and IoT)

With artificial intelligence and the Internet of Things, workplace monitoring systems have reached a level of sophistication that enables predictive and proactive safety solutions. Through IoT, disparate sensors and devices become part of a larger integrated network enabling seamless data collection and communication. AI algorithms analyze this data to detect patterns, anticipate potential threats, and recommend preventive measures (Malik & Kumar, 2022).

Predictive maintenance systems is one of the best examples of which uses IoT sensors to monitor equipment conditions, identifying wear and tear before it leads to breakdown. This minimizes downtime and avoids accidents due to machinery failure. AI-driven analytics also monitor safety compliance in real-time, alerting managers to protocol breaches and generating automated safety reports. Workplace monitoring has evolved with the integration of AI with computer vision. AI algorithms in cameras identify unsafe activities like workers entering restricted zones or not wearing personal protective equipment (PPE) They can provide real-time feedback to crime violations and mitigate risks.

4.2 Ergonomic Solutions and Employee Well-Being

Technological innovations that are significant are very much beneficial to the human factor of the company. Workplace monitoring systems evaluate ergonomic risks through data collected on posture, movement, and workstation design. Sensors mounted in office furniture like chairs and desks examine posture and suggest changes to prevent repetitive strain injuries. Motion capture systems in industrial settings evaluate the biomechanics of workers during various tasks, spotting awkward movements or excessive strain. Designers use this data to re-design work processes and / equipment to improve the working environment to be safer and provide more comfort. Through AI, ergonomic solutions are personalized by customizing the recommendations to the physical characteristics and demand of each worker (Kumar et al., 2022).

4.3 Remote Monitoring and Emergency Response

Remote monitoring systems allow real-time monitoring of workplace safety, particularly in hazardous or geographically dispersed environments. For instance, drones equipped with cameras and sensors are used by mining companies to inspect underground tunnels for structural integrity and dangerous gases. Wearable devices with GPS modules, for example, allow monitoring of workers' locations in real-time, ensuring their safety in distant or isolated job sites. In an emergency scenario, workplace monitoring systems can drastically improve response times. Sensors trigger automated alerts to emergency services and pinpoint the location. By simulating evacuation scenarios, AI-powered systems can optimize response tactics and guarantee that workers can be evacuated without any delays or obstacles.

4.4 Improvement through Data and Analytics

The key benefits of workplace monitoring systems is their ability to provide actionable insights through data analytics. By analyzing historical and real-time data, organizations can identify trends, uncover root causes of accidents, and measure the impact of safety initiatives. Managers can leverage AI-generated dashboards to visualize all relevant metrics for informed decision-making and targeted improvements. Specifically, the use of updated workplace monitoring data integrated into the enterprise resource planning (ERP) systems assists the automatic order of raw materials to ensure a seamless proactive improvement process. Integrating safety initiatives into organizational goals promotes a culture of accountability and proactive safety management.

4.5 Issues and Ethical Considerations

Workplace monitoring systems offer advantages but also contend with challenges over data privacy, employee trust and system interoperability. Organizations should write transparent policies to confirm that monitoring systems respect workers' privacy and are only used for safety purposes. Interoperability standards are also required to facilitate seamless and streamlined integration of different devices and platforms. Workplace monitoring systems: a new paradigm in occupational health and safety using sensors, wearables, AI, and IoT Not only do these systems reduce accidents, they also encourage ergonomics and health monitoring at work. Workplace monitoring systems, as with many technology and emerging trends, face challenges that must be dealt with in order to continue growing within a responsible, regulated framework: privacy, interoperability, etc. They will continue to develop, and in doing so, will redefine safety standards and set new benchmarks for occupational health in the digital age (Han, 2023).

5. CASE STUDIES AND IMPLEMENTATION: HEALTHCARE SETTINGS

Wearables and AI have revolutionized patient care, recovery, and surgical techniques in medical environments. Several case studies show how these technologies are being adopted to enhance outcomes across a range of healthcare settings. Wearable Technology, Rehabilitation and Surgery Wearables: This part focuses on how wearable technologies are being used in the recovery and rehabilitation of patients and how AI-assisted surgical wearables are being used to improve precision in performing medical procedures. From helping to recover patients and for rehabilitation there have been the emergence of a wearable devices that are vital tools of these technologies providing continuous monitoring personalized feedback tailoring, real-time insights into health conditions. These devices are particularly important for the management of chronic conditions, post-surgical recovery, and physical rehabilitation.

5.1 Case Study: Cardiac Rehabilitation

Wearable gadgets such as smartwatches and chest straps are invaluable for patients recovering from cardiac surgeries because they can monitor things such as heart rate, oxygen consumption and activity. One clinical trial at a top hospital combined wearables with a telehealth platform that let cardiologists monitor patients' progress remotely. Data was collected in real time with the wearables for metrics including blood pressure and heart rate variability—allowing for early detection of unusual findings like arrhythmias. Proactive monitoring through these wearables led to a 25% decrease in hospital readmissions for the group of patients, establishing wearables as an effective alternative for cardiac rehabilitation and increasing patient outcomes.

Wearable technologies are also changing the face of rehabilitation for neurological conditions including stroke, Parkinson's disease and spinal cord injuries. Wearable gait trainers and exoskeletons are among the devices programmed to help recover mobility. Particularly, research undertaken within a neuro-rehabilitation environment illustrates the effectiveness of AI-enhanced exoskeletons for recovering walker capabilities in patients who have experienced a stroke. The devices utilized real-time motion data to adapt to users' specific gait movements, giving dynamic support and feedback to correct muscle memory and improve coordination (Raghav et al., 2024).

5.2 Physical Therapy and Orthopedic Recovery

In physical therapy, wearables integrated into braces or compression garments track joint movement, muscle activity, and range of motion. One important application featured patients who had undergone knee replacement surgery and signaled this with the use of wearabe motion sensors coupled with a mobile application. The system monitored their adherence to prescribed exercises, and AI algorithms analyzed this data to make recommendations for adjustments. As a result, recovery times decreased, and patients adhered better to therapy protocols.

5.3 AI-Driven Surgery Attire: Precision Redefined

Surgical wearables leveraging AI are shaping the future of surgical procedures by improving accuracy, minimizing errors, and enhancing patient care. Targeted tools that harness the power of augmented reality (AR), robotics, and wearable sensors provide surgeons with a full view of the surgical field, as well as real-time insights and guidance (Banerjee et al., 2020).

5.4 Robotic Assisted Surgeries: A Case Study

AI-assisted surgical wearables have a number of innovative applications, one of which is in robotic-assisted surgeries. A prime example of this is da Vinci Surgical System, which combines robotic arms capable of performing intricate operations with wearable controls designed to offer surgeons unparalleled levels of precision during minimally invasive procedures. For instance, a prominent cancer facility employed robotic-enabled wearables for prostatectomies. AI algorithms analyzed high-resolution imaging data and operated in real time, coordinating the robotic arms to avoid critical structures like nerves and blood vessels. This led to a 30 percent decrease in postoperative complications and faster recovery for patients.

5.5 Augmented Reality Technologies for Distraction-Free Setup

Examples of wearables with AR capabilities include head-mounted displays (HMD) and smart glasses, which offer 3d visualization to the surgeon to improve the quality of data during complexities of surgical procedures (Barnes & Zvarikova, 2021). As a case, one university hospital used AR wearables for orthopedic surgeries. These devices did was project 3D models of the patient's anatomy, derived from preoperative imaging scans, onto the surgical site. AI-powered analytics provided insights into areas that required accuracy, including bone alignment and implant positioning. Surgeons said their accuracy improved, and their surgery times got shorter, yielding better outcomes and fewer complications.

5.6 Feedback in Real-Time for Minimally Invasive Surgeries

AI-assisted wearables that provide real-time feedback can be particularly beneficial for minimally invasive surgeries such as laparoscopic or endoscopic procedures. One successful case study used haptic feedback gloves powered by AI algorithms. Tactile sensations were provided to surgeons performing laparoscopic removal of the gallbladder: these sensations were similar to real tissue, giving surgeons better control over their instruments while avoiding incidental damage. Notably, this technology was particularly helpful for novice surgeons when training, as it decreased the learning curve without outputting a negative impact on the patient.

5.7 Challenges and Broader Implementation

Wearable technologies and AI are being incorporated into healthcare to manage and improve patient recovery, rehabilitation, and surgical care. From real-time monitoring to tailored feedback and improved surgical accuracy, the technology has proven its worth in improving outcomes across scenarios. Wearables have proven to be effective in cardiac rehabilitation (randomized controlled trials, observational studies, and meta-analyses), neurological recovery, and minimally invasive surgeries, while AI-assisted surgical wearables have changed the meaning of precision between theatre doors as revealed through the case studies. Addressing issues of scalability, data integration, and privacy will be key to unlocking the full potential of these technologies (Desai & Shende, 2021). With healthcare systems continuing to evolve, the combination of wearables and AI are set to take an increasingly prominent position in delivering safer, more efficient, and more patient-centric healthcare. These case studies show the power of wearables and AI in healthcare, but widespread adoption has its challenges.

Scalability and Cost: Scaling up these technologies requires a high capital investment in infrastructure, training, and devices. Healthcare institutions are likely weighing these costs against potential long-term savings from fewer complications and improved efficiency.

Data Integration and Interoperability: For wearables and AI-assisted systems to be effective, they must be integrated smoothly with existing healthcare systems. However, interoperability remains a challenge, as different systems may use different data formats or simply not be compatible with each other, affecting their widespread use.

Ethical and Privacy Issues: Wearables and AI systems must be used carefully with the opportunity they bring to protect patient privacy. For data compliance, the healthcare providers follow strict regulations like GDPR, and HIPAA that ensure sensitive data is not compromised (Hurley & Popescu, 2021).

6. CHALLENGES AND LIMITATIONS

Integrating sensors, wearable technologies, and AI into the realms of healthcare and occupational safety has evolved these industries without question. However, the path to widespread adoption includes challenges and limitations that need to be overcome in order to unleash their full potential. This section explores the main challenges falling into three key categories: technical barriers, ethical and privacy concerns, as well as cost and accessibility issues (Goel et al., 2021).

6.1. Technical Barriers

While wearable technologies hold great promise for healthcare and workplace monitoring, despite these advancements, various technical limitations inhibit their usage and trustworthiness across such applications. Ensuring the accuracy and reliability of data collected by wearable devices is one of the top technical hurdles to tackle. Sensors can distort readings due to external factors (eg, environmental conditions, user movement, and device positioning). For instance, heart rate monitors and fitness trackers can be inaccurate during intense movements or if the device is worn incorrectly. Such inaccuracies have the potential to create incorrect insights and lead to misguided decisions, which in turn can threaten patient care and workplace safety. Wearable technologies, their ecosystem are fragmented where devices and platforms run on different protocols or standards (Kumar et al., 2022). A key problem is interoperability bringing together information from disparate sources under one roof which is proving a particular challenge for healthcare providers and employers. For example, a wearable glucose monitor does not connect directly to a health care provider's electronic medical record (EMR) system, making data analysis and patient management more difficult. The absence of a common denominator acts as a barrier to smooth integration of wearables into larger systems for a comprehensive approach to monitoring care and safety.

Wearables are often limited by battery life and long-term durability. This constant monitoring and data transmission requires a lot of energy and thus frequent recharging. In work environments, which often require employees to use wearables for long periods of time, poor battery life disrupts operations and creates wariness about the technology (Huang et al., 2021).

6.2. Ethical and Privacy Concerns

Wearable technology accumulates large amounts of sensitive data such as vital signs, location tracking, and activity history. Securing this data from breaches and unauthorized access is vital, but difficult. Hackers exploit connected devices vulnerabilities on a large scale that can result in extreme measures like identity theft or abuse of health information. Consider a cyberattack on a wearable heart monitor: A cyberattack in such a case could expose patients' medical histories and compromise their privacy (Malik et al., 2021).

Wearable devices are also used to monitor employees' movements, health parameters and environmental exposure in occupational health and safety. These applications, while designed to improve workplace safety, can unintentionally violate employees' privacy. Wearables that constantly track performance also may foster feelings of violation and distrust among workers. The challenge of balancing the use of technology for safety and the privacy rights of employees is a recurring ethical dilemma.

6.3 Bias in AI Algorithms

The algorithms used by artificial intelligence to analyze data from wearables can be prone to biases or unfairness. AI models trained on non-representational datasets could lead to insights that are imbalanced. For example, wearables that are designed for lighter skin tones may not accurately measure metrics like oxygen saturation in people who have darker skin tones, contributing to disparities in care (Kumar et al., 2021).

6.3. Cost and Accessibility

The biggest barriers to widespread adoption of wearable technologies is the exorbitant costs involved in developing, deploying, and maintaining the technologies, which significantly limits access to these monitoring tools, especially in underserved communities. Building more sophisticated wearables involves big investments in research, prototyping, and manufacturing. Investing in advanced features like AI analytics, real-time data processing, and seamless connectivity supercharges the cost. The cost associated with this enorme and massive effort to rewrite their existing systems to accommodate these technologies can be overwhelming for healthcare providers and organizations and this may prevent widespread adoption of these technologies. Continuing costs for device upkeep, software upgrades, and data storage also contribute to the financial burden (Kaushik et al., 2024).

Wearables, while revolutionary, are generally too expensive for low-income populations and resource-poor areas. This results in disparity where only those who could afford to have access to wearable technologies But the rural healthcare systems may not have the facilities to embed the watch data into their information systems, and thus their patients may not benefit from these advanced monitoring solutions. It is important to address this data disparity to help drive equitable healthcare delivery.

6.4 Insurance and Reimbursement Hurdles

Insurance coverage for wearable technologies is still limited, and this further reduces access. On the other hand, patients may have difficulty being reimbursed for the costs of devices they use to maintain chronic conditions, and employers need a financial incentive to invest in wearable safety solutions. To fill that gap, we must develop policies that incentivize their use, namely subsidies and insurance coverage of wearables. Sensors, wearable technologies and AI is impacting the healthcare and occupational safety, providing new opportunities for innovation in these fields. But, the technical limitations, ethical considerations, and financial constraints represent absolute challenges that need focused attention strategies (Arora et al., 2024). Together, these stakeholders technology developers, healthcare providers, employers, and policymakers can work to overcome these limitations and ensure that wearables can ultimately deliver on their promise to improve safety, health outcomes, and quality of life in a variety of settings (Kaushik et al., 2024).

7. CONCLUSION AND SUGGESTIONS

However, sensors, wearable technologies and AI is revolutionizing healthcare and occupational safety, providing innovative solutions for real-time monitoring, predictive analytics, and improved human capabilities. These technologies have proved valuable in transforming the way we care for patients, how they recover and rehabilitate, and even in increasing workplace safety. Yet widespread adoption is challenged by a variety of obstacles, including technical limitations, ethical concerns and questions of cost and accessibility (Raghav et al., 2024). Such limitations need to be addressed to really unlock the prospects of these and ensure equal access to their benefits.

So it need to innovate, multidisciplinary working is key to achieving this. Technology developers also need to concentrate on building more reliable devices, adopting standards-based interoperability and increasing energy efficiency. This is where policymakers and regulators must get it right: creating strong frameworks to protect data privacy in support of innovation. Finally, incentives like subsidies, tax benefits and public-private partnerships also play an important role in overcoming the high price of wearable technologies.

There is also a need for efforts to close the digital divide and to encourage access and inclusivity, drawing on affordable solutions for wearable healthcare and creating education programs are key to bringing this technology to underserved and rural areas. There are ethical concerns in developing monitoring systems so it is necessary for employers and healthcare providers to maintain transparency and honesty. The future of wearables and AI in healthcare and workplace safety holds great potential but also poses various challenges. Together by addressing these challenges strategically and embracing innovation responsibly, these technologies can pave the path towards a future that is safer, healthier, and more equitable for everyone.

REFERENCES

Ahirwar, R., & Khan, N. (2022). *Smart Wireless Nanosensor Systems for Human Healthcare*. CRC Press. DOI: 10.1201/9781003093534-15

Arora, M. K., Lal, S., Singh, B., & Olyaee, M. (2024). Through an Energy Lens: Examining SDGs From a Policy Perspective. In Riswandi, B., Singh, B., Kaunert, C., & Vig, K. (Eds.), *AI Applications for Clean Energy and Sustainability* (pp. 320–343). IGI Global., DOI: 10.4018/979-8-3693-6567-0.ch016

Banerjee, A., Chakraborty, C., & Rathi, M.Sr. (2020). Medical imaging, artificial intelligence, internet of things, wearable devices in terahertz healthcare technologies. In *Terahertz biomedical and healthcare technologies* (pp. 145–165). Elsevier. DOI: 10.1016/B978-0-12-818556-8.00008-2

Barnes, R., & Zvarikova, K. (2021). Artificial intelligence-enabled wearable medical devices, clinical and diagnostic decision support systems, and Internet of Things-based healthcare applications in COVID-19 prevention, screening, and treatment. *American Journal of Medical Research (New York, N.Y.)*, *8*(2), 9–22. DOI: 10.22381/ajmr8220211

Chelliah, R., Wei, S., Daliri, E. B. M., Rubab, M., Elahi, F., Yeon, S. J., Jo, K., Yan, P., Liu, S., & Oh, D. H. (2021). Development of nanosensors based intelligent packaging systems: Food quality and medicine. *Nanomaterials (Basel, Switzerland)*, *11*(6), 1515. DOI: 10.3390/nano11061515 PMID: 34201071

Desai, D., & Shende, P. (2021). Integration of Internet of Things with Quantum Dots: A State-of-the-art of Medicine. *Current Pharmaceutical Design*, *27*(17), 2068–2075. DOI: 10.2174/1381612827666210222113740 PMID: 33618640

Gaobotse, G., Mbunge, E., Batani, J., & Muchemwa, B. (2022). Non-invasive smart implants in healthcare: Redefining healthcare services delivery through sensors and emerging digital health technologies. *Sensors International*, *3*, 100156. DOI: 10.1016/j.sintl.2022.100156

Goel, S. S., Goel, A., Kumar, M., & Moltó, G. (2021). A review of Internet of Things: Qualifying technologies and boundless horizon. *Journal of Reliable Intelligent Environments*, *7*(1), 23–33. DOI: 10.1007/s40860-020-00127-w

Han, B., Tomer, V., Nguyen, T. A., Farmani, A., & Singh, P. K. (Eds.). (2020). *Nanosensors for smart cities*. Elsevier.

Han, X. (2023). A novel assimilated navigation model based on advanced optical systems (AOS), internet of things (IoT) and artificial intelligence (AI). *Optical and Quantum Electronics*, *55*(7), 655. DOI: 10.1007/s11082-023-04947-x

He, L., & Eastburn, M. (2022, August). Smart nanosensor networks for body injury detection. In 2022 IEEE International Conference on Smart Internet of Things (SmartIoT) (pp. 15-19). IEEE. DOI: 10.1109/SmartIoT55134.2022.00012

Huang, J., Wu, X., Huang, W., Wu, X., & Wang, S. (2021). Internet of things in health management systems: A review. *International Journal of Communication Systems*, *34*(4), e4683. DOI: 10.1002/dac.4683

Hurley, D., & Popescu, G. H. (2021). Medical big data and wearable internet of things healthcare systems in remotely monitoring and caring for confirmed or suspected COVID-19 patients. *American Journal of Medical Research (New York, N.Y.)*, *8*(2), 78–90. DOI: 10.22381/ajmr8220216

Jenkins, T. (2022). Wearable medical sensor devices, machine and deep learning algorithms, and internet of things-based healthcare systems in COVID-19 patient screening, diagnosis, monitoring, and treatment. *American Journal of Medical Research (New York, N.Y.)*, *9*(1), 49–64. DOI: 10.22381/ajmr9120224

Kaushik, T. K., Singh, A., Raghav, A., Singh, B., Arora, M. K., & Lal, S. (2024). Untapping Artificial Intelligence in Environmental and Sustainable Progression: Projecting Legal and Ethical Considerations. In Maintaining a Sustainable World in the Nexus of Environmental Science and AI (pp. 109-130). IGI Global.

Kaushik, T. K., Singh, A., Raghav, A., & Singh, B. (2024). Potential of Artificial Intelligence in the Agricultural Industry: A Comprehensive Review. AI Applications for Clean Energy and Sustainability, 344-365.

Kumar, P. M., Hong, C. S., Afghah, F., Manogaran, G., Yu, K., Hua, Q., & Gao, J. (2021). Clouds proportionate medical data stream analytics for internet of things-based healthcare systems. *IEEE Journal of Biomedical and Health Informatics*, *26*(3), 973–982. DOI: 10.1109/JBHI.2021.3106387 PMID: 34415841

Kumar, P. M., Khan, L. U., & Hong, C. S. (2022). Affirmative fusion process for improving wearable sensor data availability in artificial intelligence of medical things. *IEEE Sensors Journal.*

Kumar, P. M., Khan, L. U., & Hong, C. S. (2022). Notice of Violation of IEEE Publication Principles: Affirmative Fusion Process for Improving Wearable Sensor Data Availability in Artificial Intelligence of Medical Things. IEEE Sensors Journal.

Kumar, S., & Kumari, P. (2021). Flexible Nano Smart sensors. Nanosensors for Smart Manufacturing, 199.

Malik, A., & Kumar, A. (2022). assimilation of blockchain with Internet of Things (IoT) with possible issues and solutions for better connectivity and proper security. In New Trends and Applications in Internet of Things (IoT) and Big Data Analytics (pp. 187-207). Cham: Springer International Publishing.

Malik, P. K., Sharma, R., Singh, R., Gehlot, A., Satapathy, S. C., Alnumay, W. S., Pelusi, D., Ghosh, U., & Nayak, J. (2021). Industrial Internet of Things and its applications in industry 4.0: State of the art. *Computer Communications*, *166*, 125–139. DOI: 10.1016/j.comcom.2020.11.016

Manogaran, G., Alazab, M., Song, H., & Kumar, N. (2021). CDP-UA: Cognitive data processing method wearable sensor data uncertainty analysis in the internet of things assisted smart medical healthcare systems. *IEEE Journal of Biomedical and Health Informatics*, *25*(10), 3691–3699. DOI: 10.1109/JBHI.2021.3051288 PMID: 33439849

Materon, E. M., Gómez, F. R., Joshi, N., Dalmaschio, C. J., Carrilho, E., & Oliveira Jr, O. N. (2021). Smart materials for electrochemical flexible nanosensors: advances and applications. Nanosensors for smart manufacturing, 347-371.

Mujawar, M. A., Gohel, H., Bhardwaj, S. K., Srinivasan, S., Hickman, N., & Kaushik, A. (2020). Nano-enabled biosensing systems for intelligent healthcare: Towards COVID-19 management. *Materials Today. Chemistry*, *17*, 100306. DOI: 10.1016/j.mtchem.2020.100306 PMID: 32835155

Nazari, A. (2020). Nanosensors for smart cities: an introduction. In *Nanosensors for smart cities* (pp. 3–8). Elsevier. DOI: 10.1016/B978-0-12-819870-4.00001-3

Oukhatar, A., Bakhouya, M., & El Ouadghiri, D. (2021). Electromagnetic-Based Wireless Nano-Sensors Network: Architectures and Applications. *Journal of Communication*, *16*(1), 8–19. DOI: 10.12720/jcm.16.1.8-19

Pradhan, M. R., Mago, B., & Ateeq, K. (2023). A classification-based sensor data processing method for the internet of things assimilated wearable sensor technology. *Cluster Computing*, *26*(1), 807–822. DOI: 10.1007/s10586-022-03605-3

Pramanik, P. K. D., Solanki, A., Debnath, A., Nayyar, A., El-Sappagh, S., & Kwak, K. S. (2020). Advancing modern healthcare with nanotechnology, nanobiosensors, and internet of nano things: Taxonomies, applications, architecture, and challenges. *IEEE Access : Practical Innovations, Open Solutions*, *8*, 65230–65266. DOI: 10.1109/ACCESS.2020.2984269

Raghav, A., Singh, B., Jermsittiparsert, K., Raghav, R., & Yadav, U. (2024). Artificial Intelligence in Environmental and Climate Changes: A Sustainable Future. In Singh, B., Kaunert, C., Vig, K., & Dutta, S. (Eds.), *Maintaining a Sustainable World in the Nexus of Environmental Science and AI* (pp. 485–506). IGI Global., DOI: 10.4018/979-8-3693-6336-2.ch019

Sahi, K. S. S., & Kaushik, S. (2022). Smart Nanosensors for Healthcare Monitoring and Disease Detection using AIoT Framework. In *Nanosensors for Futuristic Smart and Intelligent Healthcare Systems* (pp. 387–400). CRC Press. DOI: 10.1201/9781003093534-19

Suma, D. V. (2021). Wearable IoT based distributed framework for ubiquitous computing. *Journal of Ubiquitous Computing and Communication Technologies*, *3*(1), 23–32. DOI: 10.36548/jucct.2021.1.003

Udoh, E. E., Hermel, M., Bharmal, M. I., Nayak, A., Patel, S., Butlin, M., & Bhavnani, S. P. (2023). Nanosensor technologies and the digital transformation of healthcare. *Personalized Medicine*, *20*(3), 251–269. DOI: 10.2217/pme-2022-0065 PMID: 37403731

Vivekananthan, V., Khandelwal, G., Alluri, N. R., & Kim, S. J. (2022). E-Skin for Futuristic Nanosensor Technology for the Healthcare System. In Nanosensors for Futuristic Smart and Intelligent Healthcare Systems (pp. 133-157). CRC Press.

Chapter 14

The Potential of Artificial Intelligence in Enhancing Occupational Health and Safety for Urban Informal Vendors: A South African Case

Maasago Mercy Sepadi
https://orcid.org/0000-0002-7236-9160
Tshwane University of Technology, South Africa

Nicolene Asithandile Dyantyi
https://orcid.org/0009-0002-3648-939X
Tshwane University of Technology, South Africa

Kholofelo Khumo Nkwana
https://orcid.org/0009-0009-3865-226X
City of Johannesburg, South Africa

ABSTRACT

South Africa's informal sector, including street vendors, faces significant occupational health and safety challenges, including exposure to air pollution, extreme weather, and limited sanitation. Current legislative frameworks, offer limited protections for these workers, leaving substantial gaps in regulatory coverage. Artificial Intelligence (AI) presents a promising solution by enabling real-time environmental monitoring, predictive analytics, and health alerts tailored to high-risk conditions. This chapter explores various AI applications for improving vendor safety, such as wearable devices for air quality and vital signs monitoring, and mobile apps delivering real-time health information. However, barriers to implementation exist, including financial constraints, digital literacy gaps, and data privacy concerns. To address these, the chapter recommends targeted interventions like public-private partnerships and subsidies, and digital literacy initiatives alongside robust policy frameworks that expand OHS protections to include AI-driven health solutions.

DOI: 10.4018/979-8-3693-9301-7.ch014

1. INTRODUCTION

The informal sector in South Africa is a cornerstone of urban economies, employing approximately 2.5 million people, including a substantial number of street vendors (Stats SA, 2023). Street vendors provide essential goods and services to millions daily, often at affordable prices and in inaccessible locations. Yet, despite their economic importance, these vendors frequently lack adequate health and safety protections (Stats SA, 2023). Unlike their counterparts in formal employment, street vendors face a range of occupational hazards, from prolonged exposure to air pollution and harsh weather conditions to the challenges posed by insufficient infrastructure, limited sanitation facilities, and restricted access to public health resources. The sustainability of any nation is closely linked to the health and hygiene of its workforce, which, in turn, depends on a clean and safe environment. In South Africa, legislative frameworks such as the *Occupational Health and Safety Act* (OHSA, 1993) and various Municipal By-Laws underscore the importance of safeguarding the health and safety of all workers, including those in informal sectors. These frameworks are designed to reduce environmental and occupational hazards, thus fostering a healthier work environment. In line with these objectives, the Environmental Health National Norms and Standards, established under the National Health Act of 2003 and supported by the *Constitution of the Republic of South Africa* (1996), mandate environmental monitoring as a fundamental public health measure. These standards assert that all citizens, regardless of employment sector, have the right to work in safe environments (Sepadi & Nkosi, 2023).

However, in practice, street vendors continue to encounter significant occupational health and safety (OHS) challenges. Urban air pollution, exacerbated by traffic congestion and industrial emissions, poses a severe health risk to vendors stationed in high-traffic zones. Prolonged exposure to pollutants such as particulate matter ($PM_{2.5}$) and nitrogen dioxide (NO_2) has been shown to increase respiratory illnesses, a risk amplified by the lack of protective infrastructure around vending areas. Studies indicate that vendors in these settings are disproportionately affected by respiratory ailments, cardiovascular diseases, and other pollution-related health issues (Sepadi & Nkosi, 2023; Salamone et al., 2021). Beyond air pollution, vendors also endure exposure to extreme weather conditions, ranging from intense summer heat to cold winters, further compounded by the absence of shelter or shaded areas. In addition to environmental hazards, street vendors face substantial challenges due to inadequate sanitation facilities. Many operate without access to clean water or proper waste disposal systems, which raises the risk of foodborne illnesses and exacerbates public health concerns in densely populated trading areas. These conditions not only impact vendors' personal health but also pose a risk to the broader public, especially in urban centers where informal vending contributes significantly to daily food consumption.

Noise pollution and psychosocial stressors add further complexity to the OHS landscape for street vendors. The nature of informal work is often marked by economic uncertainty, lack of legal protection, and social stigma, contributing to heightened levels of stress among vendors. In light of these multifaceted challenges, innovative solutions are imperative. Emerging technologies, particularly Artificial Intelligence (AI), offer transformative potential for addressing these issues. AI has the capacity to revolutionize OHS for street vendors by providing real-time monitoring of environmental conditions, predictive analytics for anticipating health risks, and tailored training programs to equip vendors with essential health and safety knowledge. This chapter explores the potential of AI to enhance the OHS landscape for street vendors in South Africa.

2. METHODOLOGICAL APPROACH

This chapter adopts a conceptual and literature-based analytical approach to explore how AI technologies can enhance OHS for urban informal street vendors. The study relied on a combination of secondary data sources, including peer-reviewed articles, government reports, environmental monitoring standards, and case studies from South Africa and comparable global contexts. Literature was identified through academic databases such as Scopus, Google Scholar, and ScienceDirect, using keywords including "AI in public health," "informal sector OHS," "urban street vendors," and "environmental health monitoring." Selected sources were published between 2018 and 2024 and included national policy documents, empirical studies, and thematic reviews.

The chapter uses a thematic synthesis to group findings into key areas: (1) environmental and occupational risks; (2) potential AI solutions; (3) ethical, social, and infrastructural challenges; and (4) policy frameworks and stakeholder implications. Although the study did not include primary fieldwork, the analysis highlights the need for participatory research involving vendors to validate AI-based interventions.

3. HISTORICAL CONTEXT OF INFORMAL VENDING IN SOUTH AFRICA

The roots of informal vending in South Africa are deeply entwined with the country's history of racial segregation, exclusionary urban planning, and labour marginalization. During the apartheid era, policies such as the *Group Areas Act* (1950) and the *Urban Areas Act* (1923) enforced strict racial zoning, forcibly relocating Black populations to peripheral townships while restricting their access to formal employment in urban centers. Post-1994 urban development strategies focused heavily on formalization and economic growth but largely failed to integrate informal traders into mainstream infrastructure planning. Furthermore, the regulation and weak enforcement of labour protections continued to leave informal traders exposed to unsafe working conditions (Skinner & Haysom, 2016).

4. CURRENT OCCUPATIONAL HEALTH AND SAFETY CHALLENGES IN URBAN INFORMAL VENDING

4.1. Occupational Health Risks for Urban Informal Vendors

Urban street vendors face significant environmental and occupational hazards. In their study, Sepadi and Nkosi (2023) demonstrated that informal vendors are vulnerable to respiratory issues due to prolonged exposure to particulate matter (PM2.5) and nitrogen dioxide (NO2). These pollutants are particularly concentrated in urban areas with heavy traffic and industrial activities, exacerbating health risks. Street vendors operating outdoors are disproportionately affected by these pollutants, which are especially high during the winter and spring seasons. Similar studies have confirmed the health risks associated with such environmental exposures, showing increased cases of respiratory diseases and cardiovascular issues among those exposed to high pollution levels (Yi et al., 2022; Salamone et al., 2021).

In addition to air pollution, extreme weather conditions pose severe risks to street vendors. Heat stress, dehydration, and cold-related illnesses are common due to vendors' prolonged exposure to these elements. The lack of sanitation facilities further aggravates these risks by promoting unhygienic practices, leading to foodborne illnesses. According to Kreps et al. (2018), the absence of proper sanitation infrastructure creates an unsafe working environment that compromises public health.

Despite these occupational hazards, many vendors lack access to healthcare and preventive services, largely due to financial constraints and the informal nature of their work. This has created a gap in public health protection, necessitating innovative approaches like AI-driven solutions to monitor and predict health risks, enabling preventive and tailored interventions (Olawade et al., 2023).

4.1.1. Health and Safety Concerns in the South African Informal Sector

Street vendors in South Africa operate under challenging conditions that expose them to various occupational health and safety risks. Informal vending is a vital economic activity, especially in urban centers like Johannesburg, Cape Town, and Durban, where a large population depends on this sector for livelihood. However, due to insufficient infrastructure, lack of regulatory oversight, and environmental challenges, vendors frequently encounter hazards that pose significant health risks.

4.1.1.1. Respiratory Health Risks Due to Air Pollution

Air pollution is a critical issue in urban areas of South Africa, exacerbated by traffic congestion, industrial activities, and dense population centers. Street vendors are often stationed near busy roads or industrial zones, where they are exposed to high levels of pollutants such as particulate matter ($PM_{2.5}$) and nitrogen dioxide (NO_2). Studies in South Africa have demonstrated a link between prolonged exposure to air pollution and increased respiratory issues among informal workers (Sepadi & Nkosi, 2023; Salamone et al., 2021). According to recent data from Stats SA, Johannesburg, with its high traffic density and limited green spaces, records $PM_{2.5}$ levels that frequently exceed WHO safety standards, especially during winter months when air stagnation is more pronounced. For instance, a study conducted in the Johannesburg inner city found that informal vendors operating near main roads exhibited higher rates of respiratory illnesses, including chronic bronchitis and asthma, than those working in less polluted areas. These findings align with global research showing that $PM_{2.5}$ and NO_2 exposure heightens the risk of respiratory infections, chronic obstructive pulmonary disease (COPD), and cardiovascular conditions, posing a severe health burden for street vendors.

4.1.1.2. Impact of Inadequate Sanitation Facilities on Health

The lack of adequate sanitation facilities is another pressing challenge for informal vendors in South Africa. Many vendors operate without access to clean water, handwashing stations, or toilets, especially in informal trading areas that lack municipal support. This scarcity not only affects vendors' personal hygiene but also creates public health risks, as vendors handling food are unable to adhere to basic hygiene practices, increasing the potential for foodborne illnesses. A study on urban informal trading in Johannesburg and Cape Town found that limited access to sanitation significantly impacted vendors' health and contributed to the spread of communicable diseases. Without proper facilities, vendors face increased risks of gastrointestinal infections, skin diseases, and vector-borne illnesses, which further compromise their well-being and ability to work effectively. The lack of sanitation also poses broader public health risks, as it can lead to the contamination of food and water sources in the surrounding area (Stats SA, 2023).

4.1.1.3. Extreme Weather Conditions and Heat Stress

In South Africa's varied climate, street vendors are frequently exposed to extreme weather conditions, including high temperatures in summer and cold, dry winters. Vendors working in open-air environments are particularly vulnerable to heat stress, dehydration, and UV exposure, which are common during the summer months. According to a 2022 report from the South African Weather Service, heatwaves in urban areas have become increasingly frequent, directly impacting vendors who lack shaded or air-conditioned workspaces. For example, in Pretoria, where summer temperatures can exceed 35°C, vendors often report symptoms of heat exhaustion, dehydration, and fatigue. The absence of adequate cooling infrastructure exacerbates these risks, as many vendors must continue working despite the adverse conditions to maintain their livelihood. Such prolonged exposure to extreme weather increases the risk of heat-related illnesses, particularly among elderly vendors or those with pre-existing health conditions (South African Weather Service, 2022).

4.1.1.4. Noise Pollution and Psychosocial Stress

The informal trade environment is also marked by high noise levels from nearby traffic, public announcements, and other urban sounds (Sepadi & Nkosi, 2023). Continuous exposure to noise pollution can lead to stress, hearing impairment, and sleep disturbances, further impacting vendors' overall health. Additionally, the financial instability and insecurity associated with informal vending contribute to heightened psychosocial stress. Vendors often face harassment, limited legal protection, and unpredictable income, all of which can contribute to mental health challenges. Recent studies highlighted that those vendors working near bus and taxi ranks in Johannesburg and Durban reported increased anxiety and sleep-related issues due to chronic noise exposure and workplace insecurity. This psychosocial stress not only affects their mental well-being but can also lead to physical health issues, including hypertension and weakened immunity.

4.2. The Current Environmental Health Administrative Monitoring Systems

In South Africa, environmental health administrative monitoring systems are governed by a framework designed to ensure public health protection across various food premises. According to the South African National Environmental Health Norms and Standards for Premises and the Acceptable Monitoring Standards for Environmental Health Practitioners (EHPs), outlined in the *National Health Act*, (2003), regular inspections of food premises are essential to safeguard food safety, handling practices, and regulatory compliance. These inspections play a crucial role in hazard identification and implementing risk-based food safety management plans, ensuring that areas with the highest health risks receive proper oversight and intervention.

4.2.1. Food and Water Safety Standards and Monitoring

Food safety management is a key aspect of these standards. All food premises, whether formal or informal, are required to follow structured protocols for handling and storage. This includes developing food safety plans that focus on identifying and mitigating hazards that could compromise public health. These protocols also extend to water quality monitoring. Routine water sampling is mandated to evaluate the chemical and microbiological safety of water, with regular monitoring programs to ensure compliance with safety standards. By adhering to these sanitation, waste, and pollution protocols, health authorities aim to create an environment that minimizes health risks from contaminated food and water sources, thus safeguarding public health.

However, a study by Sepadi & Nkosi (2023) indicates a disparity in the enforcement of these standards between formal and informal sectors. While food sampling, sanitation oversight, and health inspections are stringently applied to formal businesses, informal vendors often operate outside this regulatory framework. Many street vendors face significant challenges in meeting these standards due to limited infrastructure, lack of resources, and the absence of consistent administrative oversight. This inconsistency creates unchecked health risks in informal settings, where foodborne illness outbreaks can go undetected and untreated. This presents a challenge for EHPs, who are tasked with protecting public health by assessing risks and ensuring compliance with health regulations. The informal sector's lack of formal systems makes it difficult for EHPs to carry out their duties effectively. This gap in oversight highlights the need for enhanced support and tailored interventions for informal food vendors to ensure that public health is protected, regardless of the operating environment.

In particular, it is mandatory to establish food safety plans on food premises, with a focus on hazard identification and risk-based approaches. This ensures proper food safety management where risks are highest. The same standards need to be adhered to when it comes to water quality monitoring; water sampling is essential for evaluating the chemical and microbiological quality of water, and routine monitoring programs are required to ensure water sources meet safety standards. These food and water safety measures, as part of sanitation, waste, and pollution protocols, are designed to protect public health across both formal and informal premises.

4.2.2. Challenges for Environmental Health Practitioners (EHPs) in the Informal Sector

Environmental Health Practitioners (EHPs) are tasked with protecting public health through risk assessment, compliance enforcement, and regular monitoring. However, the informal sector's lack of formal systems presents a unique challenge for EHPs, who are often unable to conduct consistent inspections due to limited resources and logistical constraints. EHPs in South African municipalities are more likely to focus on regulated premises, which often leads to informal traders receiving little to no attention. Without a formal infrastructure for food safety and sanitation practices, EHPs struggle to implement public health protections effectively, leaving a significant gap in oversight that places both vendors and consumers at risk.

For example, street vendors in crowded areas like Johannesburg's Hillbrow or Durban's Warwick Junction typically sell perishable goods without access to basic sanitation facilities. These conditions exacerbate health risks, as vendors have limited options to adhere to safe food handling practices. This reality underscores the need for tailored interventions that cater to the specific needs of the informal sector, such as mobile health inspection units or portable sanitation solutions that can be deployed in high-density trading zones.

4.2.3. Regulatory Gaps and Exemptions for Informal Vendors

Under current regulations, informal street vendors who sell unprocessed agricultural products at local authority markets are often exempt from obtaining certificates of acceptability, as per Regulation 14 of Regulation R638 under the *Foodstuffs, Cosmetics, and Disinfectants Act* (1972). This exemption, while intended to reduce bureaucratic barriers, results in regulatory gaps that leave vendors operating outside formal health inspections. Without such certificates, many street vendors lack documentation that would otherwise subject them to regular monitoring and compliance checks. This regulatory gap leaves a significant portion of the informal economy vulnerable to unmonitored risks of foodborne illness, especially given that these vendors often lack the facilities needed for safe food handling.

Furthermore, informal vendors are usually unaware of regulatory standards or lack the training required to meet them, which only heightens the risk of contamination and illness. Studies in other countries with large informal economies, such as India and Kenya, show that unregulated food handling is a major contributor to public health risks, particularly in densely populated urban areas. In response, South African municipalities could explore adaptive models from these regions, such as periodic health workshops or on-site training sessions for vendors to improve hygiene practices and awareness.

5. AI-DRIVEN SOLUTIONS

Given these pressing health challenges, innovative solutions such as Artificial Intelligence (AI) have emerged as promising tools to mitigate these risks, local authorities should reassess the existing regulations (including municipal by-laws) and consider expanding the certification requirements to include informal traders (Sepadi & Nkosi, 2023) (Table 5.1). In this regard, awareness campaigns can play a crucial role in educating vendors on the importance of food safety and the potential health hazards of non-compliance with existing regulations. Alongside these efforts, the development of enhanced monitoring systems that include informal traders would help improve public health outcomes. AI could serve a critical role here, offering scalable and real-time solutions to monitor environmental conditions and food safety practices in both formal and informal sectors (Table 1). This approach could revolutionize how municipal health services oversee and support all food vendors, ensuring safer food handling across the country (Salamone et al., 2021)

Investing in resilient AI deployment strategies such as battery-operated IoT devices, offline AI models, and community-based digital hubs can help bridge the infrastructure gap. Governments and technology developers must prioritize scalable, cost-effective solutions that do not rely solely on high-speed internet or expensive smart devices. By integrating low-tech innovations into AI-driven OHS interventions, informal vendors can benefit from technological advancements without being excluded due to digital inequalities.

Table 1. AI vs. low-tech interventions

Challenge	AI Solution	Low-Tech Alternative	Cost Implication
Air pollution	IoT air sensors + wearables	Subsidized cloth masks; shaded vending zones	AI: High / Masks: Low
Food safety	AI voice assistants for hygiene	Peer-to-peer hygiene workshops	AI: Medium / Workshops: Low
Heat stress	Real-time AI heat alerts	Mobile handwashing & shaded canopies	AI: Medium / Shade: Medium
Inspection	AI-assisted drones & sensors	Mobile EHP units, paper logs	AI: High / EHP Units: Medium

5.1. AI-Driven Occupational Exposure Monitoring for Street Vendors

5.1.1. AI in Environmental Health Monitoring for Street Vendors

AI has the potential to revolutionize environmental health monitoring by offering real-time data analysis of environmental hazards. AI algorithms can process vast datasets from sources such as weather stations, traffic cameras, and air quality sensors to assess environmental risks in real-time. For street vendors, various AI innovative applications can be beneficial by providing real-time air quality monitoring, where AI analyses data from environmental sensors to provide timely information about pollution levels. This capability allows street vendors to make informed decisions about when to operate, helping them avoid high pollution periods that could adversely affect their health (Adefemi et al., 2023).

For example, Salamone et al. (2021) emphasized how wearable devices connected to AI systems could monitor air quality, notifying vendors when pollution levels reach hazardous thresholds. This real-time feedback would, provide street vendors with timely information about pollution levels, enabling them to make informed decisions, such as relocating to safer areas or adjusting their operations to avoid high pollution periods, ultimately protecting their health (Adefemi et al., 2023). AI systems can also integrate weather data and provide predictive models, warning vendors of extreme heat or cold. This can be particularly useful in helping vendors prepare for seasonal changes that may affect their health, as seen in studies on air pollution and vendor health (Yi et al., 2022).

5.1.1.1. Initiating Pilot Projects: Monitoring Air Quality in Informal Trading Zones

Initiatives should be focused on using IoT sensors to monitor air quality in high-density trading areas where street vendors operate. These pilot programs can be implemented by the City's Environmental Health Departments, by deploying sensors that measure levels of particulate matter (PM2.5), nitrogen dioxide (NO_2), and volatile organic compounds (VOCs) in real time. This data is critical for street vendors, who are exposed daily to traffic pollution and emissions from nearby industrial activities, particularly in areas like the Kwa-Mai Mai in Johannesburg and Grand Parade and Nyanga Junction, both busy trading zones in Cape Town. This data will allow authorities to issue warnings to vendors during high-risk periods, advising them to limit their exposure or temporarily relocate to less polluted areas. The program also provides insights for city planners to consider alternative site locations or infrastructure improvements to mitigate the effects of air pollution effects on vendors. This initiative serves as a model for using AI and IoT in informal sectors by integrating health data with real-time environmental monitoring. The IoT sensors are part of a broader smart city project that seeks to improve public health and urban sustainability, demonstrating the potential of AI-driven solutions to support health and safety in the informal economy.

5.1.1.2. Innovative Approaches for Bridging Gaps in Environmental Health Monitoring

To address these gaps, South African municipalities could leverage innovative strategies to extend environmental health services to the informal sector. For instance, the integration of AI and mobile health applications has been shown to assist EHPs in conducting inspections more efficiently by identifying high-risk areas and prioritizing resource allocation. Such digital tools can allow for real-time data collection and analysis, enabling EHPs to monitor sanitation and food safety practices in informal markets more systematically.

Another potential solution involves deploying portable environmental health monitoring units, especially in markets with high vendor concentrations. Mobile units could be equipped with tools for food and water testing, waste disposal, and hygiene training, thereby providing vendors with accessible and on-the-spot health services. A pilot project in Cape Town's Grand Parade area explored the use of these portable units, which significantly improved hygiene compliance among vendors by providing easy access to sanitation facilities and health information (City of Cape Town Environmental Report, 2023). Scaling such programs across South African cities could help reduce public health risks associated with informal vending.

5.1.1.3. Recommendations for Enhanced Environmental Health Monitoring in Informal Markets

To improve environmental health monitoring for informal vendors, several key recommendations could be implemented:

- Mandatory Health Training and Certification: Introducing basic food safety training and certification for informal vendors could significantly improve compliance with health standards. Certification programs could be run in collaboration with municipal health departments and funded through public-private partnerships.
- Mobile Inspection Units: Municipalities could deploy mobile health inspection units, particularly in high-density trading zones, to provide regular health monitoring and sanitation support. These units would allow EHPs to conduct on-site inspections and training, especially in hard-to-reach areas.
- AI-Enabled Risk Assessment: Integrating AI-based predictive analytics to assess health risks in informal markets can aid EHPs in prioritizing inspections. Real-time data from mobile devices or IoT sensors could identify potential hotspots for contamination, enabling timely interventions.
- Periodic Health Workshops: Municipal health services could conduct health workshops in partnership with local NGOs to educate vendors on hygiene practices, food safety, and sanitation. These workshops could be held at regular intervals, making it easier for vendors to stay informed about safety standards.
- Flexible Regulatory Frameworks: Re-evaluating current regulations to include informal traders in health monitoring without imposing excessive costs or administrative burdens could bridge the regulatory gap. This could include tiered certifications based on the types of goods sold or trading locations.

5.1.2. Predictive Analytics for Occupational Health Risk Management

AI's predictive analytics capabilities offer significant advantages for managing health risks in the street vendor sector. By analysing historical environmental data alongside vendor health records, AI can identify patterns and forecast future health risks. For example, Olawade et al. (2023) highlighted how AI could predict foodborne illness outbreaks by correlating environmental data, such as temperature fluctuations and market hygiene conditions, with vendor health outcomes. AI systems can also facilitate communication between health authorities and street vendors, providing updates on health regulations, and environmental conditions (Adefemi et al., 2023), and, as well as alerting vendors of high-risk conditions, allowing them to implement preventive measures such as wearing appropriate protective equipment or adjusting their work hours. These proactive interventions are essential in reducing the overall health burden faced by street vendors, especially in high-risk urban environments (Adefemi et al., 2023; Olawade et al.,2023).

5.1.3. Wearable AI Technology and IoT for Real-Time Monitoring

Wearable AI devices, coupled with Internet of Things (IoT) technology, offer the transformative potential for occupational health monitoring through a collection of detailed information about personal movements, physiological measurements, and spatial data from environmental sensors (Fisher & Rosella, 2022). These devices can continuously track vendors' vital signs and environmental exposures, providing real-time data on air quality, temperature, and noise levels (Salamone et al., 2021). Such systems with the integration of AI algorithms enhance the utility of this data by generating personalized insights tailored to the individual's unique health profile which will create specific and holistic alerts to vendors to evacuate or take precautionary actions when hazardous conditions are detected, such as during high pollution days or extreme weather events. Moreover, AI can analyse historical data from wearable devices to predict potential health risks, enabling vendors to take preventive measures. This predictive capability helps vendors make more informed decisions regarding their operations, ensuring that they remain in safer working environments. This holistic approach considers not only physiological metrics but also social and environmental determinants of health, leading to a more nuanced understanding of health risks and enabling more effective management strategies (Fisher & Rosella, 2022).

5.1.4. Enhancing Communication and the Environmental Health Information System

AI can significantly enhance communication and data sharing between street vendors and municipal health services. Mobile applications powered by AI could facilitate real-time reporting of health concerns, environmental hazards, and food safety issues. Kreps et al. (2018) demonstrated that digital platforms can improve environmental health literacy and foster quicker responses to public health risks. By incorporating AI into these platforms, municipal health departments could analyse vendor-reported data to identify trends, allocate resources more effectively, and intervene in areas where health risks are highest. This would help close the gap in regulatory oversight for informal traders, particularly those excluded from traditional health and safety monitoring systems.

AI can be integrated with environmental health information systems to predict potential public health risks before they escalate (Guerra & Johnson, 2024). In this context, predictive models could analyse historical data from both formal and informal food premises to forecast outbreaks of foodborne illnesses, water contamination, or sanitation issues. This would allow municipal health services to take preventive action, minimizing the risk to public health. For Instance, AI could identify supply chain vulnerabilities, or emerging trends that might lead to an increase in food safety violations or environmental hazards.

AI-Assisted Inspections as described by (Einizinab, S et al. 2023); AI-enhanced tools like drones, thermal imaging, and IoT sensors could assist municipal health inspectors known as EHPs in monitoring large or hard-to-reach areas more efficiently. These tools could scan for environmental hazards, such as unsanitary conditions or improper waste disposal near informal vendors, providing real-time data for inspections. This would streamline the inspection process, ensuring that informal traders, who often operate in dynamic environments, are monitored without requiring constant on-site visits.

5.1.5. Connecting Environmental Health to Public Health

AI has the potential to connect environmental health data with public health systems, allowing for a more integrated approach to disease prevention. Public health clinics could collaborate with environmental health departments to monitor and report illness patterns related to environmental exposures. This would provide critical insights into how environmental factors, such as air pollution or food safety violations, impact vendor and client health (Olawade et al., 2023) Through the use of powerful and accessible application programming interfaces (APIs), AI can streamline the integration of data from environmental and public health sources. This includes linking public health data with environmental spatial data, administrative records, electronic health records, and census and survey data. By connecting these diverse data sources, AI has the potential to enhance the targeting of health interventions and policies, ensuring they reach the populations most in need. Additionally, health promotion efforts can be better tailored for maximum impact (Fisher & Rosella, 2022).

5.1.5.1. AI-Powered Integration of Food Businesses with Environmental Health Departments and Communities

By connecting public health and environmental health data, municipalities can ensure more coordinated efforts in managing health risks for both formal and informal businesses. AI-powered platforms can bridge the gap between food businesses, environmental health departments, and communities, creating a more responsive and transparent system for managing food safety; Furthermore, they can create seamless communication between food vendors and environmental health authorities, promoting food safety and public health. For example, vendors and consumers could use AI-driven mobile applications to report food spoilage or raise safety concerns. Once flagged, these reports can be automatically forwarded to relevant health authorities for further investigation. This system would allow real-time data sharing between public health departments, environmental health officers, and the community, ensuring rapid responses to potential hazards (Kreps et al., 2018).

In addition to reporting, AI can be integrated into food traceability systems. AI systems could also verify the origin of food products by scanning barcodes, allowing users to check if a product indeed comes from a certified manufacturer. Applications like IBM's Food Trust and Alibaba's supply chain platform have demonstrated how AI can track food from manufacturer to consumer, ensuring that products are fresh and safe. Such platforms could alert both vendors and health authorities if expired or recalled products enter the market, preventing public health risks. AI could also authenticate the origin of food products, helping vendors verify that they are sourced from reputable manufacturers and meet safety standards (Salamone et al., 2021).

To enhance food safety monitoring in informal markets, there can be utilising AI algorithms to analyse historical data on foodborne illnesses and environmental conditions in popular trading areas. By correlating factors such as temperature, humidity, and food handling practices, the AI system can identify periods and conditions that elevate the risk of foodborne disease outbreaks. Data from this predictive model can help municipal health inspectors target inspections more effectively, focusing on periods of high risk, such as warmer months when food spoilage is more likely.

This integration of AI into food businesses not only benefits vendors by ensuring compliance with health regulations but also empowers communities with tools to safeguard their health. By connecting public health data with environmental monitoring systems, municipalities can coordinate more effectively to manage health risks for both formal and informal sectors. This real-time reporting system would empower both vendors and consumers to actively participate in food safety monitoring, creating a community-driven approach to public health (Olawade et al., 2023). This interconnected system would ensure that food safety protocols are consistently followed, improving overall public health outcomes. By integrating these capabilities into public health systems, municipalities, and health departments can ensure better coordination in managing food safety risks. The combination of AI-driven reporting, real-time alerts, and product verification could significantly reduce the incidence of foodborne illnesses, improving overall public health outcomes for both formal and informal food vendors (Ullo & Sinha, 2020). This approach would also help health authorities allocate resources more effectively, focusing on high-risk areas and preventing food safety incidents before they escalate.

5.1.5.2. AI in Health Monitoring for Informal Workers

South Africa can provide a smart city initiative that includes AI-powered mobile health platforms that allow informal workers, including street vendors, to report health symptoms and environmental hazards in real time. Partnering with public health clinics or district health, the city can implement a pilot program in informal trading zones, where vendors can submit data via mobile apps, which is then analysed to identify health risk trends. This program, which includes symptom tracking for respiratory issues and gastrointestinal illnesses, has provided city health officials with early warnings about potential outbreaks. By linking environmental data (such as air quality and water safety) with self-reported health data, the program has successfully alerted officials to emerging health threats, enabling quicker response times. This approach illustrates how mobile AI solutions can support public health in informal settings (International Labour Organization, 2014), a model that South African cities could adopt to enhance their own OHS initiatives.

5.1.6. Enhancing Training Through AI

AI-powered training tools, including virtual and augmented reality (VR/AR), offer interactive, scenario-based learning experiences that improve vendors' preparedness for health hazards like foodborne illness and chemical exposure (AlGerafi et al., 2023). Personalized modules based on predictive data help vendors adopt safer practices, with reported improvements in food hygiene compliance and reductions in illness (Wang & Li, 2024). AI also enables continuous updates to the training content, ensuring relevance with current OHS standards (Adefemi et al., 2023; Wang et al., 2024). By adapting to diverse learning styles and real-world risks, these tools enhance engagement and long-term retention of health and safety knowledge.

5.2. Integration of AI into Local Public Health Policies and Policy Adaptations

The South African Department of Health and the Department of labour should establish and implement the Occupational Health and Safety Norms and Standards for Informal Sector Workers. Additionally, integrating AI into public health policies would foster greater accountability and streamline the management of health risks in urban environments (Sepadi & Nkosi, 2023). Integrating AI into OHS and public health policies increases accountability for managing health risks. By embedding AI in policy frameworks, the management of OHS for street vendors becomes a more transparent, systematic process that prioritizes vendor health. Municipalities can work with the private sector to create AI-powered reporting platforms for environmental hazards. Regulatory bodies like the South African Department of Labour and the National Department of Health could collaborate to set up these AI tools within existing frameworks, providing funding options or subsidies to enhance adoption.

5.3. Strengthening Real-World Case Examples AI in Enhancing Occupational Health

Platforms like IBM's Watson Health are already being used to predict health risks by analysing environmental data and individual health metrics. This predictive capability could be applied to street vending, allowing vendors to receive real-time health advice tailored to their specific working conditions. Such systems could notify vendors about impending weather changes, high pollution days, or sanitation risks in their areas, prompting them to take appropriate precautions (Olawade et al., 2023). The use of wearable AI devices, such as Fitbit or other health-monitoring gadgets, can serve as a foundation for similar technologies tailored to street vendors. By monitoring air quality and physiological data like heart rate or body temperature, these wearables can provide real-time feedback to vendors about their health status, allowing them to take proactive measures to avoid heat stress, dehydration, or respiratory problems. Integrating these wearables with IoT-enabled smart sensors for environmental monitoring can further enhance their utility, providing comprehensive safety measures for vendors (Salamone et al., 2021).

6. WORLD CASE STUDIES AND COMPARATIVE GLOBAL LESSONS

Real-world applications of AI in occupational health offer valuable models for adaptation in South Africa's informal sector. These examples highlight how wearable technology, environmental monitoring, and predictive analytics are being integrated to safeguard informal workers across diverse contexts. Platforms such as IBM Watson Health have been deployed globally to forecast health risks by analysing environmental and personal health data. As demonstrated in studies from Nigeria and South Africa, such AI systems can be tailored to monitor street vendors' exposure to urban hazards like air pollution and extreme heat (Olawade et al., 2023). These systems can generate real-time alerts on weather shifts, high pollution levels, or sanitation risks, prompting vendors to take timely protective actions.

In Italy, the use of wearable AI devices for environmental monitoring is gaining traction. Salamone et al. (2021) evaluated devices like Fitbit and air-quality monitors in built environments to assess physiological health risks. These wearables, when integrated with IoT sensors, can provide continuous feedback on body temperature, heart rate, or pollutant exposure. A similar framework adapted for street vendors in South Africa could mitigate risks of heat stress, dehydration, and respiratory illnesses through proactive alerts and real-time health data.

7. CHALLENGES FOR AI IMPLEMENTATION: CASE STUDIES AND VENDOR VOICES

While AI holds great promise for improving occupational health and safety among street vendors, its implementation faces several challenges. Key barriers include limited digital literacy, high technology costs, poor infrastructure, and concerns around data privacy and cultural acceptance. Overcoming these issues is critical to ensuring AI adoption is inclusive, accessible, and effective in South Africa's informal sector.

7.1. Limited Digital Literacy

Digital literacy is a significant barrier to AI adoption among South African street vendors, many of whom have limited exposure to digital tools. According to Stats SA (2022), only about 35% of informal workers in South Africa report proficiency with smartphones and internet-based applications, highlighting a considerable gap in digital skills. This low digital literacy rate impacts vendors' ability to effectively use AI-powered applications or wearable devices, which are often complex and require some technical knowledge.

Furthermore, many vendors may not fully understand the health benefits of AI technologies or how to operate AI-enabled health monitoring devices. Vendors accustomed to traditional work methods may feel apprehensive about using new technologies, leading to a reluctance to adopt AI solutions even when they are available. This challenge underlines the importance of incorporating digital literacy training programs specifically designed for informal workers to ensure that they can fully benefit from AI innovations.

7.2. High Cost of AI Technology and Cost of Implementation

One of the main barriers is the high cost associated with AI devices, such as wearable technology and IoT sensors. Many street vendors lack the financial resources to invest in such technologies, making it difficult to adopt these solutions on a large scale (Olawade et al., 2023). The high cost of AI devices, such as wearable health monitors, IoT sensors, and smart applications, presents another challenge. Many vendors operate with slim profit margins and cannot afford the upfront or maintenance costs associated with these technologies. For example, a basic wearable device capable of monitoring air quality and vital signs can cost upwards of R1,500 ($100), which is a substantial expense for street vendors (Ullo & Sinha, 2020). One of the main obstacles is the socio-economic disparity within the informal sector. Street vendors often operate in low-income areas where investing in advanced technology, such as wearable devices or AI platforms, is not a priority due to financial constraints (Ullo & Sinha, 2020). In many cases, vendors lack the necessary infrastructure, such as reliable internet access and smartphones, which further complicates the effective use of AI-driven solutions (Salamone et al., 2021).

7.3. Accessibility Issues: Infrastructure and Internet Access

Moreover, access to reliable internet connectivity is often required to support real-time data sharing, yet data costs in South Africa remain among the highest in Africa. Furthermore, access to reliable internet and digital devices is limited in many low-income areas, posing an additional hurdle for vendors. A 2023 report from Research ICT Africa found that South Africa's average mobile data costs are around R85 per gigabyte, a cost that can quickly add up when using AI applications that require continuous data access. These financial barriers limit the practicality of AI for many informal workers, underscoring the need for government subsidies, cost-sharing initiatives, or corporate partnerships to reduce these costs.

7.4. Management of Health-Sensitive Data

Leveraging interoperability between environmental and public health data brings both opportunities and challenges, particularly regarding data privacy and ethical use. As AI advances, personal information faces greater risks. Adefemi et al. (2023) highlighted that AI's role in disease surveillance and predictive analytics represents a transformative leap, offering early warnings, optimizing resource allocation, and improving health system responsiveness. However, integrating AI in disease surveillance requires careful management of sensitive health data to ensure privacy and compliance with regulations.

The lack of digital infrastructure, particularly in urban informal areas, significantly impedes the deployment of AI technology. South Africa's major cities, including Johannesburg and Durban, have pockets with poor internet connectivity, especially in densely populated informal settlements where many street vendors operate. According to Stats SA (2022), fewer than 40% of informal workers in urban areas have reliable access to Wi-Fi or mobile data, which makes it challenging to maintain AI systems that rely on continuous internet connectivity for real-time monitoring and updates. Additionally, even when internet access is available, the quality and speed of connections are often insufficient for data-intensive applications. This limitation restricts the potential for real-time data analytics and notifications, diminishing the effectiveness of AI systems designed to alert vendors about environmental hazards or health risks. Expanding digital infrastructure to underserved areas should be a priority for local municipalities, as improved connectivity is essential for integrating AI technologies into informal workplaces.

7.5. Public Awareness and Cultural Resistance and Trust Issues

Public awareness and trust are also crucial, as a lack of understanding can lead to fear and resistance, hindering AI adoption in health systems (Balogun et al., 2023). Moreover, cultural resistance to adopting new technologies is a considerable challenge. Cultural resistance to new technologies also presents a challenge, as vendors may be hesitant to adopt unfamiliar systems. Many vendors are unfamiliar with AI and may mistrust or feel overwhelmed by technological tools that seem too complex or foreign to their traditional business practices (Kreps et al., 2018). This reluctance is compounded by low digital literacy rates in many informal sectors, making it difficult for vendors to navigate AI platforms or mobile applications without proper training and support. Cultural resistance and trust are also significant obstacles to AI adoption among informal workers. Many vendors rely on traditional knowledge and practices passed down over generations and may view AI technologies as unnecessary or invasive. In addition to a lack of familiarity, some vendors may also have cultural or personal reservations about sharing health data, especially in communities where health information is typically kept private. Building trust in AI requires extensive community engagement, education programs, and demonstrations of the practical benefits of these technologies. Collaboration with local organizations and trusted community leaders can help bridge this gap, promoting a more positive reception of AI.

7.6. Regulatory and Policy Challenges

The regulatory framework in South Africa for AI, especially in the informal sector, is still developing. While the National Department of Health and other bodies recognize the potential of AI in public health, there is limited guidance on how AI solutions should be implemented, monitored, and regulated for informal workers. This regulatory gap creates challenges for vendors and developers alike, as there are uncertainties about compliance, funding support, and enforcement mechanisms.

For example, South African health regulations primarily address formal workplaces, leaving informal sectors with limited guidance on occupational health standards. The lack of specific AI-related OHS policies for informal workers means that vendors may be excluded from the protections that AI-driven OHS solutions could provide. Policymakers must work to establish clear guidelines and standards for AI use in informal sectors, enabling the safe and equitable deployment of these technologies.

8. ETHICAL CONSIDERATIONS IN AI USE

AI deployment in the informal sector, especially in surveillance, health monitoring, and data management, presents several ethical risks. While AI-driven monitoring tools such as CCTV cameras, drones, and environmental sensors could improve vendor safety, they also raise concerns about surveillance overreach and data privacy. In many cases, surveillance technologies have been misused for punitive enforcement, resulting in increased fines, evictions, or harassment rather than actual OHS improvements. Without proper oversight and vendor involvement, AI surveillance could reinforce marginalization rather than protection. Additionally, the integration of AI in disease surveillance and environmental monitoring brings data privacy risks. Adefemi et al. (2023). While AI-driven analytics can predict outbreaks and optimize public health responses, they also require careful regulation to prevent the misuse of sensitive health and location data. Public awareness and trust in AI systems are essential; without transparency, vendors may resist AI adoption, fearing increased scrutiny rather than support (Balogun et al., 2023). Without proper safeguards, such tools can deepen social inequities and erode public trust. To address these ethical concerns, strong AI governance frameworks must be implemented. Adopting South Africa's AI Ethics Guidelines (2022) provides a foundation for governance, emphasizing non-discrimination, transparency, and participatory design. Applying these principles to informal vending requires: Anonymized data collection to prevent tracking and targeting of individuals, Vendor oversight committees to ensure AI tools are used for OHS improvements, not punitive enforcement, and Privacy-by-design AI models with clear data-sharing protections.

8.1. Policy Related to Liability and Accountability for AI Technology

Successfully integrating AI into South Africa's informal sector requires robust legal and policy frameworks that address liability, data ownership, and vendor protection. Liability concerns, particularly for AI malfunctions, can be guided by the *Consumer Protection Act* (CPA, 2008) and the *Public Finance Management Act* (PFMA, 1999). Data ownership and privacy, especially concerning health and location data, must align with the *Protection of Personal Information Act* (POPIA, 2013), ensuring vendors retain control and consent. The extension of the *Occupational Health and Safety Act* (OHSA, 1993) to cover AI-driven tools could protect informal workers, who often lack formal labor protections. Additionally, South Africa's *AI Policy Framework* (2021) should be expanded to include informal sector provisions. Global models such as the EU's *General Data Protection Regulation* (GDPR) and Kenya's *Digital Economy Blueprint* (Ministry of ICT, 2019) offer valuable templates for inclusive digital governance. Adopting these best practices would ensure ethical, transparent, and equitable AI deployment for street vendors.

9. RECOMMENDATIONS FOR AI IMPLEMENTATION

The successful integration of AI in occupational health and safety (OHS) for informal vendors requires addressing financial, infrastructural, socio-cultural, and ethical barriers. Addressing these challenges requires collaboration among government entities, researchers, policymakers, technology companies, and public health professionals to create a supportive ecosystem for AI in the health system (Balogun et al., 2023). Governments can play a key role by subsidizing the cost of AI devices and developing digital literacy programs tailored to the needs of informal traders. One of the biggest obstacles is the high cost of AI tools, such as wearable health monitors, IoT sensors, and digital reporting platforms.

9.1. Participatory Design: Co-Creating AI Tools with Vendors

Many street vendors operate in low-income environments, where investing in smart technology is not feasible (Olawade et al., 2023). Additionally, poor digital infrastructure, including unreliable internet and limited smartphone access, restricts engagement with AI-driven solutions (Ullo & Sinha, 2020). Collaborative efforts between governments, tech companies, and non-governmental organizations (NGOs) could result in the development of affordable AI solutions tailored to the unique needs of street vendors (AlGerafi et al., 2023). Municipalities can invest in building the necessary infrastructure, such as expanding internet access to underserved areas and ensuring that AI solutions are accessible to everyone, regardless of income level.

However, for AI systems to be equitable and effective in informal environments, participatory design must be central to their development. Participatory design emphasizes collaboration with end users and street vendors, in this case, throughout the technology design, testing, and implementation process. This can include co-design workshops where vendors collaboratively prototype app interfaces, wearable functions, or alert mechanisms. Followed by feedback Loops where real-time reporting tools are built with two-way feedback (e.g., "Was this alert helpful?") to refine AI predictions and services. Then, there should be a vendor oversight committee that includes vendor leaders in governance bodies overseeing AI deployments, data policies, and surveillance tools. The participation design can close off with users testing the system in real conditions, which can be done through pilot AI tools in real urban vending environments, not just lab settings, to capture dynamic worksite challenges.

9.2. Sustainability of AI in Informal OHS

Aligning AI solutions with global goals like SDG 3 (Good Health) and SDG 8 (Decent Work) can unlock international funding and highlight South Africa's leadership in inclusive health innovation. Integrating AI into public health systems enhances risk management and accountability (Sepadi & Nkosi, 2023). As illustrated in Figure 1, the AI-OHS workflow from IoT data collection to government response demonstrates how vendor-centered design can transform AI tools into empowering, not controlling, solutions.

Figure 1. AI-OHS monitoring workflow diagram

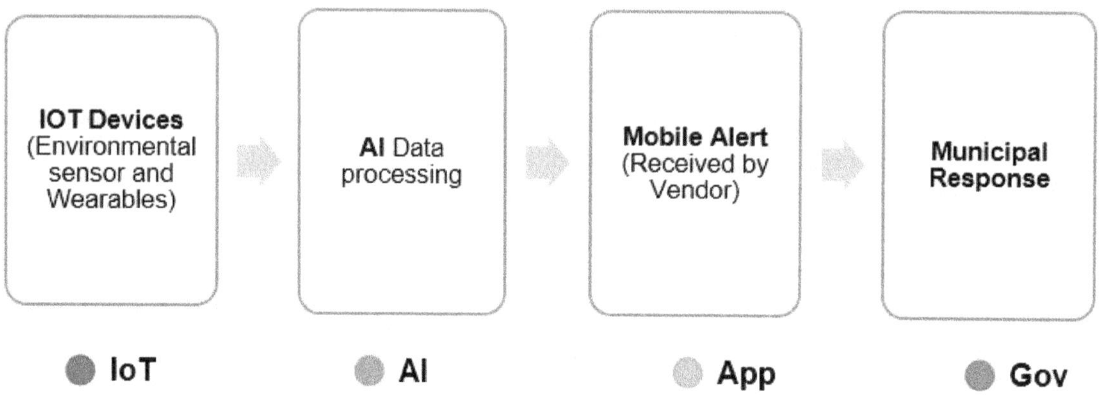

Figure 1: AI-OHS Monitoring Workflow Diagram

9.2.1. Government-Led Financial and Digital Support Initiatives

Subsidizing AI Devices and Resources: Addressing these challenges requires collaboration among government entities, researchers, policymakers, technology companies, and public health professionals to create a supportive ecosystem for AI in the health system (Balogun et al., 2023). Governments can play a key role by subsidizing the cost of AI devices and developing digital literacy programs tailored to the needs of informal traders. This includes materials such as wearable monitors and IoT sensors, which can improve safety in high-risk street vending environments. This approach aligns with the various literature on informal vendors, which emphasizes lowering financial barriers to enhance health outcomes among underserved populations. For example, partnerships between governments, tech companies, and NGOs could lead to the development of affordable, user-friendly AI tools specifically designed for street vendors. Governments could also provide grants or loans to vendors for purchasing technology that improves safety, such as wearable devices or IoT sensors (Olawade et al., 2023).

Digital Literacy Programs for Informal Vendors: Tailoring digital literacy programs for informal vendors ensures they can utilize AI tools effectively. Through these programs, vendors gain the skills to operate mobile applications, understand sensor readings, and leverage predictive analytics in their daily activities.

9.2.2. Public-Private Partnerships to Develop Vendor-Specific AI Tools

Collaboration with Technology Companies and NGOs: Partnerships between municipalities and local businesses is crucial. Collaborative efforts between governments, tech companies, and non-governmental organizations (NGOs) could result in the development of affordable AI solutions tailored to the unique needs of street vendors (AlGerafi et al., 2023). Such partnerships can yield affordable, scalable AI solutions that are designed with the practical and occupational realities of informal vendors in mind.

Grants and Loans for Technology Adoption: Financial support through grants or low-interest loans enables vendors to purchase essential AI-driven safety equipment. For instance, AI-powered wearable devices or IoT sensors can help vendors monitor environmental risks in real-time, thereby fostering a safer workplace.

9.2.3. Municipality-Driven Infrastructure Development

Expanding Internet and Digital Infrastructure: Municipalities can invest in building the necessary infrastructure, such as expanding Internet access to underserved areas and ensuring that AI solutions are accessible to everyone, regardless of income level. This foundational step ensures that street vendors have the connectivity needed to fully engage with AI technologies, reducing digital inequity and enhancing access to AI-driven health interventions.

Infrastructure and Resource Allocation for Informal Vendors: Local businesses and NGOs can contribute to the development of sanitary trading areas and provide necessary health resources, ensuring that vendors can operate in a healthier environment. These collaborative efforts bolster the creation of safer, cleaner trading spaces, aligned with the One Health model's emphasis on sanitary environments.

9.2.4. Ongoing Education and Training for Sustainable Adoption

Comprehensive AI Training for Vendors: Providing continuous education on AI applications in health and safety empowers vendors to make informed decisions and sustain safe practices. Training initiatives should include practical, hands-on modules that cover everything from interpreting sensor data to responding to health alerts.

Engaging Vendors in Digital Skills Enhancement: Engaging vendors directly in digital skills enhancement initiatives promotes the long-term success of AI-driven health interventions. This approach fosters self-reliance and reduces the digital divide, ensuring that vendors can operate safely in the modern urban environment.

9.3. Policy Roadmap

Implementing AI-driven OHS for informal vendors requires not just technology, but also legal reform, policy integration, and stakeholder collaboration. Existing laws like the OHS Act and POPIA often overlook informal workers, creating enforcement gaps. A three-phase policy roadmap, starting with pilot programs and progressing to national integration offers a path to sustainable, inclusive AI adoption. Embedding vendor needs and cross-sector coordination into this process is essential for equitable public health innovation.

Table 2. Phased policy roadmap for integrating AI into informal sector OHS initiatives

Policy Phase	Timeline	Actions	Stakeholders
Phase 1: Pilot Programs	2025–2026	Test AI health monitors in 3 major informal markets; collect vendor feedback	Municipalities, NGOs, Tech Firms
Phase 2: Legal Integration	2027–2028	Amend the South African OHS Act and R638 to recognize informal vendors and create an informal vendor registry;	National & Provincial Health Departments
Phase 3: Scaling & Infrastructure	2029 onward	Expand infrastructure (e.g., public internet hubs), subsidize wearables, and establish a national AI-OHS oversight council.	Treasury, Health Ministry, Private Sector

10. RECOMMENDATIONS FOR FUTURE STUDIES

To address the limitations identified in this chapter and further advance the understanding of AI's role in OHS for informal workers, future research should focus on the following areas:

Conduct Field-Based Empirical Studies: Field-based empirical research, such as interviews, surveys, and observations, is essential to understand street vendors' awareness of OHS risks and their readiness to adopt AI technologies. These studies should assess actual hazard exposure, digital literacy levels, trust in AI, and concerns around data privacy. Pilot programs involving AI tools can offer valuable feedback on usability and acceptance, ensuring interventions are both practical and socially aligned with vendors' needs.

Explore AI Applications Across Different Informal Work Environments: Future studies should expand beyond street vending to explore the potential of AI in other informal work settings, such as waste picking, transportation, and small-scale manufacturing. Each sub-sector within the informal economy faces unique health and safety challenges, and research that examines AI's applicability across these environments could reveal sector-specific insights and solutions.

Investigate Policy and Legal Frameworks for AI in Informal Economies: Future research should delve into the policy and legal implications of implementing AI in informal sectors, including issues of data ownership, vendor liability, and regulatory compliance. Studies that examine best practices for AI regulation, data privacy frameworks, and ethical AI use in other countries could guide the development of policies tailored to South Africa's informal economy.

Assess Long-Term Impacts of AI on Occupational Health and Safety: Finally, longitudinal studies are needed to evaluate the long-term effects of AI interventions on vendors' health, productivity, and quality of life. By tracking health outcomes, exposure levels, and behavioural changes over time, future research could provide evidence of AI's sustainability and effectiveness in improving OHS among informal workers, helping to justify further investment in these technologies.

11. CONCLUSION

The integration of AI in OHS for street vendors is not merely an option but a necessity to foster healthier urban environments and has the potential to transform the OHS landscape for urban informal vendors. By leveraging AI for environmental health monitoring, predictive analytics, real-time communication, and training, we can create safer and healthier working conditions for street vendors. However, the successful implementation of these technologies requires overcoming socio-economic, infrastructural, and cultural barriers. With strong governmental support, multi-sectoral collaboration, and targeted interventions, AI can become a powerful tool for improving the health and safety of street vendors. Ultimately, these innovations will not only enhance vendor well-being but also contribute to the broader goal of creating sustainable, healthy urban environments. The successful integration of AI in occupational health for street vendors will serve as a model for other sectors of informal labour globally, showcasing how technology can foster inclusivity and equity in public health.

REFERENCES

Adefemi, A. (2023). Artificial intelligence in environmental health and public safety: A comprehensive review of USA strategies. *World Journal of Advanced Research and Reviews, 20*(3), 1420–1434. DOI: 10.30574/wjarr.2023.20.3.2591

AlGerafi, M., Zhou, Y., Oubib, M., & Wijaya, T. T. (2023). Unlocking the potential: A comprehensive evaluation of augmented reality and virtual reality in education. *Electronics (Basel), 12*(18), 3953. DOI: 10.3390/electronics12183953

Balogun, A.-F., Ogundairo, M., Okongwu, B., Babarinde, S., & Sodamade, P. (2023). Integration of artificial intelligence into health informatics for enhanced public health in Africa: Opportunities and challenges. *International Medical Science Research Journal, 3*(3), 127–144. DOI: 10.51594/imsrj.v3i3.643

City of Cape Town. (2023). *Integrated Annual Report 2022/2023*. Retrieved from https://resource.capetown.gov.za/documentcentre/Documents/City%20research%20reports%20and%20review/CCT_Integrated_Annual_Report_2022-2023.pdf

Department of Communications and Digital Technologies. South Africa. (2021). *South Africa's Artificial Intelligence (AI) Planning*. Retrieved from. https://www.dcdt.gov.za/images/phocadownload/AI_Government_Summit/National_AI_Government_Summit_Discussion_Document.pdf

Einizinab, S., Khoshelham, K., Winter, S., Christopher, P., Fang, Y., Windholz, E., Radanovic, M., & Hu, S. (2023). Enabling technologies for remote and virtual inspection of building work. *Automation in Construction, 156*, 105096. DOI: 10.1016/j.autcon.2023.105096

Fisher, S., & Rosella, L. (2022). Priorities for successful use of artificial intelligence by public health organizations: A literature review. *BMC Public Health, 22*(2146), 2146. Advance online publication. DOI: 10.1186/s12889-022-14422-z PMID: 36419010

Government of Kenya, Ministry of ICT. (2019). *Digital economy blueprint: Powering Kenya's transformation*. Retrieved from https://dial.global/wp-content/uploads/2020/10/SmartAfrica-DIAL_DigitalEconomyInAfrica2020-v7_ENG.pdf

Guerra, K., & Johnson, V. (2024). *AI adoption: Integrating TOE, Implementation Science, and Ethics*. AMCIS 2024 TREOs. Retrieved from https://aisel.aisnet.org/treos_amcis2024/64

Kreps, G.L., Wright, K., & Burke-Garcia, A. (2018). The use of digital communication channels to enhance environmental health literacy. *Environmental Health Literacy*. 265-283. https://doi.org/DOI: 10.1007/978-3-319-94108-0_10

Olawade, D. B., Wada, O. J., Olawade, A. C. D., Kunonga, E., Abaiere, O., & Ling, J. (2023). Using artificial intelligence to improve public health: A narrative review. *Frontiers in Public Health, 11*, 1196397. DOI: 10.3389/fpubh.2023.1196397 PMID: 37954052

Salamone, F., Masullo, M., & Sibilo, S. (2021). Wearable devices for environmental monitoring in the built environment: A systematic review. *Sensors (Basel), 21*(14), 4727. DOI: 10.3390/s21144727 PMID: 34300467

Sepadi, M. M., & Nkosi, V. (2023). Strengthening Urban Informal Trading and Improving the Health of Vendors: An Integrated Management Model. *International Journal of Environmental Research and Public Health, 20*(6), 4836. DOI: 10.3390/ijerph20064836 PMID: 36981746

Skinner, C., & Haysom, G. (2016). *The informal sector's role in food security: A missing link in policy debates?* PLAAS Working Paper Series, 44. Retrieved from: https://www.wiego.org/wp-content/uploads/2025/04/The-informal-sectors-role-in-food-security-A-missing-link-in-policy-debates.pdf

South Africa. (1923). *Natives (Urban Areas) Act No. 21 of 1923*. Government Gazette of the Union of South Africa. Retrievedd from https://www.sahistory.org.za/article/natives-urban-areas-act-1923

South Africa. (1950). *Group Areas Act No. 41 of 1950*. Government Gazette of the Union of South Africa. Retrieved from https://www.sahistory.org.za/archive/group-areas-act-1950

South Africa. (1993). *Occupational Health and Safety Act 85 of 1993*. Government Gazette. Retrieved from https://www.gov.za/documents/occupational-health-and-safety-act

South Africa. (2013). *Protection of Personal Information Act 4 of 2013*. Government Gazette. Retrieved from https://www.gov.za/documents/protection-personal-information-act

South African Government. (2003). *National Health Act, No. 61 of 2003*. Retrieved from https://www.gov.za/documents/national-health-act

South African Government. (2008). *Consumer Protection Act, No. 68 of 2008*. Retrieved from https://www.gov.za/documents/consumer-protection-act

South African Weather Service. (2022). *Annual Climate Report 2022*. South African Weather Service. Retrieved from https://www.weathersa.co.za/Documents/AnnualReports/SAWS_ANNUAL_REPORT_-_Reduced_File_Size-1_27092022093113.pdf

Statistics South Africa (Stats SA). (2022). *Annual Report 2021/2022 (Book 1)*. Retrieved from https://www.stassa.gov.za/publications/AnnualReport/Stats_SA_Annual_Report_Book.pdf

Statistics South Africa (Stats SA). (2023). *Employment in the informal sector: Quarterly Labour Force Survey*. Retrieved from http://www.statssa.gov.za

Ullo, S. L., & Sinha, G. R. (2020). Advances in smart environment monitoring systems using IoT and sensors. *Sensors (Basel), 20*(11), 3113. DOI: 10.3390/s20113113 PMID: 32486411

Wang, J., & Li, J. (2024). Artificial intelligence empowering public health education: Prospects and challenges. *Frontiers in Public Health, 12*, 1389026. Advance online publication. DOI: 10.3389/fpubh.2024.1389026 PMID: 39022411

Yi, A. P. J., Sumedha, , & Ramalingam, V. (2022). Prevalence of Respiratory Symptoms and Associated Risk Factors among Street Food Vendors in Klang Valley, Malaysia. *Journal of Experimental Biology and Agricultural Sciences, 10*(3), 533–538. DOI: 10.18006/2022.10(3).533.538

KEY TERMS AND DEFINITIONS

Occupational Health and Safety (OHS): Refers to the policies, practices, and tools aimed at ensuring safe, healthy, and dignified working conditions for individuals in the workplace, including those operating in informal, unregulated environments.

Informal Economy: A segment of economic activity that is not regulated or protected by the state, often characterized by unregistered businesses, lack of formal contracts, and absence of labour protections.

Artificial Intelligence (AI): A field of computer science that uses algorithms, machine learning, and data processing to simulate human intelligence and decision-making in solving complex problems, such as real-time environmental monitoring.

Wearable Sensors: Devices worn on the body that collect real-time physiological or environmental data, such as heart rate, temperature, or air quality, used in health risk detection and prevention.

Digital Inequality: Disparities in access to digital tools, internet infrastructure, and technical literacy, which can exclude marginalized populations from benefiting fully from technological innovations.

Participatory Design: An inclusive design process where end users such as street vendors actively contribute to the development of tools and solutions to ensure cultural relevance and usability.

Spatial Apartheid: A legacy of South African urban planning under apartheid that spatially segregated populations by race, leading to unequal access to infrastructure, services, and economic opportunity effects that persist today.

Environmental Exposure: The condition of being exposed to physical, chemical, or biological hazards in the environment, such as air pollutants, heat, or contaminated water that can negatively affect health over time.

Chapter 15
The Role of AI in Revolutionising Risk Management for Moving and Handling Tasks

Tiago Manuel Horta Reis da Silva
https://orcid.org/0000-0001-5220-1718
King's College London, UK

ABSTRACT

This chapter explores how Artificial Intelligence (AI) is transforming risk management in moving and handling tasks, particularly within nursing and geriatric care. By integrating AI-powered technologies—such as wearable sensors, predictive analytics, and real-time decision support systems—organisations can identify biomechanical hazards, predict musculoskeletal injuries, and personalise care strategies. The chapter offers clinical insights from nursing practice, including safe patient handling in long-term care facilities, and illustrates how AI enhances ergonomic assessment, staff training, and risk mitigation. Drawing on current research and international practice guidelines, it positions AI as a crucial innovation in safeguarding both patients and healthcare workers. Practical applications, ethical considerations, and case studies from eldercare nursing are critically examined to showcase how AI aligns with occupational health and safety (OHS) standards.

1. INTRODUCTION

The healthcare sector is recognised for its intricate workflows and vital patient interactions, exposing healthcare professionals to various occupational hazards, particularly musculoskeletal disorders (MSDs) resulting from manual handling practices (Horta Reis da Silva, 2022; Reis da Silva, 2023a). The World Health Organization underscores the prevalence of these injuries in healthcare settings, highlighting a compelling imperative for enhanced safety protocols and ergonomic practices to alleviate these challenges (Beinert et al., 2018; Ambeba et al., 2015). Gudavalli et al., (2015) delineate that activities such as lifting, transferring, and repositioning patients significantly contribute to the high incidence of these

DOI: 10.4018/979-8-3693-9301-7.ch015

injuries among healthcare workers, particularly in nursing and gerontological care environments where physical demands are exacerbated by the limited mobility of patients.

The unique physical demands in contexts such as geriatric care, where caregivers often assist older adults with significant mobility limitations, require thoughtful integration of innovative solutions like Artificial Intelligence (AI) within occupational health and safety (OHS) frameworks (Reis da Silva, 2025a). The potential of AI systems extends beyond mere data analytics; they are increasingly viewed as vital tools for risk assessment and real-time feedback regarding manual handling practices (Nyman & Armstrong, 2015; Reis da Silva, 2025b). By deploying such technological advancements, it is posited that healthcare professionals can receive immediate guidance on effective strategies to minimise physical strain during patient interactions (Indovina et al., 2016; Reis da Silva, 2025c). This proactive approach signifies a transformational shift towards enhancing workers' safety and improving patient care quality, with AI serving as a pivotal facilitator (Beinert et al., 2018; Gudavalli et al., 2015).

Artificial Intelligence's adoption in healthcare settings manifests in various applications, from predictive analytics that help anticipate injury risks to smart assistive technologies that refine manual handling procedures (Nyman & Armstrong, 2015; Indovina et al., 2016). Recent studies highlight the promise of AI-driven wearable devices that monitor healthcare professionals' physical exertion levels, issuing alerts before they face the risk of injury (Wickramasinghe et al., 2024; Reis da Silva, 2025d). The rise of intelligent ergonomic solutions signifies not only a methodological advance in injury prevention but also a deeper commitment to creating safer working environments, which ultimately bolsters the overall well-being of patients and caregivers alike (Chung et al., 2014).

Moreover, research indicates that integrating real-time feedback through technologically advanced systems enhances the educational and operational dynamics within healthcare settings. For instance, real-time patient experience surveys indicate the increasing incorporation of immediate feedback mechanisms that can significantly improve healthcare delivery and subsequent patient outcomes (Park et al., 2021). Jointly, these advancements promote a culture of continuous learning and improvement, enabling healthcare workers to refine their skills while ensuring that patient care practices keep pace with modern healthcare demands (Chung et al., 2014; Cortegiani et al., 2017).

Diverging slightly from direct applications of AI, pertinent investigations also focus on augmenting the efficacy of manual handling techniques through rigorous training supported by real-time feedback (Mendelsohn et al., 2020; Khoury et al., 2019). The literature emphasises the importance of delivering feedback during skill acquisition, particularly in high-stakes environments such as those involved in healthcare. Real-time feedback is shown to greatly enhance the learning curve for healthcare professionals, leading to better retention of skills and improved safety practices (Hovell et al., 2019; Khoury et al., 2019). This paradigm not only assists in reducing the incidence of occupational injuries but may also contribute to greater procedural adherence and efficiency in patient care (Mendelsohn et al., 2020; Gupta et al., 2016). In the quest to mitigate the risks associated with MSDs, the evolution of AI technologies, especially in the realm of wearable tech, offers pivotal advantages. Such devices can monitor physical strain continuously, empowering healthcare professionals with the knowledge to adjust their practices proactively (Nyman & Armstrong, 2015; Wickramasinghe et al., 2024). The continuous analysis provided by these devices enhances ergonomic assessments, thus fostering environments that prioritise both employee safety and optimal patient outcomes (Wickramasinghe et al., 2024; Cortegiani et al., 2017).

Moreover, scholarly activity surrounding smart assistive technologies within this domain is growing exponentially. New methodologies facilitated by AI, encompassing ergonomic assessments and targeted training systems, show great promise in transforming the landscape of manual patient handling

(Mendelsohn et al., 2020; Khoury et al., 2019). Studies underscore the necessity of combining these technologies with robust training protocols that emphasize practical applications, ensuring that healthcare professionals can adapt to varying patient needs effectively and safely (Hovell et al., 2019; Iskrzycki et al., 2018). Beyond mere efficiency, the integration of AI and real-time feedback also emphasizes a more humane approach to healthcare delivery. Studies have shown that, by prioritising safety through advanced technology, organisations not only enhance their operational frameworks but also cultivate a supportive environment that can lead to higher job satisfaction among healthcare workers (Chung et al., 2014; Park et al., 2021). The confluence of safety, efficiency, and employee welfare engenders an ethos where both caregiver and patient needs are effectively addressed, establishing a symbiotic relationship that beneficently shapes healthcare delivery systems.

As we look forward, the synthesis of AI within healthcare offers profound implications for the future, particularly in enhancing ergonomic practices. The convergence of technology-driven solutions and actionable feedback mechanisms emphasises the evolving role of AI in shaping preventive strategies against occupational injuries and enhancing the quality of care provided to patients (Beinert et al., 2018; Gudavalli et al., 2015; Nyman & Armstrong, 2015). This progressive integration reflects a vital societal need to elevate healthcare standards while simultaneously protecting those at the forefront of delivering care, ensuring an equitable and sustainable healthcare system (Indovina et al., 2016; Cortegiani et al., 2017).

Therefore, the collaborative efforts among stakeholders—healthcare workers, OHS researchers, and technology developers—are crucial for innovating practical solutions that effectively address the myriad challenges posed by occupational hazards in healthcare settings. Additionally, as we forge ahead in this digital age, the commitment to nurturing environments that prioritise both patient safety and healthcare worker welfare will undeniably form the backbone of a robust and responsive healthcare infrastructure (Beinert et al., 2018; Gudavalli et al., 2015).

1. CONCEPTUAL FRAMEWORK

Definitions

To explore the intersection of AI and manual handling in healthcare, it is essential to clarify several key concepts. AI is conventionally defined as the simulation of human intelligence within machines that are designed to think and perform tasks similarly to humans (Reis da Silva and Mitchell, 2024; Reis da Silva, 2025e). Within the healthcare context, AI embodies various technologies such as machine learning, natural language processing, and computer vision, all of which enable the analysis of complex data sets to inform better decision-making processes (Beinert et al., 2018; Ambeba et al., 2015; Gudavalli et al., 2015). This technological framework provides healthcare professionals with actionable insights that can optimise manual handling practices, significantly mitigating occupational injuries among staff (Wynn et al., 2025).

Risk management, a critical component of healthcare operations, refers to the systematic identification, assessment, and prioritisation of risks coupled with the coordinated efforts to minimise their impact (Nyman & Armstrong, 2015; Indovina et al., 2016). In the realm of manual handling, effective risk management is paramount, as it can markedly reduce health risks associated with physically intensive tasks (Wickramasinghe et al., 2024). Healthcare environments often necessitate that professionals engage in lifting, moving, and repositioning patients, actions that are inherently linked to musculoskeletal injuries (Wickramasinghe et al., 2024; Chung et al., 2014). Therefore, understanding the union of AI and robust risk management frameworks can yield substantial improvements in occupational safety and health outcomes (Park et al., 2021).

Moving and handling practices capture the spectrum of techniques utilised for the safe transport and repositioning of patients within clinical infrastructures (Reis da Silva, 2023a). These practices are critical for safeguarding the physical health of healthcare workers (Cortegiani et al., 2017). In addition to reducing injury risks, these practices are essential for ensuring that patients receive dignified and safe care. This dual responsibility presents an opportunity for AI applications aimed specifically at enhancing the safety and efficacy of manual handling, thereby benefiting healthcare professionals and patients alike (Mendelsohn et al., 2020; Khoury et al., 2019).

Theoretical Models

Integrating AI technologies within the frameworks addressing manual handling and risk management requires reliance on established theoretical models. One fundamental tool is the Risk Matrix, which assists healthcare administrators in identifying and evaluating the probability and potential impact of various risks, effectively guiding the prioritization of necessary interventions (Hovell et al., 2019; Gupta et al., 2016). Utilising the Risk Matrix facilitates a structured approach to deploying AI solutions that can predict and mitigate risks associated with manual handling tasks (Gupta et al., 2016) (figure 1).

Figure 1. Risk matrix

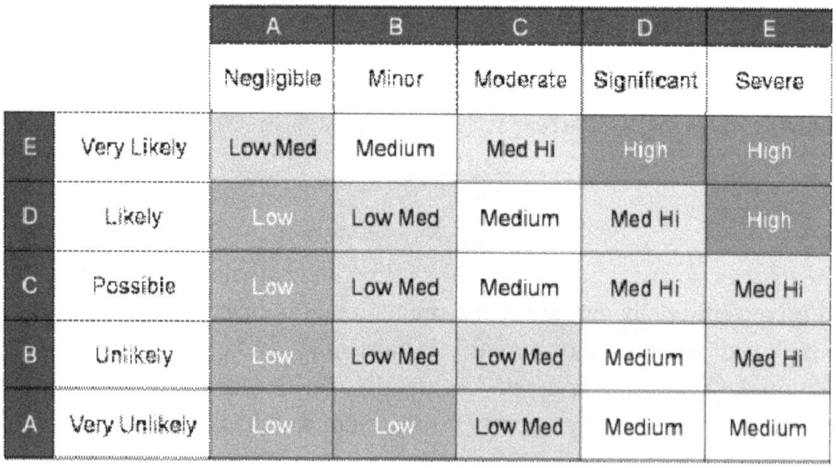

		A	B	C	D	E
		Negligible	Minor	Moderate	Significant	Severe
E	Very Likely	Low Med	Medium	Med Hi	High	High
D	Likely	Low	Low Med	Medium	Med Hi	High
C	Possible	Low	Low Med	Medium	Med Hi	Med Hi
B	Unlikely	Low	Low Med	Low Med	Medium	Med Hi
A	Very Unlikely	Low	Low	Low Med	Medium	Medium

Furthermore, models such as the Ergonomic Stress Index provide critical insights into the physical strain encountered during manual handling activities (Iskrzycki et al., 2018). By identifying specific ergonomic hazards, this model supports the creation of safer workplace environments and practices, enabling the design of interventions that minimize physical stress on healthcare personnel (Iskrzycki et al., 2018; Ouanes, 2024). Similarly, Nursing Workload Models serve as analytical tools to evaluate how workload pressures impact nurse performance and overall wellbeing (Ouanes, 2024). These models may integrate AI solutions that optimize task allocation and management, thus contributing to healthier work environments (Sharifi et al., 2024; Turchioe et al., 2024).

The amalgamation of AI technologies within these frameworks not only enhances operational efficacy in healthcare settings but also fortifies the wellbeing of healthcare professionals and enhances patient care outcomes. By systematically analysing workloads and identifying ergonomic risks via AI, clinical settings can substantially lessen the incidence of operational injuries (Hovell et al., 2019; Gupta et al., 2016).

Human-AI Interaction in Care Environments

A critical component of successfully implementing AI technologies in healthcare environments lies in understanding the interaction dynamics between humans and AI systems (Reis da Silva, 2025a; Reis da Silva, 2025c). Human-AI interaction focuses on how healthcare professionals engage collaboratively with AI systems to achieve shared objectives, particularly in manual handling scenarios (Salikutluk et al., 2023). This collaboration must sustain the human element crucial to care, ensuring that while AI can assist in manual tasks, it does not detract from the compassionate, empathetic aspects inherent in healthcare provision (Abhari et al., 2024).

Research indicates that effective human-AI collaboration can significantly enhance task performance while simultaneously reducing cognitive load for healthcare professionals (Al-Hashimi & Hamdan, 2021). The establishment of a trusting relationship between AI systems and healthcare workers forms the backbone of operational safety and efficiency, deeply impacting patient outcomes (Reis da Silva, 2025a). As AI technologies continue to evolve, refining interaction models that seamlessly adapt to human users' needs will be paramount in operationalising AI within healthcare frameworks (Aldhoayan, 2022; Janssen et al., 2024).

The alignment of AI capabilities with human intuitive practices further enhances the capacity for safer, more effective healthcare delivery models, especially in the context of manual patient handling (Jeelani et al., 2024; Reis da Silva, 2025e). This synergy is becoming increasingly necessary as healthcare systems grapple with rising patient demands and increasingly complex care requirements, making the role of AI not just beneficial but essential (Petersson et al., 2023).

2. OCCUPATIONAL RISKS IN MOVING AND HANDLING

Occupational risks, particularly musculoskeletal disorders (MSDs), are significant concerns for nurses who frequently engage in physically demanding activities in their caregiving roles. These injuries can be exacerbated by the nature of their work, particularly when caring for frail and dependent older adults. In healthcare settings, these disorders compromise the physical well-being of nurses and, subsequently, the quality of care they provide to their patients (Ozaki et al., 2017; Weathers et al., 2016).

Overview of Musculoskeletal Disorders (MSDs) in Nurses

Musculoskeletal disorders represent a broad category of injuries specifically affecting muscles, tendons, ligaments, and joints. In the nursing profession, these injuries often arise from repetitive motions and poor ergonomic practices during tasks such as lifting, transferring, and repositioning patients

(Hinsliff-Smith et al., 2015). Evidence suggests that nursing staff are at a heightened risk for developing MSDs, particularly in their lower back, shoulders, and neck (Weathers et al., 2016). Research indicates that a significant proportion of nurses report experiencing back pain during their careers, highlighting the necessity for preventative measures and interventions (Ozaki et al., 2017; Weathers et al., 2016).

Furthermore, the complexities in caring for older adults—who frequently exhibit varying levels of frailty—intensify the risks faced by healthcare workers. Frail individuals often require special adaptations in care routines, complicating the physical demands placed upon nurses (Harada et al., 2017; Reis da Silva, 2024a). As they navigate unpredictable patient behaviours and varying mobility levels, nurses must employ special techniques to ensure not only their safety but also that of the patients they are tasked with caring for (Rodríguez-Mañas et al., 2019; Reis da Silva, 2023b; Reis da Silva, 2024b).

The impact of improper lifting techniques frequently accounts for the high prevalence of these disorders, necessitating a critical reassessment of pre-existing protocols in patient handling and risk management (Ringer et al., 2017; Reis da Silva, 2023a). Current interventions, such as ergonomic training and manual handling equipment, have shown efficacy in reducing MSD incidents among nursing staff; however, their implementation remains inconsistent across different healthcare settings (Korfage et al., 2015).

Special Considerations in Caring for Frail and Dependent Older Adults

Caring for frail and dependent older adults poses unique challenges that exacerbate the risk of occupational injuries. These patients often exhibit limited mobility, compromised strength, and increased falls risk, all of which necessitate careful handling (Reis da Silva, 2023b). The physical demands of assisting patients in activities of daily living (ADLs)—such as bathing, dressing, and dining—can create occupational hazards for healthcare providers (Harada et al., 2017; Mallery et al., 2019).

Furthermore, frail patients often have comorbidities that can affect their stability and necessitate specialised lifting and transferring techniques (Reis da Silva, 2024c). For example, the presence of cognitive impairments can complicate communication and cooperation during manual handling, further escalating the risk for both patients and caregivers (Wen et al., 2021). As a result, nurses must be well-trained in both the physical aspects of manual handling and in understanding the unique needs of these vulnerable populations (Vicente et al., 2014). Given the specific challenges associated with caring for frail and dependent older adults, employing technology-enhanced solutions, such as AI-assisted lifting devices or patient monitoring systems, has the potential to further mitigate risks associated with MSDs (Shahsavarloo et al., 2020). Researching and implementing these solutions may offer significant improvements in efficiency and safety within care environments, ultimately enhancing the quality of care for older adults (Linn et al., 2021).

Current Limitations of Traditional Risk Assessment Tools

Despite the acknowledgment of significant occupational risks in nursing, traditional risk assessment tools have limitations that can hinder effective mitigation strategies. Tools such as TILE (Task, Individual, Load, Environment), ELITE (Equipment, Load, Individual, Task, Environment), MAC (Manual Handling Assessment Charts), and RULA (Rapid Upper Limb Assessment) are commonly employed to evaluate manual handling risks (Rodríguez-Mañas et al., 2014; Liotta et al., 2019; Reis da Silva, 2023a).

However, these instruments primarily focus on static assessments without considering the dynamic and complex caregiving environments that nurses encounter (Lu et al., 2019).

For instance, while TILE and ELITE provides a structured framework for analysing tasks involved in manual handling, it may not adequately account for the nuances of individual patient interactions or the unpredictable nature of a frail patient's health status (Reis da Silva, 2023a). There exists a potential disconnect between the static evaluation of ergonomic principles and the dynamic, multifaceted realities of patient care (Lee et al., 2021). Furthermore, traditional tools often fail to consider environmental factors, such as staffing levels and time constraints, which can contribute significantly to occupational risks (Spiers et al., 2019; Yu, 2016).

As a result, the integration of more comprehensive and adaptable methodologies—potentially informed by data analytics and AI—into existing risk assessment frameworks may lead to better protection for healthcare workers (Bleijenberg et al., 2016). Transitioning from traditional risk assessment tools to more dynamic, real-time evaluation methods could offer a more nuanced understanding of the risks involved in manual handling (Gazineo et al., 2020). Consequently, healthcare institutions would be better positioned to develop effective interventions tailored to the distinct challenges faced by nursing professionals.

3. AI-POWERED RISK ASSESSMENT TOOLS

The intersection of AI technology with the biomechanical assessment of healthcare workers in moving and handling has great potential in reducing workplace injuries, particularly musculoskeletal disorders (MSDs). Various AI-powered tools, such as wearables and smart garments that measure biomechanical loads, are at the forefront of this evolution. These tools use sophisticated sensors to collect real-time data on the physical strains encountered by healthcare professionals while managing patients (Stefana et al., 2021). For instance, the use of wearable devices can continuously monitor biomechanics during manual handling tasks, providing valuable feedback that can be utilized for ergonomic assessments (Stefana et al., 2021; Reis da Silva, 2025b).

Wearables, when integrated with AI algorithms, can assess risk factors by analysing the forces and motions experienced by healthcare workers during patient transfers (Reis da Silva, 2025c). This data contributes to identifying whether the lifting techniques applied during specific tasks adhere to safe ergonomic practices (Stefana et al., 2021). Comprehensive studies have shown that actively monitoring biomechanical loads through these devices helps in analysing postures and enhances awareness among healthcare workers regarding their movements (Stefana et al., 2021). Consequently, this proactive monitoring enables targeted interventions that mitigate injury risks before they manifest into more serious conditions.

In addition to wearables, computer vision has emerged as a vital technology for posture detection and movement analysis within healthcare settings (Vanegas et al., 2020). Utilising cameras and advanced imaging techniques, computer vision systems can detect posture inaccuracies and alert personnel in real time, enabling immediate corrective actions (Vanegas et al., 2020). The application of computer vision in analysing movements during lifting and transferring tasks provides an objective measure, allowing healthcare facilities to assess and modify workflows accordingly to reduce injury risk (Vanegas et al., 2020). Machine learning models are also being developed specifically to predict injury risks based on data collected from wearable devices and computer vision systems (Belen et al., 2020; Reis da Silva, 2025e). These models can analyse historical data combined with real-time inputs to identify hazardous movement patterns before they lead to injuries. For example, machine learning can be trained to recognise indicators of improper lifting techniques or unsafe postures, offering insights into preventive measures tailored for individual caregivers (Belen et al., 2020; Reis da Silva and Mitchell, 2024). As a result, healthcare facilities can transition from reactive to proactive safety measures, ultimately fostering safer work environments.

Furthermore, real-time data collection in clinical settings is becoming increasingly efficient due to advancements in AI technology (Guerzhoy & Hertzmann, 2014). This capability enables the continuous monitoring of movement patterns, assisting in the development of immediate corrective strategies and safety protocols. As real-time data streams into decision support systems, it presents an invaluable opportunity for healthcare managers to optimize nurse workflows, allocate resources effectively, and improve patient care delivery (Scott et al., 2020).

Case Scenario

A salient case example highlighting the implementation of AI-based lift planning is illustrated in a nursing home in the UK, where AI-powered systems were employed to assist staff in strategically planning patient lifts (Ralfs et al., 2022). By analysing the biomechanical loads incurred in various lifting techniques, these systems provided tailored guidelines for caregivers. The outcomes from this initiative showed not only a reduction in reported injuries and strains among staff but also smoother operations concerning patient transfers (Ralfs et al., 2022). This case exemplifies how integrating AI into healthcare operations can enhance both worker safety and the quality of patient care.

4. PREDICTIVE ANALYTICS AND DECISION SUPPORT SYSTEMS

Advancements in AI technology have maintained a pivotal role in predictive analytics and decision support systems, particularly in healthcare settings. AI systems are being increasingly employed in early warning systems for hazardous movement patterns (Abir et al., 2021). By utilising algorithms that analyse historical data and real-time inputs, these systems can identify potential risks and initiate alerts before injuries occur. This capability is vital in environments where the physical demands on workers can lead to rapid fatigue or improper lifting techniques (Wang et al., 2021).

Integration with Electronic Health Records (EHRs) plays an essential role in enhancing personalised care as it allows healthcare providers to tailor interventions based on individual patient data and caregiver capabilities (Danilov et al., 2024). Examples abound in injury prevention strategies, particularly in predicting falls and dynamically scoring lifting risks (Reis da Silva, 2024b). Predictive models leveraging AI can analyse not only the behavioural patterns of the healthcare provider but also patient-specific characteristics such as mobility levels and prior histories of falls, enabling customized and pre-emptive approaches that significantly enhance patient safety (Tali et al., 2022; Reis da Silva, 2025a).

Case Study

One notable case example involves the use of AI-assisted monitoring systems within rehabilitation units to predict transfer-related falls in older adults (Danilov et al., 2024). These systems use data from wearables and EHRs to assess patient movement patterns and identify risks associated with specific transfer activities (Reis da Silva, 2025a). By actively monitoring patient behaviour during rehabilitation exercises, healthcare professionals receive timely insights that can be used to alter interventions, thus mitigating risks before they lead to actual incidents. This predictive capability is critical for maintaining the safety and dignity of frail patients while addressing the workload of nursing staff concurrently (Veta et al., 2016).

5. TRAINING, EDUCATION, AND SIMULATION

The integration of Artificial Intelligence into training and education for manual handling in healthcare settings presents a transformative opportunity for enhancing practices among nursing staff (Reis da Silva and Mitchell, 2024). AI-enabled virtual simulations have emerged as a powerful tool for manual handling training, allowing nurses to practice essential skills in safe, controlled environments. This method not only mitigates the risk of injury during training but also enhances the learning experience by providing immersive, realistic scenarios that can be tailored to various healthcare settings (Chen et al., 2020; Reis da Silva and Mitchell, 2024).

Advanced AI systems facilitate customised feedback loops, enabling adaptive learning for nurses during virtual simulations. For instance, these systems can analyse individual performance in real-time, adjusting the complexity of tasks or altering scenarios based on the learner's skill level and performance history (Ayton et al., 2017). This adaptive approach ensures that each nurse receives personalised training experiences that can help develop competence in manual handling techniques essential for preventing musculoskeletal disorders and other injuries (Chen et al., 2020).

Moreover, AI tools can be employed for competency assessment in moving and handling tasks. They enable healthcare organisations to objectively evaluate a nurse's proficiency in essential skills, ensuring that staff members are prepared to handle the physical demands of their roles (Hasnain et al., 2019). For example, demonstrating proficiency in lifting, transferring, and repositioning patients can be effectively monitored and assessed through AI-powered simulations that capture and analyse performance metrics (Emrich-Mills et al., 2019).

A case example illustrating the practical application of these technologies is the use of virtual reality (VR) scenarios designed specifically for student nurses (Reis da Silva and Mitchell, 2024). In these scenarios, student nurses practice bed-to-chair transfers for older patients, experiencing realistic patient responses and challenges associated with mobility limitations (Zhou et al., 2019). This simulation not only builds their confidence in executing patient transfers safely but also fosters a deeper understanding of the unique considerations necessary when handling frail and older patients (Roquilly et al., 2014).

6. ETHICAL, LEGAL, AND ORGANISATIONAL CONSIDERATIONS

While the benefits of AI in training and education are clear, there are essential ethical, legal, and organisational considerations that must be addressed. Data privacy and staff surveillance concerns occupy a prominent place in discussions surrounding the implementation of AI systems in healthcare settings. The collection and analysis of data on nursing activities via monitoring systems raise substantial questions about consent, confidentiality, and the potential for misuse of information (Oreskovic et al., 2016; Gyamfi et al., 2020). It is paramount for healthcare organisations to ensure that robust measures are in place to protect sensitive personal data and comply with privacy regulations such as the General Data Protection Regulation (GDPR) (Greenwood et al., 2015).

The acceptability of AI interventions among older patients and caregivers also merits significant consideration. Ensuring that technology is user-friendly and effectively communicated to patients and their families is crucial for fostering trust and acceptance (Greenwood et al., 2017). Participatory approaches should be encouraged, allowing patients and caregivers to express concerns and contribute to the design of AI solutions that impact their care (Schouten & Mugge, 2018). Furthermore, the effectiveness of AI interventions must continually be evaluated to ensure they meet the needs and expectations of users, particularly vulnerable populations.

Regulatory frameworks, such as the UK Manual Handling Operations Regulations (MHOR) 1992, also outline the necessary legal standards for handling patients safely, emphasising the importance of training and employing safe practices in healthcare environments (Vaismoradi et al., 2020). Organisations utilising AI should harmonise these regulations with technological advancements to create a comprehensive approach that prioritises safety for both patients and healthcare staff.

Additionally, the procurement and implementation of AI technologies within healthcare organisations must be guided by thorough deliberations involving stakeholders at all levels. Initiatives do not succeed solely through technological advances; they must also consider the organisational culture, staff readiness, and available resources (Pusic et al., 2021). Training and continuous professional development opportunities should accompany the introduction of AI solutions, ensuring that staff are adequately equipped to integrate these changes into their practice settings effectively (Bowley et al., 2018).

8. IMPLEMENTATION CHALLENGES AND ENABLERS

The successful implementation of AI technologies in healthcare settings encounters various challenges and enablers. One prominent challenge is the technological infrastructure within healthcare facilities. Insufficient infrastructure can hinder the deployment and integration of AI systems, as noted by Mosavi and Santos (2021). Healthcare institutions often require significant investments in advanced systems that can support AI applications, which may not be feasible in resource-constrained environments (Mosavi & Santos, 2021). The necessity for robust hardware, reliable internet connectivity, integration with existing electronic health records (EHRs), and ongoing maintenance presents a complex multifaceted challenge that healthcare facilities must navigate (Agha-Mir-Salim & Sarmiento, 2020).

Interprofessional collaboration plays a critical role in fostering the digital literacy required for effective implementation. As digital literacy is integral to utilising AI tools effectively, it is crucial for collaborative strategies that involve nurses, doctors, administrators, and AI system developers. Vervloet et al. (2023) highlight the importance of integrating digital solutions with the existing dynamics of the healthcare workforce, advocating for comprehensive training programs to enhance digital competencies among all team members. This collaboration not only facilitates smoother transitions into AI-dependent workflows but also enhances overall patient care quality as teams align towards common objectives.

Cost-effectiveness and return on investment (ROI) considerations also present significant hurdles. While AI technologies promise to streamline processes and improve patient outcomes, scepticism regarding their net financial impact is common, as indicated by various studies that reveal uneven returns (Mosavi & Santos, 2021). The upfront costs associated with implementing AI systems—including technology purchases, training, and ongoing support—can be considerable. Organisations need clear evidence of long-term savings and enhanced efficiency to motivate stakeholders towards adoption (Bowley et al., 2018; Mosavi & Santos, 2021).

9. FUTURE DIRECTIONS

The future of AI in healthcare presents exciting advancements, particularly in the areas of robotics and AI co-pilots in manual handling (Sudha et al., 2024). Robotics can significantly enhance manual handling processes, as AI co-pilots can assist nursing staff in patient mobility, reducing physical strain and the risk of injuries among caregivers (Sudha et al., 2024). These innovations provide dual benefits: enhancing efficiency and safety during patient transfers while also preserving the dignity and comfort of patients receiving care (Huby, 2023).

Human-centred design offers another avenue for the development of gerontology-focused AI solutions. Emphasising usability and user experience, human-centred design principles ensure that AI applications are tailored to meet the needs of older adults, facilitating widespread adoption and use (Boy, 2017). A focus on the end-users in the design process can lead to improvements in technology acceptance rates and ultimately result in better health outcomes for older populations (Boopathi, 2023).

Moreover, there are substantial opportunities for research in AI-driven occupational health and safety practices. Continued exploration in this domain is essential for advancing safety measures among healthcare providers. As the landscape of AI evolves, researchers should investigate the efficacy of various applications in real-world settings, analysing their impact on reducing occupational hazards and developing best practices for integrating these technologies (Kumar et al., 2024; Rahman & Khatun, 2023).

10. CONCLUSION

The integration of AI technologies within the frameworks addressing manual handling and risk management in healthcare proves to be a multifaceted endeavour. By harnessing the power of AI to enhance risk assessments, optimise ergonomic practices, and facilitate smoother human-AI interactions, healthcare organisations can work towards creating safer environments for their personnel without compromising the quality of care provided to patients. As the landscape of healthcare continues to evolve, both AI and ergonomic principles must be strategically aligned to navigate the complexities of manual handling and occupational injury prevention (Beinert et al., 2018; Ambeba et al., 2015; Gudavalli et al., 2015). The burgeoning field of AI presents exciting opportunities that promise to transform healthcare delivery, enhancing both worker safety and patient care quality. Continued exploration and research into these arenas will be essential as we strive to develop integrated solutions that address the dual challenges of enhancing healthcare outcomes while safeguarding the wellbeing of healthcare professionals.

Addressing occupational risks associated with MSDs in nursing, particularly in the context of caring for frail older adults, requires a multifaceted strategy. Emphasising education, technology integration, and the adaptation of risk assessment methodologies will foster safer work environments for nurses while ensuring optimal care delivery for patients. Continued research and innovation in these areas are crucial to overcoming the inherent challenges present in the nursing profession.

The integration of AI-powered risk assessment tools and predictive analytics into healthcare aims to reduce the incidence of occupational risks among caregivers and fosters a culture of safety and proactivity in patient care. By adopting such technologies, healthcare facilities can ensure optimal work practices that support the well-being of both patients and workers, ultimately leading to improved outcomes and enhanced quality of care overall.

While AI holds immense potential to enhance training, education, and safety in manual handling, ethical, legal, and organisational challenges remain paramount. Healthcare providers must navigate these issues carefully to develop practices that respect patient dignity and protect healthcare workers while leveraging the benefits of innovative technologies. The integration of AI into healthcare not only represents a critical advancement for nursing practice but also necessitates a collaborative effort across disciplines, fostering an environment where caregiving is enriched by technological innovation, ultimately leading to improved quality of care and patient safety.

10.1. Summary

The transformative potential of AI in reducing harm in nursing practice is evident. By enhancing training, providing mechanisms for real-time assessment, and addressing the physical demands placed upon nurses, AI can significantly lower the incidence of musculoskeletal disorders and other occupational injuries (Agha-Mir-Salim & Sarmiento, 2020). The implications of these findings extend beyond immediate health outcomes, informing discussions regarding policy, nursing education, and clinical leadership.

To harness the full benefits of AI technologies, healthcare organisations must develop comprehensive strategies encompassing regulatory compliance, ethical considerations, digital literacy improvements, and stakeholder engagement. As AI continues to permeate healthcare, policies need to evolve to safeguard patient data while embracing innovation, ensuring a future where technology enhances, rather than complicates, care delivery (Vervloet et al., 2023; Kari et al., 2020).

10.2 Call for Action

As healthcare systems globally grapple with the dual pressures of an ageing population and increasing occupational health demands, the integration of Artificial Intelligence (AI) into moving and handling practices represents a transformative solution. Nurses, healthcare leaders, educators, and policymakers must proactively invest in AI-driven strategies that prioritise workforce safety, patient dignity, and operational sustainability. There is a pressing need to embed intelligent risk management tools into everyday clinical practice—particularly in the care of older adults—by fostering interdisciplinary collaboration, digital upskilling, and ethical innovation. By championing the use of AI in occupational health, stakeholders can align clinical excellence with global health, safety, and sustainability agendas.

10.3. Linking with Sustainable Development Goals

The application of Artificial Intelligence (AI) in risk management for moving and handling tasks in healthcare is significantly aligned with the United Nations Sustainable Development Goals (SDGs), particularly SDG 3 (Good Health and Well-being), SDG 8 (Decent Work and Economic Growth), and SDG 9 (Industry, Innovation and Infrastructure) (da Silva and Rodrigues, 2023). By integrating AI-driven technologies that specifically address and mitigate musculoskeletal injuries among nurses, there exists the potential to improve not only the safety and well-being of healthcare staff but also patient handling practices within critical sectors such as eldercare and rehabilitation (Reis da Silva, 2025a).

Moreover, the focus on AI integration supports SDG 10: Reduced Inequalities and SDG 12: Responsible Consumption and Production, especially through its capacity to reduce care disparities in long-term settings and minimise resource wastage. For example, predictive tools that reduce hospital readmissions due to lifting injuries or falls in older adults represent a sustainable intervention with economic, clinical, and ecological benefits. By empowering nurses with intelligent, context-aware technologies, we can reduce physical strain, improve retention, and ensure equitable care delivery for vulnerable populations. As such, embedding AI in risk management is not merely a clinical improvement—it is a strategic lever for achieving health equity, resilience, and sustainability on a global scale.

Contribution to SDGs

SDG 3 (Good Health and Well-being): The implementation of AI technologies to minimise work-related morbidity represents a direct contribution to enhancing overall health conditions among nursing staff, thereby fostering a healthier work environment. AI can help identify risky behaviours and conditions before they lead to injuries. By promoting safer working conditions, the healthcare system can lower injury rates, thus leading to better health outcomes not only for healthcare workers but also for patients.

SDG 8 (Decent Work and Economic Growth): Utilising AI in risk management promotes decent work by ensuring that employees are protected from injuries that could lead to career-long health issues or job loss (Reis da Silva, 2024d). When nurses are equipped to perform their duties without the heightened risk of injury, their job satisfaction increases, potentially leading to better workforce retention rates—a current challenge in the healthcare sector (Reis da Silva, 2025f; Reis da Silva, 2025g). Moreover, as nurses experience fewer work-related injuries, healthcare facilities may see a reduction in costs associated with employee turnover and training new staff (Reis da Silva, 2025h).

SDG 9 (Industry, Innovation and Infrastructure): The integration of AI technologies supports innovation within healthcare by endorsing the development of more efficient processes and infrastructures that benefit both healthcare workers and patients. AI-driven tools can automate repetitive tasks, assist in complex decision-making processes, and ensure optimal resource allocation—a significant advancement for healthcare systems under pressure. By investing in these technologies, healthcare organisations are enhancing their operational capacities (Reis da Silva, 2025c; Reis da Silva, 2025i).

Additionally, AI's focus on reducing inequalities (SDG 10) and promoting responsible consumption and production (SDG 12) is evident through its ability to address disparities in patient care provisions, particularly in long-term care settings (Reis da Silva, 2024e; Reis da Silva, 2024f). Predictive analytics tools designed to prevent incidents of falls or injuries during patient transfers can minimise resource wastage while improving clinical outcomes. For instance, predictive tools informed by AI can help prevent hospital readmissions that result from lifting injuries or falls, representing sustainable intervention methods with significant economic, clinical, and ecological benefits.

Empowering Healthcare Workers

Empowering nurses with intelligent, context-aware technologies allows for a considerable reduction in physical strain associated with patient handling. In turn, this empowerment contributes to improved job satisfaction and retention, which is essential for ensuring equitable care delivery, especially to vulnerable populations, such as older adults with complex care needs. Therefore, the embedding of AI in risk management extends beyond clinical improvements; it serves as a strategic lever to achieve health equity, resilience, and sustainability globally.

REFERENCES

da Silva, T. H. R., & Rodrigues, E. C. P. (2023). Body Image Related Discrimination. In Leal Filho, W., Azul, A. M., Brandli, L., Lange Salvia, A., Özuyar, P. G., & Wall, T. (Eds.), *Reduced Inequalities. Encyclopedia of the UN Sustainable Development Goals*. Springer., DOI: 10.1007/978-3-319-71060-0_61-1

Horta Reis Da Silva, T. (2022). Moving and Handling. In Curr, S., & Fordham-Clarke, C. (Eds.), *Clinical Skills at Glance* (pp. 20–21). Wiley.

Reis da Silva, T. H. (2024a). Chapter 11 - Integrating business essentials into Gerontological Nursing: Enhancing Care for Older Adults in Diverse Settings. In Sedky, A. Resiliency Strategies for Long-Term Business Success. Pp. 283-316. IGI Global. DOI: https://doi.org/DOI: 10.4018/979-8-3693-9168-6.ch011

Reis da Silva, T. H. (2025a). Integrating Artificial Intelligence in Geriatric Care: Enhancing Physical and Mental Health Outcomes. In Jermsittiparsert, K., & Marzo, R. R. (Eds.), *Physical Health, Mental Health, and Human Well-Being in the Age of AI*. IGI Global Scientific Publishing., DOI: 10.4018/979-8-3693-6190-0.ch11

Reis da Silva, T. H. (2025c). Promoting Emotional Well-Being in Older Adults: The Role of AI in Supporting Emotional Intelligence and Mental Health. In Jermsittiparsert, K., & Marzo, R. R. (Eds.), *Physical Health, Mental Health, and Human Well-Being in the Age of AI* (pp. 137–167). IGI Global Scientific Publishing., DOI: 10.4018/979-8-3693-6190-0.ch8

Reis da Silva, T. H. (2025d). AI-Powered Emotional Intelligence in Nursing: Bridging the Gap in Older People Care. In Jermsittiparsert, K., & Marzo, R. R. (Eds.), *Physical Health, Mental Health, and Human Well-Being in the Age of AI*. IGI Global Scientific Publishing., DOI: 10.4018/979-8-3693-6190-0.ch9

Reis da Silva, T. H. (2025e). Emotional Intelligence and AI in Geriatric Nursing: Bridging Technology and Compassionate Care. In Jermsittiparsert, K., & Marzo, R. R. (Eds.), *Physical Health, Mental Health, and Human Well-Being in the Age of AI*. IGI Global Scientific Publishing., DOI: 10.4018/979-8-3693-6190-0.ch10

Reis da Silva, T. H., & Mitchell, A. (2024). Integrating Digital Transformation in Nursing Education: Best Practices and Challenges in Curriculum Development. In Lytras, M., Serban, A. C., Alkhaldi, A., Malik, S., & Aldosemani, T. (Eds.), *Digital Transformation in Higher Education, Part B Cases, Examples and Good Practices*. Emerald Publishing Limited.

Reis da Silva, T. M. (2025b). Integrative Approaches to Geriatric Care: Enhancing Physical and Mental Health Through AI-Driven Insights. In Jermsittiparsert, K., & Marzo, R. (Eds.), *Physical Health, Mental Health, and Human Well-Being in the Age of AI* (pp. 113–136). IGI Global Scientific Publishing., DOI: 10.4018/979-8-3693-6190-0.ch007

Reis da Silva, T. M. (2025g). Cultivating Emotionally Intelligent Leadership: Strategies for Enhancing Authentic Engagement and Organisational Impact. In Sayed, Z. (Ed.), *Emotionally Intelligent Methods for Meaningful Leadership* (pp. 119–148). IGI Global Scientific Publishing., DOI: 10.4018/979-8-3693-7372-9.ch006

Reis da Silva, T. M. (2025h). Fostering Emotional Resilience and Mindful Leadership in Gerontology Nursing: A Model for Change and Innovation. In Baez, M. (Ed.), *Strategic Approaches to Mindful Leadership and Change Management* (pp. 259–280). IGI Global Scientific Publishing., DOI: 10.4018/979-8-3693-7066-7.ch009

Reis da Silva, T. M. (2025i). The Interplay Between Ethical Work Climate and Employee Well-Being: Navigating the Path to Organisational Integrity and Success. In Ige-Olaobaju, A., Ganiyu, I., Atiku, S., & Olarewaju, O. (Eds.), *Advances in Ethical Work Climate and Employee Well-Being* (pp. 243–268). IGI Global Scientific Publishing., DOI: 10.4018/979-8-3693-8819-8.ch012

Reis da Silva, T. M. H. (2025f). The Role of Emotional Intelligence in Promoting Mental Peace, Healthy Work Environments, and Emotional Well-Being Among Entrepreneurs. In Tunio, M. N. (Ed.), *Supporting Psychological and Emotional Wellbeing Among Entrepreneurs.* IGI Global Scientific Publishing., DOI: 10.4018/979-8-3693-3673-1.ch21

Wynn, M., Reis da Silva, T. H., & Pearson-Jenkins, J. (2025). Introduction to digital nursing and nursing theory. In Wynn, M. (Ed.), *Digital Nursing: Shaping Practice and Identity in the Age of Informatics.* Routledge. DOI: 10.4324/9781032714547-1

Reis da Silva Tiago. (2024d) The Value of Emotional Intelligence in Midwifery: Enhancing Care and Outcomes for Mothers and Infants through Sustainable Development Goals and Leadership. Journal of Womens Healthcare & Midwifery Research. SRC/JWHMR-133. DOI: https://doi.org/ Link: https://www.onlinescientificresearch.com/articles/the-value-of-emotional-intelligence-in-midwifery-enhancing-care-and-outcomes-for-mothers-and-infants-through-sustainable-developme.pdfDOI: 10.47363/JWHMR/2024(3)119

Ambeba, E., Ye, L., Sereika, S., Styn, M., Acharya, S., Sevick, M., Ewing, L. J., Conroy, M. B., Glanz, K., Zheng, Y., Goode, R. W., Mattos, M., & Burke, L. (2015). The use of mhealth to deliver tailored messages reduces reported energy and fat intake. *The Journal of Cardiovascular Nursing*, *30*(1), 35–43. DOI: 10.1097/JCN.0000000000000120 PMID: 24434827

Ayton, D., Barker, A., Morello, R., Brand, C., Talevski, J., Landgren, F., Melhem, M. M., Bian, E., Brauer, S. G., Hill, K. D., Livingston, P. M., & Botti, M. (2017). Barriers and enablers to the implementation of the 6-pack falls prevention program: A pre-implementation study in hospitals participating in a cluster randomised controlled trial. *PLoS One*, *12*(2), e0171932. DOI: 10.1371/journal.pone.0171932 PMID: 28207841

Beinert, K., Lutz, B., Zieglgänsberger, W., & Diers, M. (2018). Seeing the site of treatment improves habitual pain but not cervical joint position sense immediately after manual therapy in chronic neck pain patients. *European Journal of Pain (London, England)*, *23*(1), 117–123. DOI: 10.1002/ejp.1290 PMID: 29999203

Belen, R., Bednarz, T., Sowmya, A., & Favero, D. (2020). Computer vision in autism spectrum disorder research: A systematic review of published studies from 2009 to 2019. *Translational Psychiatry*, *10*(1), 333. Advance online publication. DOI: 10.1038/s41398-020-01015-w PMID: 32999273

Bleijenberg, N., Drubbel, I., Schuurmans, M., Dam, H., Zuithoff, N., Numans, M., & Wit, N. (2016). Effectiveness of a proactive primary care program on preserving daily functioning of older people: A cluster randomized controlled trial. *Journal of the American Geriatrics Society*, *64*(9), 1779–1788. DOI: 10.1111/jgs.14325 PMID: 27459236

Chen, H., Feng, H., Liao, L., Wu, X., Zhao, Y., Hu, M., Li, H., Hu, H., & Yang, X. (2020). Evaluation of quality improvement intervention with nurse training in nursing homes: A systematic review. *Journal of Clinical Nursing*, *29*(15-16), 2788–2800. DOI: 10.1111/jocn.15289 PMID: 32279376

Chung, E., Lee, B., & Hwang, S. (2014). Core stabilization exercise with real-time feedback for chronic hemiparetic stroke: A pilot randomized controlled trials. *Restorative Neurology and Neuroscience*, *32*(2), 313–321. DOI: 10.3233/RNN-130353 PMID: 24398718

Cortegiani, A., Russotto, V., Montalto, F., Iozzo, P., Meschis, R., Pugliesi, M., Mariano, D., Benenati, V., Raineri, S. M., Gregoretti, C., & Giarratano, A. (2017). Use of a real-time training software (laerdal qcpr®) compared to instructor-based feedback for high-quality chest compressions acquisition in secondary school students: A randomized trial. *PLoS One*, *12*(1), e0169591. DOI: 10.1371/journal.pone.0169591 PMID: 28056076

Emrich-Mills, L., Collier, P., & West, J. (2019). The role of nurse prescribers in memory services and their continuing professional development: A review of the literature. *Journal of Clinical Nursing*, *28*(9-10), 1422–1432. DOI: 10.1111/jocn.14796 PMID: 30667577

Gazineo, D., Godino, L., Decaro, R., Calogero, P., Pinto, D., Chiari, P., Zoli, M., & Ambrosi, E. (2020). Assisted walking program on walking ability in in-hospital geriatric patients: A randomized trial. *Journal of the American Geriatrics Society*, *69*(3), 637–643. DOI: 10.1111/jgs.16922 PMID: 33184855

Greenwood, D., Blozis, S., Young, H., Nesbitt, T., & Quinn, C. (2015). Overcoming clinical inertia: A randomized clinical trial of a telehealth remote monitoring intervention using paired glucose testing in adults with type 2 diabetes. *Journal of Medical Internet Research*, *17*(7), e178. DOI: 10.2196/jmir.4112 PMID: 26199142

Greenwood, D., Gee, P., Fatkin, K., & Peeples, M. (2017). A systematic review of reviews evaluating technology-enabled diabetes self-management education and support. *Journal of Diabetes Science and Technology*, *11*(5), 1015–1027. DOI: 10.1177/1932296817713506 PMID: 28560898

Gudavalli, M., Vining, R., Salsbury, S., Corber, L., Long, C., Patwardhan, A., & Goertz, C. (2015). Clinician proficiency in delivering manual treatment for neck pain within specified force ranges. *The Spine Journal*, *15*(4), 570–576. DOI: 10.1016/j.spinee.2014.10.016 PMID: 25452013

Gupta, A., Hilliard, R., Mudie, K., & Clothier, P. (2016). Does providing real-time augmented feedback affect the performance of repeated lower limb loading to exhaustion? *Gait & Posture*, *44*, 204–208. DOI: 10.1016/j.gaitpost.2015.12.034 PMID: 27004659

Gyamfi, J., Allegrante, J., Iwelunmor, J., Williams, O., Plange-Rhule, J., Blackstone, S., Ntim, M., Apusiga, K., Peprah, E., & Ogedegbe, G. (2020). Application of the consolidated framework for implementation research to examine nurses' perception of the task shifting strategy for hypertension control trial in ghana. *BMC Health Services Research, 20*(1), 65. Advance online publication. DOI: 10.1186/s12913-020-4912-5 PMID: 31996195

Harada, K., Park, H., Lee, S., Shimada, H., Yoshida, D., Anan, Y., & Suzuki, T. (2017). Joint association of neighborhood environment and fear of falling on physical activity among frail older adults. *Journal of Aging and Physical Activity, 25*(1), 140–148. DOI: 10.1123/japa.2016-0082 PMID: 27620962

Hasnain, M., Levi, C., Ryan, A., Hubbard, I., Hall, A., Oldmeadow, C., Grady, A., Jayakody, A., Attia, J. R., & Paul, C. (2019). Can a multicomponent multidisciplinary implementation package change physicians' and nurses' perceptions and practices regarding thrombolysis for acute ischemic stroke? an exploratory analysis of a cluster-randomized trial. *Implementation Science : IS, 14*(1), 98. Advance online publication. DOI: 10.1186/s13012-019-0940-0 PMID: 31771599

Hinsliff-Smith, K., Feakes, R., Whitworth, G., Seymour, J., Moghaddam, N., Dening, T., & Cox, K. (2015). What do we know about the application of the mental capacity act (2005) in healthcare practice regarding decision-making for frail and older people? a systematic literature review. *Health & Social Care in the Community, 25*(2), 295–308. DOI: 10.1111/hsc.12310 PMID: 26611194

Indovina, K., Keniston, A., Reid, M., Sachs, K., Zheng, C., Tong, A., Hernandez, D., Bui, K., Ali, Z., Nguyen, T., Guirguis, H., Albert, R. K., & Burden, M. (2016). Real-time patient experience surveys of hospitalized medical patients. *Journal of Hospital Medicine, 11*(4), 251–256. DOI: 10.1002/jhm.2533 PMID: 26777721

Iskrzycki, Ł., Smereka, J., Rodríguez-Núñez, A., Furelos, R., Gomez, C., Kamińska, H., & Ładny, J. (2018). The impact of the use of a cprmeter monitor on quality of chest compressions: A prospective randomised trial, cross-simulation. *Kardiologia Polska, 76*(3), 574–579. DOI: 10.5603/KP.a2017.0255 PMID: 29297195

Khoury, A., Luca, A., Sall, F., Pazart, L., & Capellier, G. (2019). Ventilation feedback device for manual ventilation in simulated respiratory arrest: A crossover manikin study. *Scandinavian Journal of Trauma, Resuscitation and Emergency Medicine, 27*(1), 93. Advance online publication. DOI: 10.1186/s13049-019-0674-7 PMID: 31640797

Korfage, I., Rietjens, J., Overbeek, A., Jabbarian, L., Billekens, P., Hammes, B., & Heide, A. (2015). A cluster randomized controlled trial on the effects and costs of advance care planning in elderly care: Study protocol. *BMC Geriatrics, 15*(1), 87. Advance online publication. DOI: 10.1186/s12877-015-0087-z PMID: 26198573

Lee, J., Yanagawa, B., An, K., Arora, R., Verma, S., & Friedrich, J. (2021). Frailty and pre-frailty in cardiac surgery: A systematic review and meta-analysis of 66,448 patients. *Journal of Cardiothoracic Surgery, 16*(1), 184. Advance online publication. DOI: 10.1186/s13019-021-01541-8 PMID: 34172059

Linn, N., Goetzinger, C., Régnaux, J., Schmitz, S., Dessenne, C., Fagherazzi, G., & Aguayo, G. (2021). Digital health interventions among people living with frailty: A scoping review. *Journal of the American Medical Directors Association, 22*(9), 1802–1812.e21. DOI: 10.1016/j.jamda.2021.04.012 PMID: 34000266

Liotta, G., Gilardi, F., Orlando, S., Rocco, G., Proietti, M., Asta, F., De Sario, M., Michelozzi, P., Mancinelli, S., Palombi, L., Marazzi, M. C., & Scarcella, P. (2019). Cost of hospital care for the older adults according to their level of frailty. a cohort study in the Lazio region, Italy. *PLoS One, 14*(6), e0217829. DOI: 10.1371/journal.pone.0217829 PMID: 31185033

Lu, Y., Niti, M., Yap, K., Tan, C., Nyunt, M., Feng, L., & Ng, T. (2019). Assessment of sarcopenia among community-dwelling at-risk frail adults aged 65 years and older who received multidomain lifestyle interventions. *JAMA Network Open, 2*(10), e1913346. DOI: 10.1001/jamanetworkopen.2019.13346 PMID: 31617926

Mallery, L., MacLeod, T., Allen, M., McLean-Veysey, P., Rodney-Cail, N., Bezanson, E., Steeves, B., LeBlanc, C., & Moorhouse, P. (2019). Systematic review and meta-analysis of second-generation antidepressants for the treatment of older adults with depression: Questionable benefit and considerations for frailty. *BMC Geriatrics, 19*(1), 306. Advance online publication. DOI: 10.1186/s12877-019-1327-4 PMID: 31718566

Mendelsohn, A., Kim, C., Song, J., Singh, A., Le, T., Abiri, A., Berke, G. S., & Geoghegan, R. (2020). Transoral robotic surgical proficiency via real-time tactile collision awareness system. *The Laryngoscope, 130*(S6). Advance online publication. DOI: 10.1002/lary.29034 PMID: 32865822

Nyman, E.Jr, & Armstrong, C. (2015). Real-time feedback during drop landing training improves subsequent frontal and sagittal plane knee kinematics. *Clinical Biomechanics (Bristol, Avon), 30*(9), 988–994. DOI: 10.1016/j.clinbiomech.2015.06.018 PMID: 26144663

Ozaki, K., Kondo, I., Hirano, S., Kagaya, H., Saitoh, E., Osawa, A., & Fujinori, Y. (2017). Training with a balance exercise assist robot is more effective than conventional training for frail older adults. *Geriatrics & Gerontology International, 17*(11), 1982–1990. DOI: 10.1111/ggi.13009 PMID: 28295912

Park, H., Nam, K., Lim, J., Yeo, S., Lee, J., & Hwang, J. (2021). Real-time interactive digital healthcare system for post-operative breast cancer patients: Study protocol for a randomized controlled trial. *Trials, 22*(1), 549. Advance online publication. DOI: 10.1186/s13063-021-05535-8 PMID: 34412658

Pusic, A., Temple, L., Carter, J., Stabile, C., Assel, M., Vickers, A., Niehaus, K., Ancker, J. S., McCready, T., Stetson, P. D., & Simon, B. (2021). A randomized controlled trial evaluating electronic outpatient symptom monitoring after ambulatory cancer surgery. *Annals of Surgery Open : Perspectives of Surgical History, Education, and Clinical Approaches, 274*(3), 441–448. DOI: 10.1097/SLA.0000000000005005 PMID: 34132697

Reis da Silva, T. (2024e). Advancing Gender Equity In Nursing Care For Older Adults: A Pathway To Achieving The United Nations Sustainable Development Goals. *J Comm Med and Pub Health Rep, 5*(12). Advance online publication. DOI: 10.38207/JCMPHR/2024/JUL051201105

Reis da Silva, T. (2024f). Gender Equity In Healthcare: Integrating Emotional Intelligence To Achieve The United Nations Sustainable Development Goals. *J Comm Med and Pub Health Rep*, *5*(12). Advance online publication. DOI: 10.38207/JCMPHR/2024/JUL051202106

Reis da Silva, T. H. (2023a). Moving and Handling in the Community. *British Journal of Community Nursing*, *28*(8), 369. DOI: 10.12968/bjcn.2023.28.8.369 PMID: 37527217

Reis da Silva, T. H. (2023b). Falls assessment and prevention in the nursing home and community. *British Journal of Community Nursing*, *28*(2), 68–72. DOI: 10.12968/bjcn.2023.28.2.68 PMID: 36735363

Reis da Silva, T. H. (2024b). Falls prevention in older people and the role of nursing. *British Journal of Community Nursing*, *29*(7), 335–339. DOI: 10.12968/bjcn.2024.0005 PMID: 38963269

Ringer, T., Hazzan, A., Agarwal, A., Mutsaers, A., & Παπαϊωάννου, A. (2017). Relationship between family caregiver burden and physical frailty in older adults without dementia: A systematic review. *Systematic Reviews*, *6*(1), 55. Advance online publication. DOI: 10.1186/s13643-017-0447-1 PMID: 28292313

Rodríguez-Mañas, L., Bayer, A., Kelly, M., Zeyfang, A., Izquierdo, M., Laosa, O., Hardman, T. C., & Sinclair, A. (2014). An evaluation of the effectiveness of a multi-modal intervention in frail and pre-frail older people with type 2 diabetes - the mid-frail study: Study protocol for a randomised controlled trial. *Trials*, *15*(1), 34. Advance online publication. DOI: 10.1186/1745-6215-15-34 PMID: 24456998

Rodríguez-Mañas, L., Laosa, O., Vellas, B., Paolisso, G., Topinková, E., Oliva, J., & Sinclair, A. (2019). Effectiveness of a multimodal intervention in functionally impaired older people with type 2 diabetes mellitus. *Journal of Cachexia, Sarcopenia and Muscle*, *10*(4), 721–733. DOI: 10.1002/jcsm.12432 PMID: 31016897

Roquilly, A., Broquet, A., Jacqueline, C., Masson, D., Segain, J., Braudeau, C., Vourc'h, M., Caillon, J., Altare, F., Josien, R., Retière, C., Villadangos, J., & Asehnoune, K. (2014). Hydrocortisone prevents immunosuppression by interleukin-10+ natural killer cells after trauma-hemorrhage. *Critical Care Medicine*, *42*(12), e752–e761. DOI: 10.1097/CCM.0000000000000658 PMID: 25289930

Shahsavarloo, Z., Atashzadeh-Shoorideh, F., Gobbens, R., Ebadi, A., & Harouni, G. (2020). The impact of interventions on management of frailty in hospitalized frail older adults: A systematic review and meta-analysis. *BMC Geriatrics*, *20*(1), 526. Advance online publication. DOI: 10.1186/s12877-020-01935-8 PMID: 33272208

Spiers, G., Matthews, F., Moffatt, S., Barker, R., Jarvis, H., Stow, D., Kingston, A., & Hanratty, B. (2019). Does older adults' use of social care influence their healthcare utilisation? a systematic review of international evidence. *Health & Social Care in the Community*, hsc.12798. Advance online publication. DOI: 10.1111/hsc.12798 PMID: 31314142

Stefana, E., Marciano, F., Rossi, D., Cocca, P., & Tomasoni, G. (2021). Wearable devices for ergonomics: A systematic literature review. *Sensors (Basel)*, *21*(3), 777. DOI: 10.3390/s21030777 PMID: 33498904

Vaismoradi, M., Tella, S., Logan, P., Khakurel, J., & Vizcaya-Moreno, M. (2020). Nurses' adherence to patient safety principles: A systematic review. *International Journal of Environmental Research and Public Health*, *17*(6), 2028. DOI: 10.3390/ijerph17062028 PMID: 32204403

Vanegas, E., Igual, R., & Plaza, I. (2020). Sensing systems for respiration monitoring: A technical systematic review. *Sensors (Basel)*, *20*(18), 5446. DOI: 10.3390/s20185446 PMID: 32972028

Vicente, V., Svensson, L., Sundström, B., Sjöstrand, F., & Castrén, M. (2014). Randomized controlled trial of a prehospital decision system by emergency medical services to ensure optimal treatment for older adults in Sweden. *Journal of the American Geriatrics Society*, *62*(7), 1281–1287. DOI: 10.1111/jgs.12888 PMID: 24916953

Weathers, E., Ó'Caoimh, R., Cornally, N., Fitzgerald, C., Kearns, T., Coffey, A., Daly, E., O'Sullivan, R., McGlade, C., & Molloy, D. (2016). Advance care planning: A systematic review of randomised controlled trials conducted with older adults. *Maturitas*, *91*, 101–109. DOI: 10.1016/j.maturitas.2016.06.016 PMID: 27451328

Wen, C., Chang, S., & Ho, H. (2021). Adverse health effects of frailty: Systematic review and meta-analysis of middle-aged and older adults with implications for evidence-based practice. *Worldviews on Evidence-Based Nursing*, *18*(4), 282–289. DOI: 10.1111/wvn.12508 PMID: 34075676

Yu, D. (2016). Effects of a health and social collaborative case management model on health outcomes of family caregivers of frail older adults: Preliminary data from a pilot randomized controlled trial. *Journal of the American Geriatrics Society*, *64*(10), 2144–2148. DOI: 10.1111/jgs.14259 PMID: 27550619

Abhari, S., Fatahi, S., Saragadam, A., Chumachenko, D., & Morita, P. (2024). A road map of prompt engineering for chatgpt in healthcare: a perspective study.. DOI: 10.3233/SHTI240578

Abir, F., Faisal, M., Shahid, O., & Ahmed, M. (2021). Contactless human activity analysis: an overview of different modalities., 83-112. DOI: 10.1007/978-3-030-68590-4_3

Agha-Mir-Salim, L. and Sarmiento, R. (2020). Health information technology as premise for data science in global health: a discussion of opportunities and challenges., 3-15. DOI: 10.1007/978-3-030-47994-7_1

Aldhoayan, M. (2022). The role of artificial intelligence and machine learning during the covid-19 pandemic: a review.. DOI: 10.3233/SHTI220651

Al-Hashimi, M. and Hamdan, A. (2021). Artificial intelligence and coronavirus covid-19: applications, impact and future implications., 830-843. DOI: 10.1007/978-3-030-69221-6_64

Boopathi, S. (2023). Securing healthcare systems integrated with IoT., 186-209. DOI: 10.4018/978-1-6684-6894-4.ch010

Bowley, C., Mattingly, M., Barnas, A., Ellis-Felege, S., & Desell, T. (2018). Detecting wildlife in unmanned aerial systems imagery using convolutional neural networks trained with an automated feedback loop., 69-82. DOI: 10.1007/978-3-319-93698-7_6

Boy, G. (2017). A human-centered design approach., 1-20. DOI: 10.1201/9781315557380-1

Danilov, G., Kostyumov, V., Pilipenko, O., Ilyushin, E., Pitskhelauri, D., Zelenova, A., … & Bykanov, A. (2024). Computer vision for assessing surgical movements in neurosurgery.. DOI: 10.3233/SHTI240564

Guerzhoy, M. and Hertzmann, A. (2014). Learning latent factor models of travel data for travel prediction and analysis., 131-142. DOI: 10.1007/978-3-319-06483-3_12

Hovell, M., Bellettiere, J., Liles, S., Nguyen, B., Berardi, V., Johnson, C., … & Hughes, S. (2019). Randomised controlled trial of real-time feedback and brief coaching to reduce indoor smoking. Tobacco Control, tobaccocontrol-2018-054717. DOI: 10.1136/tobaccocontrol-2018-054717

Huby, G. (2023). The bridge of knowledge: infrastructure for the coordination of health and social care or an easy fix?., 35-51. DOI: 10.23865/noasp.196.ch1

Janssen, A., Kavisha, S., Johnson, A., Marinic, A., Teede, H., & Shaw, T. (2024). Implementation of artificial intelligence applications in Australian healthcare organisations: environmental scan findings.. DOI: 10.3233/SHTI231142

Jeelani, O., Njie, M., & Korzhuk, V. (2024). Methods and algorithms of ensuring data privacy in ai-based healthcare systems and technologies.. DOI: 10.3233/SHTI240640

Kari, T., Sell, A., Makkonen, M., Wallin, S., Walden, P., Carlsson, C., … & Carlsson, J. (2020). Implementing a digital wellness application into use – challenges and solutions among aged people., 310-328. DOI: 10.1007/978-3-030-50249-2_23

Kumar, A., Bag, A., Anand, A., Saha, S., Mohapatra, H., & Kolhar, M. (2024). Examining healthcare services utilizing cloud technology in intelligent urban environments., 77-98. DOI: 10.4018/979-8-3693-7225-8.ch004

Mosavi, N. and Santos, M. (2021). Implementation considerations for the applied business intelligence in health care., 183-189. DOI: 10.1007/978-981-16-2502-2_19

Ouanes, K. (2024). Transforming medical and health sciences education with gamification.. DOI: 10.5772/intechopen.1005500

Petersson, L., Svedberg, P., Nygren, J., & Larsson, I. (2023). Healthcare leaders' perceptions of the usefulness of ai applications in clinical work: a qualitative study.. DOI: 10.3233/SHTI230235

Rahman, M. and Khatun, F. (2023). Challenges and prospective of ai and 5g-enabled technologies in emerging applications during the pandemic.. DOI: 10.5772/intechopen.109450

Ralfs, L., Hoffmann, N., & Weidner, R. (2022). Approach of a decision support matrix for the implementation of exoskeletons in industrial workplaces., 165-176. DOI: 10.1007/978-3-030-74032-0_14

Reis da Silva, T. H (2024c). Oncology and Cancer Medicine: Understanding the complexities in Older Patients. Biomed J Sci & Tech Res 55(3)-2024. DOI: https://doi.org/DOI: 10.26717/BJSTR.2024.55.008720

Salikutluk, V., Koert, D., & Jäkel, F. (2023). Interacting with large language models: a case study on ai-aided brainstorming for guesstimation problems.. DOI: 10.3233/FAIA230081

Schouten, A. and Mugge, W. (2018). Closed-loop identification to unravel the way the human nervous system controls bodily functions., 617-621. DOI: 10.1007/978-3-030-01845-0_123

Scott, J., Ravichandran, B., Funk, C., Collins, R., & Liu, Y. (2020). From image to stability: learning dynamics from human pose., 536-554. DOI: 10.1007/978-3-030-58592-1_32

Sharifi, S., Namvar, M., Intezari, A., & Akhlaghpour, S. (2024). Healthcare llms go to market: a realist review of product launch news.. DOI: 10.3233/SHTI240513

Sudha, K., Balakrishnan, C., Varun, C., & Subramanıan, R. (2024). Advancements in medical robotics and ai-assisted diagnostics., 23-46. DOI: 10.4018/979-8-3693-3218-4.ch002

Tali, R., Borra, S., & Mahmud, M. (2022). Detection and classification of leukocytes in blood smear images., 1099-1130. DOI: 10.4018/978-1-6684-7544-7.ch057

Turchioe, M., Pepingco, C., Lytle, K., & Austin, R. (2024). Nurses' roles in artificial intelligence implementation: results from a mixed-methods study.. DOI: 10.3233/SHTI240140

Vervloet, T., Ribeiro, F., Batista, P., & Vesco, J. (2023). Technology and innovation in enhancing primary health care: the role of digital solutions in strengthening healthcare systems.. DOI: 10.56238/globalhealthprespesc-022

Veta, M., Diest, P., & Pluim, J. (2016). Cutting out the middleman: measuring nuclear area in histopathology slides without segmentation., 632-639. DOI: 10.1007/978-3-319-46723-8_73

Wang, K., Oramas, J., & Tuytelaars, T. (2021). In defense of lstms for addressing multiple instance learning problems., 444-460. DOI: 10.1007/978-3-030-69544-6_27

Wickramasinghe, N., Ulapane, N., Sloane, E., & Gehlot, V. (2024). Digital twins for more precise and personalized treatment.. DOI: 10.3233/SHTI230961

Zhou, D., Zeng, J., Zeng, X., Li, Y., Wu, Z., Wan, X., … & Su, X. (2019). A novel p53/pomc/gas/sash1 autoregulatory feedback loop and pathologic hyperpigmentation.. DOI: 10.5772/intechopen.81567

Chapter 16
Using AI to Address Demographic-Specific Challenges in Manual Handling Safety

Tiago Manuel Horta Reis da Silva
https://orcid.org/0000-0001-5220-1718
King's College London, UK

ABSTRACT

This chapter explores the application of Artificial Intelligence (AI) in addressing demographic-specific challenges in manual handling safety, focusing on age, gender, and physical capability variations in the workforce. The chapter examines AI-driven ergonomic solutions, predictive analytics, and adaptive training programs. It highlights case studies showcasing AI's role in reducing injury rates and enhancing safety protocols tailored to diverse worker demographics. The discussion concludes with the potential for AI to revolutionise occupational health and safety, ensuring equitable and personalised interventions in manual handling practices.

1. INTRODUCTION

1.1 Overview of Manual Handling Challenges in Diverse Workforce Demographics

Manual handling tasks are a significant source of workplace injuries, particularly in industries that rely heavily on physical labour. The challenges associated with manual handling are exacerbated by the diverse demographics of the workforce, which includes variations in age, gender, and physical capability. Older workers, for instance, may experience a decline in physical strength and flexibility, making them more susceptible to injuries during manual handling tasks (Liu et al., 2020; Horta Reis da Silva, 2022a). Similarly, gender differences can influence physical capabilities and ergonomic needs, with studies indicating that women may face unique challenges in manual handling due to differences in body mechanics and strength compared to their male counterparts (Mirbabaie et al., 2021). Furthermore, workers with

DOI: 10.4018/979-8-3693-9301-7.ch016

varying levels of physical capability, including those with disabilities, may require tailored approaches to manual handling to ensure their safety and effectiveness in the workplace (Pishgar et al., 2021; Horta Reis da Silva, 2022b). The implications of these demographic variations are profound, as they necessitate a reevaluation of existing manual handling protocols and safety measures. Traditional one-size-fits-all approaches to manual handling training and safety may not adequately address the specific needs of a diverse workforce, potentially leading to increased injury rates and decreased productivity (Guzman et al., 2022). Therefore, understanding the demographic-specific challenges in manual handling is crucial for developing effective occupational health and safety strategies that promote the well-being of all workers (Horta Reis da Silva, 2022a).

1.2 Introduction to AI's Role in Occupational Health and Safety

Artificial Intelligence (AI) has emerged as a transformative force in various sectors, including occupational health and safety (OHS). AI technologies can analyse vast amounts of data to identify patterns and predict potential hazards, thereby enhancing workplace safety (Shankar et al., 2022). For instance, AI-driven predictive analytics can be employed to assess the risk factors associated with manual handling tasks, allowing organisations to implement preventive measures tailored to the specific demographics of their workforce (Kim, 2020). Moreover, AI can facilitate the development of adaptive training programs that cater to the unique needs of different worker demographics, ensuring that all employees receive the necessary skills and knowledge to perform manual handling tasks safely (Sharma, 2023). The integration of AI into OHS practices also holds the potential to revolutionise how organisations approach safety management. By leveraging AI technologies, companies can create more dynamic and responsive safety protocols that evolve based on real-time data and feedback from workers (Wagner & Schöne, 2020). This adaptability is particularly important in diverse work environments, where the needs and capabilities of the workforce can vary significantly. As such, AI not only enhances the effectiveness of safety interventions but also promotes a culture of safety that is inclusive and equitable for all employees (Howard, 2024).

1.3 Purpose and Scope

The purpose of this chapter is to explore the application of AI in addressing demographic-specific challenges in manual handling safety. By examining the intersections of age, gender, and physical capability within the workforce, this chapter aims to highlight the importance of tailored safety interventions that consider the unique needs of diverse worker populations. The scope of the chapter includes an analysis of AI-driven ergonomic solutions, predictive analytics, and adaptive training programs designed to enhance manual handling safety across various demographic groups (Fisher et al., 2023). Additionally, this chapter will showcase case studies that illustrate the successful implementation of AI technologies in reducing injury rates and improving safety protocols. These case studies will provide concrete examples of how AI can be leveraged to create safer work environments that accommodate the diverse needs of the workforce (Fukumura et al., 2021). Ultimately, the chapter will conclude with a discussion on the potential for AI to revolutionise occupational health and safety practices, ensuring that all workers, regardless of their demographic characteristics, can perform manual handling tasks safely and effectively (Mariani & Lozada, 2023).

2. LITERATURE REVIEW

Manual handling safety has been a focal point of occupational health research, particularly due to its significant contribution to workplace injuries. Studies have consistently highlighted the ergonomic risks associated with manual handling tasks, which can lead to musculoskeletal disorders (MSDs) among workers (Pishgar et al., 2021; Horta Reis da Silva, 2022c; Reis da Silva, 2023a). Research indicates that improper lifting techniques and inadequate training are primary factors contributing to the high incidence of injuries in manual handling scenarios (Reis da Silva, 2024a; Howard, 2024). Furthermore, the physical demands of manual handling can vary significantly across different demographics, necessitating tailored safety protocols to accommodate these variations (Pishgar et al., 2021). The literature also emphasises the importance of implementing effective training programs that are not only comprehensive but also adaptable to the specific needs of diverse worker populations. For example, Marinaccio et al. (2020) discuss the role of occupational factors in shaping injury risk, particularly during the COVID-19 pandemic, which has underscored the need for robust manual handling safety protocols. Additionally, Pishgar et al. (2021) present a framework for integrating AI into occupational safety, suggesting that AI-driven solutions can enhance training and ergonomic assessments, thereby reducing injury rates associated with manual handling.

Moreover, the intersection of manual handling safety and organisational culture has been explored extensively. Research indicates that a strong safety culture within organisations can significantly mitigate the risks associated with manual handling tasks. This includes fostering an environment where workers feel empowered to report unsafe practices and participate in safety training (Fisher et al., 2023). The literature suggests that organisations that prioritise safety culture not only reduce injury rates but also enhance overall employee satisfaction and productivity (Acemoğlu et al., 2022; Reis da Silva, 2023a).

2.1 The Intersection of AI and Occupational Health

The integration of Artificial Intelligence (AI) into occupational health and safety practices represents a paradigm shift in how organisations approach worker safety. AI technologies have the potential to revolutionise manual handling safety by providing real-time data analysis, predictive analytics, and personalised training solutions. For instance, Howard (2024) discusses the challenges and opportunities presented by AI in managing workplace safety, highlighting its capacity to analyse vast datasets to identify potential hazards before they result in injuries. This proactive approach is particularly beneficial in manual handling scenarios, where the risks can be mitigated through timely interventions. Furthermore, AI can enhance the effectiveness of ergonomic assessments by utilising machine learning algorithms to analyse worker movements and identify risk factors associated with manual handling tasks. This capability allows organisations to tailor safety protocols to the specific needs of their workforce, taking into account individual differences in age, gender, and physical capability (Shah, 2024). Research by Shah (2024) emphasises the advancements in AI technologies that can reshape workplace safety, particularly in preventing occupational diseases and enhancing safety solutions.

The literature also highlights the ethical considerations surrounding the use of AI in occupational health. As AI systems become more integrated into workplace practices, concerns regarding data privacy, algorithmic bias, and the potential for job displacement have emerged (Ronquillo et al., 2021). It is crucial for organisations to address these ethical implications to ensure that AI technologies are implemented responsibly and equitably. For instance, Fisher et al. (2023) discuss the importance of understanding the social structures that influence the development and implementation of AI technologies in the workplace, emphasising the need for inclusive practices that consider the diverse demographics of the workforce. Moreover, the role of AI in enhancing mental health support for workers has gained attention in recent research. AI-driven tools can provide real-time mental health assessments and support, addressing the psychological aspects of manual handling safety (Hasas, 2024). This integration of mental health support into occupational safety frameworks is essential, as it acknowledges the interconnectedness of physical and mental well-being in the workplace.

3. DEMOGRAPHIC-SPECIFIC CHALLENGES IN MANUAL HANDLING

3.1 Age-Related Challenges

Age-related challenges in manual handling are significant, particularly as the workforce ages and the prevalence of older workers increases. Research indicates that manual dexterity and physical capabilities decline with age, impacting workers' ability to perform manual handling tasks effectively (Carment et al., 2018; Reis da Silva, 2023b; Reis da Silva, 2024a). For instance, studies have shown that older adults often experience reduced grip strength and slower reaction times, which can hinder their ability to lift, carry, or manipulate objects safely (Carment et al., 2018; Reis da Silva, 2023b; Reis da Silva, 2024b). This decline in physical capability is compounded by age-related health issues, such as arthritis and other musculoskeletal disorders, which further increase the risk of injury during manual handling activities (Coman et al., 2018; Horta Reis da Silva, 2022c; Reis da Silva, 2023c; Reis da Silva, 2024b).

Moreover, the literature highlights that older workers are more susceptible to specific injuries, particularly low back pain (LBP), due to the cumulative effects of physical strain over their careers (Amer, 2020; Cowley et al., 2023). A systematic review found that factors such as age, body mass index, and gender significantly contribute to the risk of LBP among healthcare workers, emphasising the need for targeted interventions to mitigate these risks (Amer, 2020). Additionally, the physical demands of manual handling tasks can lead to fatigue, which is more pronounced in older workers, thereby increasing the likelihood of accidents and injuries (Lind et al., 2020).

The design of work environments and the implementation of ergonomic interventions are crucial in addressing age-related challenges. For example, Coman et al. (2018) discuss the importance of environmental modifications in aged care settings to enhance mobility and reduce the risk of injury among older workers. Such modifications can include the use of assistive devices, ergonomic tools, and training programs tailored to the specific needs of older employees. By adopting these strategies, organisations can create safer work environments that accommodate the physical limitations of older workers and promote their well-being.

3.2 Gender-Specific Considerations

Gender-specific considerations in manual handling are essential for understanding the unique challenges faced by male and female workers. Research indicates that women often encounter different physical demands and risks compared to their male counterparts, primarily due to physiological differences and societal roles (Kugler, 2024). For instance, women may have less upper body strength on average, which can impact their ability to perform heavy lifting tasks effectively (Sauter et al., 2021). This disparity can lead to increased vulnerability to musculoskeletal injuries, particularly in occupations that require frequent manual handling.

Furthermore, gender roles in the workplace can influence the types of tasks assigned to male and female workers. Studies have shown that women are often tasked with caregiving roles, which may involve lifting and repositioning patients or clients, thereby exposing them to higher risks of injury (Vaara et al., 2021). The literature also highlights that women may be less likely to report injuries or seek help due to social stigma or fear of job loss, which can exacerbate the issue of workplace safety (Bremer & Cairney, 2018). To address these gender-specific challenges, organisations must implement training programs that consider the unique physical capabilities and limitations of both male and female workers. For example, Kugler (2024) emphasises the importance of teaching manual handling through risk assessment, which empowers nursing teams to provide safe mobility-related care tailored to their specific needs. Additionally, fostering an inclusive workplace culture that encourages open communication about safety concerns can help mitigate the risks associated with gender disparities in manual handling tasks.

3.3 Physical Capability and Individual Differences

Physical capability and individual differences play a crucial role in manual handling safety, as workers exhibit a wide range of abilities and limitations. Factors such as body size, strength, and overall fitness level can significantly influence a worker's capacity to perform manual handling tasks safely (Williams et al., 2016). For instance, research has shown that individuals with higher levels of physical fitness and strength are better equipped to handle heavy loads and perform repetitive lifting tasks without sustaining injuries (Sebastjan et al., 2017). Conversely, workers with lower physical capabilities may struggle with these tasks, leading to increased risks of musculoskeletal disorders and other injuries. Moreover, individual differences in experience and training can also impact manual handling safety. Workers who have received comprehensive training in safe lifting techniques and ergonomic practices are generally more adept at performing manual handling tasks without injury (Yan, 2024). However, those lacking proper training may resort to unsafe practices, increasing their risk of injury (Ranavolo et al., 2020). Therefore, organisations must prioritise training and education to ensure that all workers, regardless of their physical capabilities, are equipped with the knowledge and skills necessary to perform manual handling tasks safely.

Additionally, the implementation of assistive technologies and ergonomic tools can help accommodate individual differences in physical capability. For example, the use of powered lifting devices or adjustable workstations can reduce the physical strain associated with manual handling tasks, making them more accessible for workers with varying abilities (Saroya, 2024). By recognising and addressing the diverse physical capabilities of their workforce, organisations can create safer and more inclusive work environments that promote the health and well-being of all employees.

4. AI APPLICATIONS IN MANUAL HANDLING SAFETY

4.1 AI-Driven Ergonomic Assessments

AI-driven ergonomic assessments represent a significant advancement in the field of manual handling safety. These assessments use machine learning algorithms and data analytics to evaluate the physical demands of manual handling tasks and identify potential ergonomic risks (Eetvelde et al., 2021). By analysing data collected from wearable sensors, cameras, and other monitoring devices, AI systems can provide real-time feedback on workers' movements and postures, allowing for immediate adjustments to reduce the risk of injury (Pant et al., 2021). For instance, Eetvelde et al. (2021) highlight the effectiveness of machine learning methods in predicting injury risks associated with specific movements during manual handling tasks. These AI-driven assessments can analyse individual worker data, such as body mechanics and movement patterns, to tailor ergonomic interventions that meet the specific needs of each worker. This personalised approach not only enhances safety but also improves overall productivity by ensuring that workers are operating within their physical capabilities (Padula, 2024). Moreover, the integration of AI in ergonomic assessments allows for continuous monitoring and evaluation of manual handling practices. By employing predictive analytics, organisations can identify trends and patterns in injury occurrences, enabling them to proactively implement preventive measures (Bittencourt et al., 2016). This shift from reactive to proactive safety management is crucial in reducing the incidence of musculoskeletal disorders (MSDs) associated with manual handling tasks (Cho et al., 2023).

4.2 Predictive Analytics for Injury Prevention

Predictive analytics has emerged as a powerful tool for preventing injuries in manual handling contexts. By utilising historical data and advanced statistical algorithms, organisations can identify risk factors associated with manual handling tasks and predict potential injury occurrences (Hewett et al., 2016). This proactive approach enables organisations to implement targeted interventions before injuries occur, thereby enhancing workplace safety. Research by Jiang et al. (2022) demonstrates the effectiveness of predictive analytics in identifying high-risk individuals in various settings, which can be extrapolated to manual handling scenarios. By analysing data related to worker demographics, physical capabilities, and past injury records, organisations can develop predictive models that highlight individuals at greater risk for injuries during manual handling tasks. This targeted approach allows for the allocation of resources and training to those who need it most, ultimately reducing injury rates (Xu et al., 2023). Furthermore, the application of predictive analytics extends beyond individual assessments. Organisations can analyse aggregate data to identify trends and patterns in injury occurrences across different departments or job roles (Mousavi-Shalmaei, 2023). This information can inform organisational policies and training programs, ensuring that safety measures are aligned with the specific risks associated with various manual handling tasks (Koklesová et al., 2021). The use of predictive analytics also facilitates the continuous improvement of safety protocols. By regularly updating predictive models with new data, organisations can refine their injury prevention strategies and adapt to changing workforce dynamics (Thisani, 2024). This iterative process is essential for maintaining a culture of safety and ensuring that manual handling practices remain effective in mitigating risks. In conclusion, predictive analytics serves as a vital component of injury prevention strategies in manual handling contexts. By leveraging data-driven insights, organisations can proactively address potential risks and enhance the overall safety of their workforce.

4.3 Adaptive AI-Based Training Programs

Adaptive AI-based training programs represent a transformative approach to enhancing manual handling safety. These programs utilise artificial intelligence to tailor training content and delivery methods to the individual needs of workers, ensuring that each employee receives the most relevant and effective training (Pathak, 2023). By analysing data on workers' performance, learning styles, and physical capabilities, AI systems can customise training modules that address specific ergonomic risks associated with manual handling tasks (Dar et al., 2022). Research indicates that personalised training programs significantly improve knowledge retention and skill acquisition compared to traditional one-size-fits-all training approaches (Tranæus et al., 2021). For example, Tama et al. (2022) found that adaptive training interventions led to a marked reduction in injury rates among healthcare workers engaged in manual handling tasks. By providing targeted training that aligns with workers' unique needs, organisations can enhance their employees' ability to perform manual handling tasks safely and effectively. Moreover, adaptive AI-based training programs can incorporate real-time feedback mechanisms, allowing workers to receive immediate guidance on their performance during training exercises (Wine, 2024).

This interactive approach not only reinforces safe practices but also fosters a culture of continuous learning and improvement within the organisation (Zhang et al., 2022). The implementation of AI-driven training programs also facilitates ongoing assessment and evaluation of training effectiveness. By analysing data on training outcomes and injury incidents, organisations can refine their training content and delivery methods to ensure that they remain relevant and effective (Kolenia & Domaradzki, 2021). This data-driven approach to training enhances the overall safety culture within organisations and empowers workers to take ownership of their safety practices.

5. CASE STUDIES

Case Study 1: AI Implementation in a Multigenerational Workforce

The integration of Artificial Intelligence (AI) into manual handling safety protocols has been particularly beneficial in organisations with a multigenerational workforce. For instance, a large healthcare facility in the United States implemented an AI-driven ergonomic assessment tool designed to cater to the diverse physical capabilities of its employees, ranging from younger staff to older, more experienced workers. This tool used machine learning algorithms to analyse the lifting techniques and postures of employees during patient handling tasks, providing real-time feedback and personalised recommendations for improvement (Choi & Brings, 2016).

The facility's management noted a significant reduction in work-related musculoskeletal disorders (WMSDs) following the implementation of this AI system (Horta Reis da Silva, 2022c). By tailoring ergonomic interventions to the specific needs of different age groups, the organisation was able to enhance safety and efficiency in manual handling tasks (Reis da Silva, 2023a). Older workers, who often face age-related physical limitations, benefited from customised training modules that emphasised safe lifting techniques and the use of assistive devices (Coman et al., 2018). Meanwhile, younger employees received training focused on developing strength and endurance to handle physically demanding tasks effectively.

Moreover, the AI system facilitated ongoing monitoring and evaluation of manual handling practices, allowing the organisation to adapt its training programs based on emerging trends and injury data. This proactive approach not only improved worker safety but also fostered a culture of continuous learning and adaptation within the multigenerational workforce. Overall, the case study highlights the potential of AI to bridge generational gaps in the workplace by providing tailored solutions that enhance manual handling safety for all employees.

Case Study 2: Gender-Specific AI Solutions in Manual Handling

In another case study, a manufacturing company in Europe adopted gender-specific AI solutions to address the unique challenges faced by its male and female workforce in manual handling tasks. Recognising that women often encounter different physical demands and risks compared to men, the company implemented an AI-driven training program that tailored its content to the specific needs of female employees (Hegewald et al., 2018).

The AI system analysed data on the physical capabilities and injury histories of female workers, allowing the company to develop training modules that focused on safe lifting techniques and the use of ergonomic tools designed for smaller body frames (Reis da Silva, 2025a). This approach was particularly important in a manufacturing environment where heavy lifting and repetitive motions were common, leading to a higher incidence of musculoskeletal injuries among female workers (Brusco et al., 2023; Horta Reis da Silva, 2022c).

Following the implementation of these gender-specific training programs, the company reported a notable decrease in injury rates among female employees. Additionally, the AI system provided ongoing assessments of workers' performance, enabling the company to refine its training content continually and ensure that it remained relevant to the needs of its workforce. This case study underscores the importance of recognising gender differences in manual handling safety and the potential of AI to create tailored solutions that enhance worker safety and well-being.

Case Study 3: AI-Based Customisation for Workers with Physical Limitations

A notable case study involved a logistics company that implemented AI-based customisation strategies to accommodate workers with physical limitations. The company recognised that a significant portion of its workforce included individuals with varying degrees of physical capability, including those with disabilities or chronic health conditions that affected their ability to perform manual handling tasks (Das, 2023; Reis da Silva, 2024c; Reis da Silva, 2024d).

To address these challenges, the company developed an AI-driven platform that assessed individual workers' physical capabilities and provided customised recommendations for manual handling tasks (Reis da Silva, 2025b; Reis da Silva, 2025c). The platform used data from wearable sensors to monitor workers' movements and identify ergonomic risks associated with specific tasks. Based on this analysis, the AI system suggested alternative methods for handling loads, such as using assistive devices or modifying lifting techniques to minimise strain (Ranavolo et al., 2020; Reis da Silva, 2025d; Reis da Silva, 2025e).

The implementation of this AI-based customisation not only improved safety for workers with physical limitations but also enhanced overall productivity within the organisation. Workers reported feeling more empowered and capable of performing their tasks safely, leading to increased job satisfaction and retention rates. Furthermore, the company observed a reduction in injury claims related to manual handling, demonstrating the effectiveness of personalised interventions in promoting workplace safety. This case study illustrates the transformative potential of AI in creating inclusive work environments that accommodate the diverse needs of all employees.

Case Study 4: Addressing Elder Abuse in Manual Handling through AI in Nursing Care

Elder abuse is a significant and often underreported issue that affects the well-being of older adults, particularly those in nursing care settings (Reis da Silva, 2024e). The COVID-19 pandemic has exacerbated the prevalence of elder abuse, with studies indicating that a substantial proportion of elder abuse cases identified during this period were serious in nature (Chang & Levy, 2021). As healthcare providers, nurses play a crucial role in identifying and addressing elder abuse, yet many report feeling inadequately prepared to intervene effectively (Mydin & Othman, 2017; Reis da Silva, 2024e). The case study focuses on a nursing home in the United States that serves a diverse population of older adults, many of whom have complex physical and psychological needs. The facility has recently adopted AI-driven tools to assist nursing staff in manual handling tasks, with the dual aim of improving safety and reducing the risk of elder abuse (Reis da Silva, 2024f).

The nursing home implemented an AI-based ergonomic assessment system designed to monitor manual handling practices among staff (Reis da Silva, 2025b). This system utilises wearable sensors to track the movements and postures of nursing staff during patient transfers and other manual handling tasks. The AI algorithms analyse this data in real-time, providing feedback on safe lifting techniques and alerting staff to potentially harmful practices that could lead to injuries for both caregivers and residents (Sousa et al., 2021). In addition to ergonomic assessments, the AI system includes a reporting feature that allows nursing staff to document any observed signs of elder abuse or neglect. This feature is integrated with the facility's electronic health records (EHR), enabling seamless communication among healthcare providers and ensuring that any concerns are promptly addressed. Staff members receive training on how to use the AI tools effectively, with a focus on recognizing the signs of elder abuse and understanding the appropriate reporting protocols (Wang et al., 2020).

The implementation of AI technologies in the nursing home has led to several positive outcomes. First, the ergonomic assessment system has significantly reduced the incidence of work-related injuries among nursing staff, which has, in turn, improved the quality of care provided to residents. With fewer injuries, staff members are better able to engage with residents and provide attentive care, reducing the likelihood of frustration and burnout that can contribute to elder abuse (Ribeiro et al., 2023). Moreover, the AI reporting feature has increased awareness of elder abuse among nursing staff. Training sessions have emphasised the importance of recognizing and reporting abuse, leading to a culture of vigilance and accountability within the facility. As a result, the nursing home has seen an increase in reported cases of suspected elder abuse, allowing for timely interventions and support for affected residents (Roberto et al., 2020).

Despite the positive outcomes, the nursing home faced challenges in the implementation of AI technologies. Some staff members expressed concerns about the surveillance aspect of the wearable sensors, fearing that they would be monitored excessively (Fang et al., 2022; Reis da Silva, 2025d). To address these concerns, the facility organised open discussions with staff to clarify the purpose of the technology and emphasise its role in enhancing safety rather than punitive measures. Additionally, the integration of AI tools into existing workflows required ongoing training and support for nursing staff. Ensuring that all employees were comfortable using the technology and understood its benefits was essential for successful adoption (Combes et al., 2021).

6. BENEFITS AND LIMITATIONS OF AI IN MANUAL HANDLING SAFETY

6.1 Advantages of AI Integration

The integration of Artificial Intelligence (AI) into manual handling safety protocols offers numerous advantages that can significantly enhance workplace safety and efficiency. One of the primary benefits is the ability of AI systems to conduct real-time ergonomic assessments. By using machine learning algorithms and data analytics, AI can analyse workers' movements and postures during manual handling tasks, providing immediate feedback and recommendations for safer practices (Pishgar et al., 2021). This proactive approach helps to identify potential risks before they result in injuries, thereby reducing the incidence of work-related musculoskeletal disorders (WMSDs) (Reis da Silva, 2023a; Nweke, 2024).

Additionally, AI can facilitate predictive analytics for injury prevention. By analysing historical data on workplace injuries and worker demographics, AI systems can identify patterns and risk factors associated with manual handling tasks (Reis da Silva, 2023a). This information allows organisations to implement targeted interventions tailored to the specific needs of their workforce, ultimately enhancing safety and productivity (Qadhi, 2024). For instance, predictive models can help organisations allocate resources more effectively, ensuring that training and ergonomic tools are directed toward high-risk groups (Nweke, 2024).

Moreover, AI-driven adaptive training programs can be customised to meet the unique needs of individual workers. These programs utilise data on workers' performance and learning styles to deliver personalised training content, ensuring that each employee receives the most relevant and effective instruction (Bankins & Formosa, 2023; Reis da Silva and Mitchell, 2024). Research has shown that personalised training significantly improves knowledge retention and skill acquisition, leading to safer manual handling practices (Köbis & Mehner, 2021).

6.2 Ethical Considerations and Privacy Concerns

Despite the numerous benefits of AI integration, ethical considerations and privacy concerns pose significant challenges. As AI systems collect and analyse vast amounts of data on workers' movements and behaviours, issues related to data privacy and consent become paramount (Reis da Silva, 2025d). Workers may feel uncomfortable with the extent of surveillance required for AI-driven assessments, raising concerns about their autonomy and privacy rights (Waheed, 2024; Reis da Silva, 2025c). It is essential for organisations to establish clear policies regarding data collection, usage, and storage to ensure that workers' personal information is protected (Reis da Silva, 2025d).

Furthermore, the potential for algorithmic bias in AI systems presents ethical dilemmas that must be addressed (Reis da Silva, 2025b). If AI algorithms are trained on biased data, they may inadvertently perpetuate existing inequalities in the workplace, leading to unfair treatment of certain demographic groups (Chen et al., 2022). For example, if an AI system is primarily trained on data from younger, physically fit workers, it may not accurately assess the risks faced by older or differently-abled employees, resulting in inadequate safety measures for these groups (Kooli & Muftah, 2022). To mitigate these ethical concerns, organisations must adopt a comprehensive approach to AI ethics that includes transparency, accountability, and inclusivity in the development and deployment of AI systems. Engaging workers in discussions about AI implementation and ensuring that diverse perspectives are considered can help foster trust and acceptance of AI technologies in the workplace (Valerio, 2024).

6.3 Limitations and Challenges in AI Adoption

The adoption of AI in manual handling safety is not without its limitations and challenges. One of the primary barriers to AI implementation is the high initial cost associated with developing and deploying AI systems. Organisations may face significant financial constraints that hinder their ability to invest in advanced technologies, particularly small and medium-sized enterprises (SMEs) (Yazdani, 2023). Additionally, the costs associated with training employees to use AI systems effectively can further complicate the adoption process (Singh, 2024).

Another challenge is the potential resistance from workers who may be apprehensive about the introduction of AI technologies in their workplace. Concerns about job displacement and the perceived threat of automation can lead to scepticism and reluctance to embrace AI solutions (Ayoun et al., 2015). It is crucial for organisations to communicate the benefits of AI integration clearly and involve workers in the decision-making process to alleviate fears and foster a culture of collaboration (Birkhoff et al., 2021). Moreover, the complexity of AI systems can pose challenges in terms of implementation and maintenance. Organisations may struggle to integrate AI technologies with existing systems and processes, leading to disruptions in workflow and productivity (Abukhadijah, 2024). Additionally, the need for ongoing monitoring and updates to AI algorithms can place a strain on organisational resources, particularly in industries with rapidly changing conditions (Reis da Silva, 2025f).

7. FUTURE DIRECTIONS

7.1 Innovations in AI for Occupational Health

The future of occupational health is poised for significant transformation through the continued integration of Artificial Intelligence (AI) technologies. Innovations in AI are expected to enhance the precision and efficiency of health monitoring systems, enabling real-time assessments of worker health and safety. For instance, AI algorithms can analyse data from wearable devices to monitor physiological parameters such as heart rate, body temperature, and movement patterns, providing immediate feedback to workers and managers about potential health risks (Matheny et al., 2020; Reis da Silva, 2025f). This proactive approach can facilitate early interventions, reducing the likelihood of work-related injuries and illnesses.

Moreover, advancements in natural language processing (NLP) and machine learning can enhance the analysis of unstructured data, such as incident reports and employee feedback, to identify trends and areas for improvement in workplace safety (Rilkoff, 2024). By leveraging these technologies, organisations can develop more effective safety protocols and training programs tailored to the specific needs of their workforce. Additionally, AI can support the development of predictive models that forecast potential health risks based on historical data, allowing organisations to implement preventive measures before issues arise (Bécue, 2024).

As AI technologies continue to evolve, their application in occupational health will likely expand to include more sophisticated tools for mental health monitoring and support. AI-driven platforms can provide personalised mental health assessments and interventions, helping organisations address the psychological well-being of their employees (Doki et al., 2021; Reis da Silva, 2025a). This holistic approach to worker health, encompassing both physical and mental aspects, is essential for fostering a safe and productive work environment.

7.2 Potential for AI to Create Safer, More Inclusive Work Environments

The potential for AI to create safer and more inclusive work environments is significant. By using AI-driven tools, organisations can better accommodate the diverse needs of their workforce, including those of older workers, individuals with disabilities, and employees from various demographic backgrounds (Reis da Silva, 2025c). For example, AI can assist in designing ergonomic workspaces that adapt to the physical capabilities of individual workers, thereby reducing the risk of injuries associated with manual handling tasks (Serag et al., 2019; Reis da Silva, 2025f).

Furthermore, AI can facilitate the development of inclusive training programs that consider the unique learning styles and needs of different employee groups. By providing personalised training experiences, organisations can ensure that all workers are equipped with the knowledge and skills necessary to perform their jobs safely (Saadati, 2023). This approach not only enhances safety but also promotes a culture of inclusivity and respect within the workplace.

Additionally, AI can play a crucial role in identifying and mitigating biases in workplace practices. By analysing data on hiring, promotions, and training opportunities, AI systems can help organisations uncover disparities and implement strategies to promote equity and diversity (Matheny et al., 2020). This commitment to inclusivity is essential for fostering a positive work environment where all employees feel valued and supported.

7.3 Recommendations for Policymakers and Industry Stakeholders

To maximise the benefits of AI in occupational health and safety, policymakers and industry stakeholders must collaborate to establish clear guidelines and standards for AI implementation. This includes developing regulations that ensure data privacy and security, as well as ethical considerations surrounding the use of AI technologies in the workplace (Doki et al., 2021). Policymakers should prioritise the creation of frameworks that promote transparency and accountability in AI systems, ensuring that workers' rights are protected. Moreover, investment in education and training programs is essential to equip the workforce with the skills needed to effectively utilize AI technologies. Industry stakeholders should collaborate with educational institutions to develop curricula that focus on AI literacy and its applications in occupational health (Lee et al., 2019; Reis da Silva and Mitchell, 2024). By fostering a workforce that is knowledgeable about AI, organisations can enhance the successful adoption and integration of these technologies.

Finally, ongoing research and evaluation of AI applications in occupational health are crucial for understanding their impact and effectiveness. Policymakers and industry stakeholders should support initiatives that assess the outcomes of AI-driven interventions, providing valuable insights that can inform future practices and innovations (Islam, 2024). By prioritizing research and collaboration, stakeholders can ensure that AI technologies are leveraged to create safer, healthier, and more inclusive work environments.

8. CONCLUSION

8.1 Summary of Key Findings

This chapter has explored the application of Artificial Intelligence (AI) in addressing demographic-specific challenges in manual handling safety. Key findings indicate that AI-driven ergonomic assessments, predictive analytics for injury prevention, and adaptive training programs can significantly enhance workplace safety for diverse worker populations. The integration of AI technologies has the potential to reduce injury rates, improve training effectiveness, and foster a culture of safety that accommodates the unique needs of all employees.

8.2 Contribution to the Sustainable Development Goals

In this chapter, it was examined how AI innovations have transformed various aspects of occupational health and safety (OHS), with a focus on predictive analytics, machine learning algorithms, and real-time monitoring systems. These technologies have significantly improved risk management, incident reporting, and compliance monitoring across diverse industries. The integration of AI in OHS practices has not only enhanced workplace safety but also contributed to sustainable business operations by minimizing health risks and promoting a safer working environment.

The current chapter extends this discussion by aligning AI-driven solutions in manual handling with the United Nations Sustainable Development Goals (SDGs), particularly SDG 3 (Good Health and Well-being) and SDG 8 (Decent Work and Economic Growth) (da Silva and Rodrigues, 2023). AI technologies, when applied to demographic-specific challenges in manual handling, can foster healthier workplaces by reducing the incidence of work-related musculoskeletal disorders (WMSDs) (Horta Reis da Silva, 2022c). This directly supports SDG 3 by enhancing the well-being of workers through targeted interventions and adaptive training programs.

Moreover, by creating safer and more inclusive working conditions, AI aligns with SDG 8, which emphasises the promotion of safe and secure working environments for all workers, including those in vulnerable situations such as older adults and individuals with physical limitations (Reis da Silva, 2023). The use of AI in tailoring safety protocols to meet the specific needs of diverse demographic groups ensures that economic growth is not achieved at the expense of worker health and safety, thereby promoting equitable and sustainable development.

In this context, AI not only addresses immediate safety concerns but also contributes to the broader agenda of sustainable development by fostering environments that prioritise the health, well-being, and dignity of all workers. This approach underscores the importance of leveraging advanced technologies in pursuit of both corporate and global sustainability objectives.

8.3 Implications for the Future of Manual Handling Safety

The implications of these findings for the future of manual handling safety are profound. As organisations increasingly adopt AI technologies, they can expect to see improvements in worker safety, productivity, and overall job satisfaction. By leveraging AI to create tailored interventions that address the specific challenges faced by different demographic groups, organisations can enhance their safety protocols and promote a more inclusive work environment.

Moreover, the ongoing evolution of AI technologies will likely lead to further innovations in occupational health and safety practices. As AI systems become more sophisticated, their ability to analyse complex data sets and provide actionable insights will empower organisations to make informed decisions that prioritise worker health and safety (Ibrahim et al., 2021). This proactive approach to safety management is essential for adapting to the changing dynamics of the modern workforce.

8.4 Final Thoughts on the Transformative Potential of AI in Occupational Health

In conclusion, the transformative potential of AI in occupational health is immense. By harnessing the capabilities of AI technologies, organisations can create safer, more inclusive work environments that prioritize the well-being of all employees. As the field of occupational health continues to evolve, it is imperative for stakeholders to embrace AI innovations and collaborate to establish ethical guidelines and best practices for their implementation. By doing so, they can ensure that the benefits of AI are realized while safeguarding the rights and dignity of workers in the evolving landscape of work.

REFERENCES

Abukhadijah, H., & Nashwan, A. J. (2024). Transforming hospital quality improvement through harnessing the power of artificial intelligence. *Global Journal on Quality and Safety in Healthcare, 7*(3), 132–139. DOI: 10.36401/JQSH-24-4 PMID: 39104802

Acemoğlu, D., Autor, D., Hazell, J., & Restrepo, P. (2022). Artificial intelligence and jobs: Evidence from online vacancies. *Journal of Labor Economics, 40*(S1), S293–S340. DOI: 10.1086/718327

Amer, H. (2020). Low back pain prevalence and risk factors among health workers in Saudi Arabia: A systematic review and meta-analysis. *Journal of Occupational Health, 62*(1), e12155. Advance online publication. DOI: 10.1002/1348-9585.12155 PMID: 32710807

Ayoun, B., Rowe, L., & Yassine, F. (2015). Is workplace spirituality associated with business ethics? *International Journal of Contemporary Hospitality Management, 27*(5), 938–957. DOI: 10.1108/IJCHM-01-2014-0018

Bankins, S., & Formosa, P. (2023). The ethical implications of artificial intelligence (ai) for meaningful work. *Journal of Business Ethics, 185*(4), 725–740. DOI: 10.1007/s10551-023-05339-7

Bécue, A., Gama, J., & Brito, P. Q. (2024). Ai's effect on innovation capacity in the context of industry 5.0: A scoping review. *Artificial Intelligence Review, 57*(8), 215. Advance online publication. DOI: 10.1007/s10462-024-10864-6

Birkhoff, D., Dalen, A., & Schijven, M. (2021). A review on the current applications of artificial intelligence in the operating room. *Surgical Innovation, 28*(5), 611–619. DOI: 10.1177/1553350621996961 PMID: 33625307

Bittencourt, N., Meeuwisse, W., Mendonça, L., Nettel-Aguirre, A., Ocarino, J., & Fonseca, S. (2016). Complex systems approach for sports injuries: Moving from risk factor identification to injury pattern recognition—narrative review and new concept. *British Journal of Sports Medicine, 50*(21), 1309–1314. DOI: 10.1136/bjsports-2015-095850 PMID: 27445362

Bremer, E., & Cairney, J. (2018). The interrelationship between motor coordination and adaptive behavior in children with autism spectrum disorder. *Frontiers in Psychology, 9*, 2350. Advance online publication. DOI: 10.3389/fpsyg.2018.02350 PMID: 30538659

Brusco, N., Haines, T., Taylor, N., Rawson, H., Boyd, L., Ekegren, C., & Graven, C. (2023). In Australian hospitals and residential aged care facilities, how do we train nursing and direct care staff to assist patients and residents to move? a national survey. *Australian Health Review, 47*(3), 331–338. DOI: 10.1071/AH22296 PMID: 37211193

Carment, L., Abdellatif, A., Lafuente-Lafuente, C., Pariel, S., Maier, M., Belmin, J., & Lindberg, P. (2018). Manual dexterity and aging: A pilot study disentangling sensorimotor from cognitive decline. *Frontiers in Neurology, 9*, 910. Advance online publication. DOI: 10.3389/fneur.2018.00910 PMID: 30420830

Chang, E., & Levy, B. (2021). High prevalence of elder abuse during the covid-19 pandemic: Risk and resilience factors. *The American Journal of Geriatric Psychiatry, 29*(11), 1152–1159. DOI: 10.1016/j.jagp.2021.01.007 PMID: 33518464

Chen, H., Lin, S., & Chen, I. (2022). Better safe than sorry: The role of anticipated regret and organizational ethical climate in predicting workplace safety behavior. *Chinese Management Studies, 18*(1), 48–70. DOI: 10.1108/CMS-10-2021-0446

Cho, I., Kim, M., Song, M., & Dykes, P. (2023). Evaluation of an approach to clinical decision support for preventing inpatient falls: A pragmatic trial. *JAMIA Open*, *6*(2), ooad019. Advance online publication. DOI: 10.1093/jamiaopen/ooad019 PMID: 37033322

Choi, S., & Brings, K. (2016). Work-related musculoskeletal risks associated with nurses and nursing assistants handling overweight and obese patients: A literature review. *Work (Reading, Mass.)*, *53*(2), 439–448. DOI: 10.3233/WOR-152222 PMID: 26835850

Coman, R., Caponecchia, C., & McIntosh, A. (2018). Manual handling in aged care: Impact of environment-related interventions on mobility. *Safety and Health at Work*, *9*(4), 372–380. DOI: 10.1016/j.shaw.2018.02.003 PMID: 30559984

Combes, S., Forbes, G., Gillett, K., Norton, C., & Nicholson, C. (2021). Development of a theory-based intervention to increase cognitively able frail elders' engagement with advance care planning using the behaviour change wheel. *BMC Health Services Research*, *21*(1), 712. Advance online publication. DOI: 10.1186/s12913-021-06548-4 PMID: 34284759

Cowley, S. A., Tzouvara, V., & Horta Reis da Silva, T. (2023). Public Health: healthy ageing and wellbeing. In Redfern's Nursing Older People. Fifth edition. Editors: Ross, Harris, Fitzpatrick and Abley. Elsevier.

da Silva, T. H. R., & Rodrigues, E. C. P. (2023). Body Image Related Discrimination. In Leal Filho, W., Azul, A. M., Brandli, L., Lange Salvia, A., Özuyar, P. G., & Wall, T. (Eds.), *Reduced Inequalities. Encyclopedia of the UN Sustainable Development Goals*. Springer., DOI: 10.1007/978-3-319-71060-0_61-1

Dar, J., Aijaz, M., Almanjahie, I., & Warke, A. (2022). Estimation of heat diffusion in human tissue at adverse temperatures using the cylindrical form of bioheat equation. *Mathematics*, *10*(20), 3820. DOI: 10.3390/math10203820

Das, B. (2023). Adverse health effects and perceived musculoskeletal pain in the sawmill workers of west Bengal, India. *Toxicology and Industrial Health*, *40*(1-2), 9–22. DOI: 10.1177/07482337231210331 PMID: 37877376

Doki, S., Sasahara, S., Hori, D., Oi, Y., Takahashi, T., Shiraki, N., Ikeda, Y., Ikeda, T., Arai, Y., Muroi, K., & Matsuzaki, I. (2021). Comparison of predicted psychological distress among workers between artificial intelligence and psychiatrists: A cross-sectional study in Tsukuba science city, Japan. *BMJ Open*, *11*(6), e046265. DOI: 10.1136/bmjopen-2020-046265 PMID: 34162646

Eetvelde, H., Mendonça, L., Ley, C., Seil, R., & Tischer, T. (2021). Machine learning methods in sport injury prediction and prevention: A systematic review. *Journal of Experimental Orthopaedics*, *8*(1), 27. Advance online publication. DOI: 10.1186/s40634-021-00346-x PMID: 33855647

Fang, B., Li, D., Yan, E., Zhou, Y., Yu, Z., & Hu, J. (2022). Associated factors of discrepancy between older adults and their family caregivers in reporting elder abuse. *Journal of Clinical Nursing*, *32*(5-6), 688–700. DOI: 10.1111/jocn.16283 PMID: 35289011

Fisher, E., Flynn, M., Pratap, P., & Vietas, J. (2023). Occupational safety and health equity impacts of artificial intelligence: A scoping review. *International Journal of Environmental Research and Public Health, 20*(13), 6221. DOI: 10.3390/ijerph20136221 PMID: 37444068

Fukumura, Y., Gray, J., Lucas, G., Becerik-Gerber, B., & Roll, S. (2021). Worker perspectives on incorporating artificial intelligence into office workspaces: Implications for the future of office work. *International Journal of Environmental Research and Public Health, 18*(4), 1690. DOI: 10.3390/ijerph18041690 PMID: 33578736

Guzman, J., Recoco, G., Pandi, A., Padrones, J., & Ignacio, J. (2022). Evaluating workplace safety in the oil and gas industry during the covid-19 pandemic using occupational health and safety vulnerability measure and partial least square structural equation modelling. *Cleaner Engineering and Technology, 6*, 100378. DOI: 10.1016/j.clet.2021.100378 PMID: 35013732

Hasas, A., Hakimi, M., Shahidzay, A. K., & Fazil, A. W. (2024). Ai for social good: Leveraging artificial intelligence for community development. J. Communit. Service. Society. *Empower., 2*(02), 196–210. DOI: 10.59653/jcsse.v2i02.592

Hegewald, J., Berge, W., Heinrich, P., Staudte, R., Freiberg, A., Scharfe, J., Girbig, M., Nienhaus, A., & Seidler, A. (2018). Do technical aids for patient handling prevent musculoskeletal complaints in health care workers?—A systematic review of intervention studies. *International Journal of Environmental Research and Public Health, 15*(3), 476. DOI: 10.3390/ijerph15030476 PMID: 29522440

Hewett, T., Myer, G., Ford, K., Paterno, M., & Quatman, C. (2016). Mechanisms, prediction, and prevention of ACL injuries: Cut risk with three sharpened and validated tools. *Journal of Orthopaedic Research, 34*(11), 1843–1855. DOI: 10.1002/jor.23414 PMID: 27612195

Horta Reis Da Silva, T. (2022a). Moving and Handling. In Curr, S., & Fordham-Clarke, C. (Eds.), *Clinical Skills at Glance* (pp. 20–21). Wiley.

Horta Reis Da Silva, T. (2022b). Moving and Handling: turning in bed, transfer and hoisting. In Curr, S., & Fordham-Clarke, C. (Eds.), *Clinical Skills at Glance* (pp. 22–23). Wiley.

Horta Reis Da Silva, T. (2022c). Muskuloskeletal minor injuries: assessment and treatment. In Curr, S., & Fordham-Clarke, C. (Eds.), *Clinical Skills at Glance* (1st ed., pp. 128–129). Wiley. [55]

Howard, J., & Schulte, P. (2024). Managing workplace ai risks and the future of work. *American Journal of Industrial Medicine, 67*(11), 980–993. DOI: 10.1002/ajim.23653 PMID: 39223704

Ibrahim, H., Liu, X., Rivera, S., Moher, D., Chan, A., Sydes, M., Calvert, M. J., & Denniston, A. (2021). Reporting guidelines for clinical trials of artificial intelligence interventions: The spirit-ai and consort-ai guidelines. *Trials, 22*(1), 11. Advance online publication. DOI: 10.1186/s13063-020-04951-6 PMID: 33407780

Islam, M. (2024). Exploring the impact of artificial intelligence in healthcare. *JAIGS, 2*(1), 228–238. DOI: 10.60087/jaigs.v2i1.109

Jiang, Z., Hao, Y., Jin, N., & Li, Y. (2022). A systematic review of the relationship between workload and injury risk of professional male soccer players. *International Journal of Environmental Research and Public Health, 19*(20), 13237. DOI: 10.3390/ijerph192013237 PMID: 36293817

Kim, K. (2020). Exploring the influence of workplace violence and bystander behaviour on patient safety in Korea: A pilot study. *Journal of Nursing Management, 28*(3), 735–743. DOI: 10.1111/jonm.12991 PMID: 32124510

Köbis, L., & Mehner, C. (2021). Ethical questions raised by ai-supported mentoring in higher education. *Frontiers in Artificial Intelligence, 4*, 624050. Advance online publication. DOI: 10.3389/frai.2021.624050 PMID: 33997774

Koklesová, L., Samec, M., Líšková, A., Zhai, K., Büsselberg, D., Giordano, F., Kubatka, P., & Golunitschaja, O. (2021). Mitochondrial impairments in aetiopathology of multifactorial diseases: Common origin but individual outcomes in context of 3p medicine. *The EPMA Journal, 12*(1), 27–40. DOI: 10.1007/s13167-021-00237-2 PMID: 33686350

Kolenia, D., & Domaradzki, J. (2021). Prediction and injury risk based on movement patterns and flexibility in a 6-month prospective study among physically active adults. *PeerJ, 9*, e11399. DOI: 10.7717/peerj.11399 PMID: 34046260

Kooli, C., & Muftah, H. (2022). Artificial intelligence in healthcare: A comprehensive review of its ethical concerns. *Technological Sustainability, 1*(2), 121–131. DOI: 10.1108/TECHS-12-2021-0029

Kugler, H., Brusco, N., Slade, S., Boyd, L., & Taylor, N. (2024). Teaching manual handling through risk assessment empowers the nursing team to provide safe mobility-related care: A qualitative analysis. *Focus on Health Professional Education a Multi-Professional Journal, 25*(1), 51–68. DOI: 10.11157/fohpe.v25i1.656

Lee, J., Suh, T., Roy, D., & Baucus, M. (2019). Emerging technology and business model innovation: The case of artificial intelligence. *Journal of Open Innovation, 5*(3), 44. DOI: 10.3390/joitmc5030044

Lind, C., Diaz-Olivares, J., Lindecrantz, K., & Eklund, J. (2020). A wearable sensor system for physical ergonomics interventions using haptic feedback. *Sensors (Basel), 20*(21), 6010. DOI: 10.3390/s20216010 PMID: 33113922

Liu, S., Nkrumah, E., Akoto, L., Gyabeng, E., & Nkrumah, E. (2020). The state of occupational health and safety management frameworks (OHSMF) and occupational injuries and accidents in the Ghanaian oil and gas industry: assessing the mediating role of safety knowledge. Biomed Research International, 2020(1). DOI: 10.1155/2020/6354895

Mariani, K., & Lozada, F. (2023). The use of ai and algorithms for decision-making in workplace recruitment practices. *Journal of Student Research, 12*(1). Advance online publication. DOI: 10.47611/jsr.v12i1.1855

Marinaccio, A., Boccuni, F., Rondinone, B., Brusco, A., D'Amario, S., & Iavicoli, S. (2020). Occupational factors in the covid-19 pandemic in Italy: Compensation claims applications support establishing an occupational surveillance system. *Occupational and Environmental Medicine, 77*(12), 818–821. DOI: 10.1136/oemed-2020-106844 PMID: 32967988

Matheny, M., Whicher, D., & Israni, S. (2020). Artificial intelligence in health care. *Journal of the American Medical Association, 323*(6), 509. DOI: 10.1001/jama.2019.21579 PMID: 31845963

Mirbabaie, M., Brünker, F., Möllmann, N., & Stieglitz, S. (2021). The rise of artificial intelligence – understanding the ai identity threat at the workplace. *Electronic Markets, 32*(1), 73–99. DOI: 10.1007/s12525-021-00496-x

Mousavi-Shalmaei, S., Hosseinnia, M., Mohtasham-Amiri, Z., Rad, E. H., & Khodadadi-Hassankiadeh, N. (2023). Helmet use and jaw and tooth injuries in motorcyclists admitted to a referral hospital. *Journal of Maxillofacial and Oral Surgery, 22*(3), 603–608. DOI: 10.1007/s12663-023-01934-3 PMID: 37362880

Mydin, F., & Othman, S. (2017). Elder abuse and neglect intervention in the clinical setting: Perceptions and barriers faced by primary care physicians in Malaysia. *Journal of Interpersonal Violence, 35*(23-24), 6041–6066. DOI: 10.1177/0886260517726411 PMID: 29294874

Nweke, G., & Nweke, O. C. (2024). Empowering the workforce in the ai era: Lessons from the UK's consultative approach for a global legal framework. *Beijing Law Review, 15*(01), 219–230. DOI: 10.4236/blr.2024.151014

Padula, W., Armstrong, D. G., Pronovost, P. J., & Saria, S. (2024). Predicting pressure injury risk in hospitalised patients using machine learning with electronic health records: A us multilevel cohort study. *BMJ Open, 14*(4), e082540. DOI: 10.1136/bmjopen-2023-082540 PMID: 38594078

Pant, P., Mytton, J., Dharel, M., Dangi, A., Rai, W., & Joshi, S. (2021). The prevention of – and first response to – injuries in Nepal: A review of policies and legislation. *Health Research Policy and Systems, 19*(1), 65. Advance online publication. DOI: 10.1186/s12961-021-00686-1 PMID: 33853626

Pathak, P., & Joshi, S. K. (2023). Epidemiology of unintentional childhood injuries in urban and rural areas of Nepal- a comparative study. *PLoS One, 18*(10), e0287487. DOI: 10.1371/journal.pone.0287487 PMID: 37847700

Pishgar, M., Issa, S., Sietsema, M., Pratap, P., & Darabi, H. (2021). Redeca: A novel framework to review artificial intelligence and its applications in occupational safety and health. *International Journal of Environmental Research and Public Health, 18*(13), 6705. DOI: 10.3390/ijerph18136705 PMID: 34206378

Qadhi, S., Alduais, A., Chaaban, Y., & Khraisheh, M. (2024). Generative ai, research ethics, and higher education research: Insights from a scientometric analysis. *Information (Basel), 15*(6), 325. DOI: 10.3390/info15060325

Ranavolo, A., Ajoudani, A., Cherubini, A., Bianchi, M., Fritzsche, L., Iavicoli, S., Sartori, M., Silvetti, A., Vanderborght, B., Varrecchia, T., & Draicchio, F. (2020). The sensor-based biomechanical risk assessment at the base of the need for revising of standards for human ergonomics. *Sensors (Basel), 20*(20), 5750. DOI: 10.3390/s20205750 PMID: 33050438

Reis da Silva, T. H. (2023a). Moving and Handling in the Community. *British Journal of Community Nursing, 28*(8), 369. DOI: 10.12968/bjcn.2023.28.8.369 PMID: 37527217

Reis da Silva, T. H. (2023b). Falls assessment and prevention in the nursing home and community. *British Journal of Community Nursing, 28*(2), 68–72. DOI: 10.12968/bjcn.2023.28.2.68 PMID: 36735363

Reis da Silva, T. H. (2023c). Ageing in place: Ageing at home and in the community. *British Journal of Community Nursing*, *28*(5), 213–214. DOI: 10.12968/bjcn.2023.28.5.213 PMID: 37130715

Reis da Silva, T. H. (2024a). Chapter 11 - Integrating business essentials into Gerontological Nursing: Enhancing Care for Older Adults in Diverse Settings. In Sedky, A. Resiliency Strategies for Long-Term Business Success. Pp. 283-316. IGI Global. DOI: DOI: 10.4018/979-8-3693-9168-6.ch011

Reis da Silva, T. H. (2024b). Falls prevention in older people and the role of nursing. *British Journal of Community Nursing*, *29*(7), 335–339. DOI: 10.12968/bjcn.2024.0005 PMID: 38963269

Reis da Silva, T. H (2024c). Oncology and Cancer Medicine: Understanding the complexities in Older Patients. Biomed J Sci & Tech Res 55(3)-2024. DOI: https://doi.org/DOI: 10.26717/BJSTR.2024.55.008720

Reis da Silva, T. H. (2024d). Chapter 6 – Navigating Healthcare Complexity: Integrating Business Fundamentals into Nursing Leadership. In Sedky, A. Resiliency Strategies for Long-Term Business Success. Pp. 145-168. IGI Global. https://doi.org/DOI: 10.4018/979-8-3693-9168-6.ch006

Reis da Silva, T H (2024e). Prevalence of elder abuse: a narrative review. British journal of community nursing vol. 29,9 (2024): 442-446. doi: https://doi.org/DOI: 10.12968/bjcn.2024.0004

Reis da Silva, T. H. (2024f). The Nursing Process in Geriatric Care: A Comprehensive Approach. *International Journal of Biomedical Research*, *3*(5). Advance online publication. DOI: 10.31579/2834-5029/064

Reis da Silva, T. H. (2025a). AI-Powered Emotional Intelligence in Nursing: Bridging the Gap in Older People Care. In Jermsittiparsert, K., & Marzo, R. R. (Eds.), *Physical Health, Mental Health, and Human Well-Being in the Age of AI*. IGI Global Scientific Publishing., DOI: 10.4018/979-8-3693-6190-0.ch9

Reis da Silva, T. H. (2025b). Integrating Artificial Intelligence in Geriatric Care: Enhancing Physical and Mental Health Outcomes. In Jermsittiparsert, K., & Marzo, R. R. (Eds.), *Physical Health, Mental Health, and Human Well-Being in the Age of AI*. IGI Global Scientific Publishing., DOI: 10.4018/979-8-3693-6190-0.ch11

Reis da Silva, T. M. (2025c). Integrative Approaches to Geriatric Care: Enhancing Physical and Mental Health Through AI-Driven Insights. In Jermsittiparsert, K., & Marzo, R. (Eds.), *Physical Health, Mental Health, and Human Well-Being in the Age of AI* (pp. 113–136). IGI Global Scientific Publishing., DOI: 10.4018/979-8-3693-6190-0.ch007

Reis da Silva, T. M. (2025d). Designing for Longevity: Economic Perspectives on Age-Friendly Housing and Urban Development. In Gölçek, A. (Ed.), *Perspectives on the Economics of Aging* (pp. 151–176). IGI Global Scientific Publishing., DOI: 10.4018/979-8-3693-7753-6.ch006

Reis da Silva, T. H. (2025e). Promoting Emotional Well-Being in Older Adults: The Role of AI in Supporting Emotional Intelligence and Mental Health. In Jermsittiparsert, K., & Marzo, R. R. (Eds.), *Physical Health, Mental Health, and Human Well-Being in the Age of AI* (pp. 137–167). IGI Global Scientific Publishing., DOI: 10.4018/979-8-3693-6190-0.ch8

Reis da Silva, T. H. (2025f). Emotional Intelligence and AI in Geriatric Nursing: Bridging Technology and Compassionate Care. In Jermsittiparsert, K., & Marzo, R. R. (Eds.), *Physical Health, Mental Health, and Human Well-Being in the Age of AI*. IGI Global Scientific Publishing., DOI: 10.4018/979-8-3693-6190-0.ch10

Reis da Silva, T. H., & Mitchell, A. (2024). Integrating Digital Transformation in Nursing Education: Best Practices and Challenges in Curriculum Development. In Lytras, M., Serban, A. C., Alkhaldi, A., Malik, S., & Aldosemani, T. (Eds.), *Digital Transformation in Higher Education, Part B Cases, Examples and Good Practices*. Emerald Publishing Limited.

Ribeiro, D., Carreira, L., Salci, M., Marques, F., Gallo, A., Baccon, W., Baldissera, V., & Laranjeira, C. (2023). The institutionalisation of brazilian older abused adults: A qualitative study among victims and formal carers. *Geriatrics (Basel, Switzerland)*, *8*(3), 65. DOI: 10.3390/geriatrics8030065 PMID: 37367097

Rilkoff, H., Struck, S., Ziegler, C., Faye, L., Paquette, D., & Buckeridge, D. (2024). Innovations in public health surveillance: An overview of novel use of data and analytic methods. *Canada Communicable Disease Report = Relevé des Maladies Transmissibles au Canada*, *50*(3/4), 93–101. DOI: 10.14745/ccdr.v50i34a02 PMID: 38716410

Roberto, K., Teaster, P., Lindberg, B., & Blancato, R. (2020). A first (and disturbing) look at the relationship between the opioid epidemic and elder abuse: Insights of human service professionals. *Journal of Applied Gerontology*, *40*(10), 1231–1235. DOI: 10.1177/0733464820947279 PMID: 32772619

Ronquillo, C., Peltonen, L., Pruinelli, L., Chu, C., Bakken, S., Beduschi, A., Cato, K., Hardiker, N., Junger, A., Michalowski, M., Nyrup, R., Rahimi, S., Reed, D. N., Salakoski, T., Salanterä, S., Walton, N., Weber, P., Wiegand, T., & Topaz, M. (2021). Artificial intelligence in nursing: Priorities and opportunities from an international invitational think-tank of the nursing and artificial intelligence leadership collaborative. *Journal of Advanced Nursing*, *77*(9), 3707–3717. DOI: 10.1111/jan.14855 PMID: 34003504

Saadati, S. (2023). The need for more attention to the validity and reliability of ai-generated exercise programs. HN, 1(1), 77-81. DOI: 10.61838/hn.1.1.12

Saroya, K., Gupta, A., Shrivastava, R., Mehta, N., & Goyal, A. (2024). Powered versus manual toothbrushes for plaque removal and gingival health amongst 55 and older individuals: A systematic review and meta-analysis. *Special Care in Dentistry*, *44*(4), 979–989. DOI: 10.1111/scd.12974 PMID: 38348549

Sauter, M., Barthelme, J., Müller, C., & Liebers, F. (2021). Manual handling of heavy loads and low back pain among different occupational groups: Results of the 2018 bibb/baua employment survey. *BMC Musculoskeletal Disorders*, *22*(1), 956. Advance online publication. DOI: 10.1186/s12891-021-04819-z PMID: 34781946

Sebastjan, A., Skrzek, A., Ignasiak, Z., & Sławińska, T. (2017). Age-related changes in hand dominance and functional asymmetry in older adults. *PLoS One*, *12*(5), e0177845. DOI: 10.1371/journal.pone.0177845 PMID: 28558047

Serag, A., Ion-Mărgineanu, A., Qureshi, H., McMillan, R., Martin, M., Diamond, J., & Hamilton, P. (2019). Translational ai and deep learning in diagnostic pathology. *Frontiers in Medicine*, *6*, 185. Advance online publication. DOI: 10.3389/fmed.2019.00185 PMID: 31632973

Shah, I., & Mishra, S. D. (2024). Artificial intelligence in advancing occupational health and safety: An encapsulation of developments. *Journal of Occupational Health, 66*(1), uiad017. Advance online publication. DOI: 10.1093/joccuh/uiad017 PMID: 38334203

Shankar, J., Lai, D., Chen, S., Turin, T., Joseph, S., & Mi, E. (2022). Highly educated immigrant workers' perspectives of occupational health and safety and work conditions that challenge work safety. *International Journal of Environmental Research and Public Health, 19*(14), 8757. DOI: 10.3390/ijerph19148757 PMID: 35886609

Sharma, V., Eissa, G., Newman, A., Lester, S. W., & Pandey, J. (2023). Psychological entitlement and moral disengagement as antecedents of compliance with covid-19 workplace safety protocols and the moderating role of moral identity. *Applied Psychology, 73*(2), 698–722. DOI: 10.1111/apps.12496

Singh, A., & Pandey, J. (2024). Artificial intelligence adoption in extended hr ecosystems: Enablers and barriers. an abductive case research. *Frontiers in Psychology, 14*, 1339782. Advance online publication. DOI: 10.3389/fpsyg.2023.1339782 PMID: 38327504

Sousa, R., Araújo, G., Souto, R., Santos, R., Leal, C., & Nascimento, N. (2021). Interventions to prevent elder abuse in the community: a mixed-methods systematic review. Revista Da Escola De Enfermagem Da Usp, 55. https://doi.org/DOI: 10.1590/s1980-220x2019033203677

Tama, C., Syaifullah, R., Putro, B., Purnama, S., Sabarini, S., & Nuryadin, I. (2022). Profile of injury prevent and treatment in Indonesia basketball wheelchair national team during the 11th asean para games preparation., 84-89. DOI: 10.2991/978-2-494069-79-4_12

Thisani, S. (2024). Developing a high-performance sports results prediction artificial neural network: Case study on world championship boxing. *International Journal of Computer Science in Sport, 23*(2), 1–21. DOI: 10.2478/ijcss-2023-0008

Tranæus, U., Ivarsson, A., Johnson, U., Weiss, N., Samuelsson, M., & Skillgate, E. (2021). The role of the results of functional tests and psychological factors on prediction of injuries in adolescent female football players. *International Journal of Environmental Research and Public Health, 19*(1), 143. DOI: 10.3390/ijerph19010143 PMID: 35010400

Vaara, J., Groeller, H., Drain, J., Kyröläinen, H., Pihlainen, K., Ojanen, T., Connaboy, C., Santtila, M., Agostinelli, P., & Nindl, B. (2021). Physical training considerations for optimizing performance in essential military tasks. *European Journal of Sport Science, 22*(1), 43–57. DOI: 10.1080/17461391.2021.1930193 PMID: 34006204

Valerio, A. (2024). Anticipating the impact of artificial intelligence in higher education: Student awareness and ethical concerns in Zamboanga city, Philippines. *Cognizance Journal of Multidisciplinary Studies, 4*(6), 408–418. DOI: 10.47760/cognizance.2024.v04i06.024

Wagner, A., Schöne, L., & Rieger, M. A. (2020). Determinants of occupational safety culture in hospitals and other workplaces—Results from an integrative literature review. *International Journal of Environmental Research and Public Health, 17*(18), 6588. DOI: 10.3390/ijerph17186588 PMID: 32927758

Waheed, M., & Liu, L. (2024). Perceptions of family physicians about applying ai in primary health care: Case study from a premier health care organization. *JMIR AI, 3*, e40781. DOI: 10.2196/40781 PMID: 38875531

Wang, Z., Xing, Y., Yan, W., Sun, X., Zhang, X., Huang, S., & Li, L. (2020). Effects of individual, family and community factors on the willingness of institutional elder care: A cross-sectional survey of the elderly in China. *BMJ Open, 10*(2), e032478. DOI: 10.1136/bmjopen-2019-032478 PMID: 32075825

Williams, K., Pennathur, P., Bossen, A., & Gloeckner, A. (2016). Adapting telemonitoring technology use for older adults: A pilot study. *Research in Gerontological Nursing, 9*(1), 17–23. DOI: 10.3928/19404921-20150522-01 PMID: 26020575

Wine, B., & Newcomb, E. T. (2024). A blocking and distance management staff training intervention for torso- and head-directed aggression. *Journal of Applied Behavior Analysis, 57*(3), 668–675. DOI: 10.1002/jaba.1089 PMID: 38767337

Xu, X., Rioux, T., Friedl, K., González, J., & Castellani, J. (2023). Development of interactive guidance for cold exposure using a thermoregulatory model. *International Journal of Circumpolar Health, 82*(1), 2190485. Advance online publication. DOI: 10.1080/22423982.2023.2190485 PMID: 36934425

Yan, Z., Dube, V., Heselton, J., Johnson, K., Yan, C., Jones, V., Blaskewicz Boron, J., & Shade, M. (2024). Understanding older people's voice interactions with smart voice assistants: A new modified rule-based natural language processing model with human input. *Frontiers in Digital Health, 6*, 1329910. Advance online publication. DOI: 10.3389/fdgth.2024.1329910 PMID: 38812806

Yazdani, A. (2023). The impact of ai on trends, design, and consumer behavior. aitechbesosci, 1(4), 4-10. DOI: 10.61838/kman.aitech.1.4.2

Zhang, X., Ma, L., Chen, N., Wu, D., & Yan, Y. (2022). Trend analysis and prediction of injury death in Xi'an city, China, 2005-2020. *Archives of Public Health = Archives Belges de Santé Publique, 80*(1), 238. Advance online publication. DOI: 10.1186/s13690-022-00988-y PMID: 36403065

Compilation of References

Aaron, V., V. Rohan, E. Konguvel and R. Sivakumar. (2024) An IoT-Controlled Robotic Hand for Hazardous Material Handling. *Advances in transdisciplinary engineering.*

Abatan, A., Obiuto, N. C., Ninduwezuor-Ehiobu, N., Ani, E. C., Olu-lawal, K. A., & Ugwuanyi, E. D. (2024). Integrating advanced technologies for enhanced hse management in the FMCG sector. *Engineering Science & Technology Journal, 5*(4), 1270–1280. DOI: 10.51594/estj.v5i4.1017

Abbas Khan, M., Khan, H., Omer, M. F., Ullah, I., & Yasir, M. (2024). Impact of artificial intelligence on the global economy and technology advancements. In *Artificial General Intelligence (AGI) Security: Smart Applications and Sustainable Technologies* (pp. 147–180). Springer Nature Singapore.

Abbasinia, M., & Mohammadfam, I. (2022). Identifying, evaluating and prioritizing the causes of occupational accidents in the construction industry using fuzzy AHP and fuzzy TOPSIS. *Work (Reading, Mass.), 72*(3), 933–940. DOI: 10.3233/WOR-210024 PMID: 35634821

Abdous, M.-A., Delorme, X., Battini, D., & Berger-Douce, S. (2022). Multi-objective collaborative assembly line design problem with the optimisation of ergonomics and economics. *International Journal of Production Research, 61*(22), 7830–7845. DOI: 10.1080/00207543.2022.2153185

Abdulkadir, M. K. (2020). Quality Assurance in Medical Imaging: A Review of Challenges in Nigeria. *Journal of Radiology Nursing, 39*(3), 238–244. DOI: 10.1016/j.jradnu.2020.02.005

Abdulkareem, M., & Petersen, S. E. (2021). The Promise of AI in Detection, Diagnosis, and Epidemiology for Combating COVID-19: Beyond the Hype. *Frontiers in Artificial Intelligence, 4*, 4. DOI: 10.3389/frai.2021.652669 PMID: 34056579

Abhari, S., Fatahi, S., Saragadam, A., Chumachenko, D., & Morita, P. (2024). A road map of prompt engineering for chatgpt in healthcare: a perspective study.. DOI: 10.3233/SHTI240578

Abhaysinh, R. S., Swapnil, D., Neenu, P. R., & Shalini, T. (2024). Public health risk assessment and speciation of air-borne microorganisms in an office building. *Journal of Aerosol Science, 179*, 106362. DOI: 10.1016/j.jaerosci.2024.106362

Abir, F., Faisal, M., Shahid, O., & Ahmed, M. (2021). Contactless human activity analysis: an overview of different modalities., 83-112. DOI: 10.1007/978-3-030-68590-4_3

Abukhadijah, H., & Nashwan, A. J. (2024). Transforming hospital quality improvement through harnessing the power of artificial intelligence. *Global Journal on Quality and Safety in Healthcare, 7*(3), 132–139. DOI: 10.36401/JQSH-24-4 PMID: 39104802

Acemoğlu, D., Autor, D., Hazell, J., & Restrepo, P. (2022). Artificial intelligence and jobs: Evidence from online vacancies. *Journal of Labor Economics*, *40*(S1), S293–S340. DOI: 10.1086/718327

Adefemi, A. (2023). *Artificial Intelligence in Environmental Health and Public Safety: A Comprehensive Review of USA Strategies*. World Journal of Advanced Research and Reviews., DOI: 10.30574/wjarr.2023.20.3.2591

Adepoju, O., & Esan, O. (2023). Risk Management Practices and Workers Safety in University of Medical Sciences Teaching Hospital, Ondo State Nigeria. *Open Journal of Management Science (Issn 2734-2107)*. DOI: 10.52417/ojms.v4i1.491

Aderamo, A. T., Olisakwe, H. C., Adebayo, Y. A., & Esiri, A. E.Adeoye Taofik AderamoHenry Chukwuemeka OlisakweYetunde Adenike AdebayoAndrew Emuobosa Esiri. (2024a). AI-driven HSE management systems for risk mitigation in the oil and gas industry. *Comprehensive Research and Reviews in Engineering and Technology*, *2*(1), 1–22. DOI: 10.57219/crret.2024.2.1.0059

Aderamo, A. T., Olisakwe, H. C., Adebayo, Y. A., & Esiri, A. E.Adeoye Taofik AderamoHenry Chukwuemeka OlisakweYetunde Adenike AdebayoAndrew Emuobosa Esiri. (2024b). AI-enabled predictive safeguards for offshore oil facilities: Enhancing safety and operational efficiency. *Comprehensive Research and Reviews in Engineering and Technology*, *2*(1), 23–43. DOI: 10.57219/crret.2024.2.1.0060

Adiga, U. (2023). Enhancing occupational health and ergonomics for optimal workplace well-being: A review. *International Journal of Chemical and Biochemical Science*, *24*(4), 157–164.

Afzal, M., Shafiq, M. T., & Al Jassmi, H. (2021). Improving construction safety with virtual-design construction technologies—A review. *Journal of Information Technology in Construction*, *26*, 319–340. DOI: 10.36680/j.itcon.2021.018

Agbehadji, I. E., Awuzie, B. O., Ngowi, A. B., & Millham, R. C. (2020). Review of big data analytics, artificial intelligence and nature-inspired computing models towards accurate detection of COVID-19 pandemic cases and contact tracing. In *International Journal of Environmental Research and Public Health* (Vol. 17, Issue 15, pp. 1–16). MDPI AG. DOI: 10.3390/ijerph17155330

Aggarwal, A. N., Mishra, A., Tabassum, N., Young-Mog, K., & Khan, F. (2024). Detection of Mycotoxin Contamination in Foods Using Artificial Intelligence: A Review. *Foods*, *13*(20), 3339. DOI: 10.3390/foods13203339 PMID: 39456400

Aggeri, F., Micheaux, H., & Ntsondé, J. Special Issue 23| 2021 Industry and Waste: Toward the Circular Economy.

Agha-Mir-Salim, L. and Sarmiento, R. (2020). Health information technology as premise for data science in global health: a discussion of opportunities and challenges., 3-15. DOI: 10.1007/978-3-030-47994-7_1

Ahirwar, R., & Khan, N. (2022). *Smart Wireless Nanosensor Systems for Human Healthcare*. CRC Press. DOI: 10.1201/9781003093534-15

Ahmed, S., R. Alam, M. R. Hossain, M. M. Islam, M. I. Hossain and T. Tabassum (2022). An IoT based Smart Robot that Aids in the Prevention of COVID19 Spread: 1-6.

Ahmed, I., Ahmad, M., Rodrigues, J. J. P. C., Jeon, G., & Din, S. (2021). A deep learning-based social distance monitoring framework for COVID-19. *Sustainable Cities and Society*, *65*, 102571. DOI: 10.1016/j.scs.2020.102571 PMID: 33163330

Ahmed, S., Alam, R., Hossain, M. R., Islam, M. M., Hossain, M. I., & Tabassum, T. (2022) An IoT based Smart Robot that Aids in the Prevention of COVID19 Spread. *4th International Conference on Sustainable Technologies for Industry 4.0 (STI), Dhaka, Bangladesh*: 1-6. DOI: 10.1109/STI56238.2022.10103253

Ahmed, T., Hoque, A. S. M., Karmaker, C. L., & Ahmed, S. (2023). Integrated approach for occupational health and safety (OHS) risk Assessment: An Empirical (Case) study in Small enterprises. *Safety Science*, *164*, 106143. DOI: 10.1016/j.ssci.2023.106143

Aiken, L. H., Clarke, S. P., Sloane, D. M., Sochalski, J. A., Busse, R., Clarke, H., Giovannetti, P., Hunt, J., Rafferty, A. M., & Shamian, J. (2001). Nurses' reports on hospital care in five countries. *Health Affairs*, *20*(3), 43–53. DOI: 10.1377/hlthaff.20.3.43 PMID: 11585181

Akbar, S., Wei, Y., & Zhang, M. Q. (2022). RNA Interference: Promising Approach to Combat Plant Viruses. *International Journal of Molecular Sciences 2022, Vol. 23, Page 5312*, *23*(10), 5312. DOI: 10.3390/ijms23105312

Akgun, S., & Greenhow, C. (2022). Artificial intelligence in education: Addressing ethical challenges in K-12 settings. *AI and Ethics*, *2*(3), 431–440. DOI: 10.1007/s43681-021-00096-7 PMID: 34790956

Akinsemoyin, A., Awolusi, I., Chakraborty, D., Al-Bayati, A. J., & Akanmu, A. (2023). Unmanned Aerial Systems and Deep Learning for Safety and Health Activity Monitoring on Construction Sites. *Sensors (Basel)*, *23*(15), 6690. Advance online publication. DOI: 10.3390/s23156690 PMID: 37571475

Aladhadh, S., & Mahum, R. (2023). Knee osteoarthritis detection using an improved CenterNet with pixel-wise voting scheme. *IEEE Access : Practical Innovations, Open Solutions*, *11*, 22283–22296. DOI: 10.1109/ACCESS.2023.3247502

AlAli, R. (2024). Opportunities and Challenges of Integrating Generative Artificial Intelligence in Education. *International Journal of Religion*. DOI: 10.61707/8y29gv34

Alaya, I. B., & Mars, M. (2020). Automatic Analysis of ACR Phantom Images in MRI. *Current Medical Imaging*, *16*(7), 892–901. DOI: 10.2174/1573405615666190903145343 PMID: 33059559

Aldhoayan, M. (2022). The role of artificial intelligence and machine learning during the covid-19 pandemic: a review.. DOI: 10.3233/SHTI220651

AlGerafi, M., Zhou, Y., Oubib, M., & Wijaya, T. T. (2023). Unlocking the potential: A comprehensive evaluation of augmented reality and virtual reality in education. *Electronics (Basel)*, *12*(18), 3953. DOI: 10.3390/electronics12183953

Alhamd, M. W., Jary, A. M., Atiyah, S. N., & Abbood, N. A. (2021). Improve X-ray images using quality assurance tests. *Journal of Physics: Conference Series*, *2114*(1), 012034. DOI: 10.1088/1742-6596/2114/1/012034

Al-Hashimi, M. and Hamdan, A. (2021). Artificial intelligence and coronavirus covid-19: applications, impact and future implications., 830-843. DOI: 10.1007/978-3-030-69221-6_64

Ali, O., Cecilia, T., Edward, K., & Arijit, P. (2024). *Leaping into the Future: Artificial Intelligence for Health*. Safety and Environmental Management.

Alkaissy, M., Arashpour, M., Ashuri, B., Bai, Y., & Hosseini, R. (2020). Safety management in construction: 20 years of risk modeling. *Safety Science*, *129*, 104805. DOI: 10.1016/j.ssci.2020.104805

Almakky, R. (2023). The Influence of the International Labour Organization on International Law and State Practice: An Analytical Study. *Arab Journal for Scientific Publishing (AJSP). ISSN*, *2663*, 5798.

Almeida, V., Mendes, L., Doneda, D., & Almeida, V. (2023). On the Development of AI Governance Frameworks. *IEEE Internet Computing*, *27*(1), 70–74. DOI: 10.1109/MIC.2022.3186030

Al-Naser, Y. A. (2023). The impact of artificial intelligence on radiography as a profession: A narrative review. *Journal of Medical Imaging and Radiation Sciences*, *54*(1), 162–166. DOI: 10.1016/j.jmir.2022.10.196 PMID: 36376210

Alsadik, B., & Khalaf, Y. H. (2022). Potential use of drone ultra-high-definition videos for detailed 3d city modeling. *ISPRS International Journal of Geo-Information*, *11*(1), 34. DOI: 10.3390/ijgi11010034

Alvi, A. (2023). Exploring the Ethical Challenges of Ai in Personalised Marketing in Context of Beauty and Wellness. *International Journal of All Research Education & Scientific Methods*. DOI: 10.56025/IJARESM.2023.120124482

Ambeba, E., Ye, L., Sereika, S., Styn, M., Acharya, S., Sevick, M., Ewing, L. J., Conroy, M. B., Glanz, K., Zheng, Y., Goode, R. W., Mattos, M., & Burke, L. (2015). The use of mhealth to deliver tailored messages reduces reported energy and fat intake. *The Journal of Cardiovascular Nursing*, *30*(1), 35–43. DOI: 10.1097/JCN.0000000000000120 PMID: 24434827

Amer, H. (2020). Low back pain prevalence and risk factors among health workers in Saudi Arabia: A systematic review and meta-analysis. *Journal of Occupational Health*, *62*(1), e12155. Advance online publication. DOI: 10.1002/1348-9585.12155 PMID: 32710807

Amershi, S., Weld, D., Vorvoreanu, M., Fourney, A., Nushi, B., Collisson, P., Suh, J., Iqbal, S., Bennett, P. N., & Inkpen, K. (2019). Guidelines for human-AI interaction. *Proceedings of the 2019 chi conference on human factors in computing systems*. DOI: 10.1145/3290605.3300233

Aminbakhsh, S., Gunduz, M., & Sonmez, R. (2013). Safety risk assessment using Analytic Hierarchy Process (AHP) during planning and budgeting of construction projects. *Journal of Safety Research*, *46*, 99–105. DOI: 10.1016/j.jsr.2013.05.003 PMID: 23932691

Amore, A. (2023). Artificial Intelligence in Food Biotechnology: Trends and Perspectives. *Front. Ind. Microbiol.* DOI: 10.3389/finmi.2023.1255505

Amugongo, L. M., Kriebitz, A., Boch, A., & Lütge, C. (2023). Operationalising AI ethics through the agile software development lifecycle: A case study of AI-enabled mobile health applications. *AI and Ethics*, •••, 1–18.

Ananth, M., M. Vanapalli, J. Shanthilal and R. Madhavi. (2024) Robotics Autonomous Systems (RAS) in Food Laboratories are the Future of Food Processing Industries: A Review. *Journal of advances in food science & technology*, 11: 17 - 26.

Andeobu, L., Wibowo, S., & Grandhi, S. (2022). Artificial intelligence applications for sustainable solid waste management practices in Australia: A systematic review. *The Science of the Total Environment, 834*, 155389. DOI: 10.1016/j.scitotenv.2022.155389 PMID: 35460765

Angelopoulos, A., Cahoon, J. F., & Alterovitz, R. (2024). Transforming science labs into automated factories of discovery. *Science Robotics, 9*(95), eadm6991. DOI: 10.1126/scirobotics.adm6991 PMID: 39441898

Aniket, W., A. Sampson and M. Vritik. (2024) Data-Driven Real-Time Surveillance System for Tracking Disease Outbreaks: A Case Study of Lassa Fever Outbreak. 344 - 349.

Ankolekar, A., Eppings, L., Bottari, F., Pinho, I. F., Howard, K., Baker, R., Nan, Y., Xing, X., Walsh, S. L., Vos, W., Yang, G., & Lambin, P. (2024). Using artificial intelligence and predictive modelling to enable learning healthcare systems (LHS) for pandemic preparedness. *Computational and Structural Biotechnology Journal, 24*, 412–419. DOI: 10.1016/j.csbj.2024.05.014 PMID: 38831762

Anna, G.-P. (2022). Biological Factors in the Workplace—Current Threats to Employees, the Effects of Infections, Prevention Options. *International Journal of Environmental Research and Public Health, 19*(9), 5592. DOI: 10.3390/ijerph19095592 PMID: 35564987

Annalaura, C., Gabriele, D., Lorenzo, C., Ileana, F., Roberto, L., & Marco, V. (2018). Quantitative Microbial Risk Assessment for Workers Exposed to Bioaerosol in Wastewater Treatment Plants Aimed at the Choice and Setup of Safety Measures. *International Journal of Environmental Research and Public Health, 15*(7), 1490. DOI: 10.3390/ijerph15071490 PMID: 30011925

Antonio, P. J. A., Delmo, J. A. B., Sevilla, R. V., Ligayo, M. A. D., & Montesines, D. L. (2022). Deep transfer network of knee osteoarthritis progression rate classification in MR imaging for medical imaging support system. *2022 International Conference on Decision Aid Sciences and Applications (DASA)*, 285–289. DOI: 10.1109/DASA54658.2022.9765065

Anuja, R., S. Sumisha, J. Sachin Shaju, R. Riya Ann, J. Stephin, J. Laura and V. Devi. (2024) An Automated Alert System for Monitoring the Hygiene in Restaurants Using Machine Vision.

Aqueveque, P., Gutiérrez, C., Rodríguez, F., Pino, E., Morales, A., & Wiechmann, E. (2017). Monitoring physiological variables of mining workers at high altitude. *IEEE Transactions on Industry Applications, 53*(3), 2628–2634. DOI: 10.1109/TIA.2017.2675360

Arigbabu, A. T. (2024). Data Governance in AI - Enabled Healthcare Systems: A Case of the Project Nightingale. *Asian Journal of Research in Computer Science*. DOI: 10.9734/ajrcos/2024/v17i5441

Arnold & Porter. (2024). *AI is Transforming Life Sciences but Raising Risk Concerns, New Benchmark Report Finds | News*. News & Perspectives. https://www.arnoldporter.com/en/perspectives/news/2024/11/ai-is-transforming-life-sciences-but-raising-risk-concerns-new-benchmark-report-finds?utm_source=chatgpt.com

Arora, M. K., Lal, S., Singh, B., & Olyaee, M. (2024). Through an Energy Lens: Examining SDGs From a Policy Perspective. In Riswandi, B., Singh, B., Kaunert, C., & Vig, K. (Eds.), *AI Applications for Clean Energy and Sustainability* (pp. 320–343). IGI Global., DOI: 10.4018/979-8-3693-6567-0.ch016

Arshad, S., Akinade, O., Bello, S., & Bilal, M. (2023). Computer vision and IoT research landscape for health and safety management on construction sites. *Journal of Building Engineering*, *76*, 107049. DOI: 10.1016/j.jobe.2023.107049

Aruna, S., Rafeekher, M., Gowda, P. P., Anil, A. S., & Anjaly, V. (2022). Double Haploids for Vegetable Crop Improvement: A Review. *Agricultural Reviews (Karnal)*, (Of). Advance online publication. DOI: 10.18805/ag.R-2300

As low As reasonably Achievable Guidelines. (n.d.).

Asa'd, O., & Levesque, M. (2024). Digital technologies for energy efficiency and decarbonization in mining. *CIM Journal*, *15*(1), 1–20. DOI: 10.1080/19236026.2023.2203068

Assadullah, M. M. (2019). Barriers to artificial intelligence adoption in healthcare management: A systematic review. *Available atSSRN* 3530598. DOI: 10.2139/ssrn.3530598

Austin, A. W. (2017) Robot-Human Collaboration for Improving Patient Care in Infectious Disease Environments. *Human-Robot Interaction*: 385 - 386.

Ayoun, B., Rowe, L., & Yassine, F. (2015). Is workplace spirituality associated with business ethics? *International Journal of Contemporary Hospitality Management*, *27*(5), 938–957. DOI: 10.1108/IJCHM-01-2014-0018

Ayton, D., Barker, A., Morello, R., Brand, C., Talevski, J., Landgren, F., Melhem, M. M., Bian, E., Brauer, S. G., Hill, K. D., Livingston, P. M., & Botti, M. (2017). Barriers and enablers to the implementation of the 6-pack falls prevention program: A pre-implementation study in hospitals participating in a cluster randomised controlled trial. *PLoS One*, *12*(2), e0171932. DOI: 10.1371/journal.pone.0171932 PMID: 28207841

Aziz, A., Ahmed, S., & Khan, F. I. (2019). An ontology-based methodology for hazard identification and causation analysis. *Process Safety and Environmental Protection*, *123*, 87–98. DOI: 10.1016/j.psep.2018.12.008

Babalola, A., Manu, P., Cheung, C., Yunusa-Kaltungo, A., & Bartolo, P. (2023). Applications of immersive technologies for occupational safety and health training and education: A systematic review. *Safety Science*, *166*, 106214. DOI: 10.1016/j.ssci.2023.106214

Baki, N. U. (2023). Integrating Artificial Intelligence in Human Resource Functions: Challenges and Opportunities. *International Journal of Academic Research in Business & Social Sciences*, *13*(8). Advance online publication. DOI: 10.6007/IJARBSS/v13-i8/18071

Balaji, K. (2023). Blockchain based banking transactions enabled by big data. 2023 5th International Conference on Energy, Power and Environment (ICEPE), 1–6. DOI: 10.1109/ICEPE57949.2023.10201613

Balaji, K., & Rao, P. S. (2024). Artificial intelligence and chatbots: Transforming user experience in e-tailing. 2024 9th International Conference on Communication and Electronics Systems (ICCES), 1375–1379. DOI: 10.1109/ICCES63552.2024.10859474

Balaji, K. (2023). Unlocking the potential of BI-enhancing banking transactions through AI & ML tools. *2023 International Conference on Applied Intelligence and Sustainable Computing (ICAISC)*, 1–6. DOI: 10.1109/ICAISC58445.2023.10200018

Balaji, K. (2024). Artificial intelligence for enhanced anti-money laundering and asset recovery: A new frontier in financial crime prevention. *2024 Second International Conference on Intelligent Cyber Physical Systems and Internet of Things (ICoICI)*, 1010–1016. DOI: 10.1109/ICoICI62503.2024.10696100

Balaji, K. (2024). Charting the path to global prosperity: Unveiling the impact and promise of sustainable development. In Ordóñez de Pablos, P., Anshari, M., & Almunawar, M. (Eds.), *Harnessing green and circular skills for digital transformation* (pp. 1–22). IGI Global., DOI: 10.4018/979-8-3693-2865-1.ch001

Balaji, K. (2024). The nexus of smart contracts and digital twins transforming green finance with automated transactions in investment agreements. In Jafar, S., Rodriguez, R., Kannan, H., Akhtar, S., & Plugmann, P. (Eds.), *Harnessing blockchain-digital twin fusion for sustainable investments* (pp. 287–315). IGI Global., DOI: 10.4018/979-8-3693-1878-2.ch012

Balaji, K., & Ariwa, E. (2024). Insurtech disruption: Reshaping the future of insurance in the fintech era. In Jafar, S. H., Shakeb Akhtar, H., Khan, P. A., & El Chaarani, H. (Eds.), *The adoption of fintech: Using technology for better security, speed, and customer experience in finance* (pp. 247–266). Routledge., DOI: 10.4324/9781032644165-16

Balaji, K., & Babu, M. K. (2017). A study on the affect of technology on unplanned purchase behaviour among the customers across selected corporate retail chains of Andhrapradesh, India. *International Journal of Economic Research, 14*(4), 277–288.

Balaji, K., & Babu, M. K. (2017). A study on the role of the external and internal factors on consumer impulse buying behavior in selected retail outlets of Andhra Pradesh, India. *International Journal of Applied Business and Economic Research, 15*(4), 171–185.

Balaji, K., Karim, S., & Rao, P. S. (2024). Unleashing the power of smart chatbots: Transforming banking with artificial intelligence. *2024 International Conference on Advances in Computing, Communication and Applied Informatics (ACCAI)*, 1–7. DOI: 10.1109/ACCAI61061.2024.10602456

Balaji, K., & Kishore Babu, M. (2016). A study on consumer shopping patterns in current retail scenario across selected retail stores in Andhra Pradesh, India. *International Journal of Economic Research, 13*(4), 1629–1640.

Baldassarre, A., & Padovan, M. (2024, April 24). Regulatory and Ethical Considerations on Artificial Intelligence for Occupational Medicine. *La Medicina del Lavoro, 115*(2), e2024013. DOI: 10.23749/mdl.v115i2.15881 PMID: 38686573

Balfour, T. (2024, 7 Fen). Hearing loss concern for SA miners. *Juta Medical Brief.* https://www.medicalbrief.co.za/hearing-loss-concern-for-sa-miners/

Balogun, A.-F., Ogundairo, M., Okongwu, B., Babarinde, S., & Sodamade, P. (2023). Integration of artificial intelligence into health informatics for enhanced public health in Africa: Opportunities and challenges. *International Medical Science Research Journal, 3*(3), 127–144. DOI: 10.51594/imsrj.v3i3.643

Banerjee, A., Chakraborty, C., & Rathi, M.Sr. (2020). Medical imaging, artificial intelligence, internet of things, wearable devices in terahertz healthcare technologies. In *Terahertz biomedical and healthcare technologies* (pp. 145–165). Elsevier. DOI: 10.1016/B978-0-12-818556-8.00008-2

Banerjee, R., Bhattacharya, J., & Majumdar, P. (2021). Exponential-growth prediction bias and compliance with safety measures related to COVID-19. *Social Science & Medicine*, *268*, 113473. DOI: 10.1016/j.socscimed.2020.113473 PMID: 33130402

Banez, C., Carruthers, J. B., Gelmi, S., Kraft, A., Gaulton, C., & Hall, T. (2021). Applying Human Factors Methods to Improve Healthcare Risk Management Tools. *Proceedings of the International Symposium on Human Factors and Ergonomics in Health Care*. DOI: 10.1177/2327857921101124

Bankins, S., & Formosa, P. (2023). The ethical implications of artificial intelligence (ai) for meaningful work. *Journal of Business Ethics*, *185*(4), 725–740. DOI: 10.1007/s10551-023-05339-7

Bano, M., Zowghi, D., Gervasi, V., & Shams, R. (2023). AI for All: Operationalising Diversity and Inclusion Requirements for AI Systems. ArXiv, abs/2311.14695. https://doi.org//arXiv.2311.14695 .DOI: 10.48550

Bansal, A., Padappayil, R. P., Garg, C., Singal, A., Gupta, M., & Klein, A. (2020). Utility of Artificial Intelligence Amidst the COVID 19 Pandemic: A Review. *Journal of Medical Systems*, *44*(9), 156. DOI: 10.1007/s10916-020-01617-3 PMID: 32740678

Barda, N., Yona, G., Rothblum, G., Greenland, P., Leibowitz, M., Balicer, R., Bachmat, E., & Dagan, N. (2020). Addressing bias in prediction models by improving subpopulation calibration. *Journal of the American Medical Informatics Association : JAMIA*. Advance online publication. DOI: 10.1093/jamia/ocaa283 PMID: 33236066

Barnes, R., & Zvarikova, K. (2021). Artificial intelligence-enabled wearable medical devices, clinical and diagnostic decision support systems, and Internet of Things-based healthcare applications in COVID-19 prevention, screening, and treatment. *American Journal of Medical Research (New York, N.Y.)*, *8*(2), 9–22. DOI: 10.22381/ajmr8220211

Barredo Arrieta, A., Díaz-Rodríguez, N., Del Ser, J., Bennetot, A., Tabik, S., Barbado, A., Garcia, S., Gil-Lopez, S., Molina, D., Benjamins, R., Chatila, R., & Herrera, F. (2020). Explainable Artificial Intelligence (XAI): Concepts, taxonomies, opportunities and challenges toward responsible AI. *Information Fusion*, *58*, 82–115. DOI: 10.1016/j.inffus.2019.12.012

Basahel, A., & Taylan, O. (2016). Using fuzzy AHP and fuzzy TOPSIS approaches for assessing safety conditions at worksites in construction industry. *International Journal of Safety and Security Engineering*, *6*(4), 728–745. DOI: 10.2495/SAFE-V6-N4-728-745

Bathla, G., Bhadane, K., Singh, R. K., Kumar, R., Aluvalu, R., Krishnamurthi, R., Kumar, A., Thakur, R. N., & Basheer, S. (2022). Autonomous vehicles and intelligent automation: Applications, challenges, and opportunities. *Mobile Information Systems*, *2022*(1), 7632892. DOI: 10.1155/2022/7632892

Baxter, S. L., Bass, J. S., & Sitapati, A. M. (2020). Barriers to implementing an artificial intelligence model for unplanned readmissions. *ACI Open*, *4*(02), e108–e113. DOI: 10.1055/s-0040-1716748 PMID: 33274314

Bechinie, C., Zafari, S., Kroeninger, L., Puthenkalam, J., & Tscheligi, M. (2024). Toward human-centered intelligent assistance system in manufacturing: Challenges and potentials for Operator 5.0. *Procedia Computer Science*, *232*, 1584–1596. DOI: 10.1016/j.procs.2024.01.156

Bécue, A., Gama, J., & Brito, P. Q. (2024). Ai's effect on innovation capacity in the context of industry 5.0: A scoping review. *Artificial Intelligence Review*, *57*(8), 215. Advance online publication. DOI: 10.1007/s10462-024-10864-6

Begley, A. (2006). *Development of Internet-based mining industry database for audiograms*. Safety in Mines Research Advisory Committee.

Beinert, K., Lutz, B., Zieglgänsberger, W., & Diers, M. (2018). Seeing the site of treatment improves habitual pain but not cervical joint position sense immediately after manual therapy in chronic neck pain patients. *European Journal of Pain (London, England)*, *23*(1), 117–123. DOI: 10.1002/ejp.1290 PMID: 29999203

Belen, R., Bednarz, T., Sowmya, A., & Favero, D. (2020). Computer vision in autism spectrum disorder research: A systematic review of published studies from 2009 to 2019. *Translational Psychiatry*, *10*(1), 333. Advance online publication. DOI: 10.1038/s41398-020-01015-w PMID: 32999273

Benavides Benavides, D. S. (2024). Advancements in AI-Based Interpretation of Medical Images: Comprehensive Review. *Global Journal for Research Analysis*, *50–51*, 50–51. Advance online publication. DOI: 10.36106/gjra/8005218

Benos, L., Bechar, A., & Bochtis, D. (2020). Safety and ergonomics in human-robot interactive agricultural operations. *Biosystems Engineering*, *200*, 55–72. DOI: 10.1016/j.biosystemseng.2020.09.009

Berk, R. (2021). Artificial Intelligence, Predictive Policing, and Risk Assessment for Law Enforcement. *Annual Review of Criminology*, *4*(1), 209–237. Advance online publication. DOI: 10.1146/annurev-criminol-051520-012342

Bernardes, R. C., De Medeiros, A., da Silva, L., Cantoni, L., Martins, G. F., Mastrangelo, T., Novikov, A., & Mastrangelo, C. B. (2022). Deep-Learning Approach for Fusarium Head Blight Detection in Wheat Seeds Using Low-Cost Imaging Technology. *Agriculture*, *12*(11), 1801. DOI: 10.3390/agriculture12111801

Bernhardt, A., Suleiman, R., & Kresge, L. (2021). Data and algorithms at work: the case for worker technology rights.

Bhandari, A. (2024). Revolutionizing Radiology With Artificial Intelligence. *Cureus*. Advance online publication. DOI: 10.7759/cureus.72646 PMID: 39474591

Bhaskar, N., Ramana, S., & Kumar, G. M. (2023). Internet of Things for Green Smart City Application Based on Biotechnology Techniques. *Proceedings of the International Conference on Artificial Intelligence and Knowledge Discovery in Concurrent Engineering, ICECONF 2023*. DOI: 10.1109/ICECONF57129.2023.10083965

Biolcheva, P. (2021) The place of artificial intelligence in the risk management process. *SHS Web Conf.*, 120: 02013. DOI: 10.1051/shsconf/202112002013

Birkhoff, D., Dalen, A., & Schijven, M. (2021). A review on the current applications of artificial intelligence in the operating room. *Surgical Innovation, 28*(5), 611–619. DOI: 10.1177/1553350621996961 PMID: 33625307

Birkstedt, T., Minkkinen, M., Tandon, A., & Mäntymäki, M. (2023). AI governance: Themes, knowledge gaps and future agendas. *Internet Research, 33*(7), 133–167. Advance online publication. DOI: 10.1108/INTR-01-2022-0042

Birtalan, E., Bánhidi, A., Sanders, J. I., Balázsfi, D., & Hangya, B. (2020). Efficient Training of Mice on the 5-Choice Serial Reaction Time Task in an Automated Rodent Training System. *Scientific Reports, 10*(1), 22362. Advance online publication. DOI: 10.1038/s41598-020-79290-2 PMID: 33349672

Bittencourt, N., Meeuwisse, W., Mendonça, L., Nettel-Aguirre, A., Ocarino, J., & Fonseca, S. (2016). Complex systems approach for sports injuries: Moving from risk factor identification to injury pattern recognition—narrative review and new concept. *British Journal of Sports Medicine, 50*(21), 1309–1314. DOI: 10.1136/bjsports-2015-095850 PMID: 27445362

Bleijenberg, N., Drubbel, I., Schuurmans, M., Dam, H., Zuithoff, N., Numans, M., & Wit, N. (2016). Effectiveness of a proactive primary care program on preserving daily functioning of older people: A cluster randomized controlled trial. *Journal of the American Geriatrics Society, 64*(9), 1779–1788. DOI: 10.1111/jgs.14325 PMID: 27459236

Bogina, V., Hartman, A., Kuflik, T., & Shulner-Tal, A. (2021). Educating Software and AI Stakeholders About Algorithmic Fairness, Accountability, Transparency and Ethics. *International Journal of Artificial Intelligence in Education, 32*(3), 808–833. DOI: 10.1007/s40593-021-00248-0

Bohdan, T. (2024) Robotics and artificial intelligence: safety measures and potential threats. *Комунальне господарство міст*, 3: 250 - 258.

Bonnet, F., Nélisse, H., Nogarolli, M. A. C., & Voix, J. (2020). Individual in situ calibration of in-ear noise dosimeters. *Applied Acoustics, 157*, 107015. https://doi.org/https://doi.org/10.1016/j.apacoust.2019.107015. DOI: 10.1016/j.apacoust.2019.107015

Boopathi, S. (2023). Securing healthcare systems integrated with IoT., 186-209. DOI: 10.4018/978-1-6684-6894-4.ch010

Borchardt, M., Pereira, G. M., Milan, G. S., Scavarda, A. R., Nogueira, E. O., & Poltosi, L. C. (2022). Industry 5.0 beyond technology: An analysis through the lens of business and operations management literature. *Organizacija, 55*(4), 305–321. DOI: 10.2478/orga-2022-0020

Borgosz, L., & Dikicioglu, D. (2024). Industrial internet of things: What does it mean for the bioprocess industries? In *Biochemical Engineering Journal* (Vol. 201). Elsevier B.V., DOI: 10.1016/j.bej.2023.109122

Bosch Connected Mobility. (2023). *Predictive Maintenance in Commercial Fleets*. https://www.bosch-mobility.com

Bosse, S., Maniry, D., Muller, K.-R., Wiegand, T., & Samek, W. (2018). Deep Neural Networks for No-Reference and Full-Reference Image Quality Assessment. *IEEE Transactions on Image Processing, 27*(1), 206–219. DOI: 10.1109/TIP.2017.2760518 PMID: 29028191

Bourahmoune, K., Ishac, K., & Amagasa, T. (2022). Intelligent posture training: Machine-learning-powered human sitting posture recognition based on a pressure-sensing IoT cushion. *Sensors (Basel)*, *22*(14), 5337. DOI: 10.3390/s22145337 PMID: 35891018

Bowley, C., Mattingly, M., Barnas, A., Ellis-Felege, S., & Desell, T. (2018). Detecting wildlife in unmanned aerial systems imagery using convolutional neural networks trained with an automated feedback loop., 69-82. DOI: 10.1007/978-3-319-93698-7_6

Boy, G. (2017). A human-centered design approach., 1-20. DOI: 10.1201/9781315557380-1

Bozic, V. (2023). Integrated Risk Management and Artificial Intelligence in Hospital. *Journal of AI*, *7*(1), 63–80. DOI: 10.61969/jai.1329224

BP. (2023). BP. *Sustainability Report*, *2023*, •••. https://www.bp.com

Brady, A. P., Allen, B., Chong, J., Kotter, E., Kottler, N., Mongan, J., Oakden-Rayner, L., Dos Santos, D. P., Tang, A., Wald, C., & Slavotinek, J. (2024). Developing, purchasing, implementing and monitoring AI tools in radiology: Practical considerations. A multi-society statement from the ACR, CAR, ESR, RANZCR & RSNA. *Insights Into Imaging*, *15*(1), 16. DOI: 10.1186/s13244-023-01541-3 PMID: 38246898

Bremer, E., & Cairney, J. (2018). The interrelationship between motor coordination and adaptive behavior in children with autism spectrum disorder. *Frontiers in Psychology*, *9*, 2350. Advance online publication. DOI: 10.3389/fpsyg.2018.02350 PMID: 30538659

Brinati, D., Campagner, A., Ferrari, D., Locatelli, M., Banfi, G., & Cabitza, F. (2020). Detection of COVID-19 Infection from Routine Blood Exams with Machine Learning: A Feasibility Study. *Journal of Medical Systems*, *44*(8), 135. DOI: 10.1007/s10916-020-01597-4 PMID: 32607737

Brundage, M., Avin, S., Wang, J., Belfield, H., Krueger, G., Hadfield, G., . . . Anderljung, M. (2020). Toward trustworthy AI development: mechanisms for supporting verifiable claims. arXiv preprint arXiv:2004.07213.

Brusco, N., Haines, T., Taylor, N., Rawson, H., Boyd, L., Ekegren, C., & Graven, C. (2023). In Australian hospitals and residential aged care facilities, how do we train nursing and direct care staff to assist patients and residents to move? a national survey. *Australian Health Review*, *47*(3), 331–338. DOI: 10.1071/AH22296 PMID: 37211193

Buckley, R. P., Zetzsche, D. A., Arner, D. W., & Tang, B. W. (2021). Regulating artificial intelligence in finance: Putting the human in the loop. Sydney Law Review, The, 43(1), 43-81. GSC Advanced Research and Reviews, 2024, 18(03), 050–058 57

Bullock, J., Luccioni, A., Pham, K. H., Lam, C. S. N., & Luengo-Oroz, M. (2020). Mapping the landscape of artificial intelligence applications against COVID-19. *Journal of Artificial Intelligence Research*, *69*, 807–845.

Burzoni, S., Duquenne, P., Mater, G., & Ferrari, L. (2020). Workplace Biological Risk Assessment: Review of Existing and Description of a Comprehensive Approach. *Atmosphere (Basel)*, *11*(7), 741. DOI: 10.3390/atmos11070741

Cabitza, F., Campagner, A., Ferrari, D., Di Resta, C., Ceriotti, D., Sabetta, E., Colombini, A., De Vecchi, E., Banfi, G., Locatelli, M., & Carobene, A. (2020). Development, evaluation, and validation of machine learning models for COVID-19 detection based on routine blood tests. *Clinical Chemistry and Laboratory Medicine*, *59*(2), 421–431. DOI: 10.1515/cclm-2020-1294 PMID: 33079698

Ça layan, Ç., Barnes, S. L., Pineles, L. L., Harris, A. D., & Klein, E. Y. (2022). A Data-Driven Framework for Identifying Intensive Care Unit Admissions Colonized With Multidrug-Resistant Organisms. *Frontiers in Public Health*, *10*, 853757. DOI: 10.3389/fpubh.2022.853757 PMID: 35372195

Calvin, Z., B. Frederic, V. Zoran, S. Dragan, T. Arlex Sanchez, M. Ole, L. Zlatanovic and A. Yared Abayneh. (2023) Machine Learning for Detecting Virus Infection Hotspots Via Wastewater-Based Epidemiology: The Case of SARS-CoV-2 RNA. 7.

Camardo Leggieri, M., Mazzoni, M., Fodil, S., Moschini, M., Bertuzzi, T., Prandini, A., & Battilani, P. (2021). An electronic nose supported by an artificial neural network for the rapid detection of aflatoxin B1 and fumonisins in maize. *Food Control*, *123*, 107722. DOI: 10.1016/j.foodcont.2020.107722

Campero-Jurado, I., Sánchez, S., Gomez, J., Rodríguez, S., & Corchado, J. (2020). Smart Helmet 5.0 for Industrial Internet of Things Using Artificial Intelligence. *Sensors (Basel)*, *20*(21), 6241. Advance online publication. DOI: 10.3390/s20216241 PMID: 33139608

Caputo, F., Greco, A., Fera, M., & Macchiaroli, R. (2019). Digital twins to enhance the integration of ergonomics in the workplace design. *International Journal of Industrial Ergonomics*, *71*, 20–31. DOI: 10.1016/j.ergon.2019.02.001

Cardenas, S., & Vallejo-Cardenas, S. (2019). Continuing the Conversation on How Structural Racial and Ethnic Inequalities Affect AI Biases. *2019 IEEE International Symposium on Technology and Society (ISTAS)*, 1-7. https://doi.org/DOI: 10.1109/ISTAS48451.2019.8937853

Carley, S., & Price, S. (2021). Analyzing a human-in-the-loop's decisions for the detection of data poisoning., 11746, 1174616 - 1174616-17. https://doi.org/.DOI: 10.1117/12.2586260

Carlos, M. G. (2020). Automating the Risk Out of FarmingBy Introducing Both Flexibility and Stability, Automation can Reduce Waste and Overcome Labor Shortages in the Agriculture Industry. *Mechanical Engineering (New York, N.Y.)*, *142*, 32–37.

Carment, L., Abdellatif, A., Lafuente-Lafuente, C., Pariel, S., Maier, M., Belmin, J., & Lindberg, P. (2018). Manual dexterity and aging: A pilot study disentangling sensorimotor from cognitive decline. *Frontiers in Neurology*, *9*, 910. Advance online publication. DOI: 10.3389/fneur.2018.00910 PMID: 30420830

Carrillo-Larco, R. M., Moscoso-Porras, M., Taype-Rondan, A., Ruiz-Alejos, A., & Bernabe-Ortiz, A. (2018). The use of unmanned aerial vehicles for health purposes: A systematic review of experimental studies. *Global Health, Epidemiology and Genomics*, *3*, e13. DOI: 10.1017/gheg.2018.11 PMID: 30263137

Cebulla, A., Szpak, Z., & Knight, G. (2023). Preparing to work with artificial intelligence: Assessing WHS when using AI in the workplace. *International Journal of Workplace Health Management*, *16*(4), 294–312. DOI: 10.1108/IJWHM-09-2022-0141

Cenciarelli, O., M. Andrea, M. Marco, P. Stefano, R. Gallo, F. D. Amico, B. Carlo, R. Fiorito, A. Gucciardino and G. Pasquale. (2013) Evaluation of biohazard management of the Italian national fire brigade. 6: 33 - 41.

Chae, S., Kwon, S., & Lee, D. (2018). Predicting Infectious Disease Using Deep Learning and Big Data. *International Journal of Environmental Research and Public Health, 15*(8), 1596. DOI: 10.3390/ijerph15081596 PMID: 30060525

Chaloner, T., van Kan, J. A. L., & Grant-Downton, R. T. (2016). RNA 'Information Warfare' in Pathogenic and Mutualistic Interactions. *Trends in Plant Science, 21*(9), 738–748. DOI: 10.1016/j.tplants.2016.05.008 PMID: 27318950

Chan, A. H., Kwok, W., & Duffy, V. G. (2004). Using AHP for determining priority in a safety management system. *Industrial Management & Data Systems, 104*(5), 430–445. DOI: 10.1108/02635570410537516

Chandran, H., Meena, M., & Sharma, K. (2020). Microbial Biodiversity and Bioremediation Assessment Through Omics Approaches. *Frontiers in Environmental Chemistry, 1*, 570326. Advance online publication. DOI: 10.3389/fenvc.2020.570326

Chang, E., & Levy, B. (2021). High prevalence of elder abuse during the covid-19 pandemic: Risk and resilience factors. *The American Journal of Geriatric Psychiatry, 29*(11), 1152–1159. DOI: 10.1016/j.jagp.2021.01.007 PMID: 33518464

Channa, A., Popescu, N., Skibinska, J., & Burget, R. (2021). The rise of wearable devices during the COVID-19 pandemic: A systematic review. *Sensors (Basel), 21*(17), 5787. DOI: 10.3390/s21175787 PMID: 34502679

Chartres, N., Bero, L. A., & Norris, S. L. (2019). A review of methods used for hazard identification and risk assessment of environmental hazards. *Environment International, 123*, 231–239. DOI: 10.1016/j.envint.2018.11.060 PMID: 30537638

Chazhaev, M. (2023). Economic Potential of Biotechnologies: Challenges and Windows of Opportunity. *Bio Web of Conferences*. DOI: 10.1051/bioconf/20237610002

Che Ibrahim, C. K. I., Belayutham, S., & Mohammad, M. Z. (2021). Prevention through design (PtD) education for future civil engineers in Malaysia: Current state, challenges, and way forward. *Journal of Civil Engineering Education, 147*(1), 05020007. DOI: 10.1061/(ASCE)EI.2643-9115.0000030

Chelliah, P. R., Jayasankar, V., Agerstam, M., Sundaravadivazhagan, B., & Cyriac, R. (2023). *The Power of Artificial Intelligence for the Next-Generation Oil and Gas Industry: Envisaging AI-inspired Intelligent Energy Systems and Environments*. John Wiley & Sons. DOI: 10.1002/9781119985617

Chelliah, R., Wei, S., Daliri, E. B. M., Rubab, M., Elahi, F., Yeon, S. J., Jo, K., Yan, P., Liu, S., & Oh, D. H. (2021). Development of nanosensors based intelligent packaging systems: Food quality and medicine. *Nanomaterials (Basel, Switzerland), 11*(6), 1515. DOI: 10.3390/nano11061515 PMID: 34201071

Chen, C., Z. He, J. Zhao, X. Zhu, J. Li, X. Wu, Z. Chen, H. Chen and G. Jia. (2024) Zoonotic outbreak risk prediction with long short-term memory models: a case study with schistosomiasis, echinococcosis, and leptospirosis. *BMC Infectious Diseases,* 24.

Chen, Y., Li, J., Blasch, E., & Qu, Q. (2025). Future Outdoor Safety Monitoring: Integrating Human Activity Recognition with the Internet of Physical-Virtual Things.

Chen, C., Hu, Y., Karuppiah, M., & Kumar, P. M. (2021). Artificial intelligence on economic evaluation of energy efficiency and renewable energy technologies. *Sustainable Energy Technologies and Assessments*, *47*, 101358. DOI: 10.1016/j.seta.2021.101358

Chen, C., & Reniers, G. (2018). Risk Assessment of Processes and Products in Industrial Biotechnology. *Advances in Biochemical Engineering/Biotechnology*, *173*, 255–279. DOI: 10.1007/10_2018_74 PMID: 30244300

Chen, H., Feng, H., Liao, L., Wu, X., Zhao, Y., Hu, M., Li, H., Hu, H., & Yang, X. (2020). Evaluation of quality improvement intervention with nurse training in nursing homes: A systematic review. *Journal of Clinical Nursing*, *29*(15-16), 2788–2800. DOI: 10.1111/jocn.15289 PMID: 32279376

Chen, H., Lin, S., & Chen, I. (2022). Better safe than sorry: The role of anticipated regret and organizational ethical climate in predicting workplace safety behavior. *Chinese Management Studies*, *18*(1), 48–70. DOI: 10.1108/CMS-10-2021-0446

Chen, H., Mao, Y., Xu, Y., & Wang, R. (2023). The impact of wearable devices on the construction safety of building workers: A systematic review. *Sustainability (Basel)*, *15*(14), 11165. DOI: 10.3390/su151411165

Chetty, G., Scarvell, J., & Mitra, S. (2013). Fuzzy texture descriptors for early diagnosis of osteoarthritis. *2013 IEEE International Conference on Fuzzy Systems (FUZZ-IEEE)*, 1–6. DOI: 10.1109/FUZZ-IEEE.2013.6622439

Chevron. (2023). *Technology in Transport Safety*. Chevron Global Health, Safety & Environment Briefing.

Chien-Yu, S. and Y. Kuu-Young. (2023) Autonomous Fever Detection, Medicine Delivery, and Environmental Disinfection for Pandemic Prevention. *Applied Sciences*.

Chisholm, R. L., Denny, J., Fridsma, D., Kheterpal, S., & Ohno-Machado, L. (2015). *Opportunities and Challenges related to the use of Electronic Health Records data for research*. Northwestern University.

Cho, H.-M., Lee, C., Kim, H., Kim, Y. T., Shin, T. J., & Ahn, B. (2021). Development of length standard phantom for length measurement correction in x-ray image. *The Review of Scientific Instruments*, *92*(8), 084104. DOI: 10.1063/5.0057880 PMID: 34470429

Cho, I., Kim, M., Song, M., & Dykes, P. (2023). Evaluation of an approach to clinical decision support for preventing inpatient falls: A pragmatic trial. *JAMIA Open*, *6*(2), ooad019. Advance online publication. DOI: 10.1093/jamiaopen/ooad019 PMID: 37033322

Choi, S., & Brings, K. (2016). Work-related musculoskeletal risks associated with nurses and nursing assistants handling overweight and obese patients: A literature review. *Work (Reading, Mass.)*, *53*(2), 439–448. DOI: 10.3233/WOR-152222 PMID: 26835850

Choudhury, A., & Asan, O. (2020). Role of Artificial Intelligence in Patient Safety Outcomes: Systematic Literature Review. *JMIR Medical Informatics*, *8*(7), e18599. Advance online publication. DOI: 10.2196/18599 PMID: 32706688

Choudhury, A., & Shamszare, H. (2023). Investigating the impact of user trust on the adoption and use of ChatGPT: Survey analysis. *Journal of Medical Internet Research, 25*, e47184. DOI: 10.2196/47184 PMID: 37314848

Cho, Y. S., Hong, S. C., Choi, J., & Jung, J. H. (2019). Development of an automated wet-cyclone system for rapid, continuous and enriched bioaerosol sampling and its application to real-time detection. *Sensors and Actuators. B, Chemical, 284*, 525–533. DOI: 10.1016/j.snb.2018.12.155 PMID: 32288254

Chung, E., Lee, B., & Hwang, S. (2014). Core stabilization exercise with real-time feedback for chronic hemiparetic stroke: A pilot randomized controlled trials. *Restorative Neurology and Neuroscience, 32*(2), 313–321. DOI: 10.3233/RNN-130353 PMID: 24398718

Cihon, P. (2019). Standards for AI governance: international standards to enable global coordination in AI research & development. Future of Humanity Institute. University of Oxford, 340-342.

City of Cape Town. (2023). *Integrated Annual Report 2022/2023*. Retrieved from https://resource.capetown.gov.za/documentcentre/Documents/City%20research%20reports%20and%20review/CCT_Integrated_Annual_Report_2022-2023.pdf

Claesson, A., Fredman, D., Svensson, L., Ringh, M., Hollenberg, J., Nordberg, P., & Ban, Y. (2016). Unmanned aerial vehicles (drones) in out-of-hospital-cardiac-arrest. *Scandinavian Journal of Trauma, Resuscitation and Emergency Medicine, 24*(1), 1–9. DOI: 10.1186/s13049-016-0313-5 PMID: 27729058

Clausen, E., & Sörensen, A. (2022). Required and desired: Breakthroughs for future-proofing mineral and metal extraction. *Mineral Economics, 35*(3), 521–537. DOI: 10.1007/s13563-022-00328-0

Coman, R., Caponecchia, C., & McIntosh, A. (2018). Manual handling in aged care: Impact of environment-related interventions on mobility. *Safety and Health at Work, 9*(4), 372–380. DOI: 10.1016/j.shaw.2018.02.003 PMID: 30559984

Combes, S., Forbes, G., Gillett, K., Norton, C., & Nicholson, C. (2021). Development of a theory-based intervention to increase cognitively able frail elders' engagement with advance care planning using the behaviour change wheel. *BMC Health Services Research, 21*(1), 712. Advance online publication. DOI: 10.1186/s12913-021-06548-4 PMID: 34284759

Control Engineering. (2019). Six Use Cases for Collaborative Robots. https://www.controleng.com/articles/six-use-cases-for-collaborative-robots/

Cortegiani, A., Russotto, V., Montalto, F., Iozzo, P., Meschis, R., Pugliesi, M., Mariano, D., Benenati, V., Raineri, S. M., Gregoretti, C., & Giarratano, A. (2017). Use of a real-time training software (laerdal qcpr®) compared to instructor-based feedback for high-quality chest compressions acquisition in secondary school students: A randomized trial. *PLoS One, 12*(1), e0169591. DOI: 10.1371/journal.pone.0169591 PMID: 28056076

Costa, J., & Souto, E. (2022). A IoT device for monitoring particulate matter and gaseous pollutants in indoor industrial workstations. In *2022 IEEE International Conference on Consumer Electronics—Taiwan (ICCE-TW)* (pp. 517–518). IEEE. DOI: 10.1109/ICCE-Taiwan55306.2022.9869034

Cowley, S. A., Tzouvara, V., & Horta Reis da Silva, T. (2023). Public Health: healthy ageing and well-being. In Redfern's Nursing Older People. Fifth edition. Editors: Ross, Harris, Fitzpatrick and Abley. Elsevier.

Custers, B. (2016). Drones Here, There and Everywhere Introduction and Overview. In: Custers, B. (eds) The Future of Drone Use. Information Technology and Law Series, vol 27. T.M.C. Asser Press, The Hague. DOI: 10.1007/978-94-6265-132-6_1

da Silva, T. H. R., & Rodrigues, E. C. P. (2023). Body Image Related Discrimination. In Leal Filho, W., Azul, A. M., Brandli, L., Lange Salvia, A., Özuyar, P. G., & Wall, T. (Eds.), *Reduced Inequalities. Encyclopedia of the UN Sustainable Development Goals*. Springer., DOI: 10.1007/978-3-319-71060-0_61-1

Dalia, Y., Bharath, A., Mayya, V., & Kamath, S. S. (2021). DeepOA: Clinical decision support system for early detection and severity grading of knee osteoarthritis. *2021 5th International Conference on Computer, Communication and Signal Processing (ICCCSP)*, 250–255. DOI: 10.1109/ICCCSP52374.2021.9465522

Danilov, G., Kostyumov, V., Pilipenko, O., Ilyushin, E., Pitskhelauri, D., Zelenova, A., … & Bykanov, A. (2024). Computer vision for assessing surgical movements in neurosurgery.. DOI: 10.3233/SHTI240564

Dar, J., Aijaz, M., Almanjahie, I., & Warke, A. (2022). Estimation of heat diffusion in human tissue at adverse temperatures using the cylindrical form of bioheat equation. *Mathematics*, *10*(20), 3820. DOI: 10.3390/math10203820

Das, B. (2023). Adverse health effects and perceived musculoskeletal pain in the sawmill workers of west Bengal, India. *Toxicology and Industrial Health*, *40*(1-2), 9–22. DOI: 10.1177/07482337231210331 PMID: 37877376

Dayana, D. S., V. Thummala, A. Bhagyalakshmi, M. Tyj Naga and S. Ushasukhanya. (2024) AI-Controlled Robotics in Smart Agricultural Systems. *Advances in computer and electrical engineering book series*: 351 - 382.

Dellermann, D., Calma, A., Lipusch, N., Weber, T., Weigel, S., & Ebel, P. (2021) The future of human-AI collaboration: a taxonomy of design knowledge for hybrid intelligence systems. *arXiv preprint arXiv:2105.03354*.

Demirel, Ö., Weingärtner, S., Moeller, S., & Akçakaya, M. (2023). Improved Simultaneous Multi-slice imaging with Composition of k-space Interpolations (SMS-COOKIE) for myocardial T1 mapping. *PLoS One*, *18*(7), e0283972. DOI: 10.1371/journal.pone.0283972 PMID: 37478080

Department of Communications and Digital Technologies. South Africa. (2021). *South Africa's Artificial Intelligence (AI) Planning.* Retrieved from. https://www.dcdt.gov.za/images/phocadownload/AI_Government_Summit/National_AI_Government_Summit_Discussion_Document.pdf

Department of Minerals and Energy. (2003). *Guideline for the compilation of a mandatory code of practice for an occupational health programme for noise*. Pretoria, South Africa: Department of Minerals and Energy Retrieved from https://www.gov.za/documents/notices/mine-health-and-safety-act-guideline-compilation-mandatory-code-practice-4

Desai, D., & Shende, P. (2021). Integration of Internet of Things with Quantum Dots: A State-of-the-art of Medicine. *Current Pharmaceutical Design, 27*(17), 2068–2075. DOI: 10.2174/1381612827666210222113740 PMID: 33618640

Devi, B. R. (2018). MSO–MLP diagnostic approach for detecting DENV serotypes. *International Journal of Pure and Applied Mathematics, 118*(5), 1–6.

Dharani, N. P., N. Endluru Raga, K. Erragropula, N. Thadamalapula, S. Karanam and S. Nythappagiri. (2024) Real Time Monitoring System for Bacterial Contamination in Drinking Water using Embedded Technology. 280 - 287.

Dharmani, B. C., & Khatri, K. (2023). Deep learning for knee osteoarthritis severity stage detection using X-ray images. *2023 15th International Conference on COMmunication Systems & NETworkS (COMSNETS)*, 78–83. DOI: 10.1109/COMSNETS56262.2023.10041355

Dharmendra, V. J. and A. C. Robin (2020). Prediction of Occupational Risk at Workplace Using Artificial Neural Network—A Case Study: 769 - 776.

Dignum, V. (2023). Responsible Artificial Intelligence---From Principles to Practice: A Keynote at TheWebConf 2022. ACM SIGIR Forum, ACM New York, NY, USA.

Dikici, E., Bigelow, M., Prevedello, L. M., White, R. D., & Erdal, B. S. (2020). Integrating AI into radiology workflow: Levels of research, production, and feedback maturity. *Journal of Medical Imaging (Bellingham, Wash.), 7*(01), 1. DOI: 10.1117/1.JMI.7.1.016502 PMID: 32064302

Doki, S., Sasahara, S., Hori, D., Oi, Y., Takahashi, T., Shiraki, N., Ikeda, Y., Ikeda, T., Arai, Y., Muroi, K., & Matsuzaki, I. (2021). Comparison of predicted psychological distress among workers between artificial intelligence and psychiatrists: A cross-sectional study in Tsukuba science city, Japan. *BMJ Open, 11*(6), e046265. DOI: 10.1136/bmjopen-2020-046265 PMID: 34162646

Driver, E. (2011). *Consequentialism*. Routledge. DOI: 10.4324/9780203149256

Dudhe, S. S., Mishra, G., Parihar, P., Nimodia, D., & Kumari, A. (2024). Radiation Dose Optimization in Radiology: A Comprehensive Review of Safeguarding Patients and Preserving Image Fidelity. *Cureus*. Advance online publication. DOI: 10.7759/cureus.60846 PMID: 38910606

Duraisamy, J. (2020). Design and Analysis of Remotely Amphibious Drone. *International Journal of Innovative Technology and Exploring Engineering, 9*(5), 284–287. DOI: 10.35940/ijitee.E2137.039520

Dwivedi, Y. and P. Ritesh Arvind. (2024) AI Robots in Various Sector. *International journal of innovative science and research technology*: 1926 - 1928.

Dwivedi, Y. K., Hughes, L., Ismagilova, E., Aarts, G., Coombs, C., Crick, T., Duan, Y., Dwivedi, R., Edwards, J., Eirug, A., Galanos, V., Ilavarasan, P. V., Janssen, M., Jones, P., Kar, A. K., Kizgin, H., Kronemann, B., Lal, B., Lucini, B., & Williams, M. D. (2021). Artificial Intelligence (AI): Multidisciplinary perspectives on emerging challenges, opportunities, and agenda for research, practice and policy. *International Journal of Information Management, 57*, 10199. DOI: 10.1016/j.ijinfomgt.2019.08.002

Edwards, A., Dekker, J. J., Franz, R. M., Van Dyk, T., & Banyini, A. (2011). *Profiles of noise exposure levels in South African mining.*

Edwards, A., Van Coller, P., & Badenhorst, C. (2010). Early identification of noise induced hearing loss: a pilot study on the use of distortion product otoacoustic emissions as an adjunct to screening audiometry in the mining industry.

Eetvelde, H., Mendonça, L., Ley, C., Seil, R., & Tischer, T. (2021). Machine learning methods in sport injury prediction and prevention: A systematic review. *Journal of Experimental Orthopaedics*, *8*(1), 27. Advance online publication. DOI: 10.1186/s40634-021-00346-x PMID: 33855647

Egejuru, N. C., Ogunlade, O., & Idowu, P. A. (2019). Development of a Mobile-Based Hypertension Risk Monitoring System. *International Journal of Information Engineering and Electronic Business*. DOI: 10.5815/ijieeb.2019.04.02

Einizinab, S., Khoshelham, K., Winter, S., Christopher, P., Fang, Y., Windholz, E., Radanovic, M., & Hu, S. (2023). Enabling technologies for remote and virtual inspection of building work. *Automation in Construction*, *156*, 105096. DOI: 10.1016/j.autcon.2023.105096

Ejike Innocent, N., E. Ebube Victor, A. Mojeed Dayo, O. Janet Aderonke and M. Chukwudi Cosmos. (2024) Artificial Intelligence in predictive analytics for epidemic outbreaks in rural populations. *International Journal of Life Science Research Archive*, 7: 078 - 094.

El-Helaly, M. (2024). Artificial Intelligence and Occupational Health and Safety, Benefits and Drawbacks. *La Medicina del Lavoro*, *115*(2), 1. DOI: 10.23749/mdl.v115i2.15835 PMID: 38686574

Emrich-Mills, L., Collier, P., & West, J. (2019). The role of nurse prescribers in memory services and their continuing professional development: A review of the literature. *Journal of Clinical Nursing*, *28*(9-10), 1422–1432. DOI: 10.1111/jocn.14796 PMID: 30667577

European Agency for Safety and Health at Work (EU-OSHA). (2021). *Work-related stress, fatigue, and health in the transport sector*. https://osha.europa.eu

Evangeline, C. and H. Grant (2021). The Future of Biosecurity Surveillance: 261 - 275.

Fabio, G., Giuditta, C., Margherita, P., & Raffaeli, R. A. (2025). A human-centric methodology for the co-evolution of operators' skills, digital tools and user interfaces to support the Operator 4.0. *Robotics and Computer-integrated Manufacturing*, *91*, 102854. DOI: 10.1016/j.rcim.2024.102854

Failing, J. M., Abellán-Nebot, J. V., Benavent Nácher, S., Rosado Castellano, P., & Romero Subirón, F. (2023). A tool condition monitoring system based on low-cost sensors and an IoT platform for rapid deployment. *Processes (Basel, Switzerland)*, *11*(3), 668. DOI: 10.3390/pr11030668

Fang, B., Li, D., Yan, E., Zhou, Y., Yu, Z., & Hu, J. (2022). Associated factors of discrepancy between older adults and their family caregivers in reporting elder abuse. *Journal of Clinical Nursing*, *32*(5-6), 688–700. DOI: 10.1111/jocn.16283 PMID: 35289011

Fanti, G., Spinazzè, A., Borghi, F., Rovelli, S., Campagnolo, D., Keller, M., Borghi, A., Cattaneo, A., Cauda, E., & Cavallo, D. M. (2022). Evolution and applications of recent sensing technology for occupational risk assessment: A rapid review of the literature. *Sensors (Basel)*, *22*(13), 4841. DOI: 10.3390/s22134841 PMID: 35808337

Faradonbeh, R. S., Ryoza, M. G., & Sepehri, M. (2024). Application of artificial intelligence in distinguishing genuine microseismic events from the noise signals in underground mines. In *Applications of Artificial Intelligence in Mining and Geotechnical Engineering* (pp. 197–220). Elsevier. DOI: 10.1016/B978-0-443-18764-3.00008-4

Far, B. F. (2023). Artificial Intelligence Ethics in Precision Oncology: Balancing Advancements in Technology With Patient Privacy and Autonomy. *Exploration of Targeted Anti-tumor Therapy*, 685–689. Advance online publication. DOI: 10.37349/etat.2023.00160 PMID: 37720345

Fatima, S., Desouza, K. C., & Dawson, G. S. (2020). National strategic artificial intelligence plans: A multi-dimensional analysis. *Economic Analysis and Policy*, *67*, 178–194. DOI: 10.1016/j.eap.2020.07.008

Feki, I., Ammar, S., Kessentini, Y., & Muhammad, K. (2021). Federated learning for COVID-19 screening from Chest X-ray images. *Applied Soft Computing*, *106*, 107330. DOI: 10.1016/j.asoc.2021.107330 PMID: 33776607

Felknor, S. A., Streit, J. M., Edwards, N. T., & Howard, J. (2023). Four futures for occupational safety and health. *International Journal of Environmental Research and Public Health*, *20*(5), 4333. DOI: 10.3390/ijerph20054333 PMID: 36901347

Feng, J., Phillips, R. V., Malenica, I., Bishara, A., Hubbard, A. E., Celi, L. A., & Pirracchio, R. (2022). Clinical artificial intelligence quality improvement: Towards continual monitoring and updating of AI algorithms in healthcare. *NPJ Digital Medicine*, *5*(1), 66. DOI: 10.1038/s41746-022-00611-y PMID: 35641814

Fernando, P.-R. and V. Antonio (2013). Application of Predictive Models in Quantitative Risk Assessment and Risk Management: 87 - 97.

Ferrari, G. N., Leal, G. C. L., Galdamez, E. V. C., & de Souza, R. C. T. (2020). Prioritization of occupational health and safety indicators using the fuzzy-AHP method. *Production*, *30*, e20200054. DOI: 10.1590/0103-6513.20200054

Ferretti, L., Wymant, C., Petrie, J., Tsallis, D., Kendall, M., Ledda, A., Di Lauro, F., Fowler, A., Di Francia, A., Panovska-Griffiths, J., Abeler-Dörner, L., Charalambides, M., Briers, M., & Fraser, C. (2024). Digital measurement of SARS-CoV-2 transmission risk from 7 million contacts. *Nature*, *626*(7997), 145–150. DOI: 10.1038/s41586-023-06952-2 PMID: 38122820

Feuerstein, J., & Chasin, M. (2009). Noise exposure and issues in hearing conservation. In *Handbook of Clinical Audiology* (7th ed., pp. 678–698). Lippincott Williams & Wilkins.

Fisher, E., Flynn, M. A., Pratap, P., & Vietas, J. A. (2023). Occupational safety and health equity impacts of artificial intelligence: A scoping review. *International Journal of Environmental Research and Public Health*, *20*(13), 6221. DOI: 10.3390/ijerph20136221 PMID: 37444068

Fisher, S., & Rosella, L. (2022). Priorities for successful use of artificial intelligence by public health organizations: A literature review. *BMC Public Health*, *22*(2146), 2146. Advance online publication. DOI: 10.1186/s12889-022-14422-z PMID: 36419010

Flor-Unda, O., Fuentes, M., Dávila, D., Rivera, M., Llano, G., Izurieta, C., & Acosta-Vargas, P. (2023). Innovative Technologies for Occupational Health and Safety: A Scoping Review. *Safety (Basel, Switzerland)*, *9*(2), 35. DOI: 10.3390/safety9020035

Foromo, M. R., Chabeli, M., & Satekge, M. M. (2016). Survey on the implementation of the Occupational Health and Safety Act at an academic hospital in Johannesburg. *Curationis*, *39*(1), 1–10. DOI: 10.4102/curationis.v39i1.1524 PMID: 27796104

Fox, S., & Victores, J. G. (2024, May). Safety of Human–Artificial Intelligence Systems: Applying Safety Science to Analyze Loopholes in Interactions between Human Organizations, Artificial Intelligence, and Individual People. [). MDPI.]. *Informatics (MDPI)*, *11*(2), 36. DOI: 10.3390/informatics11020036

Franz, R. M., & Phillips, J. J. (2001). Noise and vibration. In E. R. Guild R, Johnson J & Ross M (Ed.), *Handbook of Occupational Health Practice in the South African Mining Industry* (pp. 195-232). The Safety in Mines Research Advisory Committee (SAMRAC).

Fugate, H., & Alzraiee, H. (2023). Quantitative analysis of construction labor acceptance of wearable sensing devices to enhance workers' safety. *Results in Engineering*, *17*, 100841. DOI: 10.1016/j.rineng.2022.100841

Fukumura, Y., Gray, J., Lucas, G., Becerik-Gerber, B., & Roll, S. (2021). Worker perspectives on incorporating artificial intelligence into office workspaces: Implications for the future of office work. *International Journal of Environmental Research and Public Health*, *18*(4), 1690. DOI: 10.3390/ijerph18041690 PMID: 33578736

Fu, Z., Xian, Y., Zhu, Y., Xu, S., Li, Z., Melo, G., & Zhang, Y. (2021). HOOPS: Human-in-the-Loop Graph Reasoning for Conversational Recommendation. *Proceedings of the 44th International ACM SIGIR Conference on Research and Development in Information Retrieval.* https://doi.org/DOI: 10.1145/3404835.3463247

Gabbard, J. L., Smith, M., Tanous, K., Kim, H., & Jonas, B. (2019). AR DriveSim: AnImmersive Driving Simulator for Augmented Reality Head-Up Display Research. *Frontiers in Robotics and AI*, *I*, 6. DOI: 10.3389/frobt.2019.00098 PMID: 33501113

Galetsi, P., Katsaliaki, K., & Kumar, S. (2022). The medical and societal impact of big data analytics and artificial intelligence applications in combating pandemics: A review focused on Covid-19. *Social Science & Medicine*, *301*, 114973. DOI: 10.1016/j.socscimed.2022.114973 PMID: 35452893

Gallifant, J., Zhang, J., Del Pilar Arias Lopez, M., Zhu, T., Camporota, L., Celi, L. A., & Formenti, F. (2022). Artificial intelligence for mechanical ventilation: Systematic review of design, reporting standards, and bias. *British Journal of Anaesthesia*, *128*(2), 343–351. DOI: 10.1016/j.bja.2021.09.025 PMID: 34772497

Gaobotse, G., Mbunge, E., Batani, J., & Muchemwa, B. (2022). Non-invasive smart implants in healthcare: Redefining healthcare services delivery through sensors and emerging digital health technologies. *Sensors International*, *3*, 100156. DOI: 10.1016/j.sintl.2022.100156

Gaske, M. R. (2023). Regulation Priorities for Artificial Intelligence Foundation Models. *SSRN*, *26*, 1. DOI: 10.2139/ssrn.4417565

Gauzy. (2023). *Gauzy unveils next-generation AI-powered advanced driver assistance system.* https://investors.gauzy.com

Gazineo, D., Godino, L., Decaro, R., Calogero, P., Pinto, D., Chiari, P., Zoli, M., & Ambrosi, E. (2020). Assisted walking program on walking ability in in-hospital geriatric patients: A randomized trial. *Journal of the American Geriatrics Society*, *69*(3), 637–643. DOI: 10.1111/jgs.16922 PMID: 33184855

Gemler, B. T., Mukherjee, C., Howland, C. A., Huk, D. J., Shank, Z., Harbo, L. J., Tabbaa, O. P., & Bartling, C. M. (2022). Function-Based Classification of Hazardous Biological Sequences: Demonstration of a New Paradigm for Biohazard Assessments. *Frontiers in Bioengineering and Biotechnology*, *10*, 979497. Advance online publication. DOI: 10.3389/fbioe.2022.979497 PMID: 36277394

Ghiafehdavoudi, S., & Vaillant, B. (2020). The Digital Transformation of Construction Worksite Safety How much added value would AI bring for workers and work-environment safety?.

Ghimire, B. K., Yu, C. Y., Kim, W. R., Moon, H. S., Lee, J., Kim, S. H., & Chung, I. M. (2023). Assessment of Benefits and Risk of Genetically Modified Plants and Products: Current Controversies and Perspective. *Sustainability 2023, Vol. 15, Page 1722, 15*(2), 1722. DOI: 10.3390/su15021722

Ghousi, R., Khanzadi, M., & Atashgah, K. M. (2018). A flexible method of building construction safety risk assessment and investigating financial aspects of safety program. *International Journal of Optimization in Civil Engineering*, *8*, 433–452.

Gladysz, B., Tran, T., Romero, D., van Erp, T., Abonyi, J., & Ruppert, T. (2023). Current development on the Operator 4.0 and transition towards the Operator 5.0: A systematic literature review in light of Industry 5.0. *Journal of Manufacturing Systems*, *70*, 160–185. DOI: 10.1016/j.jmsy.2023.07.008

Goel, S. S., Goel, A., Kumar, M., & Moltó, G. (2021). A review of Internet of Things: Qualifying technologies and boundless horizon. *Journal of Reliable Intelligent Environments*, *7*(1), 23–33. DOI: 10.1007/s40860-020-00127-w

Goh, Y. M., & Chua, S. (2016). Knowledge, attitude and practices for design for safety: A study on civil & structural engineers. *Accident; Analysis and Prevention*, *93*, 260–266. DOI: 10.1016/j.aap.2015.09.023 PMID: 26477455

Gómez-Ochoa, S. A., Franco, O. H., Rojas, L. Z., Romero Guevara, S. L., Echeverría, L. E., Glisic, M., & Muka, T. (2020). COVID-19 in healthcare workers: A systematic review and meta-analysis of prevalence, risk factors, clinical characteristics, and outcomes. *American Journal of Epidemiology*. PMID: 32870978

Gong, Z. (2023). Artificial Intelligence in the 21st Century. *Research on Intelligent Manufacturing and Assembly*. DOI: 10.25082/RIMA.2023.01.002

Goodfellow, I., J. Pouget-Abadie, M. Mirza, B. Xu, D. Warde-Farley, S. Ozair, A. Courville and Y. Bengio. (2020) Generative adversarial networks. *Commun. ACM*, 63(11): 139–144, 136.

Gould, G. (2019). The Impact of Robotics on Safety and Health. Wolters Kluwer. https://www.wolterskluwer.com/en/expert-insights/the-impact-of-robotics-on-safety-and-health

Government of Kenya, Ministry of ICT. (2019). *Digital economy blueprint: Powering Kenya's transformation.* Retrieved from https://dial.global/wp-content/uploads/2020/10/SmartAfrica-DIAL_DigitalEconomyInAfrica2020-v7_ENG.pdf

Graham, S., Depp, C. A., Lee, E., Nebeker, C., Tu, X., Kim, H.-C., & Jeste, D. V. (2019). Artificial Intelligence for Mental Health and Mental Illnesses: An Overview. *Current Psychiatry Reports, 21*(11), 116. Advance online publication. DOI: 10.1007/s11920-019-1094-0 PMID: 31701320

Grandi, F., Zanni, L., Peruzzini, M., Pellicciari, M., & Campanella, C. E. (2020). A Transdisciplinary digital approach for tractor's human-centred design. *International Journal of Computer Integrated Manufacturing, 33*(4), 377–397. DOI: 10.1080/0951192X.2019.1599441

Greenwood, D., Blozis, S., Young, H., Nesbitt, T., & Quinn, C. (2015). Overcoming clinical inertia: A randomized clinical trial of a telehealth remote monitoring intervention using paired glucose testing in adults with type 2 diabetes. *Journal of Medical Internet Research, 17*(7), e178. DOI: 10.2196/jmir.4112 PMID: 26199142

Greenwood, D., Gee, P., Fatkin, K., & Peeples, M. (2017). A systematic review of reviews evaluating technology-enabled diabetes self-management education and support. *Journal of Diabetes Science and Technology, 11*(5), 1015–1027. DOI: 10.1177/1932296817713506 PMID: 28560898

Gregson, N. (2023). Waste, Money and Finance: Or, how turning discard into waste turns waste into an energy resource and an asset. In *The Waste of the World* (pp. 133-163). Bristol University Press.

Grobler, L. M., Swanepoel, D. W., Strauss, S., & Eloff, P. B. Z. (2020). Occupational noise and age: A longitudinal study of hearing sensitivity as a function of noise exposure and age in South African gold mine workers. *The South African Journal of Communication Disorders = Die Suid-Afrikaanse Tydskrif vir Kommunikasieafwykings, 67*(2), 1–7. https://doi.org/a687. DOI: 10.4102/sajcd.v67i2.687 PMID: 32242440

Gualtieri, L., Palomba, I., Merati, F. A., Rauch, E., & Vidoni, R. (2020). Design of human-centered collaborative assembly workstations for the improvement of operators' physical ergonomics and production efficiency: A case study. *Sustainability (Basel), 12*(9), 3606. DOI: 10.3390/su12093606

Gudavalli, M., Vining, R., Salsbury, S., Corber, L., Long, C., Patwardhan, A., & Goertz, C. (2015). Clinician proficiency in delivering manual treatment for neck pain within specified force ranges. *The Spine Journal, 15*(4), 570–576. DOI: 10.1016/j.spinee.2014.10.016 PMID: 25452013

Guerra, K., & Johnson, V. (2024). *AI adoption: Integrating TOE, Implementation Science, and Ethics.* AMCIS 2024 TREOs. Retrieved from https://aisel.aisnet.org/treos_amcis2024/64

Guerzhoy, M. and Hertzmann, A. (2014). Learning latent factor models of travel data for travel prediction and analysis., 131-142. DOI: 10.1007/978-3-319-06483-3_12

Gunderson, D. E., & Gloeckner, G. W. (2011). Superintendent competencies and attributes required for success: A national study comparing construction professionals' opinions. *International Journal of Construction Education and Research, 7*(4), 294–311. DOI: 10.1080/15578771.2011.618964

Guo, W. (2023). Exploring the Value of AI Technology in Optimizing and Implementing Supply Chain Data for Pharmaceutical Companies. *Innovation in Science and Technology*. DOI: 10.56397/IST.2023.05.01

Gupta, A., Hilliard, R., Mudie, K., & Clothier, P. (2016). Does providing real-time augmented feedback affect the performance of repeated lower limb loading to exhaustion? *Gait & Posture*, *44*, 204–208. DOI: 10.1016/j.gaitpost.2015.12.034 PMID: 27004659

Gupta, D., & Shah, M. (2022). A comprehensive study on artificial intelligence in oil and gas sector. *Environmental Science and Pollution Research International*, *29*(34), 50984–50997. DOI: 10.1007/s11356-021-15379-z PMID: 34378133

Guzman, J., Recoco, G., Pandi, A., Padrones, J., & Ignacio, J. (2022). Evaluating workplace safety in the oil and gas industry during the covid-19 pandemic using occupational health and safety vulnerability measure and partial least square structural equation modelling. *Cleaner Engineering and Technology*, *6*, 100378. DOI: 10.1016/j.clet.2021.100378 PMID: 35013732

Gyamfi, J., Allegrante, J., Iwelunmor, J., Williams, O., Plange-Rhule, J., Blackstone, S., Ntim, M., Apusiga, K., Peprah, E., & Ogedegbe, G. (2020). Application of the consolidated framework for implementation research to examine nurses' perception of the task shifting strategy for hypertension control trial in ghana. *BMC Health Services Research*, *20*(1), 65. Advance online publication. DOI: 10.1186/s12913-020-4912-5 PMID: 31996195

Halim, H. (2024) Spl22 biological hazards in the working environment: a risk of permanent relevance. *Occupational Medicine*, 74: 0.

Han, B., Tomer, V., Nguyen, T. A., Farmani, A., & Singh, P. K. (Eds.). (2020). *Nanosensors for smart cities*. Elsevier.

Hansson, S., Belin, M., & Lundgren, B. (2021). Self-Driving Vehicles—An Ethical Overview. *Philosophy & Technology*, *34*, 1383–1408. DOI: 10.1007/s13347-021-00464-5

Han, X. (2023). A novel assimilated navigation model based on advanced optical systems (AOS), internet of things (IoT) and artificial intelligence (AI). *Optical and Quantum Electronics*, *55*(7), 655. DOI: 10.1007/s11082-023-04947-x

Harada, K., Park, H., Lee, S., Shimada, H., Yoshida, D., Anan, Y., & Suzuki, T. (2017). Joint association of neighborhood environment and fear of falling on physical activity among frail older adults. *Journal of Aging and Physical Activity*, *25*(1), 140–148. DOI: 10.1123/japa.2016-0082 PMID: 27620962

Hasas, A., Hakimi, M., Shahidzay, A. K., & Fazil, A. W. (2024). Ai for social good: Leveraging artificial intelligence for community development. J. Communit. Service. Society. *Empower.*, *2*(02), 196–210. DOI: 10.59653/jcsse.v2i02.592

Hasnain, M., Levi, C., Ryan, A., Hubbard, I., Hall, A., Oldmeadow, C., Grady, A., Jayakody, A., Attia, J. R., & Paul, C. (2019). Can a multicomponent multidisciplinary implementation package change physicians' and nurses' perceptions and practices regarding thrombolysis for acute ischemic stroke? an exploratory analysis of a cluster-randomized trial. *Implementation Science : IS*, *14*(1), 98. Advance online publication. DOI: 10.1186/s13012-019-0940-0 PMID: 31771599

Hassan, M., Kushniruk, A., & Borycki, E. (2024). Barriers to and facilitators of artificial intelligence adoption in health care: Scoping review. *JMIR Human Factors*, *11*, e48633. DOI: 10.2196/48633 PMID: 39207831

Hattinger, M., & Stylidis, K. (2023). Transforming Quality 4.0 towards resilient Operator 5.0 needs. *Procedia CIRP*, *120*, 1600–1605. DOI: 10.1016/j.procir.2023.12.002

Havaei, F., MacPhee, M., McLeod, C. B., Ma, A., Gear, A., & Sorensen, C. (2020). A provincial study of nurses' psychological health and safety in British Columbia, Canada: Final report. *UBC cIRcle.*

Havaei, F., Astivia, O. L. O., & MacPhee, M. (2020). The impact of workplace violence on medical-surgical nurses' health outcomes: A moderated mediation model of work environment conditions and burnout using secondary data. *International Journal of Nursing Studies*, *109*, 103666. DOI: 10.1016/j.ijnurstu.2020.103666 PMID: 32592889

Havaei, F., Dahinten, V. S., & MacPhee, M. (2019). Effect of nursing care delivery models on registered nurse outcomes. *SAGE Open Nursing*, *5*, 5. DOI: 10.1177/2377960819869088 PMID: 33415250

Havaei, F., & MacPhee, M. (2020). Effect of workplace violence and psychological stress responses on medical-surgical nurses' medication intake. *Canadian Journal of Nursing Research*. PMID: 32046504

He, L., & Eastburn, M. (2022, August). Smart nanosensor networks for body injury detection. In 2022 IEEE International Conference on Smart Internet of Things (SmartIoT) (pp. 15-19). IEEE. DOI: 10.1109/SmartIoT55134.2022.00012

Hegewald, J., Berge, W., Heinrich, P., Staudte, R., Freiberg, A., Scharfe, J., Girbig, M., Nienhaus, A., & Seidler, A. (2018). Do technical aids for patient handling prevent musculoskeletal complaints in health care workers?—A systematic review of intervention studies. *International Journal of Environmental Research and Public Health*, *15*(3), 476. DOI: 10.3390/ijerph15030476 PMID: 29522440

He, H., Zhang, Y., Shi, G., & Shi, G. (2023). Recent Biotechnological Advances and Future Prospective of Bacillus Licheniformis as Microbial Cell Factories. *Systems Microbiology and Biomanufacturing*, *3*(4), 521–532. Advance online publication. DOI: 10.1007/s43393-023-00162-7

Helberger, N., & Diakopoulos, N. (2022). The European AI Act and How It Matters for Research into AI in Media and Journalism. *Digital Journalism (Abingdon, England)*, *11*(9), 1751–1760. DOI: 10.1080/21670811.2022.2082505

Hew, C., Tan, R., Lee, C., Hartanty, T., Hossain, W., & Lee, Y. (2022). Development of self sustainable IoT-based low cost UV index monitoring station. In *2022 IEEE 8th International Conference on Smart Instrumentation, Measurement and Applications (ICSIMA)* (pp. 36–41). IEEE. DOI: 10.1109/ICSIMA55652.2022.9928933

Hewett, T., Myer, G., Ford, K., Paterno, M., & Quatman, C. (2016). Mechanisms, prediction, and prevention of ACL injuries: Cut risk with three sharpened and validated tools. *Journal of Orthopaedic Research*, *34*(11), 1843–1855. DOI: 10.1002/jor.23414 PMID: 27612195

Hewlett Packard Enterprise. (2025). *Pharmaceutical Companies Embrace AI in Drug Discovery Efforts - Business Insider*. AI in Action. https://www.businessinsider.com/pharmaceutical-companies-embrace-ai-in-drug-discovery-efforts-2025-3?utm_source=chatgpt.com

Heyns, S., Dekker, K., Ker-Fox, J., Oberholster, A., Claassen, N., Schoeman, J., Dube, S., van der Walt, J., Pullen, M., & Preis, E. (2021). *COE 180701 – Review The Current Sami Noise Exposure Limit And Conduct A Study On Vibration OEL In Relation To The SAMI*. Pretoria: Mine Health and Safety Council Retrieved from https://mhsc.org.za/wp-content/uploads/2021/07/CoE-180701-Final-Report-%E2%80%93-Review-The-Current-SAMI-Noise-Exposure-Limit-And-Conduct-A-Study-On-Vibration-OEL-In-Relation-To-The-SAMI.pdf

Hinsliff-Smith, K., Feakes, R., Whitworth, G., Seymour, J., Moghaddam, N., Dening, T., & Cox, K. (2015). What do we know about the application of the mental capacity act (2005) in healthcare practice regarding decision-making for frail and older people? a systematic literature review. *Health & Social Care in the Community*, *25*(2), 295–308. DOI: 10.1111/hsc.12310 PMID: 26611194

Holzinger, A., Keiblinger, K., Holub, P., Zatloukal, K., & Müller, H. (2023). AI for life: Trends in artificial intelligence for biotechnology. *New Biotechnology*, *74*, 16–24. DOI: 10.1016/j.nbt.2023.02.001 PMID: 36754147

Holzinger, A., Langs, G., Denk, H., Zatloukal, K., & Müller, H. (2019, April 02). Causability and explainability of artificial intelligence in medicine. *Wiley Interdisciplinary Reviews. Data Mining and Knowledge Discovery*, *9*(4), e1312. DOI: 10.1002/widm.1312 PMID: 32089788

Hooshmand, M. A., Toledo, C. S., Moghaddas, R., & Skordilis, E. (2022). Data Analytics for Diagnosis and Prediction of Central Line-Associated Bloodstream Infections in Critical Care Units. *Computers, Informatics, Nursing*, *40*(6), 365–372. DOI: 10.1097/CIN.0000000000000794 PMID: 35670636

Horta Reis Da Silva, T. (2022). Moving and Handling. In Curr, S., & Fordham-Clarke, C. (Eds.), *Clinical Skills at Glance* (pp. 20–21). Wiley.

Hossain, M. A., Abbott, E. L. S., Chua, D. K. H., Qui, N. T., & Goh, Y. M. (2018). Design-for-safety knowledge library for BIM-integrated safety risk reviews. *Automation in Construction*, *94*, 290–302. DOI: 10.1016/j.autcon.2018.07.010

Hou, L., Wu, S., Zhang, G., Tan, Y., & Wang, X. (2021). Literature Review of Digital Twins Applications in Construction Workforce Safety. *Applied Sciences (Basel, Switzerland)*, *11*, •••. https://doi.org/**10.3390/app11010339

Hovell, M., Bellettiere, J., Liles, S., Nguyen, B., Berardi, V., Johnson, C., … & Hughes, S. (2019). Randomised controlled trial of real-time feedback and brief coaching to reduce indoor smoking. Tobacco Control, tobaccocontrol-2018-054717. DOI: 10.1136/tobaccocontrol-2018-054717

Howard, J., & Schulte, P. (2024). Managing workplace ai risks and the future of work. *American Journal of Industrial Medicine*, *67*(11), 980–993. DOI: 10.1002/ajim.23653 PMID: 39223704

Hoxhaj, O., Halilaj, B., & Harizi, A. (2023). Ethical Implications And Human Rights Violations In The Age Of Artificial Intelligence. *Balkan Social Science Review*, *22*(22), 153–171. DOI: 10.46763/BSSR232222153h

Hsiang-Yang, S., J. C. Cynthia, B. Robert and H. Y. Daniel. (2023) Development of a Soft Sensor Using Machine Learning Algorithms for Predicting the Water Quality of an Onsite Wastewater Treatment System. *ACS Environmental Au.*

Huang, C., Zhang, Z., Mao, B., & Yao, X. (2023) Overview of Artificial Intelligence Ethics, Transactions on Artificial intelligence, vol. 4, No. 4, August 2023 799 DOI: 10.1109/TAI.2022.3194503

Huang, J., Wu, X., Huang, W., Wu, X., & Wang, S. (2021). Internet of things in health management systems: A review. *International Journal of Communication Systems*, *34*(4), e4683. DOI: 10.1002/dac.4683

Huby, G. (2023). The bridge of knowledge: infrastructure for the coordination of health and social care or an easy fix?., 35-51. DOI: 10.23865/noasp.196.ch1

Hu, D., Kong, Y., Li, W., Han, Q., Zhang, X., & Zhu, L. X.. (2020). Frontline nurses' burnout, anxiety, depression, and fear statuses and their associated factors during the COVID-19 outbreak in Wuhan, China: A large-scale cross-sectional study. *Lancet*, *24*, 100424. PMID: 32766539

Hurley, D., & Popescu, G. H. (2021). Medical big data and wearable internet of things healthcare systems in remotely monitoring and caring for confirmed or suspected COVID-19 patients. *American Journal of Medical Research (New York, N.Y.)*, *8*(2), 78–90. DOI: 10.22381/ajmr8220216

Hussain, M., Alamri, A., Zhang, T., & Jamil, I. (2024). Application of Artificial Intelligence in the Oil and Gas Industry. In *Engineering Applications of Artificial Intelligence* (pp. 341–373). Springer Nature Switzerland. DOI: 10.1007/978-3-031-50300-9_19

Hussain, S., Mubeen, I., Ullah, N., Shah, S. S. U. D., Khan, B. A., Zahoor, M., Ullah, R., Khan, F. A., & Sultan, M. A. (2022). Modern Diagnostic Imaging Technique Applications and Risk Factors in the Medical Field: A Review. *BioMed Research International*, *2022*(1), 1–19. DOI: 10.1155/2022/5164970 PMID: 35707373

Hu, W., Xia, W., Li, Y., Jiang, J., Li, G., & Chen, Y. (2022). An intelligent identification method of safety risk while drilling in gas drilling. *Petroleum Exploration and Development*, *49*(2), 428–437. DOI: 10.1016/S1876-3804(22)60036-3

Huysentruyt, K., Kjoersvik, O., Dobracki, P., Savage, E., Mishalov, E., Cherry, M. J., Leonard, E. B., Taylor, R. C., Patel, B., & Abatemarco, D. (2021). Validating Intelligent Automation Systems in Pharmacovigilance: Insights From Good Manufacturing Practices. *Drug Safety*, *44*(3), 261–272. Advance online publication. DOI: 10.1007/s40264-020-01030-2 PMID: 33523400

Hwang, B.-G., Shan, M., & Phuah, S. L. (2018). Safety in green building construction projects in Singapore: Performance, critical issues, and improvement solutions. *KSCE Journal of Civil Engineering*, *22*(2), 447–458. DOI: 10.1007/s12205-017-1961-3

Ibatulin, M. (2023) Development of System and Methods of Predictive Maintenance in Production Using Industrial Sensors. *International Conference on Industrial Engineering, Applications and Manufacturing*: 1119 - 1123.

Ibrahim, C. K. I. C., Manu, P., Belayutham, S., Mahamadu, A.-M., & Antwi-Afari, M. F. (2022). Design for safety (DfS) practice in construction engineering and management research: A review of current trends and future directions. *Journal of Building Engineering*, *52*, 104352. DOI: 10.1016/j.jobe.2022.104352

Ibrahim, H., Liu, X., Rivera, S., Moher, D., Chan, A., Sydes, M., Calvert, M. J., & Denniston, A. (2021). Reporting guidelines for clinical trials of artificial intelligence interventions: The spirit-ai and consort-ai guidelines. *Trials*, *22*(1), 11. Advance online publication. DOI: 10.1186/s13063-020-04951-6 PMID: 33407780

Ibrahim, T., & Ali, H. (2023). The Impact of Wearable IoT Devices on Early Disease Detection and Prevention. *International Journal of Applied Health Care Analytics*, *8*(8), 1–15.

Idambi, K., & Boniface, J. (2021). *An Assessment of Regulatory Compliance With International and Regional Obligations Relating To Environmental Health And Safety Standards* (Doctoral dissertation, Institute of Petroleum Studies-Kampala).

ILO. (2023). *International Labour Organization. Technical guidelines on biological hazards in the working environment*. International Labour Office.

Indovina, K., Keniston, A., Reid, M., Sachs, K., Zheng, C., Tong, A., Hernandez, D., Bui, K., Ali, Z., Nguyen, T., Guirguis, H., Albert, R. K., & Burden, M. (2016). Real-time patient experience surveys of hospitalized medical patients. *Journal of Hospital Medicine*, *11*(4), 251–256. DOI: 10.1002/jhm.2533 PMID: 26777721

Inglesby, T. V. and A. A. Adalja (2022). Global catastrophic biological risks: Nature and response: 29 - 42.

International Labour Organization (ILO). (2023). *World Social Protection Report: Occupational Fatalities by Sector*. ILO Publishing.

International Maritime Organization (IMO). (2020). *Transport of Dangerous Goods by Sea: IMDG Code*. IMO.

International Road Transport Union (IRU). (2022). *Global Survey on Digital Adoption in Road Transport*. IRU Reports.

Irawan, B., & Biyanto, T. R. (2024). Industrial Evolution: The Integration of Al in Robotics. *AI Developments for Industrial Robotics and Intelligent Drones*, 85.

Iskrzycki, Ł., Smereka, J., Rodríguez-Núñez, A., Furelos, R., Gomez, C., Kamińska, H., & Ładny, J. (2018). The impact of the use of a cprmeter monitor on quality of chest compressions: A prospective randomised trial, cross-simulation. *Kardiologia Polska*, *76*(3), 574–579. DOI: 10.5603/KP.a2017.0255 PMID: 29297195

Islam, M. (2024). Exploring the impact of artificial intelligence in healthcare. *JAIGS*, *2*(1), 228–238. DOI: 10.60087/jaigs.v2i1.109

ISO. (2018). *ISO 45001:2018 Occupational Health and Safety Management Systems – Requirements with Guidance for Use*. International Organization for Standardization.

Jabbar, S. F. (2023). Automated Stand-Alone Surgical Safety Evaluation for Laparoscopic Cholecystectomy (LC) Using Convolutional Neural Network and Constrained Local Models (CNN-CLM). *Journal of Robotics and Control (Jrc).* DOI: 10.18196/jrc.v3i6.16201

Jackson, D., Anders, R., Padula, W. V., Daly, J., & Davidson, P. M. (2020). Vulnerability of nurses and physicians with COVID-19: Monitoring and surveillance needed. *Journal of Clinical Nursing.*

Jain, A. (2021). *Impact of digitalization and artificial intelligence as causes and enablers of organizational change.* Nottingham University Business School.

Jain, A., Hassard, J., Leka, S., Di Tecco, C., & Iavicoli, S. (2021). The role of occupational health services in psychosocial risk management and the promotion of mental health and well-being at work. *International Journal of Environmental Research and Public Health, 18*(7), 3632. DOI: 10.3390/ijerph18073632 PMID: 33807352

Jaiswal, R., Sharma, S., & Kaushik, R. (2023). Ethics in AI and Machine Learning. Journal of Nonlinear Analysis and Optimization. .DOI: 10.36893/JNAO.2023.V14I1.0008-0012

Janackovic, G. L., Savic, S. M., & Stankovic, M. S. (2013). Selection and ranking of occupational safety indicators based on fuzzy AHP: A case study in road construction companies. *South African Journal of Industrial Engineering, 24*(3), 175–189. DOI: 10.7166/24-3-463

Janet Aderonke, O., M. Chukwudi Cosmos, K. Tolulope Olagoke and A. Samira. (2024) Innovations in real-time infectious disease surveillance using AI and mobile data. *International medical science research journal.*

János, P. and M. Anna. (2024) AI-Powered Microscopy Platform for Airborne Biothreat Detection. *Security informatics and law enforcement*: 117 - 127.

Janssen, A., Kavisha, S., Johnson, A., Marinic, A., Teede, H., & Shaw, T. (2024). Implementation of artificial intelligence applications in Australian healthcare organisations: environmental scan findings.. DOI: 10.3233/SHTI231142

Janssen, M., Cski, C., Lindgren, I., Loukis, E., Melin, U., Viale, P. G., Rodrguez, B., Manuel, P., & Tambouris, E. (2022). AI Systems for Occupational Safety and Health: From Ethical Concerns to Limited Legal Solutions. Electronic Government, Springer International Publishing: 499--514.

Janssen, M., Brous, P., Estevez, E., Barbosa, L. S., & Janowski, T. (2020). Data governance: Organizing data for trustworthy Artificial Intelligence. *Government Information Quarterly, 37*(3), 101493. DOI: 10.1016/j.giq.2020.101493

Jarota, M. (2021). Artificial intelligence and robotisation in the EU - should we change OHS law? *Journal of Occupational Medicine and Toxicology (London, England), 16*(18), 1–8. DOI: 10.1186/s12995-021-00301-7 PMID: 33952297

Jarota, M. (2023). Artificial intelligence in the work process. A reflection on the proposed European Union regulations on artificial intelligence from an occupational health and safety perspective. *Computer Law & Security Review, 49*, 105825. DOI: 10.1016/j.clsr.2023.105825

Jebelli, H., Choi, B., & Lee, S. (2019). Application of wearable biosensors to construction sites. I: Assessing workers' stress. *Journal of Construction Engineering and Management*, *145*(12), 04019079. DOI: 10.1061/(ASCE)CO.1943-7862.0001729

Jeebhay, M. F., Naidoo, R. N., Naidoo, S., Adams, S., Zungu, M., Kgalomono, S., Naicker, N., & Kistnasamy, B. (2023). Strengthening Social Compact and Innovative Health Sector Collaborations in Addressing COVID-19 in South African Workplaces. *New Solutions*, *32*(4), 288–303. DOI: 10.1177/10482911221150237 PMID: 36650981

Jeelani, O., Njie, M., & Korzhuk, V. (2024). Methods and algorithms of ensuring data privacy in ai-based healthcare systems and technologies.. DOI: 10.3233/SHTI240640

Jeelani, I., & Gheisari, M. (2021). Safety challenges of UAV integration in construction: Conceptual analysis and future research roadmap. *Safety Science*, *144*, 105473. Advance online publication. DOI: 10.1016/j.ssci.2021.105473

Jenkins, T. (2022). Wearable medical sensor devices, machine and deep learning algorithms, and internet of things-based healthcare systems in COVID-19 patient screening, diagnosis, monitoring, and treatment. *American Journal of Medical Research (New York, N.Y.)*, *9*(1), 49–64. DOI: 10.22381/ajmr9120224

Jermutus, E., Kneale, D., Thomas, J., & Michie, S. (2022). Influences on User Trust in Healthcare Artificial Intelligence: A Systematic Review. *Wellcome Open Research*. https://doi.org/DOI: 10.12688/wellcomeopenres.17550.1

Jiang, Z., Bakker, O., & Bartolo, P. (2022). Critical review of Industry 4.0 technologies' applications on occupational safety and health. In *2022 8th International Conference on Control, Decision and Information Technologies (CoDIT)* (pp. 1267–1272). IEEE. DOI: 10.1109/CoDIT55151.2022.9804084

Jiang, N., Liu, X., Liu, H. K., Lim, E. T., Tan, C., & Gu, J. (2022). Beyond AI-powered Context-Aware services: The Role Of human–AI Collaboration. *Industrial Management & Data Systems*. Advance online publication. DOI: 10.1108/IMDS-03-2022-0152

Jiang, X., Coffee, M., Bari, A., Wang, J., Jiang, X., Huang, J., Shi, J., Dai, J., Cai, J., Zhang, T., Wu, Z., He, G., & Huang, Y. (2020). Towards an artificial intelligence framework for data-driven prediction of coronavirus clinical severity. *Computers, Materials & Continua*, *63*(1), 537–551. DOI: 10.32604/cmc.2020.010691

Jiang, Z., Hao, Y., Jin, N., & Li, Y. (2022). A systematic review of the relationship between workload and injury risk of professional male soccer players. *International Journal of Environmental Research and Public Health*, *19*(20), 13237. DOI: 10.3390/ijerph192013237 PMID: 36293817

Jilcha, K., & Kitaw, D. (2017). Industrial occupational safety and health innovation for sustainable development. *Engineering Science and Technology, an International Journal*, *20*(1), 372–380. DOI: 10.1016/j.jestch.2016.10.011

Jin, Y., Kim, H., Jin, T., & Lee, S.-M. (2020). *Automated Fall and Pressure Injury Risk Assessment Systems*. Cin Computers Informatics Nursing., DOI: 10.1097/CIN.0000000000000696

Ji, S., Li, Q., Cao, W., Zhang, P., & Muccini, H. (2020). Quality Assurance Technologies of Big Data Applications: A Systematic Literature Review. *Applied Sciences (Basel, Switzerland), 10*(22), 8052. DOI: 10.3390/app10228052

Joan, B. R., Nynke, H., Hollmann, E. K., Panagis, K., Gertjan, M., Heather, M. M., Colleen, C. N., & Matthew, E. V. (2023). Global microbial water quality data and predictive analytics: Key to health and meeting SDG 6. *PLOS Water, 2*(8), e0000166. DOI: 10.1371/journal.pwat.0000166

John, H. and A. S. Paul. (2024) Managing workplace AI risks and the future of work. *American Journal of Industrial Medicine*.

John, M., & Shaiba, H. (2019). Main factors influencing recovery in MERS Co-V patients using machine learning. *Journal of Infection and Public Health, 12*(5), 700–704. DOI: 10.1016/j.jiph.2019.03.020 PMID: 30979679

Johnson, A., Dey, S., Nguyen, H., Groth, M., Joyce, S., Tan, L., Glozier, N., & Harvey, S. B. (2020). A review and agenda for examining how technology-driven changes at work will impact workplace mental health and employee well-being. *Australian Journal of Management, 45*(3), 402–424. DOI: 10.1177/0312896220922292

Juan José, T.-P., María Renée, H.-B., Tesifón, P.-C., & Raquel, A.-R. (2022). Biohazard Accidents, Harmful Elements to the Wellness of Healthcare Workers, and Their Risk Factors. [publication_type = article.]. *International Journal of Environmental Research and Public Health, 19*(20), 13214. DOI: 10.3390/ijerph192013214 PMID: 36293794

Julius Kewir, T., N. W. E. Mathias and N. John Ngansi. (2021) Development of a Computerized Automated System for Feed, Water and Sanitation Management in Animal Farms. *Current Journal of Applied Science and Technology*: 1 - 15.

Junker, M., Böhm, M., & Krcmar, H. (2024). Advantages and disadvantages of mobile applications for workplace health promotion: A scoping review. *PLoS One, 19*(1), e0296212. DOI: 10.1371/journal.pone.0296212 PMID: 38165989

Justin, Y. Y. L., Yanhao, M., Mark, H., & Patrick, K. H. L. (2023). Artificial intelligence-based prediction of indoor bioaerosol concentrations from indoor air quality sensor data. *Environment International, 174*, 107900. DOI: 10.1016/j.envint.2023.107900 PMID: 37012194

Kadir, B. A., & Broberg, O. (2021). Human-centered design of work systems in the transition to Industry 4.0. *Applied Ergonomics, 92*, 103334. DOI: 10.1016/j.apergo.2020.103334 PMID: 33264676

Kang, Y., Cai, Z., Tan, C. W., Huang, Q., & Liu, H. (2020). Natural language processing (NLP) in management research: A literature review. *Journal of Management Analytics, 7*(2), 139–172. DOI: 10.1080/23270012.2020.1756939

Karangara, R., Shende, A., & Kathiriya, S. (2024). Harnessing the Power of AI for Enhanced Regulatory Compliance and Risk Management in Fintech. *International Journal of Computing and Engineering. CARI Journals Limited, 5*(1), 1–11.

Kari, T., Sell, A., Makkonen, M., Wallin, S., Walden, P., Carlsson, C., … & Carlsson, J. (2020). Implementing a digital wellness application into use – challenges and solutions among aged people., 310-328. DOI: 10.1007/978-3-030-50249-2_23

Katal, S., York, B., & Gholamrezanezhad, A. (2024). AI in radiology: From promise to practice – A guide to effective integration. *European Journal of Radiology, 181*, 111798. DOI: 10.1016/j.ejrad.2024.111798 PMID: 39471551

Kaushik, T. K., Singh, A., Raghav, A., & Singh, B. (2024). Potential of Artificial Intelligence in the Agricultural Industry: A Comprehensive Review. AI Applications for Clean Energy and Sustainability, 344-365.

Kaushik, T. K., Singh, A., Raghav, A., Singh, B., Arora, M. K., & Lal, S. (2024). Untapping Artificial Intelligence in Environmental and Sustainable Progression: Projecting Legal and Ethical Considerations. In Maintaining a Sustainable World in the Nexus of Environmental Science and AI (pp. 109-130). IGI Global.

Kavadi, D. P., Patan, R., Ramachandran, M., & Gandomi, A. H. (2020). Partial derivative Nonlinear Global Pandemic Machine Learning prediction of COVID 19. *Chaos, Solitons, and Fractals, 139*, 110056. DOI: 10.1016/j.chaos.2020.110056 PMID: 32834609

Kavouras, S., Vardopoulos, I., Mitoula, R., Zorpas, A. A., & Kaldis, P. (2022). Occupational health and safety scope significance in achieving sustainability. *Sustainability (Basel), 14*(4), 2424. DOI: 10.3390/su14042424

Keeling, M. J., Hollingsworth, T. D., & Read, J. M. (2020). Efficacy of contact tracing for the containment of the 2019 novel coronavirus (COVID-19). *Journal of Epidemiology and Community Health, 74*(10), 861–866. DOI: 10.1136/jech-2020-214051 PMID: 32576605

Kesharwani, R. K., & Krishna. (2021). Biotechnology in the Modern Medicinal System. *Biotechnology in the Modern Medicinal System*. https://doi.org/DOI: 10.1201/9781003129783/biotechnology-modern-medicinal-system-rajesh-kesharwani-krishna-misra

Khalifa, M., & Albadawy, M. (2024a). AI in diagnostic imaging: Revolutionising accuracy and efficiency. *Computer Methods and Programs in Biomedicine Update, 5*, 100146. DOI: 10.1016/j.cmpbup.2024.100146

Khalil, A., Ahmed, S., Khattak, A., & Al-Qirim, N. (2020). Investigating Bias in Facial Analysis Systems: A Systematic Review. *IEEE Access : Practical Innovations, Open Solutions, 8*, 130751–130761. DOI: 10.1109/ACCESS.2020.3006051

Khalili, H., & Wimmer, M. A. (2024). Towards Improved XAI-Based Epidemiological Research into the Next Potential Pandemic. *Life (Chicago, Ill.), 14*(7), 783. DOI: 10.3390/life14070783 PMID: 39063538

Khan, W., Rehman, M., Zangoti, H., Afzal, M., Armi, N., & Salah, K. (2020). Industrial Internet of Things: Recent advances, enabling technologies and open challenges. *Computers & Electrical Engineering, 81*, 106522. DOI: 10.1016/j.compeleceng.2019.106522

Khodyreva, A. (2023). Prevention of occupational injuries of employees LLC Gazprom Dobycha Orenburg based on the risk-based approach and the modernization of local regulations.

Khoury, A., Luca, A., Sall, F., Pazart, L., & Capellier, G. (2019). Ventilation feedback device for manual ventilation in simulated respiratory arrest: A crossover manikin study. *Scandinavian Journal of Trauma, Resuscitation and Emergency Medicine*, *27*(1), 93. Advance online publication. DOI: 10.1186/s13049-019-0674-7 PMID: 31640797

Khoza-Shangase, K. (2019). Hearing function of gold miners with and without a history of tuberculosis treatment: A retrospective data review [Peer Review]. *Brazilian Journal of Otorhinolaryngology*, *88*(3), 1–6. https://doi.org/https://doi.org/10.1016/j.bjorl.2018.12.003 PMID: 30765234

Khuwuthyakorn, P., Suksatit, B., & Thinnukool, O. (2018, August). First Aid Literacy Mobile Application Development. In *Proceedings of the 8th International Conference on Information Communication and Management* (pp. 17-21)

Kim, J., & Ahn, I. (2021). Infectious disease outbreak prediction using media articles with machine learning models. *Scientific Reports*, *11*(1), 4413. DOI: 10.1038/s41598-021-83926-2 PMID: 33627706

Kim, J., Jin, J. H., Kim, H. S., Song, W., Shin, S. K., Yi, H., Jang, D. H., Shin, S., & Lee, B. Y. (2016). Fully Automated Field-Deployable Bioaerosol Monitoring System Using Carbon Nanotube-Based Biosensors. *Environmental Science & Technology*, *50*(10), 5163–5171. DOI: 10.1021/acs.est.5b06361 PMID: 27070239

Kim, J., Jo, B., Jo, J., & Kim, D. (2020). Development of an IoT-based construction worker physiological data monitoring platform at high temperatures. *Sensors (Basel)*, *20*(20), 5682. DOI: 10.3390/s20195682 PMID: 33027999

Kim, K. (2020). Exploring the influence of workplace violence and bystander behaviour on patient safety in Korea: A pilot study. *Journal of Nursing Management*, *28*(3), 735–743. DOI: 10.1111/jonm.12991 PMID: 32124510

Kimutai, E. (2024). Adoption of Biotechnology in Livestock Production. *International Journal of Livestock Policy*. DOI: 10.47941/ijlp.1965

Kiritchenko, S., Nejadgholi, I., & Fraser, K. C. (2021). Confronting abusive language online: A survey from the ethical and human rights perspective. *Journal of Artificial Intelligence Research*, *71*, 431–478. DOI: 10.1613/jair.1.12590

Kirkpatrick, P., & Baez, A. V. (1948). Formation of Optical Images by X-Rays. *Journal of the Optical Society of America*, *38*(9), 766. DOI: 10.1364/JOSA.38.000766 PMID: 18883922

Köbis, L., & Mehner, C. (2021). Ethical questions raised by ai-supported mentoring in higher education. *Frontiers in Artificial Intelligence*, *4*, 624050. Advance online publication. DOI: 10.3389/frai.2021.624050 PMID: 33997774

Koklesová, L., Samec, M., Líšková, A., Zhai, K., Büsselberg, D., Giordano, F., Kubatka, P., & Golunitschaja, O. (2021). Mitochondrial impairments in aetiopathology of multifactorial diseases: Common origin but individual outcomes in context of 3p medicine. *The EPMA Journal*, *12*(1), 27–40. DOI: 10.1007/s13167-021-00237-2 PMID: 33686350

Kolenia, D., & Domaradzki, J. (2021). Prediction and injury risk based on movement patterns and flexibility in a 6-month prospective study among physically active adults. *PeerJ*, *9*, e11399. DOI: 10.7717/peerj.11399 PMID: 34046260

Konkov, M. (2023). *Ethical issues of implementing artificial intelligence in medicine*. Digital Diagnostics., DOI: 10.17816/DD430348

Kooli, C., & Muftah, H. (2022). Artificial intelligence in healthcare: A comprehensive review of its ethical concerns. *Technological Sustainability*, *1*(2), 121–131. DOI: 10.1108/TECHS-12-2021-0029

Korfage, I., Rietjens, J., Overbeek, A., Jabbarian, L., Billekens, P., Hammes, B., & Heide, A. (2015). A cluster randomized controlled trial on the effects and costs of advance care planning in elderly care: Study protocol. *BMC Geriatrics*, *15*(1), 87. Advance online publication. DOI: 10.1186/s12877-015-0087-z PMID: 26198573

Kouabenan, D. R., Ngueutsa, R., & Mbaye, S. (2015). Safety climate, perceived risk, and involvement in safety management. *Safety Science*, *77*, 72–79. DOI: 10.1016/j.ssci.2015.03.009

Koulu, R. (2021). Crafting digital transparency: Implementing legal values into algorithmic design. *Critical Analysis L.*, *8*(1), 81–100. DOI: 10.33137/cal.v8i1.36281

Krainiuk, O., B. Yu, V. Barbashyn and Y. Mykola. (2023) Use of artificial intelligence for work safety management. *Комунальне господарство міст*, 6: 207 - 213.

Kreps, G.L., Wright, K., & Burke-Garcia, A. (2018). The use of digital communication channels to enhance environmental health literacy. *Environmental Health Literacy*. 265-283. https://doi.org/DOI: 10.1007/978-3-319-94108-0_10

Krichen, M., Abdalzaher, M. S., Elwekeil, M., & Fouda, M. M. (2024). Managing natural disasters: An analysis of technological advancements, opportunities, and challenges. *Internet of Things and Cyber-Physical Systems*, *4*, 99–109. DOI: 10.1016/j.iotcps.2023.09.002

Kroenke, K., Spitzer, R. L., & Williams, J. B. W. (2001). The PHQ-9: Validity of a brief depression severity measure. *Journal of General Internal Medicine*, *16*(9), 606–613. DOI: 10.1046/j.1525-1497.2001.016009606.x PMID: 11556941

Kugler, H., Brusco, N., Slade, S., Boyd, L., & Taylor, N. (2024). Teaching manual handling through risk assessment empowers the nursing team to provide safe mobility-related care: A qualitative analysis. *Focus on Health Professional Education a Multi-Professional Journal*, *25*(1), 51–68. DOI: 10.11157/fohpe.v25i1.656

Kukar, M., Gunčar, G., Vovko, T., Podnar, S., Černelč, P., Brvar, M., Zalaznik, M., Notar, M., Moškon, S., & Notar, M. (2021). COVID-19 diagnosis by routine blood tests using machine learning. *Scientific Reports*, *11*(1), 10738. DOI: 10.1038/s41598-021-90265-9 PMID: 34031483

Kukoyi, P. O., & Adebowale, O. J. (2021). Impediments to construction safety improvement. *Journal of Engineering, Project, and Production Management*, *11*(3), 207–214.

Kulkarni, P. A., & Singh, H. (2023). Artificial Intelligence in Clinical Diagnosis. *Journal of the American Medical Association, 330*(4), 317. Advance online publication. DOI: 10.1001/jama.2023.11440 PMID: 37410477

Kumar, A., Bag, A., Anand, A., Saha, S., Mohapatra, H., & Kolhar, M. (2024). Examining healthcare services utilizing cloud technology in intelligent urban environments., 77-98. DOI: 10.4018/979-8-3693-7225-8.ch004

Kumar, P. M., Khan, L. U., & Hong, C. S. (2022). Notice of Violation of IEEE Publication Principles: Affirmative Fusion Process for Improving Wearable Sensor Data Availability in Artificial Intelligence of Medical Things. IEEE Sensors Journal.

Kumar, S., & Kumari, P. (2021). Flexible Nano Smart sensors. Nanosensors for Smart Manufacturing, 199.

Kumar, C. B., Kumar, M. V., Gayathri, T., & Kumar, S. R. (2014). Data analysis and prediction of hepatitis using support vector machine (SVM). *International Journal of Computer Science and Information Technologies*, *5*(2).

Kumar, K. S., & Narayanan, R. (2021). Review on construction risk and development of risk management procedural index–A case study from Chennai construction sector. *Materials Today: Proceedings*, *43*, 1141–1146. DOI: 10.1016/j.matpr.2020.08.606

Kumar, P. M., Hong, C. S., Afghah, F., Manogaran, G., Yu, K., Hua, Q., & Gao, J. (2021). Clouds proportionate medical data stream analytics for internet of things-based healthcare systems. *IEEE Journal of Biomedical and Health Informatics*, *26*(3), 973–982. DOI: 10.1109/JBHI.2021.3106387 PMID: 34415841

Kumar, P. M., Khan, L. U., & Hong, C. S. (2022). Affirmative fusion process for improving wearable sensor data availability in artificial intelligence of medical things. *IEEE Sensors Journal.*

Kumar, S. R., Nathan, V. N., Ashique, S. M., Rajkumar, V., & Karthick, P. A. (2021). Productivity enhancement and cycle time reduction in toyota production system through jishuken activity–Case study. *Materials Today: Proceedings*, *37*, 964–966. DOI: 10.1016/j.matpr.2020.06.181

Kumar, Y., Koul, A., Singla, R., & Ijaz, M. F. (2023). Artificial intelligence in disease diagnosis: A systematic literature review, synthesizing framework and future research agenda. *Journal of Ambient Intelligence and Humanized Computing*, *14*(7), 8459–8486. DOI: 10.1007/s12652-021-03612-z PMID: 35039756

Kutbi, R., Saib, W., Alahmadi, A., & Jezani, M. (2023). Comparison in Reading Stability between Calibrated and Non-Calibrated Ionization Chamber. [IJSR]. *International Journal of Science and Research (Raipur, India)*, *12*(12), 1589–1594. DOI: 10.21275/SR231217161354

Kwok, K. O., Tang, A., Wei, V. W. I., Park, W. H., Yeoh, E. K., & Riley, S. (2019). Epidemic Models of Contact Tracing: Systematic Review of Transmission Studies of Severe Acute Respiratory Syndrome and Middle East Respiratory Syndrome. *Computational and Structural Biotechnology Journal*, *17*, 186–194. DOI: 10.1016/j.csbj.2019.01.003 PMID: 30809323

LaDou, J., & Harrison, R. J. (2013). In *CURRENT Diagnosis & Treatment: Occupational & Environmental Medicine, 5e*. McGraw-Hill Education. accessmedicine.mhmedical.com/content.aspx?aid=1104099264

Laï, M. C., Brian, M., & Mamzer, M. F. (2020). Perceptions of artificial intelligence in healthcare: Findings from a qualitative survey study among actors in France. *Journal of Translational Medicine*, *18*(1), 1–13. DOI: 10.1186/s12967-019-02204-y PMID: 31918710

Lake, E. T., Sanders, J., Duan, R., Riman, K. A., Schoenauer, K. M., & Chen, Y. (2019). A meta-analysis of the associations between the nurse work environment in hospitals and four sets of outcomes. *Medical Care*, *57*(5), 353–361. DOI: 10.1097/MLR.0000000000001109 PMID: 30908381

Lanctôt, N., & Guay, S. (2014). The aftermath of workplace violence among healthcare workers: A systematic literature review of the consequences. *Aggression and Violent Behavior*, *19*(5), 492–501. DOI: 10.1016/j.avb.2014.07.010

Lapitan, R. L. (2024). Precognition of Known And Unknown Biothreats: A Risk-Based Approach. *Vector Borne and Zoonotic Diseases (Larchmont, N.Y.)*, *24*(12), 795–801. DOI: 10.1089/vbz.2023.0169 PMID: 39189131

Larson, D. B., & Boland, G. W. (2019). Imaging Quality Control in the Era of Artificial Intelligence. *Journal of the American College of Radiology*, *16*(9), 1259–1266. DOI: 10.1016/j.jacr.2019.05.048 PMID: 31254491

Laschinger, H. K. S. (2008). Effect of empowerment on professional practice environments, work satisfaction, and patient care quality: Further testing the Nursing Worklife Model. *Journal of Nursing Care Quality*, *23*(4), 322–330. DOI: 10.1097/01.NCQ.0000318028.67910.6b PMID: 18431259

Laschinger, H. K. S., & Leiter, M. P. (2006). The impact of nursing work environments on patient safety outcomes: The mediating role of burnout/engagement. *The Journal of Nursing Administration*, *36*(5), 259–267. DOI: 10.1097/00005110-200605000-00019 PMID: 16705307

Lase, E., & Nkosi, F. (2023). *Human-Centric AI: Understanding and Enhancing Collaboration between Humans and Intelligent Systems*. Algorithm Asynchronous., DOI: 10.61963/jaa.v1i1.49

Lee, D., & Yoon, S. N. (2021). Application of artificial intelligence-based technologies in the healthcare industry: Opportunities and challenges. *International Journal of Environmental Research and Public Health*, *18*(1), 271. DOI: 10.3390/ijerph18010271 PMID: 33401373

Lee, J. C., Daraba, A., Voidarou, C., Rozos, G., El Enshasy, H. A., & Varzakas, T. (2021). Implementation of Food Safety Management Systems Along With Other Management Tools (HAZOP, FMEA, Ishikawa, Pareto). The Case Study of Listeria Monocytogenes and Correlation With Microbiological Criteria. *Foods*, *10*(9), 2169. Advance online publication. DOI: 10.3390/foods10092169 PMID: 34574279

Lee, J., Suh, T., Roy, D., & Baucus, M. (2019). Emerging technology and business model innovation: The case of artificial intelligence. *Journal of Open Innovation*, *5*(3), 44. DOI: 10.3390/joitmc5030044

Lee, J., Yanagawa, B., An, K., Arora, R., Verma, S., & Friedrich, J. (2021). Frailty and pre-frailty in cardiac surgery: A systematic review and meta-analysis of 66,448 patients. *Journal of Cardiothoracic Surgery*, *16*(1), 184. Advance online publication. DOI: 10.1186/s13019-021-01541-8 PMID: 34172059

Leiter, M. P., & Laschinger, H. K. S. (2006). Relationships of work and practice environment to professional burnout: Testing a causal model. *Nursing Research*, *55*(2), 137–146. DOI: 10.1097/00006199-200603000-00009 PMID: 16601626

Leiter, M. P., & Maslach, C. (2016). Latent burnout profiles: A new approach to understanding the burnout experience. *Burnout Research*, *3*(4), 89–100. DOI: 10.1016/j.burn.2016.09.001

Lemos, J., de Souza, V. B., Falcetta, F. S., de Almeida, F. K., Lima, T. M., & Gaspar, P. D. (2024). Enhancing workplace safety through personalized environmental risk assessment: An AI-driven approach in industry 5.0. *Computers*, *13*(5), 120.

Lemos, J., Gaspar, P. D., & Lima, T. M. (2022a). Environmental risk assessment and management in Industry 4.0: A review of technologies and trends. *Machines (Basel)*, *10*(9), 702. DOI: 10.3390/machines10080702

Lemos, J., Gaspar, P. D., & Lima, T. M. (2022b). Individual environmental risk assessment and management in Industry 4.0: An IoT-based model. *Applied System Innovation*, *5*(4), 88. DOI: 10.3390/asi5050088

Leso, V., Fontana, L., & Iavicoli, I. (2018). The occupational health and safety dimension of Industry 4.0. *La Medicina del Lavoro*, *110*(5), 327–338. DOI: 10.23749/mdl.v110i5.7282 PMID: 30378585

Leyma, P. D. H. (2024) Biosecurity Risk Assessment for the Use of Artificial Intelligence in Synthetic Biology. *Applied Biosafety*.

Lftta, J. G. J., Nasser, A. H. K., & Shanawa, A. N. (2024). *X-Rays and Their Uses on The Human Body*.

Li, L., & Wang, C. (2023). Microbiological Risk Assessment and Its Use in Food Industry. *International Journal of Biology and Life Sciences*. DOI: 10.54097/ijbls.v2i1.5163

Liang, C. J., Le, T. H., Ham, Y., Mantha, B. R., Cheng, M. H., & Lin, J. J. (2024). Ethics of artificial intelligence and robotics in the architecture, engineering, and construction industry. *Automation in Construction*, *162*, 105369. DOI: 10.1016/j.autcon.2024.105369

Li, B., Qi, P., Liu, B., Di, S., Liu, J., Pei, J., Yi, J., & Zhou, B. (2021). Trustworthy AI: From Principles to Practices. *ACM Computing Surveys*, *55*, 1–46. DOI: 10.1145/3379443

Li, C., Liang, W., Quigley, C., Zhao, Y., & Yu, L. F. (2017). Earthquake Safety Training through Virtual Drills. *IEEE Transactions on Visualization and Computer Graphics*, *23*(4), 1275–1284. DOI: 10.1109/TVCG.2017.2656958 PMID: 28129163

Lind, C., Diaz-Olivares, J., Lindecrantz, K., & Eklund, J. (2020). A wearable sensor system for physical ergonomics interventions using haptic feedback. *Sensors (Basel)*, *20*(21), 6010. DOI: 10.3390/s20216010 PMID: 33113922

Linn, N., Goetzinger, C., Régnaux, J., Schmitz, S., Dessenne, C., Fagherazzi, G., & Aguayo, G. (2021). Digital health interventions among people living with frailty: A scoping review. *Journal of the American Medical Directors Association*, *22*(9), 1802–1812.e21. DOI: 10.1016/j.jamda.2021.04.012 PMID: 34000266

Lin, Y., Shuya, L., & Lei, Z. (2024). The Implications of Artificial Intelligence on Infection Prevention and Control: Current Progress and Future Perspectives. [publication_type = article.]. *China CDC Weekly*, *6*, 901–904. PMID: 39233995

Liotta, G., Gilardi, F., Orlando, S., Rocco, G., Proietti, M., Asta, F., De Sario, M., Michelozzi, P., Mancinelli, S., Palombi, L., Marazzi, M. C., & Scarcella, P. (2019). Cost of hospital care for the older adults according to their level of frailty. a cohort study in the Lazio region, Italy. *PLoS One*, *14*(6), e0217829. DOI: 10.1371/journal.pone.0217829 PMID: 31185033

Liu, S., Nkrumah, E., Akoto, L., Gyabeng, E., & Nkrumah, E. (2020). The state of occupational health and safety management frameworks (OHSMF) and occupational injuries and accidents in the Ghanaian oil and gas industry: assessing the mediating role of safety knowledge. Biomed Research International, 2020(1). DOI: 10.1155/2020/6354895

Liu, B., Sträuber, H., Saraiva, J., Harms, H., Silva, S. G., Kasmanas, J. C., Kleinsteuber, S., & da Rocha, U. N. (2022). Machine Learning-Assisted Identification of Bioindicators Predicts Medium-Chain Carboxylate Production Performance of an Anaerobic Mixed Culture. *Microbiome*, *10*(1), 48. Advance online publication. DOI: 10.1186/s40168-021-01219-2 PMID: 35331330

Liu, P. T., Johnson, C. D., Miranda, R., Patel, M. D., & Phillips, C. J. (2010). A Reference Standard-Based Quality Assurance Program for Radiology. *Journal of the American College of Radiology*, *7*(1), 61–66. DOI: 10.1016/j.jacr.2009.08.016 PMID: 20129274

Liu, W., Meng, Q., Li, Z., & Hu, X. (2021). Applications of computer vision in monitoring the unsafe behavior of construction workers: Current status and challenges. *Buildings (Basel, Switzerland)*, *11*(9), 409. DOI: 10.3390/buildings11090409

Li, W., Liu, J., Xiao, Z., Zhu, D., Liao, J., Yu, W., Feng, J., Qian, B., Fang, Y., & Li, S. (2024). Automatic grading of knee osteoarthritis with a plain radiograph radiomics model: Combining anteroposterior and lateral images. *Insights Into Imaging*, *15*(1), 143. DOI: 10.1186/s13244-024-01719-3 PMID: 38867121

Li, W., Wang, S., Arundel, S. T., & Hsu, C.-Y. (2023). GeoImageNet: A multi-source natural feature benchmark dataset for GeoAI and supervised machine learning. *GeoInformatica*, *27*(3), 619–640. DOI: 10.1007/s10707-022-00476-z

Lodge, M. (2004). Accountability and transparency in regulation: critiques, doctrines and instruments. The politics of regulation: Institutions and regulatory reforms for the age of governance, 124-144.

Lu, M. H., Calandra, D., & Thawonmas, R. (2023). Artificial Reality: Immersive but Factually Dishonest AR Experience. *IEEE Consumer Electronics Magazine*, *12*(1), 8–11. DOI: 10.1109/MCE.2022.3216421

Luqman, A., Alnajjar, F., Parambil, M., Younes, M. I., Abdelhalim, Z., & Aljassmi, H. (2022). Development of YOLOv5-Based Real-Time Smart Monitoring System for Increasing Lab Safety Awareness in Educational Institutions. [publication_type = article.]. *Sensors (Basel)*, *22*(22), 8820. DOI: 10.3390/s22228820 PMID: 36433418

Lussier, R., & Sherman, H. (2022). Business, Society and Government Essentials. Business, Society and Government Essentials: Strategy and Applied Ethics, 3rd Edition. https://doi.org/DOI: 10.4324/9780203106341

Lu, Y., Karanikas, N., & Carroll, J. A. (2024). A Scoping Review of Integrating Occupational Health and Safety and Workplace Health Promotion Interventions. *Journal of Human Environment and Health Promotion*, *10*(4), 179–190. DOI: 10.61186/jhehp.10.4.179

Lu, Y., Niti, M., Yap, K., Tan, C., Nyunt, M., Feng, L., & Ng, T. (2019). Assessment of sarcopenia among community-dwelling at-risk frail adults aged 65 years and older who received multidomain lifestyle interventions. *JAMA Network Open*, *2*(10), e1913346. DOI: 10.1001/jamanetworkopen.2019.13346 PMID: 31617926

Lysaght, T., Lim, H., Xafis, V., & Ngiam, K. (2019). AI-Assisted Decision-making in Healthcare. *Asian Bioethics Review*, *11*(3), 299–314. DOI: 10.1007/s41649-019-00096-0 PMID: 33717318

Macêdo, J. B., Moura, M. C., Aichele, D., & Lins, I. D. (2022). Identification of risk features using text mining and BERT-based models: Application to an oil refinery. *Process Safety and Environmental Protection*, *158*, 382–399. DOI: 10.1016/j.psep.2021.12.025

MacPhee, M., Dahinten, V., & Havaei, F. (2017). The impact of heavy perceived nurse workloads on patient and nurse outcomes. *Administrative Sciences*, *7*(1), 7. DOI: 10.3390/admsci7010007

Maddikunta, P., Pham, Q., Prabadevi, B., Deepa, N., Dev, K., Gadekallu, T., Ruby, R., & Liyanage, M. (2022). Industry 5.0: A survey on enabling technologies and potential applications. *Journal of Industrial Information Integration*, *26*, 100257. DOI: 10.1016/j.jii.2021.100257

Made, F., & Uthembe, W. (2019). Statistical analysis methods used to assess data below the limit of detection in the South African literature, 2010-2017. *Occupational Health Southern Africa*, *25*(5), 160–164.

Mahlknecht, A., Engl, A., Piccoliori, G., & Wiedermann, C. J. (2023). Supporting primary care through symptom checking artificial intelligence: A study of patient and physician attitudes in Italian general practice. *BMC Primary Care*, *24*(1), 174. DOI: 10.1186/s12875-023-02143-0 PMID: 37661285

Malatji, S., & Stewart, J. M. (2013). *The MOSH Leading Practice Adoption System: A leading practice in its own right.* https://www.mosh.co.za/siteitems/documents/adoption%20process/The%20MOSH%20Leading%20Practice%20Adoption%20System%20-%20A%20leading%20practice%20in%20its%20own%20right.pdf

Malik, A., & Kumar, A. (2022). assimilation of blockchain with Internet of Things (IoT) with possible issues and solutions for better connectivity and proper security. In New Trends and Applications in Internet of Things (IoT) and Big Data Analytics (pp. 187-207). Cham: Springer International Publishing.

Malik, P. K., Sharma, R., Singh, R., Gehlot, A., Satapathy, S. C., Alnumay, W. S., Pelusi, D., Ghosh, U., & Nayak, J. (2021). Industrial Internet of Things and its applications in industry 4.0: State of the art. *Computer Communications, 166*, 125–139. DOI: 10.1016/j.comcom.2020.11.016

Mallery, L., MacLeod, T., Allen, M., McLean-Veysey, P., Rodney-Cail, N., Bezanson, E., Steeves, B., LeBlanc, C., & Moorhouse, P. (2019). Systematic review and meta-analysis of second-generation antidepressants for the treatment of older adults with depression: Questionable benefit and considerations for frailty. *BMC Geriatrics, 19*(1), 306. Advance online publication. DOI: 10.1186/s12877-019-1327-4 PMID: 31718566

Maltseva, K. (2020). Wearables in the workplace: The brave new world of employee engagement. *Business Horizons, 63*(4), 493–505. DOI: 10.1016/j.bushor.2020.03.007

Mamata, K. C., & Lamichhane, A. (2021). Advances in Agricultural Biotechnology. *Nepal Journal of Biotechnology*. Advance online publication. DOI: 10.3126/njb.v9i1.38643

Manogaran, G., Alazab, M., Song, H., & Kumar, N. (2021). CDP-UA: Cognitive data processing method wearable sensor data uncertainty analysis in the internet of things assisted smart medical healthcare systems. *IEEE Journal of Biomedical and Health Informatics, 25*(10), 3691–3699. DOI: 10.1109/JBHI.2021.3051288 PMID: 33439849

Manzoor, B., Othman, I., & Manzoor, M. (2021). Evaluating the critical safety factors causing accidents in high-rise building projects. *Ain Shams Engineering Journal, 12*(3), 2485–2492. DOI: 10.1016/j.asej.2020.11.025

Mariani, K., & Lozada, F. (2023). The use of ai and algorithms for decision-making in workplace recruitment practices. *Journal of Student Research, 12*(1). Advance online publication. DOI: 10.47611/jsr.v12i1.1855

Marinaccio, A., Boccuni, F., Rondinone, B., Brusco, A., D'Amario, S., & Iavicoli, S. (2020). Occupational factors in the covid-19 pandemic in Italy: Compensation claims applications support establishing an occupational surveillance system. *Occupational and Environmental Medicine, 77*(12), 818–821. DOI: 10.1136/oemed-2020-106844 PMID: 32967988

Martin, M., R. Rikard and S. David. (2024) The power of artificial intelligence for managing pandemics: A primer for public health professionals. *International Journal of Health Planning and Management.*

Martin, D., Schmidt, M., & Hillerbrand, R. (2023). Implementing AI Ethics in the Design of AI-Assisted Rescue Robots. *2023 IEEE International Symposium on Ethics in Engineering, Science, and Technology (ETHICS)*, 1-1. https://doi.org/DOI: 10.1109/ETHICS57328.2023.10155062

Martinho, A., Herber, N., Kroesen, M., & Chorus, C. (2021). Ethical issues in focus by the autonomous vehicles industry. *Transport Reviews, 41*(5), 556–577. DOI: 10.1080/01441647.2020.1862355

Martin, N., Friedewald, M., Schiering, I., Mester, B. A., Hallinan, D., & Jensen, M. (2020). *The Data Protection Impact Assessment According to Article 35 GDPR*. Fraunhofer Verlag.

Martin, P., Bladier, C., Meek, B., Bruyere, O., Feinblatt, E., Touvier, M., Watier, L., & Makowski, D. (2018). Weight of evidence for hazard identification: A critical review of the literature. *Environmental Health Perspectives, 126*(7), 076001. DOI: 10.1289/EHP3067 PMID: 30024384

Maslach, C., & Leiter, M. P. (2016). Understanding the burnout experience: Recent research and its implications for psychiatry. *World Psychiatry; Official Journal of the World Psychiatric Association (WPA), 15*(2), 103–111. DOI: 10.1002/wps.20311 PMID: 27265691

Materon, E. M., Gómez, F. R., Joshi, N., Dalmaschio, C. J., Carrilho, E., & Oliveira Jr, O. N. (2021). Smart materials for electrochemical flexible nanosensors: advances and applications. Nanosensors for smart manufacturing, 347-371.

Matheny, M., Whicher, D., & Israni, S. (2020). Artificial intelligence in health care. *Journal of the American Medical Association, 323*(6), 509. DOI: 10.1001/jama.2019.21579 PMID: 31845963

Matuka, D. O., Duba, T., Ngcobo, Z., Made, F., Muleba, L., Nthoke, T., & Singh, T. S. (2021). Occupational Risk of Airborne Mycobacterium tuberculosis Exposure: A Situational Analysis in a Three-Tier Public Healthcare System in South Africa. *International Journal of Environmental Research and Public Health, 18*(19), 10130. DOI: 10.3390/ijerph181910130 PMID: 34639431

Mayya, V., S, S. K., Kulkarni, U., Surya, D. K., & Acharya, U. R. (2023). An empirical study of preprocessing techniques with convolutional neural networks for accurate detection of chronic ocular diseases using fundus images. Applied Intelligence, 53(2), 1548-1566.

McMillan, A. B. (2020). Making Your AI Smarter: Continuous Learning Artificial Intelligence for Radiology. *Radiology, 297*(1), 15–16. DOI: 10.1148/radiol.2020202664 PMID: 32845217

Mehrabi, N., Morstatter, F., Saxena, N., Lerman, K., & Galstyan, A. (2019). A Survey on Bias and Fairness in Machine Learning. *ACM Computing Surveys, 54*(6), 1–35. DOI: 10.1145/3457607

Mehta, A., Niaz, M., Adetoro, A., & Nwagwu, U. (2024). Advancements in Manufacturing Technology for the Biotechnology Industry: The Role of Artificial Intelligence and Emerging Trends. *International Journal of Chemistry. Mathematics and Physics, 8*(2), 12–18. DOI: 10.22161/ijcmp.8.2.3

Meiyong, X., H. Zhenni, W. Anlu, M. Shitong, Z. Qian, C. Song, W. Jian Min and W. Kaimin. (2024) A Machine Learning Approach for Laboratory Safety Monitoring under Extreme Conditions. 42: 1 - 3.

Mendelsohn, A., Kim, C., Song, J., Singh, A., Le, T., Abiri, A., Berke, G. S., & Geoghegan, R. (2020). Transoral robotic surgical proficiency via real-time tactile collision awareness system. *The Laryngoscope, 130*(S6). Advance online publication. DOI: 10.1002/lary.29034 PMID: 32865822

Meng, Y., Gao, Y., Jin, J., Ruan, J., He, L., Shen, Q., & Gong, X. (2022). *Automatic No-reference Quality Assessment in Chest Radiographs Based on Deep Convolutional Neural Networks*. In Review. DOI: 10.21203/rs.3.rs-1213399/v1

Michel, O., & Liedtke, M. (2021). [ISO 1999:2013 part 1: Revised probability model for calculating noise-induced hearing loss]. *Hno, 69*(6), 510-516. (ISO 1999:2013 Teil 1: Überarbeitetes Wahrscheinlichkeitsmodell zur Berechnung des lärmbedingten Hörverlusts.)DOI: 10.1007/s00106-021-00999-1

Mihret, E. T. (2020). Robotics and Artificial Intelligence. [IJAIML]. *International Journal of Artificial Intelligence and Machine Learning*, *10*(2), 57–78. DOI: 10.4018/IJAIML.2020070104

Mikhaylov, S., Estève, M., & Campion, A. (2018). Artificial Intelligence for the Public Sector: Opportunities and Challenges of Cross-Sector Collaboration. *Philosophical Transactions. Series A, Mathematical, Physical, and Engineering Sciences*, *376*(2128), 20170357. Advance online publication. DOI: 10.1098/rsta.2017.0357 PMID: 30082303

Mine Health and Safety Act. (2016). *Mine Health and Safety Act: Regulations: Guidance note for implementation of standard threshold shift in medical surveillance of noise-induced hearing loss*. South Africa Retrieved from https://www.gov.za/documents/mine-health-and-safety-act-guidance-note-implementation-standard-threshold-shift-medical

Mine, Health, Safety, & Council. (2015). "Every Mine Worker Returning From Work Unharmed Every Day. Striving For Zero Harm" - 2014 Occupational Health and Safety Summit Milestones *J Occup Health Southern Afr*, *20*(1), 2.

Mir Mohammadzade Noudehi, Z., & Bagheri Khameneh, F. (2023, September). The Impact of Internet of Things, Blockchain, and Artificial Intelligence on Occupational Health and Safety. In *International Conference on Science, Engineering Management and Information Technology* (pp. 52-76). Cham: Springer Nature Switzerland.

Mirakhori, F., & Niazi, S. K. (2025). Harnessing the AI/ML in Drug and Biological Products Discovery and Development: The Regulatory Perspective. *Pharmaceuticals (Basel, Switzerland)*, *18*(1), 47. DOI: 10.3390/ph18010047 PMID: 39861110

Mirbabaie, M., Brünker, F., Möllmann, N., & Stieglitz, S. (2021). The rise of artificial intelligence – understanding the ai identity threat at the workplace. *Electronic Markets*, *32*(1), 73–99. DOI: 10.1007/s12525-021-00496-x

Mishra*, S. (2024). Current Trends of Artificial Intelligence in Biotechnology. *Oajda*. DOI: 10.23880/oajda-16000112

Misra, N. N., Dixit, Y., Al-Mallahi, A., Bhullar, M. S., Upadhyay, R., & Martynenko, A. (2022). IoT, Big Data, and Artificial Intelligence in Agriculture and Food Industry. *IEEE Internet of Things Journal*, *9*(9), 6305–6324. DOI: 10.1109/JIOT.2020.2998584

Mix Telematics. (2022). *Fleet Safety and Predictive Maintenance Solutions*. https://www.Mixtelematics.com

Mix Telematics. (2023). *Fleet Management with Mix Fleet Manager Premium and Mix Vision AI*. Retrieved from https://www.Mixtelematics.com

Mlodzinski, E., Wardi, G., Viglione, C., Nemati, S., Crotty Alexander, L., & Malhotra, A. (2023). Assessing barriers to implementation of machine learning and artificial intelligence–based tools in critical care: Web-based survey study. *JMIR Perioperative Medicine*, *6*, e41056. DOI: 10.2196/41056 PMID: 36705960

Moepeng, M., Soer, M., & Vinck, B. M. (2017). Distortion product otoacoustic emissions as a health surveillance technique for hearing screening in workers in the steel manufacturing industry. *Occupational Health Southern Africa*, *22*(5), 8–13.

Mohamed, S., El-Rahman Mohamed, M. A., Mahmoud, S. F., & Heggy, E. (2023). The Effect of Educational Program on Nurses' Knowledge and Attitude Regarding Artificial Intelligence. *Egyptian Journal of Health Care*. DOI: 10.21608/ejhc.2023.312617

Mohammadinia, A., Saeidian, B., Pradhan, B., & Ghaemi, Z. (2019). Prediction mapping of human leptospirosis using ANN, GWR, SVM and GLM approaches. *BMC Infectious Diseases*, *19*(1), 1–18. DOI: 10.1186/s12879-019-4580-4 PMID: 31722676

Mohsin, M., Omer, R., Huang, J., Mohsin, A., Guo, M., Qian, J., & Zhuang, Y. (2021). Advances in Engineered Bacillus Subtilis Biofilms and Spores, and Their Applications in Bioremediation, Biocatalysis, and Biomaterials. *Synthetic and Systems Biotechnology*, *6*(3), 180–191. Advance online publication. DOI: 10.1016/j.synbio.2021.07.002 PMID: 34401544

Monteith, S. (2023). Artificial Intelligence and Increasing Misinformation. *The British Journal of Psychiatry*. Advance online publication. DOI: 10.1192/bjp.2023.136 PMID: 37881016

Moradi, M., Siegel, E., Kashyap, S., Karargyris, A., Wu, J. T., Saboury, B., Morris, M., & Syeda-Mahmood, T. (2019). Artificial intelligence for point of care radiograph quality assessment. In Hahn, H. K., & Mori, K. (Eds.), *Medical Imaging 2019: Computer-Aided Diagnosis* (p. 128). SPIE., DOI: 10.1117/12.2513092

Morandini, S., Fraboni, F., De Angelis, M., Puzzo, G., Giusino, D., & Pietrantoni, L. (2023). The impact of artificial intelligence on workers' skills: Upskilling and reskilling in organisations. *Informing Science*, *26*, 39–68. DOI: 10.28945/5078

Mosavi, N. and Santos, M. (2021). Implementation considerations for the applied business intelligence in health care., 183-189. DOI: 10.1007/978-981-16-2502-2_19

Moshawrab, M., Adda, M., Bouzouane, A., Ibrahim, H., & Raad, A. (2022, October 2). Smart Wearables for the Detection of Occupational Physical Fatigue: A Literature Review. *Sensors (Basel)*, *22*(19), 7472. Advance online publication. DOI: 10.3390/s22197472 PMID: 36236570

Moshood, T., Adeleke, A., Nawanir, G., & Mahmud, F. (2020). Ranking of human factors affecting contractors' risk attitudes in the Malaysian construction industry. *Social Sciences & Humanities Open*, *2*(1), 100064. DOI: 10.1016/j.ssaho.2020.100064

Mourtzis, D., Angelopoulos, J., & Panopoulos, N. (2022b). Operator 5.0: A survey on enabling technologies and a framework for digital manufacturing based on extended reality. *Journal of Machine Engineering*, *22*(4), 43–69. DOI: 10.36897/jme/147160

Mourtzis, D., Angelopoulos, J., & Panopoulos, N. A. (2022). Literature review of the challenges and opportunities of the transition from Industry 4.0 to Society 5.0. *Energies*, *15*(17), 6276. DOI: 10.3390/en15176276

Mousavi-Shalmaei, S., Hosseinnia, M., Mohtasham-Amiri, Z., Rad, E. H., & Khodadadi-Hassankiadeh, N. (2023). Helmet use and jaw and tooth injuries in motorcyclists admitted to a referral hospital. *Journal of Maxillofacial and Oral Surgery*, *22*(3), 603–608. DOI: 10.1007/s12663-023-01934-3 PMID: 37362880

Mugabe, K. V. (2021). Barriers and facilitators to the adoption of artificial intelligence in radiation oncology: A New Zealand study. *Technical Innovations & Patient Support in Radiation Oncology*, *18*, 16–21. DOI: 10.1016/j.tipsro.2021.03.004 PMID: 33981867

Mujawar, M. A., Gohel, H., Bhardwaj, S. K., Srinivasan, S., Hickman, N., & Kaushik, A. (2020). Nano-enabled biosensing systems for intelligent healthcare: Towards COVID-19 management. *Materials Today. Chemistry*, *17*, 100306. DOI: 10.1016/j.mtchem.2020.100306 PMID: 32835155

Muñoz-Organero, M. (2022). Space-Distributed Traffic-Enhanced LSTM-Based Machine Learning Model for COVID-19 Incidence Forecasting. *Computational Intelligence and Neuroscience*, *2022*, 4307708. DOI: 10.1155/2022/4307708 PMID: 36438691

Murphy, G. T., Birch, S., MacKenzie, A., Alder, R., Lethbridge, L., & Little, L. (2012). Eliminating the shortage of registered nurses in Canada: An exercise in applied needs-based planning. *Health Policy (Amsterdam)*, *105*(2-3), 192–202. DOI: 10.1016/j.healthpol.2011.11.009 PMID: 22176731

Mustapha, Z. (2019). Contractors' Perception towards Safety and its Consequences on Construction Workers in Cape Coast Metropolis. *The Korean Journal of Food & Health Convergence*, *5*(6), 11–16.

Mustapha, Z., Aigbavboa, C. O., & Thwala, W. D. (2015, November). Occupational health and safety challenges in the Ghanaian Construction Industry. In *Fourth NMMU Construction Management Conference* (Vol. 30, pp. 15-21).

Muthukumar, A., Singaravelan, S., Arun, R., Selvakumar, V., Shunmugam, D. A., Balaganesh, S., & Gopalsamy, P. (2024). Knee osteoarthritis using hybrid deep learning approach with SqueezeNet and ResNet. *International Journal of Computational Vision and Robotics*, *1*(1), 10064577. Advance online publication. DOI: 10.1504/IJCVR.2024.10064577

Myatra, S. N., Jagiasi, B. G., Singh, N. P., & Divatia, J. V. (2024). Role of Artificial Intelligence in Haemodynamic Monitoring. *Indian Journal of Anaesthesia*, *68*(1), 93–99. Advance online publication. DOI: 10.4103/ija.ija_1260_23 PMID: 38406336

Mydin, F., & Othman, S. (2017). Elder abuse and neglect intervention in the clinical setting: Perceptions and barriers faced by primary care physicians in Malaysia. *Journal of Interpersonal Violence*, *35*(23-24), 6041–6066. DOI: 10.1177/0886260517726411 PMID: 29294874

Nagbøl, P. R., Müller, O., & Krancher, O. (2021). *Designing a Risk Assessment Tool for Artificial Intelligence Systems*. DOI: 10.1007/978-3-030-82405-1_32

Naik, A. (2024). Assessing the Impact of Climate Change on Global Crop Yields and Farming Practices. *Archives of Current Research International*. DOI: 10.9734/acri/2024/v24i5743

Naimeh, B. (2024) Risk assessment and machine learning models.

Najjar, R. (2023). Redefining Radiology: A Review of Artificial Intelligence Integration in Medical Imaging. *Diagnostics (Basel)*, *13*(17), 2760. DOI: 10.3390/diagnostics13172760 PMID: 37685300

Narmadha, D., & Pravin, A. (2020). An intelligent computer-aided approach for target protein prediction in infectious diseases. *Soft Computing*, *24*(19), 14707–14720. DOI: 10.1007/s00500-020-04815-w

Nasser, Y., Jennane, R., Chetouani, A., Lespessailles, E., & Hassouni, M. E. (2020). Discriminative regularized auto-encoder for early detection of knee osteoarthritis: Data from the Osteoarthritis Initiative. *IEEE Transactions on Medical Imaging*, *39*(9), 2976–2984. DOI: 10.1109/TMI.2020.2985861 PMID: 32286962

Nathavitharana, R. R., Mishra, H., Sullivan, A., Hurwitz, S., Lederer, P., Meintjes, J., Nardell, E., & Theron, G. (2022). Predicting Airborne Infection Risk: Association Between Personal Ambient Carbon Dioxide Level Monitoring and Incidence of Tuberculosis Infection in South African Health Workers. *Clinical Infectious Diseases*, *75*(8), 1297–1306. DOI: 10.1093/cid/ciac183 PMID: 35348657

Naushin, A. (2024). Anticipating biosecurity hazards: Distribution and recognition of biological threats. *Eurasian Journal of Applied Biotechnology*, •••, 160.

Nawaz, A., Waqar, A., Shah, S. A. R., Sajid, M., & Khalid, M. I. (2019). An innovative framework for risk management in construction projects in developing countries: Evidence from Pakistan. *Risks*, *7*(1), 24. DOI: 10.3390/risks7010024

Naz, S., Saeed, S., & Irfan, M. (2020). Approaches and Recent Advances in Protein and Peptide Drug Delivery System. *Pakistan Journal of Medical & Health Sciences*. Advance online publication. DOI: 10.47176/PJMHS.2020.257

Ndudzo, A., Sibanda Makuvise, A., Moyo, S., & Bobo, E. D. (2024). CRISPR-Cas9 genome editing in crop breeding for climate change resilience: Implications for smallholder farmers in Africa. *Journal of Agriculture and Food Research*, *16*, 101132. DOI: 10.1016/j.jafr.2024.101132

NetsPresso. (2023). *NOTA AI Driver Monitoring Platform*. https://nota.ai

Neveling, P. (2024). Occupational health and safety in the global garment industry. In *The Routledge Handbook of the Political Economy of Health and Healthcare* (pp. 177–189). Routledge. DOI: 10.4324/9781003017110-16

Nguyen Huu, P., Nguyen Thanh, D., le Thi Hai, T., Chu Duc, H., Pham Viet, H., & Nguyen Trong, C. (2022). Detection and classification knee osteoarthritis algorithm using YOLOv3 and VGG-16 models. *2022 7th National Scientific Conference on Applying New Technology in Green Buildings (ATiGB)*, 31–36. DOI: 10.1109/ATiGB56486.2022.9984096

Nguyen, C. C., Wong, S., Thai, M. T., Hoang, T. T., Phan, P. T., Davies, J., Wu, L., Tsai, D., Phan, H.-P., Lovell, N. H., & Do, T. N. (2023). Advanced user interfaces for teleoperated surgical robotic systems. *Advanced Sensor Research*, *2*(4), 2200036. DOI: 10.1002/adsr.202200036

Nicolas Bono, R., R. Luca, S. Speranza and G. Emanuele. (2023) Towards pest outbreak predictions: Are models supported by field monitoring the new hope? *Ecological Informatics*.

Niehoff, J. H., Kalaitzidis, J., Kroeger, J. R., Schoenbeck, D., Borggrefe, J., & Michael, A. E. (2023). Evaluation of the clinical performance of an AI-based application for the automated analysis of chest X-rays. *Scientific Reports*, *13*(1), 3680. DOI: 10.1038/s41598-023-30521-2 PMID: 36872333

Nikolinakos, N. T. (2023). Ethical Principles for Trustworthy AI. In *EU Policy and Legal Framework for Artificial Intelligence, Robotics and Related Technologies-The AI Act* (pp. 101–166). Springer International Publishing.

Ninoria, S., Upadhyay, R., Philip, R. S., Dwivedi, R., Micheal, G., Gupta, A., & Mishra, S. (2023). AI and Crime Prevention With Image and Video Analytics Using IoT. In *Handbook of Research on Thrust Technologies' Effect on Image Processing* (pp. 96–115). IGI Global. DOI: 10.4018/978-1-6684-8618-4.ch007

Nižetić, S., Šolić, P., Gonzalez-De, D. L. D. I., & Patrono, L. (2020). Internet of Things (IoT): Opportunities, issues and challenges towards a smart and sustainable future. *Journal of Cleaner Production*, *274*, 122877. DOI: 10.1016/j.jclepro.2020.122877 PMID: 32834567

Nnaji, C., Awolusi, I., Park, J., & Albert, A. (2021). Wearable sensing devices: Towards the development of a personalized system for construction safety and health risk mitigation. *Sensors (Basel)*, *21*(2), 682. DOI: 10.3390/s21030682 PMID: 33498311

Nota America Inc. (2023). NOTA AI for Real-Time Fatigue Detection in Commercial Drivers. https://nota.ai

Nowicki, P., Klos, J., & Kokot, Z. J. (2014). ANN and Bayesian Classification Models for Virtual Screening of Endocrine-Disrupting Chemicals. *Combinatorial Chemistry & High Throughput Screening*, *17*(5), 407–416. Advance online publication. DOI: 10.2174/1386207317666140219115635 PMID: 24547995

Ntlhakana, L. (2021). *Occupational noise-induced hearing loss in South African miners: risk assessment explored at a platinum mine in South Africa*

Ntlhakana, L., Nelson, G., & Khoza-Shangase, K. (2020). Estimating miners at risk for occupational noise-induced hearing loss: A review of data from a South African platinum mine. *South African Journal of Communication Disorders*, *67*(2, a677), 1-8. DOI: 10.4102/sajcd.v67i2.677

Ntlhakana, L., Kanji, A., & Khoza-Shangase, K. (2015). The use of hearing protection devices in South Africa: Exploring the current status in a gold and a non-ferrous mine. *Occupational Health Southern Africa*, *21*(2), 10–15.

Ntlhakana, L., Khoza-Shangase, K., & Nelson, G. (2020). Occupational noise-induced hearing loss in platinum miners: What do the data tell us? [Original research]. *Occupational Health Southern Africa*, *26*(1), 8–14.

Ntlhakana, L., Nelson, G., Khoza-Shangase, K., & Dorkin, E. (2021). Occupational hearing loss for platinum miners in South Africa: A case study of data sharing practices and ethical challenges in the mining industry. *International Journal of Environmental Research and Public Health*, *19*(1), 1. DOI: 10.3390/ijerph19010001 PMID: 35010261

Ntlhakana, L., Nelson, G., Khoza-Shangase, K., & Maposa, I. (2021). Predicting standard threshold shifts for occupational hearing loss among miners at a large-scale platinum mine in South Africa. *Journal of the Southern African Institute of Mining and Metallurgy*, *121*(8), 397–404. http://www.scielo.org.za/scielo.php?script=sci_arttext&pid=S2225-62532021000800007&nrm=iso. DOI: 10.17159/2411-9717/1318/2021

Nurlia, N. (2023). *AI Implementation Impact on Workforce Productivity : The Role of AI Training and Organizational Adaptation*. Escalate., DOI: 10.61536/escalate.v1i01.6

Nweke, G., & Nweke, O. C. (2024). Empowering the workforce in the ai era: Lessons from the UK's consultative approach for a global legal framework. *Beijing Law Review*, *15*(01), 219–230. DOI: 10.4236/blr.2024.151014

Nyman, E.Jr, & Armstrong, C. (2015). Real-time feedback during drop landing training improves subsequent frontal and sagittal plane knee kinematics. *Clinical Biomechanics (Bristol, Avon)*, *30*(9), 988–994. DOI: 10.1016/j.clinbiomech.2015.06.018 PMID: 26144663

O'Brien, J., & Nelson, C. (2020). Assessing the Risks Posed by the Convergence of Artificial Intelligence and Biotechnology. *Health Security*, *18*(3), 219–227. Advance online publication. DOI: 10.1089/hs.2019.0122 PMID: 32559154

Oglat, A. A. (2020). Acceptance experimentation and quality monitor of x-ray radiography units. *Radiation Physics and Chemistry*, *172*, 108810. DOI: 10.1016/j.radphyschem.2020.108810

Ogundeko-Olugbami, O., & Ogundeko, O. (2025). AI-enhanced predictive analytics systems combatting health disparities while driving equity in US healthcare delivery.

Ojha, A., Gautam, Y., Jebelli, H., & Akanmu, A. (2024). Physiological impact of powered back-support exoskeletons in construction: Analyzing muscle fatigue, metabolic cost, ergonomic risks, and stability. Automation in Construction, 168(Pt A), 105742.

Ojji, S. O. (2024). Digital Transformation and its Impact on Safety Culture During Organizational Change. *Valley International Journal Digital Library*, 26135-26146.

Olawade, D. B., Wada, O. J., Olawade, A. C. D., Kunonga, E., Abaiere, O., & Ling, J. (2023). Using artificial intelligence to improve public health: A narrative review. *Frontiers in Public Health*, *11*, 1196397. DOI: 10.3389/fpubh.2023.1196397 PMID: 37954052

Oliveira, A. L., & Figueiredo, M. A. (2024). Artificial Intelligence: Historical Context and State of the Art. *Multidisciplinary Perspectives on Artificial Intelligence and the Law*, 3.

Oliveira, A. L. (2019). Biotechnology, Big Data and Artificial Intelligence. *Biotechnology Journal*, *14*(8), 1800613. Advance online publication. DOI: 10.1002/biot.201800613 PMID: 30927505

Ong, K. J., Johnston, J., Datar, I., Sewalt, V., Holmes, D. C., & Shatkin, J. A. (2021). Food Safety Considerations and Research Priorities for the Cultured Meat and Seafood Industry. *Comprehensive Reviews in Food Science and Food Safety*, *20*(6), 5421–5448. Advance online publication. DOI: 10.1111/1541-4337.12853 PMID: 34633147

Onifade, M., Adebisi, J. A., Shivute, A. P., & Genc, B. (2023a). Challenges and applications of digital technology in the mineral industry. *Resources Policy*, *85*, 103978. DOI: 10.1016/j.resourpol.2023.103978

Onifade, M., Said, K. O., & Shivute, A. P. (2023b). Safe mining operations through technological advancement. *Process Safety and Environmental Protection*, *175*, 251–258. DOI: 10.1016/j.psep.2023.05.052

Onugwu, A. L., Nwagwu, C. S., Onugwu, O. S., Echezona, A. C., Agbo, C. P., Ihim, S. A., Emeh, P., Nnamani, P. O., Attama, A. A., & Khutoryanskiy, V. V. (2023). Nanotechnology based drug delivery systems for the treatment of anterior segment eye diseases. *Journal of Controlled Release, 354*, 465–488. DOI: 10.1016/j.jconrel.2023.01.018 PMID: 36642250

Ordieres-Meré, J., Gutierrez, M., & Villalba-Díez, J. (2023). Toward the industry 5.0 paradigm: Increasing value creation through the robust integration of humans and machines. *Computers in Industry, 150*, 103947. DOI: 10.1016/j.compind.2023.103947

Ouanes, K. (2024). Transforming medical and health sciences education with gamification.. DOI: 10.5772/intechopen.1005500

Oudyk, J., & Smith, P. (2020). *Preliminary results for the pandemic healthcare workers' survey*. Occupational Health Clinics for Ontario Workers.

Oukhatar, A., Bakhouya, M., & El Ouadghiri, D. (2021). Electromagnetic-Based Wireless Nano-Sensors Network: Architectures and Applications. *Journal of Communication, 16*(1), 8–19. DOI: 10.12720/jcm.16.1.8-19

Ouyang, Y., & Luo, X. (2025). Effects of physical fatigue superimposed on high temperatures on construction workers' cognitive performance. *Safety Science, 181*, 106705. DOI: 10.1016/j.ssci.2024.106705

Owen, J. (2024). AI and Robotics: Transforming Automation and Labor Productivity in the Construction Industry.

Oyeniran, K. A., Tenibiaje, M. O., Oke, M. A., Olowe, B. M., Oyeniran, O. H., & Oladunmoye, M. K. (2025). *Impact of COVID-19 on Electronic-Governance Adoption*., DOI: 10.4018/979-8-3693-7678-2.ch016

Ozaki, K., Kondo, I., Hirano, S., Kagaya, H., Saitoh, E., Osawa, A., & Fujinori, Y. (2017). Training with a balance exercise assist robot is more effective than conventional training for frail older adults. *Geriatrics & Gerontology International, 17*(11), 1982–1990. DOI: 10.1111/ggi.13009 PMID: 28295912

Padula, W., Armstrong, D. G., Pronovost, P. J., & Saria, S. (2024). Predicting pressure injury risk in hospitalised patients using machine learning with electronic health records: A us multilevel cohort study. *BMJ Open, 14*(4), e082540. DOI: 10.1136/bmjopen-2023-082540 PMID: 38594078

Pagan, N., Baumann, J., Elokda, E., Pasquale, G., Bolognani, S., & Hann'ak, A. (2023). A Classification of Feedback Loops and Their Relation to Biases in Automated Decision-Making Systems. *Proceedings of the 3rd ACM Conference on Equity and Access in Algorithms, Mechanisms, and Optimization*. https://doi.org/DOI: 10.1145/3617694.3623227

Pagano, T., Loureiro, R., Lisboa, F., Peixoto, R., Guimarães, G., Cruz, G., Araujo, M., Santos, L., Cruz, M., Oliveira, E., Winkler, I., & Nascimento, E. (2023). Bias and Unfairness in Machine Learning Models: A Systematic Review on Datasets, Tools, Fairness Metrics, and Identification and Mitigation Methods. *Big Data and Cognitive Computing, 7*(1), 15. DOI: 10.3390/bdcc7010015

Pagell, M., Johnston, D., Veltri, A., Klassen, R., & Biehl, M. (2014). Is safe production an oxymoron? *Production and Operations Management, 23*(7), 1161–1175. DOI: 10.1111/poms.12100

Palačić, D. (2024). How to assess the risks of applying Artificial Intelligence in occupational health and safety-Modelling the assessment process. *The authors are responsible for the professional and linguistic accuracy of their papers.*, 1.

Paneru, S., & Jeelani, I. (2021). Computer vision applications in construction: Current state, opportunities & challenges. *Automation in Construction*, *132*, 103940. DOI: 10.1016/j.autcon.2021.103940

Panganiban, G. G. F. (2019). E-governance in agriculture: Digital tools enabling Filipino farmers. *Journal of Asian Public Policy*, *12*(1), 51–70. DOI: 10.1080/17516234.2018.1499479

Pant, P., Mytton, J., Dharel, M., Dangi, A., Rai, W., & Joshi, S. (2021). The prevention of – and first response to – injuries in Nepal: A review of policies and legislation. *Health Research Policy and Systems*, *19*(1), 65. Advance online publication. DOI: 10.1186/s12961-021-00686-1 PMID: 33853626

Pappa, S., Ntella, V., Giannakas, T., Giannakoulis, V. G., Papoutsi, E., & Katsaounou, P. (2020). Prevalence of depression, anxiety, and insomnia among healthcare workers during the COVID-19 pandemic: A systematic review and meta-analysis. *Brain, Behavior, and Immunity*, *88*, 901–907. DOI: 10.1016/j.bbi.2020.05.026 PMID: 32437915

Park, H., Nam, K., Lim, J., Yeo, S., Lee, J., & Hwang, J. (2021). Real-time interactive digital healthcare system for post-operative breast cancer patients: Study protocol for a randomized controlled trial. *Trials*, *22*(1), 549. Advance online publication. DOI: 10.1186/s13063-021-05535-8 PMID: 34412658

Patchipala, S.Surya Gangadhar Patchipala. (2023). Tackling data and model drift in AI: Strategies for maintaining accuracy during ML model inference. *International Journal of Science and Research Archive*, *10*(2), 1198–1209. DOI: 10.30574/ijsra.2023.10.2.0855

Patel, V., Chesmore, A., Legner, C. M., & Pandey, S. (2022). Trends in workplace wearable technologies and connected-worker solutions for next-generation occupational safety, health, and productivity. *Advanced Intelligent Systems*, *4*(1), 2100099. DOI: 10.1002/aisy.202100099

Pathak, P., & Joshi, S. K. (2023). Epidemiology of unintentional childhood injuries in urban and rural areas of Nepal- a comparative study. *PLoS One*, *18*(10), e0287487. DOI: 10.1371/journal.pone.0287487 PMID: 37847700

Patil, A. R., & Salunkhe, S. S. (2024). Classification and risk estimation of osteoarthritis using deep learning methods. *Measurement. Sensors*, *35*, 101279. DOI: 10.1016/j.measen.2024.101279

Patricia, E. M. D., Jody, S., Marie, A. C., Wouter, F., Hans, K., John, W. C., & Erik, T. (2011). Validation of the inhalable dust algorithm of the Advanced REACH Tool using a dataset from the pharmaceutical industry. [publication_type = article.]. *Journal of Environmental Monitoring*, *13*(6), 1597–1606. DOI: 10.1039/c1em10189g PMID: 21544304

Paulus, J. K., & Kent, D. M. (2020). Predictably unequal: Understanding and addressing concerns that algorithmic clinical prediction may increase health disparities. *NPJ Digital Medicine*, *3*(1), 99. DOI: 10.1038/s41746-020-0304-9 PMID: 32821854

Paul, W., Hadžić, A., Joshi, N., Alajaji, F., & Burlina, P. (2020). TARA: Training and Representation Alteration for AI Fairness and Domain Generalization. *Neural Computation*, *34*(3), 716–753. DOI: 10.1162/neco_a_01468 PMID: 35016212

Peiffer-Smadja, N., Rawson, T. M., Ahmad, R., Buchard, A., Georgiou, P., Lescure, F. X., Birgand, G., & Holmes, A. H. (2020). Machine learning for clinical decision support in infectious diseases: A narrative review of current applications. *Clinical Microbiology and Infection*, *26*(5), 584–595. DOI: 10.1016/j.cmi.2019.09.009 PMID: 31539636

Perez Teixeira, R. L. (2023). *Exploring Sustainable Human Manufacturing: Industry 4.0, Manufacturing, and Green Marketing for a Balanced Future*. Concilium., DOI: 10.53660/CLM-1784-23M18

Peters, D. H. (2014). The application of systems thinking in health: Why use systems thinking? *Health Research Policy and Systems*, *12*(1), 51. DOI: 10.1186/1478-4505-12-51 PMID: 25160707

Petersson, L., Svedberg, P., Nygren, J., & Larsson, I. (2023). Healthcare leaders' perceptions of the usefulness of ai applications in clinical work: a qualitative study.. DOI: 10.3233/SHTI230235

Petya, B. (2021) The place of artificial intelligence in the risk management process. 120: 02013.

Pianykh, O. S., Langs, G., Dewey, M., Enzmann, D. R., Herold, C. J., Schoenberg, S. O., & Brink, J. A. (2020). Continuous Learning AI in Radiology: Implementation Principles and Early Applications. *Radiology*, *297*(1), 6–14. DOI: 10.1148/radiol.2020200038 PMID: 32840473

Piccarozzi, M., Silvestri, L., Silvestri, C., & Ruggieri, A. (2024). Roadmap to Industry 5.0: Enabling technologies, challenges, and opportunities towards a holistic definition in management studies. *Technological Forecasting and Social Change*, *205*, 123467. DOI: 10.1016/j.techfore.2024.123467

Piccini, D., Demesmaeker, R., Heerfordt, J., Yerly, J., Di Sopra, L., Masci, P. G., Schwitter, J., Van De Ville, D., Richiardi, J., Kober, T., & Stuber, M. (2020). Deep Learning to Automate Reference-Free Image Quality Assessment of Whole-Heart MR Images. *Radiology. Artificial Intelligence*, *2*(3), e190123. DOI: 10.1148/ryai.2020190123 PMID: 33937825

Pierce, J. D., Rosipko, B., Youngblood, L., Gilkeson, R. C., Gupta, A., & Bittencourt, L. K. (2021). Seamless Integration of Artificial Intelligence Into the Clinical Environment: Our Experience With a Novel Pneumothorax Detection Artificial Intelligence Algorithm. *Journal of the American College of Radiology*, *18*(11), 1497–1505. DOI: 10.1016/j.jacr.2021.08.023 PMID: 34597622

Pierre, K., Haneberg, A. G., Kwak, S., Peters, K. R., Hochhegger, B., Sananmuang, T., Tunlayadechanont, P., Tighe, P. J., Mancuso, A., & Forghani, R. (2023). Applications of Artificial Intelligence in the Radiology Roundtrip: Process Streamlining, Workflow Optimization, and Beyond. *Seminars in Roentgenology*, *58*(2), 158–169. DOI: 10.1053/j.ro.2023.02.003 PMID: 37087136

Pillay, M. (2020). Chemicals, noise and occupational hearing health in South Africa: A mapping study. *S Afr J Commun Disord*. https://doi.org/https://doi.org/10.4102/sajcd.v67i2.687a

Pinto-Coelho, L. (2023). How Artificial Intelligence Is Shaping Medical Imaging Technology: A Survey of Innovations and Applications. *Bioengineering (Basel, Switzerland)*, *10*(12), 1435. DOI: 10.3390/bioengineering10121435 PMID: 38136026

Pishgar, M., Issa, S. F., Sietsema, M., Pratap, P., & Darabi, H. (2021). REDECA: A novel framework to review artificial intelligence and its applications in occupational safety and health. *International Journal of Environmental Research and Public Health, 18*(13), 6705. DOI: 10.3390/ijerph18136705 PMID: 34206378

Pixley, K. V., Falck-Zepeda, J. B., Paarlberg, R. L., Phillips, P. W. B., Slamet-Loedin, I. H., Dhugga, K. S., Campos, H., & Gutterson, N. (2022). Genome-edited crops for improved food security of smallholder farmers. *Nature Genetics 2022 54:4, 54*(4), 364–367. DOI: 10.1038/s41588-022-01046-7

Płaza, G., Achal, V., & Kumari, D. (2018). Microbiological Risk Assessment and Bioprocess Engineering. *Multidisciplinary Aspects of Production Engineering, 1*(1), 233–239. DOI: 10.2478/mape-2018-0030

Poggenborg, J., Yaroshenko, A., Wieberneit, N., Harder, T., & Gossmann, A. (2021). *Impact of AI-based Real Time Image Quality Feedback for Chest Radiographs in the Clinical Routine*. Radiology and Imaging. DOI: 10.1101/2021.06.10.21258326

Pote, T., Asbeck, N., & Asbeck, A. (2023). The Ethics of Mandatory Exoskeleton Use in Commercial and Industrial Settings. *IEEE Transactions on Technology and Society, 4*(4), 302–313. DOI: 10.1109/TTS.2023.3264807

Poyade, M., Eaglesham, C., Trench, J., & Reid, M. (2021). A transferable psychological evaluation of virtual reality applied to safety training in chemical manufacturing. *Journal of Chemical Health and Safety, 28*(1), 55–65. DOI: 10.1021/acs.chas.0c00105

Pradhan, M. R., Mago, B., & Ateeq, K. (2023). A classification-based sensor data processing method for the internet of things assimilated wearable sensor technology. *Cluster Computing, 26*(1), 807–822. DOI: 10.1007/s10586-022-03605-3

Pramanik, P. K. D., Solanki, A., Debnath, A., Nayyar, A., El-Sappagh, S., & Kwak, K. S. (2020). Advancing modern healthcare with nanotechnology, nanobiosensors, and internet of nano things: Taxonomies, applications, architecture, and challenges. *IEEE Access : Practical Innovations, Open Solutions, 8*, 65230–65266. DOI: 10.1109/ACCESS.2020.2984269

Pransky, J. (2020). The Pransky interview: Dr. Matanya Horowitz, founder and CEO of AMP robotics. *The Industrial Robot, 47*(3), 319–323. DOI: 10.1108/IR-02-2020-0038

Priyank, T. and M. A. Fahad. (2024) The advancement of Artificial Intelligence (AI) in Occupational Health and Safety (OHS) across high-risk industries. *Journal of infrastructure, policy and development*, 8: 6889.

Purwanto, A., Asbari, M., & Santoso, P. B. (2019). Inovbiz Influence of Transformational and Transactional Leadership Style toward Food Safety Management System ISO 22000:2018 Performance of Food Industry in Pati Central Java. In *Inovbiz: Jurnal Inovasi Bisnis* (Vol. 7). www.ejournal.polbeng.ac.id/index.php/IBP

Pusic, A., Temple, L., Carter, J., Stabile, C., Assel, M., Vickers, A., Niehaus, K., Ancker, J. S., McCready, T., Stetson, P. D., & Simon, B. (2021). A randomized controlled trial evaluating electronic outpatient symptom monitoring after ambulatory cancer surgery. *Annals of Surgery Open : Perspectives of Surgical History, Education, and Clinical Approaches*, *274*(3), 441–448. DOI: 10.1097/SLA.0000000000005005 PMID: 34132697

Qadhi, S., Alduais, A., Chaaban, Y., & Khraisheh, M. (2024). Generative ai, research ethics, and higher education research: Insights from a scientometric analysis. *Information (Basel)*, *15*(6), 325. DOI: 10.3390/info15060325

Qi, T., Guo, J., Peng, H., Liu, P., Kang, Z., & Guo, J. (2019). Host-Induced Gene Silencing: A Powerful Strategy to Control Diseases of Wheat and Barley. *International Journal of Molecular Sciences 2019, Vol. 20, Page 206*, *20*(1), 206. DOI: 10.3390/ijms20010206

Qian, C., Murphy, S. C., Orsi, R. H., & Wiedmann, M. (2023). How Can AI Help Improve Food Safety? *Annual Review of Food Science and Technology*, *14*(1), 517–538. Advance online publication. DOI: 10.1146/annurev-food-060721-013815 PMID: 36542755

Radanliev, P., & Santos, O. (2023). Ethics and Responsible AI Deployment. ArXiv, abs/2311.14705. https://doi.org//arXiv.2311.14705.DOI: 10.33774/apsa-2023-f1fkq

Radhakrishnan, J., & Chattopadhyay, M. (2020). Determinants and barriers of artificial intelligence adoption–A literature review. In *Re-imagining Diffusion and Adoption of Information Technology and Systems: A Continuing Conversation: IFIP WG 8.6 International Conference on Transfer and Diffusion of IT, TDIT 2020, Tiruchirappalli, India, December 18–19, 2020, Proceedings, Part I* (pp. 89-99). Springer International Publishing. DOI: 10.1007/978-3-030-64849-7_9

Raghav, A., Singh, B., Jermsittiparsert, K., Raghav, R., & Yadav, U. (2024). Artificial Intelligence in Environmental and Climate Changes: A Sustainable Future. In Singh, B., Kaunert, C., Vig, K., & Dutta, S. (Eds.), *Maintaining a Sustainable World in the Nexus of Environmental Science and AI* (pp. 485–506). IGI Global., DOI: 10.4018/979-8-3693-6336-2.ch019

Rahman, M. and Khatun, F. (2023). Challenges and prospective of ai and 5g-enabled technologies in emerging applications during the pandemic.. DOI: 10.5772/intechopen.109450

Rahmat, F., Zulkafli, Z., Juraiza Ishak, A., Mohd Noor, S. B., Yahaya, H., & Masrani, A. (2020). Exploratory Data Analysis and Artificial Neural Network for Prediction of Leptospirosis Occurrence in Seremban, Malaysia Based on Meteorological Data. *Frontiers in Earth Science (Lausanne)*, *8*, 377. DOI: 10.3389/feart.2020.00377

Raj Kumar, W. (2024) The role of artificial intelligence (AI) in microbiology laboratories for diagnosis of microorganisms: A review study. 13: 383 - 388.

Rajakumar, J., & Choi, J.-H. (2023). Helmet-mounted real-time toxic gas monitoring and prevention system for workers in confined places. *Sensors (Basel)*, *23*(4), 1590. DOI: 10.3390/s23031590 PMID: 36772630

Ralfs, L., Hoffmann, N., & Weidner, R. (2022). Approach of a decision support matrix for the implementation of exoskeletons in industrial workplaces., 165-176. DOI: 10.1007/978-3-030-74032-0_14

Rama Padmaja, C. V. (2024). *The Rise of AI: A Comprehensive Research Review. Iaes International Journal of Artificial Intelligence*. Ij-Ai., DOI: 10.11591/ijai.v13.i2.pp2226-2235

Ranavolo, A., Ajoudani, A., Cherubini, A., Bianchi, M., Fritzsche, L., Iavicoli, S., Sartori, M., Silvetti, A., Vanderborght, B., Varrecchia, T., & Draicchio, F. (2020). The sensor-based biomechanical risk assessment at the base of the need for revising of standards for human ergonomics. *Sensors (Basel), 20*(20), 5750. DOI: 10.3390/s20205750 PMID: 33050438

Rane, N., Choudhary, S., & Rane, J. (2023). Artificial Intelligence (AI) and Internet of Things (IoT)-based sensors for monitoring and controlling in architecture, engineering, and construction: applications, challenges, and opportunities. *Available atSSRN* 4642197. DOI: 10.2139/ssrn.4642197

Ranjan, A., Zhao, Y., Sahu, H. B., & Misra, P. (2019). Opportunities and challenges in health sensing for extreme industrial environment: Perspectives from underground mines. *IEEE Access : Practical Innovations, Open Solutions, 7*, 139181–139195. DOI: 10.1109/ACCESS.2019.2941436

Rannertshauser, P., Kessler, M., & Arlinghaus, J. C. (2022). Human-centricity in the design of production planning and control systems: A first approach towards Industry 5.0. *IFAC-PapersOnLine, 55*(10), 2641–2646. DOI: 10.1016/j.ifacol.2022.10.108

Rathipe, M., & Raphela, S. F. (2023). Hearing loss and respiratory health symptoms among large-scale sawmill workers of the timber processing factories within the Gert Sibande District Municipality: A comparative cross-sectional study. *BMC Public Health, 23*(1), 1196. DOI: 10.1186/s12889-023-16086-9 PMID: 37340332

Raul, V., Youssef, M., Víctor, M. E., Emal, Z., Patrick, B., Joseph, S. N., Juha, H., Bradley, J. N., Ajmal, Z., & Ajmal, Z. (2021). [publication_type = article.]. *Modelling the Impact of Robotics on Infectious Spread Among Healthcare Workers., 8*, 652685.

Ravi, K., Samuel, D., Karl, P., & Lauren, E. C. (2022). Predicting infectious disease for biopreparedness and response: A systematic review of machine learning and deep learning approaches. [publication_type = article.]. *One Health, 15*, 100439. DOI: 10.1016/j.onehlt.2022.100439 PMID: 36277100

Redfern, L. K., Gardner, C. M., Hodzic, E., Ferguson, P. L., Hsu-Kim, H., & Gunsch, C. K. (2019). A new framework for approaching precision bioremediation of PAH contaminated soils. *Journal of Hazardous Materials, 378*, 120859. Advance online publication. DOI: 10.1016/j.jhazmat.2019.120859 PMID: 31327574

Reiner, B. I. (2009). Quantifying Radiation Safety and Quality in Medical Imaging, Part 3: The Quality Assurance Scorecard. *Journal of the American College of Radiology, 6*(10), 694–700. DOI: 10.1016/j.jacr.2009.05.009 PMID: 19800588

Reis da Silva Tiago. (2024d) The Value of Emotional Intelligence in Midwifery: Enhancing Care and Outcomes for Mothers and Infants through Sustainable Development Goals and Leadership. Journal of Womens Healthcare & Midwifery Research. SRC/JWHMR-133. DOI: https://doi.org/ Link: https://www.onlinescientificresearch.com/articles/the-value-of-emotional-intelligence-in-midwifery-enhancing-care-and-outcomes-for-mothers-and-infants-through-sustainable-developme.pdfDOI: 10.47363/JWHMR/2024(3)119

Reis da Silva, T H (2024e). Prevalence of elder abuse: a narrative review. British journal of community nursing vol. 29,9 (2024): 442-446. doi: https://doi.org/DOI: 10.12968/bjcn.2024.0004

Reis da Silva, T. H (2024c). Oncology and Cancer Medicine: Understanding the complexities in Older Patients. Biomed J Sci & Tech Res 55(3)-2024. DOI: https://doi.org/DOI: 10.26717/BJSTR.2024.55.008720

Reis da Silva, T. H. (2024a). Chapter 11 - Integrating business essentials into Gerontological Nursing: Enhancing Care for Older Adults in Diverse Settings. In Sedky, A. Resiliency Strategies for Long-Term Business Success. Pp. 283-316. IGI Global. DOI: https://doi.org/DOI: 10.4018/979-8-3693-9168-6.ch011

Reis da Silva, T. H. (2024d). Chapter 6 – Navigating Healthcare Complexity: Integrating Business Fundamentals into Nursing Leadership. In Sedky, A. Resiliency Strategies for Long-Term Business Success. Pp. 145-168. IGI Global. https://doi.org/DOI: 10.4018/979-8-3693-9168-6.ch006

Reis da Silva, T. (2024e). Advancing Gender Equity In Nursing Care For Older Adults: A Pathway To Achieving The United Nations Sustainable Development Goals. *J Comm Med and Pub Health Rep*, *5*(12). Advance online publication. DOI: 10.38207/JCMPHR/2024/JUL051201105

Reis da Silva, T. (2024f). Gender Equity In Healthcare: Integrating Emotional Intelligence To Achieve The United Nations Sustainable Development Goals. *J Comm Med and Pub Health Rep*, *5*(12). Advance online publication. DOI: 10.38207/JCMPHR/2024/JUL051202106

Reis da Silva, T. H. (2023a). Moving and Handling in the Community. *British Journal of Community Nursing*, *28*(8), 369. DOI: 10.12968/bjcn.2023.28.8.369 PMID: 37527217

Reis da Silva, T. H. (2023b). Falls assessment and prevention in the nursing home and community. *British Journal of Community Nursing*, *28*(2), 68–72. DOI: 10.12968/bjcn.2023.28.2.68 PMID: 36735363

Reis da Silva, T. H. (2023c). Ageing in place: Ageing at home and in the community. *British Journal of Community Nursing*, *28*(5), 213–214. DOI: 10.12968/bjcn.2023.28.5.213 PMID: 37130715

Reis da Silva, T. H. (2024b). Falls prevention in older people and the role of nursing. *British Journal of Community Nursing*, *29*(7), 335–339. DOI: 10.12968/bjcn.2024.0005 PMID: 38963269

Reis da Silva, T. H. (2024f). The Nursing Process in Geriatric Care: A Comprehensive Approach. *International Journal of Biomedical Research*, *3*(5). Advance online publication. DOI: 10.31579/2834-5029/064

Reis da Silva, T. H. (2025a). Integrating Artificial Intelligence in Geriatric Care: Enhancing Physical and Mental Health Outcomes. In Jermsittiparsert, K., & Marzo, R. R. (Eds.), *Physical Health, Mental Health, and Human Well-Being in the Age of AI*. IGI Global Scientific Publishing., DOI: 10.4018/979-8-3693-6190-0.ch11

Reis da Silva, T. H., & Mitchell, A. (2024). Integrating Digital Transformation in Nursing Education: Best Practices and Challenges in Curriculum Development. In Lytras, M., Serban, A. C., Alkhaldi, A., Malik, S., & Aldosemani, T. (Eds.), *Digital Transformation in Higher Education, Part B Cases, Examples and Good Practices*. Emerald Publishing Limited.

Reis da Silva, T. M. (2025d). Designing for Longevity: Economic Perspectives on Age-Friendly Housing and Urban Development. In Gölçek, A. (Ed.), *Perspectives on the Economics of Aging* (pp. 151–176). IGI Global Scientific Publishing., DOI: 10.4018/979-8-3693-7753-6.ch006

Reis da Silva, T. M. (2025g). Cultivating Emotionally Intelligent Leadership: Strategies for Enhancing Authentic Engagement and Organisational Impact. In Sayed, Z. (Ed.), *Emotionally Intelligent Methods for Meaningful Leadership* (pp. 119–148). IGI Global Scientific Publishing., DOI: 10.4018/979-8-3693-7372-9.ch006

Reis da Silva, T. M. (2025h). Fostering Emotional Resilience and Mindful Leadership in Gerontology Nursing: A Model for Change and Innovation. In Baez, M. (Ed.), *Strategic Approaches to Mindful Leadership and Change Management* (pp. 259–280). IGI Global Scientific Publishing., DOI: 10.4018/979-8-3693-7066-7.ch009

Reis da Silva, T. M. (2025i). The Interplay Between Ethical Work Climate and Employee Well-Being: Navigating the Path to Organisational Integrity and Success. In Ige-Olaobaju, A., Ganiyu, I., Atiku, S., & Olarewaju, O. (Eds.), *Advances in Ethical Work Climate and Employee Well-Being* (pp. 243–268). IGI Global Scientific Publishing., DOI: 10.4018/979-8-3693-8819-8.ch012

Reis da Silva, T. M. H. (2025f). The Role of Emotional Intelligence in Promoting Mental Peace, Healthy Work Environments, and Emotional Well-Being Among Entrepreneurs. In Tunio, M. N. (Ed.), *Supporting Psychological and Emotional Wellbeing Among Entrepreneurs*. IGI Global Scientific Publishing., DOI: 10.4018/979-8-3693-3673-1.ch21

Ria, A. (2023). A review of biowaste remediation and valorization for environmental sustainability: Artificial intelligence approach. *Environmental Pollution*, *324*, 121363. DOI: 10.1016/j.envpol.2023.121363 PMID: 36863440

Riad, M. H., Sekamatte, M., Ocom, F., Makumbi, I., & Scoglio, C. M. (2019). Risk assessment of Ebola virus disease spreading in Uganda using a two-layer temporal network. *Scientific Reports*, *9*(1), 16060. DOI: 10.1038/s41598-019-52501-1 PMID: 31690844

Ribeiro, D., Carreira, L., Salci, M., Marques, F., Gallo, A., Baccon, W., Baldissera, V., & Laranjeira, C. (2023). The institutionalisation of brazilian older abused adults: A qualitative study among victims and formal carers. *Geriatrics (Basel, Switzerland)*, *8*(3), 65. DOI: 10.3390/geriatrics8030065 PMID: 37367097

Riccò, M., Ranzieri, S., Vezzosi, L., Balzarini, F., & Bragazzi, N. L. (2022). Wearable Exoskeletons on the Workplaces: Knowledge, Attitudes and Perspectives of Health and Safety Managers on the implementation of exoskeleton technology in Northern Italy. *Acta Biomedica*, *92*(6), e2021310. PMID: 35075091

Ricroch, A. E., Guillaume-Hofnung, M., & Kuntz, M. (2018). The ethical concerns about transgenic crops. *The Biochemical Journal*, *475*(4), 803–811. DOI: 10.1042/BCJ20170794 PMID: 29490910

Rikhotso, O., Morodi, T. J., & Masekameni, D. M. (2022). Health risk management cost items imposed by Occupational Health and Safety Regulations: A South African perspective. *Safety Science*, *150*, 105707. DOI: 10.1016/j.ssci.2022.105707

Rilkoff, H., Struck, S., Ziegler, C., Faye, L., Paquette, D., & Buckeridge, D. (2024). Innovations in public health surveillance: An overview of novel use of data and analytic methods. *Canada Communicable Disease Report = Relevé des Maladies Transmissibles au Canada*, *50*(3/4), 93–101. DOI: 10.14745/ccdr.v50i34a02 PMID: 38716410

Ringer, T., Hazzan, A., Agarwal, A., Mutsaers, A., & Παπαϊωάννου, A. (2017). Relationship between family caregiver burden and physical frailty in older adults without dementia: A systematic review. *Systematic Reviews*, *6*(1), 55. Advance online publication. DOI: 10.1186/s13643-017-0447-1 PMID: 28292313

Rittick, M., K. Sachin, K. Mandar Bhalchandra and N. B. Sai Shibu. (2023) Automated Monitoring of Healthcare-Associated Infections in Operation Theatres Using IR Camera. 1124 - 1130.

Robert, C., Meyer, P., Séroussi, B., Leroy, T., & Bibault, J. E. (2024). Artificial intelligence and radiotherapy: Evolution or revolution? *Cancer Radiotherapie*, *28*(6-7), 503–509. DOI: 10.1016/j.canrad.2024.09.003 PMID: 39406605

Roberto, K., Teaster, P., Lindberg, B., & Blancato, R. (2020). A first (and disturbing) look at the relationship between the opioid epidemic and elder abuse: Insights of human service professionals. *Journal of Applied Gerontology*, *40*(10), 1231–1235. DOI: 10.1177/0733464820947279 PMID: 32772619

Rodríguez-Mañas, L., Bayer, A., Kelly, M., Zeyfang, A., Izquierdo, M., Laosa, O., Hardman, T. C., & Sinclair, A. (2014). An evaluation of the effectiveness of a multi-modal intervention in frail and pre-frail older people with type 2 diabetes - the mid-frail study: Study protocol for a randomised controlled trial. *Trials*, *15*(1), 34. Advance online publication. DOI: 10.1186/1745-6215-15-34 PMID: 24456998

Rodríguez-Mañas, L., Laosa, O., Vellas, B., Paolisso, G., Topinková, E., Oliva, J., & Sinclair, A. (2019). Effectiveness of a multimodal intervention in functionally impaired older people with type 2 diabetes mellitus. *Journal of Cachexia, Sarcopenia and Muscle*, *10*(4), 721–733. DOI: 10.1002/jcsm.12432 PMID: 31016897

Ronquillo, C., Peltonen, L., Pruinelli, L., Chu, C., Bakken, S., Beduschi, A., Cato, K., Hardiker, N., Junger, A., Michalowski, M., Nyrup, R., Rahimi, S., Reed, D. N., Salakoski, T., Salanterä, S., Walton, N., Weber, P., Wiegand, T., & Topaz, M. (2021). Artificial intelligence in nursing: Priorities and opportunities from an international invitational think-tank of the nursing and artificial intelligence leadership collaborative. *Journal of Advanced Nursing*, *77*(9), 3707–3717. DOI: 10.1111/jan.14855 PMID: 34003504

Roquilly, A., Broquet, A., Jacqueline, C., Masson, D., Segain, J., Braudeau, C., Vourc'h, M., Caillon, J., Altare, F., Josien, R., Retière, C., Villadangos, J., & Asehnoune, K. (2014). Hydrocortisone prevents immunosuppression by interleukin-10+ natural killer cells after trauma-hemorrhage. *Critical Care Medicine*, *42*(12), e752–e761. DOI: 10.1097/CCM.0000000000000658 PMID: 25289930

Rosak-Szyrocka, J., & Abbase, A. A. (2020). Quality management and safety of food in HACCP system aspect. *Production Engineering Archives*, *26*(2), 50–53. DOI: 10.30657/pea.2020.26.11

Rožman, M., Oreški, D., & Tominc, P. (2022). Integrating Artificial Intelligence Into a Talent Management Model to Increase the Work Engagement and Performance of Enterprises. *Frontiers in Psychology*, *13*, 1014434. Advance online publication. DOI: 10.3389/fpsyg.2022.1014434 PMID: 36506984

Rubin, D. L. (2019). Artificial Intelligence in Imaging: The Radiologist's Role. *Journal of the American College of Radiology*, *16*(9), 1309–1317. DOI: 10.1016/j.jacr.2019.05.036 PMID: 31492409

Rushton, L. (2017). The global burden of occupational disease. *Current Environmental Health Reports*, *4*(3), 340–348. DOI: 10.1007/s40572-017-0151-2 PMID: 28733964

Ryan, N. B. and T. Chuck (2021). The Biothreat Assessment as a Foundation for Biosecurity: 13 - 33.

Saadati, S. (2023). The need for more attention to the validity and reliability of ai-generated exercise programs. HN, 1(1), 77-81. DOI: 10.61838/hn.1.1.12

Sacks, R., Perlman, A., & Barak, R. (2013). Construction safety training using immersive virtual reality. *Construction Management and Economics*, *31*(9), 1005–1017. DOI: 10.1080/01446193.2013.828844

Saeed, S. U., Fu, Y., Stavrinides, V., Baum, Z. M. C., Yang, Q., Rusu, M., Fan, R. E., Sonn, G. A., Noble, J. A., Barratt, D. C., & Hu, Y. (2022). Image quality assessment for machine learning tasks using meta-reinforcement learning. *Medical Image Analysis*, *78*, 102427. DOI: 10.1016/j.media.2022.102427 PMID: 35344824

Sætra, H. S. (2022). The AI ESG Protocol: Evaluating and Disclosing the Environment, Social, and Governance Implications of Artificial Intelligence Capabilities, Assets, and Activities. *Sustainable Development*. Advance online publication. DOI: 10.1002/sd.2438

Saheb, T. (2023). Ethically contentious aspects of artificial intelligence surveillance: A social science perspective. *AI and Ethics*, *3*(2), 369–379. DOI: 10.1007/s43681-022-00196-y PMID: 35874304

Sahi, K. S. S., & Kaushik, S. (2022). Smart Nanosensors for Healthcare Monitoring and Disease Detection using AIoT Framework. In *Nanosensors for Futuristic Smart and Intelligent Healthcare Systems* (pp. 387–400). CRC Press. DOI: 10.1201/9781003093534-19

Sahoo, P., Roy, I., Ahlawat, R., Irtiza, S., & Khan, L. (2022). Potential diagnosis of COVID-19 from chest X-ray and CT findings using semi-supervised learning. *Physical and Engineering Sciences in Medicine*, *45*(1), 31–42. DOI: 10.1007/s13246-021-01075-2 PMID: 34780042

Sahu, T., Ratre, Y. K., Chauhan, S., Bhaskar, L. V. K. S., Nair, M. P., & Verma, H. K. (2021). Nanotechnology based drug delivery system: Current strategies and emerging therapeutic potential for medical science. *Journal of Drug Delivery Science and Technology*, *63*, 102487. DOI: 10.1016/j.jddst.2021.102487

Salamone, F., Masullo, M., & Sibilo, S. (2021). Wearable devices for environmental monitoring in the built environment: A systematic review. *Sensors (Basel)*, *21*(14), 4727. DOI: 10.3390/s21144727 PMID: 34300467

Salazar Rodriguez, J. D. (2024). Harnessing AI for Sustainable Architecture: A TOWS Analysis of Environmental, Economic, and Social Impacts in Design. *Economic, and Social Impacts in Design (August 29, 2024).*

Saleh, S., Woskie, S., & Bello, A. (2017). The Use of Noise Dampening Mats to Reduce Heavy-Equipment Noise Exposures in Construction. *Safety and Health at Work*, *8*(2), 226–230. DOI: 10.1016/j.shaw.2016.09.006 PMID: 28593081

Salhab, W., Ameyed, D., Jaafar, F., & Mcheick, H. (2024). A systematic literature review on ai safety: Identifying trends, challenges and future directions. *IEEE Access : Practical Innovations, Open Solutions*, *12*, 131762–131784. DOI: 10.1109/ACCESS.2024.3440647

Salikutluk, V., Koert, D., & Jäkel, F. (2023). Interacting with large language models: a case study on ai-aided brainstorming for guesstimation problems.. DOI: 10.3233/FAIA230081

Salvi Del Pero, A., Wyckoff, P., & Vourc'h, A. (2022). *Using Artificial Intelligence in the workplace: What are the main ethical risks?* OECD Publishing.

Samei, E., Dobbins, J. T.III, Lo, J. Y., & Tornai, M. P. (2005). A framework for optimising the radiographic technique in digital X-ray imaging. *Radiation Protection Dosimetry*, *114*(1–3), 220–229. DOI: 10.1093/rpd/nch562 PMID: 15933112

Sánchez, M., Rodriguez, C. S., & Manuel, J. (2020). Smart protective protection equipment for an accessible work environment and occupational hazard prevention. In *2020 10th International Conference on Cloud Computing, Data Science & Engineering (Confluence)* (pp. 581–585). IEEE. DOI: 10.1109/Confluence47617.2020.9058188

Sandbrink, J. B. (2023) Artificial intelligence and biological misuse: Differentiating risks of language models and biological design tools. *ArXiv*, abs/2306.13952.

Sarno, A., Valero, C., Tucciariello, R. M., Dukov, N., Costa, P. R., & Tomal, A. (2023). Physical and digital phantoms for 2D and 3D x-ray breast imaging: Review on the state-of-the-art and future prospects. *Radiation Physics and Chemistry*, *204*, 110715. DOI: 10.1016/j.radphyschem.2022.110715

Saroya, K., Gupta, A., Shrivastava, R., Mehta, N., & Goyal, A. (2024). Powered versus manual toothbrushes for plaque removal and gingival health amongst 55 and older individuals: A systematic review and meta-analysis. *Special Care in Dentistry*, *44*(4), 979–989. DOI: 10.1111/scd.12974 PMID: 38348549

Sattari, F., Macciotta, R., Kurian, D., & Lefsrud, L. (2021). Application of Bayesian network and artificial intelligence to reduce accident/incident rates in oil & gas companies. *Safety Science*, *133*, 104981. DOI: 10.1016/j.ssci.2020.104981

Sauter, M., Barthelme, J., Müller, C., & Liebers, F. (2021). Manual handling of heavy loads and low back pain among different occupational groups: Results of the 2018 bibb/baua employment survey. *BMC Musculoskeletal Disorders*, *22*(1), 956. Advance online publication. DOI: 10.1186/s12891-021-04819-z PMID: 34781946

Sayed, M., Karthika, R., & Makena, V. K. K. (2022). Phonoarthrography for early detection of osteoarthritis using machine learning. *2022 7th International Conference on Communication and Electronics Systems (ICCES)*, 1066–1072. DOI: 10.1109/ICCES54183.2022.9835867

Scavarelli, A., Arya, A., & Teather, R. J. (2021). Virtual reality and augmented reality in social learning spaces: A literature review. *Virtual Reality (Waltham Cross)*, *25*(1), 257–277. DOI: 10.1007/s10055-020-00444-8

Scheuerman, M., Paul, J., & Brubaker, J. (2019). How Computers See Gender. *Proceedings of the ACM on Human-Computer Interaction*, *3*(CSCW), 1–33. DOI: 10.1145/3359246

Schmidt, A., H. Alina and S. Jochen (2024). 6 Continuous biomanufacturing in upstream and downstream processing: 117 - 172.

Schouten, A. and Mugge, W. (2018). Closed-loop identification to unravel the way the human nervous system controls bodily functions., 617-621. DOI: 10.1007/978-3-030-01845-0_123

Scott, J., Ravichandran, B., Funk, C., Collins, R., & Liu, Y. (2020). From image to stability: learning dynamics from human pose., 536-554. DOI: 10.1007/978-3-030-58592-1_32

Sebastjan, A., Skrzek, A., Ignasiak, Z., & Sławińska, T. (2017). Age-related changes in hand dominance and functional asymmetry in older adults. *PLoS One*, *12*(5), e0177845. DOI: 10.1371/journal.pone.0177845 PMID: 28558047

Seibert, J. A. (2004). X-Ray Imaging Physics for Nuclear Medicine Technologists. Part 1: Basic Principles of X-Ray Production. *Journal of Nuclear Medicine Technology*, *32*(3). PMID: 15347692

Seidel, C. (2018). *Consequentialism, New Directions, New Problems*. Oxford Press.

Selb, R., Wal, J., Moreno, F. J., Løvik, M., Mills, C., Hoffmann-Sommergruber, K., & Fernandez, A. (2017). Assessment of Endogenous Allergenicity of Genetically Modified Plants Exemplified by Soybean – Where Do We Stand? *Food and Chemical Toxicology*, *101*, 139–148. Advance online publication. DOI: 10.1016/j.fct.2017.01.014 PMID: 28111299

Selestine, M., E. Youssef, K. Farid and B. Larbi. (2024) Artificial Intelligence for Infectious Disease Prediction and Prevention: A Comprehensive Review.

Sengeni, D., G. Padmapriya, S. S. Imambi, D. Suganthi, S. Ashish and B. Sampath (2023). Biomedical Waste Handling Method Using Artificial Intelligence Techniques: 306 - 323.

Sepadi, M. M., & Nkosi, V. (2023). Strengthening Urban Informal Trading and Improving the Health of Vendors: An Integrated Management Model. *International Journal of Environmental Research and Public Health*, *20*(6), 4836. DOI: 10.3390/ijerph20064836 PMID: 36981746

Serag, A., Ion-Mărgineanu, A., Qureshi, H., McMillan, R., Martin, M., Diamond, J., & Hamilton, P. (2019). Translational ai and deep learning in diagnostic pathology. *Frontiers in Medicine*, *6*, 185. Advance online publication. DOI: 10.3389/fmed.2019.00185 PMID: 31632973

Shahbazi, N., Lin, Y., Asudeh, A., & Jagadish, H. (2022). Representation Bias in Data: A Survey on Identification and Resolution Techniques. *ACM Computing Surveys*, *55*(13s), 1–39. DOI: 10.1145/3588433

Shah, I. A., & Mishra, S. (2024). Artificial intelligence in advancing occupational health and safety: An encapsulation of developments. *Journal of Occupational Health*, *66*(1), uiad017. DOI: 10.1093/joccuh/uiad017 PMID: 38334203

Shah, I. A., & Mishra, S. (2024). Reimagining occupational health and safety in the era of AI. In *A Biologist s Guide to Artificial Intelligence* (pp. 79–96). Academic Press.

Shahsavarloo, Z., Atashzadeh-Shoorideh, F., Gobbens, R., Ebadi, A., & Harouni, G. (2020). The impact of interventions on management of frailty in hospitalized frail older adults: A systematic review and meta-analysis. *BMC Geriatrics*, *20*(1), 526. Advance online publication. DOI: 10.1186/s12877-020-01935-8 PMID: 33272208

Shamshiri, A., Ryu, K. R., & Park, J. Y. (2024). Text mining and natural language processing in construction. *Automation in Construction*, *158*, 105200. DOI: 10.1016/j.autcon.2023.105200

Shandilya, S. K., Datta, A., Kartik, Y., & Nagar, A. (2024). Navigating the regulatory landscape. In *Digital Resilience: Navigating Disruption and Safeguarding Data Privacy* (pp. 127–240). Springer Nature Switzerland. DOI: 10.1007/978-3-031-53290-0_3

Shankar, J., Lai, D., Chen, S., Turin, T., Joseph, S., & Mi, E. (2022). Highly educated immigrant workers' perspectives of occupational health and safety and work conditions that challenge work safety. *International Journal of Environmental Research and Public Health, 19*(14), 8757. DOI: 10.3390/ijerph19148757 PMID: 35886609

Sharifi, S., Namvar, M., Intezari, A., & Akhlaghpour, S. (2024). Healthcare llms go to market: a realist review of product launch news.. DOI: 10.3233/SHTI240513

Sharko, A. D., Sharko, G., & Qose, S. (2024, July). Artificial Intelligence In Cybersecurity Applications. In *2024 IEEE 28th International Conference on Intelligent Engineering Systems (INES)* (pp. 000175-000180). IEEE. DOI: 10.1109/INES63318.2024.10629129

Sharma, S., Virk, S. S., & Jain, V. (2016). Detection of osteoarthritis using SVM classifications. *2016 3rd International Conference on Computing for Sustainable Global Development (INDIACom)*, 2997–3002.

Sharma, V., Eissa, G., Newman, A., Lester, S. W., & Pandey, J. (2023). Psychological entitlement and moral disengagement as antecedents of compliance with covid-19 workplace safety protocols and the moderating role of moral identity. *Applied Psychology, 73*(2), 698–722. DOI: 10.1111/apps.12496

Shaukat, N., Ali, D. M., & Razzak, J. (2020). Physical and mental health impacts of COVID-19 on healthcare workers: A scoping review. *International Journal of Emergency Medicine, 13*(1), 40. DOI: 10.1186/s12245-020-00299-5 PMID: 32689925

Shausan, A., Nazarathy, Y., & Dyda, A. (2023). Emerging data inputs for infectious diseases surveillance and decision making. *Frontiers in Digital Health, 5*, 5. DOI: 10.3389/fdgth.2023.1131731 PMID: 37082524

Shaw, G. (2001). A Clinician's Guide to Digital X-Ray Systems. *Journal of the Royal Society of Medicine, 94*(8), 391–395. DOI: 10.1177/014107680109400805 PMID: 11461982

Shell. (2022). *Driving Safer Operations with AI: Shell Transport Safety Review*. Retrieved from https://www.shell.com

Sheshadri, C., Sangeeta, K., & Hatice, K. (2022). Harnessing the Potential of Artificial Intelligence to Foster Citizens' Satisfaction: An empirical study on India. *Government Information Quarterly, 39*(4), 101621. DOI: 10.1016/j.giq.2021.101621

Shi, L., Lu, Z.-A., Que, J.-Y., Huang, X.-L., Liu, L., Ran, M.-S., Gong, Y.-M., Yuan, K., Yan, W., Sun, Y.-K., Shi, J., Bao, Y.-P., & Lu, L. (2020). Prevalence of and risk factors associated with mental health symptoms among the general population in China during the coronavirus disease 2019 pandemic. *JAMA Network Open, 3*(7), e2014053. DOI: 10.1001/jamanetworkopen.2020.14053 PMID: 32609353

Shneiderman, B. (2020). Human-Centered Artificial Intelligence: Three Fresh Ideas. *AIS Transactions on Human-Computer Interaction, 12*, 109–124. DOI: 10.17705/1thci.00131

Siddiqua, T., Rahman, M., Sanaullah, M., Mitu, Z. A., Hossain, I., & Rubai, S. S. (2021). Determination of Calibration X-Ray Beam Qualities and Establish a Set of Conversion Coefficients for Calibration of Radiation Protection Devices Used in Diagnostic Radiology. *East European Journal of Physics*, *3*(3), 55–61. DOI: 10.26565/2312-4334-2021-3-08

Simpson, L., Maharaj, M. M., & Mobbs, R. J. (2019). The role of wearables in spinal posture analysis: A systematic review. *BMC Musculoskeletal Disorders*, *20*(1), 1–14. DOI: 10.1186/s12891-019-2430-6 PMID: 30736775

Sinclair, R. R., Allen, T., Barber, L., Bergman, M., Britt, T., Butler, A., Ford, M., Hammer, L., Kath, L., Probst, T., & Yuan, Z. (2020). Occupational health science in the time of COVID-19: Now more than ever. *Occupational Health Science*, *4*(1-2), 1–22. DOI: 10.1007/s41542-020-00064-3 PMID: 32838031

Singh, A., & Pandey, J. (2024). Artificial intelligence adoption in extended hr ecosystems: Enablers and barriers. an abductive case research. *Frontiers in Psychology*, *14*, 1339782. Advance online publication. DOI: 10.3389/fpsyg.2023.1339782 PMID: 38327504

Singh, N., Gunjan, V., Chaudhary, G., Kaluri, R., Victor, N., & Lakshmanna, K. (2022). IoT enabled helmet to safeguard the health of mine workers. *Computer Communications*, *193*, 1–9. DOI: 10.1016/j.comcom.2022.06.032

Singh, T., & Matuka, O. (2013). Back to basics: Work-related infections Part 1: Risks of exposure to infectious agents in the workplace. *Occupational Health Southern Africa*, *19*(2), 4–12.

Skinner, C., & Haysom, G. (2016). *The informal sector's role in food security: A missing link in policy debates?* PLAAS Working Paper Series, 44. Retrieved from: https://www.wiego.org/wp-content/uploads/2025/04/The-informal-sectors-role-in-food-security-A-missing-link-in-policy-debates.pdf

Smuha, N. (2021). Beyond the individual: Governing AI's societal harm. *Internet Policy Review*, *10*(3). Advance online publication. DOI: 10.14763/2021.3.1574

Somaraju, P., Kulkarni, S. S., Duffy, V. G., & Kanade, S. (2024, June). Artificial Intelligence and Mobile Computing: Role of AI in Ergonomics. In *International Conference on Human-Computer Interaction* (pp. 265-281). Cham: Springer Nature Switzerland. DOI: 10.1007/978-3-031-61066-0_16

Sousa, R., Araújo, G., Souto, R., Santos, R., Leal, C., & Nascimento, N. (2021). Interventions to prevent elder abuse in the community: a mixed-methods systematic review. Revista Da Escola De Enfermagem Da Usp, 55. https://doi.org/DOI: 10.1590/s1980-220x2019033203677

South Africa. (1923). *Natives (Urban Areas) Act No. 21 of 1923*. Government Gazette of the Union of South Africa. Retrievedd from https://www.sahistory.org.za/article/natives-urban-areas-act-1923

South Africa. (1950). *Group Areas Act No. 41 of 1950*. Government Gazette of the Union of South Africa. Retrieved from https://www.sahistory.org.za/archive/group-areas-act-1950

South Africa. (1993). *Occupational Health and Safety Act 85 of 1993*. Government Gazette. Retrieved from https://www.gov.za/documents/occupational-health-and-safety-act

South Africa. (2013). *Protection of Personal Information Act 4 of 2013*. Government Gazette. Retrieved from https://www.gov.za/documents/protection-personal-information-act

South Africa. Compensation for Occupational Injuries and Diseases Act No. 130 of 1993. Circular instruction no. 171. The determination of permanent disablement resulting from hearing loss caused by exposure to excessive noise and trauma; 2001. https://www.gov.za/sites/default/files/gcis_document/201409/22296.pdf

South Africa. Mine Health and Safety Act, Act 29 of 1996. https://www.dmr.gov.za/Portals/0/mhs_act_29_of_19960_1.pdf

South African Government. (2003). *National Health Act, No. 61 of 2003*. Retrieved from https://www.gov.za/documents/national-health-act

South African Government. (2008). *Consumer Protection Act, No. 68 of 2008*. Retrieved from https://www.gov.za/documents/consumer-protection-act

South African National Standards. (2013). *The measurement and assessment of occupational noise for hearing conservation purposes* (Vol. 10083). South African National Standards.

South African Weather Service. (2022). *Annual Climate Report 2022*. South African Weather Service. Retrieved from https://www.weathersa.co.za/Documents/AnnualReports/SAWS_ANNUAL_REPORT_-_Reduced_File_Size-1_27092022093113.pdf

Spiers, G., Matthews, F., Moffatt, S., Barker, R., Jarvis, H., Stow, D., Kingston, A., & Hanratty, B. (2019). Does older adults' use of social care influence their healthcare utilisation? a systematic review of international evidence. *Health & Social Care in the Community*, hsc.12798. Advance online publication. DOI: 10.1111/hsc.12798 PMID: 31314142

Spitzer, R. L., Kroenke, K., Williams, J. B. W., & Löwe, B. (2006). A brief measure for assessing generalized anxiety disorder: The GAD-7. *Archives of Internal Medicine*, *166*(10), 1092–1097. DOI: 10.1001/archinte.166.10.1092 PMID: 16717171

Spurgeon, A. (2012). *The Contribution of the Women's Factory Inspectorate (1893-1921) to improvements in women's occupational health and safety* (Doctoral dissertation, University of Worcester).

Srihari, S. N. (2020). Explainable Artificial Intelligence. *Source: Journal of the Washington Academy of Sciences*, *106*(4), 9–38. DOI: 10.2307/27130153

Srivastava, J. N., Naraian, R., Singh Kalra, S. J., & Chandra, H. (2013). Advances in Microbial Bioremediation and the Factors Influencing the Process. *International Journal of Environmental Science and Technology*. Advance online publication. DOI: 10.1007/s13762-013-0412-z

Statistics South Africa (Stats SA). (2022). *Annual Report 2021/2022 (Book 1)*. Retrieved from https://www.stassa.gov.za/publications/AnnualReport/Stats_SA_Annual_Report_Book.pdf

Statistics South Africa (Stats SA). (2023). *Employment in the informal sector: Quarterly Labour Force Survey*. Retrieved from http://www.statssa.gov.za

Steenkamp, R. J. (2018). The Exploration of Modern Noise Control Measures for Mining Operations. Johannesburg: *Proceedings of the International Conference on Industrial Engineering and Operations Management*.

Stefana, E., Marciano, F., Rossi, D., Cocca, P., & Tomasoni, G. (2021). Wearable devices for ergonomics: A systematic literature review. *Sensors (Basel)*, *21*(3), 777. DOI: 10.3390/s21030777 PMID: 33498904

Stephanidis, C., Salvendy, G., Antona, M., Chen, J. Y., Dong, J., Duffy, V. G., Fang, X., Fidopiastis, C., Fragomeni, G., Fu, L. P., Guo, Y., Harris, D., Ioannou, A., Jeong, K. K., Konomi, S., Krömker, H., Kurosu, M., Lewis, J. R., Marcus, A., & Zhou, J. (2019). Seven HCI grand challenges. *International Journal of Human-Computer Interaction*, *35*(14), 1229–1269. DOI: 10.1080/10447318.2019.1619259

Steyvers, M., & Kumar, A. (2024). Three challenges for AI-assisted decision-making. *Perspectives on Psychological Science*, *19*(5), 722–734.

Strauß, S. (2021). Deep Automation Bias: How to Tackle a Wicked Problem of AI? *Big Data and Cognitive Computing*, *5*(2), 18. Advance online publication. DOI: 10.3390/bdcc5020018

Stypinska, J. (2023). AI ageism: A critical roadmap for studying age discrimination and exclusion in digitalized societies. *AI & Society*, *38*(2), 665–677. DOI: 10.1007/s00146-022-01553-5 PMID: 36212226

Sudha, K., Balakrishnan, C., Varun, C., & Subramanıan, R. (2024). Advancements in medical robotics and ai-assisted diagnostics., 23-46. DOI: 10.4018/979-8-3693-3218-4.ch002

Sudki, J. M., Fonseca de Oliveira, G. R., de Medeiros, A. D., Mastrangelo, T., Arthur, V., Amaral da Silva, E. A., & Mastrangelo, C. B. (2023). Fungal identification in peanuts seeds through multispectral images: Technological advances to enhance sanitary quality. *Frontiers in Plant Science*, *14*, 1112916. DOI: 10.3389/fpls.2023.1112916 PMID: 36909395

Suma, D. V. (2021). Wearable IoT based distributed framework for ubiquitous computing. *Journal of Ubiquitous Computing and Communication Technologies*, *3*(1), 23–32. DOI: 10.36548/jucct.2021.1.003

Sunarti, S., Rahman, F. F., Naufal, M., Risky, M., Febriyanto, K., & Masnina, R. (2021). Artificial intelligence in healthcare: Opportunities and risk for future. *Gaceta Sanitaria*, *35*, S67–S70. DOI: 10.1016/j.gaceta.2020.12.019 PMID: 33832631

Suriyan, J., Wai Peng, W., & Chee Peng, L. (2021). An Application of Data Envelopment Analysis and Machine Learning Approach to Risk Management. [publication_type = article.]. *IEEE Access : Practical Innovations, Open Solutions*, *9*, 85978–85994. DOI: 10.1109/ACCESS.2021.3087623

Suryadevara, M., Rangineni, S., & Venkata, S. (2023). Optimizing Efficiency and Performance: Investigating Data Pipelines for Artificial Intelligence Model Development and Practical Applications. [IJSR]. *International Journal of Science and Research (Raipur, India)*, *12*(7), 1330–1340. Advance online publication. DOI: 10.21275/SR23719211528

Tali, R., Borra, S., & Mahmud, M. (2022). Detection and classification of leukocytes in blood smear images., 1099-1130. DOI: 10.4018/978-1-6684-7544-7.ch057

Tama, C., Syaifullah, R., Putro, B., Purnama, S., Sabarini, S., & Nuryadin, I. (2022). Profile of injury prevent and treatment in Indonesia basketball wheelchair national team during the 11th asean para games preparation., 84-89. DOI: 10.2991/978-2-494069-79-4_12

Tanaka, R., Nozaki, S., Goshima, F., & Shiraishi, J. (2022). Deep learning versus the human visual system for detecting motion blur in radiography. *Journal of Medical Imaging (Bellingham, Wash.), 9*(01). Advance online publication. DOI: 10.1117/1.JMI.9.1.015501 PMID: 35106323

Tangorra, F. M., Buoio, E., Calcante, A., Bassi, A., & Costa, A. (2024). Internet of Things (IoT): Sensors Application in Dairy Cattle Farming. *Animals (Basel), 14*(21), 3071. DOI: 10.3390/ani14213071 PMID: 39518794

Technologies, H. E. R. E. (2023). *Fleet Telematics Services.* https://www.here.com

Tender, M., Fuller, P., Vaughan, A., Long, M., Couto, J. P., Damien, P., Chow, V., Silva, F., Reis, F., & Reis, R. (2022, November). Lessons from implementation of Key Technological Developments to improve occupational safety and health processes in a complex UK-based construction project. []. IOP Publishing.]. *IOP Conference Series. Earth and Environmental Science, 1101*(9), 092016. DOI: 10.1088/1755-1315/1101/9/092016

Tessandra, S., Jon, Z., & Seth, D. G. (2022). COVID-19 has illuminated the need for clearer AI-based risk management strategies. [publication_type = article.]. *Journal of Risk Research, 25*(10), 1223–1238. DOI: 10.1080/13669877.2022.2077411

Teufer, B., Ebenberger, A., Affengruber, L., Kien, C., Klerings, I., Szelag, M., & Griebler, U. (2019). Evidence-based occupational health and safety interventions: A comprehensive overview of reviews. *BMJ Open, 9*(10), e032528. DOI: 10.1136/bmjopen-2019-032528 PMID: 31831544

Thapen, N., Simmie, D., Hankin, C., & Gillard, J. (2016). DEFENDER: Detecting and Forecasting Epidemics Using Novel Data-Analytics for Enhanced Response. *PLoS One, 11*(5), e0155417. DOI: 10.1371/journal.pone.0155417 PMID: 27192059

The European Federation Of Radiographer Societies. (2020). Artificial Intelligence and the Radiographer/Radiological Technologist Profession: A joint statement of the International Society of Radiographers and Radiological Technologists and the European Federation of Radiographer Societies. *Radiography, 26*(2), 93–95. DOI: 10.1016/j.radi.2020.03.007 PMID: 32252972

Thies, M., Wagner, F., Huang, Y., Gu, M., Kling, L., Pechmann, S., Aust, O., Grüneboom, A., Schett, G., Christiansen, S., & Maier, A. (2022). Calibration by differentiation – Self-supervised calibration for X-ray microscopy using a differentiable cone-beam reconstruction operator. *Journal of Microscopy, 287*(2), 81–92. DOI: 10.1111/jmi.13125 PMID: 35638174

Thikare, V. P., & Pathak, P. S. (2024). Decoding Tomorrows Biotechnology: AI and Machine Learning Unveiled. *International Journal for Research in Applied Science and Engineering Technology, 12*(2), 727–742. Advance online publication. DOI: 10.22214/ijraset.2024.58430

Thisani, S. (2024). Developing a high-performance sports results prediction artificial neural network: Case study on world championship boxing. *International Journal of Computer Science in Sport, 23*(2), 1–21. DOI: 10.2478/ijcss-2023-0008

Thomas, S., Abraham, A., Baldwin, J., Piplani, S., & Petrovsky, N. (2021). *Artificial Intelligence in Vaccine and Drug Design.* DOI: 10.1007/978-1-0716-1884-4_6

Thrall, J. H., Li, X., Li, Q., Cruz, C., Do, S., Dreyer, K., & Brink, J. (2018). Artificial Intelligence and Machine Learning in Radiology: Opportunities, Challenges, Pitfalls, and Criteria for Success. *Journal of the American College of Radiology*, *15*(3), 504–508. DOI: 10.1016/j.jacr.2017.12.026 PMID: 29402533

Tiwari, D., Bhati, B. S., Al-Turjman, F., & Nagpal, B. (2022). Pandemic coronavirus disease (Covid-19): World effects analysis and prediction using machine-learning techniques. *Expert Systems: International Journal of Knowledge Engineering and Neural Networks*, *39*(3), e12714. DOI: 10.1111/exsy.12714 PMID: 34177035

Tompa, E., Mofidi, A., van den Heuvel, S., van Bree, T., Michaelsen, F., Jung, Y., Porsch, L., & van Emmerik, M. (2021). Economic burden of work injuries and diseases: A framework and application in five European Union countries. *BMC Public Health*, *21*(1), 49. DOI: 10.1186/s12889-020-10050-7 PMID: 33407315

TomTom Telematics. (2023). *AI Fleet Routing Solutions*. https://www.tomtom.com

TotalEnergies Zimbabwe. (2023). *PATROM Training Manual and Journey Management Protocols*. Transport Contractor Orientation.

TotalEnergies. (2023). *Health, Safety, Environment, and Quality Charter*. Retrieved from https://totalenergies.com

Tóth, Z., Caruana, R., Gruber, T., & Loebbecke, C. (2022). The dawn of the AI robots: Towards a new framework of AI robot accountability. *Journal of Business Ethics*, *178*(4), 895–916. DOI: 10.1007/s10551-022-05050-z

Touahema, S., Zaimi, I., Zrira, N., & Ngote, M. N. (2024). How can artificial intelligence identify knee osteoarthritis from radiographic images with satisfactory accuracy?: A literature review for 2018–2024. *Applied Sciences (Basel, Switzerland)*, *14*(14), 6333. DOI: 10.3390/app14146333

Toyoda, R., Russo-Abegão, F., & Glassey, J. (2022). VR-based health and safety training in various high-risk engineering industries: A literature review. *International Journal of Educational Technology in Higher Education*, *19*(1), 42. DOI: 10.1186/s41239-022-00349-3

Tranæus, U., Ivarsson, A., Johnson, U., Weiss, N., Samuelsson, M., & Skillgate, E. (2021). The role of the results of functional tests and psychological factors on prediction of injuries in adolescent female football players. *International Journal of Environmental Research and Public Health*, *19*(1), 143. DOI: 10.3390/ijerph19010143 PMID: 35010400

Trivedi, P., & Alqahtani, F. (2024). *The advancement of Artificial Intelligence (AI) in Occupational Health and Safety (OHS) across high-risk industries. Journal of Infrastructure*. Policy and Development., DOI: 10.24294/jipd.v8i10.6889

Trstenjak, M., Hegedić, M., Cajner, H., Opetuk, T., & Tošanović, N. (2024). Cognitive ergonomics in Industry 5.0. In Silva, F. J. G., Ferreira, L. P., Sá, J. C., Pereira, M. T., & Pinto, C. M. A. (Eds.), *Flexible Automation and Intelligent Manufacturing: Establishing Bridges for More Sustainable Manufacturing Systems* (pp. 763–770). Springer., DOI: 10.1007/978-3-031-38165-2_88

Tugwell, P., & Tovey, D. (2021). PRISMA 2020. *Journal of Clinical Epidemiology, 134*, A5–A6. DOI: 10.1016/j.jclinepi.2021.04.008 PMID: 34016443

Tula, S. T. (2024). *Ai-Enabled Customer Experience Enhancement in Business*. Computer Science & It Research Journal., DOI: 10.51594/csitrj.v5i2.789

Turchioe, M., Pepingco, C., Lytle, K., & Austin, R. (2024). Nurses' roles in artificial intelligence implementation: results from a mixed-methods study.. DOI: 10.3233/SHTI240140

Tursunbayeva, A., Pagliari, C., Di Lauro, S., & Antonelli, G. (2022). The ethics of people analytics: Risks, opportunities and recommendations. *Personnel Review, 51*(3), 900–921. DOI: 10.1108/PR-12-2019-0680

Tushar, K., Abhishek, S., & Wong, C. J. (2024). Survey of Artificial Intelligence for Automated Regulatory Compliance Tracking. [publication_type = article.]. *Journal of Engineering Research and Reports, 26*(7), 390–406. DOI: 10.9734/jerr/2024/v26i71217

Twigg, E., Humphris, G., Jones, C., Bramwell, R., & Griffiths, R. D. (2008). Use of a screening questionnaire for post-traumatic stress disorder (PTSD) on a sample of UK ICU patients. *Acta Anaesthesiologica Scandinavica, 52*(2), 202–208. DOI: 10.1111/j.1399-6576.2007.01531.x PMID: 18005373

Udoh, E. E., Hermel, M., Bharmal, M. I., Nayak, A., Patel, S., Butlin, M., & Bhavnani, S. P. (2023). Nanosensor technologies and the digital transformation of healthcare. *Personalized Medicine, 20*(3), 251–269. DOI: 10.2217/pme-2022-0065 PMID: 37403731

Ullo, S. L., & Sinha, G. R. (2020). Advances in smart environment monitoring systems using IoT and sensors. *Sensors (Basel), 20*(11), 3113. DOI: 10.3390/s20113113 PMID: 32486411

UNECE. (2020). *Statistics of the Transport of Dangerous Goods in Europe and Central Asia*. United Nations Economic Commission for Europe.

United Nations Economic Commission for Europe (UNECE). (2022). *UN Recommendations on the Transport of Dangerous Goods – Model Regulations*. UN Publications.

Upadhyay, A. K., & Khandelwal, K. (2019). Artificial Intelligence-Based Training Learning From Application. *Development and Learning in Organizations, 33*(2), 20–23. Advance online publication. DOI: 10.1108/DLO-05-2018-0058

Urbaniec, K., Mikulčić, H., Rosen, M. A., & Duić, N. (2017). A holistic approach to sustainable development of energy, water and environment systems. *Journal of Cleaner Production, 155*, 1–11. DOI: 10.1016/j.jclepro.2017.01.119

Urmeneta, M. (2023). Reflections on the Artificial Intelligence Transformation: Responsible Use and the Role of Institutional Research and Institutional Effectiveness Professionals. *Air Professional File*, (Fall 2023). Advance online publication. DOI: 10.34315/apf1642023

Vaara, J., Groeller, H., Drain, J., Kyröläinen, H., Pihlainen, K., Ojanen, T., Connaboy, C., Santtila, M., Agostinelli, P., & Nindl, B. (2021). Physical training considerations for optimizing performance in essential military tasks. *European Journal of Sport Science, 22*(1), 43–57. DOI: 10.1080/17461391.2021.1930193 PMID: 34006204

Vaidya, S., Ambad, P., & Bhosle, S. (2018). Industry 4.0—A glimpse. *Procedia Manufacturing, 20*, 233–238. DOI: 10.1016/j.promfg.2018.02.034

Vaismoradi, M., Tella, S., Logan, P., Khakurel, J., & Vizcaya-Moreno, M. (2020). Nurses' adherence to patient safety principles: A systematic review. *International Journal of Environmental Research and Public Health, 17*(6), 2028. DOI: 10.3390/ijerph17062028 PMID: 32204403

Valerio, A. (2024). Anticipating the impact of artificial intelligence in higher education: Student awareness and ethical concerns in Zamboanga city, Philippines. *Cognizance Journal of Multidisciplinary Studies, 4*(6), 408–418. DOI: 10.47760/cognizance.2024.v04i06.024

Valiakos, G., Papaspyropoulos, K., Giannakopoulos, A., Birtsas, P., Tsiodras, S., Hutchings, M. R., Spyrou, V., Pervanidou, D., Athanasiou, L. V., Papadopoulos, N., Tsokana, C., Baka, A., Manolakou, K., Chatzopoulos, D., Artois, M., Yon, L., Hannant, D., Petrovska, L., Hadjichristodoulou, C., & Billinis, C. (2014). Use of wild bird surveillance, human case data and GIS spatial analysis for predicting spatial distributions of West Nile virus in Greece. *PLoS One, 9*(5), e96935. DOI: 10.1371/journal.pone.0096935 PMID: 24806216

Vanegas, E., Igual, R., & Plaza, I. (2020). Sensing systems for respiration monitoring: A technical systematic review. *Sensors (Basel), 20*(18), 5446. DOI: 10.3390/s20185446 PMID: 32972028

Varghese, A. P., Naik, S., Asrar Up Haq Andrabi, S., Luharia, A., & Tivaskar, S. (2024). Enhancing Radiological Diagnosis: A Comprehensive Review of Image Quality Assessment and Optimization Strategies. *Cureus*. Advance online publication. DOI: 10.7759/cureus.63016 PMID: 39050319

Vărzaru, A. A. (2024). Unveiling Digital Transformation: A Catalyst for Enhancing Food Security and Achieving Sustainable Development Goals at the European Union Level. *Foods, 13*(8), 1226. Advance online publication. DOI: 10.3390/foods13081226 PMID: 38672898

Verdantix. (2022). Strategic Focus: Improving Safety With Robotics And Automation. https://www.verdantix.com/report/environment-health-safety/strategic-focus-improving-safety-with-robotics-and-automation

Vervloet, T., Ribeiro, F., Batista, P., & Vesco, J. (2023). Technology and innovation in enhancing primary health care: the role of digital solutions in strengthening healthcare systems.. DOI: 10.56238/globalhealthprespesc-022

Veta, M., Diest, P., & Pluim, J. (2016). Cutting out the middleman: measuring nuclear area in histopathology slides without segmentation., 632-639. DOI: 10.1007/978-3-319-46723-8_73

Vicente, V., Svensson, L., Sundström, B., Sjöstrand, F., & Castrén, M. (2014). Randomized controlled trial of a prehospital decision system by emergency medical services to ensure optimal treatment for older adults in Sweden. *Journal of the American Geriatrics Society, 62*(7), 1281–1287. DOI: 10.1111/jgs.12888 PMID: 24916953

Vilhouphrenuo, Z., Angel Elizabeth, S., Joel, M. T., Dayanand, P., Thottiam Vasudevan, R., Saqer, S. A., Robert, M., Abdullatif Bin, M., Muhammad, W., & Gulzar Ahmad, N. (2024). Revolutionizing the food industry: The transformative power of artificial intelligence-a review. [publication_type = article.]. *Food Chemistry: X, 24*, 101867. DOI: 10.1016/j.fochx.2024.101867 PMID: 39431210

Vilone, G., & Longo, L. (2021). Notions of explainability and evaluation approaches for explainable artificial intelligence. *Information Fusion, 76*, 89–106. DOI: 10.1016/j.inffus.2021.05.009

Vivekananthan, V., Khandelwal, G., Alluri, N. R., & Kim, S. J. (2022). E-Skin for Futuristic Nanosensor Technology for the Healthcare System. In Nanosensors for Futuristic Smart and Intelligent Healthcare Systems (pp. 133-157). CRC Press.

Vukicevic, A. M., Macužic, I., Djapan, M., Milicevic, V., & Shamina, L. (2021). Digital Training and Advanced Learning in Occupational Safety and Health Based on Modern and Affordable Technologies. *Sustainability (Basel), 2021*(13), 13641. DOI: 10.3390/su132413641

Wagner, A., Schöne, L., & Rieger, M. A. (2020). Determinants of occupational safety culture in hospitals and other workplaces—Results from an integrative literature review. *International Journal of Environmental Research and Public Health, 17*(18), 6588. DOI: 10.3390/ijerph17186588 PMID: 32927758

Waheed, M., & Liu, L. (2024). Perceptions of family physicians about applying ai in primary health care: Case study from a premier health care organization. *JMIR AI, 3*, e40781. DOI: 10.2196/40781 PMID: 38875531

Wahid, M. A., Bukhari, S. H. R., Daud, A., Awan, S. E., & Raja, M. A. Z. (2023). COVICT: An IoT based architecture for COVID-19 detection and contact tracing. *Journal of Ambient Intelligence and Humanized Computing, 14*(6), 7381–7398. DOI: 10.1007/s12652-022-04446-z PMID: 36281429

Wang, K., Oramas, J., & Tuytelaars, T. (2021). In defense of lstms for addressing multiple instance learning problems., 444-460. DOI: 10.1007/978-3-030-69544-6_27

Wang, Y., L. Wang and K. L. Siau. Human-Centered Interaction in Virtual Worlds: A New Era of Generative Artificial Intelligence and Metaverse. *International Journal of Human–Computer Interaction*: 1-43.

Wang, Z., Chetouani, A., Hans, D., Lespessailles, E., & Jennane, R. (2022). Siamese-Gap network for early detection of knee osteoarthritis. *2022 IEEE 19th International Symposium on Biomedical Imaging (ISBI)*, 1–4. DOI: 10.1109/ISBI52829.2022.9761626

Wang, B., & Wang, Y. (2021). Big data in safety management: An overview. *Safety Science, 143*, 105414. Advance online publication. DOI: 10.1016/j.ssci.2021.105414

Wang, F.-K., Rahardjo, B., & Rovira, P. R. (2022). Lean Six Sigma with value stream mapping in Industry 4.0 for human-centered workstation design. *Sustainability (Basel), 14*(17), 17. DOI: 10.3390/su141711020

Wangia, R. N., Tang, L., & Wang, J. S. (2019). Occupational exposure to aflatoxins and health outcomes: A review. *Journal of Environmental Science and Health. Part C, Environmental Carcinogenesis & Ecotoxicology Reviews, 37*(4), 215–234. DOI: 10.1080/10590501.2019.1664836 PMID: 31512547

Wang, J., & Li, J. (2024). Artificial intelligence empowering public health education: Prospects and challenges. *Frontiers in Public Health, 12*, 1389026. Advance online publication. DOI: 10.3389/fpubh.2024.1389026 PMID: 39022411

Wang, Q., Han, X., Song, L., Zhang, X., Zhang, B., Gu, Z., Jiang, B., Li, C., Li, X., & Yu, Y. (2024). Automatic quality assessment of knee radiographs using knowledge graphs and convolutional neural networks. *Medical Physics, 51*(10), 7464–7478. DOI: 10.1002/mp.17316 PMID: 39016559

Wang, X., Liu, S., & Zhou, C. (2022). Classification of knee osteoarthritis based on transfer learning model and magnetic resonance images. *2022 International Conference on Machine Learning, Control, and Robotics (MLCR)*, 67–71. DOI: 10.1109/MLCR57210.2022.00021

Wang, Y., Bi, Z., Xie, Y., Wu, T., Zeng, X., Chen, S., & Zhou, D. (2021). Learning from highly confident samples for automatic knee osteoarthritis severity assessment: Data from the osteoarthritis initiative. *IEEE Journal of Biomedical and Health Informatics*, *26*(3), 1239–1250. DOI: 10.1109/JBHI.2021.3102090 PMID: 34347615

Wang, Z., Xing, Y., Yan, W., Sun, X., Zhang, X., Huang, S., & Li, L. (2020). Effects of individual, family and community factors on the willingness of institutional elder care: A cross-sectional survey of the elderly in China. *BMJ Open*, *10*(2), e032478. DOI: 10.1136/bmjopen-2019-032478 PMID: 32075825

Waqar, A., Khan, M. B., Shafiq, N., Skrzypkowski, K., Zagórski, K., & Zagórska, A. (2023). Assessment of challenges to the adoption of IoT for the safety management of small construction projects in Malaysia: Structural equation modeling approach. *Applied Sciences (Basel, Switzerland)*, *13*(6), 3340. DOI: 10.3390/app13053340

Wasmann, J.-W. A., Lanting, C. P., Huinck, W. J., Mylanus, E. A., van der Laak, J. W., Govaerts, P. J., Swanepoel, D. W., Moore, D. R., & Barbour, D. L. (2021). Computational audiology: New approaches to advance hearing health care in the digital age. *Ear and Hearing*, *42*(6), 1499–1507. DOI: 10.1097/AUD.0000000000001041 PMID: 33675587

Weathers, E., Ó'Caoimh, R., Cornally, N., Fitzgerald, C., Kearns, T., Coffey, A., Daly, E., O'Sullivan, R., McGlade, C., & Molloy, D. (2016). Advance care planning: A systematic review of randomised controlled trials conducted with older adults. *Maturitas*, *91*, 101–109. DOI: 10.1016/j.maturitas.2016.06.016 PMID: 27451328

Weerts, S., Naous, D., Bouchikhi, M. E., & Clavien, C. (2022, August). AI Systems for Occupational Safety and Health: From Ethical Concerns to Limited Legal Solutions. In *International Conference on Electronic Government* (pp. 499-514). Cham: Springer International Publishing. DOI: 10.1007/978-3-031-15086-9_32

Wei, F., Zhao, W., Gao, X., Xue, P., Xu, F., Xie, H., Yang, N., Zou, H., & Qiu, W. (2025, March). (2024). Associations Between Noise Exposure Level, Noise Kurtosis, and Distortion Product Otoacoustic Emissions in Young Workers With Normal Hearing. *Ear and Hearing*, *46*(2), 483–493. Advance online publication. DOI: 10.1097/AUD.0000000000001600 PMID: 39402715

Wen, C., Chang, S., & Ho, H. (2021). Adverse health effects of frailty: Systematic review and meta-analysis of middle-aged and older adults with implications for evidence-based practice. *Worldviews on Evidence-Based Nursing*, *18*(4), 282–289. DOI: 10.1111/wvn.12508 PMID: 34075676

Wenqiang, G., Chenrui, L., Meng, G., Qiwei, Z., Xinyi, Y., & Li, Z. (2023). Innovative applications of artificial intelligence in zoonotic disease management. *Science in One Health*, *2*, 100045. DOI: 10.1016/j.soh.2023.100045 PMID: 39077042

Westhoven, M., & Herrmann, T. (2023, July). Interaction design for hybrid intelligence: the case of work place risk assessment. In International Conference on Human-Computer Interaction (pp. 629-639). Cham: Springer Nature Switzerland.

Wickramasinghe, N., Ulapane, N., Sloane, E., & Gehlot, V. (2024). Digital twins for more precise and personalized treatment.. DOI: 10.3233/SHTI230961

Williams, K., Pennathur, P., Bossen, A., & Gloeckner, A. (2016). Adapting telemonitoring technology use for older adults: A pilot study. *Research in Gerontological Nursing*, *9*(1), 17–23. DOI: 10.3928/19404921-20150522-01 PMID: 26020575

Wine, B., & Newcomb, E. T. (2024). A blocking and distance management staff training intervention for torso- and head-directed aggression. *Journal of Applied Behavior Analysis*, *57*(3), 668–675. DOI: 10.1002/jaba.1089 PMID: 38767337

Wong, B. K. M., Vengusamy, S., & Bastrygina, T. (2024). Healthcare digital transformation through the adoption of artificial intelligence. In *Artificial Intelligence, Big Data, Blockchain and 5G for the Digital Transformation of the Healthcare Industry* (pp. 87–110). Elsevier. DOI: 10.1016/B978-0-443-21598-8.00014-2

Wong, P. (2019). Democratizing Algorithmic Fairness. *Philosophy & Technology*, *33*(2), 225–244. DOI: 10.1007/s13347-019-00355-w

World Bank. (2022). *Global Road Safety Facility: Innovation and Investment Programs in Africa and Asia*. World Bank Group.

World Health Organization (WHO). (2021). *Global Status Report on Road Safety*. WHO Press.

World Health Organization. (2009). *Systems thinking for health systems strengthening* (Alliance for Health Policy and Systems Research Issue. https://apps.who.int/iris/bitstream/handle/10665/44204/9789241563895_eng.pdf?sequence=1

World Health Organization. (2021). *World report on hearing*. WHO. https://apps.who.int/iris

World Health Organization. (2024). *Ethics and governance of artificial intelligence for health: large multi-modal models. WHO guidance*. World Health Organization.

Wynn, M., Reis da Silva, T. H., & Pearson-Jenkins, J. (2025). Introduction to digital nursing and nursing theory. In Wynn, M. (Ed.), *Digital Nursing: Shaping Practice and Identity in the Age of Informatics*. Routledge. DOI: 10.4324/9781032714547-1

Xiang, L., Yang, X., Hu, A., Su, H., & Wang, P. (2022). Condition monitoring and anomaly detection of wind turbine based on cascaded and bidirectional deep learning networks. *Applied Energy*, *305*, 117925. DOI: 10.1016/j.apenergy.2021.117925

Xing, F., Peng, G., Zhang, B., Li, S., & Liang, X. (2021). Socio-technical barriers affecting large-scale deployment of AI-enabled wearable medical devices among the ageing population in China. *Technological Forecasting and Social Change*, *166*, 120609. DOI: 10.1016/j.techfore.2021.120609

Xu, D., Liu, B., Wang, J., & Zhang, Z. (2022). Bibliometric analysis of artificial intelligence for biotechnology and applied microbiology: Exploring research hotspots and frontiers. *Frontiers in Bioengineering and Biotechnology*, *10*, 998298. DOI: 10.3389/fbioe.2022.998298 PMID: 36277390

Xue, Y., & Liu, S. (2022). Towards Better Governance on Biosafety and Biosecurity: China's Advances and Perspectives in Medical Biotechnology Legislation. *Frontiers in Bioengineering and Biotechnology*, *10*, 939295. Advance online publication. DOI: 10.3389/fbioe.2022.939295 PMID: 35860327

Xu, X., Rioux, T., Friedl, K., González, J., & Castellani, J. (2023). Development of interactive guidance for cold exposure using a thermoregulatory model. *International Journal of Circumpolar Health*, *82*(1), 2190485. Advance online publication. DOI: 10.1080/22423982.2023.2190485 PMID: 36934425

Yang, C.-H. (2022). How artificial intelligence technology affects productivity and employment: Firm-level evidence from Taiwan. *Research Policy*, *51*(6), 104536. DOI: 10.1016/j.respol.2022.104536

Yang, H. S., Hou, Y., Vasovic, L. V., Steel, P., Chadburn, A., Racine-Brzostek, S. E., Velu, P., Cushing, M. M., Loda, M., Kaushal, R., Zhao, Z., & Wang, F. (2020) Routine laboratory blood tests predict SARS-CoV-2 infection using machine learning. *medRxiv*: 2020.2006.2017.20133892. DOI: 10.1101/2020.06.17.20133892

Yang, J., Liu, Y., & Morgan, P. L. (2024). Human-machine interaction towards Industry 5.0: Human-centric smart manufacturing. *Digital Engineering*, *2*, 100013. DOI: 10.1016/j.dte.2024.100013

Yang, K., Ahn, C., & Kim, H. (2020). Deep learning-based classification of work-related physical load levels in construction. *Advanced Engineering Informatics*, *45*, 101104. DOI: 10.1016/j.aei.2020.101104

Yang, X., Chen, A., PourNejatian, N., Shin, H. C., Smith, K. E., Parisien, C., Compas, C., Martin, C., Costa, A. B., Flores, M. G., Zhang, Y., Magoc, T., Harle, C. A., Lipori, G., Mitchell, D. A., Hogan, W. R., Shenkman, E. A., Bian, J., & Wu, Y. (2022). A large language model for electronic health records. *NPJ Digital Medicine*, *5*(1), 194. DOI: 10.1038/s41746-022-00742-2 PMID: 36572766

Yan, Z., Dube, V., Heselton, J., Johnson, K., Yan, C., Jones, V., Blaskewicz Boron, J., & Shade, M. (2024). Understanding older people's voice interactions with smart voice assistants: A new modified rule-based natural language processing model with human input. *Frontiers in Digital Health*, *6*, 1329910. Advance online publication. DOI: 10.3389/fdgth.2024.1329910 PMID: 38812806

Yazdani, A. (2023). *The Impact of AI on Trends, Design, and Consumer Behavior*. Aitechbesosci., DOI: 10.61838/kman.aitech.1.4.2

Yazdi, M., Zarei, E., Adumene, S., & Beheshti, A. (2024). Navigating the Power of Artificial Intelligence in Risk Management: A Comparative Analysis. *Safety (Basel, Switzerland)*, *10*(2), 42. DOI: 10.3390/safety10020042

Yelne, S., Chaudhary, M., Dod, K., Sayyad, A., & Sharma, R. (2023). Harnessing the Power of AI: A Comprehensive Review of Its Impact and Challenges in Nursing Science and Healthcare. *Cureus*. Advance online publication. DOI: 10.7759/cureus.49252 PMID: 38143615

Yi, A. P. J., Sumedha, , & Ramalingam, V. (2022). Prevalence of Respiratory Symptoms and Associated Risk Factors among Street Food Vendors in Klang Valley, Malaysia. *Journal of Experimental Biology and Agricultural Sciences, 10*(3), 533–538. DOI: 10.18006/2022.10(3).533.538

Yuan, J., Zhang, Y., Liu, S., & Zhu, R. (2023). Wearable leg movement monitoring system for high-precision real-time metabolic energy estimation and motion recognition. *Research, 6*, 0214.

Yucer, S., Akçay, S., Moubayed, N., & Breckon, T. (2020). Exploring Racial Bias within Face Recognition via per-subject Adversarially-Enabled Data Augmentation. *2020 IEEE/CVF Conference on Computer Vision and Pattern Recognition Workshops (CVPRW)*, 83-92. https://doi.org/DOI: 10.1109/CVPRW50498.2020.00017

Yu, D. (2016). Effects of a health and social collaborative case management model on health outcomes of family caregivers of frail older adults: Preliminary data from a pilot randomized controlled trial. *Journal of the American Geriatrics Society, 64*(10), 2144–2148. DOI: 10.1111/jgs.14259 PMID: 27550619

Yu, F., & Schweisfurth, T. (2020). Industry 4.0 technology implementation in SMEs—A survey in the Danish-German border region. *International Journal of Innovation Studies, 4*(3), 76–84. DOI: 10.1016/j.ijis.2020.05.001

Yu, X. (2024). Artificial Intelligence-Based Perioperative Safety Verification System Improved the Performance of Surgical Safety Verification Execution. *American Journal of Translational Research, 16*(4), 1295–1305. Advance online publication. DOI: 10.62347/PUUT2092 PMID: 38715820

Zainab, H., Khan, A. H., Khan, R., & Hussain, H. K. (2024). Integration of AI and Wearable Devices for Continuous Cardiac Health Monitoring. *International Journal of Multidisciplinary Sciences and Arts, 3*(4), 123–139.

Zebari, D. A., Sadiq, S. S., & Sulaiman, D. M. (2022). Knee osteoarthritis detection using deep feature based on convolutional neural network. *2022 International Conference on Computer Science and Software Engineering (CSASE)*, 259–264. DOI: 10.1109/CSASE51777.2022.9759799

Zenor, J. (2020). If you see something, say something: Can artificial intelligence have a duty to report dangerous behavior in the home? *DENv. L.REv., 98*, 839.

Zhang, C., Wang, X., Fang, S., & Shi, X. (2022). Construction and Application of VR-AR Teaching System in Coal-Based Energy Education. *Sustainability (Basel), 14*(23), 16033. DOI: 10.3390/su142316033

Zhang, M., Ghodrati, N., Poshdar, M., Seet, B. C., & Yongchareon, S. (2023). A construction accident prevention system based on the Internet of Things (IoT). *Safety Science, 159*, 106012. DOI: 10.1016/j.ssci.2022.106012

Zhang, M., Shi, R., & Yang, Z. (2020). A critical review of vision-based occupational health and safety monitoring of construction site workers. *Safety Science, 126*, 104658. Advance online publication. DOI: 10.1016/j.ssci.2020.104658

Zhang, S., Diao, M., Yu, W., Pei, L., Lin, Z., & Chen, D. (2020). Estimation of the reproductive number of novel coronavirus (COVID-19) and the probable outbreak size on the Diamond Princess cruise ship: A data-driven analysis. *International Journal of Infectious Diseases, 93*, 201–204. Advance online publication. DOI: 10.1016/j.ijid.2020.02.033 PMID: 32097725

Zhang, S.-E., Liu, W., Wang, J., Shi, Y., Xie, F., Cang, S., Sun, T., & Fan, L. (2018). Impact of workplace violence and compassionate behaviour in hospitals on stress, sleep quality, and subjective health status among Chinese nurses: A cross-sectional survey. *BMJ Open, 8*(10), e019373. DOI: 10.1136/bmjopen-2017-019373 PMID: 30287664

Zhang, X., Ma, L., Chen, N., Wu, D., & Yan, Y. (2022). Trend analysis and prediction of injury death in Xi'an city, China, 2005-2020. *Archives of Public Health = Archives Belges de Santé Publique, 80*(1), 238. Advance online publication. DOI: 10.1186/s13690-022-00988-y PMID: 36403065

Zhang, Y., Gao, Y., Wang, H., Wu, H., Xia, Y., & Wu, X. (2022). A secure high-order gene interaction detection algorithm based on deep neural network. *IEEE/ACM Transactions on Computational Biology and Bioinformatics*. PMID: 36251904

Zhao, Z., Wu, J., Li, T., Sun, C., Yan, R., & Chen, X. (2021). Challenges and Opportunities of AI-Enabled Monitoring, Diagnosis & Prognosis: A Review. In *Chinese Journal of Mechanical Engineering (English Edition)* (Vol. 34, Issue 1). Springer. DOI: 10.1186/s10033-021-00570-7

Zhao, H., Ou, L., Zhang, Z., Zhang, L., Liu, K., & Kuang, J. (2025). The value of deep learning-based X-ray techniques in detecting and classifying KL grades of knee osteoarthritis: A systematic review and meta-analysis. *European Radiology, 35*(1), 327–340. DOI: 10.1007/s00330-024-10928-9 PMID: 38997539

Zhao, J., & Fariñas, B. G. (2022). Artificial Intelligence and Sustainable Decisions. *European Business Organization Law Review*. Advance online publication. DOI: 10.1007/s40804-022-00262-2

Zhao, S., Xie, F., Wang, J., Shi, Y., Zhang, S., Han, X., Sun, Z., Shi, L., Li, Z., Mu, H., Liu, X., Liu, W., Gao, L., Sun, T., & Fan, L. (2018). Prevalence of workplace violence against Chinese nurses and its association with mental health: A cross-sectional survey. *Archives of Psychiatric Nursing, 32*(2), 242–247. DOI: 10.1016/j.apnu.2017.11.009 PMID: 29579519

Zheng, R., Zhou, Y., Fu, Y., Xiang, Q., Cheng, F., Chen, H., Xu, H., fu, L., Wu, X., Feng, M., Ye, L., Tian, Y., Deng, R., Liu, S., Jiang, Y., Yu, C., & Li, J. (2020). Prevalence and associated factors of depression and anxiety among nurses during the outbreak of COVID-19 in China: A cross-sectional study. *International Journal of Nursing Studies, 114*, 103809. DOI: 10.1016/j.ijnurstu.2020.103809 PMID: 33207297

Zhong, B., Pan, X., Love, P. E., Sun, J., & Tao, C. (2020). Hazard analysis: A deep learning and text mining framework for accident prevention. *Advanced Engineering Informatics, 46*, 101152. DOI: 10.1016/j.aei.2020.101152

Zhou, D., Zeng, J., Zeng, X., Li, Y., Wu, Z., Wan, X., … & Su, X. (2019). A novel p53/pomc/gas/sash1 autoregulatory feedback loop and pathologic hyperpigmentation.. DOI: 10.5772/intechopen.81567

Zhou, N., Zhang, Z., Nair, V., Singhal, H., & Chen, J. (2022). Bias, Fairness and Accountability with Artificial Intelligence and Machine Learning Algorithms. *International Statistical Review, 90*(3), 468–480. DOI: 10.1111/insr.12492

Zhou, S. K., Greenspan, H., Davatzikos, C., Duncan, J. S., Van Ginneken, B., Madabhushi, A., Prince, J. L., Rueckert, D., & Summers, R. M. (2021). A Review of Deep Learning in Medical Imaging: Imaging Traits, Technology Trends, Case Studies With Progress Highlights, and Future Promises. *Proceedings of the IEEE, 109*(5), 820–838. DOI: 10.1109/JPROC.2021.3054390 PMID: 37786449

Zhou, X. (2023). *Ieee, 2023*. Designing Navigation Tool for Immersive Analytics in AR.

Zhuang, Z., Si, L., Wang, S., Xuan, K., Ouyang, X., Zhan, Y., Xue, Z., Zhang, L., Shen, D., Yao, W., & Wang, Q. (2022). Knee cartilage defect assessment by graph representation and surface convolution. *IEEE Transactions on Medical Imaging*, *42*(2), 368–379. DOI: 10.1109/TMI.2022.3206042 PMID: 36094985

Zizic, M. C., Mladineo, M., Gjeldum, N., & Celent, L. (2022). From Industry 4.0 towards Industry 5.0: A review and analysis of paradigm shift for the people, organization and technology. *Energies*, *15*(14), 5221. DOI: 10.3390/en15145221

Zou, J., & Schiebinger, L. (2021). Ensuring That Biomedical AI Benefits Diverse Populations. *EBioMedicine*, *67*, 103358. Advance online publication. DOI: 10.1016/j.ebiom.2021.103358 PMID: 33962897

Zvarivadza, T., Onifade, M., Dayo-Olupona, O., Said, K. O., Githiria, J. M., Genc, B., & Celik, T. (2024). On the impact of Industrial Internet of Things (IIoT)-mining sector perspectives. *International Journal of Mining, Reclamation and Environment*, *38*(10), 1–39. DOI: 10.1080/17480930.2024.2347131

Zwęgliński, T. (2020). The use of drones in disaster aerial needs reconnaissance and damage assessment–three-dimensional modeling and orthophoto map study. *Sustainability (Basel)*, *12*(15), 6080. DOI: 10.3390/su12156080

About the Contributors

Martha Chadyiwa is a Senior Lecturer in the Department of Environmental Health at the University of Johannesburg. She a registered Environmental Health Practitioner with the Health Professions Council of South Africa, holding a Bachelor of Science Degree in Environmental Science. She has an MBA in Environmental Management from Twente University and completed an Honors in Leadership at the University of Johannesburg. She completed her PhD with the University of the Witwatersrand. From 2013 to 2017, she served as the HOD for the Department of Environmental Health and was involved in creating and developing content for the online Master of Public Health at the University of Johannesburg, which she currently coordinates. She has been an Adjunct lecturer at Witwatersrand University, MANCOSA and Lyceum and has published papers on occupational and environmental health in nationally and internationally accredited journals. Throughout her career, she has supervised over 20 Masters students to completion, and has received numerous accolades, including being the 2021 winner of South Africa's InspiringFifty women in STEM. She is involved in several international collaborations, including serving as vice-chair of the U21 Sustainable Development Goals committee. Her research focuses on occupational and environmental health, including how artificial intelligence impacts these fields.

***

K. Balaji is an Assistant Professor in Business and Management, Christ University, Bangalore. He did Ph.D. from KLU Business School, KL University,Vijayawada. He is having 12 years of teaching experience. He has to his credit 23 Research Articles published in reputed National and International Journals. He has participated and presented more than 12 papers in both National and International Seminars/Conferences and also attended more than 50 workshops/FDPS organized by various reputed organizations. He has also participated in more than 50 seminars / webinars organized by various reputed organizations. He has also attended in 6 Short Term Training programs.He has successfully conducted 3 webinars, one 5 day FDP and one International Conference on Reimaging marketing in New Normal. He is a ratified as Assistant Professor by both JNTUH, JNTU Anantapur and Sri Venkateswara University,Tirupati. His specialized areas include, Accounting and Financial management, Marketing Management, Retailing Management, Con

Saurabh Chandra is an accomplished legal scholar and currently serves as an Associate Professor & Assistant Dean at the School of Law, Bennett University, India. With a robust academic foundation, he earned his Bachelor of Arts and Bachelor of Laws (B.A. LL.B.) from the prestigious Aligarh Muslim University (A.M.U.). He further specialized in Business Laws, completing his Master of Laws (LL.M.) at the renowned National Law School of India University (NLSIU), Bangalore. Dr. Chandra's academic journey culminated in a Doctorate in Law (Ph.D.) from the esteemed National Law University (NLU)

Delhi.Dr. Saurabh Chandra also holds a master's degree in Management with specialization in Human Resources in Management and another in Journalism and Mass Communication. With 16 years of teaching experience, he has established himself as an expert in Business Laws, with numerous publications to his credit. Dr. Saurabh Chandra is an expert in Business Laws, with a profound understanding of the intricate legal frameworks that govern the business world.Dr. Chandra brings a wealth of experience in Academic Administration, having successfully held various key administrative positions.

Nicolene Dyantyi is a final year student for the degree program "Bachelor of Environmental Health" at Tshwane University of Technology in the Faculty of Sciences, The department of Environmental Health. She received the International Federation of Environmental Health (IFEH)'s Roy Emerson Award, which was presented at their 17th World Congress in Perth, Australia from 20 to 24 May 2024.

Tiago Horta Reis da Silva is a Lecturer in Nursing Education (AEP) at King's College London, with a range of qualifications including BSc in Nursing, BSc in Traditional Chinese Medicine, MSc in Emotional Intelligence, Counselling and NLP, a Master of Business Administration, and MSc in Traditional Chinese Medicine. He has experience in other Higher Education Institutions and NHS and is a member of the Adult Nursing department, assisting with the running, development, and administration of BSc and MSc programmes. He also assists with teaching other modules' content and assists with interviews and assessment matters for other courses. Tiago is a Senior Fellow in Higher Education, a Fellow of the Royal Society of Medicine, and a Fellow for Faculty Nursing and Midwifery at the Royal College of Southern Ireland.

Tanyaradzwa Amos Jeche is a 25 year old scholar currently in his final year of Master's studies in International Relations at Midlands State University in Zimbabwe. He holds a Bachelor's Honours Degree in Peace Studies and a bible certificate from Andrew Wommack Ministries. Tanyaradzwa is an active participant in academic and professional conferences, most recently presenting at the Women's Impact, Innovation, and Sustainability in Africa (WIISA) 2024 Conference, where he contributed to the Women and Mental Health panel. He also submitted a paper addressing important issues in this field. Additionally, he was invited to contribute a paper on women's empowerment in the context of BRICS and Africa. His research interests include human justice, youth and women empowerment, conflict resolution and recurrence, and terrorism. Tanyaradzwa is a diversified researcher focused on illuminating issues of justice and empowerment for all.

Kholofelo Khumo Nkwana, an Environmental Health Practitioner registered with the Health Professions Council of South Africa, is currently the Health Information Operational Manager for Primary Health Care and Environmental Health Services at the City of Johannesburg. With a BTech in Environmental Health from Tshwane University of Technology, a Postgraduate Diploma in Public Health from the University of Pretoria, and a Business Management Diploma from MANCOSA, he brings a strong blend of public health and management expertise. As an Academic Advisory Committee member for Tshwane University of Technology's Department of Environmental Health, Mr. Nkwana actively supports advancements in environmental health education and community health outcomes in South Africa.

Liepollo Ntlhakana is the current Head of Department (Audiology) and an Audiologist with PhD in Public Health (University of the Witwatersrand). She is a Lecturer at the University of the Witwatersrand, in the Department of Speech Pathology and Audiology. Liepollo Ntlhakana teaches and supervises audiology students at both undergraduate and postgraduate levels. Her research work extensively covers hearing conservation programmes and noise-induced hearing loss in the mines and recently with extensions in other occupational settings. Her PhD research focused on developing a predictive model for early identification of occupational noise-induced hearing loss (ONIHL) among South African miners. She is the Past President of the South African Association of Audiologists (SAAA). She serves on technical and working committees responsible for the review of hearing conservation programmes, the prevention of noise-induced hearing loss and audiometry course design and/or redesign

Muftau Kolawole Oladunmoye is a professor of pharmaceutical microbiology, his research focus is novel drug discovery and the characterisation of bioactive metabolites from plants and microorganisms sources.

Kehinde Adewole Oyeniran is a lecturer in the Department of Biological Sciences, Bamidele Olumilua University of Education Science and Technology, Ikere-Ekiti. His multidisciplinary research combines bioinformatics and gold-standard wet-lab approaches to gain insights into the molecular mechanisms underlying pathogen emergence.

Olubukola Helen Oyeniran is a lecturer in the Department of Biochemistry, Federal University Oye-Ekti. Her research focus is in the use of plants as functional foods for management of degenerative diseases using Drosophila melanogaster and Rattus norvegicus as study models.

Maasago Mercy Sepadi is an Environmental Health Practitioner by Profession and a distinguished public health professional and researcher based in South Africa, recognized for her work in environmental health and occupational safety, particularly within underserved urban communities. She Holds a Ph.D. in Public Health, and undergraduate degrees in Environmental Health. Dr. Sepadi has contributed extensively to the study of health risks faced by informal workers, including street vendors, focusing on the impact of air pollution, sanitation challenges, and urban environmental hazards on public health outcomes. She is currently a lecturer at Tshwane University of Technology.

Bhupinder Singh working as Professor at Sharda University, India. Also, Honorary Professor in University of South Wales UK and Santo Tomas University Tunja, Colombia. His areas of publications as Smart Healthcare, Medicines, fuzzy logics, artificial intelligence, robotics, machine learning, deep learning, federated learning, IoT, PV Glasses, metaverse and many more. He has 3 books, 139 paper publications, 163 paper presentations in international/national conferences and seminars, participated in more than 40 workshops/FDP's/QIP's, 25 courses from international universities of repute, organized more than 59 events with international and national academicians and industry people's, editor-in-chief and co-editor in journals, developed new courses. He has given talks at international universities, resource person in international conferences such as in Nanyang Technological University Singapore, Tashkent State University of Law Uzbekistan; KIMEP University Kazakhstan, All'ah meh Tabatabi University Iran, the Iranian Association of International Criminal law, Iran and Hague Center for International Law and Investment, The Netherlands, Northumbria University Newcastle UK,

Tanusha Singh, an Associate Professor in the Department of Environmental Health at the University of Johannesburg, holds a PhD in Clinical Microbiology and Infectious Diseases and an MBA degree. She is currently registered with the Health Professional Council of South Africa and is an NRF-rated researcher. Singh boasts over two and half decades of expertise in occupational health. Serving as the coordinator of the MPH programme, she aims to build occupational and environmental health capacity in the African region. Her research focuses on hazardous biological agents, including bioaerosols, occupational allergens, and waterborne pathogens, with a specific interest in their measurement, impact on worker health, and strategies for risk prevention. She is actively engaged in numerous research projects and has made significant scientific contributions through co-publishing in top-tier DHET-accredited journals, academic development, quality assurance, and curriculum review in alignment with the Higher Education Qualification Framework. She mentors and monitors student performance online, actively participates in the programme's research activities, and builds connections with industry and relevant stakeholders. Her contributions to departmental, faculty, and university advancement are highlighted by her national and international leadership and recognition in Environmental and Occupational Health research. Her leadership extends to various technical and research committees, including roles such as Secretary for the ICOH Scientific Committee on Biohazards and Occupational Health, member of the ICOH SC Indoor Air Quality, and technical member of multiple bodies including Centres for Disease Control and Prevention, World Health Organisation and International Labour Organisation. She has chaired several technical and research committees. She is currently a Research Associate at the National Institute for Occupational Health, serving as an expert advisor on research and teaching & training with a special interest on biohazards and occupational health; and a lecturer at the University of the Witwatersrand. She has supervised numerous postgraduates and has been the recipient of several research grants, further affirming her commitment to advancing knowledge in the field of occupational and environmental health.

Index

A

B

C

D

E

F

G

H

I

L

M

N

O

P

R

S

T

W

X

www.ingramcontent.com/pod-product-compliance
Lightning Source LLC
LaVergne TN
LVHW062108300926
849161LV00010B/2396